The Dynamics of Southern Politics

To "Nommie" Marjorie Roberts Walker (1911–2010). You never knew the South, but you knew of it through me. Thank you for your love, work ethic, and grit; they continue to motivate and inspire.

S. C. M.

The Dynamics of Southern Politics

Causes and Consequences

Seth C. McKee

Texas Tech University

FOR INFORMATION:

CQ Press
An Imprint of SAGE Publications, Inc.
2455 Teller Road
Thousand Oaks, California 91320
E-mail: order@sagepub.com

SAGE Publications Ltd.
1 Oliver's Yard
55 City Road
London EC1Y 1SP
United Kingdom

SAGE Publications India Pvt. Ltd.
B 1/I 1 Mohan Cooperative Industrial Area
Mathura Road, New Delhi 110 044
India

SAGE Publications Asia-Pacific Pte. Ltd.
3 Church Street
#10-04 Samsung Hub
Singapore 049483

Printed in the United States of America

ISBN: 978-1-4522-8727-0

This book is printed on acid-free paper.

SUSTAINABLE FORESTRY INITIATIVE
Certified Sourcing
www.sfiprogram.org
SFI-01075

Acquisitions Editor: Monica Eckman
Content Development Editor: Scott Harris
Editorial Assistant: Sam Rosenberg
Production Editor: Veronica S. Hooper
Copy Editor: Diana Breti
Typesetter: C&M Digitals (P) Ltd.
Proofreader: Dennis W. Webb
Indexer: Beth Nauman-Montana
Cover Designer: Candice Harman
Marketing Manager: Erica DeLuca

18 19 20 21 22 10 9 8 7 6 5 4 3 2 1

CONTENTS

TABLES, FIGURES, AND BOXES

Tables

Figures

Boxes

Sara Miller McCune founded SAGE Publishing in 1965 to support the dissemination of usable knowledge and educate a global community. SAGE publishes more than 1000 journals and over 800 new books each year, spanning a wide range of subject areas. Our growing selection of library products includes archives, data, case studies and video. SAGE remains majority owned by our founder and after her lifetime will become owned by a charitable trust that secures the company's continued independence.

Los Angeles | London | New Delhi | Singapore | Washington DC | Melbourne

PREFACE

N o other region of the United States has experienced the political transformation occurring in the American South. Dixie was once an almost completely Democratic party system, but it is now dominated by Republicans, the perennially moribund opposition from the late eighteenth century until the 1960s. And despite the current electoral hegemony of the Grand Old Party (GOP), there is palpable evidence that, at least in some parts of the South, the Democratic Party is poised for a comeback. This book tells the story of partisan change in the American South, starting with the great sectional divide created by the Civil War and moving to the present state of political conditions in the second decade of the twenty-first century.

So much has been written about the politics of the southern United States. Perhaps because, like its culture, the South has exhibited and continues to exhibit an exceptional political dynamic not found to the same extent in the rest of America. The foundation of this exceptionalism is rooted in the distant past when African Americans were held in bondage and the white elites who prospered from slavery shaped a political system uniquely suited to maintain white supremacy. The denial of basic human rights, and then later the resistance to black citizenship through an elaborate institutionalized structure of segregation, elevated the racial issue to the forefront of southern politics, a place from which it has never retreated and thus continues to dictate most of the partisan changes taking place to this day.

But southern politics is not just about race; economics and religion are the other two, albeit lesser, pillars that structure the party system. If race is thought of as the constant leading actor, then economics and religion at various points show up to play supportive roles in altering the structure of electoral politics. When and how economics and religion affect political behavior in conjunction with the influence of race explains the general contours of southern politics. To be sure, there are various other issues that shape the southern party system, but they rarely transcend the importance of the aforementioned "big three." Further, we will see that these issues often complement and reinforce each other to a degree that makes it very hard to disentangle their effects. For instance, some scholars contend that economics has driven southern whites into the Republican Party, and yet we know that race is highly correlated with socioeconomic status. And unlike race and economics, which have always made an imprint on southern politics, religion did not play a major role in aligning partisan loyalties until after the controversial *Roe v. Wade* abortion decision in 1973.

This account of southern politics explicitly emphasizes party competition as it changes over time, placing it within a national, sectional, subregional, and sometimes

xviii   The Dynamics of Southern Politics

a state and local context. Hindsight has proven itself to be a remarkable repository that observers of southern politics continually consult to revise their understandings of the region. This book shows that the foresight in some of the leading studies of southern partisan change was cast too cautiously and narrow, failing to see that because of the central role of race in structuring partisan politics, Dixie was gradually but inexorably moving in favor of the Republican Party.

And although the current electoral advantage of the GOP is undeniable, many recent developments provide support for the contention that Republican dominance is at, or fast approaching, a high-water mark because of demographic changes tilting toward a Democratic revival. The modernization of the South and its pleasant climate continues to make it a major draw for migrants seeking a brighter economic future, a more hospitable place to retire, and for some, a welcome return to the setting of their ancestors, who left to escape the harsh reality of Jim Crow. The migratory patterns into the region have directly contributed to a more racially and ethnically diverse population, including a large segment that hails from the much "bluer" North, many of whom are importing their Democratic affiliations. In short, the current state of southern politics appears to be undergoing a notable amount of political fluidity, and the responses of the major parties to the most pressing issues will directly impact the electoral balance now and into the future.

It is my hope that this book succeeds in accomplishing its objective of educating the student of southern politics as to why the region persists as an exceptional place because of its historical and demographic features that set it apart from the rest of the United States. An exploration and analysis of historical events, long-term trends in election results, the compositional makeup and behavior of the electorate, the location and variation of partisan strength, comparative examinations of politics within and outside of Dixie, and recent changes in the dynamics of party competition serve to illuminate the extraordinary and exceedingly rich evolution of the political system below the Mason-Dixon Line.[1]

ACKNOWLEDGMENTS

This book was a long time in the making, and reflecting upon the finished product it is clear that it took the marshaling of all the knowledge I have built up since my days in graduate school. As a PhD student in the Department of Government at the University of Texas at Austin (1999–2005), I was so fortunate to have Daron Shaw as my advisor because he let me pursue my scholarly interest in southern politics. A dissertation on southern U.S. House elections was produced, then came a book from the same project, and after that a slew of published works analyzing a variety of features contributing to the move away from a Democratic-inclined American South to an ascendant Republican version.

A great deal of my scholarly success has been achievable because of the relationships I have made over the years with a host of talented colleagues and collaborators (Trey Hood, Dan Smith, Will Hicks, Danny Hayes, Jeremy Teigen, Mark McKenzie, Richard McKenzie, Gibbs Knotts, Scott Huffmon, Antoine Yoshinaka; we have produced some really nice pieces!). Also, since my first conference in 2002, the biennial Citadel Symposium on Southern Politics has been an invaluable resource and a bottomless reservoir for all manner of political musings on Dixie. Thanks Larry Moreland, Bob Steed, DuBose Kapeluck, and Scott Buchanan for your past, present, and future efforts to sustain this priceless institution. In so many ways, this meeting has shaped my academic career. For instance, I remember asking Jonathan Knuckey if he were to write a book on southern politics, what would he write about? Jonathan said he would produce a textbook. It was this offhand comment that actually led me to pursue such a grueling endeavor. Thanks Jonathan.

I want to thank the good people at CQ Press. There was a brief moment early in my "under contract" period in which I thought about simply foregoing the commitment. The periodic checking in by my editors gave me the motivation to carry on. Thanks Charisse Kiino for believing in this enterprise and thus granting me a contract. Thank you Diana Breti for your thorough copyediting, and thank you Monica Eckman for being the publisher to spur me across the finish line. And thanks to the many conference discussants and reviewers of sections of the book. I also need to thank Texas Tech University and some of its affiliates (Dennis Patterson, Dora Rodriguez, and Brent Lindquist) who generously provided me with the resources necessary to finish. With such institutional support, the many conferences I attended in 2016–2017 made it possible to churn out most of the remaining chapters. Last but not least, thank you Esther Chao McKee, you are such an amazing companion, always believing in me and having the patience to let me pursue my scholarly dreams. I am forever indebted.

—Seth C. McKee

PUBLISHER'S ACKNOWLEDGMENTS

CQ Press wishes to thank the following reviewers who generously provided feedback during the development of this book: Zachary D. Baumann (Florida Southern College), Steve Borrelli (University of Alabama), Rosalind Cook (Tulane University), Chris Cooper (Western Carolina University), Joshua Kaplan (University of Notre Dame), Gibbs Knotts (College of Charleston), Keith Lee (Georgia College), Angie Maxwell (University of Arkansas), Vaughn May (Belmont University), Wayne Parent (Louisiana State University), Stephen Shaffer (Mississippi State University), and Phillip Stone (Wofford College).

ABOUT THE AUTHOR

Seth C. McKee is associate professor of political science at Texas Tech University. McKee is the current Editor in Chief of *Political Research Quarterly* and a member of the editorial boards of *American Politics Research* and *Political Behavior*. His primary area of research focuses on American electoral politics and especially party system change in the American South. He has published numerous articles on such topics as political participation, public opinion, voter preferences, redistricting, party switching, minority representation, strategic voting behavior, and state legislator voting behavior. McKee is the author of *Republican Ascendancy in Southern U.S. House Elections* (Routledge 2010) and the editor of *Jigsaw Puzzle Politics in the Sunshine State* (University Press of Florida 2015).

1 THE LONG ARC OF SOUTHERN POLITICAL HISTORY

In 1949, V. O. Key's masterpiece *Southern Politics in State and Nation* was published. More than six decades later this treatise on southern politics is revered as the cornerstone from which scholars continue to consult in their latest studies of the region. The depth and breadth of this work is such that no one expects there to ever be another account on the politics of the American South that can rival it. And, interestingly enough, the book came out just as the "Solid South"—the common expression for the one-party Democratic system—was on the verge of collapse. The 1948 presidential election, the last race Key chronicles, was notable for the intra-party fight between national Democrats and southern Democrats, with the latter embracing the moniker "Dixiecrats" to emphasize their fervent support of the white supremacist status quo prevailing in the region. Democratic President Harry S. Truman and Dixiecrat J. Strom Thurmond split the South's electoral votes, but 1948 would be the last time Dixie was a presidential stronghold for the Democratic Party.

After 1948, the Republican Party established a permanent presence in presidential elections in the South, and since the late 1960s, the party has routinely dominated these contests (Black and Black 1987). The 1964 election would prove to be another critical turning point in southern politics. The national parties permanently reversed positions on the race issue, with Democratic President Lyndon Johnson spearheading passage of the 1964 Civil Rights Act and his opponent, Arizona Republican Senator Barry Goldwater, voting against it (Carmines and Stimson 1989). Ever since this fateful contest, southern blacks have been firmly aligned with the Democratic Party, whereas southern whites have continued to shift in favor of the Grand Old Party (GOP). V. O. Key died in October of 1963—just short of a year before the 1964 election set in motion the southern secular realignment to the Republican Party. Thirty years after the 1964 contest, southern Republicans finally captured a majority of the U.S. House delegation; the last time they had control was in 1874. Two decades since the 1994 "Republican Revolution," the southern GOP now dominates presidential, congressional, and state legislative elections. It appears the transformation of the South from a Democratic redoubt to a Republican bastion is complete.

The current state of the southern party system highlights Republican dominance (McKee 2012a), but below the surface, Democratic promise is easy to spot. The historic election of Barack Obama in 2008 sent shockwaves across the country, and for numerous reasons beyond the obvious fact that the United States finally elected a president of color. The Obama campaign assembled a winning coalition that proved resilient by securing reelection in 2012. The assemblage of minorities, women, younger voters, and lower income earners is likely to have staying power for the Democratic Party—a coalition that, thanks to favorable demographic trends, can establish a national majority in presidential elections for years to come. This development is a national phenomenon, and it has repercussions in the South where the share of Latino residents continues to grow.

After back-to-back Republican shutouts in 2000 and 2004, in 2008 Obama carried Florida, North Carolina, and Virginia. In 2012, Obama held onto Florida and Virginia but narrowly lost North Carolina to Republican challenger Mitt Romney, which was the third most competitive state based on victory margin. These three southern states share compositional features that foretell increasing Democratic competitiveness: (1) strong in-migration of northerners who are more aligned with the Democratic Party than the GOP and (2) a growing minority population—especially Latinos, who are more inclined to back Democrats. These demographic developments create changes to the culture of these states such that their electorates are shifting in favor of the Democratic Party. As will be shown repeatedly in this book, success at the top of the ticket in presidential races reverberates to lower offices. Indeed, the general pattern of Republican growth in southern politics has been referred to as "top-down advancement" (Aistrup 1996). Likewise, expect a revival of Democratic competitiveness in presidential elections in select southern states to filter down to congressional and state legislative contests.

At present, it appears that southern politics may be moving from a position of Republican hegemony to one in which the Democratic Party finds increasing territory to be competitive and, in some places, controlling electoral outcomes. In other words, the party system is once again entering a state of flux because of substantial compositional alterations to the electorates in various southern states. It seems that the long arc of southern political history is bending slowly back to the Democratic Party. But the contemporary southern Democratic Party shares very little resemblance to its Solid South predecessor, in terms of its policy positions and adherents. In fact, it is hardly a stretch to claim that over the last century and a half, the Republican and Democratic parties have essentially traded places (Miller and Schofield 2008). This book seeks to explain the leading causes and consequences that have shaped and reshaped the southern party system since the United States was torn asunder by a bloody Civil War that forever altered the course of politics in Dixie and the nation at large.

OVERVIEW OF THE BOOK

Elections are the thread that guides this account of southern politics. The changing state of two-party competition in presidential, statewide, congressional, and even state legislative races provides the strongest signal as to how the past and present will affect future political dynamics. Elections serve to anchor the reader and signal minor and major changes to the political system, but they are far from capable of telling the richness of southern political history. And because elections are outputs, the end state of any given political cycle, they leave enormous room for interpretation. This explains why there remain several unsettled debates regarding the primary causes and consequences of the southern partisan transformation. To be clear, this book does not attempt to resolve some of the more intractable disagreements. That is not its purpose. Rather, the objective is to present the student with a broad, yet at times detailed, view of the changing state of southern politics since the 1860s. In satisfying this goal, it will be necessary to favor and advance certain perspectives over others, but this will be done with evidence, not polemics. To the extent that this work proves informative, explanatory, and empirically credible, the author will deem it a success.

Because of palpable and enduring alterations to southern politics, it seems natural to begin the textbook with four chapters (chapters 2–5) that provide historical narratives of the changing state of the southern party system from the end of the Civil War to the present. These chapters equip the student with a theoretically driven and empirically supported overview of how southern politics has transformed over the last century and a half. One must have a firm understanding of historical events before comprehending the various dynamics undergirding these occurrences. After establishing the historical narrative of political change, the next four chapters (chapters 6–9) focus more specifically on the leading factors shaping southern politics from the end of the Solid South to now. In consecutive order, these chapters assess the role that generational change, issues, geographic distinctions, and demographic trends have had in overturning a one-party Democratic system and leading to the current partisan balance, which tips overwhelmingly in favor of the GOP.

Demographic change is the major impediment to the maintenance of GOP control, and thus chapter 10 offers a detailed account of how Republican control of most southern states has enabled the party to further advantageous redistricting plans and, perhaps more notably, the recent trend among most southern state legislatures to pass laws that marginally raise the costs of voting. These restrictive measures seem extremely shortsighted and insufficient for sustaining majority status, but most southern Republicans have embraced them. Chapter 11 moves beyond the confines of Dixie in order to compare the way changes within the South reflect or vary from those found in the rest of the United States. This chapter demonstrates that even after the first decade of the new millennium, the South remains politically exceptional. Finally, chapter 12 peers down the road a bit to consider the future of southern politics. Given current conditions, most of the informed speculation centers on Republican political strategy crafted in response to the undeniable trend of a growing minority and "non-southern" population.

EXPLANATIONS OF
SOUTHERN POLITICAL CHANGE

V. O. Key (1949, 10) once made the observation that "attachments to partisan labels live long beyond events that gave them birth." In other words, much of the electorate will hold to a party affiliation even when significant changes to the positions the parties take on major issues suggest voters should reconsider their partisan loyalty. This statement is an accurate assessment of the gradual movement of southern whites in favor of the Republican Party. Indeed, the decades it took for a dominant Democratic Party to give way to an ascending and now currently superior GOP speaks directly to the tendency of most voters to hold firm in their identification with a political party (Campbell et al. 1960).

In 1955, V. O. Key wrote an article titled "A Theory of Critical Elections." In this account, he argued that there are rare occasions when the strength of the major parties can be fundamentally and permanently altered by certain pivotal elections, like 1860 (precipitating the Civil War) and 1932 (the election of Democratic President Franklin D. Roosevelt). These elections stick out because they constitute indisputable turning points in which the extant national majority party (e.g., Republicans before 1932) subsequently becomes the national minority party, whereas the previous minority party (e.g., Democrats before 1932) is now the majority party not just at the time of the noted critical election, but for many elections thereafter. This conception of critical elections as turning points that are responsible for bringing about a reversal of partisan control of the American political system (especially control of national offices like the presidency and Congress) has become the classic statement of partisan realignment in American politics.

Nonetheless, these critical/realigning elections appear to be exceedingly rare. Further, even Key doubted the veracity of such a rapidly dynamic process accounting for partisan change. In 1959, Key wrote another article titled "Secular Realignment and the Party System." By "secular" Key meant "gradual," and thus, with a look at the same data used in his 1955 article, Key reinterpreted the findings, arguing instead that partisan change may exhibit a short-term phenomenon resembling a critical election, but preceding such an event were years of incremental trends leading to the flashpoint.[1] In other words, according to Key, it can take decades (in his words, even upwards of fifty years) for a partisan realignment to run its course. This suggested length of time is well within the bounds of the secular realignment of southern whites to the GOP—sparked by a critical election in 1964 and culminating in a clear Republican electoral advantage by the mid-1990s.

Interestingly, the realignment of southern blacks into the Democratic Party is highly reminiscent of a critical election–type pattern. The swift and permanent shift of African Americans to the Democratic Party in 1964 appears to be a function of civil rights being the paramount issue for this group. Because a Democratic president (Lyndon Johnson) and the Democratic Party outside the South embraced the civil rights cause, southern African Americans overwhelmingly severed their ties with the party of Lincoln (the GOP), even though the southern Democratic Party at first, and for many years to come, resisted the move in favor of civil rights (Black and Black 2002).

Further complicating an understanding of southern political change is the fact that it often does not conform to the dynamics occurring outside the region. For instance, the national realignment in favor of the Democratic Party in 1932 took place because the party finally became electorally competitive in the North. In the South, the Democratic Party had been dominant since the end of Reconstruction (in 1876), and hence 1932 only strengthened the party's grip in Dixie. By contrast, at present the two major parties compete vigorously for control of the presidency and Congress. But the evidence of a highly competitive national party system belies considerable regional disparities in partisan strength (Black and Black 2007). Now, instead of Democrats exhibiting disproportionate electoral power in southern politics, it is the GOP that reigns supreme. Republican influence is not as great outside the South, where the Democratic Party is typically stronger than the Republican Party in the rest of the United States.

Political change involves numerous working parts, but the key to understanding the dynamic lies with the position-taking of the major parties over the small bundle of issues most salient to voters. In the South, these core issues are race, religion, and economics. Going back to the country's great sectional crisis, the Civil War, a northern Republican Party stood for free soil and free labor, and their southern Democratic opposition seceded in order to protect a slave-based economic system. The political status quo in the South held steady from the turn of the nineteenth century until the 1960s when the most significant issue, civil rights, reached a turning point because the major parties reversed course on this issue (Carmines and Stimson 1989). Similarly, the large segment of white southerners who can be labeled evangelical/born-again Christians did not show any signs of abandoning their Democratic political allegiance until the parties altered their views on a set of moral issues of tremendous importance to this group of voters after the Supreme Court declared a woman's right to an abortion in the controversial 1973 *Roe v. Wade* decision. In the 1970s and early 1980s, white religious conservatives converted to the GOP because Republicans had become the defenders of the faith-based positions (e.g., pro-life and favoring prayer in school) vociferously advocated by this substantial southern constituency.

The emphasis on issues and the manner in which the major parties and their leaders respond to them is the primary agent driving political change, and this constitutes the explanatory tool for understanding the nature of southern politics and, by extension, the American electoral system. In this book, several theories of political change will be introduced and utilized to assist the student in understanding the changing nature of southern politics. No political system remains stagnant; it will invariably change. But what distinguishes the South from the rest of the nation is that for so long one political party was in control of its electoral politics: the Democratic Party. In addition, it is perhaps even more intriguing that the party that for so long had hardly any electoral strength, the GOP, is now more powerful in Dixie than in any other section of the United States. Finally, because of demographic trends that are growing the base of Democratic supporters, there is now evidence that the Republican Party will face a real challenge in various parts of the South. The next chapter begins when the South was vanquished in a bloody civil war whose aftermath introduced a complex and unstable political arrangement that eventually succumbed to a Democratic takeover.

BEFORE A "SOLID SOUTH"

In the 1860 election, Republican Abraham Lincoln won the lion's share of electoral votes in the North and was completely shut out in the South.[1] Indeed, in Virginia—the only southern state that placed the Lincoln-Hamlin ticket on the ballot—out of 166,891 votes the Republican nominee garnered 1,887 (1.1 percent). Rather than wait to see what plans a new Republican administration would have for the overriding issue of slavery, the South forced Lincoln's hand when South Carolina seceded from the Union on December 20, 1860. Ten more states would follow suit, forming the Confederate States of America—and what is defined as the South throughout this book. Table 2.1 shows the dates the eleven states seceded and their corresponding percentage of slaves out of each state's total population. It is evident from the table that states with larger slave populations seceded earlier.

TABLE 2.1 ■ Date of Secession and Percentage of Population in Slavery			
State	Date of Secession	Number of Slaves (1860)	Percentage of Slaves (1860)
South Carolina	December 20, 1860	402,406	57
Mississippi	January 9, 1861	436,631	55
Florida	January 10, 1861	61,745	44
Alabama	January 11, 1861	435,080	45
Georgia	January 19, 1861	462,198	44
Louisiana	January 26, 1861	331,726	47
Texas	February 1, 1861	182,566	30
Virginia	April 17, 1861	490,865	31
Arkansas	May 6, 1861	111,115	26
North Carolina	May 20, 1861	331,059	33
Tennessee	June 8, 1861	275,719	25

Sources: Dates for secession are from University of Georgia Special Collections Libraries website (www.libs.uga.edu/hargrett/selections/confed/dates.html). The 1860 census data for total slaves and percentage of population were extracted from the National Historical Geographic Information System website (www.nhgis.org/).

Note: Percentage of slaves is rounded up to the nearest whole number. The bivariate correlation between the percentage of slaves and the order of secession is highly significant at $-.919$ ($p < .01$, two-tailed). This means that states with a greater portion of slaves seceded earlier.

The Civil War lasted a long four years and when it ended, roughly three-quarters of a million Union and Confederate soldiers had died in the struggle (Gugliotta 2012). On April 15, 1865, six days after Confederate General Robert E. Lee surrendered at the Appomattox Courthouse in Virginia, John Wilkes Booth assassinated President Lincoln. Vice President Andrew Johnson, a Democrat loyal to the Union, was elevated to the presidency. Like Lincoln, but perhaps even more so given his Tennessee roots, President Johnson intended for the rebellious states to reenter the Union with very little price to pay as a condition of readmission. After hostilities had ended, Johnson's leadership of Presidential Reconstruction drew the ire of northern congressional Republicans who expected the South to pay a dear price for its treason. With President Johnson leading Reconstruction in the aftermath of the war, ex-Confederates reasserted their positions of political leadership in the southern states. The leniency afforded the South culminated in a constitutional crisis pitting President Johnson against congressional Republicans.

In the first post-Civil War midterm election in 1866, House Republicans expanded their majority from 136 to 173 total seats, almost 77 percent (173 out of 226) of the lower chamber.[2] In the U.S. Senate, the GOP's majority went from 39 to 57 seats, 84 percent (57 out of 68) of the total.[3] With the southern states currently enduring political limbo, lacking congressional representation because they were not granted readmission, northern congressional Republicans decided to take over the blueprint of Reconstruction—making sure that the South would endure a costly purgatory as a condition of reunion. Setting up a showdown with President Johnson, in 1867 Congress passed (over a veto) the Tenure of Office Act, which forbade the president from firing an executive appointee without congressional approval. Directly testing enforcement of the Act, President Johnson proceeded to remove Secretary of War Edwin Stanton (a Lincoln appointee), a move that facilitated his impeachment. In the impeachment trial of 1868, President Johnson escaped removal of office by a single Senate vote.

Thanks to their impressive seat gains after the 1866 midterm, congressional Republicans possessed veto-proof majorities, and they were adamant in taking over the process of shaping southern Reconstruction. President Johnson was rendered ineffectual because a united GOP could consistently override his veto of congressional legislation. By 1867, Presidential Reconstruction was replaced by Congressional Reconstruction or Radical Reconstruction, a more apt statement of the leadership of the so-called Radical Republicans who engineered the set of conditions for southern readmission to the United States. This chapter provides the foundation for understanding the key political dynamics that began with Radical Reconstruction and ended with the advent of the Democratic Solid South. The period running from roughly 1868 to 1900 was the most politically volatile in American history. An unresolved Reconstruction process ended in an uncertain political interlude that eventually gave way to a Democratic usurpation, breathtaking in its almost absolute control of the southern party system.

1868 TO 1900: THE RELENTLESS
WORK OF DEMOCRATIC "REDEMPTION"

The preeminence of race in shaping and driving southern politics is clear from an identification of the locus of power on the eve of the Civil War. The most politically powerful southerners were those who hailed from the black belt region—distinguished by its dark and fertile soil—which contained the bulk of large-scale plantations and hence the highest percentage of slaves. Geographically, the southern black belt runs from the southeastern part of Virginia across the eastern half of North Carolina and then through the middle-to-lower portions of the Deep South states of South Carolina, Georgia, Alabama, Mississippi, and Louisiana, and then tails off in east Texas.[4] Figure 2.1 displays southern counties according to their percentage of slaves (less than 25 percent, 25 to 50 percent, and more than 50 percent), based on the 1860 census.

Due primarily to their potentially disastrous political station, black-belt whites, who resided in counties where the black population rivaled and often surpassed them in total numbers, were the undisputed elites of antebellum southern politics. Their loss of control during Reconstruction would be redeemed and restored for decades to come after extinguishing the Populist threat in the 1890s. Because they were a numerical minority in a majority black setting, black-belt whites had the most to lose if their black subjects were to ever attain political equality, a reality that was vigorously and successfully delayed until the 1960s.

Beyond their immediate confines, black-belt whites had another legitimate threat to their political power: upcountry southern whites who did not hold slaves and hence had no stake in seceding from the United States in order to protect the institution of slavery. America's original sin, the peculiar institution of slavery, led to a disastrous Civil War and in the aftermath, native southerners who aligned with the Republican Party actively resisted the resurging black belt–led white supremacist southern Democracy. These mountain Republicans, many of whom fought for the Union, were bold enough to attempt a partnership with African Americans in a burgeoning Populist Party that threatened to redistribute economic power to the impoverished mass of black and white southerners. Just as they did during the "War between the States," and hastening the demise of Reconstruction, black-belt whites found a way to steer the political agenda. Through a cunning combination of political ingenuity and outright violence, the agrarian movement of the 1890s was swiftly extinguished.

In one of the most insightful passages of *Southern Politics in State and Nation*, V. O. Key (1949, 9) had this to say about the political acumen of black-belt whites:

> This sketch of the broad outlines of the foundations of southern politics points to an extraordinary achievement of a relatively small minority—the whites of the areas of heavy Negro population—which persuaded the entire South that

FIGURE 2.1 ■ Percentage of Slaves in Southern Counties Based on 1860 Census

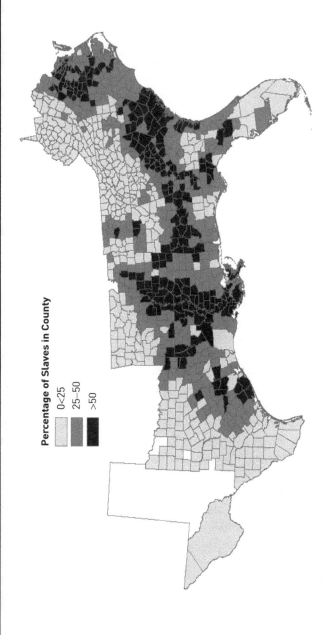

Percentage of Slaves in County

0<25

25–50

>50

Source: Shapefiles (state and county) and data on county slave populations are both from the National Historical Geographic Information System website (https://www .nhgis.org/). Figure created by the author.

it should fight to protect slave property. Later, with allies from conservatives generally, substantially the same group put down a radical movement welling up from the sections dominated by the poorer whites. And by the propagation of a doctrine about the status of the Negro, it impressed on an entire region a philosophy agreeable to its necessities and succeeded for many decades in maintaining a regional unity in national politics to defend those necessities.

But as this chapter will demonstrate, the ability of black-belt whites to control the southern political system was an arduous undertaking. The eventual establishment of a Democratic Solid South at the turn of the twentieth century was anything but a foregone conclusion, which most likely explains why Key was so impressed by the achievement.[5]

NORTHERN REPUBLICANISM IN THE SOUTH

The Grand Old Party was in its infancy when Abraham Lincoln won the White House in 1860. Although its exact origins are disputed (Gould 2003), the Republican Party came to be in 1854, as a party whose roots in the upper Midwest and its corresponding political platform would be anathema to white southerners.[6] Extolling the motto of "free soil and free labor," the rise of the GOP encroached upon the expansion of slavery in the vast territories of the western United States. The precarious and ultimately temporary North-South truce embodied in the 1820 Missouri Compromise, which only allowed for a 1-to-1 entry of free and slave states, was demolished in 1850, when Congress agreed to replace it with popular sovereignty.[7] Popular sovereignty enabled the residents of the various territories to decide for themselves whether they would become a state that would allow or forbid the peculiar institution. The 1854 Kansas-Nebraska Act, with its allowance of popular sovereignty in these two territories, foretold the imminence of a full-blown Civil War. "Bleeding Kansas," as it came to be known, was a prelude and microcosm of the coming war, as pro-slavery and anti-slavery settlers killed each other in their attempt to decide whether the Sunflower State would be free or slave.

After the Civil War, northern Republicans finally infiltrated southern politics by pushing a costly reformist agenda that demanded compliance as a necessary condition for readmission to the United States. Most famously, the Radical Republicans passed the Thirteenth (1865), Fourteenth (1868), and Fifteenth (1870) Amendments. The Thirteenth Amendment abolished slavery, the Fourteenth provided for equal protection under the law and citizenship to anyone born in the United States, and the Fifteenth outlawed racial discrimination in voting. The Fourteenth Amendment became the centerpiece for readmission of the southern states.

Reconstruction Acts

The wholesale readmission of the South created an obvious political complication. The Democratic loyalties of most white southerners, in combination with a smaller northern Democratic delegation, had the potential to comprise a national congressional majority. Rather than see reunification lead directly to the end of Republican rule, northern congressional Republicans used their majorities to pass legislation that would perpetuate their control of the political system. Two objectives were capable of maintaining northern Republican majorities. First, grant and protect the right to vote for the recently freed southern black population. Second, disfranchise numerous southern whites in order to create a Republican majority among the eligible southern electorate. Fundamental to this undertaking was requiring passage of the Fourteenth Amendment as a condition of readmission to the Union. The details of this plan were laid out in a series of Reconstruction Acts passed in the spring and summer of 1867.[8]

By passing the Fourteenth Amendment in 1866, Tennessee avoided military Reconstruction. Under the first Reconstruction Act (March 2, 1867), the other ten southern states were divided into five districts ruled by a military commander who was not below the rank of brigadier-general. Figure 2.2 displays the five Reconstruction districts, with the first consisting of Virginia; the second North Carolina and South Carolina; the third Alabama, Florida, and Georgia; the fourth Arkansas and Mississippi; and the fifth containing Louisiana and Texas. The generals in charge of each district had broad powers to enforce the laws stipulated by Congress. There was a set of chronologically ordered directives that each state had to follow in order to be readmitted. The military officer was tasked with preparing a registration of the southern population. After completion of this registration, voters would then choose delegates to participate in a convention for writing a new state constitution that would then require popular approval followed by congressional approval. Additionally, each state legislature would also have to vote in favor of the Fourteenth Amendment.

FIGURE 2.2 ■ Military Districts during Reconstruction

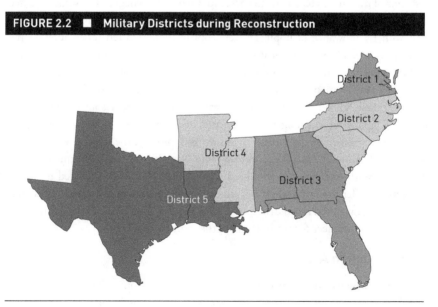

Source: Figure created by the author.

The administration of the Republican Reconstruction effort required many complex steps. The second and third Reconstruction Acts (March 23, 1867, and July 19, 1867) provided the details of the voter registration process. In practical terms, the most nettlesome issue was making sure the voter registrars were qualified to hold their positions. Because these officials were the true arbiters of who would qualify to vote, they were held to the highest standard of loyalty to the Republic, by making them take the Ironclad Oath to the Union. Essentially, under this oath individuals swore that they never took part in the rebellion nor assisted the cause in any way. The high standards of the oath proved problematic in various southern localities where it was impossible to find a resident capable of qualifying as a registrar. Undoubtedly, in some instances the oath was finessed, and in numerous others, carpetbaggers (northern immigrants to the South) were made registrars.

It was also the case that in order to register to vote, an individual was required to swear an oath of loyalty to the Union (the oath closely tracked the provisions of Section 3 of the Fourteenth Amendment, which is displayed below). This oath, found in the second Reconstruction Act, made it clear that any resident who took an active role in the rebellion and/or held any of various legislative, judicial, or executive offices in the Confederacy, was ineligible to register. Of course, holding true to the letter of the law would result in wholesale disfranchisement of the native white southern population. In reality, a raft of exceptions and loopholes were exercised so that many otherwise disqualified ex-Confederates found their way onto the voter rolls. Nonetheless, the Reconstruction Acts fulfilled their purpose of crafting a southern electorate aligned with the Republican Party. Table 2.2 presents two important statistics: (1) the size of each southern state's population of black and white males twenty-one and older (voting age) in 1860 and (2) the number of registered black and white males in the wake of the 1867 Reconstruction Acts.

It is remarkable how much the composition of these southern state voting-age populations transformed as a consequence of registration. For instance, in Alabama a clear white majority (of course, nary a single southern black was voting in 1860) in 1860 became a solidly black registered electorate in 1867. And even in those states (like in Arkansas and North Carolina) where the white majority was maintained, albeit substantially reduced, the majority of voters were decidedly Republican-leaning, thanks to a coalition of southern blacks loyal to the party of Lincoln, Republican carpetbaggers, and the segment of scalawags (native white southerners committed to the Union and GOP) who disproportionately resided in southern Appalachia (e.g., most prominently the mountain Republicans of East Tennessee and Western North Carolina).

Not surprisingly, in addition to Alabama, in the Deep South states of Louisiana, Mississippi, and South Carolina, registered black majorities foretold the most aggressive and violent white response to Reconstruction. It was in these states that the number of black officeholders was most prominent. Still, only in South Carolina did African Americans ever comprise a majority Republican state government, and due

TABLE 2.2 ■ Altering the Composition of the Southern Electorate

State	Number of White and Black Males 21 or Older (1860 Census)			Composition of Registered Electorate in 1868		
	Whites	Blacks	Comments	Whites	Blacks	Comments
Alabama	113,871	92,404	Probably safely white.	61,295	104,518	Fair white majority lost entirely.
Arkansas	70,852	22,633	Safely white.	33,047	21,207	Huge white majority cut down.
Florida	18,511	13,504	Probably safely white.	11,914	16,089	Fair white majority lost entirely.
Georgia	127,303	92,995	Probably safely white.	96,333	95,168	Good white majority almost lost.
Louisiana	94,711	92,502	Disfranchisement could Africanize.	45,218	84,436	Small white majority lost entirely.
Mississippi	80,051	89,963	Disfranchisement could Africanize.	47,434	62,091	Black majority increased.
North Carolina	138,136	71,355	Safely white.	106,721	72,932	Still safely white.
South Carolina	65,610	84,393	Safely black.	46,882	80,550	Still safely black.
Texas	103,500	36,215	Safely white.	59,633	49,497	White majority cut seriously.
Virginia	156,061	114,608	Probably safely white.	120,101	105,832	White majority endangered.

Source: Data (including comments) were reproduced from two separate tables in Russ (1934, 177).

Note: Although Russ (1934) does not emphasize this point, it must be the case that the substantial reduction in the white male registered electorate in 1868 is also directly attributable to Civil War casualties.

primarily to a sincere belief in political equality and an eye toward the consequences likely to ensue for disfranchising ex-Confederates, the black majority drew up a state constitution that tilted heavily in favor of universal male suffrage.

BOX 2.1   BLACK OFFICEHOLDERS DURING RECONSTRUCTION

During the brief period of Presidential Reconstruction (1865–1867) under Tennessean Andrew Johnson, black representation in officeholding was virtually nonexistent because the northern-led Congress (U.S. House and U.S. Senate) had not yet forced the southern states to open elective offices to African Americans. This changed with the onset of Radical Reconstruction that northern Republican members of Congress imposed on the southern states in the era of federal military control of Dixie that lasted from 1867 to 1876 (with the actual end date varying by state; see the note under Table 2.3).

The emergence of black officeholders during Reconstruction was truly a revolutionary occurrence. Although many of these officials were freeborn northern carpetbaggers, most of them were from the South and had been slaves prior to the Thirteenth Amendment's abolition of the peculiar institution. Further, due to such a small population of white Republican voters, the vast majority of black officeholders represented disproportionately black populations residing in the black-belt counties—the locus of the white ruling class that was responsible for inciting southern secession, ultimately ending Reconstruction, putting down the Populist Revolt of the 1890s, and successfully installing the Jim Crow system of legally enforced racial segregation (Key 1949).[1] Foner (1988, 355) put this remarkable development in perspective: "the spectacle of former slaves representing the Lowcountry rice kingdom or the domain of Natchez cotton nabobs epitomized the political revolution wrought by Reconstruction." Not surprisingly, for many of these black officeholders, their willingness to serve came with a costly physical price. More than 10 percent were the victims of violence, and the bulk of these assaults (roughly 80 percent) were committed in the Deep South states of Georgia, Louisiana, Mississippi, and South Carolina, which contained a large share of black-belt counties (Foner 1993, xxviii).

According to Foner (1993), during Reconstruction there were close to 2,000 African Americans who held public office in the southern states, with only fifteen affiliated with the Democratic Party; the vast remainder served as Republicans. And despite the mark of slavery afflicting most of them in the recent past, a clear majority of black officeholders were literate and accomplished in various occupations before their time spent as public servants. Nonetheless, in every southern state, white (typically northern) Republicans held the reigns of political power for the duration of Reconstruction. However, blacks in South Carolina comprised the majority of state house representatives during Reconstruction and accounted for about half of the state senate membership from 1872 to 1876 (Foner 1993, xiii).[2]

Table 2.3 presents data on the number of black officeholders during Reconstruction for each southern state who served in the U.S. Congress, state legislature (state senate and state house), major state offices, and every office at any level (federal, state, and local). These data are from Foner (1993), who indicates that he was able to account for almost 1,500 of the approximately 2,000 black officeholders who served during

(Continued)

(Continued)

TABLE 2.3 ■ Black Officeholders in the Reconstruction Era, 1867–1876					
State (end date)	Congress	State Senate	State House	State Office	Any Office
AL (1874)	3	5	66	0	167
AR (1874)	0	5	22	3	46
FL (1876)	1	12	36	2	58
GA (1871)	1	6	43	0	108
LA (1876)	1	22	105	7	210
MS (1875)	3	13	102	8	226
NC (1876)	1	10	48	0	180
SC (1876)	6	29	210	8	314
TN (1870)	0	0	0	0	20
TX (1873)	0	2	15	0	46
VA (1873)	0	8	36	0	85
Total	16	112	683	28	1,460

Source: All data are from Foner (1993).

Note: The "end date" for each state denotes when the Democratic Party regained its governing majority by controlling the governorship and both chambers of the state legislature. The total number of black officeholders does include some instances of double counting because a handful of representatives were elected in two states, and with regard to those holding a major state office (and other offices), some held more than one position at different times over the course of their careers (e.g., the only African American to hold a major state office in Florida was Jonathan C. Gibbs, who was superintendent of education and also secretary of state; thus the total equals two state officeholders for the Sunshine State). The major state offices considered by Foner (1993, xvi) and the states that had at least one black officeholder representing it during Reconstruction are governor (LA), lieutenant governor (LA, MS, SC), treasurer (LA, SC), superintendent of education (AR, FL, LA, MS), secretary of state (FL, LA, MS, SC), supreme court (SC), and state commissioner (AR, MS, SC).

Reconstruction. Of the sixteen black members of Congress, two were U.S. Senators, both of Mississippi: Blanche K. Bruce and Hiram Revels. Of the African Americans identified as holding a major state office, one briefly served as governor of Louisiana (P. B. S. Pinchback), six were lieutenant governors, two were treasurers, four were superintendents of education, nine were secretaries of state, five were state commissioners, and one served on a state supreme court (Jonathan J. Wright of South Carolina).[3] In the two states with the greatest number of black officeholders, Mississippi and South Carolina, four African American state legislators rose to the position of speaker of the house: John R. Lynch and Isaac D. Shadd in the Mississippi State House and Robert B. Elliott and Samuel J. Lee in the South Carolina State House.[4]

After Reconstruction ended in each southern state, with white Democrats native to the region winning a majority of state legislative seats and occupying the governorship (a process referred to as "Redemption," and hence these native white southerners were dubbed "the redeemers"), the number of black officeholders dropped considerably, but it did not happen all at once. The decline in black officeholders occurred at a rate reflecting the institutionalization of Jim Crow laws (Foner 1993). The removal of black voters from the southern electorate necessarily ensured the removal of black office-holders. Republican George Henry White of North Carolina was the last black member of Congress to serve in a southern state until after the Voting Rights Act was passed in 1965 (Justesen 2001). His tenure ended in 1901. Recognizing the writing on the wall, near the end of his farewell address to Congress, Representative White spoke these words, "This, Mr. Chairman, is perhaps the negroes' temporary farewell to the American Congress; but let me say, Phoenix-like he will rise up some day and come again."[5]

---

1. Given their much smaller black populations, this primarily explains why the lowest number of black officeholders resided in the Peripheral South states of Arkansas, Tennessee, and Texas (see Table 2.3).

2. As a reference point, during Reconstruction the South Carolina State Senate contained 31 members from 1868–1871 and 33 members from 1872–1876; the South Carolina State House contained 124 members (the same number to this day; see Dubin 2007, 170).

3. Perhaps to no surprise, among the major state offices, the highest number of African Americans occupied the least influential position, secretary of state, which Foner (1988) characterized as "essentially ceremonial" (354).

4. There was a fair amount of circulation among black officeholders. For instance, state house speakers John R. Lynch (MS) and Robert B. Elliott (SC) also served as U.S. House Represen-tatives in their respective state delegations.

5. The full text of Congressman White's farewell address is available online (http://docsouth .unc.edu/nc/whitegh/whitegh.html).

Given the American system of federalism, the efficacy of the Reconstruction Acts varied widely, depending on the state. For instance, as Table 2.2 shows, Georgia was the only Deep South state that kept a registered white voting majority. The Peach State simply refused to carry out the disfranchisement provisions of the Reconstruction Acts (Russ 1935). Even so, the registered white population was drastically reduced because so many whites declined to register (a common occurrence throughout the South). In short, the implementation of voter registration became the first line of defense for mold-ing a Republican electorate in the South. But this Republican bulwark exhibited variable strength, based on its application in each of the southern states. This was particularly the case once voters chose delegates to constitutional conventions that would then determine voter qualifications anew, in accordance with the provisions established in those state con-stitutions. A lengthy passage from Foner (1988, 323–324) summarizes the situation nicely:

> Many Republicans could not reconcile their party's democratic rhetoric with proposals to strip large numbers of "rebels" of the vote. Although upcountry scalawags, especially those who had suffered for their Unionist beliefs or

hailed from areas devastated by the South's internal civil war, supported disenfranchisement most vehemently, the issue followed no simple pattern, for it became embroiled in Republican divisions over the party's prospects of attracting white voters. Five states disenfranchised few or no Confederates: Georgia, Florida, and Texas, where moderates committed to luring white Conservatives into the party controlled the [convention] proceedings; South Carolina, with its overwhelming black voting majority; and North Carolina, where the party's white base appeared firm. (North Carolina's mountain delegates, however, objected to their constitution's leniency.) Alabama and Arkansas barred from voting men disqualified from office under the Fourteenth Amendment as well as those who had "violated the rules of civilized warfare" during the Civil War, and required all voters to take an oath acknowledging black civil and political equality. Even this was not enough for one delegate from the strife-torn Arkansas upcountry, who "would have disfranchised every one of them." Louisiana, where the likelihood of white support appeared bleak, disenfranchised Confederates from newspaper editors and ministers who had advocated disunion to those who had voted for the secession ordinance, but exempted men willing to swear to an oath favoring Radical Reconstruction. Mississippi and Virginia, to the chagrin of Whiggish Republicans, also barred considerable numbers of "rebels" from voting.

The key provision of the Fourteenth Amendment, which became the stumbling block for southern states' readmission to the Union, is found in Section 3:

> No person shall be a Senator or Representative in Congress, or elector of President and Vice President, or hold any office, civil or military, under the United States, or under any State, who, having previously taken an oath, as a member of Congress, or as an officer of the United States, or as a member of any State legislature, or as an executive or judicial officer of any State, to support the Constitution of the United States, shall have engaged in insurrection or rebellion against the same, or given aid or comfort to the enemies thereof. But Congress may by a vote of two-thirds of each House, remove such disability.

The provisions in this section of the Fourteenth Amendment are explicitly designed to disqualify ex-Confederate leaders from holding office, and these restrictions/disabilities often served as the basis for preventing southern whites from registering to vote. Thus, this passage of the Fourteenth Amendment was intended to prevent the old guard from returning to political power (i.e., black-belt planters). As mentioned above, however, at the stage of writing new state constitutions, the severity of voting (and officeholding) qualifications were highly variable. Yet, none of the ten southern states enduring military Reconstruction could openly disavow the direct purpose of Section 3 of the Fourteenth Amendment (denying officeholding to southerners in positions of power who previously served the Confederacy) because it had to be approved by the state legislature as a condition of readmission to the United States.

BOX 2.2   SOUTHERN STATE CONSTITUTIONS

Given the conditions enforced for readmission to the Union, it is perhaps no surprise that southern states have a higher number of state constitutions. To be clear, at any moment in time, a state only has one approved and operating constitution, and historically southern states have enacted a higher total. In addition to creating new constitutions during Reconstruction, after Reconstruction ended and the erstwhile native white ruling class managed to "redeem" political power from northern carpetbaggers and their southern scalawag co-conspirators, additional state constitutions were drawn up throughout the southern states. Because of accusations of real and perceived abuses leveled upon southern Democrats by overzealous Reconstruction-era Republican governors, in most southern states the post-Reconstruction constitutions purposely weakened the power and autonomy of the executive branch.

For instance, Florida and Texas governors share power with several statewide elected members of the executive branch, including a very powerful lieutenant governor in the latter state (the Texas lieutenant governor essentially runs the state senate). Historically, the North Carolina governor was not given the veto power, and to this day the governor cannot veto redistricting plans drafted by the state legislature (in 2012, Republicans controlled the legislature and approved a congressional map that heavily favored their party, while the Democratic governor had no power to block the plan). As V. O. Key (1949) pointed out, South Carolina's state senators ruled the Palmetto State for most of the post-Reconstruction era because each of the state's forty-six counties was represented by a single senator (since 1918; see Dubin 2007, 171) who controlled their county's local politics and combined forces with other senators to prevent ambitious governors from achieving their political objectives.

Table 2.4 shows that compared to northern states, southern states have averaged three times as many constitutions (six versus two). Of course, many northern states were recently added to the Union (e.g., Alaska, Arizona, and Hawaii) and therefore have only had one constitution since achieving statehood. Nonetheless, southern states have considerably more constitutions, even if we narrowed the comparison to northern states as old as or older than their southern counterparts. Indeed, the highest number of state constitutions in a northern state is five, in Pennsylvania, one of the original thirteen colonies. By comparison, the younger southern state of Louisiana tops them all, with a total of eleven state constitutions.

Not only do southern states typically have a higher number of state constitutions because of the Civil War, Reconstruction, and the southern response to northern Republican rule, but their constitutions also tend to be much longer, and this is partly explained by the desire to limit the powers of the state government. That is, southern state constitutions use more words to explicitly constrain the power of elected officials. The median southern state constitution contains 42,100 words, about 60 percent more than in the median northern state constitution (at 26,360 words). At close to 400,000 total words, the Alabama Constitution is an extreme outlier. The Yellowhammer State has the world's longest constitution in existence today. Perhaps surprisingly, with respect to the median number of amendments, southern states and northern states do not exhibit any notable difference (122 versus 120), but Alabama sticks out again for far exceeding its counterparts with almost 900 changes to its current constitution.

TABLE 2.4 ■ Comparing Southern and Northern State Constitutions

State/Region	Total Constitutions	Length (Words)	Amendments
Alabama	6	388,882	892
Arkansas	5	65,700	102
Florida	6	43,514	122
Georgia	10	42,100	75
Louisiana	11	73,224	184
Mississippi	4	26,229	126
North Carolina	3	17,177	32
South Carolina	7	27,421	500
Tennessee	3	13,960	43
Texas	5	86,936	491
Virginia	6	21,899	49
South	Average = 6	Median = 42,100	Median = 122
North	Average = 2	Median = 26,360	Median = 120

Source: Data are from the Council of State Government's *2016 Book of the States* (http://knowledge center.csg.org/kc/content/book-states-2016-chapter-1-state-constitutions-0).

Table 2.5 shows the date each southern state approved the Fourteenth Amendment, the date of readmission to the Union, and the rank order of readmission (a lower number means an earlier readmission date). Tennessee, the only state to escape military Reconstruction, was readmitted almost two years before the next state (Arkansas) rejoined the Union. Perhaps not surprisingly, because of its outright defiance of the Reconstruction Acts, Georgia was actually readmitted twice; by the time of its second readmission, it was the last southern state to reenter the Union. With their readmission to the United States, the southern congressional delegation was once again seated as full-fledged voting members. Curiously though, despite their readmission, military Reconstruction was not lifted. Perhaps the fear of an impending Democratic majority, led by an increasingly unified southern Democracy, compelled northern Republicans to continue their martial oversight of Dixie, but as time passed it became evident that a Republican advantage was fast deteriorating. Further, the North grew weary and disenchanted of their investment in overseeing the South's public affairs. And soon, a presidential election would provide the opening to end the nation's boldest social experiment.

TABLE 2.5 ■ Approval of Fourteenth Amendment and Readmission to United States			
State	Fourteenth Amendment	Readmission Date	Order of Readmission
Alabama	July 13, 1868	July 13, 1868	6
Arkansas	April 6, 1868	June 22, 1868	2
Florida	June 9, 1868	June 25, 1868	3
Georgia	July 21, 1868	July 15, 1870	10
Louisiana	July 9, 1868	July 9, 1868	5 (same as SC)
Mississippi	January 17, 1870	February 23, 1870	8
North Carolina	July 4, 1868	July 4, 1868	4
South Carolina	July 9, 1868	July 9, 1868	5 (same as LA)
Tennessee	July 19, 1866	July 24, 1866	1
Texas	February 18, 1870	March 30, 1870	9
Virginia	October 8, 1869	January 26, 1870	7

Sources: Fourteenth Amendment approval dates were retrieved from www.14thamendment.us/amendment/14th_amendment.html. Readmission dates were retrieved from www.infoplease.com/ipa/A0194016.html.

Notes: The Fourteenth Amendment was ratified on July 9, 1868, after 28 of the 37 states approved it. Alabama, Georgia, Mississippi, Texas, and Virginia approved the amendment after it became law. The readmission date denotes the time of restoration of representation in the U.S. Congress. The second date for Georgia's readmission is displayed. Georgia was first readmitted on July 21, 1868, but its representatives were then unseated on March 5, 1869.

THE END OF RECONSTRUCTION

The greatest threat to Republican control of southern politics was the re-enfranchisement of native white southerners who overwhelmingly aligned with the Democratic Party and could not bring themselves to acknowledge the legislated and enforced equality of the races. The sheer size of this population of southerners placed white Republicans in a bind that offered little escape over the long run. As long as the share of "unreconstructed" southern whites participating in elections could be kept at bay, then the coalition of carpetbaggers, blacks, and scalawags would prevail. But southern whites disfranchised by the Reconstruction Acts refused to go away quietly. Between 1868 and 1871, the Ku Klux Klan executed a reign of terror that inflicted unspeakable physical and psychological damage upon targeted African Americans and whites aligned with the Reconstruction program. According to Foner (1988, 425), "the Klan was a military force serving the interests of the Democratic party, the planter class, and all those who desired the restoration of white supremacy." By 1872, President Grant's administration exhibited vigorous intervention and enforcement to finally quell this episode of the most pervasive domestic terrorism in the United States. As the violence tamped down, the road to Redemption, the term used to describe the return of the political system to southern whites opposed to Reconstruction, had become decidedly shorter.

As early as 1871, "only Arkansas among the reconstructed states still retained suffrage restrictions based on Civil War loyalties" (Foner 1988, 347). And a year later, Congress nullified virtually all of the Fourteenth Amendment disabilities serving as the basis for white disfranchisement.[9] The growing number of southern white Democrats participating in elections eventually overwhelmed Republican control, and where it did not, Republicans found it politically expedient to cut deals with the Democratic opposition as the only way to remain in power. The Democratic Redeemers were forcefully taking back their governments despite the continuing presence of northern Republican oversight of southern affairs. Indeed, as pointed out by Foner (1988, 539),

> As 1873 began, however, Republicans enjoyed undisputed control of state government only in Arkansas, Louisiana, Mississippi, and South Carolina. Tennessee, Georgia, and Virginia had been "redeemed," while in Alabama, Florida, North Carolina, and Texas, Republican governors confronted hostile or divided legislatures.

The 1874 midterm marked a stunning electoral reversal in the House of Representatives. Prior to the election, the Republican majority stood at 68 percent (199 out of 292 seats). After the 1874 contests, Democrats controlled 62 percent of House seats (182 out of 293).[10] More than any other factor, the GOP was punished for holding the reins of power when the economic panic broke out in 1873—an economic downturn that would last through the end of the decade. In the South, for the first time since the end of the Civil War, Democrats constituted a majority of the U.S. House delegation—a position they would hold until 1994. Despite the resounding Democratic victory in the 1874 House elections, in 1875 large-scale violence erupted in the Deep South states of Louisiana, Mississippi, and South Carolina. Democrats perpetrated vicious attacks on blacks and white Republicans who were bold enough to show up at the polling place.[11] And if intimidation failed to keep Republicans from the polls, then Democrats were satisfied with stuffing the ballot box in their favor. Mississippi fell to the Redeemers in 1875, mainly because of Democratic violence and electoral fraud that the Grant administration refused to counter (Foner 1988). Despite the rampant undermining of the democratic process in Louisiana and South Carolina, these states did not succumb to Democratic control—a result that would materialize one year later.

Although Reconstruction had, for all political intents and purposes, run its course in most southern states by the mid-1870s, the presidential election of 1876, and its politically motivated resolution in 1877, sounded its official death knell. Republicans nominated Rutherford Hayes and Democrats chose Samuel Tilden. The major parties monopolized the Electoral College, and the official outcome was 185 votes for Hayes versus 184 for Tilden. Out of more than eight million Democratic and Republican presidential ballots, the popular vote favored Tilden by a 252,666 margin, only adding to the controversy engulfing the contest. A dearth of honest election administration in numerous southern localities cast considerable doubt as to who really won. Specifically, along with Oregon, the electoral results in Florida, Louisiana, and South Carolina were in dispute. To win the White House, Hayes would need to prevail in all four states. Given the closeness of the race, a commission was formed in February of 1877 and its job was to finally decide the victor. In the interim between Election Day and the final decision rendered by the commission, a deal was struck. In exchange for ending what remained of Reconstruction in the South, southern Democrats were agreeable to the Republican Hayes winning the presidency. Hence, the commission awarded the electoral votes of Florida, Louisiana, Oregon, and South Carolina to Hayes, which resulted in his one-vote margin Electoral College victory.

AN UNSTABLE INTERLUDE

There are two widely held myths surrounding the period following the end of Reconstruction. First, that once the northern occupation of the South ended as a result of the 1877 compromise, the Jim Crow system of racial segregation immediately took hold. Second, and closely tied to the first myth, that Jim Crow was a southern invention. In *The Strange Career of Jim Crow* (2002), C. Vann Woodward busted both of these myths. On the first point, it took decades for the Democratic Redeemers to implement the elaborate set of laws that disfranchised African Americans. On the second, Jim Crow originated in the North, not in the South. With the exception of the border states of Delaware, Kentucky, Maryland, and Missouri, northern abolition of slavery was nearly absolute twenty years before the Civil War. Although they were generally free to choose their occupation in the marketplace, in most northern states African Americans were denied suffrage, and in various settings their movements were restricted by ordinances enforcing racial segregation.[12]

The return of southern state governments to the hands of white Democrats did not guarantee Democratic hegemony and certainly not into perpetuity—a condition desired by the recently reinstated native white elites who generally resided in the black belt. For this best possible political scenario to be realized, it became clear that blacks would have to be disfranchised because their overwhelming preference for the GOP undermined Democratic rule. The continuing presence of the black vote was an obvious affront to the establishment of a white supremacist southern Democracy. Further, the black vote was often pivotal—holding the balance of power between Republicans and Democrats. White Republicans also had to consider the complicated presence of black voters. African Americans naturally aligned with the Republican Party, but some GOP leaders actually sought the support of white

Democrats if they believed such a coalition was possible while still allowing the GOP to retain the upper hand. But this sort of alienation of the black vote could back-fire, with African Americans actually shifting their support to white Democrats if they were promised a better deal. If, instead, white Republicans cultivated the black vote—the most common strategy—it typically resulted in wholesale rejection of support from white Democrats, who refused to enter such a coalition. If the black vote was necessary to control offices, then white Democrats might seek it through persuasive promises or blatant ballot fraud.

In short, the large presence of African American voters injected instability into southern electoral politics. For the GOP, black voters contributed to the party's political viability. For Democrats, black voters made the dream of a one-party Solid South unattainable. With the close of Reconstruction, southern Democrats bus-ied themselves with shaping a political system that would ultimately revoke black suffrage and, thereafter, lead to an easy victory over the smaller segment of white Republicans. Such a plan was certainly not preordained nor a foregone conclusion. As Woodward (2002) argued, the success of Jim Crow was decades in the making and events could have led to alternative political outcomes, especially if the North had instead chosen to intervene in southern affairs as opposed to turning its back on the wanton undermining of black civil rights.

As late as 1898, South Carolina had yet to succumb to the complete separation of the races in all customs and places of public accommodation. The Charleston *News and Courier* editor made a mockery of the notion that Jim Crow would someday overwhelm all aspects of race relations, by penning the following (presumed) far-fetched scenario:

> If there must be Jim Crow cars on the railroads, there should be Jim Crow cars on the street railways. Also on all passenger boats. . . . If there are to be Jim Crow cars, moreover, there should be Jim Crow waiting saloons at all stations, and Jim Crow eating houses. . . . There should be Jim Crow sections of the jury box, and a separate Jim Crow dock and witness stand in every court—and a Jim Crow Bible for colored witnesses to kiss. It would be advisable to also have a Jim Crow section in county auditors' and treasurers' offices for the accommodation of colored taxpayers. The two races are dreadfully mixed in these offices for weeks every year, especially about Christmas. . . . There should be a Jim Crow department for making returns and paying for the privileges and blessings of citizenship. Perhaps, the best plan would be, after all, to take the short cut to the general end . . . by establishing two or three Jim Crow counties at once, and turning them over to our colored citizens for their special and exclusive accommodation. (Woodward 2002, 68)

But as Woodward pointed out, almost the entirety of the editor's intended elabo-rate hyperbole came to fruition.

In resorting to the tactics of *reductio ad absurdum* the editor doubtless
believed that he had dealt the Jim Crow principle a telling blow with his
heavy irony. But there is now apparent to us an irony in his argument of
which the author was unconscious . . . Apart from the Jim Crow counties
and Jim Crow witness stand, all the improbable applications of the principle
suggested by the editor in derision had been put into practice—down to
and including the Jim Crow Bible. (Woodward 2002, 68–69)

POPULIST THREAT AND ITS REMOVAL

In the 1890s, when Democrats had made considerable progress in legislating into
existence a Jim Crow South, another threat emerged. Starting with farmers in
east Texas and soon spreading throughout various sections of Dixie and across the
Midwest and western United States, an agrarian movement took hold and threatened redistribution and economic relief for indebtedness exacerbated by the financial
panic of 1893. In its most successful political form, the unrest of organized farmers manifested itself in the Populist Party. The Populist movement or, as a leading
scholar of the phenomenon fittingly labeled it, *The Populist Moment* (Goodwyn
1978), did not have staying power but it was the last significant obstacle to the construction of a one-party Democratic Solid South.

Similar to the ruling class predating Reconstruction and the one emerging after
its conclusion, the southern political hierarchy resembled a pyramid in which only
those situated within the narrower top (the "haves") controlled the vast mass of
blacks and whites residing within the broader base (the "have-nots"). Populism, if
it were to take hold, could prove the greatest threat to Democratic hegemony, particularly where its adherents were willing to form biracial coalitions. The unification
of impoverished black and white farmers and laborers could easily overwhelm the
core of southern Democratic adherents consisting primarily of planters, merchants,
businessmen, and other professionals (e.g., doctors and lawyers). Indeed, nothing
would upend Democratic rule faster and more resoundingly than the embrace of
poor blacks and whites organizing under a single party label. This worst-case scenario never materialized because most African Americans and a smaller number of
whites continued to seek representation from the GOP. Nonetheless, the influence of
Populism was great enough to bring about fusion tickets, particularly when southern
Republicans and Populists would unite behind a single candidate.

Nationally, in the 51st Congress (1889–1891) only Democrats and Republicans
populated the Senate, whereas the House of Representatives contained only one
member not affiliated with the Democratic or Republican parties—a Labor Party
adherent. From the 52nd Congress (1891–1893) to the 57th Congress (1901–1903),
a total of 60 members who ran under the Populist Party label served in the House of
Representatives while 21 served in the Senate. By the 58th Congress (1903–1905)
not a single Populist remained.[13]

The Populist intervention peaked in 1896 when a true believer, William Jennings Bryan, managed to secure the Democratic presidential nomination (Bensel 2008). His opponent for the open presidential contest was Republican William McKinley. Bryan sought to assemble a majority coalition consisting of the working class from northeastern cities and farmers from the Midwest, West, and South. With a severely diminished Republican presidential presence in the South, Bryan swept Dixie's electoral votes and those of the interior West. But the workers of the more populous Northeast and parts of the upper Midwest did not unite behind Bryan; rather, these most vote-rich sections coalesced in favor of McKinley, delivering him the White House and in the process delivering a mortal blow to the farmers' movement.

The 1896 popular presidential vote was competitive: 51 percent for McKinley and 47 percent for Bryan (out of 13,622,945 Democratic and Republican votes). The Electoral College vote was not: 61 percent for McKinley (271 votes) and 39 percent for Bryan (176 votes). Some scholars (e.g., Burnham 1970) have interpreted the 1896 contest as a critical election because it solidified the partisan divide between the North and South, strengthening Republican loyalties in the former region and further steeling Democratic fealty in the South. The irony is that most southern Democrats did not welcome the populist agenda of William Jennings Bryan; it was as though he hijacked the Democratic presidential ticket because, at least in Dixie, the Democratic Party was actively involved in extinguishing the Populist Party. So, despite the fact that the 1896 presidential election polarized the partisan divide between the North and South, within the South, 1896 marked the apex of Populism, a height from which it would quickly topple.

In the 1896 gubernatorial election in Texas, the birthplace of southern Populism, "the Populist candidate for governor in that year polled the highest vote of any candidate in the party's history, 44.2 per cent of the total" (Key 1949, 534). And seventeen third-party candidates who aligned with the Populist movement won southern U.S. House elections. But just four years later, southern Populism, especially in the form of a party label for contesting elections, was swiftly passing from the scene. For instance, in 1900, the southern U.S. House delegation contained zero members espousing the Populist Party label. Its ninety-two members included four Republicans and eighty-eight Democrats. To be sure, at the turn of the twentieth century, southern Populism was not wholly moribund because many sympathetic to its principles simply ran as Democrats. Additionally, the Democratic Party coopted the Populist agenda in those parts of the South where the movement's ideas remained popular.

SUMMARY OF A MOST POLITICALLY VOLATILE PERIOD

This section summarizes (primarily in graphical form) the general patterns of electoral change taking place in the South from 1868 to 1900. The purpose of this review is to show the movement from a brief Republican-advantaged period to the eventual realization of a Solid South under nearly complete Democratic control. Figure 2.3

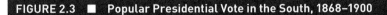

FIGURE 2.3 ■ **Popular Presidential Vote in the South, 1868–1900**

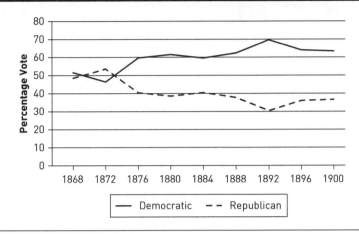

Source: Data compiled by the author from Dave Leip's *Atlas of U.S. Presidential Elections* (http://uselection atlas.org/RESULTS/).

tracks the popular presidential vote (two-party) in the South from 1868 to 1900. Interestingly, the popular vote slightly favored the Democratic Party in 1868, in the midst of Reconstruction. Only in 1872 does the GOP win the southern presidential vote. After 1872, the difference in support of the major parties considerably widens and Democratic ascendancy becomes readily apparent. For the last four contests (1888–1900) the Democratic share of the popular presidential vote is above 60 percent and just under 70 percent in 1892.

Table 2.6 presents presidential election data based on the votes cast in the Electoral College (EC). The picture looks very different from the popular vote, strongly favoring the GOP in the South in 1868 and 1872, awarding Grant 72 and 62 percent of the EC vote in these respective contests. In 1876, the last Reconstruction election, Democratic strength is on full display—even with the EC votes of Florida, Louisiana, and South Carolina going to Hayes—80 percent of the southern EC votes are won by Tilden. After 1876, Dixie assumes its status as a Democratic bastion in southern presidential elections, granting all of its EC votes to the Democratic nominee from 1880 through 1900. The solidarity of the southern Democratic presidential vote contributes to an increasingly competitive national scene as Cleveland wins in two of his three consecutive runs for the White House.

Table 2.7 tracks the presence of Populists in southern state legislatures between 1890 and 1900. In state legislatures, Populism is completely absent in 1890, but then it shows up two years later in six southern states. Alabama, in particular, experienced a notable uptick in Populist lawmakers that would gradually fade by 1900. Interestingly, in the most race-conscious states, Mississippi and South Carolina (which had the highest percentage of black residents), not one Populist served in the state legislature. Populists were most successful in North Carolina, where briefly

TABLE 2.6 ■ Electoral College Votes in the South, 1868–1900

Election	Democrat	Republican	Dem % (Votes)	Winner
1868	H. Seymour	U. Grant	28 (57)	Republican
1872	H. Greeley	U. Grant	38 (81)	Republican
1876	S. Tilden	R. Hayes	80 (95)	Republican
1880	W. Hancock	J. Garfield	100 (95)	Republican
1884	G. Cleveland	J. Blaine	100 (107)	Democrat
1888	G. Cleveland	B. Harrison	100 (107)	Republican
1892	G. Cleveland	B. Harrison	100 (112)	Democrat
1896	W. Bryan	W. McKinley	100 (112)	Republican
1900	W. Bryan	W. McKinley	100 (112)	Republican

Source: Data compiled by the author from Dave Leip's *Atlas of U.S. Presidential Elections* (http://uselection atlas.org/RESULTS/).

TABLE 2.7 ■ Populists in Southern State Legislatures, 1890–1900

State	1890	1892	1894	1896	1898	1900
Alabama	0 | 0	21 | 38	24 | 34	27 | 23	15 | 10	3 | 6
Arkansas	0 | 0	6 | 9	3 | 9	3 | 13	0 | 0	0 | 1
Florida	0 | 0	0 | 0	3 | 0	3 | 0	0 | 0	0 | 0
Georgia	0 | 0	2 | 6	11 | 27	14 | 17	0 | 3	0 | 5
Louisiana	0 | 0	0 | 0	0 | 0	3 | 14	0 | 0	0 | 0
Mississippi	0 | 0	0 | 0	0 | 0	0 | 0	0 | 0	0 | 0
North Carolina	0 | 0	6 | 8	48 | 30	48 | 29	20 | 22	6 | 2
South Carolina	0 | 0	0 | 0	0 | 0	0 | 0	0 | 0	0 | 0
Tennessee	0 | 0	3 | 5	9 | 7	0 | 4	0 | 0	0 | 0
Texas	0 | 0	3 | 6	6 | 17	6 | 5	0 | 7	0 | 1
Virginia	0 | 0	0 | 0	0 | 12	3 | 0	0 | 0	0 | 0

Source: Data compiled by the author from Dubin (2007).

Notes: Entries show the percentage of the state senate and state house, respectively (and separated by a vertical line), that consists of Populist legislators. For instance, in 1894 in Alabama, Populists were 24 percent of the state senate and 34 percent of the state house (24 | 34). For most states, the data correspond on the even year at two-year intervals, but this is not true for Louisiana (even years spaced out by four-year intervals), Mississippi (odd years spaced out by two- and then four-year intervals), and Virginia (odd years spaced out by two-year intervals). The data for Mississippi and Virginia match the odd year that precedes the even year in these states (e.g., 1897 corresponds with 1896). In Louisiana, 1896 was an even year with recorded data, and there were no Populists recorded before (in 1888 and 1892) and after this year (in 1900).

they fused with Republicans to gain control of the legislature and the governorship. In 1894 and 1896, Populists were a strong plurality of the North Carolina Senate (48 percent in both years). Indeed, so successful was the coalition of Populists and Republicans in North Carolina that Democrats halted their brief reign by executing a violent reprisal. Most notorious was the 1898 Wilmington race riot, in which white Democrats used deadly force to wrest political power from local black Republicans (Cecelski and Tyson 1998; Woodward 2002).

Figure 2.4 shows the percentage of U.S. House seats held by Democrats and Republicans out of the entire southern congressional delegation. The benefit of examining data on the House of Representatives is that the entire body faces an election every two years, which provides a sensitive barometer for assessing political change. Unlike the House, not only were Senators not popularly elected until 1913 (Seventeenth Amendment), the much smaller number of Senators and their longer terms (six years) results in a poor gauge of electoral dynamics. The Republican advantage in southern House elections is evident during most of the Reconstruction period (1868–1872). Nonetheless, even in these years Republicans did not dominate the southern delegation. Between 1872 and 1874, the Democratic seat share vaulted from 17 to almost 70 percent. After 1872, the Republican presence in southern House elections exhibits a pronounced decline until around 1878, when thereafter the GOP is no longer a viable opposition to the Democratic Party. Southern Democrats gradually build upon their impressive 1874 performance until the 1896 elections, when Populist candidates put a dent in Democratic hegemony, dropping their seat share below 80 percent for

FIGURE 2.4 ■ Southern U.S. House Seats Controlled by the Major Parties, 1868–1900

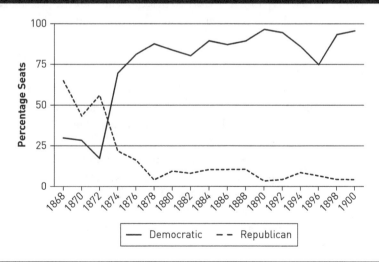

Source: Data compiled by the author from CQ Press (2005).

Note: The percentage of Democratic and Republican seats is out of the total southern U.S. House seats.

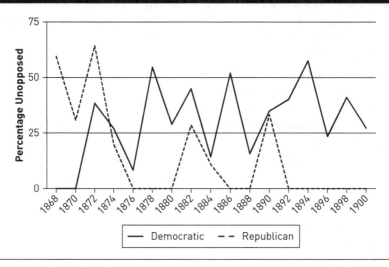

FIGURE 2.5 ■ Unopposed Southern U.S. House Seats, 1868–1900

— Democratic   – – Republican

Source: Data compiled by the author from CQ Press (2005).

the first time since 1874. The Democratic rebound is substantial in 1898 (93 percent) and reaches more than 95 percent in 1900, signaling the advent of a Solid South.

Figure 2.5 presents another way to assess electoral competition, by displaying the percentage of unopposed southern House seats held by the major parties. *Unopposed* is defined as the absence of a major party opponent (Democrat or Republican) in the general election. Bear in mind that the GOP holds a small number of southern House seats after 1876 (typically less than 10 percent), and thus the percentage of unopposed GOP seats is out of a modest total. The jagged pattern of unopposed seats closely tracks on-year (presidential) and off-year (midterm) elections, with midterms generally translating into more unopposed races. During the first three Reconstruction-era elections (1868 to 1872), Republicans were the beneficiaries of a higher percentage of unopposed contests. But after 1872, Democrats always possess a higher percentage of races without an opponent, and this is true even though Democrats hold the lion's share of House seats. From 1892 to 1900, all of the southern Republican House seats are contested.

Figure 2.6 concludes this section with a comparative examination of participation in House elections. Specifically, the turnout percentage in northern and southern House elections is tracked from 1868 to 1900. The turnout rate is a particularly important indicator of the health of electoral competition because it is generally higher when the major parties are more competitive. Similar to Figure 2.5, the zigzag pattern closely follows presidential and midterm years and unsurprisingly, turnout is higher in presidential years. In 1868–1870, turnout is higher in northern House races, but from 1870 to 1875 the regional gap is negligible. With the end of Reconstruction

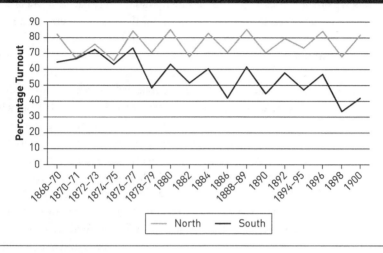

FIGURE 2.6   ■   **U.S. House Turnout in the North and South, 1868–1900**

Source: Data compiled by the author from Burnham (2010).

in 1876–1877, a clear pattern emerges, with the northern turnout rate maintaining a steady level in the 70 and 80 percentiles, whereas the southern turnout rate embarks on a gradual and substantial descent. In 1900, the North-South gap (39.8 percentage points) in House turnout reached its widest for the entire span of elections. This gap would become even more pronounced in the coming years as the southern Democracy essentially locked down its one-party system. Hence, the notable decline in southern House turnout is strongly reflective of Democratic dominance—the dearth of two-party competition translates into a reduction in participation.

CONCLUDING THOUGHTS

Congressional Reconstruction in the South was a truly radical social, economic, and political undertaking. It is remarkable to comprehend the revolutionary changes affecting southern blacks, almost all of whom were slaves before their freedom was secured by the Thirteenth Amendment in 1865. And thanks to vigorous enforcement of the Fourteenth and Fifteenth Amendments, for a brief period African Americans were not only exercising the franchise but also winning elective offices in state and federal contests. This progress was all the more impressive because in "1868, only eight Northern states allowed blacks to vote" (Foner 1988, 448). For a short time it did, indeed, appear as though the bottom rail had ascended to the top. But even as Reconstruction began, "a North Carolina Democrat" proved prescient: "When the bayonets shall depart . . . then look out for the reaction. Then the bottom rail will descend from the top of the fence" (Foner 1988, 588).

Reconstruction was doomed from within and from without. Internally, southern Democrats had no intentions of going away quietly and taking a backseat to a biracial Republican coalition of blacks, carpetbaggers, and scalawags. Southern Democrats' rapid re-enfranchisement—as a consequence of generally accommodating, newly written state constitutions—directly undermined the desire of northern Republicans to maintain a southern party system controlled by the GOP. If sheer numbers in the political arena were not enough to defeat Republicans, then extra-constitutional means were generously employed, especially violence and election fraud. From without, the North tired of enforcing the Reconstruction Acts and exercising martial law to quell disturbances. Over time, legal enforcement became less and less forthcoming, and by the time of President Grant's second term, the Republican North had become more interested in its own problems, particularly labor strife (Foner 1988).

With the end of Reconstruction secured by the bargain struck in 1877, the Redeemers busied themselves with the monumental task of locking down the political system in favor of a one-party Democratic Solid South. As discussed, it took more than two decades to remove black voters from the electorate and relegate them, in almost every way, to a second-class citizenship (Woodward 2002). And just as things appeared increasingly promising for the Redeemers and their allies, in the mid-1890s the Populist movement briefly derailed the advancement of Democratic hegemony. Because of their lengthy experience countering Republican power, southern Democrats were prepared in their response to the Populist threat and resorted to the same playbook for neutralizing the farmers' revolt: a heavy dose of intimidation, violence, and election fraud and sometimes even social ostracism (Key 1949, 553). The particulars of ushering in a Solid South will be covered at greater length in the next chapter.

3 DEMOCRATIC PAST

From the turn of the century until 1948, rarely was there a political disturbance that generated any formidable challenge to the Solid South. For almost half a century, Democratic dominance below the Mason-Dixon Line was practically absolute. Nonetheless, various developments emerged that would eventually contribute to the end of this era of southern Democracy. Most telling was the spread of Democratic strength to the North. The antithetical views on the race issue among large segments of the Democratic North versus those held by their southern Democratic counterparts gave rise to an uneasy and, ultimately, unsustainable voting coalition. Elites, especially those seeking the greatest prize, the presidency, had the platform and influence to jeopardize a national Democratic majority. Democratic President Truman accomplished as much by cultivating the votes of northern blacks, which of course stirred up many white southerners. This action permanently split the New Deal Coalition and concomitantly opened the door to a revival of the long-moribund GOP in southern presidential politics.

But before explaining how the national growth of the Democratic Party actually served to unravel the Solid South, this chapter begins with a discussion of how this political system was made possible. As discussed in chapter 2, locking down a one-party system was a formidable task, and this chapter explains the primary mechanisms shaping and undergirding the Solid South. The foundation for the Solid South was strong but never secure. As in the past, if the North found a reason to intervene in southern affairs, then its Democratic system would be imperiled. By the late 1940s, the North, specifically a northern president, decided it was time to threaten the white supremacist political status quo. Since 1948, the path to a two-party South had presented itself, and it started at the top, in presidential elections.

ORIGINS OF THE SOLID SOUTH

There is a disagreement concerning whether disfranchisement directly accounts for the dominance of southern Democrats. One perspective, advanced by Key (1949), suggests that the one-party system was already taking shape in advance of legally enforced disfranchisement measures. Citing the case of Texas, Key shows that one of the cardinal features of the Solid South, low participation, had already set in prior to the state's passage of a poll tax. The argument, then, would seem to be that intimidation, violence, and ballot fraud already were having the intended effect of closing off the political system so that those opposed to Democratic rule had tired of actively resisting the party's increasing hold over public affairs.[1] Indeed, Key viewed Democratic dominance as attaining a point where it amounted to a fait accompli–essentially a foregone conclusion that was only later fortified by a raft of disfranchisement laws.

> The evolution of suffrage restrictions differed from state to state, for some, perhaps even for all, southern states the thesis could be argued plausibly that formal disfranchisement measures did not lie at the bottom of the decimation of the southern electorate. They, rather, recorded a fait accompli brought about, or destined to be brought about, by more fundamental political processes. (Key 1949, 533)

There is a chicken-and-egg conundrum regarding the dynamic of the Democratic takeover. For instance, how was it possible for the various disfranchisement laws to pass if Democrats were not already in control of the system? And yet it seems clear, even according to Key, that most southerners, whites included, opposed these restrictive voting measures. The political historian J. Morgan Kousser disputes Key's fait accompli thesis.[2] According to his version of an impending Solid South, disfranchisement became the ultimate means to ensure Democratic control. Prior to disfranchisement, throughout the South, Democrats faced a pesky opposition in the form of Republicans and Populists (e.g., as shown by a slew of data on gubernatorial elections). Further, "extensive violence, intimidation, fraud, or a small but sufficient change in the election laws preceded passage of all major statutes and amendments" (Kousser 1974, 246). To be sure, intimidation, violence, and ballot fraud were very effective in securing a Democratic advantage, but these tactics would have to be employed over and over again, so long as resistance cropped up. Finally, such methods were obviously illegitimate and their repeated usage cast doubt on the integrity of the political system.

According to Kousser (1974), the advent of a Solid South was anything but a fait accompli because the opposition to the Democratic Party did not go away quietly. Instead, Democrats repeatedly engaged in extralegal activity to keep the opposition at bay. Besides creating the impression of instant respectability, legal disfranchisement was the most efficient and permanent way to neutralize opposition to Democratic rule. This argument is plausible because in the absence of disfranchisement it would have been impossible to contain various political uprisings that might flair up in response to Democratic governance. In other words, reliance on legal forms of disfranchisement ensured the greatest amount of electoral stability (Aldrich 1995) because it provided the most control over limiting the size of the voting electorate. Kousser (1974) argued that disfranchisement laws were an integral component for not only making a Solid South possible, but thereafter, perpetuating it for decades to come. In opposition to Key, Kousser had this to say:

To a degree, Key's fait accompli hypothesis merely states a tautology: any statute passed by any legislative body reflects the structure of power at the time. If blacks and other advocates of widespread political participation had not been somewhat suppressed already, the disfranchisers could not have pushed their laws through the assemblies. (1974, 3)

Denying that acquiescence and capitulation by the opposition had set in prior to legal disfranchisement, Kousser argued instead that

It was not necessary for the disfranchisers to decimate the opposition and end Negro voting entirely before disfranchisement. Rather, they had somehow to reduce dissent to whatever point it took to push a law through the legislature, pass an amendment at a referendum, or call a constitutional convention. (1974, 243)

A close examination of Key's (1949) and Kousser's (1974) explanations for the origins of the Solid South actually generate considerable nuance and agreement, especially with respect to the motivations and goals of the disfranchisers. The sticking point centers on the extent to which disfranchisement accounts for the hallmark features of the Solid South: low participation, rampant factionalism, poor representation, and unrivaled Democratic control. Kousser would say disfranchisement was the linchpin and Key would hedge.

We cannot resolve this disagreement over the extent to which disfranchisement was part and parcel to the making of the Solid South. But there is no denying that legal disfranchisement was the final step in the construction of Democratic hegemony. Fortunately, Key (1949) and Kousser (1974) were masterful in their accounts of disfranchisement, a process that began in the 1890s and ended in the early 1900s.

Five southern states (Alabama, Louisiana, Mississippi—it went first in 1890—South Carolina, and Virginia) held constitutional conventions for the purpose of passing disfranchisement legislation. The remaining six (Arkansas, Florida, Georgia, North Carolina, Tennessee, and Texas) resorted to referenda, statutes, and amendments to accomplish the same objective of removing from the electorate African Americans and others not aligned with the Democratic Party. The disfranchisers were open about their goal of eviscerating black suffrage, but reducing the participation of undesirable whites was typically left unsaid, although there were exceptions (see Key 1949, 543). On this point, the general silence was obvious. Since only a minority of southern whites was obsessed with implementing disfranchisement laws, and they resided primarily in the black belt, it was critical to secure enough support from whites living in majority white counties. And yet, these whites were much more likely to feel the brunt of the restrictive voting measures because of their lower social status.

As Kousser (1974) and Key (1949) both documented, the pattern of support for restricting the franchise was heavily correlated with the percentage of blacks residing

in a county. That is, the higher the proportion of blacks, the greater the support for
disfranchisement laws, among both delegates participating in constitutional conventions and those within the electorate voting on restrictive legislation. Kousser identified the core supporters of disfranchisement:

> Not only did the vast majority of the leaders reside in the black belt, almost
> all of them were affluent and well-educated, and they often bore striking
> resemblances to antebellum "patricians." Indeed, almost every one was the
> son or grandson of a large planter, and several of the older chiefs had been
> slaveholders before the war. (1974, 247)

The heavy emphasis on designing voting restrictions so that blacks would be most
disadvantaged stemmed directly from their constituting the greatest impediment to
Democratic rule. First, African Americans were almost all Republicans (Key 1949,
540) and hence their support of Democrats and Populists, or other brands, was typically insincere—often done for strategic reasons or as a consequence of Democratic
manipulation. On this latter point, Democrats made it clear that the removal of blacks
from the political system would keep politics honest because otherwise Democrats
would continue to engage in fraud and violence as the primary means of countering
the black vote. This was precisely the point made by a Virginia Republican, who
brought to light the absurdity and moral bankruptcy of the Democrats' position:

> It is now proposed to right a wrong by punishing those who have been
> defrauded of their votes to the extent of destroying their right of suffrage;
> in other words the Negro vote of this Commonwealth must be destroyed to
> prevent the Democratic elections officers from stealing their votes. (Kousser
> 1974, 258)

Because of the respect conferred upon a law, "advocates of disfranchisement
argued that substituting legal for extralegal methods of controlling politics would
reinforce the Southern political system's legitimacy in the eyes of both Northerners
and Southerners" (Kousser 1974, 262–263). In short, "Southern political institutions, then, gained legitimacy not by expanding, but by contracting the electorate"
(Kousser 1974, 263).

The primary goal of disfranchising African Americans was rooted in their
potentially pivotal status and their frequently demonstrated unpredictable presence in electoral politics. In the words of Key, "according to southern tradition
Negroes were in a position to hold the balance of power between white factions"
(1949, 541). Constricting the white vote was a more complicated proposition
because in some states and locales, unaligned whites thought it was possible to
beat back the Democratic opposition, especially if the black vote no longer existed
for Democratic manipulation. In other words, the lack of widespread evidence in

favor of reducing white participation is likely because there was no consensus on furthering this objective.

Many of the natural enemies of the black-belt whites, the whites residing in majority white counties, went along with disfranchisement if it was expected to have only a limited effect on white participation. Elimination of the black vote might, in fact, lead to a fair fight between Democrats and their white opponents. At least, that was the hope for perhaps most of the unaligned whites living outside the black belt who provided just enough support for the Democratic dream of disfranchisement to become a political reality. As Key brilliantly assessed the situation:

> It is reasonable to assert that the battle for suffrage contraction was not solely a question of the Negro's position. Although the Bourbon Democrats of the black belt were usually in the vanguard and probably expected a degree of disfranchisement of the poor whites, the exceptions of South Carolina and Georgia make it difficult to defend a general theory of conspiracy to disfranchise the lesser whites. Perhaps the sounder generalization is that the groups on top at the moment, whatever their political orientation, feared that their opponents might recruit Negro support. (1949, 550)

THE TIMING AND TOOLS OF DISFRANCHISEMENT

In 1896, the Supreme Court gave a monumental gift to the southern white Democracy. In a Louisiana case disputing a Jim Crow law that separated railway cars according to race, the plaintiff, Homer Plessy, challenged the segregation. Plessy was 7/8 white and 1/8 black (an "octoroon"), but under Louisiana law this made him black, which led to his removal from riding in the "whites only" railway car. In a sweeping decision, the Supreme Court upheld the law and in the process gave its seal of approval to Jim Crow segregation throughout the South, declaring the separation of races legal as long as the accommodations were equal. This precedent would stand until the 1954 *Brown v. Board of Education* decision.

There is little question the *Plessy* ruling emboldened the South to move forward with the business of disfranchisement. What made Plessy so important was that it sanctioned the Jim Crow system that relegated blacks to second-class citizenship. Although facilities were supposed to be equal, they almost never were. Further, by allowing the South to control its social arrangements, the Court, and by extension the North, decided not to intervene in southern affairs. The timing of *Plessy* corresponded with the disfranchisement movement and, in a way, made this activity easier because Democratic politicos expected the federal government to be less aggressive in checking for racially discriminatory voting provisions. As Kousser explained the situation,

In the eighties and early nineties, Democrats developed a panoply of restrictive measures—registration and multiple-box laws, the poll tax, the Australian [secret] ballot, and the educational qualification. Each state became in effect a laboratory for testing one device or another. Indeed, the cross-fertilization and coordination between the movements to restrict the suffrage in the Southern states amounted to a public conspiracy. (1974, 39)

Table 3.1 displays a chart with the year of passage and the type of restrictive voting law adopted by each southern state from 1889 to 1908. The grandfather clause, unlike the other laws, was actually a loophole that enabled whites otherwise disfranchised (due to the literacy test) to vote if their grandfather had been able to vote at a certain time in the past (e.g., before 1867). The other laws were clearly tailored to curtail the electorate. It should be noted, however, that the move in favor of self-registration and the secret ballot were nationwide reforms successfully promoted by Progressives, whose primary objective was to weaken political machines in northern cities (Kleppner 1982). In these settings, party bosses controlled local politics by mobilizing the support of the large and swelling immigrant communities. These impoverished newcomers were happy to exchange their votes in return for the local political machine that provided services (like waste disposal) and possibly employment. Viewing these quid pro quos as patently corrupt, Progressives managed to pass numerous electoral reforms that weakened the machines and, as a result, severely reduced the political participation of the lower-class and heavily immigrant populations.

Similarly, in the South, registration and the secret ballot upped the costs of voting. The primary hurdle was being motivated to register; second, ballots no longer provided pictures designating the party. In the privacy of the voting booth, the state-issued ballot had to be read in order for the voter to make a choice—an impossible task for the substantial segment of illiterates. Multiple-box laws separated ballots in accordance with the specific office voted on. Thus, there might be eight different boxes corresponding to eight different offices (this was the case in South Carolina, which put in place such a law in 1882). Multiple-box laws were very effective in voiding the ballots of illiterates because they could not determine which ballot went with which box.

The literacy test and understanding clause were particularly useful in culling undesirables from the electorate, and both pointed directly to the outsized power of the voting registrar. As Key put it, "In practice literacy and understanding have little to do with the acquisition of the right to vote. Whether a person can register to vote depends on what the man down at the courthouse says, and he usually has the final say" (1949, 560).[3] Indeed, similar to the case of native southern whites choosing to remove themselves from the electorate at the time of registration under Reconstruction, thousands of African Americans chose not to attempt registration. A culture quickly developed in many rural locales in Deep South states in particular, in which it was understood that African Americans would not seek to register (Key

TABLE 3.1 ■ The Timing and Type of Disfranchisement Laws in Southern States, 1889–1908

Law	1889	1890	1891	1892	1893	1894	1895	1897	1898	1899	1900	1901	1902	1903	1908
Poll tax	FL	MS, TN		AR			SC		LA		NC	AL	VA, TX		
Registration	TN				AL	SC		LA		NC					
Multiple-box	FL									NC					
Secret ballot	TN	MS	AR		AL	VA		LA						TX	
Literacy test		MS					SC		LA		NC	AL	VA		GA
Property test									LA		NC	AL	VA		GA
Understanding clause	MS						SC						VA		GA
Grandfather clause									LA		NC	AL			GA
Number of laws, by year	5	4	1	1	2	2	3	2	4	2	4	4	5	1	4

Source: Data are from Kousser (1974, 239).

Notes: Table 3.1 is a partial replication of Kousser's Table 9.1 (1974, 239). Table 3.1 has been modified both in form and years covered. Notice that 1896 is not shown nor are 1904–1907 because no southern state passed one of these restrictive laws during those years. In the original Table 9.1 created by Kousser, no years are skipped and the first entry is for 1871, when Georgia first implemented a poll tax. There were three additional poll tax entries before 1889: Georgia again in 1877, Virginia in 1875, and Virginia in 1881 (when it repealed the poll tax). Also, South Carolina passed a registration law and a multiple-box law in 1882.

1949, 566–567). Also, many whites thought better of subjecting themselves to the public ridicule of attempting to prove their literacy.

The understanding clause was a double-edged sword in the hands of meddlesome voting registrars. If an African American was bold enough to try registering, then the registrar could use his ample discretion to determine whether the passage (often a section of the state constitution) was "correctly" interpreted. On the other hand, an illiterate white might qualify to register if the registrar simply decided that understanding was "demonstrated." The property test was straightforward and was set around $300 to $500 (Key 1949, 556–557), a very large sum of money for the vast number of sharecroppers (black and white), who rarely possessed anything of value, let alone a positive cash flow (Ayers 1992).

Although it is necessarily difficult to isolate the possible vote suppressing effects of any particular disfranchisement provision, it is safe to say that the totality of their capacity to reduce the electorate was breathtaking. Regarding black turnout, according to Kousser, "The decline and proportionate reduction figures for the elections immediately before and after disfranchisement were . . . 32 percent and 62 percent, respectively. Moreover, the death of opposition parties came *after*, not *before* disfranchisement" (1974, 244; italics in original). Perhaps the most telling statement on the effectiveness of disfranchisement is Woodward's account from Louisiana:

> The effectiveness of disfranchisement is suggested by a comparison of the number of registered Negro voters in Louisiana in 1896, when there were 130,334 and in 1904, when there were 1,342. Between the two dates the literacy, property, and poll-tax qualifications were adopted. In 1896 Negro registrants were in a majority in twenty-six parishes—by 1900 in none. (Woodward 2002, 85)

Given his expertise on the matter, Kousser deserves the last word in summing up the environment of southern politics in the early twentieth century:

> All in all, the post-1900 Southern political structure was markedly different from the post-Reconstruction order. In the eighties and nineties, turnout regularly exceeded 60 percent of all adult males, and sometimes reached 85 percent. By 1910, almost no Negroes and only about half of the whites bothered to vote in the most hotly contested elections. (1974, 236)

THE (WHITE) PRIMARY SYSTEM

With their opponents effectively removed from the political system, the direct primary became the vehicle by which southern Democrats managed the spoils of their one-party monopoly. As Key (1949) emphasized, it is primarily in its relations outside the region that the South took on its one-party Democratic character. From within, because competition was bottled up within a single party, southern politics during the Solid South years more aptly resembled a "no-party" system. Hence, a fundamental feature of electoral politics was the ever-changing nature of Democratic factionalism that pervaded the southern states.[4]

With the exception of pockets of Republican viability (Heard 1952), primarily in parts of Appalachia (notably in East Tennessee, Western North Carolina, Southwestern Virginia, and the German hill country of Central Texas), because the Democratic Party was the only game in town, perhaps the single most effective deterrent to black participation was the white primary. With a justification nothing short of incredible, Democrats contended that their party was private and could therefore discriminate on the basis of race. This political farce was carried out for decades before the Supreme Court intervened in the mid-1940s. Except for Tennessee and sections of Florida and North Carolina, throughout the South the white primary was more or less operable for barring black participation and thus reinforcing the reality that in Dixie, the Democracy was a white man's party.[5]

Table 3.2 is a compilation of two tables originally displayed by Key (1949, 17–18). The top half of the table presents the percentage of the vote for the top two gubernatorial candidates in the first Democratic primary from 1920 to 1948—the core years of the Solid South era. The states are arrayed from the highest to lowest percentage of the vote garnered by the top two candidates. Thus, in Tennessee, Virginia, and Georgia, because of the high share of the vote awarded to just two candidates (their median vote exceeds 90 percent), there appears to be a bifactional pattern of Democratic competition. Moving down the rankings, it is evident that in other states the top two candidates are far from dominating gubernatorial elections. A multi-factional system prevails in states like Arkansas, South Carolina, Texas, Mississippi, and Florida. Indeed, in the case of Florida, because of the rarity of one or even two candidates collecting the lion's share of votes (the median share for the top two candidates is less than 60 percent), Key titled his chapter on the Sunshine State, "Every Man for Himself." With only a viable Democratic Party, the primary contest typically amounted to election because the outcome in the general was usually a foregone conclusion. Throughout Dixie, the jockeying for Democratic votes often amounted to a free-for-all.

The bottom half of Table 3.2 provides another way of examining the extent of factionalism in southern politics. Here, the percentage of the vote for the leading gubernatorial candidate in the first Democratic primary is presented from 1920 to 1948. The rank order is very similar to that shown in the top half of the table. The order remains the same from Arkansas down to Florida. At the top, Virginia and Tennessee switch places, as do North Carolina, Alabama, and Louisiana. In these states where fewer candidates take most of the vote (the median is more than 50 percent for the leading candidate in Virginia, Tennessee, and Georgia), the degree of factionalism is necessarily less and, to some extent, the intra-Democratic competition is more disciplined. Typically, there is a dominant faction that serves to organize the opposition against it. For instance, in Virginia it was a contest between the dominant Byrd machine and its detractors; in Tennessee, it was a fight between the Crump machine in Memphis

TABLE 3.2 ■ The Degree of Factionalism in Southern States, 1920–1948			
Total Votes Won by Top Two Gubernatorial Candidates in First Democratic Primary			
State	**Median**	**High**	**Low**
Tennessee	98.7	100.0	76.0
Virginia	98.3	100.0	82.8
Georgia	91.6	100.0	70.4
North Carolina	77.4	100.0	54.0
Alabama	75.2	100.0	52.9
Louisiana	69.1	99.7	62.4
Arkansas	64.2	99.4	46.7
South Carolina	63.2	100.0	45.4
Texas	63.2	97.1	48.3
Mississippi	62.9	86.0	59.0
Florida	57.0	93.7	30.0
Vote Won by the Top Gubernatorial Candidate in First Democratic Primary			
Virginia	72.6	86.0	61.4
Tennessee	58.8	87.3	39.2
Georgia	51.7	100.0	27.3
Alabama	43.4	78.7	27.7
Louisiana	41.5	67.1	34.9
North Carolina	40.2	100.0	31.4
Arkansas	36.3	55.7	26.0
South Carolina	35.1	100.0	25.9
Texas	33.9	68.5	27.5
Mississippi	33.5	55.3	31.4
Florida	29.5	59.4	15.7

Source: Data reproduced by the author from the two tables shown in Key (1949, 17–18).

versus the rest of the state (including an unusually strong Republican opposition in East Tennessee); in Georgia, it was the Talmadge faction versus its numerous and ever-changing opponents. Even in the most developed and stable factional settings, as Key (1949) stressed, the general absence of a second party did not allow for a political system capable of responding to the considerable needs of an impoverished southern electorate.

Nonetheless, the primary system was remarkably successful in bottling up competition within the Democratic Party. In all but two southern states (Tennessee and Virginia; see Glaser 2006, 777), if necessary, there was a runoff primary in those instances when the top vote getter in the first primary was denied a simple majority. The runoff consisted of the top two candidates from the first round. This provision provided much-needed legitimacy because of the frequency with which multiple candidates split up the vote so that no one came close to capturing a majority in the first round. Not only does the runoff provision ensure that the ultimate winner captures a majority, but an extensive analysis of primary runoffs by Glaser (2006) highlights another important aspect of this rule. In the first round, it is often the case that the most extreme candidate or one differentiated for some other notable feature (e.g., the most vocal demagogue) is able to capture a substantial share of the vote by virtue of differentiating himself from the rest of the field. But interestingly, in the runoff this candidate is more likely to lose because a majority of votes coalesce around the other, less extreme candidate making it to the runoff.

By the end of the Solid South, the runoff provision came under attack because of a perceived racial bias. In the 1960s, when African Americans reentered the southern electorate in substantial numbers, they overwhelmingly aligned with the Democratic Party because outside the South it was the party that led the charge for black civil rights (see chapter 4). With the growing number of black Democrats participating in primary contests, in many instances the black vote would unite behind a single candidate, who was often African American. A pattern clearly emerged in which the unity of the black vote could get a fellow African American candidate into the runoff, but more often than not, white voters would rally around the other (white) candidate with enough votes to deny the black candidate a runoff victory. In the days of the Solid South, however, the runoff provision was the mechanism that served to legitimize the electoral process in a region where the Republican opposition was demoralized for decades. In fact, the success of keeping voters and candidates aligned with the southern Democracy is noted by the fact that in several states, more of the electorate participated in the Democratic primary than in the ensuing general election because the latter contest was rarely competitive (Key 1949).

THE 1930S: DEMOCRACY HEADS NORTH

From the 1896 election to 1928, Republicans dominated the White House. In these nine contests, the Democratic Party prevailed in just two: 1912 and 1916—both won by Woodrow Wilson. A born and raised southerner who eventually migrated to the Northeast, Wilson prevailed in 1912 because of the rift between the Republican President Howard Taft and Teddy Roosevelt. Roosevelt ran as the nominee for the Bull Moose Progressive Party and earned more votes than Taft (88 to 8 Electoral College votes), and in the process, the cleaving of the GOP vote between these former friends opened the way for Wilson to easily capture a popular and Electoral College vote (435) majority.

From the late nineteenth century until the 1930s, the Republican Party was dominant outside the South. To be sure, the one-party/no-party system existing within the confines of Dixie was not exhibited under the GOP banner in the North. But Republicans clearly had the upper hand in elections occurring above the Mason-Dixon Line (Reiter and Stonecash 2011). As mentioned, some scholars (see Burnham 1970) considered the 1896 election as demarcating a new electoral pattern, characterized primarily by the solidification of support behind the GOP in the northern states and the advent of Democratic hegemony in the Solid South. There is no question that the GOP did grow in electoral strength in the North and one of the tried and true campaigning methods was to wave the "bloody shirt." In other words, Republican candidates harped on their party's victorious legacy going back to the Civil War and outwardly branded their Democratic opponents as complicit allies with their vanquished southern Democratic counterparts, who deserved disdain for backing the morally bankrupt institution of slavery.

In the North, the GOP also took credit for being the party in the vanguard of economic advancement, in a region where manufacturing and industrialization became the hallmarks of the capitalist system. And the economy appeared healthy and robust for most of the early 1900s, especially during the roaring twenties when Republicans had a lock on the presidency. But the laissez faire economic system had come under increasing attack from Progressives who were alarmed by the inhumane working conditions prevalent in factories that routinely worked their employees for better than half the day and employed child labor. In the South, where manufacturing was not as prevalent, the region had established a large textile industry. Textile production led to the creation of mill towns where the managers and owners provided for every need of their employees and, in the process, essentially held their labor in a form of indentured servitude (Ayers 1992).

The unbridled capitalism of the early twentieth century would receive a massive jolt in the late 1920s with the stock market crash of 1929 setting off a worldwide Great Depression that would persist until World War II. The economic repercussions transformed electoral politics in the northern United States. Republican President Herbert Hoover presided over the early years of the Great Depression, and his basic philosophy was to let the market self-correct—an approach that did not satisfy the vast and growing number of unemployed Americans. Seeking reelection in 1932, President Hoover was crushed by his Democratic opponent Franklin Delano Roosevelt (FDR). Table 3.3 presents Electoral College (EC) vote data from the 1900

TABLE 3.3 ■ Electoral College Votes in the North and South, 1900–1944					
Election	Democrat	Republican	North-Dem % (Votes)	South-Dem % (Votes)	Winner
1900	W. Bryan	W. McKinley	13 (335)	100 (112)	Republican
1904	T. Roosevelt	A. Parker	6 (356)	100 (120)	Republican
1908	W. Bryan	W. Taft	12 (363)	100 (120)	Republican
1912	W. Wilson	W. Taft	76 (405)	100 (126)	Democrat
1916	W. Wilson	C. Hughes	37 (405)	100 (126)	Democrat
1920	J. Cox	W. Harding	3 (405)	90 (126)	Republican
1924	J. Davis	C. Coolidge	2 (405)	100 (126)	Republican
1928	A. Smith	H. Hoover	6 (405)	51 (126)	Republican
1932	F. Roosevelt	H. Hoover	86 (407)	100 (124)	Democrat
1936	F. Roosevelt	A. Landon	98 (407)	100 (124)	Democrat
1940	F. Roosevelt	W. Willkie	80 (407)	100 (124)	Democrat
1944	F. Roosevelt	T. Dewey	75 (404)	100 (127)	Democrat

Source: Data compiled by the author from Dave Leip's *Atlas of U.S. Presidential Elections* (http://uselection atlas.org/RESULTS/).

to 1944 presidential elections. In addition to displaying the names of the Democratic and Republican nominees and which party won, the table shows the Democratic percentage of the EC vote garnered in the North and South.

Prior to the 1932 contest, the North was dominated by Republican presidential candidates—only in 1912 did the region give an EC vote majority to a Democrat, 76 percent for Wilson. By comparison, Democratic candidates owned the South's EC votes. In 1920, Tennessee broke from the Democratic fold, giving its EC votes to Republican Warren Harding. The only other exception to the southern Democratic EC vote monopoly occurred in 1928 with the election of Hoover. Referring to this contest in the South as "The Bolt of 1928," Key (1949, 318) showed that Hoover attracted the support of whites located outside the black-belt region where the race issue was not as salient. In these Peripheral South states (Hoover carried Florida, North Carolina, Tennessee, Texas, and Virginia), Hoover was better aligned with the moral concerns of voters who could not stomach the northern Democratic nominee Al Smith, a Catholic New Yorker who opposed prohibition. Despite his unpalatable political profile, Democrats in the Deep South stuck with the Democrat Al Smith, and most likely because solidarity was tied directly to the race issue. Even if

Al Smith possessed several characteristics and views anathema to the white southern creed, he did not upset the racist status quo prevailing in Dixie, and principally for that he was preferable to the Republican Hoover.

The 1932 presidential election marked a sea change in northern politics. FDR carried 86 percent of the North's EC votes and won no less than three-quarters of the region's votes in the next three contests. With the rise of Democratic support in the North, coupled with the party's stronghold in Dixie, the Democratic Party would dominate federal elections until the 1960s. Put simply, in the early 1930s the Democratic Party had assembled a national majority in American politics. By vowing to "muddle through" the economic catastrophe, FDR at least gave voters some hope that a solution could be found, even if it meant unprecedented political intervention in the American economy. His New Deal Coalition of political supporters constituted a diverse and ultimately unsustainable collection of voters. In the North, the Democratic Party drew its strength from African Americans, Catholics, Jews, Union members and other working class voters, and the large population of white ethnic immigrants populating large cities. In the South, the New Deal Coalition was composed of the overwhelming majority of whites (almost all of whom were Protestant), but southern blacks were shut out because of the apparatus of disfranchisement laws.

Figure 3.1 displays the percentage of northern U.S. House seats held by Democrats and Republicans from 1900 to 1948. This pattern is notably different from the one of Democratic dominance in the South (see Figure 3.4). In the early 1900s the northern GOP had a grip on U.S. House seats, but their hold was severely weakened from 1910 to 1916, a period when Democrats controlled the House of Representatives (the 62nd through 64th Congresses: 1911–1917) because of their overwhelmingly Democratic southern delegation. Then, from around 1918 to 1928 the GOP once again held most northern House seats. When FDR won the presidency in 1932, he showed impressive coattails in northern House elections, but this down-ballot Democratic strength only persisted for three election cycles (1932–1936). In fact, the resurgence of the northern GOP in the first postwar midterm in 1946 resulted in the Democratic Party's loss of its House majority for the first time since the onset of the party's national takeover in 1932. Hence, unlike the South, where the Democratic Party reigned supreme, in the North, below the presidential level, the 1930s ushered in a period of vigorous two-party competition, not one-party dominance under the Democratic label.

FDR's hold on the presidency eventually soured many white southerners and a fair number of northerners, too. He incurred the ire of his own party in a failed attempt to pack the Supreme Court with justices sympathetic to his New Deal policies. Because the Court repeatedly ruled Democratic congressional legislation unconstitutional for its regulation of the economy, in 1937 FDR proposed that for every member of the nine-member Supreme Court older than seventy, an additional justice be added. This would ensure that the Court consisted of a majority in agreement with President Roosevelt's political agenda. Most of the Congress was livid

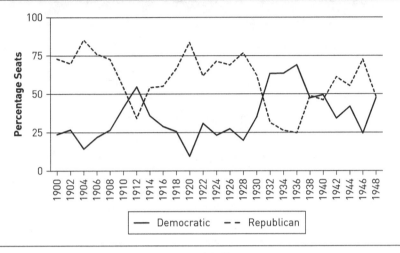

FIGURE 3.1 ■ **Northern U.S. House Seats Controlled by the Major Parties, 1900–1948**

Source: Data compiled by the author from CQ Press (2005).

Note: The percentage of Democratic and Republican seats is out of the total northern U.S. House seats.

that FDR would attempt such a power play, and the scheme was foiled by the Court itself because the threat of an expanded judiciary caused its majority to engage in an about-face, now upholding the constitutionality of New Deal legislation (Kernell et al. 2015). This famous "switch in time that saved nine" had lasting negative repercussions for the president. The effrontery to maneuver for a restructuring of the Court that clearly would weaken it at the direct expense of the executive delayed congressional assistance for bolstering the administrative apparatus necessary for the president to carry out his New Deal agenda.

Relations with southern members of Congress also took a turn for the worse in the 1938 midterms. Most likely emboldened by his impressive Democratic congressional majorities, FDR decided to target for defeat a handful of his more conservative southern Democratic congressional detractors. Like the court-packing plan, this attempted purge also failed. Democratic incumbency in southern congressional elections was nearly absolute in the days of the Solid South, and thus the president's scheme to replace conservative Democrats with more moderate-to-liberal allies was foolhardy. The deteriorating relations between FDR and the southern wing of the Democratic Party was probably inevitable because the most powerful members in Dixie were increasingly departing from the liberal tenets of the New Deal program.

Figure 3.2 provides data on the ideology of every member of the House of Representatives from the 57th Congress (1901–1903) to the 81st (1949–1951). These data are called DW-NOMINATE scores measured on the first ideological

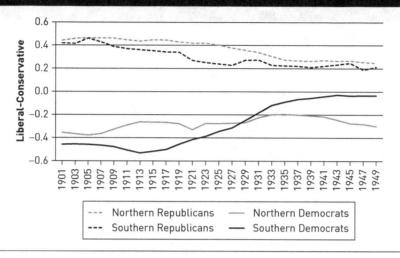

FIGURE 3.2 ■ Party Means on Liberal-Conservative Dimension, 1901–1949

Source: Data compiled by the author from the DW-NOMINATE scores website (http://www.voteview.com/dwnomin.htm).

Note: The possible range extends from −1 to +1, with negative numbers moving in a liberal direction and positive numbers moving in a conservative direction.

dimension, which essentially captures the extent to which members are classified as liberal-to-conservative based on their roll-call votes. At the extremes, the ideological range spans −1 to +1, with −1 being the most liberal and +1 being the most conservative (note, however, that the actual range shown in Figure 3.2 goes from −.6 to +.6).

By 1901, the last black Representative to serve in the southern congressional delegation had left the scene, Republican George White of North Carolina (Foner 1988). Not until the 1970s would the next African American represent a southern House seat in the U.S. Congress. Even with the absence of any African American members, in the early years of the 1900s, southern Democrats were decidedly more liberal than their northern Democratic peers. This difference persists until the start of the Great Depression in the late 1920s. An explanation for this sectional difference among Democrats is that, in the South, many Democrats took Populist positions even if they did not adopt the party label. And similar to the North, there was a strong Progressive streak that ran through southern politics from the late 1800s into the 1920s (Grantham 1983).

By the 1930s, a more familiar pattern emerges in which southern Democrats become increasingly conservative vis-à-vis northern Democrats. By the mid-1940s, northern Democrats move in a more liberal direction while southern Democrats become slightly more conservative. It is no coincidence that southern Democrats were becoming more conservative during the tenure of President Roosevelt. As FDR pushed the national agenda in a liberal direction, southern Democrats pushed back, moving in a conservative direction. With the growing rift between southern

Democrats and President Roosevelt, congressional scholars began to speak of a "conservative coalition" that consisted of an inter-party alignment of southern Democrats and northern Republicans (Shafer 2016). When this coalition formed over various issues, it was easily capable of not only blocking the liberal agenda of the president and northern Democrats, but it could even produce conservative-leaning policies. Most important for southern Democrats was that northern Republicans were regularly agreeable to assisting in blocking civil rights legislation that would chip away at the South's Jim Crow laws. The conservative coalition manifested itself fairly routinely on various congressional votes well into the 1980s.

Throughout the first half of the twentieth century, never was there a sustained regional gap in the ideological positioning of northern and southern Republicans. Even when the difference seemed substantial during the 1920s, because the number of southern Republicans was so small (typically around three to seven seats), there were not enough members to say the ideological gap was substantively important. Further, the difference between northern and southern Republicans closed during the New Deal era and the GOP was moving toward the ideological center, a trend that makes sense, given the dominance of the more liberal Democratic opposition.

Despite the tension between President Roosevelt and southern Democrats, their differences never escalated to the point of undoing the impressive national Democratic majority in federal elections. FDR was too clever to fatally undermine the base of his winning coalition: southern white voters. Indeed, a prime example of President Roosevelt appealing southern sentiments is that on various occasions an anti-lynching law was introduced in Congress and FDR and southern Democrats repeatedly blocked its passage. From the vantage of southern Democrats, it would have been sheer folly to disturb an arrangement that delivered significantly more federal dollars to the South than the amount Dixie paid in (Black and Black 2002). And this was true despite the fact that southern Democrats, as a group, were not as economically liberal as their northern co-partisans. So long as southern blacks were disfranchised, the odd but somehow workable Democratic coalition of northern African Americans and southern whites repeatedly delivered Democratic majorities in Congress and the White House. But this arrangement was clearly ephemeral. Over the long run it would prove impossible to hold together a biracial, cross-sectional coalition of voters who were diametrically opposed on the civil rights issue. The first blow to this precarious Democratic solidarity was delivered with the Supreme Court ruling in the Texas case of *Smith v. Allwright.*

THE 1948 ELECTION: A PERMANENT FISSURE IN THE SOLID SOUTH

In the 1944 *Smith v. Allwright* case, the Supreme Court finally struck down the white primary. No longer could southern Democrats contend that their party was a private club free to include or exclude whomever they wished. In the words of Black and Black (1987, 84), "the proposition that southern Democratic parties were simply private organizations with no implicit state functions was so preposterous that only small children believed it and only constitutional lawyers debated it."

In the Deep South states, particularly in Alabama, Mississippi, and South Carolina, the ruling was met with a panic. Fearing a massive infusion of black voters, Alabama passed its blatantly unconstitutional Boswell Amendment in 1946—a provision that assembled a board of examiners who quizzed potential voters to determine their fitness for exercising the franchise (Key 1949). In South Carolina, the constitution was scrubbed of any language mentioning political parties so that the Democratic Party could then legitimately be classified as a private club with the authority to choose its members. In Mississippi, a lengthy loyalty oath to the Democratic Party was required of those wanting to participate in the primary. Key cites an example from Mississippi in which two African Americans attempted the oath and failed:

Q. How do you intend to vote, Democratic or Republican?

A. Democratic.

Q. Do you believe in Communism or Fascism?

A. No.

Q. Are you in favor of F. E. P. C.?

A. Yes.

The judgment followed: "You boys are disqualified" (1949, 642).

The Fair Employment Practice Committee (FEPC) prohibited companies contracting with the federal government from discriminating on the basis of race as well as religion. Undoubtedly, these would-be voters had no idea what the FEPC was.

Despite the numerous creative efforts to evade the *Smith* ruling, it was not negotiable and eventually the Deep South states relented. The fear of an abrupt end to the white supremacist status quo was premature. The poll tax, literacy test, and understanding clause were now more heavily leaned upon to continue denying blacks the right to vote. By 1952, 80 percent of southern African Americans were still not registered to vote (Black and Black 1987, 85).

Even though the *Smith* decision did not topple the elaborate southern structure of disfranchisement, it sent a strong signal that additional outside intervention in southern affairs was likely to follow. Southern Democrats were right to be wary of the Supreme Court, but the greatest threat to the Solid South originated from the political calculations of a Democratic president. FDR died in office on April 12, 1945, and his Vice President, Harry S. Truman, assumed the presidency. After presiding over the end of World War II, President Truman decided to seek election in 1948. In hindsight, the events transpiring over the course of the 1948 presidential election set in motion the end of the Solid South (Frederickson 2001). Coming at the very end of his classic writing on southern politics, Key (1949, 329) dubbed the election "The Revolt of 1948." What made the contest historic and pivotal was that President Truman considered black votes in northern battleground states critical to winning the election.

Truman was transparent in his desire to court the black vote.[6] His most overt actions consisted of the creation of the President's Committee on Civil Rights, desegregating the military via executive order in 1948, and endorsing a strong civil rights plank in the Democratic Party's 1948 platform. The response from southern Democrats was fierce and immediate. "With the adoption of the [civil rights] platform the Mississippi delegation and half of the Alabama delegation walked out" of the Democratic National Convention in Philadelphia in protest (Key 1949, 335). Reconvening on July 17 in Birmingham, the States' Rights Democratic Party—more popularly known as the Dixiecrats—was born. South Carolina Governor J. Strom Thurmond was chosen as the presidential nominee, and his running mate was Mississippi Governor Fielding Wright.

BOX 3.1   STROM THURMOND

Some southern politicians stand out for being tremendously influential in their political careers. It is indisputable that James Strom Thurmond was one of the most influential politicians to ever represent a southern constituency. He was born on December 5, 1902, in Edgefield County, South Carolina, a county that has produced a remarkable total of 10 South Carolina governors! Thurmond became a pivotal player in southern politics because of the longevity of his time in public office and the decisions he made as the South transitioned from a Democratic stronghold to a Republican bastion (Bass and Thompson 2003).

Thurmond hastened Republican advancement in southern presidential politics by splitting the region in the 1948 election. Because Democratic President Truman was pushing a liberal civil rights agenda that had the potential to overturn the Jim Crow status quo in southern states, Thurmond, who was governor of South Carolina at the time, agreed to run as an insurgent candidate, the presidential nominee of the States' Rights Democratic Party (also known as the Dixiecrat Party; see Frederickson 2001; Key 1949). With the intention of throwing the presidential election into the House of Representatives by denying Truman (or his Republican opponent Thomas Dewey) an Electoral College majority, Thurmond managed to win the votes of four Deep South states: Alabama, Louisiana, Mississippi, and South Carolina. Truman won an Electoral College majority and hence the presidency in 1948, but since then Republicans have been competitive in southern presidential politics and usually the GOP dominates these elections.

(Continued)

(Continued)

In 1954, Thurmond made history by winning a U.S. Senate seat as a write-in candidate (a feat recently achieved by Alaska Senator Lisa Murkowski in the 2010 midterm). Three years later, Thurmond set the record for the longest filibuster, delaying the Senate's business for a total of 24 hours and 18 minutes in a failed attempt to block passage of the 1957 Civil Rights Act. He was a militant segregationist, and the national Democratic leadership on civil rights in the early 1960s directly contributed to his decision to switch to the Republican Party when its presidential standard bearer, Barry Goldwater, ran against Democratic President Johnson in 1964. Thurmond helped deliver South Carolina's electoral votes for Goldwater in 1964, and in 1968 when the segregationist Alabama Governor George Wallace ran for president under the American Independent Party label, Thurmond was instrumental in securing a Palmetto State victory for Republican Richard Nixon.

Despite being a highly representative contemporary southern Republican—as noted by his conservative positions on race, economics, and foreign policy—by the 1980s Thurmond had softened his rhetoric on civil rights. He even voted for the 25-year extension of the Voting Rights Act in 1982, and exit polls indicated that near the end of his tenure he was able to capture about 20 percent of the black vote (see Black and Black 2002) because of his colorblind legislative service to his South Carolina constituents. Thurmond last won reelection to the Senate in 1996, and by the time he retired in 2002, he was 100 years old. Thurmond died where he was born, in Edgefield, South Carolina, on June 26, 2003.

The Dixiecrats were an insurgent party that attempted to uphold the tenets of racial segregation within the larger Democratic Party. The short-term objective was to capture enough votes in the Electoral College to deny Truman an outright majority. If this were accomplished, then the contest would be decided in the House of Representatives where southern Democrats expected to have considerable bargaining power to at least reassert the legitimacy of southern segregation. In every southern state a power struggle was waged within the Democratic Party to decide whether to back Truman or Thurmond (Key 1949). It was no surprise that Thurmond exhibited more strength in the Deep South states, which always placed the race issue at the forefront of the political agenda. The Dixiecrats managed to control the ballot in Alabama, Louisiana, Mississippi, and South Carolina. Only in Georgia was Truman represented on the ballot as the official Democratic presidential nominee. In the remaining Rim South states (Arkansas, Florida, North Carolina, Tennessee, Texas, and Virginia), Truman was the preferred choice of the Democratic Party.

The 1948 election was so close that Truman famously held up a copy of the *Chicago Tribune* with the incorrect headline, "Dewey Defeats Truman."[7] Thanks to an energetic and strategic whistle-stop campaign (Holbrook 2002), Truman prevailed and even carried Illinois's 28 EC votes. Truman defeated Dewey in the Electoral College 303 to 189. The Dixiecrat Strom Thurmond won the remaining 39 EC votes, all cast in the South by the electors of Alabama, Louisiana, Mississippi, and South Carolina, and one elector in Tennessee (Truman won 11 of the 12 EC votes in the Volunteer State). Despite his liberal stance on civil rights, the rest of the South backed Truman and hence, once again the GOP was completely shut out of Dixie. But 1948 was the last time the Republican Party would come up empty in southern presidential elections. The intra-party imbroglio in 1948 exposed a deep and growing divide between the northern and southern wings of the Democracy, and it stemmed from the intractable civil rights issue.

SUMMARY OF SOUTHERN DEMOCRATIC DOMINANCE

This section recaps the dominance of southern Democrats across various elections from 1900 to 1948. Republican top-down advancement would commence in 1952, but over the first half of the twentieth century, Democratic control of the southern political system verged on absolute. Figure 3.3 presents the popular vote in southern presidential elections from 1900 to 1948. Only in 1928 and 1948 did the percentage of the Democratic vote fall below 60 percent. In most years, the Republican nominee was fortunate to crack 30 percent of the popular vote. In the first two New Deal elections (1932 and 1936), FDR won an astounding 80 percent or more of the popular southern vote. In 1912, Progressive Teddy Roosevelt polled more southern votes than Republican President Taft. And in the other notable three-way contest of 1948, even though Republican Dewey failed to tally an EC vote, he actually won a slightly higher percentage of the southern popular vote than Dixiecrat Thurmond (26.7 to 22.4 percent).

Table 3.4 displays data on the Democratic percentage of seats in southern state legislatures. For each southern state, the percentage of Democrats in the state senate and state house is shown respectively, for 1900, 1908, 1918, 1928, 1938, and 1948. Although Key's (1949) characterization of southern politics as a no-party, faction-riddled system was an accurate description within each state, Democratic legislators were ubiquitous. In 1900, Democrats comprised 95 percent of southern state senates and 94 percent of state houses. By 1948, Democratic control was even more impressive; 98 percent of upper chambers and 97 percent of lower chambers were populated by Democratic legislators. This said, some variation in the prevalence of Democratic lawmakers is worth noting. In some Deep South states (Louisiana, Mississippi, and South Carolina), the Democratic monopoly was complete. In others, the presence of mountain Republicanism cut into Democratic hegemony. This was particularly true of North Carolina, Tennessee, and Virginia.

FIGURE 3.3 ■ Popular Presidential Vote in the South, 1900–1948

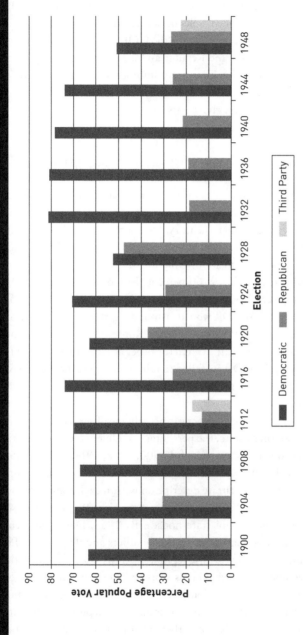

Source: Data compiled by the author from Dave Leip's *Atlas of U.S. Presidential Elections* (http://uselectionatlas.org/RESULTS/).

Notes: The popular vote is the percentage Democratic and Republican out of the two-party vote total, except for 1912 and 1948. In these elections, the vote is out of the total cast for the Democrats, Republicans, and Progressives (Teddy Roosevelt) in 1912 and the total cast for the Democrats, Republicans, and Dixiecrats (Strom Thurmond) in 1948.

TABLE 3.4 ■ Democratic Dominance in Southern State Legislatures, 1900–1948						
State	1900	1908	1918	1928	1938	1948
Alabama	97/92	97/97	97/94	100/98	100/99	100/99
Arkansas	100/97	100/100	100/95	100/98	100/98	100/98
Florida	100/100	99/100	100/100	97/98	100/100	100/100
Georgia	98/95	100/100	100/99	100/99	98/99	98/99
Louisiana	100/100	100/100	100/100	100/100	100/100	100/100
Mississippi	100/98	100/100	100/100	100/100	100/100	100/100
North Carolina	78/84	80/80	80/78	76/70	96/95	96/91
South Carolina	100/99	100/100	100/100	100/100	100/100	100/100
Tennessee	85/77	85/78	79/73	76/73	88/84	88/81
Texas	100/98	97/98	100/99	100/99	100/100	100/100
Virginia	95/93	88/86	85/88	95/95	95/97	95/94
Total	95/94	95/95	95/94	95/94	98/98	98/97

Source: Data compiled by the author from Dubin (2007).

Notes: Data show the percentage of Democrats in the state senate and state house, respectively. For example, in Alabama in 1900, 97 percent of the state senate was Democratic and 92 percent of the state house was Democratic (97/92). Because in some states the dates do not exactly correspond with the displayed year, the computation is based on the data closest to a given year.

Figure 3.4 presents the percentage of Democrats and Republicans in the southern U.S. House delegation from 1900 to 1948. This is probably the most impressive display of Democratic electoral dominance during the Solid South era. A quick look back at Figure 3.1, which presents the same data for northern U.S. House elections, reinforces the unique one-party nature of southern politics. The electoral volatility associated with two-party competition in northern congressional elections is wholly absent in the South. Democratic control of the southern House delegation manifests itself in an almost flat line that consistently hovers near 100 percent. From 1932 to 1948, the 2 Republicans in the 100-plus member southern House delegation made for a lonely political existence.

Figure 3.5 displays the percentage of unopposed House seats for southern Democrats and Republicans from 1900 to 1948. As discussed in chapter 2, the jagged pattern of contestation reflects the reality that two-party competition is more

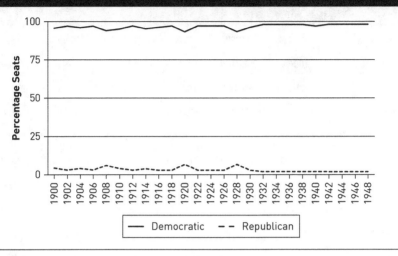

FIGURE 3.4 ■ Southern U.S. House Seats Controlled by the Major Parties, 1900–1948

Source: Data compiled by the author from CQ Press (2005).

Note: The percentage of Democratic and Republican seats is out of the total southern U.S. House seats.

FIGURE 3.5 ■ Unopposed Southern U.S. House Seats, 1900–1948

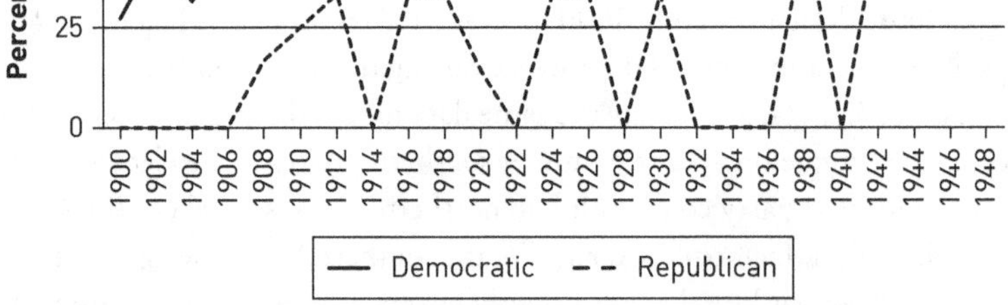

Source: Data compiled by the author from CQ Press (2005).

likely in presidential years. Even though Democrats outnumber Republicans at a rate of roughly 97 to 3, the percentage of unopposed Democratic House seats is consistently higher and trends upward. Only in 1946 is the rate of unopposed Republican

House seats greater than that for Democrats, but keep in mind there were only two Republicans in the southern House delegation.

Finally, Figure 3.6 shows turnout in U.S. House contests in the North and South from 1900 to 1948. Continuing the pattern of a substantial regional participatory gap that emerged in the latter part of the 1800s, southern turnout drops from more than 40 percent in 1900 to slightly more than 20 percent in 1948. In the North, turnout in House elections falls from more than 80 percent in 1900 to less than 60 percent in 1948. Overall, turnout exhibits a long-term decline as a consequence of the Progressive reforms (i.e., the direct primary, the secret ballot, and self-registration) that served to weaken party machines and substantially demobilize the lower class of citizens who bore the brunt of these costs. In addition to the Progressive reforms, which enjoyed universal implementation, southern turnout plummeted even farther because of the various restrictive voting laws that disfranchised most African Americans and a large segment of whites. Perhaps just as significant in reducing turnout was, of course, the Democratic Party's hold on electoral politics. It is no wonder that the eligible participating southern electorate hovered somewhere between 10 and 20 percent (in midterm and presidential years, respectively) when Democrats utterly dominated general elections. In the 1930s and 1940s the typical size of the southern Republican House delegation was two to three members—a number plenty capable of holding a caucus in a proverbial, but alas now archaic, phone booth. For participation to rebound, the Democratic Party would have to face viable electoral competition.

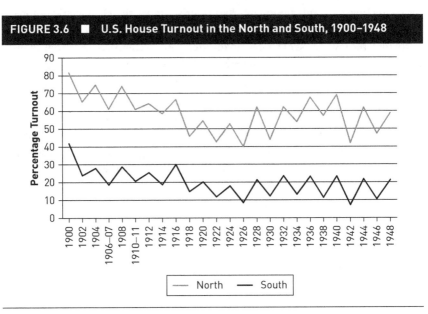

FIGURE 3.6 ■ U.S. House Turnout in the North and South, 1900–1948

Source: Data compiled by the author from Burnham (2010).

CONCLUDING THOUGHTS

The Great Depression and the advent of the New Deal Democratic Coalition forever altered party competition outside the South. The economic cleavage that came to structure politics from the early 1930s to the present advantaged Democrats because there have always been more voters inhabiting the bottom rungs of the economic ladder. FDR's success in presidential elections was so unprecedented that when Republicans captured a brief congressional majority (after the 1946 midterm), they made sure such a run would never happen again by proposing to limit presidential tenure. By 1951, the Twenty-Second Amendment was passed, limiting all future officeholders to two presidential terms. The dominance of the New Deal Coalition was on borrowed time. It was impossible to sustain a national Democratic majority in federal elections because the northern wing of the party grew stronger, eventually consisting of more congressmen than in the South, and they did not agree with Dixie's Jim Crow system of racial segregation.

In fact, the northern Republican Party was more compatible with the interests of southern Democrats. For one, the demography of the northern GOP (native-born, Protestant, upper class, and moderate-to-conservative in political views) was a much better fit with the rank-and-file southern Democrat. And as northern Democrats veered in a liberal direction (see Figure 3.2), it made sense that southern Democrats and northern Republicans formed a conservative coalition to curtail the excesses of New Deal policies. The economic cleavage that clearly divided northern party politics was muddled in the South because its one-party factional system made room for competing economic philosophies to flourish under the Democratic umbrella. Nonetheless, the southern upper class was actually more loyal to the Democratic Party than the lower class of whites, an inverted pattern compared to the one prevailing in the North (Nadeau and Stanley 1993). Hence, the GOP could, and would, attract middle- and upper-class southern whites on the basis of economics. But more significant by far was the race issue. An appeal to racial conservatism by opposing federal intervention as the vehicle for securing black civil rights was the surest way to drive a wedge into the Democratic Party and peel off southern whites (Hillygus and Shields 2009). President Truman's brazen courting of the northern black vote opened the door for the GOP to gain a foothold in Dixie. By the 1950s, it was finally time for Republicanism to head South.

4 COMPETITIVE TRANSITION

The 1950s marked an important interlude in American politics and especially in Dixie. After World War II and the 1948 presidential election, the urgency for black civil rights was reaching a boiling point. American blacks, and particularly those from the South, were exposed to a broader perspective as a result of serving in the military in various international settings, some of which were much more tolerant of racial diversity (e.g., France). Further, the undergirding principle for entering the war was to fight against, and ultimately destroy, the powers of tyranny as embodied in the regimes of Hitler in Nazi Germany, Mussolini in Fascist Italy, and Hirohito in Imperial Japan. America and its allies eventually defeated this so-called "Axis of Evil" and in the aftermath, many black veterans were anything but comfortable with returning to the second-class citizenship still enforced in the Jim Crow South. Indeed, the hypocrisy of American race relations was a major impediment to arguing for the moral superiority of the United States as it engaged in a lengthy Cold War with its primary foe, the Communist Soviet Union (Woodward 2002).

The Supreme Commander of the Allied Forces in Europe, General Dwight D. Eisenhower, chose not to retire to civilian life upon conclusion of the war. Instead, Eisenhower sought the presidency and both major parties furiously courted him as the 1952 election neared. "I like Ike" became a popular campaign slogan in the presidential race, and it was fitting because Eisenhower did not campaign on an overtly ideological agenda. As a Republican, Eisenhower acknowledged the Democratic New Deal status quo, and neither he nor his two-time Democratic opponent, Adlai Stevenson, focused attention on the civil rights issue. But it would not go away. The GOP made permanent presidential inroads into the South in the 1950s, but the southern Democracy continued to defend its white supremacist position on race relations. Dixie finally experienced the birth pangs of an impending civil rights movement in the mid-1950s, and instead of capitulating to equal rights for African Americans, the white power structure pushed back even harder and dug in its heels even deeper by massively resisting any threat to the South's status quo.

By the 1960s, the South witnessed a full-blown civil rights movement fueled by a sympathetic change in the public opinions of northern whites, many of whom reacted in horror to the scenes of violent opposition to peaceful protestors broadcast on their television screens. The major parties were changing their positions on civil rights (Feinstein and Schickler 2008), and the permanent reversal came in 1964 when Democratic President Lyndon Baines Johnson (LBJ) championed passage of the Civil Rights Act and his Republican opponent, U.S. Senator Barry Goldwater, voted against the historic legislation (Carmines and Stimson 1989). The postwar GOP had begun its initial southern ascent on the basis of economic appeals to a growing white middle class, but in the 1960s the race issue dominated the discussion and again asserted itself as the most salient in shaping American politics. By leading the charge for black civil rights, the national Democratic Party welcomed the huge influx of black southerners recently re-enfranchised by the 1965 Voting Rights Act (VRA). In contrast, under the leadership of Barry Goldwater, the Republican Party's conservative opposition to aggressive federal intervention into southern race relations sprung the door wide open for southern whites to realign to the GOP.

The post–civil rights period of the 1970s was an important transition period in southern politics. The Democratic Party was still in charge, but it was gradually ceding ground to Republicans because the difficult task of satisfying the needs of white and black Democrats proved unmanageable. Instead of countering with its own recipe for building a biracial coalition of supporters, the southern GOP chose the course of appealing almost exclusively to the white electorate (Black and Black 2002). Because of their ancestral allegiance to the southern Democracy, it would take decades to capture a majority of white voters and hence finally control the southern party system. But this goal was aided by the emergence of a charismatic Californian whose political views meshed perfectly with those held by the bulk of white southerners.

In the 1980s, President Reagan brought clarity and consistency to the major issues that divided the Democratic and Republican parties. By taking conservative positions on the most important issues capturing the attention of the American electorate, Reagan was the patron saint of contemporary partisan polarization in American politics. In the South, Reagan's opposition to social liberalism on such issues as abortion and school prayer helped turn a heretofore Democratic evangelical Christian population into Republicans. And more broadly, as Black and Black (2002) contend, Reagan was the catalyst for de-aligning white Democratic moderates while at the same time realigning white conservatives to the Republican Party. This chapter chronicles the important changes in southern politics from the 1950s through the 1980s. By examining this period in chronological order by decade, we can see how a one-party Democratic South evolved into a competitive two-party political system that was on the brink of taking a decidedly Republican turn as the 1990s approached.

THE NOT-SO PLACID 1950s

After five straight Democratic victories, the GOP finally won the White House again with the election of Republican Dwight D. Eisenhower in 1952. Although the war hero was more popular outside the South, Ike had permanently reopened the door to the GOP in southern presidential elections. Eisenhower's two terms would ultimately prove to be a temporary respite from an otherwise Democratic national party system (Campbell et al. 1960). In the North, Eisenhower took 56.6 percent of the popular vote and won 47.2 percent of the South's votes, while besting his hapless Democratic opponent Adlai Stevenson 442 to 89 in the Electoral College (EC). Four Rim South states voted for Eisenhower: Florida, Tennessee, Texas, and Virginia (57 out of 128 total southern EC votes). In 1956, President Eisenhower easily won reelection, beating the Democrat Stevenson again by an even more impressive margin: 457 to 73 in the Electoral College. Outside the South, Ike took 58.9 percent of the popular vote. In Dixie, for the first time since Grant defeated Greeley in 1872, a Republican captured a majority of the popular vote (50.6 percent) and the Electoral College vote (52 percent). In the process, Eisenhower held onto the four Peripheral South states he won in 1952 and added the Deep South state of Louisiana to his win column (67 out of 128 total southern EC votes).

Eisenhower was not interested in weighing in on the civil rights of African Americans, and perhaps somewhat surprisingly, given the aggressive courting of the black vote by President Truman, Adlai Stevenson also elided the issue. As a consequence, civil rights would only come to the fore if African Americans pressed it, and they did, forcing President Eisenhower to respond. Given Eisenhower's somewhat begrudging acceptance of the New Deal economic status quo, and the absence of an outward partisan battle over civil rights in the 1952 and 1956 presidential campaigns, the gradual movement of southern whites in favor of the GOP seemed tied more to economics than race. As Bartley and Graham (1975) have documented with precinct-level data on presidential vote returns, Eisenhower's strongest southern support came from disproportionately white and upscale urban centers fueling the region's postwar population growth. These burgeoning metropolitan centers, primarily located in the Rim South, were attractive to northern migrants who were more likely to affiliate with the Republican Party than their native southern neighbors (Scher 1997). Thus, the appeal of President Eisenhower was not premised on the race issue, but for southern whites, economics would soon mesh seamlessly with the race issue, which flared up in the mid-1950s and became a full-blown conflagration in the next decade.

From 1952 to 1960, Democrats controlled the House of Representatives in all but the 83rd Congress (1953–1955) when Eisenhower was first elected president. Thanks to such large southern Democratic majorities, their combination with Democratic-held seats in the North were usually enough to control the lower chamber. The continued dominance of southern Democrats in electoral politics and the increasing competitiveness of the Democratic Party in the North since the 1930s sustained and perpetuated a national Democratic majority in the 1950s, even though Republican President Eisenhower managed to win two terms. This is why scholars often speak of Eisenhower's success in 1952 and 1956 as representing deviating elections because a widely popular Republican won office in a Democratic era (see Campbell et al. 1960). The New Deal Coalition was still intact, but the civil rights issue generated considerable tension in a Democratic electorate most conspicuously described by the presence of southern whites and northern blacks.

In 1954, the Supreme Court handed down a monumental decision in the case of *Brown v. Board of Education*. Throughout the South and in states bordering the region, like in Kansas (where this case originated), children were separated into different schools on the basis of race. This longstanding feature of the Jim Crow era was sanctioned by the "separate but equal" doctrine established back in the 1896 case of *Plessy v. Ferguson* (see chapter 3). Chief Justice Earl Warren, an Eisenhower appointee (whom the president openly regretted appointing), knew the *Brown* case would be historic and controversial and hence he made sure to secure a unanimous decision. Basing the ruling on social science evidence that young minority children felt racially inferior when subjected to experiments that highlighted racial differences, a unified Supreme Court averred that the separation of the races was inherently unequal, thus overturning *Plessy* and directly undermining the plank that the Jim Crow South rested on.[1]

Fortunately, the *Brown* ruling was handed down not long after the American National Election Studies (ANES) had begun undertaking detailed surveys of the U.S. electorate.[2] The Court's decision created a firestorm in the South; to say that the white population was not ready for such a revolutionary alteration to Dixie's way of life would be the essence of understatement. For instance, in 1962—eight years after *Brown*—the ANES indicated that 72 percent of southern whites thought that the "government should stay out" of ensuring school integration. Ten years later, in 1972, 64 percent of southern whites still held this segregationist position (see McKee 2012b).[3] Given southern whites' massive resistance to the *Brown* decision and its obvious implication of overturning any law that imposed racial separation in public places, politicians quickly recognized that taking a firm and vocal stand against federal intervention in the South's race relations was a winning electoral strategy.

In December 1955, civil rights activist Rosa Parks boldly took a stand on a public bus in Montgomery, Alabama, by refusing to give up her seat in the front of the bus, as was expected when white passengers boarded. By not moving to the back of the bus, Ms. Parks unofficially kicked off the postwar southern civil rights movement. Her actions drew the attention of a 26-year-old Baptist preacher by the name of Martin Luther King, Jr. (MLK). MLK took this opportunity to lead a boycott of the Montgomery bus law, and in a little over a year the economic effects had inflicted enough damage that the city capitulated by removing the discriminatory conditions placed upon black bus riders. But this victory proved an isolated event because the backlash toward the *Brown* ruling was starting to set in across the South, and for the remainder of the 1950s, white massive resistance short-circuited a nascent civil rights movement. As Woodward (2002) put it, it was as though the lights were turned out throughout Dixie as southern politicians effectively evaded the Court's desegregation ruling and made it clear that securing black civil rights would be a long, hard, and violent struggle.

Expressing their disgust and purported defiance of the *Brown* decision, in 1956, most of the South's congressional delegation backed a "Southern Manifesto," which denied the authority of the federal government to intervene in Dixie's political affairs. Highly reminiscent of the doctrine of interposition, espoused by South Carolinian John C. Calhoun in the Jacksonian era (1828–1836), which claimed a state had the right to prevent federal usurpation of its laws, the Southern Manifesto was another feeble attempt by the South to deny federal control over its actions. And although the manifesto was a toothless statement of outrage, the Supreme Court was also hobbled by its Achilles' heel: the inability to enforce its rulings. It took aggressive presidential enforcement of the law to ensure state compliance, and this was not something President Eisenhower was eager to do. But events forced his hand. In 1957, Little Rock Central High School admitted nine African Americans. Local white Arkansans were apoplectic, Governor Orval Faubus rode their outrage to a string of reelection victories, and the president had to bring in the National Guard to protect the safety of the "Little Rock Nine" for the entire school year. Rather than prolong the tension, the following year Little Rock Central High School closed.

In the same year as the standoff in Little Rock, Congress passed a Civil Rights Act—the first of the twentieth century—but it was a modest provision (Black and Black 2002), placing the burden on African Americans to seek legal recourse if they believed their right to vote was denied. Nonetheless, the legislation was threatening to most southern politicians, with the exception of a few, like the Senate's Democratic Majority Leader Lyndon Johnson, who already had his sights set on a presidential run and pushed the reform to signal that a southern Democrat could lead the party forward on civil rights. More common was the stance of South Carolina Senator and former Dixiecrat nominee Strom Thurmond, who took the opportunity to filibuster the proposal for twenty-four hours and eighteen minutes (a record that stands to this day). Thurmond, like Faubus and the vast majority of southern politicians, could easily gauge the mood of an angry, overwhelmingly white electorate who demanded maximum resistance to federal intervention in Dixie's race relations.

Ten years after *Brown*, less than 10 percent of southern public schools were desegregated and in most of those that were, it was best characterized as token integration (Black and Black 1987). Virginia initially responded to the decision by simply closing its public schools and then reopening them as private schools in order to keep blacks out (Woodward 2002). In the states of the Deep South, where opposition to integration was most militant, nary a trace of desegregation occurred in the first decade after *Brown* (Black and Black 1987). White massive resistance held firm throughout the latter half of the 1950s. The white backlash to the Court's attack on the Jim Crow status quo was swift and fierce, stopping a budding civil rights movement in its tracks. Southern politicians quickly understood that the easiest path to securing elective office was to express disregard, if not open defiance, of federal intervention in race relations. Those who did not learn this lesson at first (e.g., George Wallace in his failure to win the 1958 Alabama Democratic gubernatorial primary) were likely to morph into militant segregationists (e.g., George Wallace in the 1962 Alabama Democratic gubernatorial primary) because it was the surest bet to winning office after *Brown* (Black 1976). But massive resistance would not prevail, and in the next decade the black civil rights movement would reach its stride, a pace that was remarkably swift in overturning decades of oppressive laws that prevented racial equality and the opportunity for blacks to have an influence in southern party politics.

THE TUMULTUOUS AND TRIUMPHANT 1960s

The civil rights movement heated up again in the winter of 1960 when a handful of brave African American college students decided to engage in a silent lunch counter sit-in at the Woolworth's Drugstore in Greensboro, North Carolina (blacks were protesting against the refusal to be served in these establishments). Soon, the sit-ins spread to cities all across the South, and white students from the North became active participants in these as well as various other forms of civil rights protests. The leading organizations pushing for nonviolent resistance to Jim Crow laws included the Congress of Racial Equality (CORE), the Student Nonviolent Coordinating Committee (SNCC), and the Southern Christian Leadership Conference (SCLC). CORE was the most racially integrated, with many white northerners actively involved; SNCC was a more homegrown organization consisting of numerous young, ambitious, and fearless southern blacks; SCLC was the most refined and stately outfit, that MLK and several other revered southern African American preachers led. These primary players in the civil rights movement often worked together and coordinated strategy, but in the mid-1960s, as the movement frayed, internal fighting and fundamental disagreements would lead to their demise.[4]

With the spread of lunch counter sit-ins and the galvanizing of young people, the civil rights movement revved up to a breakneck pace in the first half of the 1960s. Despite the Supreme Court striking down segregation in interstate travel, throughout the South, bus travel remained segregated and became an important target of civil rights activists who boarded buses in the upper South (e.g., North Carolina) and rode them deep into the heart of Dixie (into Alabama and Mississippi). The objective of these black and white "Freedom Riders" was to desegregate ridership and the facilities (waiting rooms and bathrooms) located in bus stations. In some settings, local law enforcement and the Ku Klux Klan would coordinate assaults on the riders when they departed the buses to enter local stations. Many riders were severely beaten and one bus was firebombed outside of Anniston, Alabama. In Jackson, Mississippi, most riders were arrested and then shipped off to Parchman, a maximum security prison in the Delta that was revived for its new inhabitants, who were forced to perform hard labor. Numerous blacks and whites, men and women alike, considered it a badge of honor to cut their teeth at Parchman, making it an effective proving ground for those who became even more committed to push for civil rights upon their release (see Arsenault 2006).

BOX 4.1   THE STRATEGY OF THE CIVIL RIGHTS MOVEMENT

As the civil rights movement progressed, the dominant strategy embraced and employed by its leaders was large-scale nonviolent protest. In the early days of the movement, such as the 1955–1956 Montgomery Bus Boycott triggered by Rosa Parks's refusal to move from the front to the back of the bus (as black passengers were expected to do), mass protests in the streets had not yet taken off. In the early 1960s, the civil rights movement was reignited by college students who exhibited tremendous courage in holding silent lunch counter sit-ins at numerous establishments throughout the South that, at the time, refused to serve black customers. In 1961, a racially integrated group of young blacks and whites (the latter of whom were almost all from the North), affiliated with the civil rights organization CORE (Congress of Racial Equality), dared to ride buses from the upper South to deep into the heart of Dixie (Alabama and Mississippi) with the objective of integrating interstate travel and desegregating the bus stations that dotted the paths of these bus routes (Arsenault 2006). The lunch counter sit-ins and so-called "Freedom Rides" of the early 1960s were highly effective in furthering integration in restaurants and mass transit, and the tactics of these participants became the blueprint for the strategy of civil rights activists.

These methodically planned protests garnered substantial media coverage because the demonstrators often endured brutal beatings at the hands of militant whites and local and state authorities who often coordinated their violent attacks. It became evident that among the local white populations, this kind of naked violence against their black neighbors or even worse, outside agitators, was easily tolerated if not condoned. Rather, the South's elaborate Jim Crow system of legally sanctioned racial segregation unraveled because of the marked shift in national public opinion toward the civil rights movement in response to the violence endured by peaceful protestors. As the public consciousness was aroused by the struggle for racial equality in Dixie, there became an opening for northern Democratic and Republican politicians to coalesce around monumental legal reforms spearheaded by President Johnson.

Martin Luther King, Jr. (MLK), obviously the most famous and influential civil rights leader, modified and retooled his political strategy by enduring a devastating failure from 1961–1962 in the small town of Albany, Georgia (Garrow 1978). It was MLK's expectation that this location would be ideal for attracting national attention through mass protests that would hopefully result in a violent response. This strategy is what has always been hard for many to comprehend and accept. Legions of civil rights activists underwent the rigors of stressful and strenuous training that simulated the kind of abuse they would receive in real, unscripted situations. Through this training, it was possible for these protestors to suffer great abuses without ever retaliating. It was this remarkable restraint under great physical cruelty that proved the key weapon in the struggle for black civil rights. In the absence of a vicious and unwarranted response, civil rights protests would be robbed of the media attention vital to influencing public opinion. It was in Albany, Georgia, where MLK met his match in Laurie Pritchett, the chief of police. Rather than play the

(Continued)

(Continued)

role of militant and violent southern segregationist, Pritchett calmly arrested one protestor after another and did so without a hint of police brutality. Pritchett simply would not be provoked, and his calmness and civility deflated MLK and the rest of the activists who expected Albany to be a powder keg. "The chief's tactics were mass arrests, the control of white racists, amiable relations with the press, and even friendly contact with King himself. Pritchett's real triumph was that he was not a credible villain" (Reston 2016, 57).

MLK desperately needed a villain after incurring the most demoralizing episode of his civil rights leadership during the futile Albany campaign. Although Pritchett refused to play MLK's game, MLK found a willing participant and the ideal foil in Eugene "Bull" Connor, the police commissioner of Birmingham, Alabama. Birmingham was arguably the most racially hostile major Deep South city, and Bull Connor played perfectly into MLK's hands because he was quick to resort to violence, even when faced with peaceful mass protests. MLK decided to deploy children in the Birmingham demonstrations and on multiple occasions Bull Connor unleashed firehoses and police dogs on the protestors. The Birmingham campaign commenced in the spring of 1963 and reached a boiling point heading into summer, when the violence (some of it committed by local black youth who were not trained in the nonviolent tactics of veteran activists) reached a level such that President Kennedy called for what would later become the Civil Rights Act of 1964, in a nationally televised address on June 11. Media coverage was ample and by 1963, most American households had a television and only three channels to choose from, which all covered the conflagration underway in Birmingham. As noted by Black and Black (1987, 110), at the start of the Birmingham protests, most Americans did not consider civil rights to be one of the nation's most pressing issues ("4 percent in early spring"), but "by early summer" 52 percent of respondents in a national Gallup poll chose "civil rights as the nation's most important problem."

The success of the Birmingham campaign and the subsequent assassination of President Kennedy in his Dallas, Texas, motorcade on November 22, 1963 galvanized enough votes in Congress for President Johnson to honor the fallen president's wishes by signing the Civil Rights Act on July 2, 1964. In the following year, the civil rights movement would achieve its greatest success with passage of the Voting Rights Act, which was signed into law by President Johnson on August 6, 1965. Just as Birmingham incited excessive, unjustified, and unwarranted violence by law enforcement that mobilized public opinion in favor of the civil rights protestors, in Selma, Alabama, Dallas County Sheriff Jim Clark played the role of Bull Connor in his unabashed violence toward peaceful demonstrators who targeted Selma because it was a heavily black town in the heart of the Alabama black belt that allowed only a handful of blacks to register to vote. Sheriff Clark was the antithesis of Laurie Pritchett—he was the perfect villain in the civil rights drama and the violence he bestowed upon a group of peaceful marchers on the Edmund Pettus Bridge on Sunday, March 7, 1965 (forever memorialized as "Bloody Sunday"), once again played seamlessly into the hands of MLK and other courageous civil rights leaders (like John Lewis, who was severely beaten on that fateful day), who used the salience of the event to gain momentum for what would be the hallmark achievement of the movement.

> In sum, nonviolent mass protest, the primary strategy of the civil rights movement, was recognized as being most effective when it was met with mass violence, especially coordinated violence undertaken by law enforcement because it undermined the credibility of local authority in the eyes of the national electorate (certainly not the view among most white southerners). In the absence of highly publicized instances of mass suffering at the hands of guilty oppressors, there is little question that the civil rights movement would have registered a much smaller effect on furthering racial equality. Hence, there is an inescapable irony. By acting recklessly, the Bull Connors and Jim Clarks actually did much more than the likes of a Laurie Pritchett to bring about the desired legal reforms sought by southern African Americans.

In the fall of 1962, African American James Meredith was approved for admission to the University of Mississippi, an action vehemently opposed by Governor Ross Barnett—making it the first high-profile attempt to block integration at a flagship institution in a Deep South state.[5] In perhaps the first large-scale violent skirmish between residents of a southern state and the federal government since the Civil War, a riot broke out on the Ole Miss campus as hundreds of students and residents from surrounding communities did battle with federal marshals. The violence left two people dead and added another permanent scar to the tragic legacy of race relations in the Magnolia State (Silver 2012). At his inauguration on a cold January day in 1963, Alabama Governor George Wallace proclaimed, "Segregation now, segregation tomorrow, segregation forever!" At the University of Alabama, Wallace "stood in the schoolhouse door" to temporarily deny the admission of African Americans James Hood and Vivian Malone. And it was in the spring of 1963 that Birmingham, Alabama, became ground zero for one of the most significant civil rights protests.

BOX 4.2 GEORGE WALLACE

George Corley Wallace, Jr. was born on August 25, 1919 in Clio, Alabama, a small town in the Wiregrass region of southeastern Alabama.[1] In his youth, he was a Golden Gloves amateur boxing champion and then served as a fighter pilot in World War II. Wallace experienced post-traumatic stress disorder that contributed to his military discharge (Carter 1995). Wallace began his foray into Alabama politics as a local judge, and by most accounts, he did not appear to harbor the racial animus that he later became notorious for. Indeed, Wallace was an understudy of "Kissing Big Jim" Folsom, the Alabama populist who clearly had no interest in stirring up racial antagonism between the poor whites and blacks who formed the base of his electoral support in his two successful nonconsecutive terms as Alabama governor in 1946

(Continued)

(Continued)

and 1954.[2] In the open Democratic gubernatorial primary of 1958, Wallace decided to succeed his mentor, but he was defeated in the runoff by Attorney General John Patterson. Wallace did not run as a militant segregationist, but Patterson did, and the lesson Wallace learned from this setback was to never "be out-nigguhed again" by a political opponent (Frady 1996, 131). The 1958 contest was the turning point when Wallace understood that taking a militant segregationist position held broad appeal to the post–*Brown v. Board of Education* (1954) white Alabama electorate.

In 1962, on the verge of the most tumultuous period of the civil rights movement, and especially in the state of Alabama, George Wallace was elected governor. With a fiery inauguration speech, from the outset Wallace made it clear that he would actively use his office to block black civil rights. He "stood in the schoolhouse door" in a futile but symbolic act of defiance against the federally enforced integration of the University of Alabama. Wallace was in charge when the city of Birmingham experienced its greatest racial turmoil in the spring and summer of 1963 (an event that led President Kennedy to advocate for a Civil Rights Act in a nationally televised address on June 11), and later that year on September 15, when four young black girls were murdered by a bomb set off in the 16th Street Baptist Church. Wallace was still in the governor's mansion when the culmination of the civil rights movement was consecrated by the peaceful march from Selma to the Alabama capital of Montgomery in March of 1965.[3]

As per state law, Wallace could not serve a consecutive term so he cajoled his wife Lurleen to run in 1966, and she won, making her the second woman to win a southern governorship since Miriam "Ma" Ferguson was elected governor of Texas in 1924. Lurleen was basically a placeholder for her ambitious husband, who decided to seek the presidency as the American Independent Party candidate in 1968. In what would prove a highly competitive presidential race during the national unrest stemming from racial tensions and Vietnam War protests fueled by the assassinations of Martin Luther King, Jr. in April and then Robert Kennedy in June (Nelson 2014), Wallace was seen as a major threat to Republican Richard Nixon's campaign because both of them appealed to white southern voters. Nixon narrowly prevailed over his Democratic opponent Hubert Humphrey (President Johnson's vice president), but in the South, Wallace and Nixon each carried the electoral votes of five states (AL, AR, GA, LA, and MS went to Wallace, and Nixon won FL, NC, SC, TN, and VA) while Humphrey only won Texas.[4]

Wallace won his second term as governor in 1970 and chose to make another run at the White House in 1972. Campaigning during the Maryland Democratic primary, Wallace was shot multiple times at close range by Arthur Bremer, and the wounds left him wheelchair bound and partially paralyzed for the rest of his life. Wallace was reelected governor in 1974, and in 1976, he ran one last time for the presidency, again seeking the Democratic nomination. Wallace dropped out early and endorsed the eventual winner, Georgia Governor Jimmy Carter. This was not the end of Wallace's political career, though; he won his fourth and final term as governor of Alabama in 1982.

Wallace was a towering figure in Alabama politics. His brand of economic populism combined with a racist appeal to the white working class resonated across the nation (Carter 1999), even if his presidential runs made him appear as little more than a regional candidate. His longevity in Alabama politics (no one else has served four terms as governor) and the fact that Wallace never contemplated a switch to the Republican Party, choosing instead to transition from a racist demagogue to a New South Democratic liberal in the mid-1970s, stunted the rise of Alabama Republicans. Indeed, it is nothing short of remarkable that the most infamous governor during the height of the civil rights movement, who proclaimed at his 1963 inauguration speech, "segregation today, segregation tomorrow, segregation forever," in the twilight of his life would seek and receive forgiveness for his transgressions against the civil rights of African Americans (Carter 1998).

1. A very informative short biography of George Wallace is available at https://www.biography .com/people/george-wallace-9522367.

2. During this time, Alabama governors could only serve one term and then had to step down before being eligible to run again.

3. A previous march from Selma to Montgomery was aborted because of the massive violence that Alabama police unleashed on the demonstrators under the direction of Dallas County Sheriff Jim Clark on the Edmund Pettus Bridge. This brutal attack on peaceful protestors occurred on Sunday, March 7, and it has forever since been referred to as "Bloody Sunday."

4. Wallace also won the vote of one North Carolina elector (the Tar Heel State had 13 electoral votes and the rest went to Nixon; Dave Leip's *Atlas of U.S. Presidential Elections*, http://uselectionatlas .org/RESULTS/).

Still brooding from his failed attempt to make national news at a protest in Albany, Georgia, MLK next decided to muster the forces of massive dissent in Birmingham, Alabama. The city seemed perfect for eliciting a violent reaction from local law enforcement and various rabble-rousers who were invariably drawn to a civil rights demonstration. Not only was Birmingham one of the most militantly segregated large southern cities, but its acting police commissioner, Eugene "Bull" Connor, had a deserved reputation for using force to stifle discontent. Unlike most campaigns, in Birmingham, MLK chose to include teens and young children in the mass protests, a move that drew criticism but also had the intended effect of garnering national attention at the sight of violence. And violence there was; Commissioner Connor unleashed firehouses and police dogs on the protestors. By 1963, almost every American household owned a television set and with only three major channels that of course covered the exact same breaking story on the nightly news, the unrest in Birmingham captured the nation's attention (Black and Black 1987).

Most telling about the effectiveness of the Birmingham campaign was the remarkable shift in public opinion. Gallup regularly asks Americans to state the nation's most important problem and at the start of the mass protests in April, 10 percent mentioned civil rights. By July of 1963, 50 percent considered civil rights to be the country's number one problem (see Kernell, Jacobson, and Kousser 2009, 167). Indeed, the mass protests and attendant violence in Birmingham reached the point that on the evening of June 11, President John F. Kennedy (JFK) issued a nationally televised address that strongly advocated for the civil rights of all Americans and his statements were the precursor to the 1964 Civil Rights Act that President Johnson heralded as fulfilling a final wish of his slain predecessor.

The next significant civil rights activity occurred in the summer of 1964 in Mississippi. Dubbed "Freedom Summer" by its proponents, hundreds of black and white college students affiliated with CORE and SNCC (and smaller allied groups) descended upon Mississippi communities in an attempt to register local black populations. As part of the Southern Regional Council's (a nonprofit organization birthed by the JFK Administration) Voter Education Project (VEP), thousands of black Mississippians took part in mock elections to demonstrate their willingness to register and vote in real contests (Parker 1990). Little progress was made in the effort to register black Mississippians because of local white resistance, and the most infamous episode of violence took place in Neshoba County, where three civil rights workers were abducted and murdered. Although the VEP was far from successful in the goal of registering black Mississippians, the attention given to Freedom Summer was added justification for President Johnson's successful leadership in pushing Congress to pass the historic 1964 Civil Rights Act in early August. The law barred racial discrimination in all places of public accommodation (i.e., stores, restaurants, hotels, theaters)—dealing a mortal blow to Jim Crow segregation.

The 1964 presidential election was shaping up to be an equally historic moment in the nation's history, for it would permanently reverse the positions of the national parties on the civil rights issue (Carmines and Stimson 1989). Riding the political momentum of his signature civil rights achievement, President Johnson realized that his embrace of this salient issue had alienated southern whites and cut off the southern Democracy from its more powerful and liberal northern wing. Hence, LBJ was a southerner who had become the leader of a party whose northern principles would take priority moving forward, and especially with respect to the civil rights of African Americans. Barry Goldwater, a Senator from Arizona, captured the Republican presidential nomination. Along with almost the entire southern congressional delegation, Goldwater voted against the 1964 Civil Rights Act, presumably disagreeing with its heavy-handed federal intervention in southern race relations. In taking a stand against the historic legislation, Goldwater sent an obvious signal to white southerners, and he was on the record for saying he would go "hunting where the ducks are." But the white ducks of the Deep South were an exotic species compared to the rest of the American electorate. In the 1964 election, LBJ won in a landslide, defeating his Republican opponent 486 to 52 in the Electoral College. Goldwater carried just six states: his native Arizona, and the entire Deep South (Alabama, Georgia, Louisiana, Mississippi, and South Carolina), where white resistance to black civil rights was, not surprisingly, the most extreme (Cosman 1966).

The 1964 election denoted a critical shift in the party identification and voting behavior of southern blacks. According to the ANES data, in 1960, the percentage of southern blacks identifying as Democrats was 60, Republicans were 32 percent, and Independents accounted for 8 percent. Four years later, with the issue of civil rights front-and-center in the 1964 presidential campaign, 86 percent of southern African Americans identified as Democrats, 6 percent were Republicans, and 8 percent were Independents. Perhaps just as impressive, among the small ANES sample of southern African American voters (well under 100, because so few were voting in the South at the time), everyone claimed to have voted for LBJ.[6] The 1964 election signaled the death of southern blacks' attachment to the party of Lincoln. The GOP had come to be viewed as the enemy of civil rights, despite the fact that most of the local resistance to the struggle for racial equality emanated from white Democratic politicians.

Goldwater's "southern strategy" of using race to divide white Democrats and hopefully lure strong support from the most racially conservative voters (see Sundquist 1983), provided a formula that was refined and perfected by future Republican nominees, most notably Richard Nixon in 1968 (Hillygus and Shields 2009; Phillips 1969) and Ronald Reagan in 1980 (Black and Black 2002). In the immediate term, the 1964 election did not move white southerners toward identifying with the GOP. For instance, the changes in white southerners' party identification barely moved between 1960 and 1964: 70.3 to 71.2 percent Democratic, 20.8 to 21.0 percent Republican, and 8.9 to 7.8 percent Independent. And with respect to presidential vote choice, white southerners were considerably more supportive of Nixon in his failed bid against Kennedy (47.6 percent voted Republican in 1960) than they were for the more extreme Goldwater in 1964 (who won 41.5 percent of the white vote).[7] But Goldwater's legacy was lasting because his direct appeal to white southerners on the civil rights issue became the primary approach to cultivating political support and building the modern Republican Party (Aistrup 1996). Indeed, 1964 was the last time a Democratic presidential nominee would capture a white majority of the two-party vote in southern presidential elections (Black and Black 2002).

Buoyed by his success in winning the 1964 election, President Johnson recognized that the civil rights issue was still hanging over the country, and more could be done. The last chapter of the southern movement took place in March 1965, in Selma, Alabama. Similar to Birmingham, the small town of Selma, located in Dallas County, deep in the Alabama black belt, had a sheriff easily moved to violence. To locals, Sheriff Jim Clark was notorious for denying the equal rights of Selma's black residents and he made sure that no one would dare register to vote. But it was his open hostility to blacks that drew the attention of civil rights organizers, who recognized that Sheriff Clark would be the perfect foil for a massive and peaceful civil rights protest. In an unseasonably cold March, the drama of Selma played out. At first, civil rights activists went en masse to the county registrar to assist local blacks who wanted to enter their names on the voting rolls. The approach was futile because Sheriff Clark repeatedly blocked these efforts to register, sometimes beating the peaceful demonstrators. But as the police violence ramped up, the protestors' nonviolent resistance gained momentum and national exposure. Sensing the weight of the moment, the leaders of the major civil rights organizations converged on Selma and it was decided that the next step would be to march from Selma to the capital city of Montgomery—in a mass (and massive) demonstration of unity impossible for Governor Wallace and the entire nation to ignore.

But it was an event that took place before the demonstrators departed Selma that captured the nation's attention and left most white northerners stunned by the actions of southern law enforcement. On Sunday, March 7, John Lewis, one of the leaders of the SNCC, placed himself at the front of a long line of protestors who gathered on the Edmund Pettus Bridge to march from Selma to Montgomery. Joined by Alabama state troopers, Sheriff Clark and his horseback-riding deputies, who were outfitted in full riot gear, ordered the marchers to stand down and disperse. The marchers stood their ground and the police force responded with a vicious assault that severely injured scores of protestors, including John Lewis, who was beaten within an inch of his life. The violent outbreak on "Bloody Sunday" was widely reported on the national news and in newspapers across the country. The outpouring of support was tremendous, as thousands of blacks and whites from all over the United States came down to Selma to join in the march to Montgomery. Two weeks later the march reconvened, and this time Governor Wallace even pledged to ensure the safety of the demonstrators as they undertook the fifty-four mile trek to the Alabama state capital.

The events in Selma provided the momentum and moral justification for passage of the Voting Rights Act (VRA), which Congress approved later that summer. A truly groundbreaking law, the 1965 VRA aggressively enforced the right to vote, even sending federal registrars into select southern counties that were found to be noncompliant in registering African Americans. It had its greatest impact in the Deep South states that were most resistant to black enfranchisement: Mississippi, Alabama, and Louisiana (Timpone 1995). In short, the 1965 VRA and its subsequent extensions quickly became the primary bulwark for re-enfranchising the southern black population and thereafter safeguarding their suffrage. Table 4.1 highlights the dramatic increase in black registration by showing data before and after passage of the VRA, in 1960, 1964, and 1968. As shown in the table, five years before the VRA, only 5 percent of black voting age Mississippians were registered to vote. But three years after the VRA, 59 percent of Mississippi's adult black population was registered to vote. The mobilization of black voters was remarkable, and especially in Deep South states like Mississippi, where black suffrage was historically low as a direct result of restrictive voting laws and physical intimidation. Now, black registration rates are commensurate with white rates throughout the South (Black and Black 1987), and in some Deep South settings African Americans control local politics (Bullock and Gaddie 2009).

TABLE 4.1 ■ Percentage of the Black Voting Age Population Registered in Southern States			
State	1960	1964	1968	Δ 1968–1960
Alabama	14	23	57	+43
Arkansas	37	49	68	+31
Florida	39	64	62	+23
Georgia	29	44	56	+27
Louisiana	31	32	59	+28
Mississippi	5	7	59	+54
North Carolina	38	47	55	+17
South Carolina	16	39	51	+35
Tennessee	59	69	73	+14
Texas	35	58	83	+48
Virginia	23	46	58	+35

Source: Table was originally published in McKee (2012b).

Notes: Data compiled by the author from Kernell, Jacobson, and Kousser (2009, Map 4–3, p. 170). Italicized states were not covered by the Voting Rights Act of 1965 (40 out of North Carolina's 100 counties were covered by the 1965 VRA). Florida (only 5 counties) and Texas (statewide coverage) became covered states with the 1972 amendment to the VRA that included language minorities. The VRA has never applied to Arkansas and Tennessee.

The Reapportionment Revolution

In the midst of a roiling civil rights movement another revolution had gotten underway. Shortly after the war, in the 1946 Supreme Court case of *Colegrove v. Green,* the justices pledged not to enter the "political thicket" of redistricting. But in the 1960s, the more liberal Court of Chief Justice Earl Warren reconsidered. In various states, and especially those in the South, congressional and state legislative district boundaries had remained in place for decades (Engstrom 2013). In Dixie, this was done on purpose because the locus of political power resided firmly in the hands of white Democrats who represented smaller rural populations (see chapter 8). In some states, the largest district might contain hundreds of times more residents than those inhabiting the smallest district (Bullock 2010). By the 1960s, the Supreme Court was no longer willing to allow such gross malapportionment to stand. The Supreme Court issued a series of rulings that all served the general purpose of complying with a one-person, one-vote principle, and hence an equal population standard was put into effect in district-based elections (Ansolabehere and Snyder 2008; Ladewig and McKee 2014).

In *Baker v. Carr* (1962), a case originating from Tennessee, the Supreme Court established the one-person, one-vote principle and in the next few years most states were ordered to redraw their congressional districts (as per the 1964 ruling in *Wesberry v. Sanders*—originally a Georgia case) and state legislative districts (as per the 1964 ruling in *Reynolds v. Sims*—originally an Alabama case) so that they were approximately equal in population. Forcing the states to equalize their district populations was a truly revolutionary decision because it immediately shifted the center of power and influence in Congress and state legislatures. Broadly speaking, because Republicans in the North were the beneficiaries of most underpopulated districts, the *Baker* ruling was a net benefit to Democrats (Cox and Katz 2002). In the South, the opposite was true: equalizing district populations took power away from rural Democrats and redistributed it to urban Democrats and Republicans who were gaining support in numerous fast-growing suburban areas. The increase in representatives from urban districts also had the general effect of altering redistributive politics, as more money would now be allocated to constituents residing in metropolitan areas (Ansolabehere, Gerber, and Snyder 2002).

In *Gray v. Sanders* (1963), the Supreme Court struck down Georgia's controversial county unit system. The county unit system was severely malapportioned because the number of votes allotted to the largest counties was not nearly commensurate with the number assigned to smaller counties (see Buchanan 1997; Key 1949, 117–123).[8] Used by Democrats in statewide primaries (and in some U.S. House primaries) going back to 1917, the county unit system bore a resemblance to the Electoral College because it allowed for the possibility of a candidate winning the popular vote but losing the primary because another candidate could win the majority of county unit votes. Such a scenario played out in 1946, when Eugene Talmadge won a majority of county unit votes and hence won the Democratic gubernatorial nomination, even though his opponent won 16,000 more popular votes (Key 1949). It is no wonder that Talmadge bragged that he never wanted to carry a county with streetcars because he didn't need to, so long as the county unit system stacked the deck in favor of rural voters. The enforcement of the equal population standard would prove difficult for many rural Democratic politicians representing districts in Deep South states like Georgia. The readjustment of district boundaries and the attendant influx of new and unfamiliar urban voters often constituted a constituency more inclined to back a Republican challenger (Fenno 2000).

The 1968 Presidential Election

Despite his impressive victory over Goldwater in 1964, LBJ sensed he had a quickly closing window of opportunity to push through some historic domestic legislation. As discussed, the Voting Rights Act passed in 1965. Viewing FDR's New Deal agenda as unfinished, President Johnson wanted to build upon this Democratic legacy by putting forth an ambitious "Great Society" program, which would wage a "war on poverty" and enact Medicare and Medicaid in 1965, the largest entitlement since FDR led congressional passage of the Social Security Act in 1935. Perhaps LBJ was prescient because his flurry of domestic achievements were done swiftly, prior to the 1966 midterm in which his Democratic House majority lost 47 seats. But even more troubling than the large midterm loss was that President Johnson was embroiled in the Vietnam conflict, a war that he said American boys would not die for. LBJ lied, and soon the press knew it and shared the lie with an increasingly anxious and volatile American electorate.

As American casualties in Vietnam mounted, draft-dodging and war protests made the national news. Growing anti-war fervor took place alongside massive unrest in the nation's inner cities as race riots erupted across the country (Woodward 2002). In the South, after the triumphant passage of the 1965 VRA, the movement seemed to grind to a screeching halt. Younger activists broke away from MLK's message and practice of nonviolence, preferring instead to advocate for "Black Power" and a curious message of racial separation that they aggressively promoted throughout the North. Turning the central message of the civil rights movement on its head, influential leaders like Huey Newton of the Black Panthers believed violence was often a necessary means to achieve racial equality and that voluntary segregation was beneficial. Needless to say, these views were not shared by most white Americans, and especially not white southerners, who considered the Black Power movement to be anathema to their well-established cultural norms (Black and Black 1987).

As the 1968 presidential election neared, the country had reached a crisis state (Nelson 2014). Although he no longer had the luxury of deploying a massive army of nonviolent disciples, MLK remained the most influential leader of the civil rights movement. After Selma, MLK had shifted to the cause of poverty and was outspoken in his criticism of LBJ and the Vietnam War. In Memphis, Tennessee, to lead a march of sanitation workers and draw national attention to poverty, on the evening of April 4, MLK was gunned down by an assassin's bullet while standing on the balcony outside his hotel room. He was 39. Just days before, on March 31, amidst the growing domestic unrest over the calamity of Vietnam, President Johnson issued a nationally televised address in which he stated, "I shall not seek, and I will not accept, the nomination of my party for another term as your president."[9]

The Democratic Party drew two anti-war candidates who actively sought the presidential nomination: Senator Bobby Kennedy of New York (and the former Attorney General of his late brother John F. Kennedy) and Senator Eugene McCarthy of Minnesota. While campaigning in early June in Los Angeles, Bobby Kennedy was assassinated. In late August, Senator McCarthy was left to carry the anti-war fight to the raucous and ultimately riotous 1968 Democratic National Convention (DNC) held in Chicago. Since the reelection of Andrew Jackson in the early 1830s, the major American parties had committed to nominating their presidential candidates in national conventions and hence the 1968 DNC was no different in this regard. But what made 1968 different was the heated backdrop of Vietnam and race riots, which Senators Kennedy and McCarthy addressed on the campaign trail while the other major contender for the Democratic nomination, Vice President Hubert Humphrey, did not actively campaign. At the convention, a behind-the-scenes power play orchestrated by President Johnson delivered the Democratic nomination to Humphrey and all hell broke loose. Enraged that the Democratic presidential nomination was essentially giftwrapped for Humphrey, a riot broke out as anti-war protestors exercised their disgust, and Mayor Richard Daley made sure they were greeted with a brutal beating at the hands of the Chicago Police.

The Republican nomination attracted a familiar face. Richard Nixon had decided to give the White House another run after coming so close against JFK in 1960. Unlike the Democratic skirmish, Nixon enjoyed an easy path to the GOP nomination. Rather than engage in a difficult conversation over the roots of racial unrest and outrage over American involvement in a controversial war, Nixon tapped into the vein of what he dubbed the "silent majority." Decoded, Nixon's strategy was to court the majority of white voters who were tired of domestic disturbances and more than anything demanded law and order during a time of tremendous political and social instability (Scammon and Wattenberg 1970). Further, Nixon understood that Goldwater's original southern strategy could be expanded to appeal to whites outside the South who were recoiling from the violence perpetrated in heavily black inner cities (Phillips 1969). Finally, without a strong challenge for the GOP mantle, Nixon invested heavily in a Madison Avenue–like image makeover with highly choreographed interactions with the electorate that were designed to cast him as stately and, above all else, as eminently presidential (McGinniss 1969).

The biggest electoral threat, as Nixon saw it, was not from a Democratic opponent, but the third-party American Independent Party bid of Alabama Governor George Wallace. As a southerner, Wallace was much more skilled in speaking to the concerns of race-conscious white voters and, of course, the vast lot of conservative white southerners whose votes Nixon coveted. In a close election, Nixon feared that Wallace would cut into his southern strategy and hand the presidency to the Democrat Hubert Humphrey. Nixon had reason to be concerned, but he also had important southern allies like South Carolina Senator Thurmond who had switched to the GOP in 1964 and four years later vowed to deliver the Palmetto State to Nixon.

Wallace caused a stir in and outside the South with his remarkable ability to prime the grievances of a disgruntled white working class that bore the brunt of the Vietnam War and was embittered by the perceived favoritism of the federal government toward minorities in the case of welfare assistance and job opportunities (Carter 1995). And it was with the white working class that the candidacies of Nixon and Wallace diverged. Whereas Nixon was happy to embrace the southern strategy, he was not a champion of the working class—his economic appeal was comfortably in line with Republican orthodoxy—attracting the support of upwardly mobile white voters. Wallace, on the other hand, was an outspoken racist demagogue with a fierce populist streak. He could best relate to, and mobilize, downscale whites with a racist chip on their shoulders.

As predicted, the 1968 presidential election turned out to be very close. Nixon won the popular vote over Humphrey by less than one percentage point (43.42 to 42.72 percent). Wallace captured more than 13 percent of the popular vote, but he failed to carry a single state outside the South. The vote breakdown in the Electoral College was 301 for Nixon (55.9 percent), 191 for Humphrey (35.5 percent), and 46 for Wallace (8.6 percent). In Dixie, the contest had, in fact, played out as a battle between Nixon and Wallace. True to his word, Thurmond helped deliver South Carolina to Nixon, but Wallace carried the other four Deep South states of Alabama, Georgia, Louisiana, and Mississippi. In addition, Arkansas went to Wallace and the state was arguably a microcosm of the politically unstable state of southern politics because the Natural State's voters engaged in a remarkable display of ticket-splitting: choosing the third-party candidate for president (Wallace), a Democrat for Senator (William Fulbright), and a Republican for Governor (Winthrop Rockefeller). Like Eisenhower, Nixon performed best in the Peripheral South states of Florida, North Carolina, Tennessee, and Virginia, with their relatively more racially tame electoral politics and larger white middle class. If not for the clout of LBJ, Humphrey would have been shut out of Dixie. Texas was the only southern state the Democratic nominee managed to win.

THE DECEPTIVELY QUIET 1970S

Perhaps it was the tumult of the 1960s that made the 1970s seem calm by comparison. But this is not an accurate description of the decade. Major electoral, institutional, and legal reforms would register a palpable impact on southern politics. A Republican president resigned before certain impeachment, and the political fallout propelled a southern Democrat to the White House. The massive re-enfranchisement of black voters was being felt in state and local southern elections, and their growing presence was a welcome reprieve for Democratic politicians who knew the white electorate was gradually turning toward the GOP. The difficult balancing act of satisfying the demands of black and white Democratic voters became nearly impossible when a smooth-talking ex-movie star decided to enter presidential politics and, in his pursuit, offered white southerners a conservative message that came across as a siren song powerful enough to embrace the party of Lincoln.

In direct response to the imbroglio at the 1968 Democratic National Convention, the McGovern-Fraser Commission enacted a set of sweeping reforms. Indeed, the changes to the process of nominating major party candidates for the presidency was so consequential that the period from 1972 forward is often called the *postreform era*. The McGovern-Fraser Commission was created to deal explicitly with the Democratic Party's nomination process, but most of its enacted reforms were also adopted by the Republican Party. Most telling was the shift from the national convention as the selection mechanism to making primaries and caucuses conducted throughout the American states the determinant for choosing the presidential nominee. Coincidentally, George McGovern, of the McGovern-Fraser Commission and a liberal Senator from South Dakota, won the Democratic presidential nomination in 1972. Branded as a candidate in favor of abortion, acid, and amnesty (for Vietnam deserters), McGovern was perhaps the most liberal candidate to ever win a major party nomination, and he was obliterated by the more centrist President Nixon. Nixon won more than 60 percent of the popular vote and took 520 of the 538 Electoral College votes. In addition to Washington, D.C., McGovern won just one state: Massachusetts. In the South, more than 80 percent of whites backed Nixon, as he became the first Republican presidential candidate to sweep the region.

Opening up the process of nominating presidential candidates to rank-and-file voters was quickly followed by an institutional reform in Congress that was clearly designed to remove power from longstanding southern Democratic committee chairs who were resistant, or at least recalcitrant, in their compliance with the national party's liberal policy agenda. Because of the lack of a strong Republican opposition in southern congressional elections, southern Democrats who served in Congress built up impressive tenure, and by virtue of their lengthy service, many of them were committee chairs in a party that controlled the House of Representatives for forty consecutive years (from 1954 to 1994). Over this long period, most of the institutional power in the U.S. House resided in the hands of committee chairs who singlehandedly set the legislative agenda in their policy domain (e.g., the House Committee on Agriculture). But in the 1970s, southern Democrats were outnumbered by their northern Democratic colleagues, and the latter did not appreciate the conservatism of the former, particularly with respect to issues like civil rights. So, instead of adhering strictly to the seniority rule that stated the longest serving member of the majority party would serve as committee chair, in early January 1973, congressional Democrats chose committee chairs by a secret ballot cast by the Democratic caucus (all Democrats serving in the U.S. House; Pearson and Schickler 2009).

The move to a secret ballot for selecting committee chairs stripped some southern Democrats of these positions and directly threatened their future ability to manage the needs of a biracial coalition of black and white supporters who frequently clashed on numerous political issues. The national Democratic Party was taking an aggressive position that pressured southern Democrats to either relinquish institutional power or shift their political philosophy in a more liberal direction that resembled the beliefs and policy views of northern Democrats (McKee 2010). This kind of heavy-handed action was just the sort that might provoke a switch to the GOP (Yoshinaka 2016). The difficult balancing act of trying to serve the needs of a biracial coalition of black and white voters had become a form of representation that former Democratic Alabama Congressman Glen Browder dubbed "Stealth Reconstruction" (see Browder and Stanberry 2010). In order to maintain a majority reelection coalition, Deep South Democrats had to be nimble and perhaps, at times, deceptive in their efforts to convince white voters that they were conservative enough, while also demonstrating to their black constituents that they were unwavering in their commitment to civil rights. Stealth Reconstruction in action might consist of advocating forcefully on issues that mattered to white voters (like lowering taxes) while making appearances in black churches or broadcasting pro-civil rights ads aired exclusively to the black community on black radio stations (Glaser 1996).

Further complicating the electoral health of southern Democrats, although the symptoms would not register for many years (Carmines and Woods 2002), was the Supreme Court's *Roe v. Wade* (1973) ruling declaring a constitutional right to an abortion. Before the decision, the major parties were basically silent on the issue, and during this period when the issue was dormant, abortions were more likely to be obtained by upscale Republican women (Stimson 2004). But in the late 1970s, conservative Christian organizations would mobilize to counter the *Roe* decision (Wilcox and Robinson 2011), and they found a willing ally in Republican presidential upstart Ronald Reagan. The partisan responses to the *Roe* decision spawned long-term effects that moved erstwhile southern Democratic religious conservative whites to the GOP (Adams 1997; more on this in chapter 7).

In 1974, southern Democrats—and the entire party, for that matter—would catch a needed break with the political fallout from the Watergate scandal. Despite the evidence that the 1972 presidential election would be a blowout, operatives for President Nixon engaged in a break-in at the Democratic National Committee headquarters at the Watergate Hotel in Washington, D.C. Thanks to a steady stream of political leaks provided by Mark Felt, a special agent working for the Federal Bureau of Investigation (FBI), *Washington Post* reporters Carl Bernstein and Bob Woodward (1974) blew the lid off of the Watergate story. Congressional investigations revved up and when it looked like impeachment was certain, President Nixon announced his resignation on August 8, 1974. Former House Minority Leader Gerald Ford had replaced Nixon's Vice President Spiro Agnew and became president upon Nixon's resignation. After being sworn in, the first major decision President Ford made was to pardon Nixon. At this time, the economy was in horrible shape with the onset of stagflation, a combination of high unemployment and high inflation. President Ford tried to boost morale with the slogan "Whip Inflation Now" (WIN), but the midterm elections, as expected, resulted in a large seat loss for the GOP. Before the 1974 elections, there were 243 Democrats and 192 Republicans in the U.S. House; after the election there were 291 Democrats and 144 Republicans. In the South, Democrats picked up five seats to control 75 percent of the region's U.S. House delegation.

As the 1976 election neared, the political environment was tailor made for the likes of a Jimmy Carter. The straight-laced peanut farmer and Georgia governor promised to restore decency and honor to the White House. By all accounts, President Ford was a good man, but the poor economy and the Nixon pardon likely sealed his unfortunate political fate. In a wide-open Democratic field, Carter ran hard and won enough primaries and caucuses to secure the Democratic presidential nomination. Perhaps it was luck, but Carter ran against the only Republican since 1960 who did not care to invoke the southern strategy of appealing to whites' racial conservatism. This helped the southern Democrat assemble a biracial coalition in Dixie's presidential contests. Even George Wallace campaigned for Carter. When the votes were counted, 1976 proved to be a razor-close election. Carter defeated Ford 297 to 240 in the Electoral College.[10] The popular two-party vote split 51 percent in favor of Carter. The South carried Carter to the White House. He won the popular votes of every southern state but Virginia and bested Ford 118 to 12 in EC votes. A biracial coalition of southerners accounted for his impressive performance because a majority of whites narrowly backed Ford (52.5 percent, according to the American National Election Study).

REAGAN AND THE 1980s TURNING POINT

Despite serving at a time of large Democratic congressional majorities in both the House and Senate, President Carter's tenure was a failure. Continued stagflation, turmoil in the Middle East that led to an oil crisis followed by an American hostage crisis in Iran, and then a failed rescue attempt, and the President's ineffectiveness in working with his own party (Pfiffner 1988), doomed the Carter Administration. As had happened to President Ford in 1976 (he faced a formidable intra-party nomination challenge from Ronald Reagan), in 1980 Senator Edward Kennedy challenged President Carter for the Democratic nomination. Senator Kennedy fell short of unseating President Carter, but his challenge signaled the incumbent's electoral vulnerability. To make matters worse, Ford's rival for the Republican nomination in 1976, Ronald Reagan, was the GOP nominee in 1980. By 1980, the former movie star, erstwhile Democrat, and former California governor had been a Republican activist for years, even giving an ideologically charged and impassioned speech ("A Time for Choosing") on behalf of Barry Goldwater in 1964. Put plainly, Reagan was a much more capable politician than the sitting president, possessing an uncanny ability to draw the support of white southerners. Indeed, Reagan would turn out to be the GOP's most successful party-builder in the American South (Black and Black 2002). Under his leadership, the South finally turned decisively in favor of the Republican Party.

Demonstrating his ability to capture the votes of white southerners, Reagan kicked off his 1980 presidential campaign at the Neshoba County Fair in Philadelphia, Mississippi.[11] Perhaps surprisingly, given such poor short-term political and economic conditions, the 1980 presidential contest appeared competitive until the final days, when it became evident that Reagan would prevail handily (Petrocik 1996). Late in the evening on Election Night, the Republican rout was widely reported. For the first time since 1954, Republicans captured a Senate majority and picked up three dozen seats in the House. Reagan won 55 percent of the popular two-party vote and defeated Carter 489 to 49 in the Electoral College.[12] Just as impressive was Reagan's southern performance. Whereas Carter won all but Virginia in 1976, he lost all but his home state of

Georgia in 1980. Reagan carried 64 percent of the white vote, won 54 percent of the popular two-party vote, and smothered Carter 118 to 12 in the Electoral College.[13]

The nation endured a recession that began not long after Reagan took office, and in 1982 it contributed to a 26-seat GOP midterm loss in the House of Representatives. But as the 1984 election neared, the economy strongly rebounded. Particularly in Dixie, but also true nationally, the 1984 presidential contest drew attention to what would be a recurrent problem with the Democratic Party: in the postreform era, its voters were prone to nominating northern liberals who lost the general election (e.g., McGovern in 1972, Mondale in 1984, Dukakis in 1988, and John Kerry in 2004). As one of these nominees, the Democrat Walter Mondale of Minnesota (and Carter's vice president) did not stand a chance against President Reagan. Like McGovern in 1972, Mondale managed to win only one state, his own (Minnesota), along with D.C.'s three EC votes. Beyond the Republican landslide in 1984, there was a more telling sign of GOP ascendancy in the American South. In 1980, the ANES showed that 32.6 percent of white southerners identified as Republicans. In 1984, Republican identifiers vaulted to 42.4 percent and ticked up to 43.7 percent in 1988. By comparison, 45.5 percent of white southerners claimed allegiance to the Democratic Party in 1988. The Democratic advantage in identification was almost gone.

The ANES data provided evidence for a large and enduring movement of white southerners to the Republican Party. Some of the leading studies at the time found evidence of both de-alignment and realignment of white southerners (Petrocik 1987; Stanley 1988). In hindsight, and with a longer data stream, it is clear that during the Reagan era, white moderates de-aligned from the Democratic Party while white conservatives realigned to the GOP (see Black and Black 2002). Further, generational replacement was a key factor in moving southern whites to the Republican Party (see Green, Palmquist, and Schickler 2002; McKee 2010; more on this in chapter 6). The last time one of the major parties controlled the presidency for three or more straight terms under different presidents was the transition from FDR to Truman. It happened again in 1988, when Vice President George H. W. Bush defeated Massachusetts Governor Michael Dukakis. Bush, a born-and-raised New England Yankee, later in life had transformed into a Texas oilman—a profile that of course most white southerners cottoned to. Bush's southern performance in the 1988 presidential election was impressive, adding another GOP sweep, but the national result was not a cakewalk reminiscent of 1984. Nonetheless, Dukakis only carried ten states (plus D.C.), lost the EC vote 111 to 426, and took only 46 percent of the popular two-party vote.[13]

The sound defeat of another northern liberal Democrat raised major concerns, which the party had already tried to address, but to no avail, in 1988. In Democratic-controlled legislatures throughout the South, the party devised Dixie's presidential nomination strategy popularly known as "Super Tuesday." The objective was to stack most (if not all) southern states' primary dates on the same day so that Dixie would be influential in shaping the nomination process. On March 8, 1988, the first ever large-scale southern Super Tuesday, with the objective of tilting the candidate selection process so a southern Democrat would be advantaged, went up in flames (Hadley and Stanley 1989). On this Super Tuesday, the South's primary votes split three ways: Jesse Jackson won the Deep South states of Alabama, Georgia, Louisiana, and Mississippi, and also Virginia; Michael Dukakis finished first in the mega states of Florida and Texas; leaving Al Gore (the preferred choice of the aspiring southern Democratic kingmakers who created Super Tuesday) the victor in Arkansas, North Carolina, and his home state of Tennessee (Bullock 1991).[14] The next presidential nomination cycle would yield a much more favorable result when a gifted politician from Arkansas sought the presidency. Perhaps it is ironic, but also true, that the only thing better for growing the southern GOP than having a Republican in the White House is to have a Democrat hold the office (Jacobson 1990), a point to be continued in the next chapter.

SUMMARY EVIDENCE OF THE COMPETITIVE TRANSITION

The 1950s to 1980s witnessed perhaps the greatest electoral change in the political history of the southern United States. The heretofore Solid Democratic South had finally given way to a competitive two-party political system (Lamis 1988) that advantaged Republicans in presidential contests (Black and Black 1992), whereas Democrats maintained an edge in all lower-level contests (Aistrup 1996; Black and Black 1987; Lublin 2004). This section briefly summarizes the competitive transition in southern politics by showing a series of tables and figures that document the shift from Democratic dominance to Republican competitiveness. In addition to election returns, the emergence of a running record of survey data cataloging the voter preferences among black and white southerners illuminates the turn toward the GOP.

Starting with presidential elections, Table 4.2 shows the Electoral College results in the South and Figure 4.1 presents the popular vote in southern presidential elections from 1952 to 1988. From 1952 to 1968, the Republican share of the EC vote in the South ranges from a low of 26 percent in 1960 to a high of 52 percent when President Eisenhower won reelection in 1956. In 1968, Nixon was held under an EC majority because of the presence of American Independent Party nominee George Wallace—the Alabama governor won four Deep South states—and the Democrat Hubert Humphrey was fortunate to win only Texas thanks to a strong assist from his former boss President Johnson. After 1968, Republicans dominate southern presidential contests. Jimmy Carter in 1976 is the only bright spot for a Democratic Party that otherwise was held to less than 10 percent of the South's EC votes from 1972 to 1988.

Because, with two exceptions (Maine and Nebraska), EC votes are winner take all, Figure 4.1 displays the popular two-party vote in southern presidential elections from 1952 to 1988. Because George Wallace registered an impressive performance in 1968, the popular vote is divided between Nixon, Humphrey, and Wallace in this election. From 1952 to 1964, the two-party split is very close and then the vote is also close

TABLE 4.2 ■ Electoral College Votes in the South, 1952–1988				
Election	Democrat	Republican	Rep % (Votes)	Winner
1952	A. Stevenson	D. Eisenhower	45 (128)	Republican
1956	A. Stevenson	D. Eisenhower	52 (128)	Republican
1960	J. Kennedy	R. Nixon	26 (128)	Democrat
1964	L. Johnson	B. Goldwater	37 (128)	Democrat
1968	H. Humphrey	R. Nixon	45 (128)	Republican
1972	G. McGovern	R. Nixon	99 (130)	Republican
1976	J. Carter	G. Ford	9 (130)	Democrat
1980	J. Carter	R. Reagan	91 (130)	Republican
1984	W. Mondale	R. Reagan	100 (138)	Republican
1988	M. Dukakis	G. Bush	100 (138)	Republican

Source: Data compiled by the author from Dave Leip's *Atlas of U.S. Presidential Elections* (http://uselection atlas.org/RESULTS/).

Note: In 1972, one unfaithful Nixon elector in Virginia cast his presidential vote for John Hospers.

among the three presidential candidates in 1968. In fact, Nixon won 34.7 percent of the popular vote and Wallace took 34.4 percent (31 percent for Humphrey). The 1972 election was a historic blowout as Nixon defeated McGovern with just under 71 percent of the popular vote. Democrats make a comeback with Jimmy Carter in 1976, but lose their advantage in 1980, when Ronald Reagan denies Carter a second term and then the GOP notches impressive popular vote margins in 1984 and 1988.

Turning to survey data, Figures 4.2 and 4.3 display the black and white vote in southern presidential elections from 1952 to 1988, respectively. Although a note of caution needs to accompany a presentation of votes cast by southern blacks from 1952 to 1964, because of such small sample sizes (fewer than 100 respondents in the ANES who said they voted for president in these years), the 1964 election clearly demarcates a permanent shift in presidential voting behavior. In 1956, a majority of southern African Americans backed Republican President Eisenhower instead of his repeat Democratic challenger Adlai Stevenson, whom southern blacks favored four years prior. Kennedy is favored over Nixon in 1960, and then the new normal in southern black voting preferences occurs in 1964 when not one African American claimed to have voted for the Republican Goldwater. The unanimous support for LBJ in 1964 set the standard for black Democratic loyalty in all subsequent presidential contests. After 1964, only once did southern blacks give significantly less than 90 percent of their votes to a Democrat (McGovern in 1972).

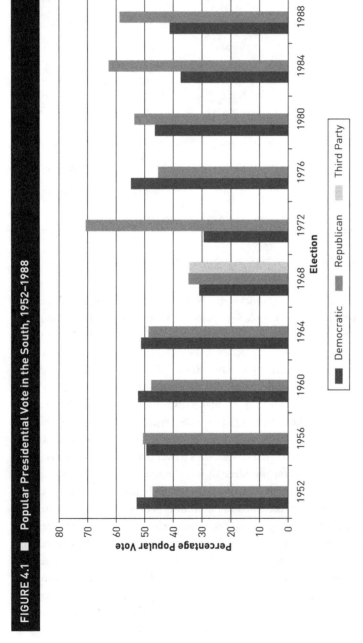

FIGURE 4.1 ■ Popular Presidential Vote in the South, 1952–1988

Source: Data compiled by the author from Dave Leip's *Atlas of U.S. Presidential Elections* (http://uselectionatlas.org/RESULTS/).

Note: The popular vote is the percentage Democratic and Republican out of the two-party vote total, except for 1968. In this election, the vote is out of the total cast for the Democrat (Humphrey), Republican (Nixon), and American Independent Party (Wallace).

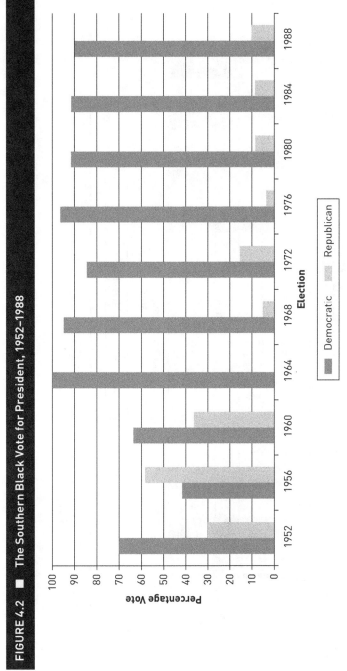

FIGURE 4.2 ■ The Southern Black Vote for President, 1952–1988

Source: Data compiled by the author from the American National Election Studies cumulative file.

Note: The vote percentage includes the third-party candidate in 1968, but no black votes were recorded for Wallace. The total self-reported votes cast by black southerners is less than 40 in 1952 (*n* = 10), 1956 (*n* = 11), 1960 (*n* = 12), 1964 (*n* = 35), and 1968 (*n* = 39).

FIGURE 4.3 ■ The Southern White Vote for President, 1952–1988

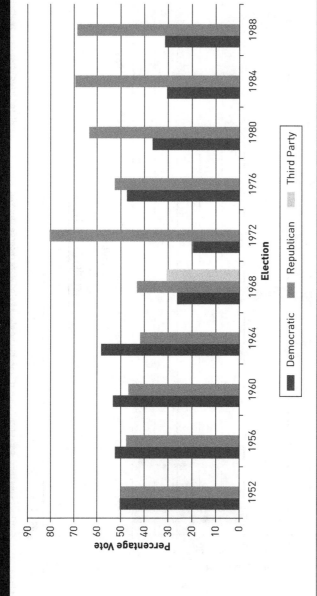

Source: Data compiled by the author from the American National Election Studies cumulative file.

Note: The vote percentage includes the third-party candidate in 1968 (Wallace).

The white vote in southern presidential elections is not the mirror opposite of black voters' preferences but it does represent a somewhat less pronounced flip side. From 1952 to 1964, white southerners are more supportive of the Democratic presidential nominee. But in the three-way 1968 contest, the Republican Nixon garners a clear plurality of the southern white vote (43 percent). After 1968, white southerners always cast a majority of their votes for the Republican presidential nominee and with the exception of 1976, the gap in favor of the GOP is very large, ranging from 27 to over 60 percentage points.

Undoubtedly, the permanent shift of southern blacks in favor of the Democratic Party and the increasing support of Republican presidential nominees exhibited by southern whites is registered in a display of these two groups' party identification from 1952 to 1988 (see Figure 4.4). In 1952, compared to blacks (79 percent Democratic), a higher percentage of whites identified as Democrats (84 percent). Conversely, more blacks were Republicans in 1952 (19 percent) than were whites (14 percent Republican). The large and permanent shift of black identification with the Democratic Party, and the gradual decline in white Democratic identification followed by a steady rise in white Republican identification commences after the 1964 election. As mentioned, by 1988 the partisan identification gap among southern whites is less than two percentage points (45.5 percent Democrats and 43.7 percent Republicans).

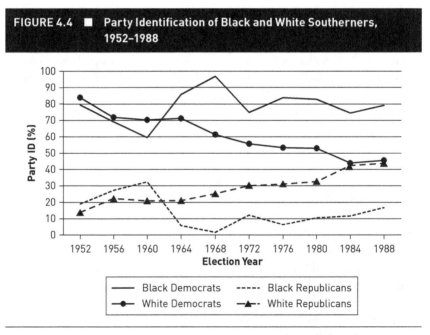

FIGURE 4.4 ■ **Party Identification of Black and White Southerners, 1952–1988**

Source: Data compiled by the author from the American National Election Studies (ANES) cumulative file.

Note: Independent leaners are classified as partisans. The percentages of Democrats and Republicans are computed out of the total number of respondents in the racial group (e.g., percentage of black Republicans = black Republicans ÷ black Republicans + black Democrats + black Independents).

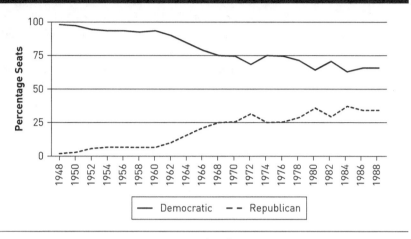

FIGURE 4.5 ■ Southern U.S. House Seats Controlled by the Major Parties, 1948–1988

Source: Data compiled by the author from CQ Press (2005).

Note: The percentage of Democratic and Republican seats is out of the total southern U.S. House seats.

Continuing the display of the major party split in southern U.S. House seats from previous chapters, Figure 4.5 shows the percentage of Democratic and Republican-held congressional districts from 1948 to 1988. For the first time since 1896, the Democratic Party no longer has a near monopoly of southern U.S. House seats. In 1948, southern Republicans held two U.S. House seats and Democrats controlled the rest (104 out of 106). But Democratic dominance was slowly receding from this high-water mark. And of course Democratic losses directly translated into Republican gains. Republican growth begins in earnest in the early 1960s and continues into the mid-1980s. In the late 1980s, Republican seat gains hold steady at around a third (34 percent) of the southern U.S. House delegation. As documented in the next chapter, a redistricting shake-up in the 1990s round of reapportionment would be a catalyst for reigniting GOP growth in southern House contests.

From the late 1960s to the 1980s, the southern party system was often characterized as a split-level alignment in which the GOP dominated presidential contests while Democrats controlled congressional elections (Lublin 2004). Election results certainly supported this description of southern politics, and individual-level data from the ANES highlights this phenomenon by documenting split-ticket voting among white southerners. Figure 4.6 presents the percentage of white southerners splitting their votes for President and the U.S. House. The black dashed line shows the percentage of individuals casting a Republican Presidential vote and a Democratic House vote (as opposed to a Republican vote for both offices). The lighter gray dashed line shows the percentage of individuals casting a Democratic Presidential vote and a Republican House vote (as opposed to a Democratic vote for both offices). Back in

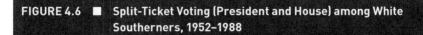

FIGURE 4.6 ■ Split-Ticket Voting (President and House) among White Southerners, 1952–1988

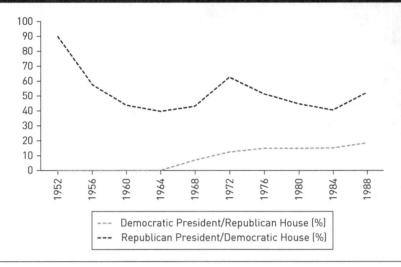

--- Democratic President/Republican House (%)
--- Republican President/Democratic House (%)

Source: Data compiled by the author from the American National Election Studies cumulative file.

Notes: The percentage shown for each type of split-ticket voting is based on the party of the presidential vote. For instance, in 1952, 89.8 percent of southern whites split their tickets in favor of a Republican presidential nominee and a Democratic House nominee (as displayed), whereas 10.2 percent voted Republican for both offices (not displayed). Likewise, in 1988, 18.5 percent of southern whites split their tickets in favor of a Democratic presidential nominee and a Republican House nominee (as displayed), whereas 81.5 percent voted Democratic for both offices (not displayed).

1952, among white southerners who voted for the Republican Eisenhower, 90 percent also voted for a Democratic House candidate—split-ticket voting of this kind was rampant—making it obvious that white southerners routinely voted Republican at the top of the ticket while voting Democratic in House elections. Even in 1988, more than half of white southerners (52 percent) who voted Republican for President cast Democratic House ballots. Interestingly, although a much rarer split-ticket pattern, after 1964, a growing number of white southerners who voted Democratic for President voted Republican for the U.S. House. By 1988, more than 18 percent of white southerners who cast Democratic votes for President also cast Republican votes for the U.S. House. The high rate of split-ticket voting among white southerners is a clear indication of a party system undergoing considerable change.

Finally, the last table in this section presents evidence of Republican growth in southern state legislatures. Rather than display data on contests for the Senate and governor (with only a third of Senate seats up for election every two years, whereas most gubernatorial contests occur in off years and in some southern states in odd years), most southern state legislative contests take place every two years, and even when this is not the case, the large number of seats and the low level of these offices

TABLE 4.3 ■ The Slow Rise of Republican State Legislators, 1950s–1980s

State	1950s		1960s		1970s		1980s	
	Senate	House	Senate	House	Senate	House	Senate	House
Alabama	0.0	0.6	1.4	0.9	0.0	1.9	11.4	13.3
Arkansas	0.0	2.0	0.0	1.2	2.3	3.2	9.1	8.4
Florida	2.1	4.8	17.3	19.8	29.3	29.0	30.0	34.7
Georgia	1.5	1.1	10.3	6.2	10.0	12.7	13.6	14.8
Louisiana	0.0	0.0	0.0	0.6	0.9	3.8	7.7	12.9
Mississippi	0.0	0.0	0.0	0.0	5.1	1.9	9.6	5.7
North Carolina	3.6	8.3	9.6	17.5	13.2	14.8	20.0	31.7
South Carolina	0.0	0.0	3.8	3.5	6.5	12.3	18.1	21.0
Tennessee	15.2	19.0	24.8	31.1	35.8	38.4	33.3	38.0
Texas	0.0	0.1	1.9	2.5	7.1	10.7	21.3	31.6
Virginia	6.7	5.6	11.3	11.4	15.0	20.4	22.5	34.0
South	2.7%	3.7%	8.7%	9.6%	12.4%	14.5%	18.8%	24.3%

Source: Data compiled by the author from Dubin (2007).

provides an excellent long-term barometer of Republican growth in southern politics. Table 4.3 shows the percentage of Republican legislators in each southern state and chamber (state Senate and state House) by decade, from the 1950s to the 1980s. Several patterns are evident. First, in the 1950s, when the GOP was hardly a presence, it showed more viability in the traditional mountain Republican sections of North Carolina, Tennessee, and Virginia (Lublin and Voss 2000). Second, the Republican presence has always been greater in the lower chamber (state House) where there are more seats to contest. Third, GOP gains were generally more substantial in Rim South states as opposed to Deep South states (McKee and Springer 2015). Finally, Republican gains have been notable, moving from well under 5 percent of seats in both chambers in the 1950s to between 6 and 7 times as many seats (depending on the chamber) in the 1980s.

CONCLUDING THOUGHTS

Starting in the 1950s, the one-party South slowly clawed its way toward a competitive two-party system. This chapter has covered a substantial amount of electoral ground in order to explain and document the steady rise of the southern Republican Party. Ultimately, this period was a transition from Democratic rule to a Republican takeover. But the pattern of GOP top-down advancement is best viewed as steady and gradual rather than swift and abrupt. Presidential politics clearly favored the Republican Party from the late 1960s forward, but below the top of the ticket Democrats remained in charge and seemed to have adjusted to cultivating biracial coalitions as a means to prolong their majority status (Lamis 1988).

But, as African Americans became a larger share of the southern Democratic coalition, more and more whites sought political refuge in the GOP rather than maintain a difficult relationship in which so many of the views of black and white southerners diverged and often directly clashed. One of the more consequential events of the 1980s was the Supreme Court ruling in the case of *Thornburg v. Gingles* (1986), which opened a path for the large-scale creation of majority-minority districts. Specifically, crafting districts with majority black populations and to a lesser extent some with majority Latino residents (and some combining blacks and Latinos to produce majority-minority district populations) directly undermined the biracial politics that furthered Democratic majorities after passage of the 1965 Voting Rights Act. Perhaps somewhat ironically, the VRA became one of the primary vehicles used to justify the creation of districts that contained enough minority voters so that the presence of whites was not substantial enough to engage in a racially integrated electoral strategy.

In the next chapter, the wholesale creation of majority-minority districts and their electoral ramifications is discussed in detail. In short, by weakening the Democratic reliance on biracial coalitions, many African Americans won elective offices while their white Democratic allies were squeezed out by the emergence of viable Republicans who targeted districts with large majority white populations (Black and Black 2002; McKee 2010). But the rise of southern Republicans in the early 1990s extended well beyond this development. Younger white southerners continued to shift in favor of the GOP and became a growing segment of the electorate with the decline in the number of older generations of white southerners who still exhibited a considerable allegiance to the Democratic Party. And, as fortune would have it, similar to the election of a white southern Democrat in 1976, the election of another white southern Democrat to the White House in 1992 proved an electoral boon for southern Republicans. The early 1990s was an electorally volatile period in southern politics. Republicans' swift and substantial increase in electoral victories provided the foundation for the long-term success of the GOP, which currently dominates Dixie's politics.

REPUBLICAN PRESENT

By the end of the 1980s, the southern Grand Old Party (GOP) was poised to take another major step in its top-down advancement as it became more competitive in U.S. House contests. Changes to redistricting would prove a major advantage to the Republican Party, and in 1992—the first elections held under new congressional and state legislative district boundaries—the GOP takeover of southern electoral politics began in earnest (McKee 2010).

This chapter begins with an examination of the changing demographics of U.S. House districts, which, to a large extent, were initially brought about by redrawing congressional boundaries in a manner that placed a greater emphasis on fostering minority representation. This development set in motion a swift increase in Republican electoral gains in district-based contests (i.e., U.S. House and state legislative contests), not only because minority voters, and especially African Americans, are decidedly Democratic in their voting behavior, but also because the incumbency advantage is rendered inoperable where Republican-leaning white voters are drawn into districts with an unfamiliar Democratic representative (Petrocik and Desposato 1998).

But the onset of Republican ascendancy in the early 1990s goes far beyond the electorally beneficial consequences of redrawing congressional and state legislative districts. Indeed, Republican success has been most impressive in statewide elections where boundaries are, of course, not subject to alteration. Simply put, the GOP has attained a dominant position in contemporary southern elections from the top of the political ladder to well near the bottom. Over the last quarter-century, Republican top-down advancement from presidential races to state legislative contests appears to have reached its completion. The only question now is whether the GOP can possibly squeeze any more electoral juice out of a southern political system that exhibits hints of a Democratic comeback; a subject broached in this chapter's concluding section. Whereas the previous chapter undertook a deep historical dive into the many events that moved the Democratic Solid South to a competitive two-party system, this chapter is heavy on data because the rise of southern Republicans is a remarkable story best told via the electoral record in federal, statewide, and state legislative contests.

UNINTENDED CONSEQUENCES?

As alluded to in the last chapter, the U.S. Supreme Court's ruling in the North Carolina case of *Thornburg v. Gingles* (1986) paved the way for a large increase in the number of congressional and state legislative districts that were drawn to further the election of minority candidates. The easiest way to ensure minority representation is to create districts with majority-minority voting populations (Lublin 1997, 1999). Because of the South's long history of racial discrimination, and the racially polarized voting behavior exhibited by its black and white citizens (Davidson 1984), in *Thornburg* the Court laid out a set of qualifications that, if met, would make it necessary to draw voting districts that encompassed a majority-minority electorate so that they would have a chance to elect a representative of their choosing. Sparing the details of the specific requirements needed to create a majority-minority district based on the *Thornburg* decision (see McKee and Shaw 2005 for a discussion of them), suffice it to say that the geographic concentration of a substantial minority population is the key ingredient for producing a majority-minority voting district.

Under the Civil Rights Division in the Department of Justice (DOJ), prior to the ruling in *Shelby County v. Holder* (2013),[1] all or parts (specific counties) of nine of the southern states (only Arkansas and Tennessee were exempt) were under supervision with respect to their drawing of voting districts. Specifically, under the Section 5 preclearance provision of the Voting Rights Act (VRA), most southern states had to receive DOJ approval of their proposed redistricting maps. On the eve of the 1992 elections, when most states would redraw their election districts, the DOJ pressured several southern states to maximize their creation of majority-minority districts (Cunningham 2001). For instance, in Georgia and North Carolina, the DOJ insisted that three majority black congressional districts be drawn in the Peach State (it had only one majority black district) and two new majority black districts in the Tar Heel State (it had no majority-minority congressional districts).

In southern states, as is still true in most states throughout the nation (Butler and Cain 1992; McDonald 2004), the state legislature is assigned the task of drawing not just their own district boundaries but also those of their congressional delegation. Before the 1992 elections, Democrats constituted the majority party in all southern state legislatures, and in only four states was the governor not a Democrat.[2] This meant that, barring a legal dispute (which was not uncommon), in most southern states the majority Democratic Party would draw the new congressional maps. But the DOJ placed a considerable check on what these plans would ultimately look like because it demanded an expansion in minority representation via the creation of majority-minority districts.

Because African Americans are the most Democratic voters, to the extent that this population is concentrated into a small number of majority black districts, it necessarily follows that neighboring district populations will have higher white populations. And given white voting preferences, districts with increased white populations advantage Republicans. So in order to get approval from the DOJ while at the same time trying to minimize the electoral harm likely to stem from the increase in majority-minority districts, Democratic legislators drew congressional boundaries with incredibly complicated and bizarre shapes (Monmonier 2001). The objective was to draw these majority-minority districts in such a fashion that overall, at least based on a generally reliable indicator like presidential vote returns, neighboring majority white districts would still be competitive. But therein lay the Democrats' insoluble problem.

Figure 5.1 demonstrates the issue Democratic line drawers faced as a consequence of drawing several new majority-minority congressional districts in southern

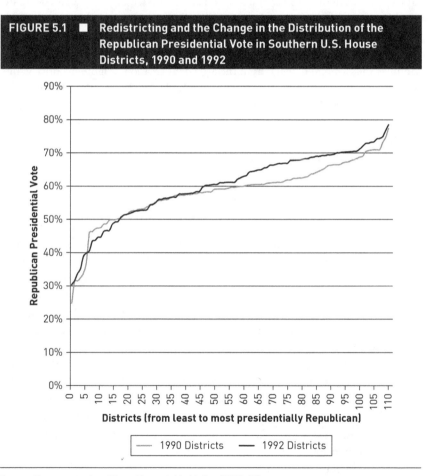

FIGURE 5.1 ■ **Redistricting and the Change in the Distribution of the Republican Presidential Vote in Southern U.S. House Districts, 1990 and 1992**

Districts (from least to most presidentially Republican)

——— 1990 Districts   ——— 1992 Districts

Source: Figure reproduced from Figure 3.1 in McKee (2010, 87).

Note: Data are the 1988 Republican share (two-party) of the district presidential vote for districts in 1990 and 1992. There are a total of 125 districts in the South in 1992, but only for 110 districts is it possible to record the 1988 Republican presidential vote in 1990 and 1992.

states. The figure is reproduced from McKee (2010) and the inspiration came from an article by political historian J. Morgan Kousser (1996), "Estimating the Partisan Consequences of Redistricting Plans—Simply." Among all the districts that retained enough of their previous boundaries to be compared before and after redistricting (this is not possible, for instance, in a state that adds a district through reapportionment because there is no district to compare it to under the previous map), the presidential vote for the most immediate contest before the redistricting can be compared for each district as it was drawn before and after being reconfigured. In Figure 5.1, the district-level 1988 Republican presidential vote is plotted from least to most Republican for the same set of districts as they were drawn in 1990 and 1992 (N = 110). It is clear to the naked eye what Democrats were up against in 1992 because there was such a substantial increase in the number of districts that were drawn to be more presidentially Republican.

Based on the data in Figure 5.1, it is hardly surprising that Democratic intentions of crafting majority-minority districts to satisfy the DOJ and at the same time minimize the electoral damage from the attendant creation of more majority white districts were not realized (Cameron, Epstein, and O'Halloran 1996; Epstein and O'Halloran 1999a, 1999b, 2000). Indeed, as one scholar put it, the vast increase in the number of majority-minority districts blew up in their Democratic creators' faces (Bullock 1995).[3] To be sure, drawing majority-minority districts accomplished the objective of electing minority candidates. But that was about the only goal that was met. The bigger picture was trying to limit the electoral harm to the Democrats' majority position in southern congressional delegations, and in this respect, Democratic line drawers failed miserably.

It proved impossible to increase the number of majority-minority districts without jeopardizing the overall competitiveness of the Democratic Party because, by the 1990s, the party had become heavily reliant, in fact dependent upon, the support of black voters. But it was not just the direct impact of concentrating the most loyal Democrats into a smaller number of districts that weakened the Democrats' electoral fortunes (Hill 1995); it was more broadly the chain reaction that race-based reapportionment set off, which catalyzed Republican ascendancy in district-based elections (McKee 2010).

Consider the following scenario that played out repeatedly in southern congressional elections. First, drawing a majority-minority district displaced (Cain 1984) the sitting white Democratic incumbent. In other words, because the white Democratic incumbent correctly anticipated that a minority candidate would win the majority-minority district, it made more sense to either retire or seek reelection in a nearby district, with a majority white electorate. The problem with this proposition is twofold: (1) southern Democratic candidates, irrespective of their own racial background, are reliant upon the support of minority voters, and (2) Democratic incumbents lose their incumbency advantage among the voters who were never represented by them in these reconfigured districts where these embattled incumbents sought reelection because they were displaced by the creation of majority-minority districts.

Hence, in most southern states, the infusion of more majority-minority districts endangered and doomed a select set of candidates: white Democratic incumbents, the perennial majority in southern politics. Indeed, redistricting was one of the culprits accounting for the historically high rate of incumbent retirements prior to the 1992 U.S. House elections (Jacobson and Carson 2016, 207). And for the many white Democratic incumbents who decided to seek another term, their chances of winning were greatly diminished the more their districts were altered to include constituents whom they never represented prior to redistricting (McKee 2010, 2013; Petrocik and Desposato 1998). The presence of a high percentage of redrawn voters (those new to the incumbent as a consequence of redistricting) was particularly electorally perilous for white Democratic incumbents because these voters, all else equal, were more inclined to vote Republican if they were not familiar with the candidates running in their district.[4] And the elite response was predictable; strong Republican challengers were more likely to run in districts with higher redrawn constituencies, which in turn made these voters even more likely to vote for GOP candidates.

Not long after the 1992 elections, in a series of southern cases (*Shaw v. Reno* in 1993; *Miller v. Johnson* in 1995; and *Bush v. Vera* in 1996), the U.S. Supreme Court determined that districts drawn expressly or primarily for the purpose of ensuring a majority-minority voting electorate would be deemed unconstitutional racial gerrymanders if their creation wholly ignored geographic considerations (Butler 2002). In other words, the byzantine cartography necessary to create *some* majority-minority districts was a violation of the *Thornburg* precedent because it was expected that the minority population was geographically concentrated, whereas in several of the majority-minority districts first created for the 1992 elections the minority populations meandered all across the state and/or were anything but a cohesive population in a given urban area.

In short, the DOJ had overstepped its authority by insisting that most southern states maximize their number of majority-minority districts irrespective of how they were drawn. So in 1996, before the ensuing elections, under court order, several southern states (Florida, Georgia, Louisiana, and Texas) redrew their congressional boundaries and some of the extant majority-minority districts were altered so that their new boundaries made them majority white (Voss and Lublin 2001). But unfortunately for the Democrats, the extensive electoral damage due to race-based redistricting had already been inflicted. After the 1994 elections, not only had Republicans achieved majority status in the southern U.S. House delegation for the first time since 1874 (Black and Black 2002), but for the first time in forty years the lower chamber of the U.S. Congress reverted back to GOP control.

BOX 5.1   THE CREATIVE CARTOGRAPHY OF CONGRESSIONAL DISTRICTS

The large increase in majority-minority districts in the 1992 elections made for some extraordinarily byzantine maps. As mentioned in this chapter, the court case of *Thornburg v. Gingles* (1986) was the impetus for increasing the number of majority-minority districts. Department of Justice oversight of redistricting plans via Section 5 preclearance under the Voting Rights Act ensured that most of the Democratic-controlled southern legislatures would draw extremely convoluted district boundaries in the hopes that minority voters could be concentrated without incurring too much electoral damage in the surrounding districts that were necessarily more Republican because of their higher percentage of white voters. Figure 5.2 shows a selection of some of the more bizarrely shaped congressional districts that were newly created for the 1992 U.S. House elections. Five districts are displayed in the figure: North Carolina District 12 (NC 12), Louisiana District 4 (LA 4), Georgia District 11 (GA 11), and Texas Districts 6 and 30 (TX 6 and TX 30). Texas Districts 6 and 30 are displayed separately and then together (with TX 6 shaded black and TX 30 shaded gray) because these two districts intersect along portions of the border between Tarrant County (city of Fort Worth) and Dallas County. Based on the black voting age population (BVAP), four of these districts were majority or plurality black (NC 12: 53% BVAP; LA 4: 63% BVAP; GA 11: 60% BVAP; TX 30: 47% BVAP and 15% Latino VAP), and one was majority white (TX 6: 92% white VAP). All four predominantly black districts elected black Democratic Representatives: Melvin Watt in NC 12, Cleo Fields in LA 4, Cynthia McKinney in GA 11, and Eddie Bernice Johnson in TX 30. The redrawn majority white TX 6 reelected Republican Congressman Joe Barton (first elected in 1984).

NC 12 was nicknamed the "I-85" district because it was once quipped that an open car door would hit half the residents located along the skinny stretch of Interstate 85 as the district snaked its way from the black neighborhoods of inner-city Charlotte to the northeast along the path of I-85, picking up heavily African American areas in the cities of Winston-Salem, Greensboro, and Durham. LA 4 was dubbed the "Mark of Zorro" district as it crisscrossed its way along the upper part of the Pelican State's boot-like shape from the Red River border with southern Arkansas, encompassing black sections of Shreveport in the northwest and then east to Monroe and then south along the Mississippi River (and border with Mississippi), turning back to the northwest to take in parts of Alexandria and then moving southeast to capture sections of Baton Rouge before finally bending southwest to Lafayette. GA 11 became known as "Sherman's March to the Sea" district, in reference to a path somewhat reminiscent of the one taken by the notorious Union Army Civil War General William Tecumseh Sherman, who wreaked havoc all along the large swath of territory his troops covered on their way from Atlanta to Savannah. The district took in black neighborhoods in Atlanta and Augusta and less populated areas in between as it narrowed into a thin band that made its way down to the port city of Savannah. Rather than give TX 6 and TX 30 distinct names, because they were so remarkably convoluted, they came to be known as "bug-splattered" districts. The lower share of African Americans in the Lone Star State vis-à-vis the aforementioned districts in North Carolina,

FIGURE 5.2 ■ Congressional Districts Shaped by Race-Based Redistricting

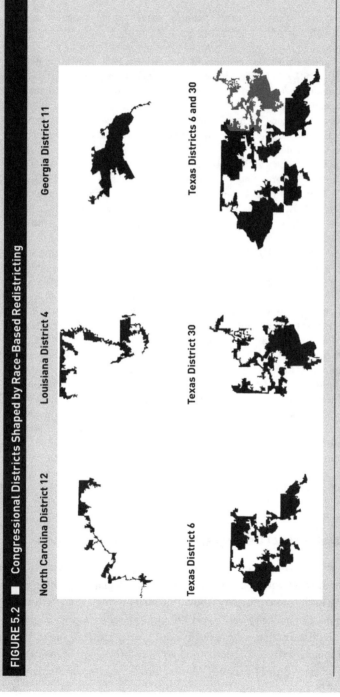

North Carolina District 12 Louisiana District 4 Georgia District 11

Texas District 6 Texas District 30 Texas Districts 6 and 30

Source: District shapefiles of the 103rd Congress (1992 U.S. House Elections) are from Lewis et al. (2013).

Note: Figure created by the author.

[Continued]

(Continued)

Louisiana, and Georgia partially accounts for the essentially indescribable contours of TX 6 and TX 30. The remainder of the reason for these districts resembling bug splats is because of the great efforts undertaken by Texas Democrats (under the direction of Congressman Martin Frost) to draw two predominantly black districts (TX 30 in Dallas and TX 18 in Houston) while minimizing the electoral harm to Anglo Democrats seeking reelection in 1992. In order to create a district in the shape of TX 30, neighboring districts like TX 6 (taking in parts of five counties in the Dallas-Fort Worth Metroplex) also took on inexplicably complex boundaries. Displaying the districts together makes it evident that each district contains various sprawling sections and tentacles with no definitive core.

These districts (along with several others) did not survive in their current form because the Supreme Court, in a series of cases (*Shaw v. Reno* 1993; *Miller v. Johnson* in 1995; and *Bush v. Vera* in 1996) ruled them unconstitutional racial gerrymanders. NC 12 was the target of the Court in *Shaw v. Reno* when Justice O'Connor likened its construction and purpose to racial apartheid. The decision that these heretofore predominantly black districts were crafted primarily to create majority-minority electorates irrespective of their geographic shapes resulted in all of them being redrawn with boundaries that were made considerably less intricate/more compact, and the constituencies in these reconfigured districts were now majority white (NC 12 in 1998, LA 4 in 1996, GA 11 in 1996) or plurality white (TX 30 in 1996). LA 4 was significantly altered in 1994 (though it remained majority black until another redrawing in 1996), and after winning reelection, Representative Fields vacated the seat for a run at the governorship in 1995 (he was defeated by Republican Mike Foster). Throughout its multiple permutations, Congressman Watt finally retired from representing NC 12 in 2014 when he resigned to become Director of the Federal Housing Finance Agency. Georgia Representative McKinney endured a very rough tenure in the House of Representatives. She was twice defeated by fellow black Democrats in highly contentious primaries in 2002 and later in 2006. Congresswoman Johnson, a Texas State Senator prior to taking office in TX 30 in 1992, still represents the latest permutation of this Dallas-based district in the U.S. Congress. In 2018, Republican Congressman Barton retired from office in TX 6, a district that now barely resembles the bug splat originally drawn in 1992.

Congressional District Demographics and Representation

Table 5.1 presents the percentage of southern congressional districts according to whether the district voting age population (VAP) is majority white, majority black, majority Latino, and plurality (those in which no single racial/ethnic group comprises the district majority VAP). In 1990, prior to redistricting, 91 percent of southern U.S. House districts were majority white. After redistricting in 1992, the percentage of majority white districts stood at 79 and the share of majority black districts jumped from 3 to 11 percent. Although there were not as many majority

Latino districts as majority black districts, the former went from 5 percent in 1990 to 7 percent in 1992. Moving forward to 2016, Table 5.1 shows that majority black districts are 8 percent and majority Latino districts are 9 percent of the southern total. The decline in the percentage of majority black districts since 1994 is primarily because of court-ordered redistricting that reduced some of these heretofore majority black district populations. By comparison, Latinos are the fastest growing minority in the South, and the steady increase in majority Latino districts has occurred exclusively in Florida and Texas, where all of these districts reside. Finally, notice that the percentage of majority white districts in 2016 was 76 percent and the portion of plurality districts has grown from only 1 percent in 1990 to 7 percent in 2016.[5]

To get a sense of the degree to which majority-minority districts favor the Democratic Party, Table 5.2 shows the number of U.S. House members, according to their race/ethnicity and party affiliation, who represent seats that are composed of a majority-minority district population. As the note under Table 5.2 explains, the definition of a majority-minority district is one in which the sum of the black and Latino VAP exceeds 50 percent. It is worth mentioning this because there was actually one additional majority-minority district in the South in 2016 that was not included in Table 5.2: Republican Pete Olson of District 22 in Texas represented a VAP that was 11.9 percent black, 22.1 percent Latino, and 16.1 percent Asian (50.1 percent majority-minority). In 1990 there were only 11 majority-minority districts based on the aforementioned definition; by 2016, there were 29 southern congressional districts that contained a majority-minority VAP based on the sum of black and Latino residents. This number is slightly down from the 32 majority-minority districts that existed from 2012 to 2014 because redistricting in Florida and Virginia reduced the number of majority-minority districts in these states. Demographic change in the form of a growing minority electorate is a principal feature of contemporary southern politics. Nonetheless, the single largest increase in the number of majority-minority districts took place not so much because of long-term demographic change, but due to the DOJ's insistence that southern states expand their number of majority-minority districts prior to the 1992 elections. Reflecting this political reality, the number of majority-minority districts went from 11 in 1990 to 26 in 1992.

Table 5.2 speaks to another reality of southern politics: with a handful of exceptions, minority politicians primarily represent district populations in which their racial/ethnic group is either the majority or plurality group (Lublin et al. 2009). And this is more often the case with Democratic Representatives because most Republicans, regardless of their race/ethnicity, represent majority white districts. For instance, in 2016 the four Latino Democrats listed in the table all represented majority Latino districts in Texas. Although there was only one additional Latino Democrat in the southern U.S. House delegation in 2016, he was the first of Puerto

TABLE 5.1 ■ Percentage of Majority White, Majority Black, Majority Latino, and Plurality Southern U.S. House Districts, 1990–2016

District	1990	1992	1994	1996	1998	2000	2002	2004	2006	2008	2010	2012	2014	2016
% Majority White	91	79	79	82	80	80	80	80	81	81	81	75	75	76
% Majority Black	3	11	11	8	7	7	7	7	7	7	7	8	8	8
% Majority Latino	5	7	7	7	7	7	8	8	8	8	8	9	9	9
% Plurality	1	2	2	2	6	6	5	5	5	5	5	9	9	7
Total Districts	116	125	125	125	125	125	131	131	131	131	131	138	138	138

Source: Data compiled by the author from the U.S. Census Bureau.

Note: Majority for each racial/ethnic category is based on the district voting age population. Plurality districts do not contain a majority voting age population for a single racial/ethnic group.

TABLE 5.2 ■ Race and Party of Representatives in Majority-Minority Southern U.S. House Districts, 1990–2016

	1990	1992	1994	1996	1998	2000	2002	2004	2006	2008	2010	2012	2014	2016
Majority-Minority Districts	11	26	26	22	25	25	26	26	25	25	25	32	32	29
Black Democrats	5	17	17	13	14	14	14	14	14	13	14	18	18	16
Latino Democrats	4	4	4	5	5	5	5	5	6	6	4	6	4	4
White Democrats	1	2	2	1	3	3	3	3	2	2	2	5	5	4
Black Republicans													1	1
Latino Republicans	1	3	3	3	3	3	4	4	3	3	4	2	3	3
Asian Republicans										1				
White Republicans											1	1	1	1
Percentage Democrats	91	88	88	86	88	88	85	85	88	84	80	91	84	83
Percentage Republicans	9	12	12	14	12	12	15	15	12	16	20	9	16	17

Source: Data compiled by the author from various editions of *The Almanac of American Politics* (1992–2016).

Note: Majority-minority districts are greater than 50 percent majority-minority based on the sum of the black and Latino voting age population.

Rican descent to serve in the Sunshine State (Anderson, Baumann, and Geras 2018, 296); Darren Soto, whose Florida District 9 in the Orlando area had a VAP that was 29.9 percent Latino and 11.2 percent black. Likewise, in 2016, of the twenty African American Democrats in the southern congressional delegation, sixteen (80 percent) represented majority-minority districts. Of the four white Democrats representing majority-minority districts in 2016, three were veteran Anglo incumbents presiding over majority Latino districts in Texas (Lloyd Doggett in District 35 with a 58 percent Latino VAP, Gene Green in District 29 with a 73 percent Latino VAP, and Beto O'Rourke in District 16 with a 78 percent Latino VAP) and the other was Jewish Congressman Steve Cohen, who represented the Memphis-based majority black District 9 in Tennessee (61 percent black VAP).

With respect to Republicans, more than half of the five representing majority-minority districts in 2016 were all Latinos, three Cuban-Americans who represented majority Latino districts in South Florida (Mario Diaz-Balart in the 75 percent Latino VAP District 25; Carlos Curbelo in the 68 percent Latino VAP District 26; Ileana Ros-Lehtinen in the 69 percent Latino VAP District 27). The two remaining Republicans, African American Will Hurd and Anglo Blake Farenthold, are both Texans who represent districts with substantial Latino populations. In fact, Hurd's District 23 has a 66 percent Latino VAP (3 percent black VAP), while Farenthold's District 27 has a 45.1 percent Latino VAP and a 5.1 percent black VAP. The takeaway from Table 5.2 is not just that the number of majority-minority districts has nearly tripled since 1990, but Democrats (and especially minority Democrats) are much more likely to occupy these seats in the southern U.S. House delegation; 83 percent Democrats versus 17 percent Republicans in 2016.[6]

Figure 5.3 presents a graphical display of the race/ethnicity of Democrats and all Republicans (regardless of their racial background) serving in the southern U.S. House delegation from 1990 to 2016. In 1990, the old southern pattern still prevailed, that is, white Democrats comprised a majority and there were hardly any minority Democrats. But due mainly to the direct and indirect electoral effects of race-based redistricting, the situation drastically changes in 1992, as the number of Republicans and black Democrats surges and the number of white Democrats plummets. In 2006 and 2008, back-to-back elections in which a strong national tide favored Democrats (Jacobson and Carson 2016), the long-term decline in white Democrats is temporarily reversed. But the Republican "tsunami" in the 2010 midterm produces an even stronger reduction in the number of white Democrats. In 2016, except for one African American and three Latinos, the rest of the 99-member southern Republican U.S. House contingent was comprised of non-Latino whites. By contrast, the 39-member southern Democratic opposition is remarkably diverse: consisting of 20 African Americans, 13 whites, 5 Latinos, and for the first time in the history of southern congressional politics, an Asian Democrat (not shown in Figure 5.3), Stephanie Murphy of Florida, who defeated veteran Republican Congressman John Mica in the redrawn Orlando-based

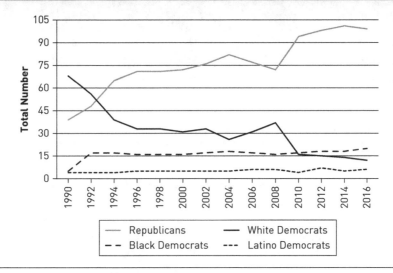

FIGURE 5.3 ■ **The Number of Republicans, White Democrats, Black Democrats, and Latino Democrats in the Southern U.S. House Delegation, 1990–2016**

Sources: Data compiled by the author from various editions of *The Almanac of American Politics* (1992–2016). The 2016 data were compiled from the *New York Times* (http://www.nytimes.com/elections/results/house).

District 7. To reiterate an observation made by southern politics scholar Earl Black (1998), "the newest southern politics" still revolves around race, but now it consists of a diverse minority coalition of Democrats (Black 2004) who do battle with a much larger and overwhelmingly white Republican majority.

REPUBLICAN CONTROL FROM TOP TO BOTTOM

The preceding foray into congressional politics is an appropriate way to start a chapter documenting Republican electoral gains in the South because the long-term shift in favor of the GOP is so palpable. Further, many of the dynamics that have played out in U.S. House contests are also present in other elections. Indeed, Republican dominance of contemporary southern politics is hardly limited to the House of Representatives. As will be shown in the sections that follow, GOP hegemony extends not just to federal elections (President, Senate, and House) but also to statewide and even state legislative races.

Table 5.3 shows just how far southern Republicans have come in the quarter-century transpiring between the 1990 and 2016 elections. Displayed is the percentage of seats won by the GOP in federal elections (Senate and House), statewide contests,

TABLE 5.3 ■ Republican Electoral Gains in the South between 1990 and 2016						
Republican (%)	U.S. Senate (*N* = 22)	U.S. House (*N* = 138 [116])	Statewide (*N* = 74 [78])	State Senate (*N* = 457)	State House (*N* = 1,325)	Total (*N* = 2,016 [1,998])
After 1990	32	34	17	24	28	27
After 2016	86	72	88	67	65	67
Difference	+54	+38	+71	+43	+37	+40

Source: Data compiled by the author.

Notes: The second number displayed in brackets (for the U.S. House, Statewide, and Total columns) accounts for the number of U.S. House districts and statewide seats in 1990. Statewide elections include gubernatorial contests but exclude U.S. Senate races.

and state legislative races (state senate and state house) after 1990 and after 2016. In 1990, Republicans had their greatest presence in U.S. House elections where they comprised 34 percent of the southern delegation. By contrast, southern Republicans were least prevalent in statewide races, holding only 17 percent of 78 total seats in 1990. Overall, at the start of the decade in 1990, across the five types of elections presented in Table 5.3, Republicans controlled a meager 27 percent of these elective offices.

Two and a half decades hence, after the 2016 elections, the political terrain in Dixie had transformed. Now, southern Republican dominance is most impressive in statewide races where the GOP occupies 88 percent of the seats. Only slightly less impressive is that Republicans hold all but three of the South's U.S. Senate seats, which amounts to 86 percent. The U.S. House delegation has become a GOP fortress with a 72 percent Republican majority, and in state legislatures two-thirds of the seats belong to Republicans. In fact, after 2016, out of a total of 2,016 seats, spanning federal, statewide, and state legislative contests, just over two-thirds of them (67 percent) were occupied by Republicans. In the 1980s, it was accurate to describe southern electoral politics as a competitive two-party system (Lamis 1988). In the mid-2010s, such a pronouncement would be utterly false. Republicans currently dominate the southern political landscape (McKee 2012a).

Table 5.3 gives the student a telling overview of the historic gains southern Republicans have notched since the start of the 1990s. Now it is time to fill in the period between 1990 and 2016 with a detailed accounting of Republican representation in federal, statewide, and state legislative elections, respectively.

FEDERAL CONTESTS

In part because they are higher profile (attracting greater attention from the media and scholars), but also because they are collectively more significant in shaping the current and future course of American politics, federal elections will be examined first. As has been stated numerous times, top-down advancement (Aistrup 1996) is the general pattern of Republican success in southern politics. Not only have GOP gains been more substantial at the top of the electoral ladder, they have typically occurred earlier at the apex of the political food chain. In chapter 4 it was documented that southern Republicans have been the dominant party in presidential politics since the late 1960s. A quick look back at Table 5.3 shows how long it has taken for the southern GOP to consolidate their presidential gains in lower level offices. Even after 1990, it is apparent that southern Democrats still maintained a firm grip on every office except the presidency.

Despite the order of Republican progression going from presidential elections to senatorial races, and then finally to House elections, the assessment of top-down advancement in federal contests will begin with the lower chamber of Congress and then go back up. This order of presentation is preferable because House contests have already been discussed at length and the greater number of seats makes for a more comprehensive understanding of the dynamics shaping these elections.

House Elections

Any discussion of the dynamics of congressional elections should start with explaining the importance of the incumbency advantage. Some scholars have actually quantified how much of an electoral bonus is associated with being the current occupant of a congressional district (Gelman and King 1990; Jacobson 2009a). There are several reasons why it is to be expected that an incumbent will have an easier time winning when seeking reelection. In other words, the advantage of being the incumbent is multifaceted. Perhaps it is easier to start with what is not a component of the incumbency advantage. Most obvious is that the partisan connection between a representative and a voter is separable from the incumbency advantage because a Republican (Democrat) is expected to vote for a Republican (Democrat). Rather, an incumbent seeks an advantage that accrues from the benefits attached to holding office apart from party affiliation. Some refer to the incumbency advantage as a "personal vote" because it is not tied to party affiliation, but instead predicated on how representative behavior is exercised to earn the support of voters (Cain, Ferejohn, and Fiorina 1987).

House incumbents engage in a variety of activities, most of which are done expressly for the purpose of winning reelection (Mayhew 1974). As Mayhew points out, keeping a high profile among constituents by advertising their activity, claiming credit for legislative accomplishments, and taking positions on issues that are expected to garner constituency support all further incumbents' objective of winning reelection. In addition, most incumbents work very hard on casework (Fiorina 1977), which means dealing with problems brought to their attention by a voter in their district; typically, these entail mishaps with the federal bureaucracy (like an undelivered Social Security check). Because incumbents are diligent in their cultivation of a personal vote on the basis of the aforementioned activities, it is no wonder that they enjoy high name recognition in their districts, and voters are much more likely to vote for the candidate they are more familiar with (Jacobson 2009a).

Ever since House members viewed their position as worthy of a political career (Polsby 1968), and probably even long before that (Carson and Roberts 2013), the basic formula for optimizing the incumbency advantage has not changed: engage in activities that attract votes. And in order to maximize the electoral advantages tied to holding office, members of Congress have designed their institution so that it can foster the goal of reelection (Mayhew 1974). This explains why most legislative activity is conducted between Tuesday and Thursday and there is essentially no budget for taking trips back to the district for the rest of the week. Likewise, the franking privilege gives members unlimited use of the postal service for mailing constituents at taxpayer expense. And finally, by dint of being the incumbent, it is much easier to raise the necessary funds to underwrite a reelection campaign because most political donors behave strategically and therefore place their financial bets on the more likely winner (the incumbent).

Since the end of World War II (specifically 1946 to 2014), in general elections House incumbents have been reelected at the impressive rate of 92 percent, whereas their Senate counterparts have won reelection 80 percent of the time (Sides et al. 2015). So obviously, the odds that an incumbent wins another term are very favorable. Nonetheless, considerable changes that have taken place since the 1970s have served to weaken the electoral bonus accruing from the incumbency advantage. Although in the short term, the electoral advantage tied to being an incumbent is highly variable (Petrocik and Desposato 2004), over time it has steadily declined because of the rise in partisan voting (Bartels 2000; Jacobson 2015; Levendusky 2009). In the 1970s, when the share of political independents in the electorate reached its postwar peak, the incumbency advantage was very high, and scores of Democrats and Republicans defected from their party identification by casting congressional votes for House incumbents of the opposing party (Cox and Katz 1996). By contrast, in the 2010s, the incumbency advantage is currently at a low point because there has been an increase in voters identifying with the major parties, and among those who do, their likelihood of voting their party affiliation in congressional elections is at a historic high (Jacobson and Carson 2016).

In the American South, a region that was thoroughly dominated by Democrats from the end of the 1800s into the early 1960s, perhaps never before or since has the incumbency advantage proved so electorally consequential in American politics. As assiduously documented by Earl and Merle Black (2002), the primary reason why there was a three-decade delay in Republican presidential success filtering down to congressional contests was principally due to the active resistance exercised by southern Democratic House and Senate incumbents, who did all they could to impede Republican advancement. But the Democratic incumbency advantage invariably weakened as more and more of the white southern electorate aligned with the GOP (Stonecash 2008) and the emergence of viable Republican candidates gave these voters a reason to stick with their party when voting in congressional elections (Bullock, Hoffman, and Gaddie 2005). With the onset of the 1990s, the split-level alignment of a Republican presidential South and a Democratic South for every election below the top electoral rung (Lublin 2004) would finally come to an end.

Figure 5.4 displays the percentage of Democrats and Republicans in the southern U.S. House delegation from 1990 to 2016. In 1990, Democrats were two-thirds of the delegation; in 2016 they were down to 28 percent. Put another way, at the beginning of the 1990s, Republicans held just a third of southern congressional districts and in 2016 the GOP occupied 72 percent, which was even better than the two-thirds of seats their Democratic opponents controlled a quarter-century earlier. The reasons behind the initial Republican surge in seat pickups between 1990 and 1992 have already been discussed, but notice that the GOP's rapid rise in southern House elections continues through 1996 and then levels off until a slight uptick in 2004. In 1992, there were twice as many open seats vacated by Democratic incumbents ($N = 10$) while Republican members and redistricting produced an additional 16 open seats. All else equal, it is easier to win an open seat because by definition the incumbency advantage is absent, and over the three election cycles (1992–1996) when the GOP surged to its majority position, Democrats left open 39 seats versus

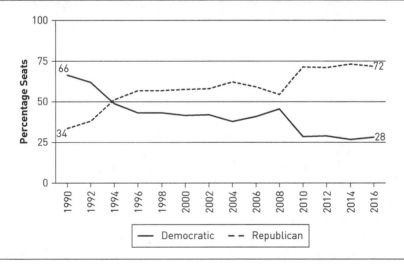

FIGURE 5.4 ■ Southern U.S. House Seats Controlled by the Major Parties, 1990–2016

Sources: Data compiled by the author from *The Almanac of American Politics* (1992–2016 editions). The 2016 data are from the *New York Times* (http://www.nytimes.com/elections/results/house).

Note: The percentage of Democratic and Republican seats is out of the total southern U.S. House seats.

14 for Republicans. From 1992 to 1996, Republicans netted a total of 32 southern House seats, and 59 percent of them were won in open-seat districts vacated by Democratic incumbents.

A new Republican electoral equilibrium seems to have set in after the 1996 House elections, and it was only slightly altered in 2004 because of events that took place in one southern state: Texas. After the 2002 elections, for the first time since the end of Reconstruction, the Texas GOP had majority control of both chambers of the legislature and occupied the governorship. With their newfound political monopoly, Republican U.S. House Majority Leader and Texas Congressman Tom DeLay (TX-22) urged his fellow Republicans in the Texas Legislature to undertake a "re-redistricting" of its congressional map (as per the decennial census, the districts were redrawn before the 2002 midterm contests). They obliged after a cumbersome delay, courtesy of Texas Democratic legislators who absconded from the state on two occasions rather than face the music of a new congressional plan designed solely to increase the number of Texas U.S. House Republicans (McKee and Shaw 2005).

The Republican remap was highly effective because it concentrated on demolishing the incumbency advantage of several Anglo Democratic incumbents by greatly altering their congressional districts (McKee 2010). In addition to overloading targeted Democrats with redrawn constituents whom the GOP knew (as did their Democratic opponents) were inclined to vote Republican (presidential vote returns made this clear), two Texas Democrats (Martin Frost and Charles Stenholm) were displaced in a manner so that their only chance of winning reelection was by defeating Republican incumbents who, of course, retained a much higher percentage of their old voters under the new plan. In the lead-up to the 2004 elections, one Democratic incumbent switched to the GOP (Ralph Hall), one retired (Jim Turner), and four of the Anglo Democratic incumbents in the GOP's crosshairs were defeated: Martin Frost, Nick Lampson, Max Sandlin, and Charles Stenholm. In sum, the 2004 Republican gerrymander in the Lone Star State accounts for the southern GOP's half-dozen seat increase in this election cycle.[7]

Although the South is, in many ways, distinct from the rest of the United States, it certainly is not immune to the electoral shockwaves produced by national conditions (Prysby 2014). Democrat Bill Clinton won the presidency in 1992 with essentially no coattails; in fact, his party lost 10 seats (Jacobson and Carson 2016), 9 of which the Democrats lost in the president-elect's native Dixie. In Clinton's first midterm, the national Democratic seat loss was 52 (Jacobson and Carson 2016), enough to relinquish Democratic control of the House of Representatives for the first time since the Eisenhower Administration in 1954. Similarly, in the strong Democratic tides running in the 2006 midterm, when Republicans lost their national congressional majority, and in 2008 with the historic election of Democrat Barack Obama,

Figure 5.4 indicates a slight drop in the number of southern Republican House seats (a 10-seat pickup for the Democratic opposition since 2004). And in the Republican wave election of 2010, fueled by an agitated and burgeoning Tea Party movement (Jacobson 2011), President Obama acknowledged that his party endured a "shellacking." The 63-seat Democratic midterm loss was the largest suffered by a President's party since President Roosevelt's Democrats hemorrhaged 71 in 1938. The reversal in 2010 was easily enough for Republicans to take back a national House majority, and in the South it seems that an even higher GOP electoral equilibrium was attained, with the party holding more than 70 percent of Dixie's congressional districts. As the electoral record indicates, in Dixie, the House GOP is much better off when a Democrat occupies the White House.

Table 5.4 shows the number of House Republicans in each southern state's delegation from 1990 to 2016. By presenting the data in this more fine-grained detail, one gets a better sense of where and when GOP gains occurred. Bracketed numbers denote a 50–50 partisan split in a state's House delegation (e.g., Louisiana in 1990), while a number in bold indicates a Republican majority. A subregional pattern of GOP advancement is evident in the table (more on this in chapter 8). With the exception of Mississippi, the Deep South has been majority Republican since the 1996 elections (Georgia and South Carolina have been since 1994). The primary explanation for this subregional pattern is the greater electoral impact of race-based redistricting on furthering Republican success in these states containing the highest percentage of African American voters. Among the Peripheral South states, Florida was already majority Republican in 1990 and has been ever since. Although North Carolina achieved a Republican House majority in 1994, it was lost in 1996, then the GOP regained control for the next four elections (1998–2004), then the Democrats had the majority from 2006 to 2010, and for the last three elections the Tar Heel State is again majority Republican. Tennessee has also experienced a similar pattern of multiple partisan reversals of majority control. The laggards to the Republican congressional takeover are Virginia, Texas, and Arkansas. Since 1990, the first Republican majority in Virginia takes place in the 2000 elections; the 2004 elections for Texas Republicans, and not until 2010 do Arkansas Republicans take a majority of the Natural State's four-member House delegation. Since 2012, the South has witnessed a Republican blackout—all of the eleven states have majority Republican House delegations since President Obama was reelected.

The ascendancy of southern U.S. House Republicans is worthy of considerable ink because it is a political transformation on par with the 1930s Democratic New Deal realignment. The contemporary southern Republican realignment also happens to share some of the same dynamics driving the rapid partisan takeover that occurred in the North in the 1930s. First, seat gains were unusually large and took place in a short span of time (a handful of election cycles). Second, because of the

TABLE 5.4 ■ The Increase in Republican U.S. House Representatives, 1990–2016

Republicans	1990	1992	1994	1996	1998	2000	2002	2004	2006	2008	2010	2012	2014	2016
Alabama	2	3	3	5	5	5	5	5	5	4	6	6	6	6
Arkansas	1	[2]	[2]	[2]	[2]	1	1	1	1	1	3	4	4	4
Florida	10	13	15	15	15	15	18	18	16	15	19	17	17	16
Georgia	1	4	7	8	8	8	8	7	7	7	8	9	10	10
Louisiana	[4]	3	3	5	5	5	4	5	5	6	6	5	5	5
Mississippi	0	0	1	3	2	2	[2]	[2]	[2]	1	3	3	3	3
North Carolina	4	4	8	[6]	7	7	7	7	6	5	6	9	10	10
South Carolina	2	[3]	4	4	4	4	4	4	4	4	5	6	6	6
Tennessee	3	3	5	5	5	5	4	4	4	4	7	7	7	7
Texas	8	9	11	13	13	13	15	21	19	20	23	24	25	25
Virginia	4	4	5	5	5	7	8	8	8	5	8	8	8	7
Total	39	48	64	71	71	72	76	82	77	72	94	98	101	99
N	116	125	125	125	125	125	131	131	131	131	131	138	138	138
Republican %	34	38	51	57	57	58	58	63	59	55	72	71	73	72

Sources: Data compiled by author from various issues of *The Almanac of American Politics* (1992–2016 editions). The 2016 data are from the *New York Times* (http://www.nytimes.com/elections/results/house).

Note: Numbers in bold indicate a Republican majority and bracketed numbers indicate a split delegation.

swift jump in electoral success, neither ascending party (northern Democrats in the 1930s and southern Republicans in the 1990s) had enough politically experienced candidates to contest most of the promising districts at the height of electoral upheaval (Canon 1990; McKee 2010). Hence, in the short term, patterns of candidate emergence were significantly altered. For instance, there was an abnormally high rate of party switching candidates (northern officeholders who switched from Republican to Democrat in the 1930s, and southern officeholders who switched from Democrat to Republican in the 1990s; see McKee et al. 2016). But perhaps even more important, because party switching among incumbent politicians is a rarity even when it ramps up (McKee and Yoshinaka 2015), was the extraordinarily high number of political amateurs who decided to make a run for Congress and actually were successful. From 1992 to 1996, when the southern GOP made its greatest gains in U.S. House contests, 56 percent of newly elected Republicans had no previous elective officeholding experience (McKee 2010, 132). As discussed, after 1996 a new Republican electoral equilibrium set in, and with this greater certainty and electoral stability, the behavior of ambitious politicians returned to a more typical pattern in which the most viable candidates (typically gauged in terms of money and previous elective experience) behaved strategically (Jacobson and Kernell 1983) by winning the lion's share of the most electorally promising congressional districts (i.e., open seats and those with vulnerable incumbents).[8]

BOX 5.2 THE IMPORTANCE OF PARTY SWITCHING TO THE GOP

Party switching among officeholders in the United States is an exceedingly rare phenomenon. Nevertheless, this uncommon event has been much more prevalent in the American South than in the rest of the nation because of the pronounced partisan realignment from Democratic hegemony to Republican dominance. At higher rungs up the electoral ladder, it is even more seldom that a sitting lawmaker will commit the ultimate act of partisan betrayal by defecting to the opposite party or going from a party affiliation to political independence. Table 5.5 displays the population of sitting members of Congress representing southern states who switched parties, from 1964 to the last occurrence in 2009. There has been a total of 17 southern congressional party switchers over this period; 3 Senators and 14 House Representatives. One of the evident distinctions in southern party switching is subregional. All of the 9 Deep South legislators switched from Democrat to Republican (D to R), whereas two of the 8 Peripheral South legislators at least initially switched from Democrat to Independent (D to I), while the other half-dozen switched from Democrat to Republican. From 1964 to 1989, 5 of the 7 switches were undertaken by Peripheral South lawmakers (the 2 Deep South switches took place

(Continued)

[Continued]

TABLE 5.5 ■ Congressional Party Switchers in the South, 1964–2009

Legislator	State	Chamber	Year of Switch	Direction of Switch
Strom Thurmond	SC	Senate	1964	D to R
Albert Watson	SC	House	1964	D to R
Harry F. Byrd, Jr.	VA	Senate	1970	D to I
Phil Gramm	TX	House	1983	D to R
Andy Ireland	FL	House	1984	D to R
Bill Grant	FL	House	1989	D to R
Tommy Robinson	AR	House	1989	D to R
Richard Shelby	AL	Senate	1994	D to R
Nathan Deal	GA	House	1995	D to R
Greg Laughlin	TX	House	1995	D to R
Billy Tauzin	LA	House	1995	D to R
Mike Parker	MS	House	1995	D to R
Jimmy Hayes	LA	House	1995	D to R
Virgil Goode, Jr.	VA	House	2000; 2002	D to I; I to R
Ralph Hall	TX	House	2004	D to R
Rodney Alexander	LA	House	2004	D to R
Parker Griffith	AL	House	2009	D to R

Source: This table has been modified from Yoshinaka (2016, 11) to show only the data on southern members of Congress.

in 1964 by South Carolinians Strom Thurmond and Albert Watson). From the 1990s to the most recent switch in 2009, when the turn to the GOP hastened in all contests below the presidential level, 70 percent (7 out of 10) of defections were carried out by Deep South lawmakers.

Recent scholarship on party switching has revealed many of the factors conditioning the likelihood of defecting. First, as mentioned, the broader political milieu in which Dixie has made a hard shift in favor of the GOP accounts for why the bulk of party switching has taken place in this region (McKee et al. 2016) and why it has overwhelmingly been of the D-to-R variety (more than 90 percent among members of Congress and state legislators; see Yoshinaka 2012, 2016; and this D-to-R defection rate almost certainly holds among southern politicians representing other offices, too). In the case of state legislators, which is a much higher number than members of Congress (more than 250 state legislative party switchers from 1980 to the present; see Yoshinaka 2012), in the narrower context of the district environment where most of these switchers find themselves, a D-to-R switch is more likely if the percentage of the minority population (black and Latino) is lower, average household income is higher, and the percentage of residents who attended college (but did not graduate) is lower (McKee and Yoshinaka 2015; Yoshinaka 2012).

In addition, expressly political factors have also played a role in the decision to switch parties. The election of a Republican governor increases the number of D-to-R switchers, and in fact, there have been several occasions when the number of switches occurring after a Republican wins the governorship has been enough to turn a Republican legislative minority into a GOP majority (some examples of this so-called pivotal switch, as dubbed by Yoshinaka 2012, 358–359, occurred in the Georgia Senate in 2002; the South Carolina House in 1994 and the South Carolina Senate in 2001; the Tennessee Senate in 1995; the Mississippi Senate in 2007; the Louisiana Senate in 2011). Party switches are also more likely to take place if the lawmaker is not a member of the majority party (McKee and Yoshinaka 2015) and during a redistricting (McKee and Yoshinaka 2015; Yoshinaka 2012).

As stated above, more than 250 state legislators have switched parties in the South since 1980, and the rate of switching picked up considerably in the 1990s, when thereafter almost 200 of these switches occurred. Similar to the dynamic found among the much smaller number of congressional party switchers, Deep South state lawmakers comprise a clear majority of defectors from 1980 onward—roughly 80 percent of all D-to-R switches (Yoshinaka 2012, 362). This subregional difference reflects the reality that in more recent decades the GOP has become much stronger in the Deep South (see chapter 8), and many of these Democratic legislators rightly realized that barring a switch they would be left behind. Further, because the southern GOP has become so dominant at most levels of elective officeholding, not surprisingly, politicians with progressive ambition (wanting to hold a higher office) are notably more likely to switch from the Democratic Party to the GOP (Yoshinaka 2012). There are numerous examples of southern politicians climbing the electoral ranks who at one time switched from Democrat to Republican (e.g., Governors Rick Perry of Texas, Sonny Perdue of Georgia, David Beasley of South Carolina, Mike Foster and Buddy Roemer of Louisiana). Indeed, prior to the 1990s when the rarity of party switching became more frequent, Canon and Sousa (1992, 358) estimate that more than 40 percent of southern members of Congress and state officeholders affiliated with the Republican Party were, at one time, Democrats.

Party switching is an infrequent occurrence because it generally comes at a considerable electoral price. Switchers are much more likely to lose vote share and reelection, compared to nonswitchers (Grose 2004; Grose and Yoshinaka 2003), as a consequence of the backlash incurred by voters who feel betrayed, and perhaps to a lesser extent because voters of the party the switcher defects to are not entirely welcoming of the newly minted party member. Perhaps former Democratic Alabama Congressman Glen Browder (not a party switcher) said it best: "switchers have a difficulty. Democrats are mad at them for leaving, Republicans fault them because they're a Johnny-come-lately. Their old friends hate them and their new

(Continued)

(Continued)

friends don't trust them" (Glaser 2001, 75). Nevertheless, some politicians take the plunge, and most likely because a long political career in southern politics has become more and more promising under the GOP label, especially if one wants to climb to the top of the electoral ladder (i.e., governor, senator) where Republicans are most dominant. Party switching is a phenomenon that is worthy of greater examination, and particularly in the context of southern politics where Yoshinaka (2012, 357) rightly claims that it is a fundamental feature of Republican "party building in the South."

Senate Elections

It is somewhat surprising to see that in Table 5.3, after 1990, the Republican share of southern U.S. Senate seats is lower than the percentage of Republican U.S. House districts (32 percent versus 34 percent). But with a much smaller total number of Senate seats ($N = 22$; there were 116 southern congressional districts in 1990), if several are up for election in the same cycle and it proves to be a favorable year for one party (e.g., Republicans in 2004), then the overall partisan composition of the Senate delegation can change markedly. Also, in keeping with the dynamic of Republican top-down advancement, historically, southern Republicans have had more success in races for the upper chamber versus those for the U.S. House (Black and Black 1987).

When Republican Ronald Reagan was elected President in 1980, he brought in a U.S. Senate majority. But the GOP majority was short-lived; when many of the 1980 freshman class stood for reelection in 1986, they were defeated and Democrats regained control. In the South, Republicans accounted for 45.5 percent of the Senate delegation in 1980 (10 total); there were 11 Democratic Senators (50 percent) and one independent, Virginia Senator Harry F. Byrd, Jr. In 1986, seven southern states (Alabama, Arkansas, Florida, Georgia, Louisiana, North Carolina, and South Carolina) had U.S. Senate contests and the GOP lost all seven! After the Democrats' clean sweep in the 1986 elections, the southern U.S. Senate delegation consisted of just 27 percent Republicans (6 out of 22). Thus, the reason the GOP held a slightly higher share of U.S. House seats than U.S. Senate seats heading into the 1990s was the unusually poor performance in the 1986 midterm.

Although the incumbency advantage also factors into Senate elections, it is not nearly as important as in House contests. Recall that from the end of World War II through 2014, House incumbents had a 92 percent reelection rate versus an 80 percent reelection rate for Senate incumbents. There are some easily identifiable reasons for why it is more difficult to maintain a Senate seat. First, Senators are more likely to face stiffer competition because most ambitious contenders would rather be U.S. Senators (1 out of 100) than U.S. House Representatives (1 out of 435). Simply put, Senators have more visibility and more power in the workings of the federal government. There is a joke that when a Senator wakes up in the morning she sees a president of the United States. Not many House members feel this way, and if they do, then they better find their way to the Senate because many more presidents have entered the White House via the Senate (most recently, Barack Obama).

Second, state boundaries are constant and, as a general rule, a state's population will be more demographically diverse than any given congressional district. With greater demographic diversity comes more variability in voter preferences, and therefore it is a taller task to satisfy the demands of a state's electorate than a district's electorate. In the South, there is not a single state in which the population is so small that it contains an at-large congressional district, which means that the district is equivalent to the boundaries of the state (there are currently seven states with at-large districts because their state populations are so small). In states with multiple congressional districts, when one party controls redistricting (like Texas Republicans in 2004), the districts can be drawn in a multitude of ways, but a common strategy for the party in charge is to concentrate the minority party opposition into a smaller number of districts where they can easily win and then maximize the number of winnable districts for the majority party. Under this scenario, the minority party casts many more "wasted" votes because their districts could still be won if their share of supporters were spread more evenly across a greater number of districts (what the majority party does with its voters). All this is to say that district boundaries are easily manipulated, and numerous House incumbents have safe districts because they are purposely drawn so that one party's voters dominate the district. As much as Senators might prefer an alteration to their constituency, it is whatever the state voting electorate happens to be when they run for reelection.

Finally, because of their higher profile, it has proven more difficult for Senators to distance themselves from the positions taken by their national party. This is a two-edged sword, and more recently it has definitely worked to the electoral advantage of southern Republicans. On the one hand, if the positions of the national party are popular and/or the election cycle is favorable to a Senator's party, then reelection is almost assured. On the other hand, and this has played out in Dixie, if one party is generally favored over the other, then association with the more unpopular party makes it much more difficult to win election. Nationally, the Democratic Party has a liberal persona and the GOP opposition is correctly characterized as very conservative (Theriault and Rohde 2011). Over the last several decades the parties have grown increasingly ideologically polarized in Congress (Fleisher and Bond 2004; Hetherington 2001), and this makes it more difficult for voters to evaluate any given Senator separately from their opinions of the incumbent's party affiliation.

In Dixie, which party a Senate candidate associates with is decidedly more important than the incumbency advantage. Incumbency matters less in southern

Senate contests because the GOP dominates most states in the region (Hayes and McKee 2008). Similar to presidential contests, which are statewide affairs, because the contemporary parties are now so ideologically differentiable (Democrats are liberals and Republicans are conservatives; Levendusky 2009), if a state clearly tilts in favor of one party, then Senate candidates of the preferred party will be advantaged irrespective of incumbency. In contemporary southern politics, there exist only a handful of battleground states, those in which statewide contests (usually thought of in terms of presidential elections) are consistently competitive. For instance, in the 2016 presidential election in the South, most political observers only considered Florida, North Carolina, and Virginia to be swing states. And in hindsight, Virginia was more aptly classified as a Democratic-leaning state than as a battleground. The remaining eight southern states were appropriately viewed as Republican locks.

To the extent that lower-level elections have come to take on the dynamics of presidential elections, this development is referred to as *nationalization*. American politics is currently experiencing a heavy dose of nationalization (Jacobson and Carson 2016), and this is especially true in the South. In fact, Republican top-down advancement in southern electoral politics is just a specific variant of nationalization. Southern Senate elections, in particular, have become extremely nationalized affairs. This explains why in 2002, with a popular Republican President George W. Bush, fellow Texan Republican Senate nominee John Cornyn boiled down his candidacy matter-of-factly: a vote for him was a vote for the president. Likewise, in 2014, when Louisiana Democratic Senator Mary Landrieu went down to defeat (the last Democratic Senator in the Deep South's delegation until Doug Jones prevailed in the 2017 special election in Alabama), it was impossible for her to escape from underneath the massively unfavorable impression that most (white) Louisiana voters harbored with respect to President Obama.

Figure 5.5 displays the percentage of southern Senate seats held by Democrats and Republicans from 1990 to 2016. The short-term Republican surge from 1992 to 1996 is reminiscent of the pattern observed in southern U.S. House elections (see Figure 5.4), but then the next notable GOP jump takes place in 2004 when there were seven contests (Alabama, Arkansas, Florida, Georgia, Louisiana, North Carolina, and South Carolina—the same seven states that proved disastrous for southern Republicans in 1986) and Republicans only lost one (Arkansas), to go from 59 percent of the southern Senate delegation in 2002 to 82 percent in 2004. Southern Republicans are reduced to 68 percent of the delegation in the 2008 Democratic tide and then recover one seat in 2010 (73 percent) and hold this number until netting 3 more seats in 2014—an 86 percent southern Senate majority maintained through 2016.

Similar to Table 5.4 for southern U.S. House elections, Table 5.6 shows the number of Republican Senate seats according to each southern state from 1990 to

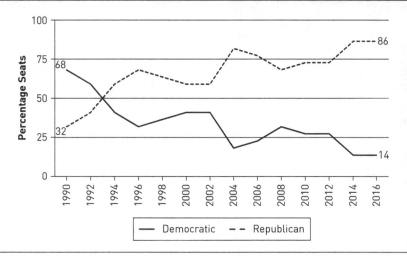

FIGURE 5.5 ■ Southern U.S. Senate Seats Controlled by the Major Parties, 1990–2016

Sources: Data compiled by the author from *The Almanac of American Politics* (1992–2016 editions). The 2016 data are from the *New York Times* (http://www.nytimes.com/elections/results/senate).

Note: The percentage of Democratic and Republican seats is out of the total southern U.S. Senate seats.

2016. It is more intuitive to make sense of the numbers in Table 5.6 as compared to Table 5.4 because there are, of course, only two U.S. Senators in every state. Therefore, a 0 denotes two Democratic Senators, a bracketed 1 indicates a split delegation (1 Democrat and 1 Republican), and a boldface 2 means that both Senators are Republicans. In 1990, only in the Deep South state of Mississippi are both Senators Republicans (Thad Cochran and Trent Lott). Five states have split delegations (Florida, North Carolina, South Carolina, Texas, and Virginia), and in the five remaining states, Democrats have a monopoly (Alabama, Arkansas, Georgia, Louisiana, and Tennessee).

After 1990, the Republican advance is set in motion. There are perhaps several different ways to discuss the rise in southern Senate Republicans in the table, but once again, the subregional distinction is useful, as is simply the general competitiveness of a state. Viewed in subregional terms, with the exception of Louisiana, where a split delegation lasts from 2004 to 2012, the other four Deep South states have been exclusively Republican in Senate elections since at least 2004: Georgia and South Carolina in 2004, Alabama in 1996, and Mississippi back in 1988. With proportionally larger African American populations and a more racially polarized electorate that has sorted along partisan lines (Hood, Kidd, and Morris 2012), contemporary Deep South politics essentially comes down to a battle between a minority Democratic Party controlled by African Americans and a majority

TABLE 5.6 ■ The Increase in Republican U.S. Senators, 1990–2016

Republicans	1990	1992	1994	1996	1998	2000	2002	2004	2006	2008	2010	2012	2014	2016
Alabama	0	0	[1]	2	2	2	2	2	2	2	2	2	2	2
Arkansas	0	0	0	[1]	[1]	[1]	0	0	0	0	[1]	[1]	2	2
Florida	[1]	[1]	[1]	[1]	[1]	0	0	[1]	[1]	[1]	[1]	[1]	[1]	[1]
Georgia	0	[1]	[1]	[1]	[1]	0	[1]	2	2	2	2	2	2	2
Louisiana	0	0	0	0	0	0	0	[1]	[1]	[1]	[1]	[1]	2	2
Mississippi	2	2	2	2	2	2	2	2	2	2	2	2	2	2
North Carolina	[1]	2	2	2	[1]	[1]	[1]	2	2	2	2	[1]	2	2
South Carolina	[1]	[1]	[1]	[1]	[1]	[1]	[1]	2	2	[1]	2	2	2	2
Tennessee	0	0	2	2	2	2	2	2	2	2	2	2	2	2
Texas	[1]	[1]	2	2	2	2	2	2	2	2	2	2	2	2
Virginia	[1]	[1]	[1]	[1]	[1]	2	2	2	[1]	0	0	0	0	0
Total	7	9	13	15	14	13	13	18	17	15	16	16	19	19
N	22	22	22	22	22	22	22	22	22	22	22	22	22	22
Republican %	32	41	59	68	64	59	59	82	77	68	73	73	86	86

Sources: Data compiled by the author from various issues of *The Almanac of American Politics* (1992–2016 editions). The 2016 data are from the *New York Times* (http://www.nytimes.com/elections/results/house).

Note: Numbers in bold indicate a Republican majority and bracketed numbers indicate a split delegation.

Republican Party that is overwhelmingly white (Black and Black 2012; McKee and Springer 2015). Under these conditions, it is very difficult, absent a political scandal, for Deep South Republican Senators to lose to Democratic challengers, especially when the challenger is African American (a more likely occurrence in Deep South Senate races).[9]

The much greater attachment of Deep South whites to the GOP consequently makes these five southern states much less competitive than most of their Peripheral South counterparts. With respect to competitiveness, Tennessee and Texas have been Republican redoubts for a long time in presidential elections and therefore, not surprisingly, these states have both consisted of strictly Republican Senate delegations since the 1994 "Republican Revolution" (Glass 2007). For most of the period under examination, Senate contests in Arkansas have been fairly competitive, but of late the state has moved in an increasingly deep red direction (Dowdle and Giammo 2014; Parry and Barth 2014). This leaves Florida, North Carolina, and Virginia; the three southern states that Democrat Barack Obama won in 2008. Due in part to the considerable northern in-migration of Democrats from the Northeast (McKee and Teigen 2016), the changing demographics in these states appear to favor the Democratic Party and they are the most competitive in statewide elections. In 2014 and 2016, the most recent elections in Table 5.6, Florida had a split Senate delegation (the typical outcome in the Sunshine State), both Virginia Senators were Democrats, and although both North Carolina Senators are Republicans, in the 2016 election the Republican incumbent Richard Burr won 53 percent of the two-party vote.

Presidential Elections

Because the GOP has dominated southern presidential politics going back to the late 1960s, there necessarily is not a notable dynamic evident in these contests from 1992 to 2016. This said, as the GOP has risen in electoral prominence below the presidential level, presidential elections since the early 1990s have actually become slightly more competitive. After two southern sweeps in 1984 and 1988, the Democratic Arkansan Bill Clinton managed to win four southern states in 1992 and 1996. But then the Republican Texan George W. Bush ran the table in Dixie in 2000 and 2004. Despite being a northerner, or as so many Republicans mistakenly believe, a Muslim and a foreigner (Jacobson 2011), but undoubtedly an exotic species of candidate for the typical southern voter, with impressive minority support, Barack Obama picked off three southern states in 2008 and two more in 2012. In 2016, the most unconventional major party nominee in American history, Republican Donald Trump, won every southern state but Virginia.

The presidency is the most politically influential office in shaping the American political system, and what happens in presidential elections has international, national, and regional implications. Because the presidency is the grandest political stage, the positions that the major party nominees take on the most important issues of the day not only guide voters in the short run, but over the long term, the party coalitions are altered as a result of the agendas pursued and championed by presidential hopefuls. For instance, the Republican southern strategy of appealing to the racial conservatism of southern white voters (Phillips 1969) began with Goldwater in 1964 and with few exceptions, it has been a winner in Dixie's presidential politics ever since. The GOP finally put down its anchor in southern electoral politics because of its success in courting the majority white electorate in presidential elections. And as the national profiles of the major parties began to reverse course on the issue of civil rights and then later on social issues, candidates for lower level federal offices and state and local offices began to adjust their positions accordingly so that presidentially induced nationalization of American politics is pervasive. Now, if a southern Democrat tries to convince a given electorate that he is more conservative than his Republican opponent it is unlikely to be a credible argument. Conversely, a southern Republican would probably be laughed at for claiming to be more liberal (or at least moderate) than her Democratic opponent. Presidential elections have been the primary driver of this contemporary partisan sorting of voters into their respective and opposing ideological camps (Levendusky 2009).

Table 5.7 presents southern presidential outcomes from 1992 to 2016 based on Electoral College (EC) data. As the Republican South was just starting to flex its muscles in elections below the presidential level, the Democrat Bill Clinton turned in two impressive political showings in 1992 and 1996. In 1988, Republican President George H. W. Bush won the EC votes of all eleven southern states, but in his 1992 reelection, Clinton defeated Bush in his home state of Arkansas, his

TABLE 5.7 ■ Electoral College Votes in the South, 1992–2016				
Election	Democrat	Republican	Rep % (Votes)	Winner
1992	B. Clinton	G. Bush	74 (147)	Democrat
1996	B. Clinton	B. Dole	65 (147)	Democrat
2000	A. Gore	G. W. Bush	100 (147)	Republican
2004	J. Kerry	G. W. Bush	100 (153)	Republican
2008	B. Obama	J. McCain	64 (153)	Democrat
2012	B. Obama	M. Romney	74 (160)	Democrat
2016	H. R. Clinton	D. Trump	91 (160)	Republican

Source: Data compiled by the author from Dave Leip's *Atlas of U.S. Presidential Elections* (http://uselectionatlas.org/RESULTS/).

Note: In 2016, there were two unfaithful Trump electors in Texas; one cast his presidential vote for John Kasich and the other for Ron Paul.

running mate Al Gore's native Tennessee, and also in the Deep South states of Georgia and Louisiana. Four years later, President Clinton held onto Arkansas, Tennessee, and Louisiana, but he lost Georgia while picking up the largest and hence most coveted battleground state: Florida. Bush Senior's son George W. Bush emerged as a natural fit for the white southern electorate in 2000, defeating Al Gore in every southern state, including Tennessee. In 2004, with his approval rating still high but steadily receding from the historic boost from his response to the terrorist attacks on 9/11/01 (Jacobson 2007a), President Bush easily dispatched his Yankee Democratic opponent, Senator John Kerry of Massachusetts. The Texan made history for being the only Republican to ever sweep Dixie's EC votes in both of his successful presidential runs.

In 2008 and 2012, with respect to his share of EC votes, the Democrat Barack Obama was as competitive as his southern Democratic predecessor Bill Clinton was. But unlike Clinton, a southerner capable of appealing to a nontrivial share of white southerners, the emergence of Barack Obama ushered in a more polarizing dynamic with respect to the southern presidential electorate. Whereas Bill Clinton made deep inroads with southern white rural voters (McKee 2007), this population could not stomach Barack Obama (Arbour and Teigen 2011). Instead, Obama forged a formidable coalition among minorities, women, the young, the highly educated, and Democratic-inclined northern transplants. In 2008 this political formula proved successful in southern states with an abundance of these groups: Florida, North Carolina, and Virginia. Four years hence, Obama carried Florida and Virginia, but he came up short in North Carolina, a true battleground state that has nonetheless experienced a hard-right turn in its state and local politics.

With the presidential election open for the first time in eight years, former first lady, New York Senator, and Secretary of State Hillary Clinton did her best to reassemble the vaunted "Obama coalition," but in a year in which a very disgruntled and active Republican opposition mobilized for change, she came up short against the Republican (and erstwhile Democrat) real estate mogul and celebrity entertainer Donald Trump. In the South, Clinton only managed to carry her running mate Tim Kaine's Virginia, which makes sense because in statewide elections it has emerged as the most competitive southern state (Rozell 2018). Indeed, the Old Dominion is best characterized as light blue and getting darker. Trump's 91 percent haul of Dixie's 160 EC votes is reminiscent of the more typical dominant showing turned in by Republican presidential nominees.

Because, in every state but Maine and Nebraska, EC votes are awarded in a winner-take-all fashion, it is necessary to examine the popular vote breakdown to get a more accurate sense of how competitive southern presidential elections have been from 1992 to 2016. Figure 5.6 presents the South-wide popular vote cast for the major party presidential candidates for the aforementioned span of elections, and because of Ross Perot's impressive popular showings in 1992 and 1996, the popular vote is parceled three ways in these two contests.[10] In 1992, Perot won 16 percent of

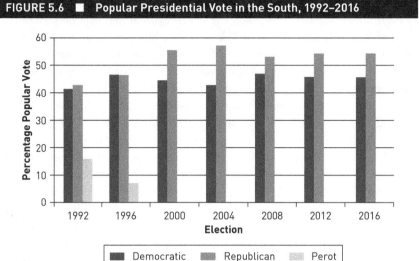

FIGURE 5.6 ■ Popular Presidential Vote in the South, 1992–2016

Source: Data compiled by the author from Dave Leip's *Atlas of U.S. Presidential Elections* (http://uselectionatlas.org/RESULTS/).

Note: The popular vote is the percentage of Democratic and Republican out of the two-party vote total except for 1992 and 1996. In these elections, the vote is out of the total cast for the Democrat (Clinton), Republican (Bush/Dole), and Independent/Reform Party (Perot).

Dixie's presidential votes and thus denied either major party candidate of coming close to a majority (Bush was the plurality winner with 43 percent). Perot was no longer the darling outsider in 1996, and his decline in the popular vote reflects this (7 percent), but a generally overlooked fact in Clinton's reelection (but see Lamis 1999) is that although Clinton won just 35 percent of Dixie's EC votes, he was actually the plurality popular vote winner (outperforming his Kansan Republican opponent Bob Dole by a sliver: 24,229 votes separating the two candidates out of over 24 million cast).

The competitiveness of the 1992 and 1996 presidential elections receded in 2000 and 2004 when Republican George W. Bush not only twice swept the South's EC votes, but in doing so he won 56 and 57 percent of the popular vote in these respective years. Although in 2000 Bush easily won the popular vote in most southern states, the presidency hung in the balance, based on the outcome in Florida (Ceaser and Busch 2001). Whoever won the Sunshine State would become the next President because its 25 EC votes would be enough to deliver an EC majority (a minimum of 270 EC votes). In a bitterly disputed vote recount followed by a Supreme Court decision (*Bush v. Gore*) that halted the counting of presidential ballots in the Sunshine State, a month after Election Day George W. Bush was declared the winner with a jaw-dropping 537 two-party popular vote margin that gave the Republican 271 total EC votes.

In 2008 and 2012, Democrat Barack Obama managed to reduce the southern Republican popular presidential vote shares in these contests (Republicans John McCain won 53 percent in 2008 and Mitt Romney won 54 percent in 2012). And interestingly, in 2016, in terms of the percentage of the popular presidential vote, Donald Trump virtually mirrored Romney's 2012 performance. Of course, 2016 was anything but a typical year in presidential politics. The rise of Trump took the entire political class by surprise. And with respect to election outcomes, 2016 will go down as another one of those rarities where, as was true in 2000, the popular vote winner (Gore in 2000; Clinton in 2016) was not the EC victor (Bush in 2000; Trump in 2016). Unlike Bush before him, Trump did not owe his election to the South; it was made possible by a surprising Republican shift in three states that had not been won by the GOP since the 1980s (Michigan, Pennsylvania, and Wisconsin). However, the fairly competitive popular vote in the South is not really a sign of Republican vulnerability, if viewed through a national lens. Although Trump won 57 percent of the total votes cast in the EC, Clinton won 51 percent of the national popular two-party vote. So, even though Trump's national popular vote share was underwater (below 50 percent), in Dixie he outperformed his overall popular vote share by 5.5 percentage points.

STATEWIDE CONTESTS

Although not as nationalized as U.S. Senate elections have become (McKee and Sievert 2017), southern gubernatorial contests clearly exhibit the impressive forward march of the contemporary GOP. As the most important and politically influential office in the context of state politics, the governorship is sort of like a miniature version of the American presidency. With its executive role and command over the laws in each state, perhaps it is no wonder that the most promising path to the White House has been via the governor's mansion, and several southern chief executives have made this transition (e.g., Jimmy Carter in 1976; Bill Clinton in 1992; George W. Bush in 2000).

Primarily due to the electoral threat that Republican presidential success would have in boosting the performances in down-ballot races like gubernatorial elections, the timing of most of these contests has served as a barrier to the possible contagion effects of presidential politics. Thus, in the 1960s to 1980s, southern Democratic leaders understood that holding gubernatorial elections in "off-years" was a wise idea (Black and Black 1987). In fact, North Carolina is the only southern state to hold it governor's race in a presidential year; the rest either hold their contests in even-numbered midterms (Alabama, Arkansas, Florida, Georgia, South Carolina, Tennessee, and Texas), odd-numbered midterms prior to presidential years (Louisiana and Mississippi), or odd-numbered midterms after presidential years (Virginia). The length of term for all southern governors is four years (this has not always been true;

e.g., Arkansas used to have two-year terms for governor) and except for Virginia, which has a one-term limit, the other ten southern states allow for a consecutive two-term limit.[11] Texas is the only southern state without a gubernatorial term limit, and most recently, Republican Governor Rick Perry served from 2000 to 2014, the longest serving executive in Lone Star State history.

There are such a large number of southern congressional districts that it is sensible to present data on them for every two years when all U.S. House seats are up for election. And with 22 southern U.S. Senate seats, displaying changes in two-year increments is feasible even though only a third of the seats are up because of the equal staggering of these six-year term offices. However, there are only 11 southern governorships and therefore, in Figure 5.7, Republican success rates are displayed according to decade, starting with the 1960s. The ascendancy of the GOP is palpable as the percentage of Democratic wins exhibits a step-down pattern in each decade while the share of Republican victories steps upwards over the same period. Out of a total of 32 southern gubernatorial elections in the 1960s, the GOP came away with only 5 victories. By contrast, in the 2010s (through 2016), out of 21 governor's races, Republicans have won all but 4.

Currently, in the eleven-governor southern delegation, there are three Democrats: Louisiana's John Bel Edwards, North Carolina's Roy Cooper, and

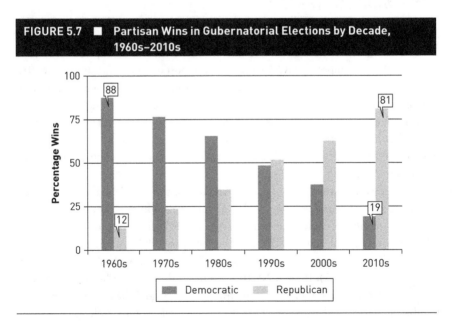

FIGURE 5.7 ■ Partisan Wins in Gubernatorial Elections by Decade, 1960s–2010s

Source: Data compiled by the author.

Notes: For each decade, the total number of contests is as follows: 1960s = 32; 1970s = 34; 1980s = 26; 1990s = 31; 2000s = 24; and 2010s = 21. The data run through 2016, and thus the Democratic gubernatorial victory in 2017 in Virginia is not included in the 2010s data displayed in the figure.

Virginia's Ralph Northam. Although not accounted for in the figure, in the first southern gubernatorial election since Trump was elected President in 2016, in Virginia's 2017 open-seat contest, Northam handily beat his Republican opponent Ed Gillespie by 9 percentage points (54.5 to 45.5 percent of the two-party vote). Whereas Virginia is clearly trending blue, the election of Edwards and Cooper, however, speak to the importance of short-term political conditions that aided these Democrats. Particularly in the deep red Pelican State, it now takes a situation very favorable for Democrats to be competitive in statewide elections. This was so in 2015 when Edwards triumphed because, by all accounts, the departing Republican Governor Bobby Jindal was one of the main reasons why the state was reduced to financial ruin. In addition, Edwards' Republican rival was the highly unpopular and scandal-plagued Senator David Vitter.[12] Likewise, in the Tar Heel State, Cooper was the benefactor of running against the polarizing and controversial incumbent Republican Pat McCrory who, among several missteps, provoked national outrage over his defense of a "bathroom bill" that made it a crime for transgendered persons to use a facility that did not match the sex on their birth certificate.

Usually examinations of statewide elections start and end with the gubernatorial office. Fortunately, there are numerous other statewide nonjudicial elective offices that are up for election at the same time as the governorship.[13] And the range in the number of offices is considerable. For instance, in Tennessee the governorship is the only statewide elective office, but every other southern state has at least three statewide elective offices (the modal number is seven); and with a total of ten, North Carolina has the most. Because of some changes (like changing an elective position to appointed, as was the case for Florida's Secretary of State position in 2002), the total number of southern statewide elective offices has slightly varied from 1990 to 2016, but the sum has never been less than 74.

Figure 5.8 documents the percentage of southern Democrats and Republicans in statewide elective offices from 1990 to 2016. Including gubernatorial contests along with all the other statewide elective positions reveals an astounding partisan transformation. As late as 1990, Republicans held only 17 percent of statewide elective offices and their Democratic opposition controlled the other 83 percent. The first Republican seat majority surfaces in the 2002 midterm, and the GOP has not looked back since. In 2016, the GOP had reached its apex in southern statewide elective officeholding—88 percent of 74 positions, thus leaving Democrats with a total of nine seats. Of all the data presented in this chapter, the partisan reversal in southern statewide elective officeholding are the most remarkable. Among the current Democratic total of nine seats, seven of them reside in the Peripheral South. In the entire 39-seat Deep South delegation, prior to John Bel Edwards' Louisiana gubernatorial victory in 2015, for the previous four years, Mississippi Democratic Attorney General Jim Hood was the only statewide-elected Democrat.

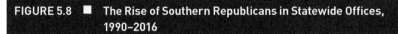

FIGURE 5.8   ■   The Rise of Southern Republicans in Statewide Offices, 1990–2016

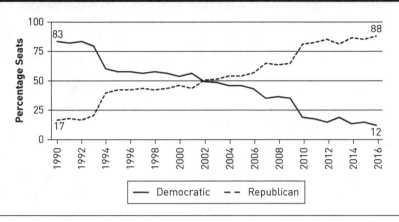

Sources: Data collected by the author from Secretary of State websites and *The Green Papers* (www .thegreenpapers.com/).

Notes: From 1990 to 2001, there were a total of 78 statewide offices (40 in the Deep South and 38 in the Peripheral South). Florida and Louisiana altered their number of statewide elective offices after 2001, so that there were 75 in 2002 (40 in the Deep South and 35 in the Peripheral South). Since 2003, there are a total of 74 statewide offices (39 in the Deep South and 35 in the Peripheral South). A list of all statewide offices for each state will be made available by the author upon request.

STATE LEGISLATIVE ELECTIONS

Outside of truly local elections like county commissioner, state legislative contests are often considered the bottom rung of the electoral ladder for those politicians who harbor progressive ambition (Schlesinger 1966). But in the aggregate, these elections are very important because they are a perennial stepping stone to other offices (Yoshinaka and McKee 2017), and particularly the U.S. House, where typically half of that body's members come from state legislatures (Jacobson 2009a). In the heyday of the Democratic Solid South, there was never a fear in any southern state legislative delegation that the GOP would wrest majority control of the seats. And this viewpoint was correct; it took many years after southern Republicans won majority control of U.S. Senate and U.S. House seats for southern state legislative seats to follow suit. Specifically, it was not until the 2010 midterm that southern Republicans managed to win a resounding majority of state senate and state house seats. State legislative elections were the last political domino to fall into the hands of southern Republicans.

Although there is considerable variation in statutory provisions applicable to state legislative elections (e.g., the timing of elections, term lengths, term limits, multimember/single-member districts, number of legislators in the upper and lower chambers), the sheer size of the southern state legislative delegation (1,782 total seats) makes it easy to justify looking at the data in even-year two-year increments despite the fact that, as pointed out with regard to gubernatorial elections, many states hold these contests in odd years. As shown in Figure 5.9, southern Democrats in 1990 controlled 73 percent of state legislative seats (upper and lower chambers combined) versus just 27 percent for the GOP. It was not until the new millennium that Republican electoral parity materialized, and thereafter the two major parties held an almost even number of seats until a Republican margin opened up in 2010. Since 2010, the GOP has expanded upon its state legislative seat majority with 66 percent in 2016 as compared to 34 percent for Democrats.

In line with the data displayed for U.S. House seats (Table 5.4) and U.S. Senate seats (Table 5.6), Tables 5.8 and 5.9 show the number of Republican state legislators in each southern state legislative delegation from 1990 to 2016 for the state senate and state house, respectively. Once again, bracketed numbers indicate a split delegation and boldface numbers denote a GOP majority. Beginning with the southern state senate delegation, in 1990 there was not a single state with a Republican majority. The Florida GOP led the way to a majority, achieving a split delegation in 1992 and then Republican control in 1994. In 1996, Texas Republicans were the next to topple the Democratic state senate majority. Virginia Republicans followed in 1998, but their Democratic opponents won back a senate majority for two cycles and then there was a split delegation in 2012 that finally reverted back to GOP control in 2014. The

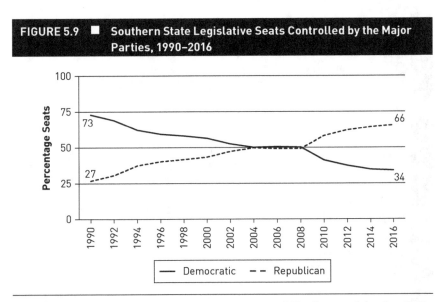

FIGURE 5.9 ■ Southern State Legislative Seats Controlled by the Major Parties, 1990–2016

Sources: Data compiled by the author from various issues of *The Almanac of American Politics* (1992–2016 editions). The 2016 data are from the National Conference of State Legislatures (http://www.ncsl.org/research/about-state-legislatures/partisan-composition.aspx).

Note: The percentage of Democratic and Republican seats is out of the total southern state legislative seats.

TABLE 5.8 ■ The Increase in Republican State Senators, 1990–2016

Republicans	1990	1992	1994	1996	1998	2000	2002	2004	2006	2008	2010	2012	2014	2016
Alabama	7	8	12	12	12	11	10	10	12	13	22	23	26	26
Arkansas	4	5	7	7	6	8	8	8	8	8	15	21	24	26
Florida	17	[20]	21	23	25	25	26	26	26	26	28	26	26	25
Georgia	11	15	21	22	22	24	30	34	34	34	36	38	38	38
Louisiana	6	6	7	14	14	14	13	15	15	15	20	24	26	25
Mississippi	9	14	15	18	18	18	23	24	27	25	27	32	32	32
North Carolina	14	11	23	20	15	15	22	21	19	20	31	32	34	35
South Carolina	11	16	18	20	22	24	25	27	26	27	27	28	28	28
Tennessee	14	14	15	15	15	15	15	17	[16]	19	19	26	28	28
Texas	8	13	14	17	16	16	19	19	20	19	19	19	20	20
Virginia	10	18	18	[20]	21	21	23	24	23	19	18	[20]	21	21
Total	111	140	171	188	186	191	214	225	226	225	262	289	303	304
N	457	457	457	457	457	457	457	457	457	457	457	457	457	457
Republican %	24	31	37	41	41	42	47	49	49	49	57	63	66	67

Sources: Data compiled by the author from various issues of *The Almanac of American Politics* (1992–2016 editions). The 2016 data are from the National Conference of State Legislatures (http://www.ncsl.org/research/about-state-legislatures/partisan-composition.aspx).

Note: Numbers in bold indicate a Republican majority and bracketed numbers indicate a split chamber.

TABLE 5.9 ■ The Increase in Republican State Representatives, 1990–2016

Republicans	1990	1992	1994	1996	1998	2000	2002	2004	2006	2008	2010	2012	2014	2016
Alabama	23	23	32	34	36	37	42	42	43	43	**66**	**66**	**72**	**72**
Arkansas	8	10	12	14	25	30	30	28	25	28	45	**51**	**63**	**76**
Florida	46	49	57	**61**	**72**	**77**	**81**	**84**	**79**	**76**	**81**	**74**	**81**	**79**
Georgia	35	52	66	74	78	75	73	**99**	**106**	**105**	**113**	**119**	**114**	**118**
Louisiana	18	16	17	27	27	34	34	37	41	50	52	58	58	**60**
Mississippi	18	27	31	36	37	33	35	47	47	48	50	**63**	67	**72**
North Carolina	38	42	**68**	**61**	54	58	[60]	57	52	52	**67**	77	**74**	74
South Carolina	42	50	**63**	**69**	**65**	**70**	**73**	**74**	**73**	**71**	**75**	**78**	**77**	**80**
Tennessee	42	36	40	38	40	41	45	46	46	49	**64**	70	72	74
Texas	57	59	61	68	72	72	**88**	**87**	**81**	**76**	**101**	**95**	**98**	**94**
Virginia	39	41	47	46	49	**52**	**65**	**60**	**57**	**53**	**59**	**67**	**67**	**66**
Total	366	405	494	528	555	579	626	661	650	651	773	818	843	865
N	1,325	1,325	1,325	1,325	1,325	1,325	1,325	1,325	1,325	1,325	1,325	1,325	1,325	1,325
Republican %	28	31	37	40	42	44	47	50	49	49	58	62	64	65

Sources: Data compiled by the author from various issues of *The Almanac of American Politics* (1992–2016 editions). The 2016 data are from the National Conference of State Legislatures (http://www.ncsl.org/research/about-state-legislatures/partisan-composition.aspx).

Note: Numbers in bold indicate a Republican majority and bracketed numbers indicate a split chamber.

Deep South states of South Carolina and Georgia registered Republican state senate majorities in 2000 and 2002, respectively. Tennessee in 2004 and then Mississippi in 2006 experience their first taste of GOP state senate control, which is then temporarily lost in the next election cycle and then regained thereafter. Not until 2010 do state senate Republicans in Alabama, Louisiana, and North Carolina assume majority control. And finally, pulling up the rear is Arkansas, which first attains a Republican state senate majority in 2012. After 2012, every single southern state senate delegation is majority Republican.

Although the state patterns of Republican advancement in southern state house delegations in Table 5.9 are somewhat different from those prevailing in the southern state senate elections displayed above, the generally steady and gradual rise is very similar. As was the case in the state senate, from 1990 to 1992 there is no southern state house delegation with a Republican majority. Rather than systematically discuss the order in which each southern state attains majority Republican status in the South's lower legislative chamber, notice that the overall percentage of state house Republicans closely tracks the share of their GOP state senate colleagues for every given two-year increment (e.g., 67 percent of southern state senators are Republicans in 2016 and 65 percent of southern state house representatives are Republicans in 2016). Since 2012, Republicans comprise the majority of state house members in all eleven southern states.

THE PEAK OF REPUBLICAN HEGEMONY?

In the 1980s, the cigarette company Virginia Slims placed billboards along Interstate 95 that showed an attractive female sunbather enjoying a nice smoke, with the headline "You've Come a Long Way, Baby." And since then, so have southern Republicans. As discussed in chapter 4, the deep GOP inroads paved by the likes of presidential hopefuls and presidents-elect, from Barry Goldwater in 1964 to Ronald Reagan in 1980, led to the rise of southern Republicans in all manner of lower level elective offices chronicled in this chapter. Simply put, the electoral evidence of GOP dominance in contemporary southern politics is incontrovertible. In fact, it makes one question whether GOP hegemony has finally reached its apex. Of course, only time will tell, but considering the general demographic trends in the southern electorate, in some states at least (like the battlegrounds of Florida and North Carolina and Democratic-leaning Virginia), there is reason for Democrats to be optimistic about their prospects for reclaiming a competitive position in district-based contests (U.S. House and state legislative elections).

But before considering the extent to which demographic changes can translate into a Democratic advantage (a subject explored in chapter 9), let us first consider why the southern GOP has come to dominate the political landscape. Mortality is a universal condition and it can be the primary driver contributing to the rise and decline of political parties. In the South, as the national parties reversed themselves on civil rights in the 1960s and then later battled over other salient issues of concern to voters (e.g., abortion in the 1970s), the natural passing of each generation of southerners proved a major problem for the ruling Democratic Party. As will be demonstrated in the next chapter, as early as the 1950s, subsequent generations of southerners loosened their attachment to the Democratic Party, and eventually a critical mass of white southerners came to identify with the GOP. The manifestation of a southern white Republican voting majority via the process of generational change made it possible for the party to capture overwhelming political majorities in the various offices featured in this chapter, and that is the dynamic to which we now turn.

6 GENERATIONAL CHANGE AND GOP GROWTH

Time never stands still. The aging of the American electorate can lead to lasting changes in the political system. In the American South, perhaps the greatest threat to Democratic hegemony was the mortality of the white population as big political changes took place. There is compelling evidence that a massive disruption to the status quo in the party system would have to transpire for older voters to consider altering their party identification. But the tumult of the civil rights movement in the late 1950s to mid-1960s was the kind of event that catalyzed and solidified the permanent alignment of southern blacks to the Democratic Party while their white counterparts decided to vote Republican in presidential contests after 1964 and gradually shift their partisanship in favor of the GOP thereafter.

Changes to the positions staked out by the major parties on the most salient issues impacting southerners directly set in motion the remarkable partisan transformation of this section of the United States. No issue looms larger than race, and by the national parties reversing themselves on civil rights, with Democrats embracing the liberal end of the political continuum and their Republican opposition staking out the conservative side, it became readily apparent that black southerners would quickly embrace the erstwhile white supremacist party of Dixie, while their white neighbors would recognize and seize upon the political imperative to affiliate with the party of Lincoln (Carmines and Stimson 1989). For southern African Americans, the 1964 election constituted such a powerful period effect that regardless of age, this group moved en masse toward the Democratic Party. Southern whites, on the other hand, exhibited a more secular transition in favor of the GOP—with many in this group initially dealigning from a Democratic identification, while the advent of newer generations of white southerners would be needed to complete the realignment to the Republican Party.

In this chapter, the long-term changes to the party identification of southerners are documented. Because party identification is the most influential factor in shaping voter preferences (Campbell et al. 1960), the distribution of Democrats and Republicans in the electorate determines the relative strength of the major parties in electoral politics. With the use of American National Election Study (ANES) data from 1952 to 2012, the party identification of black and white southerners is assessed. Because African Americans are almost uniformly Democratic, the ascendancy of the Republican Party is almost entirely due to changes in the party identification of white southerners. The remainder of the chapter considers the role of generational change in contributing to the growing strength of the southern GOP. Through the use of cohort analysis and a rare but extremely valuable survey that tracks the political behavior of the same individuals over a long span of time, it is possible to gauge the importance of how the white realignment in favor of the Republican Party was fueled by the entrance of younger voters whose more malleable partisanship realigned to the GOP as they aged during a political time when the Republican Party was electorally ascendant.

THE IMPORTANCE OF PARTY IDENTIFICATION

After World War II, a team of researchers at the University of Michigan collaborated on a series of surveys designed to better understand the behavior of American voters. In 1960, these scholars—Angus Campbell, Philip Converse, Warren Miller, and Donald Stokes—produced the aptly titled book, *The American Voter*. In this tour de force examination of political attitudes and political activity among the mass electorate, the authors came to a fairly definitive conclusion about the typical American citizen: politics is not an endeavor that ranks very high on the list of everyday priorities. In fact, going back to an economic theory of politics proposed by Downs (1957), Campbell et al. (1960) would agree that most Americans' lack of political interest is tied to having better things to pay attention to, and therefore the avoidance of seeking out political information is purposive; Downs called it "rational ignorance." But if voters pay politics little attention, then how are they able to navigate the political world?

Campbell et al. (1960) had a simple answer for the aforementioned question: party identification. In the political milieu of American politics, no other factor carries as much weight and especially with respect to vote choice. To be sure, not all voters affiliate with one of the two major parties, but a clear majority do; particularly when we make the fair assumption that with respect to voting behavior, individuals who claim to be politically independent but lean toward either the Democratic or Republican Party behave very similar to people who express a "not very strong" affiliation with one of the major parties (Keith et al. 1992). In other words, as long as analysts have tracked party identification, only a small share of the American public claims to be wholly independent of the major parties. Because most voters either affiliate with or are inclined toward the Democratic or Republican labels, this fact goes a long way toward explaining their political behavior. Indeed, for most voters, absent a party label they could not make sense of their choices in any given election. Party identification is the primary cue voters rely upon to interpret their political surroundings (Bartels 2002), and it is certainly the main indicator for guiding voter preferences (Campbell et al. 1960).

Detailed examination of survey data, with questions asked repeatedly over many years, made it apparent to the authors of *The American Voter* that only a small segment of the mass public harbors anything close to what we would describe as a well-defined worldview of politics in which clear linkages are made with respect to their positions on a multitude of issues (Converse 1964). In other words, most voters are not ideological; they do not make clear connections between issues in a fashion that political scientists would call conservative or liberal. For example, the typical American voter does not recognize that a contemporary conservative position on the death penalty is to be in favor of its enforcement while a conservative position on abortion is to be pro-life, whereas a typical liberal takes the opposing positions on both issues. Most liberals and conservatives take these stated positions but most Americans are moderate, and they lack a high level of issue consistency in the manner demonstrated by their more ideological peers. As Converse (1964) pointed out decades ago, where one *should* position oneself on issues as disparate as the death penalty and abortion, or say gun control and school prayer, are socially constructed arrangements that party elites have concocted. That is, the dominant conservative faction of Republicans tells the American voter that a conservative favors gun rights and school prayer, whereas the liberal wing of Democrats lets us know that a liberal favors more gun control and keeping God out of public schools.

Instead of ruminating on the question of why conservatives are pro-gun and pro-God, and why what it means to be a conservative or a liberal has changed over the course of American history, most voters lean on their party affiliation in order to figure out essentially what their party says about what goes with what. Put another way, because most voters are not ideological but most are partisan, the party label usually guides them with respect to how they view any salient issue making noise in the body politick (Carsey and Layman 2006; Levendusky 2009). For instance, to the extent that a typical Democratic voter realizes that his party supports greater intervention in the economy in terms of regulation and wealth redistribution, while that same party takes a hands-off approach with respect to the private behavior of individuals, the connection in Democratic positions is rarely made explicit to this voter. Rather, most Democrats just come to recognize that their party has taken these stances and not that there is any underlying liberal ideology linking them together. Simply put, party affiliation is what guides the political behavior of most voters and the signals they receive from party elites help shape the dynamics of the American political system.

Because two major parties have always dominated American politics, whether it is Federalists versus Jeffersonian-Republicans, Democrats versus Whigs, and finally Democrats versus Republicans, the party affiliation of the voter is the most telling indicator of voting behavior. Campbell et al. (1960) utilized a seven-point scale for determining party identification. The construction of the scale consists of two questions: the first establishes identification, and the second assesses the degree of attachment to a party. Campbell et al. measured party identification among a representative sample of the American electorate in what came to be known as the American National Election Study (ANES), and the ANES has been conducted continuously for every presidential election from 1952 to the present (see note 2 in chapter 4 for additional information on the ANES).

The first question asked of an ANES respondent is as follows: "Generally speaking, do you usually think of yourself as a Republican, a Democrat, an Independent, or what?" This question determines identification or lack thereof because a respondent states affiliation with a major party or political independence and, in the case of a minuscule share of the electorate, one can also state identification with another party (hence the "or what" option—because this portion of the electorate is so small, it is excluded from examination). If only this question was asked, then party identification would divide into Republican, Democrat, and Independent; the two major party identifiers and those unaffiliated with the major parties. But the follow-up question seeks to determine how strong is the attachment to a political party, and hence it asks, "Would you call yourself a strong Republican (Democrat) or not very strong Republican (Democrat)?" Likewise, in the case of respondents who state they are Independent on the first question, the accompanying follow-up question is "Do you think of yourself as closer to the Republican or Democratic party?"

The sequencing of these questions allows the researcher to build the seven-point party identification scale. Instead of classifying partisan identifiers as "not very strong," this label is altered to "weak." Briefly, if a respondent first states identification with the Democratic Party, then the follow-up is whether he is a "strong" or "not very strong" (weak) Democrat. And if a respondent states political independence, then the follow-up is whether he is closer to the Republican or Democratic Party. Importantly, this Independent can state he is closer to neither major party, and this would make him a pure Independent. Under these scenarios is the possibility of a strong Democrat, weak Democrat, Independent-leaning Democrat, pure Independent, and Independent-leaning Republican. If the respondent stated he was a Republican for the initial question, then the follow-up question provides us with the possibility of either a strong or weak Republican. Hence, the seven-point scale is: 1 = Strong Democrat (SD); 2 = Weak Democrat (WD); 3 = Independent-leaning Democrat (ID); 4 = Independent (I); 5 = Independent-leaning Republican (IR); 6 = Weak Republican (WR); 7 = Strong Republican (SR).

The seven-point party identification scale may seem simplistic, but it encapsulates a lot of information. First, the party identification question starts with the language, "Generally speaking, do you usually think of yourself as . . ." Prefacing the question in this manner is designed to capture the conception of party identification as an attachment to a political party that is believed to be enduring. That is, individuals are rarely quick to change their party affiliation (Campbell et al. 1960; Green, Palmquist, and Schickler 2002). Second, unlike exit polls that merely ask a voter to indicate Democrat, Republican, Independent, or something else, by offering the follow-up question to assess the degree of attachment to a party (or whether or not an Independent leans toward a party), the ANES measure of party identification captures not just identification (or lack thereof) with a party, but the strength of that attachment (e.g., strong Democrat, weak Democrat). By accounting for the degree of attachment to a party, some prefer the term *partisanship* to *party identification* because the former term better captures the intensity of identification. For our purposes, however, partisanship and party identification will be treated as synonymous, interchangeable concepts.

Not surprisingly, the most loyal partisans are strong partisans, and it is often the case that the share of weak partisans who vote for their party is not much different from the portion of independent leaners who side with the party they lean toward (Keith et al. 1992). The empirical evidence that shows the voting behavior of weak partisans and leaning independents to be very similar has led numerous scholars to treat the latter group as if they were actually partisans, which means that only pure Independents are considered unaffiliated with one of the major parties. In some of the analyses that follow, leaning independents will be classified as partisans.

To give the student a sense of the powerful relationship between party identification and vote choice, consider the 2012 ANES data on southern respondents. For the major party presidential vote (Democrat Barack Obama versus Republican Mitt Romney), 99 percent of strong Democrats voted for Obama; 88 percent of weak Democrats supported Obama; 91 percent of Independent-leaning Democrats went with the Democratic president; 52 percent of pure Independents voted for Romney; 92 percent of Independent-leaning Republicans went with the Republican challenger; 90 percent of weak Republicans supported Romney; and 99 percent of strong Republicans voted for Romney. In 2012, the loyalty exhibited by partisans and independent leaners, in favor of the presidential candidate sharing their affiliation, is simply extraordinary. In fact, in the history of modern survey sampling, going back to at least the 1950s, partisan loyalty in this presidential election reached an all-time high (see Jacobson 2014). Notice also that weak partisans and Independent leaners are basically indistinguishable in their voting behavior, though the leaners are a little bit more loyal than their weak partisan counterparts.

Because of the importance of party identification in affecting the outcome of elections, the distribution of partisans in the electorate is the most critical factor in accounting for the relative electoral strength of the major parties. As discussed in previous chapters, because the Democratic Party once dominated southern politics, it necessarily followed that the vast majority of voters identified as Democrats. The rise of southern Republicans would not have been possible unless the southern electorate turned away from its ancestral Democratic heritage and instead eventually came to embrace the GOP. But given the tremendous significance of race, the movement toward the Republican Party has been almost entirely due to an alteration in the party affiliation of white southerners. By contrast, black southerners went in the opposite direction, rapidly shifting in favor of the Democratic Party at around the same time that their white neighbors began to abandon it (Hood, Kidd, and Morris 2012). The next two sections of the chapter document the longitudinal changes in party identification among black and white southerners, respectively. These patterns need to be presented before taking the next step of illustrating and explaining how generational change registers as the primary mechanism through which GOP growth has occurred.

PARTY IDENTIFICATION OF BLACK SOUTHERNERS

Before passage of the 1965 Voting Rights Act (VRA), the much lower percentage of registered and hence participating African Americans in the southern states also mitigated the strength of their affiliation with either major party. Nonetheless, because of the legacy of President Lincoln and a Republican Party that once upon a time vigorously defended the rights of black southerners during the Reconstruction era, allegiance with the Democratic Party was malleable prior to the 1964 election. The 1964 presidential contest proved a pivotal and historic turning point in the political behavior of southern blacks. To be sure, the Democratic Party under the leadership of Presidents Roosevelt and Truman made deep inroads with the black electorate because of their actions that furthered the interests of African Americans, but it was not until the 1964 election that a permanent period of political reckoning transpired. As Carmines and Stimson (1989) thoroughly explicate, 1964 became the critical moment in a racial issue evolution that eventually realigned southern whites in favor of the GOP while fostering an attendant and uncharacteristically rapid and abiding shift of black southerners to the Democratic Party.

The major party presidential nominees treaded lightly on the civil rights issue in the 1950s (Republican Dwight Eisenhower vs. Democrat Adlai Stevenson in 1952 and 1956) and also in 1960 when Republican Richard Nixon favored a me-too position, and therefore voters had trouble distinguishing any difference between his position on the issue as compared to the stance of his Democratic opponent John F. Kennedy. The 1964 election was different because civil rights became an issue that rose to the forefront of American politics as the civil rights movement was cresting due to the demonstrations taking place throughout the South (Black and Black 1987). Indeed, on June 11, 1963, President Kennedy was compelled to offer a poignant plea for racial equality in a nationally televised address in reaction to the latest racial unrest in Birmingham, Alabama. After Kennedy was assassinated on November 22, 1963, the newly sworn-in President Lyndon Baines Johnson (LBJ) recognized the opportunity to fulfill the fallen president's wish by passing a major civil rights act. After months of unrelenting negotiation with a reluctant Congress (Whalen and Whalen 1985), LBJ's effort finally passed into law in August of 1964.

Most likely, passage of the 1964 Civil Rights Act would have had a much more limited political impact if not for the fact that LBJ's Republican opponent for the presidency, U.S. Senator Barry Goldwater of Arizona, was one of a minority of Senate Republicans who voted against this major piece of civil rights legislation (Carmines and Stimson 1989; Stimson 2004). By voting against this historic legal reform, Goldwater sent a bright signal, particularly to black and white southerners, which essentially was interpreted simply as the Republican presidential nominee opposing black interests.

Figure 6.1 displays ANES data on the party identification of black southerners in order to highlight their pronounced and enduring shift to the Democratic Party. Leaning Independents are classified as partisans, and thus only pure Independents are labeled as Independents. Although 80 percent of southern blacks affiliated with the Democratic Party in 1952, in the next two elections black Democratic identification drops considerably (69 percent in 1956 and then to 60 percent in 1960). But in 1964, the drastic ascent of black alignment with the Democratic Party occurs and then attains its apex in 1968. In 1964, 86 percent of black southerners identified as Democrats, a dramatic increase over 1960. In 1968, with the presence of a reinvented Republican Richard Nixon (McGinniss 1969), who now fully embraced Goldwater's "southern strategy" (Phillips 1969), and Alabama governor and American Independent Party candidate George Wallace, an "unreconstructed" race-baiting demagogue, black Democratic affiliation reached an astounding 97 percent. The 1968 contest may have been the peak of black Democratic identification, but it remains somewhere in the 80th percentile. For instance, in 2012, black Democratic identification was 88 percent—2 percentage points higher than where it stood in that fateful 1964 election. Conversely, black Republicanism has been essentially moribund ever since 1964 (6 percent; 5 percent in 2012).

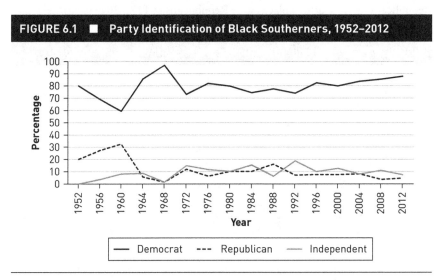

FIGURE 6.1 ■ Party Identification of Black Southerners, 1952–2012

Source: Data compiled by the author from the American National Election Studies (ANES) *Time Series Cumulative Data File (1948–2012).*

Notes: All Independent-leaning partisans are classified as partisans (e.g., an Independent who leans toward the Democratic/Republican party is classified as a Democrat/Republican). Because of a large oversample of African American respondents in the 2008 and 2012 ANES, the data for these years were weighted to more accurately reflect the racial composition of the southern subsample. In 1960 the sample for black southerners consists of only 37 respondents; in all other years the sample size is greater than 50. Hispanics are excluded.

The overwhelming allegiance of blacks to the Democratic Party is a cardinal feature of contemporary southern politics, and thanks to the availability of ANES data going back to 1952, the dramatic shift to the erstwhile party of southern white supremacy can be pinpointed to the political events of the mid-1960s. Further, because southern African Americans typically vote upwards of 90 percent in favor of Democratic candidates (see Black 1998; Black and Black 2002; Bullock and Gaddie 2009), for all intents and purposes, this segment of the southern electorate has played no part in the growth of the contemporary southern GOP, a dynamic almost entirely due to the changing behavior of white southerners, the segment of Dixie's electorate that we will focus on for the remainder of this chapter.

PARTY IDENTIFICATION OF WHITE SOUTHERNERS

Compared to party identification among black southerners, the changing pattern of party identification among white southerners is a much more gradual transformation in the direction of Republicanism. Figure 6.2 charts the party identification of southern whites from 1952 through 2012. Four years after Strom Thurmond's Dixiecrat presidential bid was undertaken to defend the South's Jim Crow system of racial segregation, southern white Democratic affiliation remained at a Solid South level, with fully 85 percent claiming allegiance and just 14 percent identifying as Republicans (more southern blacks were Republicans in 1952: 20 percent).

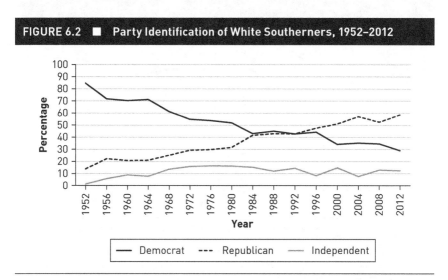

FIGURE 6.2 ■ Party Identification of White Southerners, 1952–2012

Source: Data compiled by the author from the American National Election Studies (ANES) *Time Series Cumulative Data File (1948–2012).*

Notes: All Independent-leaning partisans are classified as partisans (e.g., an Independent who leans toward the Democratic/Republican party is classified as a Democrat/Republican). Because of a large oversample of African American respondents in the 2008 and 2012 ANES, the data for these years were weighted to more accurately reflect the racial composition of the southern subsample. Hispanics are excluded.

From the vantage of Democratic affiliation, Figure 6.2 exhibits a notable lag effect in its decline. For example, Republican Eisenhower splits the South in 1952, but a strong drop in white Democratic identification occurs during his reelection bid in 1956 (72 percent Democratic). Likewise, in the pivotal 1964 election, white Democratic identification holds steady and then drops 10 percentage points in 1968 (from 71 to 61 percent). And although most southern whites opposed Democratic President Carter in 1980, the marked decline in Democratic affiliation takes place in 1984 (from 52 percent in 1980 to 43 percent in 1984). Finally, instead of a sharp decline in white Democratic identification between 1992 and 1996, when the House Democrats lost 52 seats in the 1994 midterm, a significant drop manifests in 2000 (going from 44 percent in 1996 to 34 percent Democratic in 2000).

Not surprisingly, as white Democratic affiliation has declined, white Republican identification has increased. But unlike the swift shift of southern blacks to the Democratic Party, in the case of southern whites, many are not going directly from Democratic to Republican; a large component of white southerners are, instead, not identifying with either party (Beck 1977). Especially in the late 1960s to around 1980, a nontrivial share of the decline in white Democratic identification is transferred to southern whites identifying as pure independents. This dealigning pattern does not keep pace with the even greater increase in Republican identification. By 2012, the share of white Republicans tops out at 59 percent and white Democrats reach their nadir at 29 percent (with 12 percent pure independents).

To provide additional insight on the pattern of white party identification, Table 6.1 displays the percentage of white southerners in each category along the seven-point scale from 1952 to 2012. Boxes are placed around each classification in the seven-point scale for the year(s) when it attains its maximum value. Starting with 1952, this year is the high-water mark for Democratic identification, registering 39 percent for both strong and weak identifiers. It is interesting that the highest share of Independent-leaning Democrats (15 percent) registers more than fifty years later, in 2008. Comporting with Figure 6.2, the greatest share of pure Independents (16 percent) materializes from 1972 to 1980, the peak period of white southern dealignment. Importantly, from 1972 to 1980, the share of pure Independents was greater than the portion of white southerners identifying as Independent-leaning Republican, weak Republican, or strong Republican. The highest percentage of Republican affiliates (leaning, weak, and strong) shows up near the end of the time series, which of course coincides with the current period of GOP electoral dominance in southern politics. By 2012, the share of Republicans, whether leaning, weak, or strong, is greater than any other category along the seven-point scale.

By tracing the alteration of party identification among southern whites, it seems that the more gradual pattern of change contains a pronounced generational replacement component. To be sure, there are notable drops and concomitant ascents that register for several of the four-year intervals shown in Figure 6.2 (e.g., between 1964 and 1968), but most of these ANES samples are not very large (sampling variability

TABLE 6.1 ■ Partisanship of White Southerners, 1952–2012

PID	1952	1956	1960	1964	1968	1972	1976	1980	1984	1988	1992	1996	2000	2004	2008	2012	Change
SD	39	33	31	36	20	13	16	18	15	14	15	16	12	11	11	8	–31
WD	39	36	36	30	30	33	29	23	21	19	15	18	12	14	9	10	–29
ID	7	4	3	6	11	9	9	11	7	12	13	11	10	11	15	11	+4
I	1	6	9	8	14	16	16	16	15	12	15	8	15	8	13	12	+11
IR	3	7	4	6	12	10	8	9	16	16	16	14	16	12	13	19	+16
WR	7	10	8	7	8	11	14	15	15	11	14	19	15	19	16	16	+9
SR	4	6	9	8	5	8	8	8	11	16	12	15	21	27	23	24	+20
N	295	341	236	281	310	544	426	360	406	382	477	387	386	219	440	930	6,420

Source: Data compiled by the author from the American National Election Studies (ANES) *Time Series Cumulative Data File (1948–2012)*.

Notes: Data shown are the percentage of respondents classified in each partisanship category along the seven-point scale for each year (columns sum to 100% except when rounding to the whole number slightly alters the total). SD = Strong Democrat; WD = Weak Democrat; ID = Independent-leaning Democrat; I = Independent; IR = Independent-leaning Republican; WR = Weak Republican; SR = Strong Republican. Boxes around numbers highlight the highest percentage(s) in the specific partisanship category for the time series (1952–2012). Because of a large oversample of African American respondents in the 2008 and 2012 ANES, the data for these years were weighted to more accurately reflect the racial composition of the southern subsample. Hispanics are excluded.

can be an issue; see Green, Palmquist, and Schickler 2002). Overall, the pattern of growing white Republican identification is gradual; it certainly does not take place in the span of a handful of years, which was the case for southern blacks; who permanently align with the Democratic Party in the mid-1960s. Indeed, the black pattern of party identification makes it obvious that the 1960s induced a distinct period effect: a political moment that registered a deep and lasting transformation for all southern African Americans, from young to old. By contrast, the secular trend away from Democratic identification to political independence and eventually to Republicanism suggests that newer generations of southern whites are contributing to the long-term realignment in favor of the GOP. The ANES data can be examined to confirm this expectation.

LIFE-CYCLE, PERIOD, AND GENERATION EFFECTS

In *The American Voter,* Campbell et al. (1960) spoke about the evidence for a life-cycle effect. Basing their understanding of the American electorate on the events of the 1950s (the 1952 and 1956 elections), the authors claimed that there was a general pattern among individuals such that aging produced the effect of strengthening identification with a political party. Hence, younger voters displayed a higher propensity to *not* identify with a political party and if they did, then they were more likely to be weak rather than strong partisans. As these voters aged, however, the data suggested that their attachment to a political party strengthened. Therefore, Campbell et al. posited that a fundamental dynamic of party identification is a life-cycle effect in which the aging process strengthens affiliation with a political party.

In hindsight, it appears that Campbell et al. overstated the evidence for the sort of life-cycle effect discussed above. Although there is evidence that irrespective of the generation, as individuals get older they will become more partisan (Converse 1976; Flanigan et al. 2015; Green, Palmquist, and Schickler 2002), this type of life-cycle effect can be greatly diminished by a dynamic that was heavily present in the political milieu of white southerners: dealignment. Scholars following in the footsteps of Campbell et al. have come to view the 1950s as a stable period for party identification. In fact, even though Eisenhower won the 1952 and 1956 presidential elections as a Republican, Campbell et al. coined the term "deviating election" because in these two contests the American electorate remained overwhelmingly Democratic in party identification despite the fact that the Republican candidate prevailed. In other words, party identification in the 1950s was in a steady state, with most voters identifying with the major parties and Democrats substantially outnumbering their Republican counterparts.

Party identification began to wane in the mid-1960s, and by the 1970s, all across the United States and especially in the South a period of dealignment had set in. With the exception of African Americans, the general pattern of longitudinal change in partisanship was for voters to move away from being partisans in favor of political independence. Hence, in the 1970s a notable period effect occurred; one in which white voters exhibited a weakening in their party identification, irrespective of age, although older voters were more likely to be partisan. The work of Abramson (1976) convincingly showed that the purported life-cycle effect of a strengthening attachment to a political party was overridden by the competing period effect of dealignment (see also Abramson 1979). Therefore, as younger generations aged, they were not significantly more likely to increase their attachment to a political party. In his examination of the increase in the share of the white electorate moving in favor of political independence from 1952 to 1974, Abramson concluded that

> In developing the life-cycle explanation, Campbell and his colleagues did not take politics adequately into account. Partisan loyalties might grow stronger throughout the life-cycle, *if* [italics in original] political conditions reinforce party ties; conditions in postwar America did not. (Abramson 1976, 478)

In other words, Abramson discovered that because there were not clear differences between the major parties that helped signal to voters why they should be Democrats or Republicans, many instead ended up identifying with neither party or weakening their attachment to their preferred party (e.g., going from strong Democrat to weak Democrat). So if new generations of voters come of political age in an environment where the differences between the major parties are not sharply defined across a range of salient issues, then there is no reason why as one ages one *should* become more attached to a political party. The generation effect of younger voters entering the electorate during a period when the attachment to political parties reached a low point was the most powerful factor accounting for the absence of a strengthening of partisanship when these voters aged.

A year after Abramson, Beck (1977) published an article that focused specifically on the high degree of dealignment found among white southerners. The movement away from Democratic identification and toward political independence among this segment of the electorate was palpable (as shown above in Table 6.1), but without the benefit of a longer passage of time, Beck repeatedly overstated the expectation that white southerners would continue to dealign but not realign toward the GOP.[1] In fairness, when Beck undertook his study there really was no empirical evidence that white southerners would move from political independence to Republican affiliation. Nonetheless, the issue reshaping white partisan allegiances since 1964 was the reversal of the major parties on civil rights, and therefore it probably should have been anticipated that because the GOP had become the more conservative party on racial issues (Carmines and Stimson 1989), as younger generations of white southerners entered the electorate and their more Democratic elders exited, the Republican Party would disproportionally gain affiliates. This is exactly what transpired. For white southerners, the entry of new generations of younger voters pushed the southern party system from dealignment to realignment.

In the 1980s, with the passage of time and more data, it was becoming more apparent that the evolution in white southern identification suggested a gradual movement away from dealignment in favor of the road to Republican realignment (Petrocik 1987; Stanley 1988). Relying on his conception of realignment as a marked transformation in the demographic composition of the social groups comprising the major party coalitions (Petrocik 1981), Petrocik (1987) recognized that the robust decline in white southerners who claimed allegiance to the Democratic Party portended a realignment to the GOP. In a lengthy footnote, Petrocik (1987, 350) perceptively articulated the dynamic of white southern realignment to the Republican Party:

> The connection between dealignment and realignment may be quite strong. It is possible that the early period of the transformation of a party system will be characterized by a general loosening of the partisan attachments of the electorate. This dealignment might persist until subsequent events facilitate the reestablishment of a stable equilibrium. The common expectation was that the dealignment of the 1970s would create a party politics marked by nonpartisanship and a peripheral electorate for the indefinite future. The apparently greater partisanship of young voters since 1980 and the southern realignment cast doubt on this prediction of a dealigned, peripheral electorate. It also suggests that there might be merit in examining the extent to which dealignment is a harbinger of realignment.

BOX 6.1   GENERATIONAL CHANGE AND PARTY IDENTIFICATION

There are many variants of cycling theories in political science. For instance, Skowronek (2011) has advanced a theory of presidential effectiveness that is closely tied to the time in which a president serves because of a cycling pattern with respect to the relative power of the two parties and whether the officeholder is affiliated with the ruling regime or opposed to it. Some presidents, like Franklin Roosevelt, are highly effective because they act as regime builders when their party assumes governing power (the Democratic Party in 1932), whereas fellow Democrat Jimmy Carter was considered highly ineffective, in part because he served when the Democratic regime was crumbling (in the late 1970s). Likewise, Dodd (2015) has constructed an elaborate theory that argues in favor of a cyclical pattern of congressional effectiveness that is intimately linked to longitudinal changes in the level of congressional polarization (at the moment, the U.S. Congress is highly polarized). Burnham (1970) has also viewed the timing of critical elections as being fundamentally rooted in a cyclical pattern, with partisan realignments expected to unfold approximately every thirty to forty years.

There has been a considerable amount of scholarly criticism of cyclical theories of American politics (see Carmines and Stimson 1989; Mayhew 2002), but whether

(Continued)

(Continued)

one is a believer or a skeptic, generational change is a key component of almost any theory of partisan change. The reason for this is fairly straightforward. First, as the authors of *The American Voter* (Campbell et al. 1960) demonstrated decades ago, party identification is the main driver of voting behavior and particularly vote choice. Second, the primary factor accounting for the party affiliation of voters is the identification possessed by their parents. In other words, parental transmission of party identification looms large in the American context. But this also means that when parents do not share the same party affiliation and/or they are not strongly aligned to one of the major parties, their offspring are more likely to be weak partisans or political independents (Flanigan et al. 2015).

Beck (1977) probably went the farthest in elaborating a theory of how party identification is altered as a consequence of generational change. Writing during the height of partisan dealignment among white southerners in the post–World War II South, Beck explained how real political events occurring at the time a generation comes of political age can set in motion a long-term pattern of party identification (or lack thereof). Using the example of white southerners, Beck found that the youngest generation of voters in the 1970s was the least Democratic and most politically independent in partisan allegiance. This could be accounted for by understanding that the salient political events reinforcing their parents' attachment to the southern Democracy held less appeal and relevance to the youngest generation of voters. Although the Democratic Party became the bulwark of the white South in the aftermath of the demolition of the Populist Revolt in the 1890s, and with it the implementation of racial segregation and black disfranchisement, later generations would have to seize upon a more current political crisis to either reinforce their partisanship or possibly erode it. The Great Depression was just the kind of major event that spawned an economic and political crisis capable of reinforcing white allegiance to the Democratic Party, particularly among the youngest generation of voters who came of age when the economy collapsed.

After the Great Depression, however, American politics entered a new era in which the reason for aligning with the Democratic Party became thoroughly muddled. Operating under Beck's (1977) thesis, consider the cross-pressure placed upon younger generations of white southerners for whom the Great Depression amounted to little more than a bedtime story told by their grandparents, while the more relevant issue of their formative political years was the civil rights movement. A reversal in party positioning on civil rights left legions of white southerners pondering whether they should continue to identify as Democrats or shift toward the Republican Party because its more conservative position on race seemed a better fit with their own views. Figure 6.5 in this chapter strongly indicates that most white southerners who came of political age during the peak of the civil rights movement (in 1965) did, in fact, dealign from their initial parentally transmitted Democratic identification, and by the 1990s most were Republicans or leaned toward the Republican Party. Ultimately, it is probably not a cyclical pattern of predictable change; rather, the reality of how pivotal political events unfold when generations come of political age informs many of the large-scale changes occurring within the American party system.

Cohort Differences in Republican Identification

The definition of a generation can be a rather malleable concept. So instead of offering a rigid demarcation of the necessary time needed to elapse in order to distinguish one generation from the next, for our purposes, any reasonable gap in the year of birth should establish the requisite and evident differences in the party identification of white southerners on the basis of age. This said, Abramson (1974, 99) provides a very useful definition to keep in mind: "A political generation is 'a group of persons who have undergone the same basic historical experiences during their formative years'" (quoting Rintala 1968). By making use of the ANES Cumulative Data File (1952–2012), the increase in Republican identification among white southerners can be tracked over time according to birth cohorts.

Table 6.2 splits the ANES sample of white southerners into eight separate birth cohorts: born before 1895; 1895–1910; 1911–1926; 1927–1942; 1943–1958; 1959–1974; 1975–1990; and 1991–now. In later years (starting with the 1927–1942 cohort), because the sample size may be too small, the initial election for which the most recent cohort registers may be several years after many individuals attained voting age (e.g., not until 1968 is the sample large enough to register the percentage of Republican identifiers for those survey respondents born from 1943 to 1958). The election year descends down the rows from earliest to latest (1952 to 2012) and the total sample size for all respondents is shown in the far right column. Finally, the last row shows the change in the percentage of Republican affiliates (strong plus weak) between the latest and earliest election year.

Despite the fact that in some instances the subsample of birth cohorts may be quite small (fewer than 50 respondents), the general pattern of growing Republicanism tied to generational change is palpable. For instance, consider the oldest generation—those individuals born prior to 1895—in 1952, only 6 percent identified with the GOP and when this generation exited the electorate in 1968, 21 percent were Republicans. By comparison, among the cohort born between 1975 and 1990, 19 percent were Republican when the sample was large enough to register in the table (in 2000) and by 2012, 38 percent of this cohort claimed a Republican identification.

Beyond the expected pattern of newer generations displaying a greater Republican affiliation, notice that every generation becomes more Republican with the passage of time (from 1952 to 2012). This is evidence of a life-cycle effect favoring the GOP; as each cohort of white southerners ages, it becomes more Republican. However, given this division of cohorts, the most Republican generation is not the latest; instead, it would seem that individuals born between 1927 and 1942 are as Republican, if not more so, than any subsequent birth cohort. The youngest individuals in this cohort would have reached voting age right at the peak of the civil rights movement, in 1963[2]; definitely a political moment (period effect) that could drastically affect the partisan loyalty of a white southerner who most likely was born to parents affiliated with the Democratic Party (Abramowitz and Saunders 1998; Black and Black 1987).

TABLE 6.2 ■ Percentage of White Southerners Who Were Strong or Weak Republicans from 1952 through 2012, by Years of Birth

Birth Years	Before 1895	1895–1910	1911–1926	1927–1942	1943–1958	1959–1974	1975–1990	1991–now	Total	Cases
Election										
1952	6	14	10	—	—	—	—	—	10	267
1956	26	15	15	9	—	—	—	—	16	336
1960	20	18	15	16	—	—	—	—	17	236
1964	15	16	12	14	—	—	—	—	14	274
1968	21	20	9	11	31	—	—	—	15	310
1972	—	21	19	19	15	—	—	—	18	525
1976	—	25	16	21	24	—	—	—	21	416
1980	—	20	19	28	28	—	—	—	25	329
1984	—	29	15	24	30	25	—	—	25	405
1988	—	—	23	18	28	38	—	—	27	366
1992	—	—	16	25	28	29	—	—	26	460
1996	—	—	30	34	39	30	—	—	34	359
2000	—	—	26	41	35	39	19	—	35	380
2004	—	—	—	46	54	55	26	—	47	206
2008	—	—	—	45	34	50	29	—	40	420
2012	—	—	—	47	38	41	38	30	40	915
Change	+15	+15	+16	+38	+7	+16	+19		+30	N = 6,204

Source: Data compiled by the author from the American National Election Studies (ANES) *Time Series Cumulative Data File (1948–2012).*

Republican Identification Spanning Five Political Eras

For white southerners born from 1927 until the most recent period of time displayed in Table 6.2 (1991–now), Republican identification appears to have leveled off. Rather, there seems to be some evidence of convergence around a fairly stable rate of Republican identification for most of the white southern electorate (irrespective of birth cohort) by the time of the 2012 election. Additional evidence of this phenomenon can be illustrated in Figure 6.3. Unlike Table 6.2, Figure 6.3 includes Independent-leaning Republicans as Republican identifiers. Also, the eight birth-year cohorts in Table 6.2 have been collapsed into five, on the basis of a more historically relevant reclassification of when white southerners came of political age. Specifically, individuals born before 1895 and up to 1926 are part of the "Solid South" generation; those born from 1927 to 1942 are the "Postwar" generation; those born from 1943 to 1958 are the "Civil Rights" generation; those born from 1959 to 1974 are the "Reagan" generation; and those born from 1975 to the most recent date for being voting eligible (in the ANES) are the "Republican" generation.

Moving from left to right (1952 to 2012) across the rows and bar graphs for each of the aforementioned generations, it is once again apparent that every generation of white southerners shows a general pattern of growing Republican identification as they age. For example, among Solid South respondents, in 1952 just 14 percent were Republican, but by 2000, 38 percent of this generation identified with the GOP. In 2000, 32 percent of the Republican generation affiliated with the party bearing its name; by 2012, 58 percent of this most recent generation affiliated with the GOP.

Returning to the evidence of generational convergence, in 2012, regardless of generation (except for the Solid South, which has exited the electorate), Republican identification only varies by about 2 percentage points: a high of 60 percent for the Postwar generation, 59 percent for the Reagan generation, and 58 percent for the Civil Rights and Republican generations. Again, it would seem that the Postwar generation (born between 1927 and 1942) is consistently the most Republican, but later generations exhibit similar Republican proclivities by the end of the time series.

TRACKING GENERATIONAL CHANGE AND PARTY IDENTIFICATION

The analysis in the last section is informative, but it admittedly conveys a somewhat amorphous, if not distorted, picture of how generational replacement has led to the growth of the southern GOP. The issue is that the ANES relies on a cross-section of respondents who are almost all part of a brand new sample from one election cycle to the next. That is, we are not tracking changes (if any) in party identification for the same individuals over a long span of time. Perhaps this is not that big of a problem if the slice of respondents for any given year is representative of the population of white southerners born around the same time (this should be the case).

FIGURE 6.3 ■ Percentage of White Southerners Identifying with the Republican Party According to Generation, 1952–2012

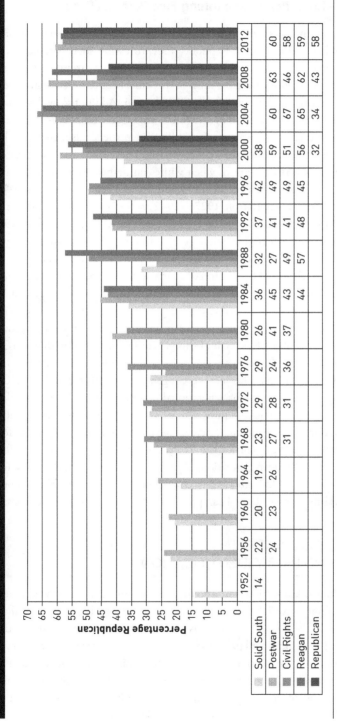

	1952	1956	1960	1964	1968	1972	1976	1980	1984	1988	1992	1996	2000	2004	2008	2012
Solid South	14	22	20	19	23	29	29	26	36	32	37	42	38			
Postwar		24	23	26	27	28	24	41	45	27	41	49	59	60	63	60
Civil Rights					31	31	36	37	43	49	41	49	51	67	46	58
Reagan									44	57	48	45	56	65	62	59
Republican													32	34	43	58

Source: Data compiled by the author from the American National Election Studies (ANES) *Time Series Cumulative Data File (1948–2012).*

But there is another obvious shortcoming with the aforementioned cohort analysis. Consider the postwar generation of white southerners born between the years 1927 and 1942. That is a fairly large window of time (fifteen years); someone born in 1927 would come of voting age in the 1948 election (recall that most states still operated under a minimum 21-year-old voting age), whereas a newborn in 1942 would first cast a presidential ballot in 1964. Put simply, it is a stretch to say that these two voters are of the same generation. The first voter came of political age when the Solid South just began to fissure, while the second voter would have been exposed to the most tumultuous period of the civil rights movement and attained the franchise when the national parties reversed their positions on race, and henceforth the New Deal Democratic coalition would experience the exodus of its base of white southerners (Petrocik 1981).

Finally, as time moves on, the survey respondents born closer to 1927 will exit the electorate at a faster rate than those born nearer to 1942. This means that the profile of voters is gradually changing within each cohort as the older part of it succumbs to Father Time. This reality can cast serious doubt with respect to the representativeness of generations born within each cohort category because it is likely that the oldest and youngest voters do not exhibit the same party identification. Fortunately, there exists a survey that also makes use of the seven-point party identification scale and specifically tracks the same respondents over a long span of time. Further, the timing of these interviews and the age of the respondents are practically ideal for seeing whether there has been a pronounced shift in the partisanship of white southerners.

The Youth-Parent Socialization Panel Study[3] conducted a series of interviews with a representative sample of high school seniors and their parents in 1965 and reinterviewed the youth component of the sample (1965 high school seniors) three more times: in 1973, 1982, and 1997. The parent component of the sample was reinterviewed in 1973 and 1982. The panel design of the survey ensures that only the original respondents interviewed in 1965 are the sample from which future interviews would be conducted in 1973, 1982, and 1997 (in the case of the youth subsample). With these data it is possible to isolate white southerners who were high school seniors along with their parents in 1965 and then track their partisanship for either two (the parents) or three additional moments in time, to determine whether their partisanship has undergone a notable transformation.

In the following two figures, the partisanship of the white southern parents will be displayed as they reported it in 1965, 1973, and 1982 (Figure 6.4) and then the self-reported partisanship of their children will be shown in 1965, 1973, 1982, and 1997 (Figure 6.5). Respondents identified as white southerners were those who grew up in the South and lived in a southern state at the time of the 1973 and 1982 surveys. Even with some necessary attrition in the sample size due to mortality and nonresponse rates, tracing the panel of white southern youth from 1965 to 1997 results in a sample size of 136 and a total of 171 white southern parents from 1965 to 1982. With regard to the parents, in 1965 most were in their mid-forties to early fifties and, of course, their high school senior children display very little range in their ages, between 17 and 18 years old in 1965.

Beginning with the parents, Figure 6.4 displays an indisputable pattern of partisan stability. By capturing a fairly narrow age range that starts when these respondents were already middle-aged, it is apparent that these white southerners were, for lack of a better choice of words, too old to shift their partisanship (see Green, Palmquist, and Schickler 2002) even though several consequential political events transpired in the seventeen years following 1965. The only real appreciable shift that catches the naked eye is a decline in the portion of strong Democrats between 1965 and 1973 (going from 30 percent to 22 percent)—some evidence of dealignment. Nonetheless, in 1965, 57 percent of these white southern parents were Democrats (strong or weak) and in 1982, 53 percent remained affiliated with the Democratic Party. By tracking the same sample of middle-aged white southerners as they entered their golden years, there is no question that their partisan identity had already calcified by the mid-1960s, and therefore this cohort was not a primary driver of the southern realignment to the Republican Party.

Their children, on the other hand, are clearly some of the primary agents responsible for southern Republican ascendancy (see Figure 6.5). In 1965, a plurality of these white southern high school seniors identified themselves as weak Democrats (26 percent), followed by strong Democrats at 18 percent. By comparison, combining strong and weak Republican identifiers amounted to a total of 19 percent of the 1965 high school senior sample. Remember that these white southerners are reaching political adulthood at the peak of the civil rights movement when three of the most consequential events took place: passage of the 1964 Civil Rights Act, the pivotal 1964 presidential election, followed less than a year later by the 1965 Voting Rights Act. In their late teens at the time of these historic events, there is little question they would make a lasting impression and register in terms of party identification.

But before many of these 1965 high school seniors would shift their Democratic affiliations toward the GOP, there is ample evidence of dealignment preceding Republican realignment. In 1965, already 17 percent of the high school seniors were pure Independents, and this portion ballooned to 26 percent in 1973 (a plurality of the sample), right around the height of the period of partisan dealignment. Pure political independence proved an ephemeral condition for most of these white southerners because by 1997, when these individuals were 50 years old, less than 4 percent remained wholly unaffiliated with either major party. In 1965, at 7 percent, Independent-leaning Republicans were the smallest category of identifiers; in 1997 they were the largest, at 24 percent. In 1965, each Democratic category of identification (including leaners) outnumbered its Republican counterpart. In 1997, every Republican category of identification outnumbered its Democratic counterpart. Combining leaners with partisans, in 1965, 57 percent of white southern high school seniors were aligned with the Democratic Party. In 1997, among these same individuals, now having lived a half century, 57 percent identified with the Republican Party.

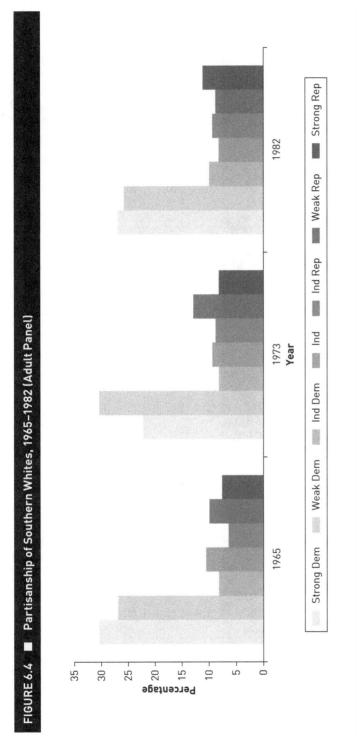

FIGURE 6.4 ■ Partisanship of Southern Whites, 1965–1982 (Adult Panel)

Strong Dem   Weak Dem   Ind Dem   Ind   Ind Rep   Weak Rep   Strong Rep

Source: Data compiled by the author from the Youth–Parent Socialization Panel Study (IICPSR 4037).

FIGURE 6.5 ■ Partisanship of Southern Whites, 1965–1997 (Youth Panel)

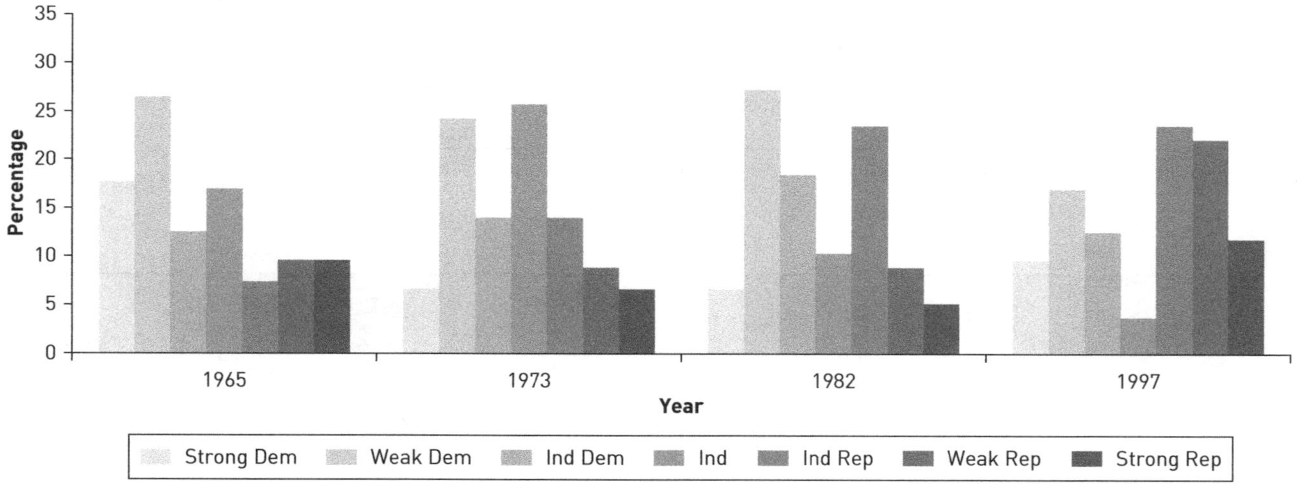

Legend: Strong Dem | Weak Dem | Ind Dem | Ind | Ind Rep | Weak Rep | Strong Rep

X-axis (Year): 1965, 1973, 1982, 1997

Y-axis: Percentage (0, 5, 10, 15, 20, 25, 30, 35)

Source: Data compiled by the author from the Youth–Parent Socialization Panel Study (ICPSR 4037).

Thanks to the Youth-Parent Socialization Panel Study, we have incontrovertible evidence of a dynamic and long-term shift in the partisan allegiances of a generation of white southerners who came of political age in the mid-1960s. By contrast, their parents' partisanship was essentially immune to alteration, even when faced with some of the most disruptive political moments to transpire in their lifetimes. They were simply too old to reconsider their party identification. For southern Republicans to deepen their inroads in electoral politics, their message would have to be embraced by a younger generation who, by the inexperience of youth, were impressionable enough to consider altering their partisanship to align with a rising Republican Party.

CONCLUDING THOUGHTS

In their influential book, *Partisan Hearts and Minds* (2002), Green, Palmquist, and Schickler offer a strong defense of the main findings of *The American Voter* (Campbell et al. 1960). In their view, decades of political change have not debunked the core dynamics of party identification as elucidated by Campbell et al. (but for a different perspective on party identification, see Fiorina 1981; MacKuen, Erikson, and Stimson 1989). Nonetheless, the partisan transformation of the American South was such a dramatic and atypical phenomenon that Green, Palmquist, and Schickler devoted an entire chapter (Chapter 6: "Party Realignment in the American South") to explain the factors responsible for the movement of an overwhelmingly Democratic white electorate to a heretofore electorally moribund Republican opposition. In their rigorous examination of the realignment of white southerners to the GOP, Green, Palmquist, and Schickler (2002, 141) concluded that "roughly half of the Southern realignment is due to cohort replacement, not individual-level change." Although this chapter does not assign an exact weight to how much of the white shift in favor of the GOP was a direct consequence of generational replacement, the evidence suggests that it was indeed a primary driver.

In *Southern Politics in State and Nation,* Key (1949, 10) brilliantly observed that "attachments to partisan labels live long beyond events that gave them birth." This can explain why many older white southerners affiliated with the Democratic Party would remain so, even after the 1964 presidential election, passage of the 1965 VRA, and the rise of Ronald Reagan. To them, the Democratic Party would always be the conservative party on racial issues because that is what it was when these white southerners grew up, and throughout so many localities the southern Democracy persisted in its defense of racial conservatism. Their image of the Democratic Party was crystalized in a political period when southern Democrats provided a unified front in defense of Jim Crow against would-be agitators from outside the region, and especially in massive resistance to a native black population that eventually took a stand for racial equality.

But as time passed, so did the share of unreconstructed Democrats, and in their place rose new generations of white southerners whose image of the major parties was very different according to party positioning on salient issues assuming the national stage in presidential politics. By the 1980s, with the clear and opposing stands taken by Democrats and Republicans on not only race, but also on national security and moral values (Abramowitz 1994), it was nearly impossible for a white southerner not to comprehend that the GOP had become the more politically conservative party.[4] With an image of the major parties delineated along a more pronounced ideological cleavage, it was much easier for younger generations of white southerners to align with the Republican Party, and this they did.

7 ISSUES: RACE, ECONOMICS, AND RELIGION

Back when V. O. Key was elucidating the dynamics of southern politics in the still–Solid Democratic South of the late 1940s, he quoted a Florida county judge who said, "Issues? Why, son, they don't have a damn thing to do with it" (1949, 94). Among the eleven southern states, Florida ranked as one of the highest with respect to its level of factionalism within the dominant Democratic Party. As was true in the Sunshine State, it was a general pattern across the region that Democratic Party–controlled elections were often reduced to local popularity contests won by those contenders who garnered more support among their "friends and neighbors."

But as Dixie slowly turned more politically competitive, the significance of personal associations with politicians became less important as issues began to rise to the forefront of voters' minds. Indeed, Key (1949) was able to demonstrate that "friends and neighbors" voting patterns weakened and often were absent in certain parts of the South where sectional political divisions formed around salient issues. The emergence of more issue-based voting patterns in various sections of the South could be witnessed within the Democratic Party (e.g., the Mississippi Delta versus the Mississippi Hills; likewise the Lowcountry versus the Piedmont/Upcountry in South Carolina), and in some places there was notable inter-party competition (Republicans in East Tennessee versus Democrats in the rest of the state; Republicans in Western North Carolina versus the more Democratic piedmont and eastern section of the state).

To the extent that issues could supplant the politics of personality and demagoguery, Key (1949) viewed this as a welcome sign of political modernization. In fact, Key hoped that ultimately the economic issue, in particular, might be able to overtake the lasting prejudice engrained in the issue of race, so that maybe someday a marriage of lower class black and white voters would finally wrest control of southern electoral politics. This expectation, however, has clearly not come to pass. Nonetheless, issues have definitely become the primary shaper of contemporary southern politics, even if the relationship between specific policy prescriptions and political behavior is admittedly flimsy. Nonetheless, voters have come to view clear differences in the ideological positioning of Democrats and Republicans and this, in turn, has led to their sorting into the proper partisan homes (Levendusky 2009).

There are arguably three perennial issues that pervade southern culture: race, economics, and religion. These are not issues in a narrowcast sense; rather, the general subjects of race, economics, and religion are factors that have broadly shaped southern culture, have strongly resonated throughout history, and at different times have played a critical role in shaping the political behavior of southern voters. Not surprisingly, race, economics, and religion are the main drivers involved in the contemporary partisan transformation of southern politics. Race occupies a perennial role, whereas economics proved especially consequential in the Populist uprising of the late 1800s but was essentially held in check until the 1950s, when a class cleavage began to alter white southerners' partisan loyalties and voting behavior. Religion, interestingly, has historically exhibited the least impact on structuring political behavior. This finally changed in the late 1970s with the emergence of the Religious Right in American politics (Wilcox and Robinson 2011).

This chapter starts with a discussion of the broader picture of the interaction between issues, ideology, and political sophistication (or lack thereof). With this theoretical groundwork established, the empirical analysis begins with an accounting of the sorting and polarization that has occurred within the southern electorate. Next, the focus turns specifically to the issues of race, economics, and religion. Wherever feasible, given sample sizes, the data are limited to voters (self-reported voters in many instances and those participating in exit polls; see chapter 9 for more details on the datasets). Similar to the previous chapter, because of the important effect of party identification on political behavior (especially voter preferences), this variable is given considerable attention. But unlike chapter 6, throughout this chapter (and those that follow) party identification is always measured so that only Democratic and Republican identifiers are classified as partisans (independent leaners are treated as Independents). Finally, with regard to voting behavior, the data show voter preferences in presidential elections. The advantage of using presidential elections is that every southern voter is faced with the choice of the two major party nominees, which means that the evaluation of several decades of political change in voter preferences is based on a consistent metric.

ISSUES, IDEOLOGY, AND POLITICAL SOPHISTICATION

In *The American Voter,* Campbell et al. (1960) painted a somewhat grim view of the mass electorate (see also Converse 1964). Contrary to the musings of ancient political theorists, who described the model citizen as one busily engaged in political activity and therefore well-informed about political issues, the survey data collected after World War II (and particularly the revered American National Election Studies spearheaded by Campbell et al.) told a very different story. Based on repeated surveys of the mass public, a profile emerged in which the typical voter was not only minimally informed of the political news of the day, but the vast majority of voters did not condition their voting preferences on the basis of issues per se. Instead, whichever political party the voter aligned with was the driving force behind his or her political behavior and especially his or her vote choice.

In perhaps one of the longest, and certainly one of the most important, book chapters examining political sophistication, Philip Converse (1964; one of *The American Voter* coauthors) demonstrated that only a small segment of the American electorate exhibited a substantial awareness of political issues. Based on open-ended responses to American National Election Studies (ANES) questions asking voters about what they liked and disliked about the Democratic and Republican parties, Converse generated levels of conceptualization (political sophistication) among the American mass public. From the top to the bottom of the scale were the ideologues, near-ideologues, group-benefit, nature-of-the-times, and no-issue-content voters.[1]

The most politically sophisticated ideologues were classified as such because they not only discussed the political parties in ideological language; they went a step further by describing how it was that one (or both) of the parties was conservative/liberal with respect to a political issue (e.g., "the Democratic Party is more liberal in its approach to using economic policy to assist poor people"). Near-ideologues used ideological terms but did not apply them to a specific demonstration of a liberal/conservative position taken by one of the major parties (e.g., "I prefer the Republican Party because it's more conservative"). Group-benefits voters expressed their views in nonideological terms, stating something like the party was either in favor or against delivering benefits to a certain group within the American electorate (e.g., "the Republican Party only cares about the rich"; "the Democratic Party looks out for the worker"). Nature-of-the-times voters expressed their opinions of the major parties based on the immediate short-term conditions prevailing in the political environment (e.g., after 9/11/2001, a voter would say, "I favor the Republican Party because it's tougher on fighting terrorists"). No-issue-content voters remark on the political parties in such a manner that there is no association made between the party and its positioning on issues (e.g., "I am a Democrat because my daddy was a Democrat").

Based on Converse's (2006, 17) results from the 1956 ANES, the percentage distribution was 3.5 percent ideologues, 12 percent near-ideologues, 45 percent group-benefit, 22 percent nature-of-the-times, and 17.5 percent no-issue-content voters. Obviously, only a small component of the electorate occupies a spot at the top of the political sophistication hierarchy as developed by Converse. More recent studies have updated Converse's work and discovered that there are now more voters who seem to belong in the ideologue/near-ideologue categories, but it remains true that the vast majority of the public falls well short of being deemed very politically sophisticated (see Flanigan et al. 2015, 172).

The empirical evidence that most voters are not very knowledgeable about politics (Delli Carpini and Keeter 1996) and therefore not heavily involved in political pursuits (beyond the most common expression of voting) actually is not terribly surprising. As Downs (1957) argued long ago, rational ignorance is a pervasive behavior in just about any context. That is, most people only learn as much as they need to know when navigating any subject matter. Hence, most voters only learn enough to cast a vote that satisfies their preferences. Outside of politicians and groups who possess strong political interests because they are vested in the governmental distribution of goods and services, most of the public cares very little about politics because they receive very little reward for paying much attention to the political arena.

Given the aforementioned political reality within which most American voters find themselves, it is no wonder that party identification holds such an enormous value. The Democratic and Republican parties have taken it upon themselves to determine where they stand on the issues of most concern to the American voter. As viewed by Downs (1957), the political parties have constructed elaborate ideologies that consist of bundled issue positions packaged in a manner designed to maximize votes and, therefore, win political office. Apart from the political elite (e.g., partisan officeholders and party activists), as mentioned, only a sliver of the American electorate maintains a highly ideological understanding of politics such that they can connect their positions across a wide range of issues along a single liberal/conservative dimension (Lupton, Myers, and Thornton 2015).

Converse (1964) referred to the ability of voters to accurately piece together partisan issue positions on a variety of matters—some related (in the same issue domain, e.g., social issues like prayer in school and abortion) and some not (e.g., gun control and school vouchers)—as "constraint." Voters possessing a high level of constraint tend to be the most ideologically sophisticated because they have figured out "what goes with what." In other words, a liberal ideologue is pro-choice, pro-economic regulation, opposed to war, and supports gay rights, among other things. By contrast, a conservative ideologue would embrace the opposite position on all of the above-mentioned issues. Of course, most voters are neither very liberal nor very conservative. Instead, they are more pragmatic and do not make the ideological connection with respect to most political issues. They are what we would call ideological moderates, and as Converse (1964) showed, they are not as politically knowledgeable or interested in politics. Among this great mass of the electorate there is little to no strong connection made across issues (they appear unrelated), and over time the positions that most voters hold on any given issue lack stability (their views change almost to the point of being randomly selected).

Fortunately, voter disinterest in politics does not mean that political outcomes are determined at random—far from it (MacKuen, Erikson, and Stimson 1989; Page and Shapiro 1992). There is a tremendous incentive for political elites (especially elected officeholders, who owe their jobs to voters) to help steer the direction of the mass public (Aldrich 1995). Further, voters are quite adept at using political cues and short-cuts to help them vote in a manner aligned with their preferences (Baum and Jamison 2006; Lau and Redlawsk 1997; Lau, Andersen, and Redlawsk 2008; Lupia 1994; Popkin 1991). And there is no better cue and shortcut than party identification. Party affiliation alone is the most reliable indicator of how one should vote because on most of the major issues voters care about, the parties have taken opposing sides. Further, although most voters do not recognize what is necessarily the liberal or conservative position on a specific issue, in contemporary politics there has been a growing consistency and polarization (more on this in the next section) in the ideological positioning of the major parties across a broad spectrum of issues.

Finally, even though, for instance, only 46 percent of southern voters knew that the Democratic Party was the national majority in the House of Representatives before the 2008 election (based on an examination of ANES data), there exists a host of "big" political issues that almost every voter registers an opinion on, and political knowledge is not relevant because positions on these issues do not require a correct answer. These big issues also happen to be what political scientists characterize as "easy" issues as opposed to "hard" issues (see Carmines and Stimson 1980). An easy issue is salient (high profile and important) to the voter, and it is not difficult to register an opinion on. In contrast, a hard issue is necessarily complicated and therefore requires some more specific knowledge in order to render an informed judgment. The civil rights of African Americans would constitute an easy issue (i.e., oppose/support), whereas the medical application of stem cell research is a hard issue (fraught with extremely complex scientific and difficult moral implications). In this chapter, there are three big issues assessed in detail: race, economics, and religion. The word *big* was originally placed in quotes because these issues are not distilled into more policy-specific areas like, say, affirmative action in the case of the race issue. Further, voters are not assessed in terms of their specific opinions on racial, economic, and religious issues. Rather the political behavior of southern voters is examined within the prism of race, economics, and religion. That is, specifically, how does party identification and presidential vote choice vary with respect to race, income, and religion?

But before the aforementioned central question can be examined, it is necessary to document the extent to which the southern electorate has sorted and polarized over the last several decades. Investigating this dynamic entails a look at the relationship between ideology and party identification. As the Democratic Party has become positioned in a more liberal direction on race, economics, and religion, while its Republican counterpart has staked out a more conservative stance on these issues, the changing political profile of southern voters should be reflective of this development.

SORTING AND POLARIZATION WITHIN THE SOUTHERN ELECTORATE

With the growing divide between elected Democrats and Republicans across a panoply of political issues, a substantial literature has sprung up to assess the causes and consequences of partisan polarization (for an excellent review, see Hetherington 2009). The most common form of polarization examined by scholars is couched in ideological terms. Consider an ideological distribution of Congress that resembles a bell-shaped curve with the great bulk of the middle composed of moderates and the smaller left- and right-end tails of the distribution occupied by the most liberal and conservative members. Based on roll-call voting behavior, for decades this is what the ideological distribution of Congress looked like. For instance, there were many Democrats (particularly southern Democrats) who were positioned to the right of Republicans, and vice versa (moderate Republicans from the Northeast positioned to the left of southern Democrats).

Eventually, though, through a combination of member replacement (a liberal Democrat taking the place of a conservative Democrat) and conversion (a conservative

Democrat shifting positions to align with the liberal direction of the party, or more extreme and rare, a conservative Democrat switching to the more conservative Republican opposition), the ideological distribution of Democratic and Republican members of Congress has become very polarized (Fleisher and Bond 2004). Now, a much smaller number of Democrats and Republicans occupy a position on the ideological distribution that would be deemed moderate, and all Democrats (Republicans) are situated to the left (right) of their Republican (Democratic) colleagues.

There is no dispute over the pronounced ideological polarization of members in the contemporary Congress, but scholars have disagreed with respect to the extent that the mass public has followed suit (cf. Abramowitz and Saunders 2008; Fiorina, Abrams, and Pope 2008). Nonetheless, there is plenty of evidence that some polarization among the electorate has transpired (see Jacobson 2004), and it would be hard not to become polarized because voters have recognized the growing political distance between the major parties (Hetherington 2001). Among those political observers skeptical that the typical voter has done much polarizing (see Fiorina, Abrams, and Pope 2008), the more plausible explanation for changes in the mass electorate is referred to as "sorting." Unlike polarization, which reduces the share of ideological moderates via replacement or conversion and thus increases the share of liberals and conservatives, sorting occurs when the overall share of political moderates remains the same, but ideological incongruence gives way to ideological congruence. In other words, in the setting of contemporary American politics, sorting occurs when the number of moderates is constant, but among Democrats a decline in conservatives is directly offset by an increase in liberals (or conversely, among Republicans a decline in liberals is directly offset by an increase in conservatives). These days, conservative Democrats and liberal Republicans are ideologically incongruent with their respective parties' positions, and hence there are now fewer of them.

BOX 7.1 COMPARING SOUTHERN PARTY ACTIVISTS TO THE MASS ELECTORATE

Party activists are critical conduits in the dissemination of information regarding the positioning of their party on salient issues. And activists are particularly influential when party positions change because of the shifting of issue positions as promulgated by candidates (Carmines and Stimson 1989; Stimson 2004). As a fundamental go-between for officeholders and voters (Carmines 1991), party activists tend to be more extreme than the mass electorate, particularly with regard to political ideology. With the long-term trend of the Democratic Party moving in a liberal direction while its Republican counterparts have moved in a conservative direction, there is no question that party activists have become considerably more ideologically extreme.

Table 7.1 presents data comparing the ideological distribution (percentage liberal, moderate, and conservative) of party activists in comparison to that of voters, in the early 1990s and early 2000s. The data are delineated by major party, Democrats and then Republicans, showing the ideological frequency distribution of Democratic (Republican) activists and then Democratic (Republican) voters.

In the early 1990s, a time when southern Republican ascendancy really began to accelerate (McKee 2010; McKee and Yoshinaka 2015), the distribution of Democratic activists was closely parceled between liberals (39 percent) and moderates (35 percent), and more than a quarter (26 percent) were conservatives. By comparison, 29 percent of voters were liberals, and half (50 percent) were moderates, with 22 percent conservatives. The disparity in liberals is the key difference, with Democratic activists 10 percentage points more liberal than rank-and-file Democratic voters. The greatest gap is in the moderate category, with markedly fewer activists placing themselves in the middle of the ideological spectrum. Interestingly, a decade later the share of Democratic moderate voters was somewhat higher at 56 percent. Some ideological sorting is evident because the percentage of conservatives declined to 18 percent, but it is also the case that the percentage of liberals declined two points to 27 percent. In contrast, the new millennium witnessed tremendous ideological sorting among Democratic activists (and some polarization because of the decline in moderates), with fully 57 percent now liberals, 28 percent moderates, and 15 percent conservatives. With the much greater ideological sorting among Democratic activists, the gap in liberal identification between activists and voters widened from 10 to 30 percentage points.

A comparison between Republican activists and voters is notably different because the GOP has long been much more ideological. Even in the early 1990s, a clear majority of Republican voters (55 percent) were conservatives. Nonetheless, the share of conservative GOP activists is markedly higher, at 86 percent. Hardly any Republicans are liberals; 2 percent of activists and 6 percent of voters. Just 12 percent of GOP activists are moderates, whereas a substantial 40 percent of Republican voters are moderates. Ten years hence, more than nine out of ten activists (91 percent) are conservatives, leaving just 7 percent moderates and 2 percent liberals. There is also some ideological sorting among Republican voters because the share of moderates hardly changes (39 percent), while the percentage of conservatives increased to 57 percent and the share of liberals declined to 4 percent. Similar to Democrats in the key category of liberals, for Republican activists and voters, the ideological gap has widened in the key category of conservatives, increasing from 31 to 34 percentage points.

TABLE 7.1 ■ The Greater Ideological Extremism of Party Activists: 1991–1992 and 2000–2001					
1991–1992	**Democrats**		**2000–2001**	**Democrats**	
Ideology	**Activists (%)**	**Voters (%)**	**Ideology**	**Activists (%)**	**Voters (%)**
Liberal	39	29	Liberal	57	27
Moderate	35	50	Moderate	28	56
Conservative	26	22	Conservative	15	18

(Continued)

(Continued)

1991–1992 Ideology	Republicans Activists (%)	Republicans Voters (%)	2000–2001 Ideology	Republicans Activists (%)	Republicans Voters (%)
Liberal	2	6	Liberal	2	4
Moderate	12	40	Moderate	7	39
Conservative	86	55	Conservative	91	57

Sources: Data on 1991–1992 party activists are from Hadley, Charles D., and Lewis Bowman. Southern Grassroots Party Activists Project, 1991–1992: [United States] [Computer file]. 2nd ICPSR version. New Orleans, LA: Charles D. Hadley and Lewis Bowman [producers], 1993. Ann Arbor, MI: Inter-university Consortium for Political and Social Research [distributor], 1997. Data on 2001 party activists are from Clark, John A., and Charles Prysby. Southern Grassroots Party Activists Project, 2001. ICPSR04266-v1. Ann Arbor, MI: Inter-university Bibliographic Citation: Consortium for Political and Social Research [distributor], 2006-03-17. http://doi.org/10.3886/ICPSR04266.v1. The data on voters in 1992 are from the Voter Research and Surveys: National Election Day Exit Poll, 1992. The data on voters in 2000 are from Voter News Service General Election Exit Polls, 2000.

Notes: The 1991–1992 data on southern party activists comprise a representative sample of county-level political party committee members and chairpersons as well as a sample of 1992 national convention delegates. The 2001 data on southern party activists is a large weighted sample consisting primarily of Democratic and Republican county chairs and county committee members and also precinct presidents/chairs and other activists (depending on the state). Whereas the exit poll data on voters simply parcels survey respondents according to liberal, moderate, and conservative, the party activist data was originally based on a five-point scale: very liberal, somewhat liberal, moderate, somewhat conservative, and very conservative. To make comparisons between voters and activists, the five-point scale was collapsed so that the "very" and "somewhat" categories were combined into just liberal/conservative.

Table 7.2 presents data on the overall ideological distribution of the southern electorate according to voters who self-identify as liberal, moderate, or conservative. The data are partitioned by decade, starting in the 1970s (the ANES first asked the ideological self-placement question in 1972) and ending in the 2000s (2008, to be exact). In addition, the partisan distribution is displayed for liberal, moderate, and conservative voters, respectively. Starting with the ideological distribution of the southern electorate, the constancy of the relative share of liberals, moderates, and conservatives is remarkable. In the 1970s, the percentage of liberal voters was 16, moderate voters were 45 percent, and conservative voters were 39 percent of the southern electorate. Three decades later, the overall ideological distribution of the southern electorate remains the same. In terms of the distribution of voters according to ideology, if there are changes in the relationship between party identification and ideology, then at the macro level it is due to sorting and not polarization.

TABLE 7.2 ■ Ideology and Party Identification of Southern Voters					
Southern Voters	**1970s**	**1980s**	**1990s**	**2000s**	**Difference**
Ideology					
Liberal	16	15	17	16	0
Moderate	45	46	45	45	0
Conservative	39	40	38	39	0
Liberals PID					
Democratic	66	67	71	70	+4
Independent	22	20	17	18	−4
Republican	12	13	12	12	0
Moderates PID					
Democratic	54	50	46	44	−10
Independent	30	26	27	25	−5
Republican	16	24	27	31	+15
Conservatives PID					
Democratic	39	28	20	16	−23
Independent	32	26	21	16	−16
Republican	29	45	59	69	+40

Sources: The 1972–1974 data are from the American National Election Studies (ANES); the remaining data, from 1976 to 2008, are all from the national exit polls.

Notes: The ANES data are limited to southern respondents who self-reported voting in the 1972 and 1974 national elections. Under each category of voters (e.g., "Ideology") the sum of the column of voters is equal to 100 percent (barring rounding). PID stands for party identification. The 1970s = 1972, 1974, 1976, 1978; 1980s = 1980, 1982, 1984, 1986, 1988; 1990s = 1990, 1992, 1994, 1996, 1998; 2000s = 2000, 2002, 2004, 2006, 2008. "Difference" equals the data for the 2000s minus the data for the 1970s.

Among liberal voters, the slight increase in the percentage of Democratic voters (from 66 percent in the 1970s to 70 percent in the 2000s) is mainly due to a reduction in the share of independents (from 22 percent in the 1970s to 18 percent in the 2000s). With respect to moderate voters, the long-term pattern is a shift away from Democratic identification (from 54 percent in the 1970s to 44 percent in the 2000s) and political independence (from 30 percent in the 1970s to 25 percent in the 2000s) in favor of greater Republican affiliation (from 16 percent in the 1970s to 31 percent in the 2000s). Still, although no longer a majority (54 percent in the 1970s), in the 2000s a comfortable plurality of southern moderates (44 percent) remain affiliated with the Democratic Party. Finally, conservative voters have moved strongly in favor of the GOP. Among this segment of the southern electorate, a pronounced decline in Democratic adherents (from 39 percent in the 1970s to 16 percent in the 2000s) and political independents (from 32 percent in the 1970s to 16 percent in the 2000s) translates into a 40-percentage point increase in Republican conservative voters (going from 29 percent in the 1970s to 69 percent in the 2000s).

Table 7.3 shows that southern voters are cognizant of the ideological polarization occurring among the Democratic and Republican parties. Compared to the 1970s, more voters in the 2000s viewed the Democratic Party as liberal (70 versus 75 percent). By comparison, the increasing perception of the Republican Party as conservative is even more evident as 61 percent of voters held this view in the 1970s, whereas 75 percent considered the GOP conservative in the 2000s. Notice that the changing ideological perceptions of the major parties is in part due to a decline in the share of voters viewing either party as ideologically moderate, an acknowledgment of ideologically driven partisan polarization. In the 2000s, 75 percent of voters viewed the Democratic Party as liberal and the Republican Party as conservative. The last two rows of the table show the difference in the percentage of voters who view the GOP as

TABLE 7.3 ■ Southern Voters' Ideological Perceptions of the Major Parties

Democratic Party Viewed As . . .	1970s	1980s	1990s	2000–12	Difference
Liberal	70	58	64	75	+5
Moderate	17	17	15	12	−5
Conservative	13	25	21	12	−1
Republican Party Viewed As . . .	**1970s**	**1980s**	**1990s**	**2000–12**	**Difference**
Liberal	18	18	16	14	−4
Moderate	20	11	11	11	−9
Conservative	61	71	73	75	+14
Republican Conservative Margin	+48	+47	+52	+63	+15
Republican Liberal Margin	−51	−41	−48	−61	−10

Source: ANES Time Series Cumulative Data File.

Notes: Self-reported voters. "Republican Conservative Margin" is the percentage of respondents who view the Republican Party as conservative for a certain time period (e.g., 1970s) minus the percentage of respondents who view the Democratic Party as conservative for that same time period (e.g., 61 percent minus 13 percent equals +48 for the 1970s). "Republican Liberal Margin" is calculated the same way (e.g., 16 percent minus 64 percent equals −48 for the 1990s; there is some rounding error due to whole numbers for some of the computed margins).

conservative versus those who view the Democratic Party as conservative (Republican Conservative Margin) and similarly, the difference in the percentage of voters who view the Republican Party as liberal versus those who view the Democratic Party as liberal (Republican Liberal Margin). In the 2000s, the Republican Conservative Margin was +63 percentage points (75 percent of voters viewed the GOP as conservative minus the 12 percent of voters who viewed the Democratic Party as conservative). Likewise, in the 2000s the Republican Liberal Margin was −61 percentage points (14 percent of voters viewed the GOP as liberal minus the 75 percent of voters who viewed the Democratic Party as liberal).

Figure 7.1 presents the Republican Conservative Margin and Republican Liberal Margin data from Table 7.3 in graphical form in order to highlight the visual evidence of increasingly ideologically polarized perceptions of the Democratic and Republican parties. From the 1970s to the 2000s, the Republican Conservative Margin goes from 48 to 63 percentage points while the Republican Liberal Margin moves ten points in favor of the Democratic Party (from −51 to −61 percentage points).

Table 7.4 presents data on the changing ideological distribution of Democratic and Republican voters. This provides an opportunity to see to what extent, if any, that not just sorting but also polarization has occurred among Democratic and Republican voters. Changes to the long-term ideological distribution of Democratic voters are almost wholly due to sorting. In the 1970s there were more conservative

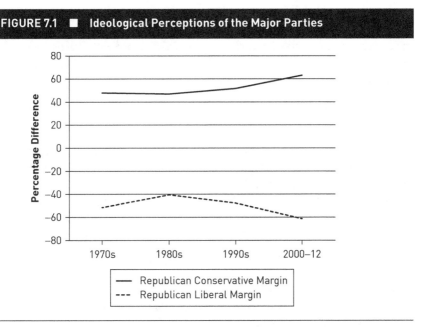

FIGURE 7.1 ■ Ideological Perceptions of the Major Parties

— Republican Conservative Margin
--- Republican Liberal Margin

Source: ANES Time Series Cumulative Data File.

Note: Data shown are the plotted results in the last two rows of Table 7.3 (not including the "Difference" column).

TABLE 7.4 ■ Ideology of Democratic and Republican Voters in the South					
Democratic Voters	**1970s**	**1980s**	**1990s**	**2000–12**	**Difference**
Liberal	29	28	41	48	+19
Moderate	36	38	33	35	–1
Conservative	35	34	26	17	–18
Republican Voters	**1970s**	**1980s**	**1990s**	**2000–12**	**Difference**
Liberal	6	7	4	4	–2
Moderate	28	18	17	14	–14
Conservative	66	75	79	82	+16
Republican Conservative Margin	+31	+41	+52	+64	+33
Republican Liberal Margin	–22	–21	–37	–44	–22

Source: ANES Time Series Cumulative Data File.

Notes: Data were calculated in the same manner as those for Table 7.2 (see the note under Table 7.2). Margins might appear to be slightly off due to rounding to the whole number in the table.

Democrats than liberal Democrats (35 versus 29 percent). But in 2000–2012, the greater share of liberal Democrats (48 percent) was almost entirely due to a decline in the percentage of conservative Democrats (down to 17 percent). Practically none of the rise in liberal Democratic voters was a consequence of a reduction in moderates (36 percent in the 1970s and 35 percent in 2000–2012), and therefore ideological sorting was the primary driver of this transformation.

By contrast, the Republicans' growing share of conservative adherents is primarily due to ideological polarization. It has never been the case that liberals comprised more than a modest share of the Republican electorate (for the data shown, they peak at 7 percent in the 1980s). Instead, it used to be the case that there were many moderates who identified with the GOP—28 percent of Republican voters in the 1970s. But by 2000–2012, the percentage of moderate Republicans was cut in half to 14 percent, and the share of conservative Republican voters went from 66 percent in the 1970s to 82 percent in 2000–2012.

Similar to Table 7.3, Table 7.4 also presents data on the Republican Conservative Margin and the Republican Liberal Margin. As a higher percentage of Republican voters have self-identified as conservatives while Democratic conservatives have declined, the Republican Conservative Margin has necessarily increased. Likewise, the increase in liberal Democratic voters and the decline in liberal Republicans have expanded the deficit for the Republican Liberal Margin. Figure 7.2 displays the Republican Conservative Margin and the Republican Liberal Margin data from

FIGURE 7.2 ■ Ideological Differentiation of Democratic and Republican Voters

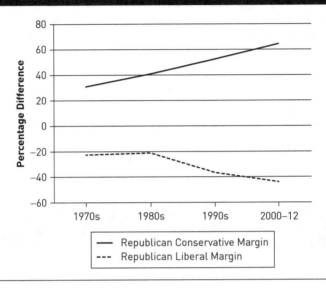

Source: ANES Time Series Cumulative Data File.

Note: Data shown are the plotted results in the last two rows of Table 7.4 (not including the "Difference" column).

Table 7.4. The Republican Conservative Margin has shown a very pronounced upward trajectory since the 1970s. The Republican Liberal Margin, however, remained the same in the 1970s and 1980s, but it grew substantially in favor of the Democratic Party after that. Because conservatives dominate the Republican Party (82 percent in 2000–2012) to a much greater extent than do liberals associated with the Democratic Party (under a majority at 48 percent in 2000–2012), the Republican Conservative Margin is much larger (+64 percentage points) than the corresponding deficit for the Republican Liberal Margin (−44 percentage points).

This section concludes with a look at voters' thermometer ratings of liberals and conservatives and the major parties. The ANES includes a battery of questions that assess the degree to which an individual feels favorable or unfavorable toward a specific group. These thermometer scales range from 0 to 100. Respondents are told that a rating of 50 indicates a neutral feeling toward a specific group (lukewarm), whereas a rating of 0 is the most unfavorable (ice cold) and a rating of 100 is necessarily the most favorable (white hot). The top half of Table 7.5 presents data on voters' thermometer ratings of liberals and conservatives, respectively. The ratings of liberals and conservatives are shown for Democratic and Republican voters and liberal and conservative voters (beginning in the 1970s). Additionally, the rating margin is always displayed with respect to the voter category more favorably disposed to the group being rated (e.g., Democratic voters rating liberals or liberal voters rating liberals).

With the thermometer rating data for liberals and conservatives dating back to 1964, it is evident that Democratic voters have become more favorably disposed toward liberals (from 52 to 64) while Republicans have become less favorable (going from 42 to 35). Likewise, but not to as great an extent, Republican voters rate conservatives higher in 2000–2012 than in the 1960s (from 70 to 74), while Democratic voters have become somewhat less favorable toward conservatives over this period (from 58 to 54). Liberal voters' rating of liberals has declined a bit (going from 72 to 68), whereas conservative voters' rating of liberals has become much less favorable, dropping 15 points from the 1970s to 2000–2012. Over time the rating of conservatives among liberal and conservative voters has not experienced as much change, but again the opposite group (in this case, liberal voters) registers a larger decline in its thermometer rating (liberal voters rate conservatives a 51 in the 1970s, and this declines to 45 in 2000–2012).

TABLE 7.5 ■ Voters' Thermometer Ratings of Liberals and Conservatives and the Major Parties

Rating Liberals	1960s	1970s	1980s	1990s	2000–12	Difference
Democrats	52	62	65	65	64	+12
Republicans	42	52	41	37	35	−7
Democratic Margin	10	10	24	28	29	+19
Rating Liberals						
Liberals	—	72	69	70	68	−4
Conservatives	—	58	54	48	43	−15
Liberal Margin	—	14	15	22	25	+11
Rating Conservatives						
Democrats	58	65	65	61	54	−4
Republicans	70	73	74	73	74	+4
Republican Margin	12	8	9	12	20	+8
Rating Conservatives						
Liberals	—	51	52	50	45	−6
Conservatives	—	75	72	71	71	−4
Conservative Margin	—	24	20	21	26	+2

Rating Democratic Party			1980s	1990s	2000–12	Difference
Democrats			81	79	78	−3
Republicans			43	39	29	−14
Democratic Margin			38	40	49	+11
Rating Democratic Party						
Liberals			72	72	72	0
Conservatives			65	58	45	−20
Liberal Margin			7	14	27	+20
Rating Republican Party						
Democrats			48	45	30	−18
Republicans			78	75	75	−3
Republican Margin			30	30	45	+15
Rating Republican Party						
Liberals			47	41	28	−19
Conservatives			63	62	61	−2
Conservative Margin			16	21	33	+17

Source: ANES Time Series Cumulative Data File.

Notes: The thermometer ratings for Liberals and Conservatives began with the 1964 ANES, but classifying liberal and conservative voters begins in 1972 (when the ideology question is first asked). The party ratings (the Democratic and Republican parties) began in 1978, but the data in the table start with the 1980 ANES. The top part of the table displays the thermometer ratings registered by Democratic and Republican voters for Liberals and Conservatives, respectively. The bottom part of the table displays the ratings registered by Democratic and Republican voters for the Democratic Party; the ratings registered by Liberal and Conservative voters for the Democratic Party; the ratings registered by Democratic and Republican voters for the Republican Party; the ratings registered by Liberal and Conservative voters for the Republican Party. "Difference" equals the data for 2000–12 minus the data for the 1960s/1970s/1980s. The "Margin" values are computed to register positive values because the category of voter labeled in the margin line is always more supportive of the subject being rated (e.g., the Democratic margin for rating Liberals; the Conservative margin for rating the Republican Party).

The bottom half of Table 7.5 examines voters' thermometer ratings of the Democratic and Republican parties. Starting with the Democratic Party, ratings of the party are first displayed for partisans (Democratic and Republican voters) and then for liberal and conservative voters. Then the thermometer rating for the Republican Party is shown for Democratic and Republican voters and finally for liberal and conservative voters. Beginning with the Democratic Party ratings, it is probably no surprise that Democratic voters' ratings of their own party hardly change over time, going from 81 in the 1980s to 78 in 2000–2012. But notice the strong drop in Republican voters' rating of the Democratic Party, going from 43 in the 1980s to 29 in 2000–2012. And although liberal voters are naturally more aligned with the Democratic Party and their rating is a constant 72 from the 1980s to 2000–2012, conservative voters have become markedly less favorable in their rating of the Democratic Party, going from 65 in the 1980s to 45 in 2000–2012.

With respect to rating the GOP, Democratic voters have become much less favorable, moving from 48 in the 1980s to 30 in 2000–2012. Similar to Democratic voters rating the Democratic Party, Republican voters rating the Republican Party, as expected, show very little movement (going from 78 in the 1980s to 75 in 2000–2012). A similar dynamic manifests with respect to liberal and conservative voters rating the Republican Party. Just as liberal voters remain constant in their rating of the Democratic Party, so, too, do conservative voters in their rating of the GOP (63 in the 1980s and 61 in 2000–2012). And just as conservatives exhibited a notable drop in their favorability toward the Democratic Party, it is the case that liberal voters have become markedly less favorable toward the Republican Party (going from a thermometer rating of 47 in the 1980s to 28 in 2000–2012).

The reason for displaying so much data on voters' thermometer ratings of liberals and conservatives and the major parties in Table 7.5 is to emphasize a simple but important point. Over time, partisans have become more favorable toward the ideological group more aligned with their party (e.g., increasing Republican affinity with conservatives and increasing Democratic affinity with liberals) and less favorable toward the ideological out-group (e.g., Democratic/Republican ratings of conservatives/liberals). And this growing antagonism toward the perceived political opposition is even more pronounced with regard to voters' thermometer ratings of the major parties. Republican and conservative voters have become much less favorable in their rating of the Democratic Party, and similarly, Democratic and liberal voters have become much less favorable in their rating of the Republican Party. Perhaps this development is not a surprise but it is strong evidence for why elected Democrats and Republicans so often choose conflict over compromise. If the political opposition is increasingly viewed in a negative light then there is little incentive to extend the olive branch.

THE BIG THREE: RACE, ECONOMICS, AND RELIGION

Race, economics, and religion are cardinal features of the American South. Historically, and to this day, the region has always contained a higher share of African Americans. The institution of slavery, with its much greater prevalence in southern states of course, explains why Dixie has a considerably larger African American population.

Race, more than any other issue, is the primary architect shaping the contours of southern politics. It is the most enduring, deepest, and consequential political fault line. And unlike economics and religion, which are both malleable, race is an ascriptive trait determined by birth. In other words, race is hereditary and this single feature, which no voter can alter, is the most important factor influencing political behavior.

Economics is an issue that is difficult to wholly separate from race because the economically disadvantaged have always been disproportionally African American. The legacy of slavery undoubtedly contributes to the persisting lower economic station of southern blacks. Nonetheless, because of a greater dependency on agriculture, which limited opportunities for upward mobility, poor whites have historically been a decidedly larger population in southern states. In fact, if not for the deep racial division in southern politics, it seems plausible that the region would not be as politically conservative if lower class African Americans and whites were able to unite in common cause. With urbanization, in-migration, modernization, economic diversification, and a more business-friendly environment, the South has come a long way from the days of widespread sharecropping and tenant farming. Regional disparities in wealth and income have closed considerably as the South embraced and fostered economic growth and innovation.

To this day, not only is the South more racially diverse and economically impoverished, it is also the most devout region of the United States. For instance, there is a humorous poster that caricaturizes different parts of the country, and placed over the southern states in large letters is the word "Jesusland." Funny and true; the share of Christians is much larger in the South. This is in part due to the ancestral lineage of blacks and whites. White southerners were historically one of the least ethnically diverse groups to settle in the United States. Unlike the markedly more diverse immigration streams of white Europeans to various northern states, in the South, white European migrants were primarily limited to English, Irish, and Scots-Irish descent. The predominant strain of Protestantism found among these immigrants was impressed upon African slaves, and over time, both southern whites and blacks were overwhelmingly Christian, if not necessarily Protestant, although the marked prevalence of Protestantism endures.

Race has always maintained a leading role in shaping southern politics, and its paramount importance has generally served to downplay the significance of economics and religion. With respect to African Americans, neither economics nor religion add that much explanatory power for understanding their political behavior because this group moved virtually en masse in favor of the Democratic Party when President Johnson championed the cause of black civil rights in the mid-1960s (Black 1998; Black and Black 1987; Bullock and Gaddie 2009; Carmines and Stimson 1989; Fauntroy 2007). Hence, because race alone is such an overpowering factor influencing the political behavior of southern blacks, the following sections on economics and religion are assessed only with respect to southern whites. White political behavior is further influenced by economics and religion, as both play a notable role in the shift of southern whites from the Democratic Party to the GOP.

RACE

It is perhaps nothing short of amazing that it has taken up to seven chapters to finally quote the most frequently cited passage of V. O. Key's *Southern Politics in State and Nation:*

> In its grand outlines the politics of the South revolves around the position of the Negro. It is at times interpreted as a politics of cotton, as a politics of free trade, as a politics of agrarian poverty, or as a politics of planter and plutocrat. Although such interpretations have a superficial validity, in the last analysis the major peculiarities of southern politics go back to the Negro. Whatever phase of the southern political process one seeks to understand, sooner or later the trail of inquiry leads to the Negro. (1949, 5)

The entire paragraph is quoted because Key is clearly arguing that race trumps economics with respect to its importance in structuring southern politics. Despite some scholarship that elevates the role of economics in furthering the realignment of southern whites to the Republican Party (Lublin 2004; Shafer and Johnston 2001, 2006), the bulk of the survey evidence and election returns seven decades after Key, strongly support the contention that race remains the fundamental driver of southern politics.

Table 7.6 presents a series of bivariate correlations that assess the relationship between race and several other variables like ideology, the Republican share of the two-party presidential vote, income, and religion. With respect to race, blacks are coded 1 and otherwise 0. Likewise, whites are coded 1 and otherwise 0. Ideology is based on an individual's self-placement on a seven-point scale ranging from 1 = extremely liberal to 7 = extremely conservative. Income is a three-point scale: 1 = the lowest third of family income, 2 = the middle third of family income, and 3 = the highest third of family income. Protestant is coded 1 and otherwise 0. For additional details refer to the note below Table 7.6.

For the student unfamiliar with correlations, their purpose is to measure the degree of association between two variables. Unlike a regression analysis, which designates which variable is affected (the dependent variable) by another (the independent variable), a bivariate correlation simply determines whether two variables are related but not in a directional fashion (e.g., variable X influences variable Y). Correlations range from negative one (−1) to positive one (+1) and a value of zero (0) indicates no relationship between two variables. For example, a perfect negative correlation would mean that a step in a positive direction is always offset by a step in the negative direction. If the race variable took on a value of 1 for an African American and otherwise 0, and the presidential vote variable took on a value of 1 for a Republican vote and a 0 for a Democratic vote, if every time the race variable was 1 for African American and the corresponding value for Republican presidential vote was 0 (Democratic vote) then this would be a perfectly negative correlation.

TABLE 7.6 ■ The Relationship between Race and Party Identification, Ideology, Presidential Vote, Income, and Religion						
Correlation	1950s	1960s	1970s	1980s	1990s	2000–12
Party ID						
Blacks	+.06*	−.12*	−.23*	−.27*	−.31*	−.44*
Whites	−.06*	+.12*	+.21*	+.26*	+.29*	+.42*
Ideology						
Blacks	—	—	−.29*	−.12*	−.12*	−.17*
Whites	—	—	+.26*	+.14*	+.09*	+.22*
Rep Pres. Vote						
Blacks	−.01	−.27*	−.45*	−.43*	−.41*	−.47*
Whites	+.01	+.26*	+.43*	+.43*	+.39*	+.49*
Income						
Blacks	−.35*	−.32*	−.30*	−.26*	−.21*	−.19*
Whites	+.35*	+.32*	+.28*	+.26*	+.25*	+.21*
Protestant						
Blacks	+.06*	+.08*	+.11*	+.14*	+.23*	+.17*
Whites	−.06*	−.07*	−.02	+.14*	+.05*	+.06*

Source: ANES Time Series Cumulative Data File.

Notes: Displayed are pairwise correlation coefficients. For respondent race: black = 1, otherwise = 0; white = 1, otherwise = 0. Party identification is the seven-point scale: 1 = Strong Democrat; 2 = Weak Democrat; 3 = Independent-leaning Democrat; 4 = Independent; 5 = Independent-leaning Republican; 6 = Weak Republican; 7 = Strong Republican. Ideology is the seven-point scale: 1 = Extremely Liberal; 2 = Liberal; 3 = Somewhat Liberal; 4 = Moderate; 5 = Somewhat Conservative; 6 = Conservative; 7 = Extremely Conservative (the ideology question was first asked on the 1972 ANES and that is why there is no data for the 1950s and 1960s). Two-party presidential vote: 1 = Republican, 0 = Democratic. Income is a three-point scale: 1 = low income; 2 = middle income; 3 = high income. Protestant = 1, otherwise = 0. A plus sign indicates one's race is positively related to the Republican Party ("Party ID"); a more conservative ideology; a Republican presidential vote; a higher income; the Protestant denomination. * = significant at $p < .05$.

In addition to measuring whether a correlation is negative or positive, its level of statistical significance can also be determined. Statistical significance is typically assessed in terms of probability values, or p-values for short. All of the correlations are evaluated at the most common cutoff for statistical significance: $p < .05$. Because .05 is the same as saying a 5 percent probability, if the generated p-value is less than .05, then there is less than a 5 percent likelihood that the relationship between two variables is due to chance as opposed to it being a real relationship (statistically significant). In other words, when a p-value is .05 or less, then at least 95 out of 100 times the correlation between two variables is statistically significant and not merely due to chance.

Returning to the results in Table 7.6, in almost every instance the correlations between race and the aforementioned variables are statistically significant at the $p < .05$ level. Further, except for the last three time periods, when the correlation for blacks and Protestant and the correlation for whites and Protestant is positive, in every other instance the correlations for blacks and whites are signed in opposite directions and almost always statistically significant (exceptions include the correlations for Republican presidential vote in the 1950s and the correlation between whites and Protestant in the 1970s). Going across the rows and starting at the top with the correlation between race and party identification, it is notable that in the 1950s African Americans exhibit a statistically significant and positive relationship in the Republican direction (recall that 1 = strong Democrat and 7 = strong Republican). By comparison, whites exhibit a statistically significant and negative relationship with party identification, meaning they are more likely to identify as Democrats. After the 1950s these relationships are permanently reversed and growing in statistical strength based on the absolute size of the correlation coefficients. By 2000–2012, African Americans are much more likely to identify with the Democratic Party while whites are much more likely to identify with the GOP.

With respect to ideology, it is always the case that blacks are significantly more likely to place themselves on the liberal end of the seven-point ideological scale (1 = extremely liberal and 7 = extremely conservative). Whites, on the other hand, exhibit a positive relationship with ideology, meaning they are more likely to place themselves on the conservative end of the scale. The relationship between ideology and race was strongest in the 1970s. In the 1950s, when the sample of African American voters is admittedly miniscule ($n = 22$ respondents), there is no relationship between race and Republican presidential vote. But thereafter, the expected pattern emerges (blacks are significantly less likely to vote Republican whereas whites are significantly more likely to vote Republican) and the correlation between race (for blacks and whites) and presidential vote is strongest in 2000–2012.

As expected, the correlation between black and income is negative and the correlation between white and income is positive. Over time, however, reflecting an increase in the standard of living of both black and white southerners, these correlations have reduced in absolute size (down to −.19 for blacks in 2000–2012 and reduced to +.21 for whites in 2000–2012) but remain statistically significant. Lastly, the relationship between race and Protestant is documented. In every time period, African Americans are significantly more likely to be Protestants. In contrast, whites in the 1950s and 1960s are significantly less likely to be Protestants, then demonstrate no relationship with Protestantism in the 1970s and thereafter show a positive and statistically significant association with Protestantism (although at +.06 in

TABLE 7.7 ■ Race of Voter and Party Identification, Ideology, Presidential Vote, Income, and Religion in the 2012 Election				
Correlation	Black Voter	White Voter	Black Voter	White Voter
Party ID	−.42*	+.37*	Strong Democrat	Leans Republican
Ideology	−.17*	+.15*	Moderate	Somewhat Conservative
Rep Pres. Vote	−.40*	+.38*	5%	62%
Income	−.15*	+.13*	$20K < $30K	$30K < $40K
Born Again	+.14*	−.07*	61%	43%

Source: Data are from the 2012 Cooperative Congressional Election Study (CCES).

Notes: Displayed are pairwise correlation coefficients. For respondent race: black voter = 1, otherwise = 0; white voter = 1, otherwise = 0. Party identification is the seven-point scale: 1 = Strong Democrat; 2 = Weak Democrat; 3 = Independent-leaning Democrat; 4 = Independent; 5 = Independent-leaning Republican; 6 = Weak Republican; 7 = Strong Republican. Ideology is the seven-point scale: 1 = Extremely Liberal; 2 = Liberal; 3 = Somewhat Liberal; 4 = Moderate; 5 = Somewhat Conservative; 6 = Conservative; 7 = Extremely Conservative. Income is a twelve-point scale (1 = < $10K; 12 = $150K+). Born Again = 1, otherwise = 0. A plus sign indicates one's race is positively related to the Republican Party ("Party ID"); a more conservative ideology; a Republican presidential vote; a higher income; being born again. The last two columns for black and white voters display the median variable category with respect to Party ID, Ideology, and Income. Data are limited to self-reported voters in the 2012 national election. * = significant at $p < .05$.

2000–2012, the absolute value of the correlation coefficient is much smaller than the +.17 correlation coefficient for African Americans).

With data from the 2012 Cooperative Congressional Election Study (CCES), Table 7.7 takes another look at the relationship between race and the same set of characteristics displayed in Table 7.6, with one exception: instead of Protestant, here the religious classification is now Born Again. Wilcox and Robinson (2011, 209) define born again as an "experience common in evangelical churches in which an individual repents of his or her sin, accepts Christ as his or her personal savior, and is redeemed by grace." As will be demonstrated in the upcoming section on religion, based on their party identification and voting behavior, born again white southerners comprise a core group in the modern Republican coalition. Given the very large sample size for the 2012 CCES (more than 11,000 southern voters), all of the data in Table 7.7 are limited to black and white respondents who self-reported voting in the 2012 national elections.

The first two columns of results display correlation coefficients for black and white voters, respectively. The last two columns then display the median value for a black and white voter with respect to party identification, ideology, and income.

Finally, the distribution of the Republican presidential vote and the share of those born again are shown for black and white voters. All of the correlations for black and white voters are statistically significant and signed in opposite directions. Speaking to the deep racial divide in southern politics, the strongest relationships are between race and party identification and between race and presidential vote choice. Black voters are strongly affiliated with the Democratic Party and much more likely to vote Democratic for president. White voters exhibit the opposite relationship.

Breathing substantive life into these relationships, the placement of the African American voter along the seven-point party identification scale at exactly the middle of the distribution of black voters (the median value) is equivalent to a strong Democrat. By comparison, the median placement of a white voter on the party identification scale is equivalent to an independent leaning Republican. According to the 2012 CCES data, 99.5 percent of African American southern voters who identified as strong Democrats cast a Democratic presidential vote. In stark contrast, 96.3 percent of white southern voters who identified as independent-leaning Republicans cast a Republican presidential vote.

The median black voter is an ideological moderate and the median white voter is somewhat conservative. Based solely on race, the black vote for the Republican presidential nominee was just 5 percent, while 62 percent of white voters cast presidential ballots for the GOP standard bearer. The median black voter has a family income between $20,000 and $30,000, whereas the median white voter resides in the next highest income category (between $30,000 and $40,000). Finally, the born-again experience is prevalent among black and white southern voters, and especially in the former group, with 61 percent of African Americans claiming to have undergone this religious conversion.

The most palpable schism between black and white southerners manifests in party identification and voting behavior and therefore the remainder of this section will take a closer look at the party identification and voting behavior of African Americans and whites from the 1950s forward. Beginning with party identification, Table 7.8 shows the percentage of white and black voters who identify with the Republican and Democratic Parties by decade, starting with the 1950s and moving through the 2010s (2010–2014). In addition, the bottom row for Republican and Democratic identifiers displays the white margin in Republican identification and the white margin in Democratic identification, respectively. Coming at the tail end of the Solid Democratic South, the 1950s show a pattern of party identification by race that has never appeared again. In percentage terms, black Republicans (24 percent) outnumber white Republicans (14 percent) and white Democrats (73 percent) outnumber black Democrats (69 percent). But from the 1960s forward, Republican affiliation is much more prominent among white voters and Democratic identification is much more popular among African American voters.

TABLE 7.8 ■ Party Identification of Black and White Southern Voters							
Republicans (%)	**1950s**	**1960s**	**1970s**	**1980s**	**1990s**	**2000s**	**2010s**
Whites	14	17	22	34	43	52	42
Blacks	24	8	6	7	7	4	4
White Margin	−10	+10	+16	+27	+36	+48	+38
Democrats (%)	**1950s**	**1960s**	**1970s**	**1980s**	**1990s**	**2000s**	**2010s**
Whites	73	61	48	39	32	26	22
Blacks	69	83	76	80	80	84	79
White Margin	+4	−22	−28	−41	−49	−57	−57

Source: ANES data from 1952–1974; national exit polls from 1976 to 2008; CCES data from 2010 to 2014.

Notes: Self-reported voters for the ANES and CCES data. Republicans include strong and weak identi-fiers; Democrats include strong and weak identifiers. "White Margin" is the percentage of white identifiers minus the corresponding percentage of black identifiers (e.g., 42 percent white Republicans in the 2010s minus 4 percent black Republicans in the 2010s equals a white margin of +38 percentage points). Margins might appear to be slightly off due to rounding to the whole number in the table.

Figure 7.3 depicts the white Republican margin and white Democratic margin data from Table 7.8. After the 1950s, the disparity in Republican identifiers by race and the corresponding disparity in Democratic identifiers by race becomes a veritable chasm. The white Democratic margin is negatively signed because black Democratic voters outnumber white Democratic voters. The absolute size of this disparity is consistently larger than the white Republican margin. For instance, in the 2010s, 42 percent of white voters identified with the GOP versus only 4 percent of black voters, which results in a +38 percentage-point white Republican margin. By comparison, 22 percent of white voters identified with the Democratic Party versus 79 percent of black voters who identified as Democrats, which results in a −57 percentage-point white Democratic margin. As has been the case since the 1960s, African American voters are much more Democratic than white voters are Republican.

Table 7.9 displays the percentage of the major party presidential vote cast by black and white southerners from the 1950s to 2012. Despite small sample sizes in the 1950s, even in this final Solid Democratic South decade, African Americans are somewhat less likely than whites to vote Republican and somewhat more likely than whites to vote Democratic for president. Voting behavior is often described as a leading indicator of political change (Black and Black 2002), whereas party affiliation, because of its more lasting hold on a voter's political identity (Campbell et al. 1960; Green, Palmquist, and Schickler 2002), is slower to adjust. The evidence in Table 7.9 strongly supports this dynamic. For instance, in the 1970s only 22 percent of white voters identified with the GOP (48 percent identified as Democrats; see Table 7.8), but 57 percent of

FIGURE 7.3 ■ Differences in Party Identification of Black and White Southern Voters

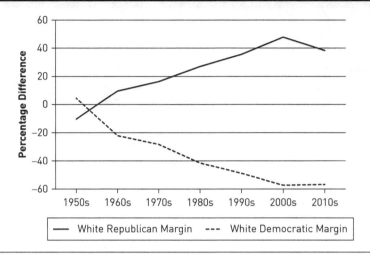

Source: Data are from the 2012 Cooperative Congressional Election Study (CCES).

Notes: The data are the plotted results for the white Republican margin and white Democratic margin shown in Table 7.8. A positive margin indicates more white identifiers for that party (Republican Party after the 1950s), whereas a negative margin indicates more black identifiers for that party (Democratic Party after the 1950s).

TABLE 7.9 ■ Democratic and Republican Presidential Vote Cast by Black and White Southerners

Republican Vote (%)	1950s	1960s	1970s	1980s	1990s	2000s	2012
Whites	49	49	57	67	60	70	62
Blacks	45	10	17	10	11	6	5
White Margin	+4	+39	+40	+57	+49	+64	+57
Democratic Vote (%)	**1950s**	**1960s**	**1970s**	**1980s**	**1990s**	**2000s**	**2012**
Whites	51	51	43	33	40	30	38
Blacks	55	90	83	90	89	94	95
White Margin	−4	−39	−40	−57	−49	−64	−57

Source: ANES data from 1952 to 1974; national exit polls from 1976 to 2008; CCES data in 2012.

Notes: Republican and Democratic presidential vote percentages are based on the votes cast for the major parties only (no third party/independent votes). "White Margin" is the percentage of white presidential votes cast minus the corresponding percentage of black presidential votes cast (e.g., 62 percent white Republican presidential vote cast in 2012 minus 5 percent black Republican presidential vote cast in 2012 equals a white margin of +57 percentage points). Because the data are confined to black and white voters and based on the two-party presidential vote, the white Republican margin and white Democratic margin are the exact converse of each other.

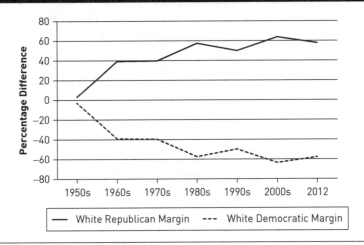

FIGURE 7.4 ■ Differences in Presidential Vote of Black and White Southern Voters

Source: ANES data from 1952 to 1972; national exit polls from 1976 to 2008; CCES data from 2010 to 2014.

Notes: The data are the plotted results for the white Republican margin and white Democratic margin shown in Table 7.9. A positive margin indicates more white presidential votes cast for that party (Republican Party), whereas a negative margin indicates more black presidential votes cast for that party (Democratic Party).

white southerners voted Republican in presidential elections. Black voter loyalty to the Democratic nominee in presidential elections is striking. After the 1950s typically 90 percent or more African Americans vote Democratic and black Democratic voting reaches its apex in the most recent contests because of the added incentive to vote for Barack Obama, the first African American major party presidential nominee.

Figure 7.4 displays the white Republican margin and the white Democratic margin for the two-party presidential vote data from Table 7.9. Unlike the data on party identification in Table 7.8 and graphed in Figure 7.3, the margin data in Figure 7.4 are perfectly symmetrical because it is based on the two-party presidential vote, whereas the party identification data accounted for the share of political independents (they are factored into the denominator when calculating the percentage of Democrats and Republicans). For example, if the white Republican presidential vote margin is +57 percentage points in 2012 then conversely the white Democratic presidential vote margin is –57 percentage points in 2012. Black and white southerners are miles apart with respect to their voting preferences, and this gulf is rooted in their contrary partisan allegiances.

ECONOMICS

The Republican reign in national politics came to a swift end in the late 1920s when the stock market crash ushered in an impending economic Great Depression of international proportions. The GOP assumed a long-term minority status with the 1932 election of Democratic President Franklin D. Roosevelt. And for the first time since before the Civil War, a major party had pieced together a national political majority by becoming electorally competitive in the North and South (Black and Black 2002). This vaunted New Deal Coalition made for some of the strangest of political bedfellows: southern (and Protestant) whites, northern blacks, Catholics and Jews, union workers, the poor, and liberal intellectuals. What helped keep the coalition intact was the literal distance between some of its constituents who were diametrically opposed on the civil rights issue (e.g., northern blacks versus southern whites) as well as President Roosevelt's recognition that the race issue was best left alone.

But the New Deal Coalition was ultimately unsustainable because the cleavage on civil rights eventually grew large enough to split it apart as southern whites abandoned the cause when the national Democratic Party went all-in on championing black civil rights in the movement politics of the 1960s. While it lasted, in the 1930s through 1950s, the New Deal Coalition was chiefly undergirded by a widely embraced position in favor of economic relief, even if that meant pervasive governmental intervention of private enterprise. Indeed, the class cleavage was the most palpable division between Democrats and Republicans, at least outside the South. In Dixie, however, the overriding significance of race served to suppress the class cleavage. After all, in the vast majority of southern localities the Republican opposition was a farce. In most settings, the GOP was a nominal party and hence whatever class division emerged, did so within the factionalism of the southern Democracy (e.g., there emerged a notable economic division within the Texas Democratic Party).

It was a gradual process, but eventually the economic division between lower class Democrats and middle to upper class Republicans in the North, seeped its way into southern politics. After World War II, Republican growth south of the Potomac was necessarily more viable in those areas where the race issue held less sway—primarily in Peripheral South settings because they contained smaller black populations. Furthermore, because the Jim Crow system of legalized racial segregation was relatively less oppressive, rigid, and suffocating in the Rim South as compared to the Deep South, the former section managed to attract a much greater number of northern in-migrants and political entrepreneurs who helped fuel urbanization and economic advancement (Black and Black 1987). In the more industrious and enterprising Peripheral South, economic growth fostered greater social mobility and with it followed an attraction to the more business friendly Republican Party.

When Eisenhower won the presidency in 1952, the first Republican to do so since Herbert Hoover in 1928, he made it clear that he would not spend his precious political capital fighting to roll back New Deal policies. Instead, he accepted the New Deal's policy prescriptions and even spearheaded a massive government-led infrastructure program: the construction of the interstate highway system. Nonetheless, Eisenhower was still a Republican and, therefore, in comparison to the Democratic opposition, the president was viewed as more accepting of and favorable toward a market economy and the Republican philosophy of economic individualism. In his two successful presidential bids in 1952 and 1956, Eisenhower won the popular votes from a total of five different southern states and only one was located in the Deep South (Louisiana in 1956). Precinct analyses of the southern presidential vote in the 1950s revealed evidence of a burgeoning economic divide, as Eisenhower garnered more support in heavily urban and higher income areas ("silk-stocking" districts; see Bartley and Graham 1975).

Although the turbulence of the 1960s pushed the racial issue firmly to the forefront of southern politics, it remains the case that among white voters the class-based partisan cleavage that emerged during the Eisenhower Administration continues to play a role in conditioning political behavior. Figure 7.5 displays the distribution of white southerners according to level of family income: low income equals the lowest third of the income scale, middle income equals the middle third of the income scale, and high income equals the highest third of the income scale. In the 1950s a large plurality (44 percent) of white southerners occupy the low income category. Moving forward in time, however, the percentage of low-income individuals declines and the three income categories bunch closer together, so that in 2000–2012 the three income classifications constitute roughly a third of white southerners (32 percent low income, 35 percent middle income, and 33 percent high income).

The next three figures display in succession the changing partisanship of low-income, middle-income, and high-income white southerners, respectively. Starting

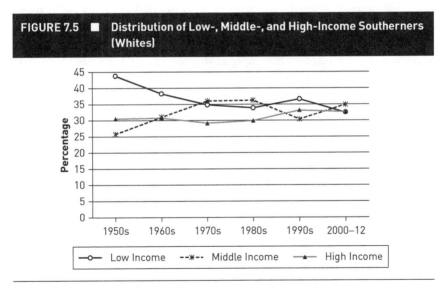

FIGURE 7.5 ■ Distribution of Low-, Middle-, and High-Income Southerners (Whites)

Source: ANES Time Series Cumulative Data File.

Notes: Data are confined to white (non-Latino) southerners. "Low Income" consists of respondents whose income resides in the lower third of family incomes; "Middle Income" consists of respondents whose income resides in the middle third of family incomes; "High Income" consists of respondents whose income resides in the highest third of family incomes.

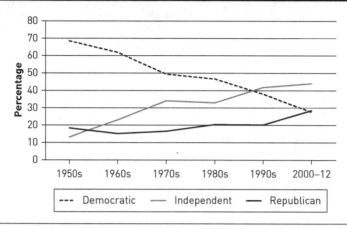

FIGURE 7.6 ■ Party Identification of Low-Income Southerners (Whites)

Source: ANES Time Series Cumulative Data File.

Note: Data are confined to white (non-Latino) southerners. "Low Income" consists of respondents whose income resides in the lower third of family incomes.

with low-income whites, in Figure 7.6 there is an obvious long-term decline in Democratic identification. But the drop in Democratic affiliates is primarily compensated for by an increase in the share of political independents, who go from 13 percent in the 1950s to a 44 percent plurality in 2000–2012. By comparison, Republican identification increases from 18 percent in the 1950s to 29 percent in 2000–2012, reaching parity with the share of Democratic identifiers (28 percent). At the end of the time series it is apparent that the long-term pattern of partisan change is from overwhelming Democratic affiliation to dealignment because most low-income whites are now political independents.

The partisan distribution of middle-income white southerners is displayed in Figure 7.7. Similar to low-income whites, there is a pronounced descent in Democratic identifiers, who comprised an impressive 77 percent of middle-income whites in the 1950s (compared to 69 percent of low-income whites in the 1950s). By 2000–2012, Democrats comprise the smallest share of middle-income whites (just 19 percent), whereas the rest of the distribution is split between Republicans (40 percent) and political independents (41 percent).

The movement away from Democratic identification and toward Republican affiliation is most pronounced in the case of high-income whites. As shown in Figure 7.8, in the 1950s Democrats constituted 72 percent of high-income whites while the remainder of the high-income population was roughly split between political independents (15 percent) and Republicans (13 percent). The Democratic share of identifiers is now the lowest among high-income whites, who in 2000–2012 comprise only 18 percent of this group. Political independents are now 38 percent of high-income whites and Republican identifiers constitute a 44-percent plurality.

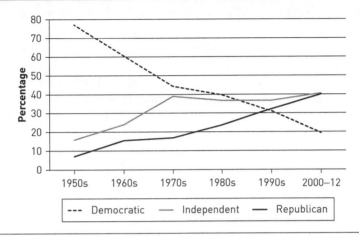

FIGURE 7.7 ■ Party Identification of Middle-Income Southerners (Whites)

Source: ANES Time Series Cumulative Data File.

Note: Data are confined to white (non-Latino) southerners. "Middle Income" consists of respondents whose income resides in the middle third of family incomes.

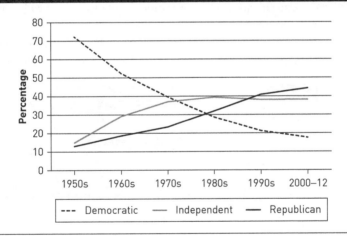

FIGURE 7.8 ■ Party Identification of High-Income Southerners (Whites)

Source: ANES Time Series Cumulative Data File.

Note: Data are confined to white (non-Latino) southerners. "High Income" consists of respondents whose income resides in the highest third of family incomes.

Despite some notable variation in the changing partisan distribution of southern whites with respect to income level, the general pattern exhibits remarkable consistency. In every income category (low income, middle income, high income) the long-term decline in Democratic identification is massive (ranging from a reduction of 41 to 58 percentage points). In addition, since the 1950s, and at least through the 1980s, the Democratic decline in identification is offset more by a rise in political independents than Republican adherents. Stated slightly differently, for most of the period under examination, southern whites, irrespective of income level, were dealigning from Democratic identification more than they were realigning in favor of the GOP.

Table 7.10 presents bivariate correlations of party identification and income. The first row shows the relationship between party identification (seven-point scale; 1 = strong Democrat and 7 = strong Republican) and family income (three-point scale; 1 = low, 2 = middle, and 3 = high income). In keeping with the historical narrative, in the 1950s there is indeed evidence of an inverted class relationship among southern whites because a higher income is associated with a Democratic affiliation (by contrast, in the 1950s for northern whites the correlation is positive and significant [+.051 and $p < .05$], indicating that a higher income is associated with a Republican affiliation). But from the 1960s forward, higher income southern whites are more likely to be Republican identifiers.

The next three rows of Table 7.10 examine the correlation between party identification and each income level. For low-income whites, the inverted pattern shows up in the 1950s because there is a positive association between low income and GOP identification. In every subsequent time period, low income is negatively correlated with Republican affiliation. In the case of middle-income whites, in the 1950s there is a negative correlation with party identification (middle-income whites are more likely to identify with the Democratic Party). But after the 1950s, there is never a statistically significant relationship between middle-income whites and party identification. Finally, for high-income whites in the 1950s there is no correlation with

TABLE 7.10 ■ Relationship between Party Identification and Income (Whites)						
Correlation	1950s	1960s	1970s	1980s	1990s	2000–12
Family Income	−.07*	+.09*	+.09*	+.18*	+.22*	+.16*
Low Income	+.09*	−.06*	−.07*	−.13*	−.20*	−.16*
Middle Income	−.10*	−.03	−.02	−.02	+.01	+.04
High Income	+.003	+.08*	+.09*	+.16*	+.19*	+.11*

Source: ANES Time Series Cumulative Data File.

Notes: Displayed are pairwise correlation coefficients for party identification and income. Data are confined to white (non-Latino) southerners. "Family Income" is coded 1 = Low Income, 2 = Middle Income, 3 = High Income. Party identification is the seven-point scale: 1 = Strong Democrat; 2 = Weak Democrat; 3 = Independent-leaning Democrat; 4 = Independent; 5 = Independent-leaning Republican; 6 = Weak Republican; 7 = Strong Republican. A plus sign indicates income is positively related to Republican identification; * = significant at $p < .05$.

party identification. But in every time period since, high-income whites are significantly more likely to identify with the Republican Party.

This section concludes with a brief look at presidential voting behavior as it relates to income. Figure 7.9 displays the Republican share of the two-party presidential vote from the 1950s to 2012, according to white southerners' income level (low, middle, and high). In the 1950s and 1960s, only high-income whites cast a majority of their presidential votes for the GOP nominee. However, in the 1970s there is a substantial rise in Republican presidential voting across all three income levels (including a 20-point surge in the case of middle-income whites). In the 1980s Republican support declines among low-income whites (going from 61 percent Republican in the 1970s to 52 percent Republican in the 1980s), it holds steady at 66 percent for middle-income whites, and climbs to 80 percent for high-income whites.

In the two economically prosperous President Clinton terms in the 1990s, Republican presidential voting drops off considerably among each income level (a 10-point decline for low-income whites, an 11-point decline for middle-income whites, and a 17-point decline for high-income whites). For the first time since the 1960s, a Democratic presidential candidate won a majority of the vote from a sizable segment of the white electorate according to income level, specifically low-income whites, who cast 58 percent of their presidential vote for Clinton in the 1992–1996 elections. But after Clinton leaves the presidency, a decisive Republican presidential

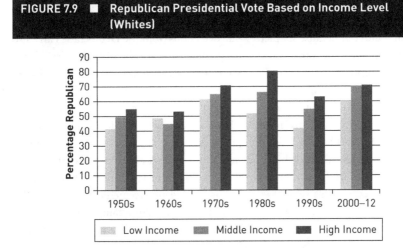

FIGURE 7.9 ■ Republican Presidential Vote Based on Income Level (Whites)

Source: ANES Time Series Cumulative Data File.

Notes: Data are confined to white (non-Latino) southerners. "Low Income" consists of respondents whose income resides in the lower third of family incomes; "Middle Income" consists of respondents whose income resides in the middle third of family incomes; "High Income" consists of respondents whose income resides in the highest third of family incomes. The percentage Republican vote is out of the votes cast for the major parties (two-party vote).

advantage returns. In the 2000–2012 presidential elections, 60 percent of low-income whites voted Republican while middle- and high-income whites backed the GOP presidential nominees over these same years at a rate of 70 and 71 percent, respectively.

With regard to voting behavior in presidential contests, perhaps the most interesting finding is the high rate of Republican support exhibited by whites residing in the lowest third of income level. At least with respect to the two-party vote share, Black and Black (2002) consider a 60-percent haul as translating into an electoral landslide. Another intriguing development is that the typical tiered pattern of higher Republican voting rates corresponding with higher income categories (which manifests in the 1950s, 1970s, 1980s, and 1990s) goes away in the most recent contests (2000–2012) because Republican voting rates for middle- and high-income whites are virtually indistinguishable.

RELIGION

Compared to the role of race and economics in shaping southern politics, religion has been afforded relatively meager consideration. At least with respect to elections scholars, perhaps they can be forgiven for this oversight because religion has historically registered very minimal effects, especially with regard to structuring the party system. Since the 1950s and especially from the late 1970s to the present, religion has become an important factor influencing party competition due to alterations in the composition of religious groups aligning with the Democratic and Republican parties.

Prior to the 1960 presidential election, which pitted the Catholic Democrat John F. Kennedy against the Protestant Republican Richard Nixon, the 1928 presidential election stands out because southern white defections from the Democratic Party also appeared in part to be rooted in religious prejudice toward the Catholic New Yorker Al Smith. Support for Smith's Protestant Republican opponent Herbert Hoover was particularly strong in Rim South states where the race issue was not as likely the determining factor in vote choice (Key 1949). Smith easily carried the Deep South states where the race issue trumped religion (i.e., a show of political solidarity for the white supremacist Democratic Party), but he was bested by Hoover in the Peripheral South states of Florida, North Carolina, Tennessee, Texas, and Virginia (Smith won Arkansas). Southern Democratic defections to Hoover in 1928 appeared to be an isolated event because this type of voting behavior did not reemerge for decades. But thanks to hindsight, it is also true that southern white Protestant support for a co-believer (Hoover) in 1928 was indicative, if not a harbinger, of the future alignment of southern white Protestants to the Republican Party.

More than half a century after the 1928 presidential election, a pivotal shift occurred with respect to a specific group that was at the time still firmly situated within the fold of the Democratic Party. Evangelical Protestants, who comprised the majority of southern whites and were often distinguished by their profession of having undergone a deeply spiritual "born again" religious conversion, were about to undertake a mass exodus in favor of the GOP. The backdrop to this story arguably begins with the U.S. Supreme Court's controversial pro-choice ruling in *Roe v. Wade* (1973). The decision mobilized a variety of heretofore apolitical or at least politically dormant, Christian conservative groups, who eventually came to be known as the Religious Right (Wilcox and Robinson 2011).

The Moral Majority, a politically active Religious Right pressure group founded by Baptist Minister Jerry Falwell of Lynchburg, Virginia, became one of the most visible organizations amidst a chorus of such groups that sprang to life to counter-mobilize against their secular and liberal opponents whom the Religious Right viewed as waging a war on the Judeo-Christian values the nation was built upon. There is a bit of irony to the movement of Christian conservatives from out of the Democratic Party and into the GOP. In the late 1970s when the Religious Right became a growing and visible force in American politics, Southern Baptist Georgia Governor Jimmy Carter (who happened to enjoy teaching Sunday School), won the Democratic nomination and then the presidency in 1976.

The religious profile of President Carter would seem to hold a strong attraction among Religious Right supporters but this was not the case. In the 1980 election, Carter's Republican opponent, the former actor and governor of California, Ronald Reagan, who incidentally hardly ever darkened the door of a church, became the darling of the Religious Right. Reagan captivated the Religious Right because he embraced and championed their issues, something Carter refused to do. As a Democrat, Carter did not stray from the secular stances of the contemporary and dominant northern wing of his party. Whereas Carter's administration upheld the principle of a separation between church and state, his Republican opponent openly courted the Religious Right by wholeheartedly espousing their agenda, as evidenced by Reagan's vociferous opposition to abortion and his support for bringing back prayer in public schools.

Since the late 1970s, it is obvious that the major parties underwent an "issue evolution" (Carmines and Stimson 1989) with respect to their positions on moral/social issues of great concern to Christian conservatives (see Adams 1997). Now, it is clear that within the white electorate, those who value a privileged position for Christianity in the public square are strongly aligned with the Republican Party, whereas those who think religion and politics should not mingle or are themselves not religious, are much more likely to side with the Democratic Party. In short, there is a religious divide that is manifested in the coalitions of Democratic and Republican supporters. The significance of this development is hard to ignore. For example, because of the alignment of Christian conservatives with the GOP, the abortion issue is now a litmus test for presidential hopefuls. Pro-choice Republicans are essentially politically dead on arrival (see the case of Republican presidential hopeful Rudy Giuliani in 2008) and likewise, pro-life Democrats have no chance of winning their party's presidential nomination (Stimson 2004). Finally, at least for the time being, the religious sorting of southern white voters has advantaged the Republican Party because of the substantial size of this component of the electorate (Green et al. 2014).

Going back to the 1950s, the American National Election Studies times series data partition survey respondents into the following four major religious groups: Protestant, Catholic, Jewish, and Other/None. It is unfortunate that there was not further partitioning of these religious categories because "Other" can refer to any other religious faith, including other Christians and non-Christians such as Muslims or Hindus. And "None" refers primarily to respondents who either don't know how to respond to the question or more likely do not harbor a religious faith (e.g., atheists and agnostics). In short, the Other/None classification serves as a residual catchall category in the case of respondents who are not Protestant, Catholic, or Jewish. This is troublesome to the extent that other believers and nonbelievers captured in the Other/None category do not exhibit the same political behavior (which is likely the case). Further, Jewish believers have never been a sizable population within the southern electorate, and because of this, their party identification and voting behavior can only be examined in more recent surveys with very large sample sizes (not a possibility with the ANES).

With the principal limitations of the ANES data fully disclosed, Figure 7.10 displays the distribution of southern whites from the 1950s to 2000–2012 according

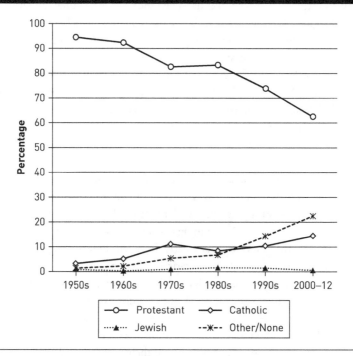

FIGURE 7.10 ■ Distribution of Religious Preferences (Whites)

Source: ANES Time Series Cumulative Data File.

Note: Data are confined to white (non-Latino) southerners. Because of the small sample size, the "Other/None" category is essentially a catchall residual classification for any religious preference outside of Protestant, Catholic, Jewish (including other Christian and non-Christian faiths, e.g., Muslims and/or nonbelievers (atheists, agnostics).

to religious group: Protestant, Catholic, Jewish, and Other/None. In the 1950s Protestants are the prohibitive majority of southern whites, comprising 95 percent. By comparison, the three other religious groups account for a trivial share of the population. However, after the 1950s the percentage of white Protestants declines while the share of Catholics and Other/None respondents rises. By 2000–2012, white Protestants comprise 63 percent of the religious distribution and the Other/None group is the next most prominent, accounting for 23 percent, while Catholics constitute 14 percent. There is no long-term change in the scintilla of southern white Jews, who register at under 1 percent in 2000–2012.

Similar to the progression of figures displayed in the previous section on economics, the next three figures chart the changing partisan distribution of the three major religious categories (Protestant, Catholic, and Other/None, respectively). Figure 7.11 shows the partisan distribution of Protestants in the 1950s to 2000–2012. In the 1950s, almost three-quarters (72 percent) of white Protestants identify with the Democratic Party, while independents and Republicans each comprise 14 percent. Just as most of the long-term decline in Democratic identification was met with a pattern of dealignment (increasing political independents) preceding Republican realignment in the previous section on economics, the same dynamic occurs among white Protestants. This said, by the end of the time period, in 2000–2012 most white Protestants are now Republicans (43 percent) followed by independents (36), who greatly outnumber Democrats (now only 21 percent).

As shown in Figure 7.12, in the 1950s 63 percent of white (non-Latino) Catholics identified with the Democratic Party and there were slightly more Catholic Republicans (20 percent) than Catholic independents (17 percent).

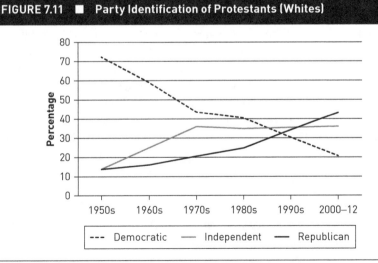

FIGURE 7.11 ■ Party Identification of Protestants (Whites)

Source: ANES Time Series Cumulative Data File.

Note: Data are confined to white (non-Latino) southerners.

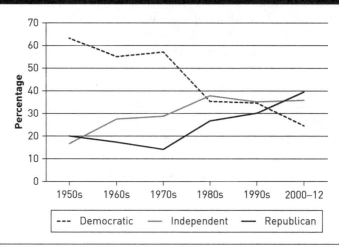

FIGURE 7.12 ■ Party Identification of Catholics (Whites)

Source: ANES Time Series Cumulative Data File.
Note: Data are confined to white (non-Latino) southerners.

There is a drop in the share of Democrats in the 1960s, but this lower percentage persists into the 1970s when the portion of Democrats takes another notable decline in the 1980s and then holds steady through the 1990s only to decline further in 2000–2012. For most of the years of Democratic decline, there is a rise in the share of independents, but eventually, by the end of the time series, most Catholics are now Republican (40 percent) followed by independents (36 percent) and then Democrats (25 percent).

Among whites who profess a faith that is neither Protestant nor Catholic, or harbor no faith at all, the distribution of this group's party identification is very different. To be sure, as Figure 7.13 shows, like Protestants and Catholics, in the 1950s Other/None whites were decidedly Democratic (62 percent). But unlike their Protestant and Catholic peers (both were less than 20 percent independent), even in the 1950s a sizable share of Other/None whites were political independents (31 percent), and very few were Republicans (8 percent). Like Protestants and Catholics, there has been a long-term decline in Democratic identifiers. But instead of most Other/None whites gradually becoming Republicans, the majority of this group is politically independent and has been so since the 1970s. Other/None whites are a dealigned segment of the southern white electorate. In 2000–2012, 55 percent of them were independents, 25 percent were Republicans, and 20 percent were Democrats.

Table 7.11 shows bivariate correlations for the relationship between party identification and religious group. In the first two decades (the 1950s and 1960s) there is no statistically significant relationship between party identification and any of the three groups. In the 1970s, however, Protestantism is positively correlated with Republican

FIGURE 7.13 ■ Party Identification of Other/None Religious Category (Whites)

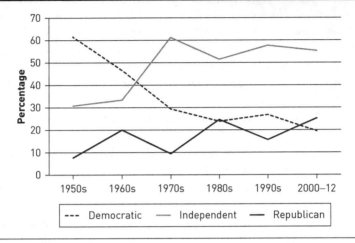

Source: ANES Time Series Cumulative Data File.

Note: Data are confined to white (non-Latino) southerners.

TABLE 7.11 ■ The Relationship between Party Identification and Religion (Whites)

Religion	1950s	1960s	1970s	1980s	1990s	2000–2012
Protestant	−.043	−.010	+.073*	−.036	+.091*	+.112*
Catholic	+.035	+.005	−.080*	+.022	−.019	−.006
Other/None	+.001	+.013	+.002	+.042	−.075*	−.110*

Source: ANES Time Series Cumulative Data File.

Notes: Displayed are pairwise correlation coefficients. Data are limited to white (non-Latino) southerners. Party identification is the seven-point scale: 1 = Strong Democrat; 2 = Weak Democrat; 3 = Independent-leaning Democrat; 4 = Independent; 5 = Independent-leaning Republican; 6 = Weak Republican; 7 = Strong Republican. A positive sign indicates the religious preference aligns in the direction of the Republican Party, and a negative sign indicates the religious preference aligns in the direction of the Democratic Party. * = significant at $p < .05$.

identification whereas Catholicism is negatively correlated with Republican identification (more likely to identify with the Democratic Party). In the 1980s, again there is no relationship between party identification and religious classification. But in the last two decades white Protestants are more likely to identify with the GOP and this relationship has strengthened since the 1990s (from +.091 to +.112). By contrast, Other/None whites are significantly less likely to identify as Republicans and this negative relationship has strengthened since the 1990s (from −.075 to −.110).

Historically, there has been a tension between Catholic and Protestant southerners manifested in a fight over dogma, as opposed to a dispute over economic resources (a scenario much more prevalent among Catholics and Protestants living in northern cities). The much larger Protestant population has viewed Catholicism with a heavy dose of skepticism and in many cases downright dismissive disrespect. But over time, as the national GOP has come to be viewed as the party of believers and the Democratic Party as the secular alternative, religious commitment (or devotion) has proved a unifying ecumenical force for growing the ranks of Republican identifiers.

Evidence of the relationship between religious commitment and Republican identification is presented in Table 7.12. Religious commitment is operationalized in terms of frequency of church attendance. With ANES data on church attendance going back to the 1970s, it is apparent that Republican identification used to show no variation with respect to the frequency of going to church. This dynamic eventually changes so that in 2000–2012, high-attendance Protestants and Catholics (attend church every/almost every week) are markedly more likely to identify as Republicans: 49.9 percent Republican among highly committed Protestants and 51.1 percent Republican for Catholics claiming a commensurate rate of church attendance.

TABLE 7.12 ■ Church Attendance and Republican Identification (Whites)				
Church Attendance	**1970s**	**1980s**	**1990s**	**2000–2012**
Protestants	Republican %	Republican %	Republican %	Republican %
1. Every/Almost Every Week	19.9	27.5	37.6	49.9
2. Once or Twice a Month	22.0	24.3	36.1	38.1
3. Few Times a Year/ Never	20.4	22.1	28.5	36.0
Catholics	Republican %	Republican %	Republican %	Republican %
1. Every/Almost Every Week	14.9	37.0	31.4	51.1
2. Once or Twice a Month	13.6	4.5	31.8	38.6
3. Few Times a Year/ Never	12.9	22.7	27.8	28.4

Source: ANES Time Series Cumulative Data File.

Note: Data are limited to white (non-Latino) southerners.

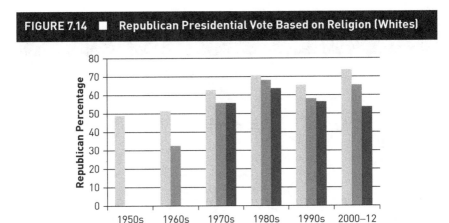

FIGURE 7.14 ■ Republican Presidential Vote Based on Religion (Whites)

Source: ANES data from 1952 to 1972; national exit polls from 1976 to 2008; CCES data in 2012.

Note: The percentage Republican vote is out of the two-party vote.

Figure 7.14 concludes the examination of the three largest southern white religious categories with a bar chart displaying the Republican share of the presidential vote from the 1950s to 2000–2012. Because of the small samples, the ANES data for the 1952–1972 presidential elections are limited to showing only the Protestant vote in the 1950s and the Protestant and Catholic vote in the 1960s. National exit poll data, with its much larger samples, is used for the 1976–2008 elections, and the CCES survey (a very large sample) is used for the 2012 election. Thus, beginning in the 1970s the samples for Other/None presidential voters are substantial.

In the 1950s and 1960s, the two-party presidential vote cast by white Protestants was split almost right down the middle. In the 1960s, only a third of white Catholics voted Republican for president. In the 1970s, the Republican presidential advantage among all three groups materializes and Protestants always exhibit the highest GOP proclivity. After the 1970s, there is a consistent tiered voting pattern with Protestants the most presidentially Republican followed by Catholics. The across-the-board decline in the Republican presidential vote in the 1990s reflects a similar drop found among income groups (recall Figure 7.9). Perhaps this pervasive decline in southern white presidential voting in the 1990s should be dubbed the Clinton effect because the rate of Republican voting among Protestants and Catholics rebounds in the new millennium (just like it does for low-, middle-, and high-income white southerners). By contrast, the rate of Republican presidential voting among Other/None whites reaches its lowest level (54 percent) in 2000–2012. As the Other/None group becomes comprised of more and more nonbelievers (which is the trend), support for the Republican presidential nominee should continue to decline.

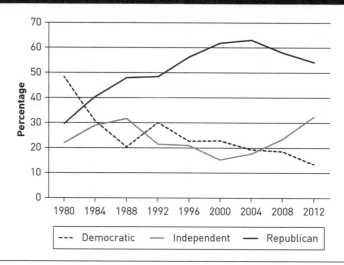

FIGURE 7.15 ■ Party Identification of Born Again/Evangelical Voters (Whites)

Source: National exit polls from 1980 to 2008; CCES data in 2012.

Notes: Data from 1980 to 2008 are from national exit polls; question asks "born again" for 1980, 1984, 1992, 2004, 2008; question asks "evangelical Christian/fundamentalist: in 1988; question asks if Respondent is "part of Religious Right movement" in 1996 and 2000. CCES data in 2012, and the question asks "born again" (self-reported voters).

Finally, because born again/evangelical Christians have become a stalwart Republican faction, and given their impressive size within the southern electorate (see Table 7.7), their political behavior warrants a closer look. Born again/evangelical Christians were the segment of white southerners most activated by the Religious Right counter-mobilization of the late 1970s and early 1980s. The marriage between the Religious Right and the Republican Party birthed a legion of born again Republican offspring. Figure 7.15 shows the party identification of white born again southern voters in presidential years from 1980 to 2012. It is unfortunate that the 1976 national exit poll did not ask the born again question, but nonetheless, in 1980 when Reagan took on Carter a strong plurality of born again voters identified with the Democratic Party (48 percent). But four years later in 1984, when President Reagan cruised to a second term, the percentage of born again Democrats dropped to 31 percent and Republican identifiers accounted for a 40 percent plurality. Since the mid-1990s, a majority of born again white southerners have identified with the GOP, while in 2012, as Figure 7.15 shows, the percentage of born again Democrats reached its nadir (13 percent).

Lastly, Figure 7.16 shows the Republican and Democratic percentage of the two-party presidential vote cast by white born again southerners from 1980 to 2012. These data provide another instance in which voting behavior is a strong leading

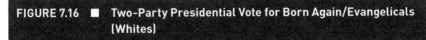

FIGURE 7.16 ■ Two-Party Presidential Vote for Born Again/Evangelicals (Whites)

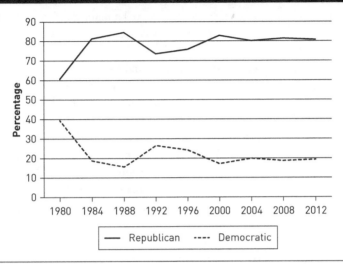

Source: National exit polls from 1980 to 2008; CCES data in 2012.

Notes: Data from 1980 to 2008 are from national exit polls; question asks "born again" for 1980, 1984, 1992, 2004, 2008; question asks "evangelical Christian/fundamentalist" in 1988; question asks if Respondent is "part of Religious Right movement" in 1996 and 2000. CCES data in 2012, and the question asks "born again" (self-reported voters).

indicator of partisan change. In 1980, when born again Democrats were a substantial 48 percent plurality of the white evangelical electorate, 61 percent of born again voters backed Reagan. In the elections since, only Clinton managed to keep the born again Republican presidential vote under 80 percent. African Americans are undeniably the most loyal Democratic group within the southern and national electorate. By contrast, with respect to the Republican coalition, born again/evangelical voters come the closest to rivaling African Americans according to the lopsided support they render to GOP candidates.

SUMMARY

This chapter began with a discussion of the role of issues in shaping political behavior. It was argued that only a small segment of the electorate actually votes in response to the specifics of policy prescriptions; instead, most rely on cues and shortcuts to register their preferences. Party identification is the most important and pervasive cue/shortcut in the American electoral environment, and because the parties have undergone an ideologically driven polarization it is easier for voters to recognize partisan differences. Although it is true that party elites exhibit a much greater degree of ideological polarization, voters are aware of the growing divide between the parties and have, in turn, sorted into the appropriate partisan camp. In the milieu of southern politics, the most enduring and salient issues are race, economics, and religion. At different times, each of these issues has exerted a marked effect on the political behavior of Dixie's citizenry and, as a consequence, altered the current and future path of the political system.

A detailed examination of race, economics, and religion was undertaken in order to demonstrate how these cardinal features of the southern electorate have influenced political behavior. Although the transformation occurred in various stages, the Republican Party has become consistently more conservative in its approach to dealing with racial, economic, and religious issues whereas the Democratic Party, in almost every instance, has found itself taking the opposing and more liberal side on each of these issues. Interestingly, for decades the overall ideological distribution of the southern electorate has remained constant, but what has changed is the increasing liberal issue positioning of the Democratic Party and the even more pronounced conservative issue positioning of the GOP. Partisan elites have provided a level of ideological clarity that makes it possible for voters to sort themselves into the more politically congruent party and this restructuring of the southern electorate, at least for now, has contributed to contemporary Republican dominance.

8 SECTIONAL AND LOCATIONAL DIFFERENCES

I t matters where one lives. Such a simple statement can have profound effects on political behavior and hence electoral outcomes. During the Democratic Solid South era, one of the main pillars propping up the one-party political system was an extreme form of malapportionment that directly favored the Democratic politicians of the black-belt counties and their Democratic allies representing similar grossly underpopulated rural communities. Although federal and state constitutions prescribe the task of periodic reapportionment, and with it the redistricting of political boundaries to accommodate changes to congressional and state legislative district populations, in most southern states this exercise was not performed until the U.S. Supreme Court enforced compliance through its momentous "one person, one vote" ruling in the 1962 case of *Baker v. Carr* (see chapter 4).

Because urban populations were not reallocated and dispersed via redistricting, with the passage of time these metropolitan constituencies grew at a much greater rate than their rural, primarily black-belt-centered counterparts. By concentrating urban populations in a much smaller number of districts, urban political representation, and by extension the political clout of urban politicians, was greatly diminished. Consider Table 8.1, which shows both the population ratio of the largest versus smallest state legislative district in each southern state in 1960 and the minimum percentage of each state's population in 1955 needed to elect a simple majority of the state house and state senate. Florida will be highlighted because the Sunshine State was the worst offender in state legislative malapportionment. In the state house in 1960, the largest district contained more than one hundred times (108.7) more constituents than the least populated district. Likewise, the state senate's largest district had 98 times more inhabitants than the least populous district. In terms of apportionment, this meant that about 17 percent of Florida's total population was enough to seat a majority of lawmakers in both the state house and state senate![1] As H. C. Nixon (1948, 412) put it, "The typical southern legislature . . . is chiefly a body of Democratic, small-town or rural, white men, a majority of whom represent a minority of the population of the state."

Although not nearly as malapportioned as state legislative districts, southern congressional districts were also far from equal in their number of constituents.[2]

TABLE 8.1 ■ Malapportionment in Southern State Legislatures				
	Population Ratio		1955 Apportionment	
State	State House	State Senate	State House	State Senate
Alabama	15.6	41.2	27.2	28.2
Arkansas	6.4	2.3	37.5	47.0
Florida	108.7	98.0	17.2	17.7
Georgia	98.8	42.6	26.3	26.9
Louisiana	17.4	8.0	25.6	34.1
Mississippi	16.7	8.8	32.7	34.6
North Carolina	19.0	6.0	30.2	40.1
South Carolina	3.1	25.1	46.7	26.6
Tennessee	23.0	6.0	30.1	33.3
Texas	6.7	9.4	39.9	36.8
Virginia	7.1	5.5	43.7	43.9

Source: Data compiled by the author from Table 2.1 presented by Bullock (2010, 30–31).

Notes: Population ratio is the largest district population divided by the smallest district population in the 1960 Census, as calculated by David and Eisenberg (1961). As stated by Bullock (2010, 31), the 1955 Apportionment measure is the "minimum percentage of the population needed to elect a majority of the chamber using the apportionment plan in place following the 1950 Census."

Table 8.2 presents total district populations for the largest and smallest districts, this corresponding ratio, and the correlation between total district population and urban district population for each southern state based on 1960 Census data. Once again Florida is notable because, out of a total of eight U.S. House districts, it had the largest in the South (982,968 residents). With six total congressional districts, Arkansas contained Dixie's least populous (182,314 inhabitants). The motivation for the overrepresentation of small-town, rural, white, Democratic, southern state lawmakers to not redraw district boundaries becomes obvious based on the correlations shown in the last column of the table. The positive relationship between total district population and urban district population is statistically significant in every southern state but Arkansas. South-wide, this correlation is almost a perfect 1-to-1 relationship, meaning that more populated districts almost always contain more urban constituencies.

The Lone Star State contains the second-most urban population (behind Florida) and in Table 8.2, in 1960, it possessed the highest ratio (4.40) of largest-to-smallest congressional district population in the South's most numerous U.S. House

TABLE 8.2 ■ Largest and Smallest Southern Congressional Districts in 1960 and Correlation between Total Population and Urban Population

State	Largest	Smallest	Ratio	Correlation Urban
Alabama (9)	634,864	236,216	2.69	+0.99***
Arkansas (6)	360,183	182,314	1.98	+0.28
Florida (8)	982,968	239,992	4.11	+0.89***
Georgia (10)	823,680	272,154	3.03	+0.99***
Louisiana (8)	536,029	263,850	2.03	+0.71*
Mississippi (6)	460,100	237,887	1.93	+0.76*
North Carolina (12)	487,159	253,511	1.92	+0.62**
South Carolina (6)	531,555	272,220	1.95	+0.77*
Tennessee (9)	627,019	223,387	2.81	+0.67**
Texas (22)	951,527	216,371	4.40	+0.99***
Virginia (10)	539,618	312,890	1.72	+0.58*
South (106)	982,968 (FL)	182,314 (AR)	5.39	+0.99***

Sources: District population data are from the 1960 decennial census. The correlation of total population and urban population data are from the 87th Congress (1961–1962) file created by E. Scott Adler and made available on his website: https://sites.google.com/a/colorado.edu/adler-scott/data/congressional-district-data.

Notes: The number in parentheses next to each state is the total U.S. House districts. The correlation coefficients are significant at the following levels: * = $p < .10$, ** = $p < .05$, *** = $p < .01$ (two-tailed). See the discussion of bivariate correlations (like those shown here) in chapter 7.

delegation (22 districts). At this time, the smallest Texas district (216,371 persons) was represented by the longest serving U.S. House Speaker in American history: Democrat Sam Rayburn. The most populous Texas district (951,527 persons) was represented by Republican Bruce Alger, and at the time he was the only Republican member of the Texas U.S. House delegation. Figure 8.1 shows a map of Texas congressional districts in 1960, highlighting Rayburn's District 4 and Alger's neighboring District 5. The more geographically expansive but markedly less populated District 4 runs from the Red River border with Oklahoma to the south and east of the more urban and densely populated District 5. District 5's borders were equivalent to Dallas County and its burgeoning city of the same name. This example captures the significance of malapportioned southern politics in 1960, while also offering a window into the region's future. Speaker Rayburn of rural District 4 was not fond of his urbane Republican neighbor and House colleague Bruce Alger in District 5,

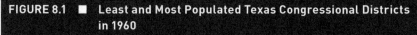

FIGURE 8.1 ■ **Least and Most Populated Texas Congressional Districts in 1960**

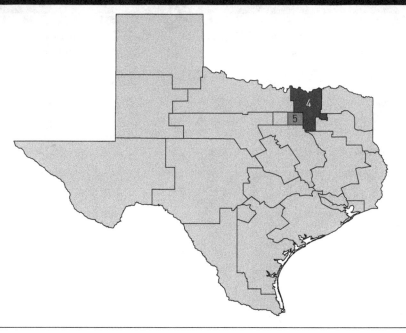

Source: Figure created by the author. District shapefiles of the 87th Congress (1960 U.S. House Elections) from the following source: Jeffrey B. Lewis, Brandon DeVine, Lincoln Pitcher, and Kenneth C. Martis. (2013) *Digital Boundary Definitions of United States Congressional Districts, 1789–2012.* Retrieved from http://cdmaps.polisci.ucla.edu [accessed October 21, 2017].

Note: District 4 was the least populated and District 5 was the most populated.

whose business background and metropolitan-based constituency would eventually represent the most common type of district for Grand Old Party (GOP) advancement in contemporary southern U.S. House elections (Black and Black 2002).

This chapter emphasizes the spatial dimension of southern politics. The manipulation of district boundaries and hence district populations can register a substantial impact on electoral outcomes. And there remains broad leeway in terms of how election district boundaries are drawn, but since the landmark reapportionment decisions handed down by the U.S. Supreme Court in the 1960s, in most states district populations (for Congress and the state legislature) are now roughly equivalent (Ansolabehere and Snyder 2008). Nevertheless, this chapter is not concerned with the electoral effects of redistricting (see chapters 5 and 10 for this kind of analysis). Instead, the focus is on demographic and political variation tied to sectional and locational differences. In this context, the term sectional refers to the longstanding subregional distinction between the states of the Deep South (Alabama, Georgia, Louisiana, Mississippi, and South Carolina) and those of the Peripheral/Rim South (Arkansas, Florida, North Carolina,

Tennessee, Texas, and Virginia). As a conceptually smaller unit of geographic aggregation, the term locational refers specifically to the relative density of populations. Thus, location is considered with respect to either an urban/rural categorization or a three-prong classification of residents inhabiting an urban, suburban, or rural place.

The chapter proceeds as follows. The next section documents the growing urbanization of southern states and counties. Next, the enduring subregional division between the Deep and Rim South is assessed over a lengthy period of time and with respect to white voting behavior across various offices in recent elections. Then, locational differences are evaluated over time and through the lens of racial/ethnic and partisan differences. Finally, voter preferences are analyzed with respect to locational differences. The chapter concludes with some final thoughts regarding the role of place in shaping southern politics.

SOUTHERN URBANIZATION

In *Southern Politics in State and Nation,* V. O. Key (1949, 85) examined 1940 Census data to show that only Florida had a state population more urban (55.1 percent) than rural, and more than 1 out of every 7 residents (16.1 percent) still lived on a farm, which was a rate lower than twice that of the next state (Texas, with a 33.7 percent farm population). Table 8.3 shows the percentage urban/rural population of each

TABLE 8.3 ■ The Rising Southern Urban Population			
State	1950: Urban–Rural %	2000: Urban–Rural %	2010: Urban–Rural %
Alabama	44–**56**	55–45	59–41
Arkansas	33–**67**	53–47	56–44
Florida	65–35	89–11	91–9
Georgia	45–**55**	72–28	75–25
Louisiana	55–45	73–27	73–27
Mississippi	28–**72**	49–**51**	49–**51**
North Carolina	34–**66**	60–40	66–34
South Carolina	37–**63**	60–40	66–34
Tennessee	44–**56**	64–36	66–34
Texas	63–37	83–17	85–15
Virginia	47–**53**	73–27	75–25
Deep South	43–**57**	64–36	67–33
Rim South	51–49	77–23	80–20
South	48–**52**	73–27	77–23

Source: All data are from the corresponding decennial census (1950, 2000, 2010).

Note: Data are in bold where the state population is majority rural.

southern state, according to southern subregion (Deep versus Rim), and for the entire South, based on data from the 1950, 2000, and 2010 decennial censuses. The table shows the percent urban followed by a dash and then the percent rural. Further, rural percentages are highlighted in bold where they exceed 50 percent.

In 1950, Florida, Texas, and Louisiana were the only states with majority urban populations. The Deep South was 57 percent rural, whereas the Rim South, thanks in part to the presence of Texas, was slightly more urban (51 percent) than rural. And for the entire region, the South was 52 percent rural in 1950. At the dawn of the new century, Mississippi remained the only southern state with a majority rural population (51 percent) and this condition held ten years later in 2010. By 2010, more than three-quarters (77 percent) of the southern population resided in an urban area and both subregions were majority urban (67 percent urban in the Deep South versus 80 percent urban in the Rim South), but interestingly, the urban gap between the Rim and Deep South went from 8 points in 1950 to 13 points in 2010.[3] The mega-states of Florida and Texas are the pacesetters with respect to their overwhelmingly urban populations (91 and 85 percent, respectively), whereas the two least populous southern states of Arkansas and Mississippi are also not surprisingly the least urban at 56 and 49 percent, respectively.

Figure 8.2 displays a county level map of the South in 1950, with the percent urban delineated in varying shades of gray for three intervals of urban: (1) 0–20 percent, (2) > 20–50 percent, and (3) > 50 percent. Going from states to counties, it is still evident to the naked eye that the Sunshine State and the Lone Star State contain the most urban populations. Outside of Florida and Texas, majority urban counties are considerably scarcer. Indeed, in the middle of the twentieth century, most of the majority urban southern populations were confined to the counties or cluster of counties containing Dixie's major cities (e.g., Atlanta, Birmingham, Charlotte, Memphis, New Orleans) or the smattering of smaller counties experiencing urbanization despite not being part of a major metropolitan area (like some of the counties in middle Georgia, south of Atlanta). In 1950, 17.6 percent of the South's counties were majority urban.

A sea change in urbanization is highlighted in Figure 8.3, which shows the county level percent urban in 2010, while employing the same shading for counties with urban populations of 0–20 percent, > 20–50 percent, and > 50 percent. Florida and Texas easily remain the southern leaders in urban population. The lower two-thirds of the Florida peninsula is almost completely majority urban at the county level. There remain several North Florida counties that are still majority rural in 2010. Despite the vast expanses of territory in Texas, among its South-leading 254 counties, in every section of the state there reside majority urban counties. Even among the relatively small populations located in the Texas Panhandle there are majority urban counties. To a much greater extent than in the 1950s, the rise of southern urbanization displays a clear clustering pattern in growing metropolitan centers like the counties of Central Texas running from north of Austin (Travis County)

FIGURE 8.2 ■ Urban Percentage of Southern County Residents in 1950

Urban County Percentage

- 0–20
- >20–50
- >50

Source: Figure created from 1950 Census data and a 1950 county shapefile available from the National Historical Geographic Information System (NHGIS) website (https://www.nhgis.org/) [accessed October 21, 2017].

FIGURE 8.3 ■ Urban Percentage of Southern County Residents in 2010

Urban County Percentage

- 0–20
- >20–50
- >50

Source: Figure created from 2010 Census data and a 2010 county shapefile available from the National Historical Geographic Information System (NHGIS) website (https://www.nhgis.org/) (accessed October 21, 2017).

down to San Antonio (Bexar County); the greater New Orleans and Baton Rouge areas of Louisiana; Little Rock in Central Arkansas, the Nashville area in Central Tennessee; the counties encapsulating Richmond in Virginia; the Jackson metropolitan area in Mississippi; the clustering of counties in the Charleston, South Carolina, Lowcountry; and of course the explosion of majority urban counties in the greater Atlanta, Georgia, area. In 2010, 38.1 percent of the South's counties were majority urban, a 116 percent increase over 1950.

Perhaps as much as any other factor, the transition from a Democratic Solid South to a contemporary Republican-dominant political system was made possible by urbanization. The "Old South" that conservative white Democrats controlled was composed of overwhelmingly small-town, rural constituencies. Obtaining GOP electoral traction was much easier, especially initially, by cutting into Democratic margins in urban settings with growing white middle-class populations more receptive to the Republican message of fiscal conservatism and economic advancement through individual achievement—the kind of mindset that flourishes in places like the Rim South's Dallas-Fort Worth metroplex. With respect to southern subregions, urbanization has been much more rapid in the Peripheral South states and this is one of the primary reasons why Republican inroads were established earlier there. Nonetheless, with regard to explaining the persistent political differences between the Deep and Rim South, there is much more to the story than urbanization, and the next section tackles this subject.[4]

DEEP VERSUS PERIPHERAL SOUTH: AN ENDURING DIVIDE

Contrary to a scholarly pronouncement that the political distinction between the Deep and Peripheral South is merely a "myth" (see Shafer and Johnston 2006), it is anything but; the political differences found in the cardinal sectional division of Dixie are palpable and enduring. As will be shown, the voter preferences of southern whites are much more divergent in terms of subregion (Deep and Rim South) than they are with respect to location (urban, suburban, and rural). In various passages of *Southern Politics in State and Nation*, Key (1949, 5) emphasizes the primary shaper of southern political behavior:

> The character of the politics of individual states will vary roughly with the Negro proportion of the population. The truth of that proposition will be abundantly illustrated as the story progresses.

To this day, it remains the case that every Deep South state contains a higher percentage of African Americans (30 percent black) than every Rim South state (16 percent black).[5] This simple subregional distinction in the size of the black constituency, is the fundamental driver of the evolution of two-party competition in the Deep and Peripheral South (McKee 2017).

Assessing southern politics from the time of V. O. Key (1949) up through the mid-1980s, in their seminal work *Politics and Society in the South,* Earl and Merle Black (1987) identify the leading correlates of Republican growth in southern elections. They make it clear that over the period they analyze, Republican electoral gains came at a much faster rate in the Rim South because of its history of mountain Republicanism (particularly in East Tennessee, Western North Carolina, and Southwestern Virginia), greater urbanization and northern in-migration, and a burgeoning white, college-educated middle class. These were the main ingredients for the rise of southern Republicans in subpresidential politics from the 1950s through the 1980s (Black and Black 1987, 2002).[6]

As demonstrated and explained by Black and Black (1987), after passage of the 1964 Civil Rights Act and the 1965 Voting Rights Act, black southerners wanted nothing to do with the GOP. White southern Republicans obliged by writing off black votes and instead focused almost exclusively on building their party brand by courting whites. Initially, this strategy was more successful in the Rim South because the lower percentage of overwhelmingly Democratic, black voters meant that it took a lower share of the white vote for Republicans to be victorious. The New Deal class cleavage in national politics dating back to the 1930s, in which the Democratic Party became the home of the have-littles and have-nots versus the middle- and upper-class Republican opposition, finally made an impression in Dixie in the 1950s when the Republican Eisenhower broke through the Democratic Solid South in his two successful presidential runs in 1952 and 1956. This early GOP success in southern presidential elections was based primarily on appeals to class as opposed to race, and for the first time since the days of Reconstruction, the Republican Party showed vigorous signs of life, as multitudes of middle- and upper-class whites in the growing urban centers found disproportionally in the Peripheral South, cast their votes for Eisenhower (Bartley and Graham 1975; also see the discussion in chapter 7).

Thus, as the New Deal class divide finally penetrated the South, Republican gains were mainly associated with the natural fit between a more economically conservative GOP and a growing white middle class whose upward mobility aligned better with the political philosophy of the erstwhile moribund Republican Party. An insightful passage by Black and Black (1987, 313) captures the leading perception of the southern GOP, which prevailed even into the 1980s:

> Southern Republicanism increasingly epitomizes the values and beliefs of the most affluent white southerners, as well as those who aspire to such status and rewards. Though its mass base includes some working-class southerners, in terms of real influence and control the GOP is preeminently the vehicle of upper-middle-class, well-educated, conservative whites. Southern Republicanism is the party of *Southern Living,* if that magazine

could be imagined to possess an explicit political philosophy. The appeal of the southern version of the American Dream is palpable, but the party's firm grounding in the upper middle class also entails serious risks and liabilities for southern Republicanism as a potential majority party.

The caveat at the end of the aforementioned quote, regarding the possibility of the southern GOP narrowcasting itself by not broadening its coalition of white voters to include many of those lower down the economic scale has, hence and heretofore, been successfully avoided.

The 1964 presidential election turned explicitly on the salient and volatile issue of civil rights. With the national partisan reversal on this issue (Carmines and Stimson 1989)—as the Republican presidential nominee, Senator Goldwater embraced a conservative position (voting against the 1964 Civil Rights Act), whereas the Democratic Party under President Johnson championed black legal equality— there was now not only an economic appeal, but a clear race-based appeal for white southerners to align with the Republican Party. Of course, with respect to voting behavior, Deep South whites defected in droves for the Republican Goldwater in 1964, and despite President Johnson winning in a landslide, Goldwater managed to carry his home state of Arizona and all five Deep South states, which were clearly ignited by the issue of race. Henceforth, in two-party presidential contests, a majority of white southerners have supported the Republican nominee (Black and Black 1987, 1992, 2002). But when a third-party candidate emerged and appealed to racial conservatism, like American Independent Party and Alabama Governor George Wallace did in 1968, he garnered considerable Deep South backing. In hindsight, the 1968 presidential contest was a harbinger for the contemporary southern GOP's remarkably successful coalition of voters.

In 1968, the Republican Nixon's greatest appeal was among the "*Southern Living*" white voters, whereas Wallace drew most of his votes from the white working class. Nixon carried only one Deep South state in 1968 (South Carolina) and principally because the recent party switcher (in 1964) and most influential politician in the Palmetto State, Republican Senator Thurmond, favored him. The raw, racial rhetoric and economic populism of Wallace carried him to victory in the rest of the Deep South (Alabama, Georgia, Louisiana, and Mississippi) and Arkansas. Nixon took the Rim South states of Florida, North Carolina, Tennessee, and Virginia, while the Democrat and former Vice President under President Johnson, Hubert Humphrey, only managed to win Texas (thanks to Johnson). The overwhelmingly white southern vote that split between Nixon and Wallace comprised just the kind of winning combination the GOP needed and eventually obtained, throughout most of the South in subsequent presidential contests and eventually in various down-ballot races. As characterized by Black and Black (1987, 289), the winning Republican coalition consists of "the Nixon voters and the Wallace voters, the educated conservatives and the uneducated conservatives, the uptown church members and the fundamentalists, the middle-class conservatives and the working-class conservatives." In short, the southern GOP had consummated the political marriage between whites residing in the penthouse and socializing at the country club with whites living in modest small-town and suburban settings where gatherings take place at the roadhouse and the sports bar.

By widening its appeal to capture the support of both economic and cultural/racial conservatives, the southern GOP eventually became formidable in both the Rim and Deep South. And because of the primacy of the race issue, now the Republican Party is stronger in the Deep South than in its Peripheral South neighbor. Figure 8.4 nicely tracks the long-term ascendancy of the southern GOP by presenting a ten-year moving average of the Republican index of party strength from 1950 to 2016. Importantly, because the Deep South immediately expressed a greater affinity for Republican presidential nominees starting in 1964 (in two-party matchups), the index shown in the figure does not include presidential returns; rather, it consists of votes cast for governor, U.S. senator, and U.S. house representative, with each office constituting a third of the computed index (see the note under the figure). In Figure 8.4, the GOP index is shown for the entire South and separately for each subregion.

True to the narrative, for most of the time spanning the 1950s to 1980s, the southern GOP is notably more successful in high-profile subpresidential contests in the Rim South. But subregional electoral parity manifests in the 1990s as the GOP index for the Deep and Rim South converges. Around 2006, the subregional dynamic alters so that the Republican Party is now electorally stronger in the Deep South. It took decades for this latest development to materialize and primarily because below the presidential level conservative Democratic officeholders in the Deep South proved much more resistant to conceding the race issue to their likewise racially conservative Republican opponents (Black and Black 2012). Over time, however, these conservative Deep South Democrats either moderated their positions to suit a growing black electorate, were defeated by more racially liberal Democrats in primary contests, retired, switched parties, or lost to the increasing number of quality Republican candidates who took conservative positions on race and economics (and religion too).

Based on the very large samples in the Cooperative Congressional Election Study (CCES) surveys administered for the 2006–2016 elections, the difference in white voting behavior according to subregion is palpable. Table 8.4 shows the percentage of whites voting Republican for President, Governor, U.S. Senate, and U.S. House, on the basis of southern subregion. From 2006 to 2016, in every election year (and contest) a higher percentage of Deep South whites voted Republican. In fact, out of 18 subregional comparisons across these four offices, over this decade, in only two instances (the U.S. House in 2008 and the U.S. Senate in 2010) is the subregional gap in Republican voting under double digits (+6 points more Republican in the Deep South). In 2016, more than three-quarters of Deep

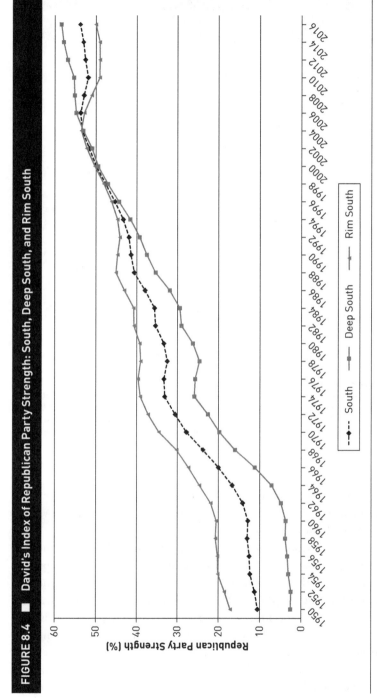

FIGURE 8.4 ■ David's Index of Republican Party Strength: South, Deep South, and Rim South

- - ◆ - - South   ■ Deep South   ▲ Rim South

Source: Data compiled and computed by the author and Trey Hood at the University of Georgia.

Notes: The percentage of Republican Party strength is based on David's (1972) Composite B Index, which is the Republican percentage of the vote summed in thirds for gubernatorial, U.S. Senate, and U.S. House contests [percentage Republican Vote [Gubernatorial Election] + percentage Republican Vote [Senate Election] + percentage Republican Vote [Average Republican U.S. House Vote]] / 3. In this case [for David's Index], the Republican vote is out of all votes cast, not just the two-party vote. The data shown in the figure are based on a ten-year moving average in order to smooth out any short-term fluctuations that may disproportionally favor one party.

TABLE 8.4 ■ Republican Percentage of the Two-Party Vote Cast by Deep and Rim South Whites in the 2006–2016 Elections

Office	Subregion	2006	2008	2010	2012	2014	2016
President	Deep	—	75	—	73	—	77
	Rim		61		59		63
	Difference		+14		+14		+14
Governor	Deep	67	—	73	—	75	—
	Rim	53	61**	58	68**	65	54**
	Difference	+14		+15		+10	
U.S. Senate	Deep	75*	73	79	79*	79	76
	Rim	53	58	73	57	66	61
	Difference	+22	+15	+6	+22	+13	+15
U.S. House	Deep	66	67	82	75	80	77
	Rim	54	61	68	63	69	64
	Difference	+12	+6	+14	+12	+11	+13

Source: All data are from the Cooperative Congressional Election Study (2006, 2008, 2010, 2012, 2014, and 2016 common content CCES surveys).

Notes: Data show the Republican share of the two-party vote cast for a given office (not taking into account whether a particular race was contested by both major parties). *Only accounts for Mississippi voters; the only Deep South state with a U.S. Senate contest in 2006 and 2012. **Only accounts for North Carolina voters because no other southern state holds its gubernatorial election in a presidential year. The "Difference" is simply the Deep South share of the Republican vote minus the Rim South share of the Republican vote for a specific office (e.g., the subregional difference for the U.S. House in 2016 was +13 percentage points).

South whites voted Republican for President, U.S. Senate, and U.S. House; while the highest rate of Republican voting among their Rim South counterparts was 64 percent in U.S. House elections.[7]

At the time of this writing, the growing racial and ethnic diversity of the Rim South electorate (see chapter 9) and this subregion's politicians (see chapter 5), finds a clear contrast with the overriding black and Democratic, versus white and Republican, politics of the Deep South. African Americans comprise a *majority* of the *minority* population of Democratic state lawmakers in every Deep South legislature (state house and state senate), all but one governor is a Republican, all but one non-judicial statewide officeholder is a Republican, every U.S. House member is either a white Republican (30 total) or a black Democrat (8 total), all but one U.S. Senator is a Republican (including African American South Carolina Senator Tim Scott), and the last time a Deep South state gave its electoral votes to a Democratic presidential nominee was two decades ago when Arkansan Bill Clinton won Louisiana in 1996. As summarized by McKee (2010, 201):

> Relative to the Peripheral South, given the greater presence of African Americans in the Deep South, race always was and still remains a greater issue to Deep South whites. It is a primary reason why racial polarization in voting behavior is consistently more pronounced in the Deep South.

LOCATION AND A CHANGING SOUTH, 1950–2000

To this point, location has only been examined in a binary fashion, showing the percentage urban/rural for the entire South, its subregions, and counties. The urbanization of Dixie since 1950 has been very impressive, and it is a pattern that is likely to persist far into the future. But the dichotomous classification between urban and rural overlooks considerable political variation within urban populations and therefore it is useful to differentiate a step further between urban and suburban residents. From the 1950s (starting in 1952) until 2000, the American National Election Studies (ANES) categorized respondents as living in a city (urban), suburban, or small-town/rural setting. Before proceeding, there is admittedly some discretion in these locational categories, but in terms of population density the aim is to account for possible differences in the political behavior of those living in the most concentrated areas (urban), those somewhere in the middle (suburbia), versus those residents of the sparsest locations (rural). Additionally, different data sources (like exit polls and the surveys from the Pew Research Center) employ somewhat different definitions for urban, suburban, and rural settings, and in comparison, the ANES data display a relatively greater share of rural respondents.

Figure 8.5 charts the percentage of southerners living in urban, suburban, and rural areas by decade, starting in the 1950s and ending with the last decade of the twentieth century (1992–2000). It is evident from the parsing of the three-category ANES definition of residential density, that the rural classification is defined fairly liberally, given its substantial size compared to urban and suburban dwellers. Nevertheless, the locational trends are in the anticipated direction, with rural residents declining and suburban and urban denizens increasing. From 1952 to 1960, more than two-thirds (68 percent) of southerners resided in a small-town/rural location, 23 percent in the suburbs, and only 10 percent in a central city (urban setting). Four decades hence, from 1992 to 2000, the share of rural residents has dropped 23 points to a 45-percent locational plurality, and the greatest gain is among urban residents, who now comprise 26 percent of southerners. Suburbanites exhibit a more modest 6-point long-term increase, going from 23 percent to 29 percent of the southern population.

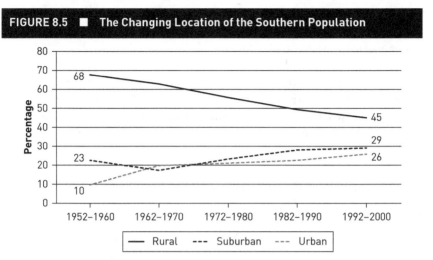

FIGURE 8.5 ■ The Changing Location of the Southern Population

Source: Data are from the American National Election Studies cumulative file.

Table 8.5 displays the two-party identification (ID) of southerners from 1952 to 2000, based on location. In addition, the Republican share of the two-party presidential vote is displayed according to location from the 1950s to 2000. Starting with party ID and location, in the earliest decade (1952–1960), there is no discernible difference in the share of Democratic identifiers according to location. Conversely though, among GOP affiliates, they are more prevalent in suburban (20 percent) and rural (18 percent) locations than in urban (6 percent) areas. Four decades later, only in urban settings do Democrats remain the majority of identifiers, at 51 percent in 1992–2000. In suburban and rural locations, Democratic ID has essentially cratered; a 31-point decline among rural residents (from 68 percent to 37 percent) and a 38-point decline in the suburbs, where there are more Republicans at 30 percent. From 1992 to 2000, Democrats still retain a double-digit identification advantage in rural locations (+13 points) and a substantial 32-point margin in urban settings.

The bottom three rows of Table 8.5 assess how location translates into Republican presidential preferences. Interestingly, among urban voters, even though Democratic ID has declined from 68 percent in the 1950s to 51 percent in the 1990s, the share of the GOP presidential vote goes from a 55-percent majority to a decided 29-percent Republican minority share of the two-party vote. Although not to the same extent, the Republican vote in southern suburbia was quite a bit higher in the 1950s (62 percent) than in the 1990s (53 percent). It is only among rural voters where a slight uptick can be found in Republican presidential voting from the 1950s (42 percent Republican) to the 1990s (46 percent Republican).

TABLE 8.5 ■ Southern Party Identification and Republican Presidential Vote by Location

Location	Party Identification	1952–1960	1962–1970	1972–1980	1982–1990	1992–2000
Urban	Democrats	68	56	57	48	51
	Republicans	6	11	9	16	19
	Difference	+62	+45	+48	+32	+32
Suburban	Democrats	66	52	41	39	28
	Republicans	20	19	18	23	30
	Difference	+46	+33	+23	+16	–2
Rural	Democrats	68	61	46	47	37
	Republicans	18	16	20	19	24
	Difference	+50	+45	+26	+28	+13

Location	Presidential Vote	1952–1960	1962–1970	1972–1980	1982–1990	1992–2000
Urban	Republican (%)	55	41	33	39	29
Suburban	Republican (%)	62	54	60	65	53
Rural	Republican (%)	42	37	61	52	46

Source: Data are from the American National Election Studies cumulative file.

Notes: Democratic and Republican identification is the percentage of each party affiliate out of all respondents claiming a major party identification or political independence (respondents who lean toward the Democratic/Republican Party are classified as independents). Republican percentage of the presidential vote is out of the total votes cast for the major parties (Democratic and Republican nominees). The "Difference" is the percentage of Democratic identifiers minus the percentage of Republican identifiers.

Disparities between the share of major party identifiers and the GOP percentage of the presidential vote are partly explained by differences in the racial/ethnic composition of residents in urban, suburban, and rural areas. The ANES samples are only large enough to examine southern white respondents separately, but this is a revealing exercise. Table 8.6 presents the same analysis as that shown in Table 8.5, except the data are limited to white southerners. In the waning days of the Solid Democratic South (1952–1960), there is not much variation in white Democratic identification on the basis of location, but white Republicans are a rare species in urban settings (just 4 percent). By the 1990s, white affiliation with the Democratic Party has plunged across the board: a 35-point drop among urbanites, a 39-point decline for rural residents, and a whopping 44-point dive in the case of suburban dwellers. By looking only at white southerners, irrespective of location, they are no longer anywhere close to majority

TABLE 8.6 ■ Party Identification and Republican Presidential Vote by Location for White Southerners						
Location	**Party Identification**	**1952–1960**	**1962–1970**	**1972–1980**	**1982–1990**	**1992–2000**
Urban	Democrats	70	47	50	32	35
	Republicans	4	13	13	24	32
	Difference	+66	+34	+37	+8	+3
Suburban	Democrats	64	45	39	34	20
	Republicans	21	21	20	27	37
	Difference	+43	+24	+19	+7	−17
Rural	Democrats	69	58	44	42	30
	Republicans	16	17	22	23	30
	Difference	+53	+41	+22	+19	0
Location	**Presidential Vote**	**1952–1960**	**1962–1970**	**1972–1980**	**1982–1990**	**1992–2000**
Urban	Republican (%)	57	60	54	65	53
Suburban	Republican (%)	62	65	69	75	65
Rural	Republican (%)	43	44	67	67	56

Source: Data are from the American National Election Studies cumulative file.

Notes: Democratic and Republican identification is the percentage of each party affiliate out of all respondents claiming a major party identification or political independence (respondents who lean toward the Democratic/Republican Party are classified as independents). Republican percentage of the presidential vote is out of the total votes cast for the major parties (Democratic and Republican nominees). The "Difference" is the percentage of Democratic identifiers minus the percentage of Republican identifiers.

Democratic in their party identification by the last decade of the twentieth century. Even in urban areas, the margin in Democratic identification in the 1990s is a mere +3 points; whereas in suburbia the Republican affiliation advantage is +17 points; and in rural places—the backbone of the old Democratic Solid South—by the 1990s Democrats and Republicans were perfectly split at 30 percent apiece.

The bottom three rows of Table 8.6 display results that are much more intuitive than those shown at the bottom of Table 8.5 because white voting behavior is considerably more partial to Republican presidential nominees. When only white urban voters are evaluated, there is only a 4-point drop in the GOP presidential vote from the 1950s (57 percent) to the 1990s (53 percent). Recall the drop over the same period among all urbanites in Table 8.5 was from 55 percent to 29 percent Republican. In suburban locales, the white Republican presidential vote increases slightly by 3 points from 62 percent in the 1950s to 65 percent in the 1990s. Lastly, whereas a majority of rural whites favored Democratic presidential nominees in the 1950s, their shift toward the GOP in the 1990s has been the most impressive (+13 points), and since the 1970s (1972–1980), white southerners in all three locational categories have cast a majority Republican presidential vote. Singling out southern white voters in presidential elections highlights their much greater Republican support, no matter whether these individuals live in an urban, suburban, or rural setting.

LOCATION IN THE NEW MILLENNIUM

Unfortunately, after 2000, the ANES no longer classified survey respondents based on whether they resided in an urban, suburban, or rural place. More recently (beginning in 2000), however, the Pew Research Center has administered numerous polls of the American public with sample sizes that are typically larger than the ANES and contain a locational classification for respondent residence (urban, suburban, rural).[8] For most of these surveys there are enough respondents to examine the location of racial/ethnic groups in the South, though it is still wise (based on the number of cases) to confine an examination of location and party ID to just white southerners. The data in this section come from Pew Research Center surveys conducted either in October or November of an election year, running from 2002 to 2016 (see the source note under Figure 8.6).

Similar to Figure 8.5, Figure 8.6 shows the percentage of southerners residing in urban, suburban, and rural locations from 2002 to 2016. These data show that suburban settings are predominant, with 49 percent of southerners in suburbia in

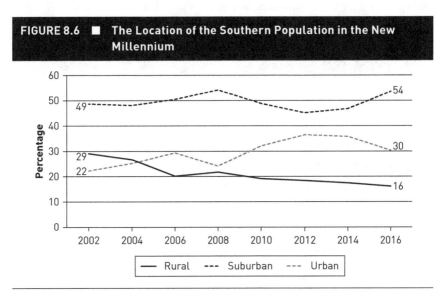

FIGURE 8.6 ■ The Location of the Southern Population in the New Millennium

Sources: Data are from the following Pew Research Center surveys: November 2002 Election Weekend Survey, Election Weekend 2004, October 2006 Survey on Electoral Competition, Mid October 2008 Political Survey, October 2010 Political Survey, November 2012 Election Weekend Survey, October 2014 Political Survey, and October 2016 Political Survey.

2002, and a 54 percent majority of suburbanites in 2016. As mentioned, because of differences across data sources with respect to how locations are defined, the Pew surveys are not comparable with the ANES data shown previously. Nevertheless, the downward trend in rural residents persists from 2002 to 2016. In 2002, 29 percent of southerners lived in a rural setting, but by 2016 rural dwellers account for 16 percent of the southern population. In contrast, the share of urban southerners goes from 22 percent in 2002 to 30 percent in 2016.

Race and Ethnicity by Location

There is notable variation in the location of the major racial/ethnic groups in southern politics: whites, blacks, and Latinos. Figure 8.7 displays the distribution of white southerners according to location, from 2002 to 2016. Reflecting the overall locational pattern, most southern whites inhabit suburban settings; 52 percent in 2002 and 56 percent in 2016. Once again there is a pronounced decline in the percentage of rural residents, going from 30 percent in 2002 to 19 percent in 2016. The drop in rural denizens is partially offset by the increase in urban white southerners who go from 18 percent in 2002 to 26 percent in 2016.

The locational pattern among African Americans (see Figure 8.8) looks very different. Though it is likely a smaller sample size for blacks that partially explains the bunching of the data in 2002 when African Americans show a roughly equal propensity to reside in urban, suburban, and rural places, the full extent of the longitudinal coverage reveals a discernible pattern. In keeping with the general trend, and also found among whites, there is a marked decline in the share of African Americans living in

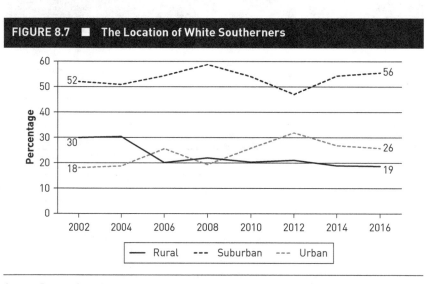

FIGURE 8.7   ■   The Location of White Southerners

Sources: Data are from the following Pew Research Center surveys: November 2002 Election Weekend Survey, Election Weekend 2004, October 2006 Survey on Electoral Competition, Mid October 2008 Political Survey, October 2010 Political Survey, November 2012 Election Weekend Survey, October 2014 Political Survey, and October 2016 Political Survey.

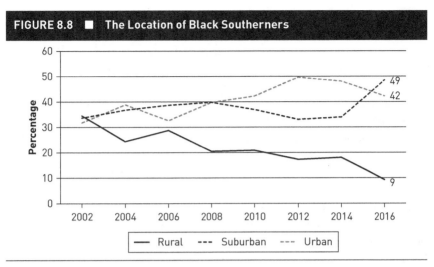

FIGURE 8.8 ■ The Location of Black Southerners

Sources: Data are from the following Pew Research Center surveys: November 2002 Election Weekend Survey, Election Weekend 2004, October 2006 Survey on Electoral Competition, Mid October 2008 Political Survey, October 2010 Political Survey, November 2012 Election Weekend Survey, October 2014 Political Survey, and October 2016 Political Survey.

rural locations, going from a slight 35-percent plurality in 2002 to an obvious 9-percent minority in 2016. Since 2002, most African Americans reside in either urban or suburban places. Whereas a clear majority of whites live in suburbia, in 2016 blacks show a fairly equal distribution of urban (42 percent) and suburban residents (49 percent).

The locational pattern of southern Latinos (see Figure 8.9) has come to look fairly similar to that of African Americans. Latinos are the only group among the

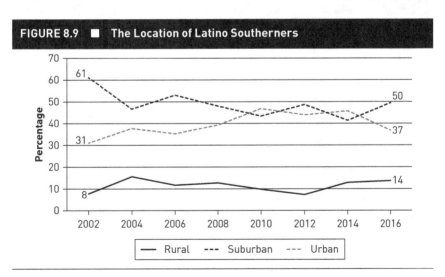

FIGURE 8.9 ■ The Location of Latino Southerners

Sources: Data are from the following Pew Research Center surveys: November 2002 Election Weekend Survey, Election Weekend 2004, October 2006 Survey on Electoral Competition, Mid October 2008 Political Survey, October 2010 Political Survey, November 2012 Election Weekend Survey, October 2014 Political Survey, and October 2016 Political Survey.

three examined, in which the rank-order of the locational distribution does not alter for 2002 versus 2016. In 2002, the locational distribution of southern Latinos was 61 percent suburban, 31 percent urban, and 8 percent rural. In 2016, most Latinos still reside in suburbia but their share has declined to 50 percent, while the percentages of urban (37 percent) and rural (14 percent) residents have both increased since 2002. Compared to whites and blacks, in 2002 Latinos are decidedly less prevalent in rural areas. On the other hand, it is only among Latinos that the percentage of rural dwellers actually increases; going from 8 percent in 2002 to 14 percent in 2016.

Table 8.7 takes the data displayed in the previous three figures and shows the distribution of each racial/ethnic group according to location from 2002 to 2016. The distribution of each individual racial/ethnic group across the three locations (urban, suburban, rural) sums to 100 percent. Showing the data in this fashion provides a picture of the relative distribution of each racial/ethnic group on the basis of location. Though the share of urban whites has gone up from 18 percent in 2002 to 26 percent in 2016, a relatively higher percentage of minorities reside in urban places; 37 percent of Latinos and 42 percent of African Americans in 2016. Among suburbanites, whites and Latinos are more prominent in this location as compared to blacks, going back to 2002. But by 2016, most white (56 percent), black (49 percent), and Latino (50 percent) southerners live in suburbia. Finally, the overall decline in rural residents from 2002 to 2016 figures prominently in the pronounced drop among whites

TABLE 8.7 ■ Race/Ethnicity of Southerners by Location

Location	Race/Ethnicity	2002	2004	2006	2008	2010	2012	2014	2016
Urban	Whites	18	19	26	19	26	32	27	26
	Blacks	32	39	33	40	42	50	48	42
	Latinos	31	38	35	39	47	44	46	37
Suburban	Whites	52	51	54	59	54	47	54	56
	Blacks	34	37	39	40	37	33	34	49
	Latinos	61	47	53	48	43	49	41	50
Rural	Whites	30	30	20	22	20	21	19	19
	Blacks	35	24	29	21	21	17	18	9
	Latinos	8	16	12	13	10	7	13	14

Sources: Data are from the following Pew Research Center surveys: November 2002 Election Weekend Survey, Election Weekend 2004, October 2006 Survey on Electoral Competition, Mid October 2008 Political Survey, October 2010 Political Survey, November 2012 Election Weekend Survey, October 2014 Political Survey, and October 2016 Political Survey.

(30 to 19 percent) and blacks (35 to 9 percent), while Latinos are the one group whose rural presence has grown (8 to 14 percent).

Party Identification by Location

From 2002 to 2016, the Pew surveys show an overall decline in the share of southern partisans (the percentage of Democrats and Republicans among all southerners). As displayed in Table 8.8 the percentage of urban partisans (Democrats plus Republicans) went from 80 in 2002 to 62 in 2016. The share of suburban partisans drops from 80 percent in 2002 to 63 percent in 2016, and the proportion of rural partisans goes from 70 percent in 2002 to 59 percent in 2016. Among partisans, between 2002 and 2016, there is a relatively greater decline in urban Republicans (−11 points) and suburban Republicans (−10 points) vis-à-vis urban Democrats (−7 points) and suburban Democrats (−7 points). Hence the partisan gap favoring urban Democrats has gone from +10 points in 2002 to +14 points in 2016, while the partisan advantage among suburban Republicans has been reduced from +10 points in 2002 to +7 points in 2016. Contrary to the *relative* gains in Democratic affiliates versus Republican identifiers among an overall declining proportion of urban and suburban partisans, in the shrinking rural South the GOP has made notable inroads. In 2002, the partisan gap in favor

Location	Party ID	2002	2004	2006	2008	2010	2012	2014	2016
TABLE 8.8 ■ Party Identification by Location									
Urban	Democrats	45	49	32	39	41	42	36	38
	Republicans	35	30	29	22	26	26	24	24
	Difference	+10	+19	+3	+17	+15	+16	+12	+14
Suburban	Democrats	35	27	29	29	28	28	25	28
	Republicans	45	45	35	45	36	37	37	35
	Difference	−10	−18	−6	−16	−8	−9	−12	−7
Rural	Democrats	33	36	37	29	28	34	28	19
	Republicans	37	42	33	39	28	36	36	40
	Difference	−4	−6	+4	−10	0	−2	−8	−21

Sources: Data are from the following Pew Research Center surveys: November 2002 Election Weekend Survey, Election Weekend 2004, October 2006 Survey on Electoral Competition, Mid October 2008 Political Survey, October 2010 Political Survey, November 2012 Election Weekend Survey, October 2014 Political Survey, and October 2016 Political Survey.

Note: Democratic and Republican identification is the percentage of each party affiliate out of all respondents claiming a major party identification or political independence (respondents who lean toward the Democratic/Republican Party are classified as Independents).

of Republican identifiers was +4 points, but in 2016 the share of Democratic affiliates has plummeted from a third (33 percent in 2002) to 19 percent. Over this same period, the percentage of GOP identifiers ticked up from 37 to 40 percent, which expanded the partisan gap favoring Republicans to a substantial +21 points.

With the considerable subsample of white respondents in the Pew surveys, Table 8.9 displays the party ID of white southerners by location, from 2002 to 2016. Once again there is a general decline in partisans (the percentage of Democrats and Republicans among all southerners) for each location from 2002 to 2016 (80 to 61 percent in urban areas, 80 to 64 percent in suburban locales, and 66 to 61 percent in rural places). In 2002, white Republicans generously outnumbered white Democrats in all three aforementioned locations (52 to 28 percent in urban places, 51 to 29 percent in suburban settings, and 46 to 20 percent in rural areas). Only a slight decline in urban Democrats from 2002 to 2016 (−4 points) contrasts with a marked decline in urban Republicans over this same period (−15 points), which has narrowed the GOP partisan advantage from +24 points in 2002 to +13 points in 2016. In 2016, white Republicans are more prevalent in suburban and rural locations, where the relative percentage of Democrats has declined −10 points and −9 points, respectively, in these settings from 2002 to 2016. With a smaller decline in suburban Republicans

TABLE 8.9 ■ Party Identification by Location for White Southerners									
Location	Party ID	2002	2004	2006	2008	2010	2012	2014	2016
Urban	Democrats	28	31	33	30	22	26	30	24
	Republicans	52	45	36	37	34	39	39	37
	Difference	−24	−14	−3	−7	−12	−13	−9	−13
Suburban	Democrats	29	22	21	23	22	21	20	19
	Republicans	51	52	42	51	44	46	47	45
	Difference	−22	−30	−21	−28	−22	−25	−27	−26
Rural	Democrats	20	30	24	26	15	20	18	11
	Republicans	46	48	46	46	33	47	53	50
	Difference	−26	−18	−22	−20	−18	−27	−35	−39

Sources: Data are from the following Pew Research Center surveys: November 2002 Election Weekend Survey, Election Weekend 2004, October 2006 Survey on Electoral Competition, Mid October 2008 Political Survey, October 2010 Political Survey, November 2012 Election Weekend Survey, October 2014 Political Survey, and October 2016 Political Survey.

Note: Democratic and Republican identification is the percentage of each party affiliate out of all respondents claiming a major party identification or political independence (respondents who lean toward the Democratic/Republican Party are classified as Independents).

(−6 points), in this location the GOP affiliation advantage has grown from +22 points in 2002 to +26 points in 2016. Finally, the most impressive alteration in the partisan gap has taken place among the declining population of rural white southerners. The share of rural Democrats goes from 20 percent in 2002 to 11 percent in 2016 (−9 points), while rural Republicans increase from 46 percent in 2002 to 50 percent in 2016 (+4 points), which expands the Republican affiliation margin from +26 points in 2002 to a remarkable +39 points in 2016.

Overall, from 2002 to 2016, Democrats have increased their relative partisan advantage in urban areas while cutting into the Republican partisan advantage in suburban locations. Among the declining southern rural population, the Republican partisan advantage has grown substantially. Limiting the data to whites, between 2002 and 2016, the favorable Republican margin in identifiers in urban locales has been greatly reduced. In contrast, the partisan gap in suburban places has slightly increased in favor of the GOP, while Republicans now dominate in rural areas, where they outnumbered Democrats 50 to 11 percent in 2016.

VOTER PREFERENCES BY SUBREGION AND LOCATION

This section turns to yet another data source to examine voter preferences with respect to subregion and location. Exit polls are perhaps the most reliable self-reports of vote choice because respondents are interviewed shortly after leaving the voting booth. Further, exit polls contain large samples (several thousand respondents) and therefore are reliable even when the data are partitioned with respect to southern subregion, location, and limiting the analysis to white voters. Last, in three consecutive presidential years, 2000, 2004, and 2008, the national exit polls included respondents from all eleven southern states.

Table 8.10 displays the southern Republican share of the presidential and U.S. House vote by location and subregion, in the 2000, 2004, and 2008 elections. Among all voters, there is a consistent decline in the Republican percentage of the presidential and U.S. House vote from 2000 to 2008. In addition, except for 2004, a majority of urban voters supported Democrats for president and U.S. House. By comparison, despite a decline in the GOP vote since 2000, a majority of suburban and rural voters backed Republican presidential and U.S. House candidates from 2000 to 2008. Turning to location on the basis of subregion does not reveal any major sectional differences in voter preferences beyond the fact that urban Deep South voters consistently prefer Democratic presidential and U.S. House nominees from 2000 to 2008. Likewise, in 2008, urban Rim South voters favor Democrats in presidential and U.S. House contests. Finally, between 2000 and 2008, suburban and rural voters, irrespective of subregion, always prefer Republicans for president and U.S. House.

Table 8.11 limits the data to white voters in the 2000–2008 elections. South-wide, white southern voters' robust support for the GOP is evident regardless of location. In

TABLE 8.10 ■ Voters' Preferences by Subregion and Location in Presidential and U.S. House Elections				
Location		2000 Republican (%)	2004 Republican (%)	2008 Republican (%)
South				
Urban	President	47	55	45
	U.S. House	49	55	43
Suburban	President	59	57	56
	U.S. House	60	56	55
Rural	President	66	64	58
	U.S. House	60	59	52
Deep South				
Urban	President	43	49	47
	U.S. House	41	47	47
Suburban	President	58	69	57
	U.S. House	51	61	55
Rural	President	69	61	57
	U.S. House	62	58	54
Rim South				
Urban	President	49	58	45
	U.S. House	53	59	41
Suburban	President	59	54	56
	U.S. House	63	55	55
Rural	President	63	66	59
	U.S. House	59	60	51

Sources: Data are from the 2000 Voter News Service national exit poll; the 2004 National Election Pool national exit poll; and the 2008 National Election Pool national exit poll.

Note: Data show the Republican share of the two-party vote cast for a given office (not taking into account whether a particular U.S. House race was contested by both major parties). In all three of these exit polls (2000, 2004, and 2008), respondents were interviewed in all eleven southern states.

TABLE 8.11 ■ White Voters' Preferences by Subregion and Location in Presidential and U.S. House Elections

Location		2000 Republican (%)	2004 Republican (%)	2008 Republican (%)
South				
Urban	President	66	71	65
	U.S. House	67	71	65
Suburban	President	68	66	69
	U.S. House	68	66	67
Rural	President	74	79	74
	U.S. House	67	73	65
Deep South				
Urban	President	70	78	77
	U.S. House	66	75	77
Suburban	President	73	83	84
	U.S. House	60	74	77
Rural	President	83	93	78
	U.S. House	73	91	73
Rim South				
Urban	President	64	68	61
	U.S. House	68	70	60
Suburban	President	65	61	65
	U.S. House	71	63	64
Rural	President	67	72	72
	U.S. House	63	65	61

Sources: Data are from the 2000 Voter News Service national exit poll; the 2004 National Election Pool national exit poll; and the 2008 National Election Pool national exit poll.

Note: Data show the Republican share of the two-party vote cast for a given office (not taking into account whether a particular U.S. House race was contested by both major parties). In all three of these exit polls (2000, 2004, and 2008), respondents were interviewed in all eleven southern states.

2008, around two-thirds or more of the southern white vote is given to Republican presidential and U.S. House nominees. The only outlier from a lack of variation in white Republican voting according to location, is the almost three-quarters (74 percent) of rural residents who supported GOP presidential nominee John McCain in 2008. Turning to the relationship between location and subregion, it is the Deep versus Rim South sectional divide that accounts for the variation in southern white voting behavior. In other words, the variation in Republican voting by location in each subregion does not differ nearly as much as the variation in GOP support across subregions, no matter the location. Similar to the findings presented in Table 8.4, Deep South whites exhibit a much more pronounced proclivity for voting Republican. In 2008, more than 70 percent of Deep South whites voted Republican for president and U.S. House in all three locations (urban, suburban, rural), including an 84-percent suburban Republican presidential vote. In contrast, there is only one instance in which Rim South whites vote more than 70-percent Republican in 2008: rural voters in the presidential contest. Indeed, compared to their counterparts residing in the same location, in 2008, it is only among rural presidential voters where the Deep South Republican margin does not reach double digits (a 78-percent GOP presidential vote in the Deep South versus a 72-percent GOP presidential vote in the Rim South).

Finally, Table 8.12 displays the Republican percentage of the 2016 presidential vote for the six southern states included in the National Election Pool exit polls. The GOP presidential vote is displayed with respect to a voter's location (urban, suburban, rural). The pattern of the vote by location is generally in accordance with expectations. With the exception of South Carolina, the share of the urban Republican

TABLE 8.12 ■ The Republican Presidential Vote in the 2016 Election by Location			
State	Urban %	Suburban %	Rural %
Florida	41 [46]	53 [45]	61 [9]
Georgia	29 [18]	51 [58]	67 [23]
North Carolina	35 [37]	60 [39]	58 [24]
South Carolina	46 [35]	62 [55]	40 [10]
Texas	42 [43]	58 [48]	70 [8]
Virginia	34 [30]	48 [51]	56 [19]

Source: Data are from the 2016 National Election Pool state exit polls (accessible online: http://www.cnn.com/election/results/exit-polls/national/president).

Notes: The percentage of the Republican presidential vote is out of the two-party vote (Republican Donald Trump and Democrat Hillary Clinton) as well as other (e.g., Libertarian Gary Johnson and Green Jill Stein) and no answer. The share of voters in each location for each state is shown in brackets ([urban%] + [suburban%] + [rural%] = [100%]).

presidential vote is the lowest among the three locations, and it is always under a GOP majority (a low of 29 percent in Georgia and a high of 46 percent in South Carolina). Without having additional details regarding the South Carolina exit poll sample, it is safe to assume that the share of black voters in the rural subsample was substantial and accounts for why the rural Republican presidential vote was just 40 percent. In addition to rural voters in South Carolina, Democratic-leaning Virginia is the only other instance in which suburban or rural voters fail to register a majority Republican presidential vote (a 48-percent GOP presidential vote cast by suburban Virginians). In four of the six states (Florida, Georgia, Texas, and Virginia), rural voters are the most Republican in their presidential preferences. Nationally, Trump's greatest support was among rural voters, and this dynamic generally holds for the six southern states in Table 8.12.[9]

CONCLUDING THOUGHTS

The fateful 1964 presidential election set in motion the Republican Party's "southern strategy." Henceforth, the national GOP embraced the more conservative position on civil rights and by extension, race issues in general (Carmines and Stimson 1989). Though Senator Goldwater was never branded a racist for voting no on the 1964 Civil Rights Act, in the minds of many white southerners his action was interpreted as a white supremacist overture and therefore a perfectly good reason to vote Republican in the 1964 presidential election. With the exception of Louisiana siding with the Republican Eisenhower in 1956 (Parent and Perry 2018), the last time a Deep South state went Republican prior to 1964 was in another fateful election: the disputed 1876 contest, which was resolved in a compromise that brought an end to Reconstruction in exchange for awarding the presidency to the Republican Rutherford Hayes.[10]

In 1964, Democratic President Johnson crushed his Republican opponent Goldwater, winning more than 60 percent of the popular vote and 90 percent in the Electoral College. But the champion of black civil rights was shut out of the Deep South where Goldwater had his only success in addition to carrying his home state of Arizona. The most telling sign that the race issue turned white southerners to the GOP was the 87-percent Republican vote cast in the most race-conscious and racially reactive state: Mississippi.[11] But it would take another forty years for the Deep South to consolidate its Republican support below the presidential level, with its white residents exhibiting a rate of GOP loyalty that by the mid-2000s surpassed that of their white Rim South counterparts. As this chapter has shown, the sectional divide between the Deep South and Peripheral South remains a persistent shaper of southern white political behavior and this subregional distinction is palpable with regard to voter preferences (see also McKee and Springer 2015; White 2014).

Figures 8.10 and 8.11 are presented as an illustrative way to capture the extraordinary growth of the GOP in southern presidential politics since 1964. Figure 8.10

FIGURE 8.10 ■ Southern County-Level Republican Presidential Vote in 1964

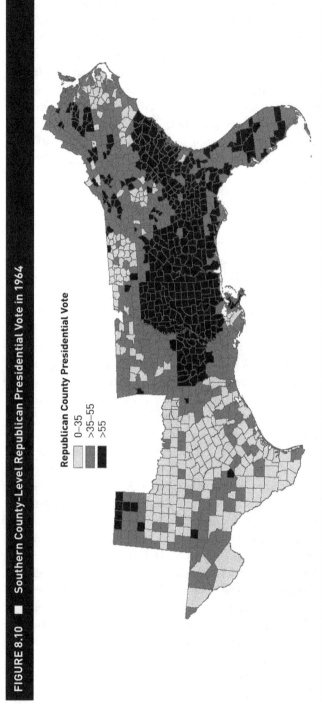

Republican County Presidential Vote

- 0–35
- >35–55
- >55

Sources: Figure created by the author. County shapefile for 1960 is from the National Historical Geographic Information System (NHGIS) website: (https://www.nhgis.org/) [accessed October 21, 2017]. Presidential vote data are from Dave Leip's *Atlas of U.S. Presidential Elections*.

Note: In Alabama, the Republican percentage of the vote includes those cast for unpledged electors.

FIGURE 8.11 ■ Southern County-Level Republican Presidential Vote in 2016

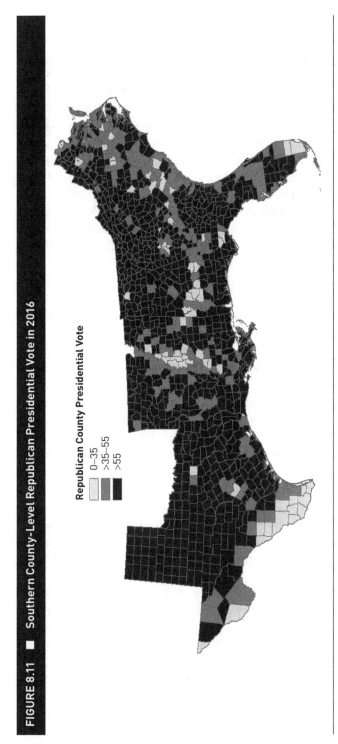

Republican County Presidential Vote

- 0–35
- >35–55
- >55

Sources: Figure created by the author. County shapefile for 2015 is from the National Historical Geographic Information System (NHGIS) website: (https://www.nhgis.org/) [accessed October 21, 2017]. Presidential vote data are from Dave Leip's *Atlas of U.S. Presidential Elections.*

Note: As was the case in Figure 8.10, the Republican county percentage is out of all votes cast.

shows the county level percentage of the 1964 Republican presidential vote cast in the South, and Figure 8.11 presents the same analysis for the 2016 presidential election. The GOP share of the vote is partitioned in darker shades for 0–35 percent, > 35–55 percent, and > 55 percent. In 1964, the Republican Goldwater's dominance of Deep South counties manifests in a wide dark band (more than 55 percent Republican) running from South Carolina in the east to the northern half of Louisiana in the west. Based on evidence from the 1964 ANES survey, not only were the southern votes for Goldwater exclusively cast by whites, but in most Deep South states, black disenfranchisement was the predominant condition, and this was particularly acute in the heavily African American counties located in the heart of the black belt where Goldwater garnered his most lopsided support.

More than a half-century later, the 2016 presidential election illustrates the far-reaching geographic dominance of the Republican Party in southern politics. In 1964, Goldwater won more than 55 percent of the vote in 34.5 percent of the South's counties; in 2016, Trump won more than 55 percent of the vote in 74 percent of the South's counties. With the removal of Jim Crow–era barriers to black participation (still prevalent in 1964), in the remaining quarter of southern counties in 2016 that registered a Republican vote of 55 percent or less, the racial and ethnic composition of the county is the most obvious indicator of Democratic support. In contrast to 1964 when the black-belt counties were most fervent for Goldwater and most of their African American residents were denied the vote, in 2016 many of the black-belt counties are the least supportive of Trump because their heavily black constituencies are now voting, and voting overwhelmingly Democratic. Similarly, the dominant presence of Latinos in South Texas translates into a one-sided Democratic presidential vote, whereas the middle part of Florida (the "I-4" corridor running from St. Petersburg in the west to Tampa, Orlando, and finally Daytona on the east coast) is the most competitive section of the state and it contains a burgeoning population of Puerto Ricans who favor the Democratic Party.[12]

By comparison, Republican presidential gains have been impressive among rural and heavily white counties, and particularly those running along the spine of Appalachia from Virginia in the east to Tennessee and west across the northern part of Arkansas. In 1964, President Johnson did well among this section of the South, but many of these counties share a history of mountain Republicanism dating back to the Civil War when the whites of the highlands were shut out of the slave economy and thus had no desire to fight for slave owners' interests (Key 1949). In the new millennium, the descendants of these southern whites have greatly favored Republican presidential candidates (Arbour and Teigen 2011) and this was clearly the case in 2016.

The urbanization of the modern South is another factor altering two-party competition. In the less dense suburban areas, the GOP has a decided advantage (McKee and Shaw 2003; McKee and Teigen 2009), but the party is losing ground in denser urban cities that are growing in population. As thoroughly demonstrated in this chapter, white voting behavior does not vary substantially depending on location (urban, suburban, rural), but because growing minority populations are locating disproportionally in urban areas, these settings are veering in a Democratic direction. This development is evident in the county-level presidential election returns in Figure 8.11. For instance, in deep red Texas, Democratic presidential candidates now carry the most urban centers of the state, which contain racially and ethnically diverse populations in Dallas County (Dallas), Travis County (Austin), Bexar County (San Antonio), and Harris County (Houston). On net, due to demographic changes that show the southern minority electorate outpacing the majority segment that is non-Latino white, urban growth and rural decline is a dynamic that bodes well for the Democratic Party in electoral politics.

In sum, sectional and locational differences are factors that greatly contribute to the shaping of southern politics. The subregional distinction between the Deep and Rim South, centers primarily on cultural differences that have been formed around the role of African Americans (Key 1949; Matthews and Prothro 1966). Given their much greater presence in the Deep South, the perceived and sometimes actual threat of blacks to the white ruling elite, has resulted in the most racially polarized politics in the contemporary United States (Black and Black 2012; Hood, Kidd, and Morris 2012). Locational differences, on the other hand, are not so much imbued with cultural habits that date back to the antebellum period; rather residential density affects political behavior primarily in terms of the racial and ethnic composition of these places. That is, the Republican Party performs better in rural and suburban areas because these populations contain much higher shares of white voters vis-à-vis urban locations. Of course, it is not possible to completely divorce locational factors from the broader context of whether an urban, suburban, or rural community resides in the Deep or Peripheral South. Furthermore, because of vast alterations to certain locations in these subregions, like the Deep South cities of Atlanta, Georgia, and Charleston, South Carolina, subregional sectionalism is also undergoing notable changes. In fact, based on recent presidential election returns, it already appears that considerable locational changes in certain parts of the Deep and Rim South are eroding sectional differences in political behavior (see Box 8.1).

BOX 8.1   A NEW SOUTHERN SECTIONALISM?

This chapter has placed considerable emphasis on the subregional political differences between the Deep South and Peripheral South, but there is another southern sectional pattern that has recently emerged in presidential elections. And, as stated throughout this book, presidential elections are an excellent indicator of broader political trends. Table 8.13 provides clear evidence of an Eastern

(Continued)

[Continued]

TABLE 8.13 ■ An Eastern Seaboard Pattern of Presidential Competitiveness in Recent Elections (Lowest to Highest Margin)

1996	2000	2004	2008	2012	2016	1996–2004	2008–2016	1996–2016
Georgia	Florida	Florida	North Carolina	Florida	Florida	Florida	Florida	Florida
Virginia	Tennessee	Virginia	Florida	North Carolina	North Carolina	Virginia	North Carolina	Virginia
Tennessee	Arkansas	Arkansas	Georgia	Virginia	Georgia	Tennessee	Virginia	North Carolina
North Carolina	Louisiana	North Carolina	Virginia	Georgia	Virginia	Georgia	Georgia	Georgia
Texas	Virginia	Tennessee	South Carolina	South Carolina	Texas	North Carolina	South Carolina	South Carolina
Mississippi	Georgia	Louisiana	Texas	Mississippi	South Carolina	Arkansas	Texas	Tennessee
South Carolina	North Carolina	Georgia	Mississippi	Texas	Mississippi	Louisiana	Mississippi	Mississippi
Florida	Alabama	South Carolina	Tennessee	Louisiana	Louisiana	South Carolina	Louisiana	Texas
Alabama	South Carolina	Mississippi	Louisiana	Tennessee	Tennessee	Mississippi	Tennessee	Louisiana
Louisiana	Mississippi	Texas	Arkansas	Alabama	Arkansas	Alabama	Alabama	Arkansas
Arkansas	Texas	Alabama	Alabama	Arkansas	Alabama	Texas	Arkansas	Alabama

Source: Data calculated by the author from Dave Leip's *Atlas of U.S. Presidential Elections* (http://uselectionatlas.org/RESULTS/).

Notes: Data show the rank order of competitiveness based on the two-party presidential vote margin from the lowest margin/most competitive (top row) to the highest margin/least competitive (bottom row). The vote margin was calculated as follows: the absolute value of the difference in the two-party presidential vote cast, divided by the total two-party vote cast, and multiplied by 100. For instance, in 1996 Georgia had the following most competitive/narrowest margin: Absolute Value of [1,053,849 (Dem votes) − 1,080,843 (Rep votes)] / [1,053,849 + 1,080,843] * 100 = 1.26 percent.

Seaboard pattern of voting in contemporary southern presidential elections. The table shows the rank order for each southern state from most competitive (top row) to least competitive (bottom row) based on the absolute value of the two-party presidential vote margin for the last twenty years of presidential contests, 1996 to 2016.

The Eastern Seaboard pattern refers specifically to presidential voting behavior being more similar among the five southern states that border the Atlantic Ocean from north to south: Virginia, North Carolina, South Carolina, Georgia, and Florida. The common characteristic possessed by these states is the recent in-migration flow of northeasterners.[1] Among the eleven southern states, the five located along the Eastern Seaboard contain the highest percentage of northeastern in-migrants based on one-year 2012 American Community Survey (ACS) data. According to the 2012 ACS data, the share of in-migrants from the Northeast out of all in-migrants (coming from outside the South), from highest to lowest, in the Eastern Seaboard southern states was: 52 percent in Virginia, 48 percent in South Carolina, 46 percent in North Carolina, 46 percent in Florida, and 30 percent in Georgia (McKee and Teigen 2016, 229). Only in Georgia is it the case that the stream of in-migrants from the Northeast was not the largest in percentage terms (38 percent of Georgia in-migrants hailed from the Midwest; see McKee and Teigen 2016, 229).

Recent northeastern in-migration is a significant development in southern politics because the Northeast is one of the most presidentially Democratic regions of the United States (Black and Black 2007). Thus, greater streams of northeastern migrants to the South turn sections of these states in a more Democratic and hence competitive direction (Hillygus, McKee, and Young 2016) because the southern states have been Republican presidential strongholds dating back to the late 1960s (Black and Black 1992). The data in the table highlight a changing pattern of presidential competitiveness in which the first three elections (1996–2004) are notably different from the last three contests (2008–2016). From 1996 to 2004, in each of these presidential elections, at least one Eastern Seaboard state was ranked the eighth most competitive (Florida in 1996 and South Carolina in 2004) based on presidential vote margin, and South Carolina was the ninth most competitive in 2000.

In 2008 and 2012, the five Eastern Seaboard states were the five most competitive in these presidential years. In 2016, there was one exception to the pattern, Texas was more presidentially competitive (in the fifth spot) than South Carolina, which was the sixth most competitive state. It is difficult to say that Texas is likely to be more competitive than at least one of the five Eastern Seaboard states in future presidential contests, because in 2016, Republican Donald Trump was decidedly less popular than his Republican predecessors in the Lone Star State, where two presidential electors did not cast votes for the Republican nominee (one voted for John Kasich and the other for Ron Paul).

Averaging the presidential vote margin from 1996 to 2004, shows that South Carolina is the eighth most competitive state. In contrast, averaging the presidential vote margin from 2008 to 2016 reveals that the five Eastern Seaboard states are

(Continued)

(Continued)

also the five most presidentially competitive. Further, averaging the presidential vote margin over the entire span of presidential elections, 1996 to 2016, shows once again that the Eastern Seaboard pattern of presidential competitiveness holds. Notice that from 2008 to 2016 and from 1996 to 2016, the three most presidentially competitive states are Florida, North Carolina, and Virginia. Of course, Democratic nominee Barack Obama won all three of the aforementioned states in 2008 and two of the three in 2012 (Florida and Virginia), while Democratic nominee Hillary Clinton carried Virginia in 2016. The movement of Virginia from second most competitive from 1996 to 2016 to third most competitive from 2008 to 2016 most likely reflects the fact that the state is shifting in a Democratic direction and if this continues, then, eventually the Old Dominion will become even less competitive because it is the most presidentially Democratic southern state, and recall that it also was the only one based on the 2012 ACS data with a majority of in-migrants from the Northeast (52 percent).

---

1. Based on the definition used by Black and Black (2007), the Northeast consists of the following states (plus the District of Columbia): Connecticut, Delaware, Maine, Maryland, Massachusetts, New Hampshire, New Jersey, New York, Pennsylvania, Rhode Island, and Vermont.

9 THE CHANGING SOUTHERN ELECTORATE

I n his final chapter in *Southern Politics in State and Nation,* V. O. Key remarked on the fluidity of the political system in spite of the common perception that Democratic dominance was as certain as the sunrise. In his own words:

> Not only is there diversity within the South; the region is also changing. Its rate of evolution may seem glacial, but fundamental shifts in the conditions underlying its politics are taking place. (Key 1949, 664)

Key closed his masterpiece with an anticipation that the American South would find its way out of its repressive Jim Crow system of lawfully enforced racial segregation and elitist-driven politics by expecting Dixie to take on a brand of politics more in line with its neighbors to the North. But unlike the rest of the nation, because the southern wing of the Democratic Party still stood for a vigorous internal and external defense of the tenets of white supremacy (most recently manifested in the Dixiecrat presidential campaign waged a year prior to Key's book making its way into print), the class-based partisan cleavage had yet to take hold below the Mason-Dixon Line.

Into the 1950s it remained true that upper-class whites were even more wedded to the southern Democracy than their lower-class white counterparts (see Nadeau and Stanley 1993 and the evidence presented in chapter 7). And although Key envisioned a marriage between lower-class whites and blacks, and the liberalization of southern politics via growing urbanization, this potentially powerful coalition has never fully materialized. It is the stickiness of racial and economic conservatism that continues to deny a transformation of southern politics that would redistribute the bulk of electoral clout to the greatest common denominator of southern voters. To this day white southerners, irrespective of their socioeconomic status and geographic location (city, town, and country), are distinct from whites in the rest of the United States because they are notably less likely to vote in a manner similar to minority voters of a commensurate class (Bartels 2008).

Nonetheless, a massive partisan transformation, and one not entirely understood nor anticipated by many scholars writing on southern political change, has finally come to fruition.[1] Simply put, the modern southern party system is best characterized by Republican hegemony as demonstrated throughout chapter 5. As stated by Merle Black, "the emergence of the Republican party as a realistic alternative to the Democrats is the most dramatic story in southern politics during the late twentieth and early twenty-first centuries" (2004, 1001). Similarly, Hood, Kidd, and Morris

(2012, 3) aver that, "from the late 1940s to the present day, the South has undergone the most dramatic political transformation of any region in the country."

Figure 9.1 displays perhaps the single most important visual of the macro-level picture of party politics in the South. With the exception of the 1954 midterm,[2] the percentage of Democratic and Republican voters in the South is shown from 1952 to 2016. In this figure and in many that follow, the time series begins in 1952, a time when it was evident that the Democratic Solid South was still alive. In 1952, 78 percent of southern voters identified as Democrats while slightly less than 11 percent expressed an affiliation with the Grand Old Party (GOP). Never again would such a large share of the southern electorate align with the Democratic Party. Partisan parity nears in the mid-1980s, and by the new millennium the GOP enjoys a brief plurality position (2002–2006). Since 2008, there has been very little separation between the share of Democratic and Republican voters. It is important to note that neither party now even approaches majority status with respect to their share of identifiers (this was last achieved by Democratic voters at 51 percent in 1982). In 2016, the last year the data cover, Democrats were 36 percent and Republicans were 35 percent of voters in the American South. With such a large portion of the electorate identifying with neither major party, this should be cause for great concern, and especially for the GOP because most of the recent population growth is attributable to groups more partial to the Democratic Party.

This chapter details the tremendous alteration of southern politics by illustrating how the electorate has changed with respect to the party identification of its most prominent demographic groups: whites, blacks, and Latinos. Further, partisan distinctions are made with respect to race and gender. Not only are the southern Democratic and Republican coalitions examined in terms of these demographic classifications for voters in general elections, the analysis takes an additional step by looking at the remarkable partisan transformations transpiring among voters in primary elections. Finally, the chapter concludes with a brief but important note on the electoral implications of the changing demography of southern in-migration.

It is difficult to digest the bigger picture of the current partisan evolution of southern politics without coming to the conclusion that as impressive as the contemporary Republican run has been, it is likely that the Democratic opposition will gradually reassert itself. And it is this impending reality, however faint in many southern locales (e.g., the Deep South), that probably best accounts for why the southern GOP remains busily engaged in using their majority position to craft and implement legislation that curtails voting in a manner intended to weaken the growing Democratic coalition—a subject taken up in the next chapter.

A NOTE ON THE DATA

Before launching into a discussion of the various figures presented in the sections following this one, it is necessary to clearly outline the data analyzed so that the student has an understanding of what they do (and don't) show. First, most of the

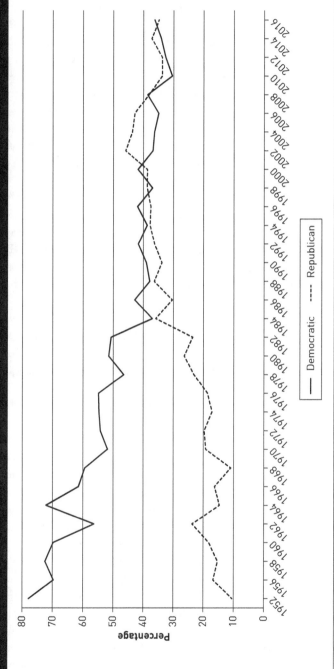

FIGURE 9.1 ■ Party Identification of Southern Voters, 1952–2016

Democratic —— Republican ----

Sources: American National Election Studies (ANES) data from 1952 to 1974 (self-reported voters in national elections); National Exit Poll data from 1976 to 2008 (South includes eleven-state ex–Confederate definition plus Kentucky and Oklahoma from 1976 to 1982; only Confederate South after 1982); Cooperative Congressional Election Study (CCES) data from 2010 to 2016 (self-reported voters in national elections).

Notes: All national exit poll and CCES data were properly weighted. Strong and weak identifiers are classified as partisans and independent-leaning voters are classified as independents. Due to the reliance on self-reported turnout for the ANES and CCES data, it is very likely that the share of Democratic and Republican voters is actually higher because nonvoters are not as likely to identify with a major party (i.e., many respondents who reported voting did not in fact vote).

data are on survey respondents who are classified as voters. That is, these individuals reported that they voted in a national election in a midterm or presidential year and did so in either a general contest or a presidential party primary. Why just voters? The simple answer is that voters are obviously the group that matters in deciding the outcome of elections. And perhaps not surprisingly, many studies of representation (e.g., Verba and Nie 1987) indicate that politicians exhibit a bias in their behavior to the extent that they are more responsive to voters than those who sit on the sidelines. Consider Virginia back in the day when Key (1949) wrote about the Old Dominion's politics. The conservative Democratic political machine, under its leader Harry F. Byrd, had stifled competition to the point that from 1920–1946 a mere 10 percent of Virginians voted in gubernatorial elections (Key 1949, 493, Figure 57). When an electorate is shrunken to 1 out of 10 potential voters, it strains credulity to believe they are representative of the legions of abstainers.

Second, with regard to the classification of voters, this is somewhat problematic for some of the data. There are three primary sources of survey data used in this chapter: the American National Election Studies (ANES), the exit polls, and the Cooperative Congressional Election Study (CCES). For two of the three survey outfits, the ANES and the CCES, whether someone is classified as a voter is based on their self-report. In other words, respondents are queried as to whether they voted in the election, but their responses are not validated by checking the voting record to confirm whether they did in fact vote. There has never been (and one can easily venture to say never will be) evidence of self-reported turnout in any respectable survey ever being less than the actual validated turnout rate. Stated another way, a nontrivial share of the eligible electorate consistently lies when asked about voting (Bernstein, Chadha, and Montjoy 2001), and this is expected because saying one participated is the socially desirable response (Traugott, Traugott, and Presser 1992; Phillips and Clancy 1972). With this in mind, it is definitely the case that some portion of the ANES and CCES respondents who are categorized as voters are really nonvoters who said they voted. By comparison, for the exit poll data, there is no self-reported voting issue because individuals are surveyed about their voting behavior upon leaving their polling place. Thus, the exit poll samples definitely consist almost entirely of actual voters.

Now if nonvoters and voters essentially exhibited the same political behavior then the inclusion of large samples of self-reported voters would not matter. Unfortunately, it is often the case that voters and nonvoters are statistically different on a host of characteristics (Ansolabehere and Hersh 2012; McKee, Hood, and Hill 2012) and with respect to the matter at hand it is true that their levels of partisanship are not commensurate. As Bartels (2000) demonstrated with ANES data, self-reported voters are more likely to identify with a major party than are nonvoters. It should naturally follow, then, that self-reported voters are likely to be less partisan (more politically independent) than a sample consisting entirely of actual voters (i.e., exit poll respondents). This makes sense from what has long been known about political participation, partisans are more motivated to vote because they care more about who is elected

(Campbell et al. 1960), much like sports fans exhibit more loyalty and interest in rooting for their team (Green, Palmquist, and Schickler 2002). Therefore, a word of caution should be exercised when examining the transition from one data source to the next and particularly when going from the exit polls to the CCES. Both of these surveys are based on very large samples, and it is probable that the presence of many nonvoters in the CCES reduces the percentage of Democratic and Republican voters and hence inflates the share of political independents. This means that evidence of a decline in the number of partisans for the CCES component of the time series is likely in part at least an artifact of many nonvoters who claimed to be voters. The good news is that even if the portion of partisans is understated, there is no reason to think that there is a bias in the share of Democratic versus Republican identifiers; they may be underrepresented but this underrepresentation should affect both groups equally.

In most of the time series of data on party identification, the sequencing starts with the ANES data (from 1952 to 1974), then moves to the exit poll data (1976–2008), and the CCES data are employed for the most recent elections (2010–2016). This progression matches that of Black (2004), except that his analysis ends with the 2002 exit poll data and therefore never made use of the CCES.[3] And like Black (2004, 1003), from 1976 to 1982 the exit polls did not include a state indicator and the region for the South in these years was a bit more expansive than the eleven ex-Confederate state classification, including Kentucky and Oklahoma. For all of the ANES data, the exit polls after 1982 and for the CCES data, the eleven-state South is employed. Lastly, party identification is based on the initial question of whether one is a Democrat, Republican, Independent or something else. Although the wording is somewhat more elaborate for the ANES and CCES (they use the same exact question), there should not be an issue regarding responses to this question because the exit polls only ask the initial party identification question. By contrast, the ANES and CCES provide the branching questions to build the seven-point party identification scale (for details, see chapter 6). This is not necessary in this chapter because independent leaners (e.g., an independent who leans toward the Republican Party) are classified as Independents. There is broad consensus that independent leaners behave very much like weak partisans (see Keith et al. 1992), but they are not, in fact, partisans because they refuse to call themselves such, and this is relevant in assessing the relative strength of the major parties as expressed by their supporters in the electorate (Miller 1991).

RACIAL AND ETHNIC COMPOSITION OF THE GENERAL ELECTORATE

Throughout most of the South, whites and blacks remain the predominant groups, but more recently the region has experienced an impressive rise in Latino residents (Stanley 2010). It is certainly true that some localities are also home to a substantial number of Asians (e.g., Houston, TX, is 7 percent Asian),[4] but in assessing large-scale changes to the southern electorate, whites, blacks, and Latinos comprise the vast majority of Democratic and Republican voters, and therefore these are the racial and ethnic categories of interest. In the election data, *race* refers to white or black, whereas Latino is treated as an ethnic classification so that Latinos can be of any race. In all of the data presented, white voters are not Latino and black voters are not Latino, but Latinos can include either of the aforementioned races or any other racial combination for that matter (the distinction is never made explicit).

Historically, southern politics boiled down to a simple racial formula of blacks versus whites, with the latter group firmly in charge. In most Deep South states it remains a politics of black and white (Black and Black 2012; see chapter 8), but the burgeoning Latino population in many Peripheral South states has added a new dimension to coalitional politics. Parceling the composition of the southern Democratic and Republican parties according to race and ethnicity is particularly useful because these demographic features play such an outsized role in sorting party loyalties. Further, to the extent that race and ethnicity exhibit minimal overlap, almost the entirety of the Democratic and Republican coalitions can be partitioned this way, but like Black (2004), gender is another leading demographic that will be added to the analysis.

For now, looking at just a simple racial bifurcation of the southern electorate, Figure 9.2 shows the percentage of white and nonwhite voters in presidential years from 1952 to 2016. In 1952, the southern voting electorate was an astounding 94 percent white and the meager 6 percent nonwhite component was entirely

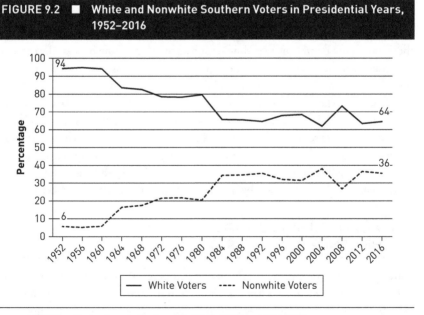

FIGURE 9.2 ■ White and Nonwhite Southern Voters in Presidential Years, 1952–2016

Source: ANES Time Series Cumulative Data File (1948–2012) and 2016 ANES.

Note: Self-reported voters in presidential years and White means non-Latino white with every other category of voter classified as Nonwhite.

African American. Over six decades later, white voters account for 64 percent of the southern electorate and, conversely, nonwhite voters have grown to 36 percent. This 36 percent nonwhite segment of southern voters is, of course, very diverse, but as mentioned, consists mainly of blacks and Latinos.

The changing racial composition of the southern voting electorate is a strong indicator of the future direction of southern politics because a more racially diverse (read "less white") population of voters is more Democratic in its voting preferences. The next three sections look at the partisan transformations taking place among white, black, and Latino voters based primarily on their population size and, hence, their electoral clout.

WHITE VOTERS

In order to increase the reliability of the results and thus reduce the random variability associated with smaller samples based on a single year, the data on party identification are displayed by decades (e.g., 1960s = 1960, 1962, 1964, 1966, 1968). Starting with white voters, Figure 9.3 charts the gradual and permanent reversal in the share of Democrats and Republicans. Once again, in the 1950s white southerners are overwhelmingly Democratic (73 percent) whereas only 14 percent claim allegiance to the GOP (an almost 60 percentage point difference). But in each subsequent decade the percentage

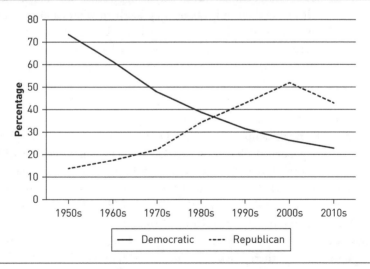

FIGURE 9.3 ■ Party Identification of White Voters in the South

Sources: American National Election Studies (ANES) data from 1952 to 1974 (self-reported voters in national elections); National Exit Poll data from 1976 to 2008 (South includes eleven-state ex-Confederate definition plus Kentucky and Oklahoma from 1976 to 1982; only Confederate South after 1982); Cooperative Congressional Election Study (CCES) data from 2010 to 2016 (self-reported voters in national elections).

Note: White means non-Latino white. Only strong and weak identifiers are classified as partisans.

of Democratic voters declines and the portion of Republicans rises through the 2000s, when Republican voters constitute a 52 percent majority of the voting electorate.

Republican voters first outnumber Democrats in the 1990s, and since then the likelihood of white Democrats recovering their majority status has been slim. The largest difference favoring Republicans is in the 2000s (26 percentage point margin), and even though the relative share of Republican voters drops in the 2010s (43 percent Republicans), the GOP still maintains an impressive 20 percentage point advantage over Democrats. The long-term decline in white Democratic voters and the concomitant growth in white Republicans is the main storyline of contemporary southern politics. It is nothing short of stunning how the share of Democratic voters has consistently dropped since the 1950s, producing a 69 percent overall decline by the 2010s. Notice however, that the slope of Democratic decline appears to level off after the 1970s. It would seem improbable that the share of white Democratic voters will drop even more in subsequent years if, in fact, white Republicanism reached its apex in the 2000s.

BLACK VOTERS

The efforts of the Franklin Roosevelt Administration to court the support of northern African Americans surely did not go without notice among the massive disenfranchised population of southern blacks. What made the New Deal Democratic coalition unique was that two of its largest groups, northern blacks and white southerners (the single largest segment), were basically at loggerheads since the furtherance of black civil rights was vehemently opposed by southern whites and this conflict ultimately dissolved the national Democratic majority. Unlike the gradual decline of white Democratic voters in the South, their African American peers were already strongly Democratic in the 1950s and then became even more so in the 1960s when the national Democratic Party under the leadership of President Johnson took a clear stand in favor of civil rights as most saliently demonstrated with the passage of the 1964 Civil Rights Act and the 1965 Voting Rights Act.[5]

Based on the small sample of southern black voters in the 1950s displayed in Figure 9.4 (29 respondents), 69 percent were Democrats versus 24 percent affiliated with the GOP. In the 1960s the pattern of overwhelming black allegiance to the Democratic Party takes hold with almost 84 percent of black voters identifying with the party in the vanguard of furthering their cause outside of Dixie. By contrast, the share of black Republican voters drops below 10 percent (8 percent) in the 1960s and undergoes a long-term decline to reach it lowest share in the 2000s and 2010s, when a paltry 4 percent of southern black voters identify with the GOP.

The long-term pattern of southern black party identification is distinct from that of southern whites and Latinos. African Americans display a loyalty to the Democratic Party that is properly characterized as monolithic (Black 1998; Black and Black 1987, 2002; Bullock and Gaddie 2009; Fauntroy 2007). The importance

FIGURE 9.4 ■ Party Identification of Black Voters in the South

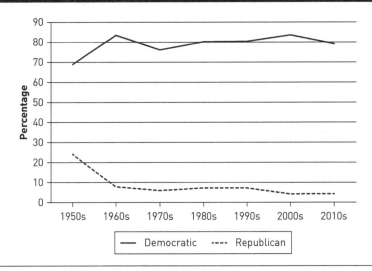

Sources: American National Election Studies (ANES) data from 1952 to 1974 (self-reported voters in national elections); National Exit Poll data from 1976 to 2008 (South includes eleven-state ex-Confederate definition plus Kentucky and Oklahoma from 1976 to 1982; only Confederate South after 1982); Cooperative Congressional Election Study (CCES) data from 2010 to 2016 (self-reported voters in national elections).

Note: Black means non-Latino black. Only strong and weak identifiers are classified as partisans.

of civil rights galvanized black Democratic identification in the 1960s and this group's one-sided allegiance to the Democratic Party has held firm ever since (in the 2010s, black Democrats comprise 79 percent of the black voting electorate). In short, African Americans constitute the base of the contemporary southern Democratic Party and any efforts at restoring the party to majority status will be accomplished with considerable deference to this most important and influential group in the Democratic coalition.

LATINO VOTERS

Outside of Texas and Florida, the two southern states with historically sizable Latino populations, the growth of this group in the remainder of the region really began to take off in the 1990s. As discussed, by treating the Latino classification as an ethnicity, it consists of a considerable degree of racial diversity and more important than this, the origins of Latinos are notably varied. This last point bears emphasis because immigration constitutes a large component of the burgeoning southern Latino population. For instance, among the 38 percent Latino population in Texas (2010 Census data), fully 86 percent is of Mexican origin. By comparison, among the 22 percent Latino population in Florida, 29 percent is Cuban, 20 percent is Puerto

Rican, 15 percent is Mexican, and another 17 and 11 percent originally hails from South America and Central America, respectively.[6]

With the exception of Puerto Ricans, who are born American citizens, because the fairly recent uptick in Latino voters is heavily contingent upon citizenship (noncitizens cannot vote in national elections), there is a large disparity in the overall percentage of southern Latinos versus their citizen voting age population. In addition, compared to southern blacks and whites, the Latino population is considerably younger (under voting age), which further diminishes their electoral strength. Table 9.1 shows the percentage of the southern Latino population from the 1980 Census to the most recent conducted in 2010. Specifically, the Latino population is broken down into their overall share of the population, their voting age population (VAP), and then their percentage of the citizen voting age population (CVAP).

In 1980, Latinos constitute 7 percent of the southern population, and thirty years later they had become almost 18 percent. But over these three decades, the Latino citizen voting age population lags far behind; a CVAP of 5 percent in 1980 has increased to 10 percent in 2010. So, despite the CVAP doubling from 1980 to 2010, the still relatively small share of the southern Latino population goes a long way in accounting for why this group has yet to register broad political influence in southern electoral politics, and especially in Deep South states where their share of the electorate and lack of citizenship renders them almost a nonfactor in party politics (Bullock and Hood 2006).

Nonetheless, despite their relatively smaller portion of the southern electorate, the Latino population is growing at a faster rate than the likes of whites and African Americans, and therefore the changing political behavior of this group warrants attention. Figure 9.5 displays the percentage of Democratic and Republican Latino voters from the 1970s (when their numbers are large enough to document) to the 2010s. Initially, the Democratic Party enjoys a large advantage among the Latino electorate with 61 percent of these voters identifying as Democrats versus 22 percent as Republicans. The partisan difference widens in the 1980s to a 47 percentage-point gulf (64 percent Democrats and 17 percent Republicans). But since 1980, Democratic affiliates have declined (just below 50 percent in the 1990s), though the downward trend has tapered off from the 2000s to 2010s (going from 47 to 45 percent Democratic). By comparison, there is an obvious increase in Republicans from the 1980s to 2000s (from 17 to 28 to 35 percent Republican). But in the 2010s the share of Republicans drops back to its 1990s level (28 percent) and this most recent drop undoubtedly reflects the recent positioning of a substantial share of Republican leaders who have taken a hard line on issues of great concern to the Latino community (e.g., immigration). Supporting this explanation is the growing margin between Democratic and Republican voters in the 2010s as compared to the 2000s (an 11.8 percentage point difference in the 2000s widens to a 16.8-point disparity in the 2010s). In the future, it bears watching whether Latino Democrats can expand upon their plurality status, which currently stands at 45 percent of the Latino voting electorate.

TABLE 9.1 ■ The Southern Latino Population, 1980–2010					
	1980 %	1990 %	2000 %	2010 %	2010 %–1980 %
Latino Population	7.0	9.0	13.1	17.6	10.6
Latino VAP	6.1	8.2	11.8	15.6	9.5
Latino CVAP	4.9	8.6	8.1	10.1	5.2

Source: Data are from the U.S. Census Bureau.

Note: VAP = voting age population and CVAP = citizen voting age population.

FIGURE 9.5 ■ Party Identification of Latino Voters in the South

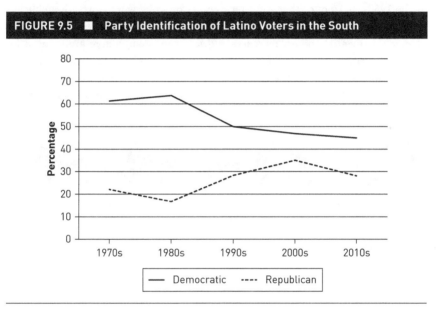

Sources: American National Election Studies (ANES) data from 1970 to 1974 (self-reported voters in national elections); National Exit Poll data from 1976 to 2008 (South includes eleven-state ex-Confederate definition plus Kentucky and Oklahoma from 1976 to 1982; only Confederate South after 1982); Cooperative Congressional Election Study (CCES) data from 2010 to 2016 (self-reported voters in national elections).

Note: Latinos can be of any racial group. Only strong and weak identifiers are classified as partisans.

RACE AND GENDER

Beginning in the 1980s, American politics scholars noticed the emergence of a gender gap in the voting behavior of men and women (Box-Steffensmeier, De Boef, and Lin 2004). But there is a longstanding misconception of how to understand gender differences in party affiliations. As Kaufmann and Petrocik (1999) correctly argue, the manifestation of a gender gap in voting preferences is primarily a consequence of men becoming more Republican than a result of women becoming more Democratic. Furthermore, from a regional perspective, race must be considered with respect to how it interacts with the party identification of men and women over time. Whereas African American men and women are decidedly Democratic, their white counterparts are markedly more Republican. But, as will be shown, both white and black men are notably less Democratic than their co-racial women peers.

Figure 9.6 presents the percentage of Democratic and Republican white voters according to gender from the 1950s to the 2010s. As the core of the Democratic Solid South electorate, in the 1950s, 77 percent of white men were Democrats. Almost 70 percent of white women voters in the 1950s affiliated with the Democratic Party. By contrast, neither sex accounted for even 20 percent Republican voters in the 1950s, but notice that a greater number of white women were Republicans (16 percent versus 12 percent for white men). After the 1950s, the secular decline in Democratic identification commences and it is consistently more pronounced for white men. Since the 1960s, the Democratic gender gap is ever present, with more white women voters affiliating with the Democratic Party than is the case for white men. In the 2010s, close to 26 percent of white women voters identified as Democrats versus 20 percent of white men.

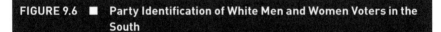

FIGURE 9.6 ■ Party Identification of White Men and Women Voters in the South

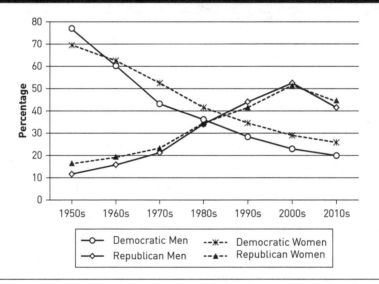

Sources: American National Election Studies (ANES) data from 1952 to 1974 (self-reported voters in national elections); National Exit Poll data from 1976 to 2008 (South includes eleven-state ex-Confederate definition plus Kentucky and Oklahoma from 1976 to 1982; only Confederate South after 1982); Cooperative Congressional Election Study (CCES) data from 2010 to 2016 (self-reported voters in national elections).

Note: White means non-Latino white. Only strong and weak identifiers are classified as partisans.

An examination of the trend in white Republican men and women voters reveals a definitive conclusion: among white southern voters there is no tangible gender gap in GOP identification (see Kaufmann 2006). By the 1970s, white Republican women are only slightly more Republican than white Republican men (23 percent versus 21 percent). Over four decades later, when pluralities of white women and white men identify with the GOP, there is only a modest difference in their rates of Republican affiliation (less than 3 percentage points; white women voters are 44.2 percent Republican and white men are 41.5 percent Republican).

Turning to African American men and women voters in Figure 9.7, the general pattern is not surprising because of their solid allegiance to the Democratic Party. However, there is a persistent gender gap among both Democratic and Republican black men and women. First, among the much smaller share of Republican voters, black men have always been somewhat more Republican than black women. In the 2010s, there is a 4.2 percentage point difference between the portion of black Republican men and women; 7.1 percent of black men were Republicans and a paltry 2.9 percent of black women voters identified with the GOP.

Among the vastly greater share of Democratic black men and women, in the 1960s there was no gender gap (83.6 percent of black women voters were Democrats and 83.3 percent of black men voters were also Democrats). The Democratic gender

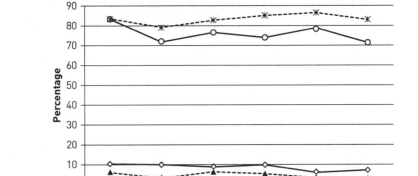

FIGURE 9.7 ■ Party Identification of Black Men and Women Voters in the South

Sources: American National Election Studies (ANES) data from 1952 to 1974 (self-reported voters in national elections); National Exit Poll data from 1976 to 2008 (South includes eleven-state ex-Confederate definition plus Kentucky and Oklahoma from 1976 to 1982; only Confederate South after 1982); Cooperative Congressional Election Study (CCES) data from 2010 to 2016 (self-reported voters in national elections).

Note: Black means non-Latino black. Only strong and weak identifiers are classified as partisans.

gap emerges in the 1970s (black women voters were 79.2 percent Democratic and black men were 71.8 percent Democratic), and thereafter, black Democratic women voters always comprise more than 80 percent of their gender participating in southern elections. By comparison, in no decade after the 1960s does the share of Democratic black men reach the eightieth percentile. In the 2010s the black Democratic gender gap was almost 12 percentage points (83.0 percent of black women voters were Democrats and 71.4 percent of black men were Democrats). Black women are the hardcore of the African American base of the modern southern Democratic Party. Not only are they substantially more Democratic than black men, but African American women are also significantly more likely to register and vote in national elections (Ansolabehere and Hersh 2013).[7]

THE DEMOCRATIC AND REPUBLICAN COALITIONS, THEN AND NOW

Now that the party identification of whites, blacks, and Latinos has been examined separately for each group, while race and party affiliation was further subdivided by gender, it is time to consider the composition of the southern Democratic and Republican coalitions from the 1950s to today (the 2010s). Given their much larger sample sizes, the portion of white men and women voters will be shown, but the percentage of black and Latino voters are not further parceled by gender. Confining the southern electorate to white men, white women, black, and Latino voters, provides a realistic portrait of how the relative size of each group has changed within the southern Democratic and Republican coalitions from the middle of the twentieth century to the present.

Figure 9.8 displays the demographic composition of the southern Democratic coalition from the 1950s to the 2010s. Starting in the 1950s, at 54 percent, white men were clearly the predominant group in the Solid South Democratic Party. White women comprised 41 percent of southern Democrats, whereas the still heavily disenfranchised African American population accounted for the remaining 5 percent of Democratic voters. By the 1970s, Latino voters register a presence in the Democratic coalition (at about 2 percent) and now white women are the most prevalent group (41 percent of Democratic voters). By the 1990s, black voters are finally more prominent than white men (30 percent versus 28 percent). In the new millennium the most current and probably stable pattern materializes: black voters are the plurality group in the southern Democratic coalition, followed by white women then white men and finally Latinos. In the 2010s the relative size of the aforementioned groups in the Democratic coalition was: 36 percent African Americans, 30 percent white women, 25 percent white men, and 9 percent Latinos.

The remarkable transformation of the southern Democratic coalition of voters starkly contrasts with the almost demographically static nature of its southern

FIGURE 9.8   ■   The Southern Democratic Coalition, 1950s–2010s

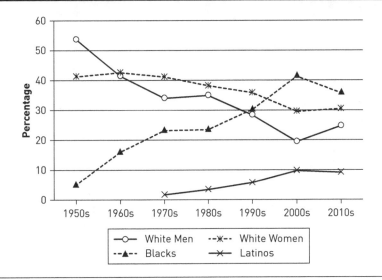

Sources: American National Election Studies (ANES) data from 1952 to 1974 (self-reported voters in national elections); National Exit Poll data from 1976 to 2008 (South includes eleven-state ex-Confederate definition plus Kentucky and Oklahoma from 1976 to 1982; only Confederate South after 1982); Cooperative Congressional Election Study (CCES) data from 2010 to 2016 (self-reported voters in national elections).

Note: Data show the size of each group (in percentage terms) in the southern Democratic coalition (sums to 100 percent).

Republican counterpart. Figure 9.9 displays the demographic composition of the southern GOP coalition from the 1950s to the 2010s. In the 1950s, white women were the most prominent group of Republican voters (at 49 percent) and remain so for the next two decades. White men were 42 percent of the 1950s GOP coalition while African American voters comprised the remaining 9 percent. After the 1950s, black voters begin their exit of the southern Republican coalition, amounting to less than 2 percent by the 2010s. In the 1970s, Latino voters register a Republican presence (1.6 percent) and constitute 5.1 percent of Republican voters in the 2010s. Although white women are considerably more prevalent than white men in the 2000s (49 versus 42 percent), in the 2010s there is no discernible difference in their share of the Republican coalition. In the 2010s, the relative size (rounding up) of the four demographic groups in the southern Republican coalition was: 47 percent white women, 46 percent white men, 5 percent Latinos, and 2 percent African Americans. The southern GOP's small coalition in the 1950s was dominated by white voters (91 percent) while its much larger current version is still ruled by a disproportionally large white voter contingent (93 percent).

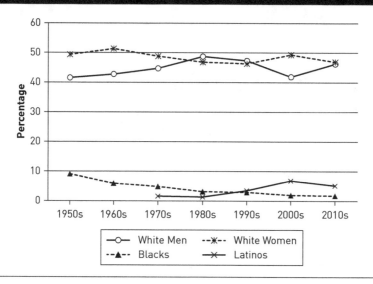

FIGURE 9.9 ■ The Southern Republican Coalition, 1950s–2010s

Sources: American National Election Studies (ANES) data from 1952 to 1974 (self-reported voters in national elections); National Exit Poll data from 1976 to 2008 (South includes eleven-state ex-Confederate definition plus Kentucky and Oklahoma from 1976 to 1982; only Confederate South after 1982); Cooperative Congressional Election Study (CCES) data from 2010 to 2016 (self-reported voters in national elections).

Note: Data show the size of each group (in percentage terms) in the southern Republican coalition (sums to 100 percent).

THE PRIMARY ELECTORATE

Given the importance of primary elections as a leading indicator of partisan change (Stimson 2004), it is more than a little bit curious that there is comparably very little scholarship on the changing nature of party coalitions in primary electorates. The preferences of primary voters ultimately determine which candidates succeed in securing their party nomination and hence shaping the direction of their party in general elections. In other words, primaries are the testing grounds for defining and redefining the images of the major parties.

In the South, the longstanding participation advantage in Democratic presidential primary electorates persisted until 2000, the first election in which more voters participated in Republican presidential primaries (McKee and Hayes 2010). Figure 9.10 captures the sea change in the rate of Republican participation by comparing the size of the Republican presidential primary electorate of each southern state in 1988 versus 2016. Beyond occurring almost three decades apart, in both of these elections there was competition in both major party primaries because the White House was open (President Reagan was term limited in 1988 and President Obama was term limited in 2016).[8]

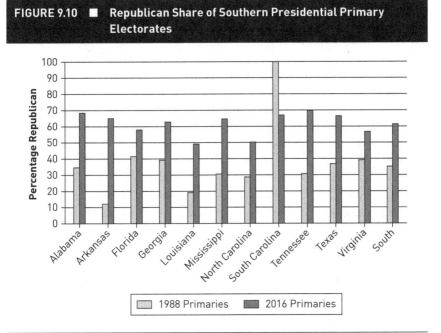

FIGURE 9.10 ■ Republican Share of Southern Presidential Primary Electorates

☐ 1988 Primaries   ■ 2016 Primaries

Sources: Presidential primary vote data for the 1988 contests are from CQ Press's *Guide to U.S. Elections* (Kalb 2016); data for the 2016 presidential primaries are from Dave Leip's *Atlas of U.S. Presidential Elections* (http://uselectionatlas.org/RESULTS/).

Notes: In 1988 only the South Carolina GOP held a primary (South Carolina Democrats held a caucus and that is why 100 percent of primary votes were cast in the Republican primary). Percentage Republican is the Republican share of primary votes cast out of all Democratic and Republican votes cast in these respective major-party presidential primaries. South-wide, the total Democratic and Republican votes cast in 1988 were, respectively: 7,134,576 and 3,859,766; in 2016, the total Democratic and Republican votes cast in southern presidential primaries were 7,736,011 and 12,257,718.

In each state, the graph shows the percentage of GOP presidential primary votes cast out of the two-party total. For example, in the 1988 Democratic and Republican presidential primary contests held in Mississippi, 31 percent of the votes were cast in the GOP race. In 2016, 65 percent of presidential primary votes in Mississippi were cast in the Republican contest. The comparison of Republican primary vote shares over this three-decade span is possible in every southern state but South Carolina because only the Republican Party conducted a presidential primary in the Palmetto State in 1988 (South Carolina Democrats held a caucus).

In 1988, every southern state (excluding South Carolina for the reason stated above) had a majority Democratic presidential voting primary electorate. Twenty-eight years later, only in Louisiana did Democrats cast a higher portion of the presidential primary vote (51 percent). North Carolina was the state where the GOP presidential primary vote margin was the smallest at 0.3 percentage points. The participation gap was greatest in Tennessee where 70 percent of presidential primary voters participated in the Republican contest. The biggest reversal in the share of Republican presidential primary votes took place in Arkansas. In 1988 only 12 percent of Arkansan presidential primary votes were cast in the GOP race, but in 2016, 65 percent of the two-party presidential primary vote total was delivered to Republican contenders.

Overall, in 1988 the Republican portion of presidential primary votes was 35 percent; in 2016 the GOP share vaulted to 61 percent. Put another way, in 1988 almost 11 million presidential primary votes were cast in the South and over 7 million went to Democratic candidates; in 2016 almost 20 million presidential primary votes were cast in Dixie and over 12 million went to Republican aspirants. Finally, one last way to comprehend the shift in favor of Republican presidential primary participation is that between 1988 and 2016 the total number of Democratic votes increased by 8.4 percent while the total number of Republican votes increased by 218 percent.

Racial and Ethnic Composition of the Primary Electorate

Similar to the assessment of the racial and ethnic composition of the southern Democratic and Republican coalitions in general elections, Table 9.2 displays the racial composition of presidential primary electorates (the percentage of voters who are white, black, and Latino) for each southern state in 1988 and 2016. All of these data are from exit polls conducted among a sample of each state's Democratic and Republican presidential primary voters. Starting with the Democratic presidential primary electorate, in 1988 every southern state had a majority white Democratic coalition (ranging from a low of 54 percent in Mississippi to a high of 86 percent in Arkansas).

By 2016, in every Deep South state (Alabama, Georgia, Louisiana, Mississippi, and South Carolina) the Democratic presidential primary electorate is majority black (ranging from a low of 51 percent in Georgia to a high of 71 percent in Mississippi). In addition to the growing black segment of the Democratic presidential primary electorate, the practically nonexistent Latino component in every southern state in 1988 (with the exception of Texas) has become notable in Georgia (7 percent) and the Peripheral South states of Florida (20 percent), Texas (32 percent), and Virginia (7 percent). Only in the Rim South mega-states of Florida and Texas is the Democratic presidential primary electorate no longer majority white, and the rise of Latino voters is principally responsible for this development.

The racial and ethnic makeup of the southern Republican presidential primary electorate is, to put it gently, challenged in the diversity department. In 1988, white voters comprised well over 90 percent of the GOP presidential primary electorate in every southern state (ranging from a low of 93 percent in Florida and Texas to a high of 98 percent in the Deep South states of Alabama, Mississippi, and South Carolina). Twenty-eight years hence, seven of the eleven southern states still have

TABLE 9.2 ■ Racial Composition of Southern Presidential Primary Electorates, 1988 versus 2016

Primary	Percentage White		Percentage Black		Percentage Latino	
Democratic	1988	2016	1988	2016	1988	2016
Alabama	55	40	45	54	<1	1
Arkansas	86	67	13	27	1	3
Florida	80	48	17	27	1	20
Georgia	63	38	35	51	<1	7
Louisiana	62	[36]	37	[61]	<1	[?]
Mississippi	54	24	45	71	1	1
North Carolina	71	62	29	32	<1	3
South Carolina	N/A	35	N/A	61	N/A	2
Tennessee	72	63	27	32	<1	2
Texas	65	43	22	19	10	32
Virginia	64	63	34	26	<1	7
Republican	1988	2016	1988	2016	1988	2016
Alabama	98	93	2	4	<1	1
Arkansas	96	96	3	2	<1	1
Florida	93	78	2	3	5	16
Georgia	97	88	2	7	<1	3
Louisiana	96	[96]	3	[1]	1	[?]
Mississippi	98	93	2	6	<1	1
North Carolina	97	94	3	2	<1	1
South Carolina	98	96	2	1	<1	1
Tennessee	97	94	2	2	<1	1
Texas	93	82	3	3	3	10
Virginia	97	86	2	9	1	2

Source: Data compiled by the author from the 1988 CBS/New York Times state primary exit polls for every state but South Carolina (an ABC News exit poll for Republican primary voters; there was no South Carolina Democratic primary and therefore N/A denotes not applicable). All of the summary data for the state presidential primaries in 2016 are available at the following CNN website: http://www.cnn.com/election/primaries/polls.

Notes: There was not an exit poll for Louisiana in 2016, but some of the data can be determined because the state provides turnout data for registered voters according to race (white, black, and other) and party, and holds closed presidential primaries (i.e., only registered Democrats can vote in the Democratic presidential primary and only registered Republicans can vote in the Republican presidential primary). Data on Latino registration and turnout are not available (indicated by a question mark). The 2016 Louisiana data are bracketed and in bold to indicate that they are not from an exit poll.

90-percent plus majority white GOP presidential primary coalitions. Because of the increase in the share of Latino voters in Florida (from 5 percent to 16 percent) and Texas (from 3 percent to 10 percent), these states have the lowest percentage of white voters (78 percent in Florida and 82 percent in Texas). Interestingly, the reduction in the white share of voters in Virginia and Georgia is mainly attributable to a nontrivial increase in the portion of black voters (increasing from 2 to 9 percent in Virginia and rising from 2 to 7 percent in Georgia).

The Primary Gender Gap

The analysis of southern presidential primary electorates can be taken a step further by considering the portion of women voters participating in each major party coalition. As shown in Table 9.3, in 1988, for every southern state holding a Democratic presidential primary (recall that only South Carolina did not), women voters were the majority. In 2016, an across-the-board development surfaces: the share of women Democratic presidential primary voters increases significantly in every state (ranging from a low of a 5 percentage point increase in Arkansas, Florida, Tennessee, and Virginia to an impressive 11 percentage point jump in Mississippi). Women are the clear majority gender in Democratic presidential primary electorates, and in four Deep South states (most likely all five, but there is no exit poll data on Louisiana) 60 percent or more of the Democratic coalition consists of women. The reason for women constituting an especially large portion of Democratic presidential primary voters in Deep South states is that, among this majority black coalition, black women are much more prevalent than black men.[9]

In contrast to the markedly greater presence of women voters in southern Democratic presidential primary electorates, the gender differences among Republican presidential primary voters have become much more balanced in 2016. In 1988, men were the majority of Republican primary voters in six of the eleven southern states (Alabama, Florida, Georgia, South Carolina, Tennessee, and Texas). In 2016, women comprised at least half of the Republican presidential primary coalition in a minimum of seven southern states (again, no exit poll data on Louisiana). The greatest changes between 1988 and 2016 took place in Arkansas (7 percentage point decline in women voters) and Virginia (5 percentage point decline in women voters) where majority female electorates are now majority male. Reflecting the absence of a gender gap among white Republican men and women in general elections, in Republican presidential primaries most southern states are evenly balanced in their share of men and women voters.

A Look at South Carolina

South Carolina offers an insightful example of a changing primary electorate. The Palmetto State makes primary data on registered voters available according to

TABLE 9.3 ■ Gender Composition of Southern Presidential Primary Electorates, 1988 versus 2016			
Primary	**Percentage Women in Presidential Primary**		
Democratic	**1988**	**2016**	**2016–1988**
Alabama	53	60	+7
Arkansas	52	57	+5
Florida	53	58	+5
Georgia	52	62	+10
Louisiana	52	N/A	—
Mississippi	53	64	+11
North Carolina	52	58	+6
South Carolina	N/A	61	—
Tennessee	53	58	+5
Texas	52	58	+6
Virginia	52	57	+5
Republican	**1988**	**2016**	**2016–1988**
Alabama	47	51	+4
Arkansas	55	48	–7
Florida	49	51	+2
Georgia	49	51	+2
Louisiana	51	N/A	—
Mississippi	53	50	–3
North Carolina	52	50	–2
South Carolina	46	49	+3
Tennessee	48	50	+2
Texas	48	50	+2
Virginia	52	47	–5

Source: Data compiled by the author from the 1988 CBS/New York Times state primary exit polls for every state but South Carolina (an ABC News exit poll for Republican primary voters; there was no South Carolina Democratic primary and therefore N/A denotes not applicable). All of the summary data for the state presidential primaries in 2016 are available at the following CNN website: http://www.cnn.com/election/primaries/polls.

Note: See the note on Louisiana under Table 9.2.

race (white/nonwhite) and gender. For decades now, South Carolina has been the first state in the South to hold its presidential primaries (see Huffmon, Knotts, and McKee 2017) and therefore it acts as the initial electoral barometer of southern voter preferences.

As shown with the exit poll data above in Table 9.2, 61 percent of South Carolina Democratic presidential primary voters in 2016 were African American. On the basis of a white/nonwhite racial division, the percentage of registered South Carolina voters participating in the last two open-seat presidential elections (2008 and 2016) can illustrate the change in the racial composition of the Democratic primary coalition. And because African Americans comprise the lion's share of South Carolina's nonwhite registered electorate, it is a serviceable proxy for African Americans (recall that the exit poll data put the share of Latino Democratic presidential primary voters in 2016 at 2 percent and just 1 percent for Latino GOP presidential primary voters; see Table 9.2).

In the 2008 South Carolina Democratic presidential primary, 56 percent of the voting electorate was nonwhite, and their support for Barack Obama set him on an early path to the Democratic nomination. Ironically, the minority electorate that so overwhelmingly favored Obama over Hillary Clinton in 2008 was extremely partial to Clinton in her matchup against Bernie Sanders in 2016 (see Huffmon, Knotts, and McKee 2017). Further, the share of nonwhite voters participating in the 2016 South Carolina Democratic presidential primary reached a record-high 66 percent. By comparison, the nonwhite share of the South Carolina Republican presidential primary electorate voting in the 2008 and 2016 contests went from 1.4 percent to 2.1 percent.

With respect to gender, in the 2008 Democratic presidential primary, 61 percent of voters were women. In 2016, women were 63 percent of the Democratic presidential primary voting electorate. By contrast, and in line with the general pattern that prevails in Republican presidential primary electorates, there was no discernible gender gap in political participation. In 2008, 49 percent of GOP primary voters were women and in 2016 women constituted 51 percent of Republican presidential primary voters in South Carolina.

Two elections held eight years apart are suggestive, but not enough evidence to confirm a pattern. Therefore, it is necessary to turn to South Carolina's data on voters in nonpresidential party primary elections. In South Carolina, state party primaries do not take place on the same date as their presidential primaries. For instance, in 2016 the Democratic and Republican presidential preference primaries were conducted in February but on different days (2/20 for the GOP and 2/27 for the Democrats). The state party primary date for both major parties was not until June 14.[10] The Palmetto State provides the same kind of data on registered voters in both presidential primaries and state primary elections. These data are available from 1984 to 2016 for each state primary election occurring every two years.

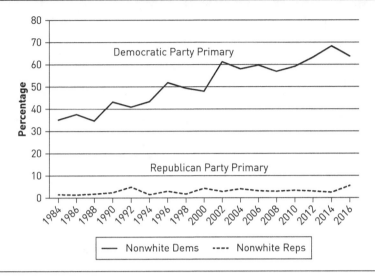

FIGURE 9.11 ■ **Percentage of Nonwhite Primary Voters in South Carolina**

Source: Data compiled from the South Carolina Election Commission voter history statistics website (https://www.scvotes.org/data/voter-history.html).

Note: Data display the percentage of nonwhite registered voters out of all registered voters (nonwhite and white) who turned out in each major party (Democratic and Republican) primary in South Carolina from 1984 to 2016. These are not presidential primary data.

Beginning with race, Figure 9.11 documents the percentage of nonwhite registrants who participated in the Democratic Party primary or the Republican Party primary from 1984 to 2016. The trend for an increasing nonwhite voting electorate in the Democratic Party primary is palpable. In 1984, nonwhite voters accounted for 35 percent of the Democratic Party primary electorate. Thirty-two years later (in 2016), nonwhites had taken over the South Carolina Democratic primary coalition, comprising 64 percent of its voters. The GOP primary electorate, by comparison, appears frozen with respect to its racial composition. In 1984, 1.5 percent of Republican primary voters were nonwhite. In 2016, the nonwhite share of GOP primary voters had peaked at a whopping 5.5 percent.

Figure 9.12 displays the share of women voters participating in the Democratic and Republican state primary elections in South Carolina from 1984 to 2016. Similar to the data displayed in Table 9.3 and discussed with regard to the increase in women voters between the 2008 and 2012 South Carolina Democratic presidential primary contests, there is a clear pattern of an increasing share of women voters from 1984 to 2016 in Palmetto State Democratic primary elections. In 1984, women accounted for almost 55 percent of Democratic primary voters. In 2016, women constituted 60 percent of the voters participating in the Democratic primary elections. As for Republicans, from 1984 to 2016, there has essentially been

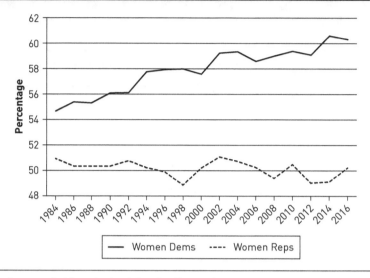

FIGURE 9.12 ■ Percentage of Women Primary Voters in South Carolina

Women Dems   ---- Women Reps

Source: Data compiled from the South Carolina Election Commission voter history statistics website (https://www.scvotes.org/data/voter-history.html).

Note: Data display the percentage of registered women voters out of all registered voters (women and men) who turned out in each major party (Democratic and Republican) primary in South Carolina from 1984 to 2016. These are not presidential primary data.

no long-term change (though some evident short-term fluctuations) in the gender composition of voters in GOP primaries. In 1984, 50.9 percent of Republican primary voters were women; in 2016, 50.2 percent of GOP primary participants were women.

Although there is hardly any detectable alteration in the demographic composition of the South Carolina Republican primary electorate from 1984 to 2016 (at least with respect to race and gender), there has been a transformation nothing short of a game changer. Consider that in 1984 the number of registered voters participating in the South Carolina Republican primary was 48,494. By comparison, 373,258 registered voters participated in the 1984 South Carolina Democratic primary. In 1984, 11.5 percent of registered South Carolinians chose to vote in the GOP primary while the remaining 88.5 percent made their vote count in the Democratic primary. In 2016, 260,612 registered voters participated in the Republican primary versus 158,959 registered voters who chose to cast a ballot in the Democratic primary. In other words, Republican primary voters comprised 62 percent of all major party voters in 2016.[11] The racial sorting of minority voters into the Democratic primary coalition has been more than offset by the tremendous rise in the share of white voters aligning with the GOP opposition—a very familiar pattern manifested in all Deep South states.

WELCOME BACK CARPETBAGGERS!
SOUTHERN IN-MIGRANTS

There is a consensus view among scholars that the early waves of post–World War II immigration to the American South advanced the Grand Old Party (Hood, Kidd, and Morris 2012; Scher 1997), even if it only did so marginally in most locations because the size of these migration streams tended to be rather small vis-à-vis the much larger native population. Over time, however, the political contribution of new arrivals appears to have registered a different impact on the partisan tenor of southern politics. Since the end of World War II, the partisan balance in various parts of the United States has been fundamentally altered, and of course more so in the South than in any other region. Nonetheless, consider that the locus of GOP political strength used to reside in New England, but now this northernmost section of the Northeast is decidedly Democratic. Likewise, before the 1990s, California was a Republican state in presidential elections (straight Republican from 1968 to 1988), but after 1988 it has only voted Democratic.

Once the unrivaled epicenter of the Democratic Party, now the southern United States are unquestionably the most staunchly Republican. As Dixie has turned into a very deep shade of red, most of the northern states above it, and especially those situated closer to the Atlantic Seaboard (the Northeast as opposed to the Midwest), have morphed into a more distinctive blue. In other words, the South has become more Republican as most of the states outside the region have become more Democratic. This geographic sorting of the American electorate (Bishop and Cushing 2008) means that the most recent arrivals to Dixie tend to be less Republican than the native population. For example, in 2008 Barack Obama managed to win three southern states: Florida, North Carolina, and Virginia. It is no coincidence that in the South, these states contain some of the largest populations of in-migrants from the heavily Democratic Northeast (McKee 2010; McKee and Teigen 2016). It was not just a surge in black support that won Obama these three states, it was also the votes he received from the more Democratically inclined in-migrant residents.

Indeed, scholarship on the most recent white migrants to the South clearly demonstrates that they are not as likely to identify as Republicans and they are also more likely to vote Democratic in presidential elections (Hillygus, McKee, and Young 2017). Parsing the same ANES data analyzed by Hillygus, McKee, and Young (2017), McKee and Teigen (2016) found that in dividing the nation into the five sections defined by Black and Black (2007), white in-migrants from the Northeast and Midwest (but not from the Mountains/Plains or Pacific Coast)—the regions closest to the South and responsible for most of the recent in-migration, were significantly more likely than native white southerners to vote for Barack Obama in 2008 (even when party identification and several other voter characteristics were taken into account). In an in-depth case study of North Carolina, Hood and McKee (2010a) found that in-migrants to the Tar Heel State were more likely to register as political independents and these in-migrants were much more likely to vote for Barack Obama in 2008 than native North Carolinians who otherwise shared a similar political profile (apart from the migration distinction).

BOX 9.1   WAKE COUNTY, NORTH CAROLINA: A WINDOW INTO SOUTHERN CHANGE

In the county containing the capital city of Raleigh, North Carolina, demographic change has occurred at a mind-numbing rate. Wake County, located in the center of the state in the North Carolina piedmont, is witnessing a remarkable political transformation due primarily to the compositional changes among the population residing in this booming area. The significant alteration of the Wake County population is a development that clearly favors the Democratic Party, and it can be viewed as a microcosm of the kind of population change occurring in many southern settings (MacManus 2011). Table 9.4 documents several features indicating how Wake County has changed over the last two decades. First, the registered voter population has increased nearly 100 percent, going from 349,854 registrants in 1997 to 697,093 in 2017. Much of this population growth is attributable to the in-migration of northerners and especially those from the Northeast (McKee and Teigen 2016). Compared to native North Carolinians, these residents are much more likely to register as independents and vote Democratic (Hood and McKee 2010a). In 1990, 42 percent of Wake County residents were born outside of the state. In 2015, the U.S. Census Bureau estimated that 56 percent of Wake County residents were born outside of North Carolina.

In the South, North Carolina is one of three states (Florida and Louisiana are the other two) with voter registration that documents party affiliation, race/ethnicity, and gender. As shown in Table 9.4, the share of registered Democrats and Republicans has declined 10 and 9 percentage points, respectively, from 1997 to 2017. Unaffiliated registrants are now only 3 points shy of attaining parity with Democratic registrants who are now just a slight plurality (38 percent) of registrants, whereas twenty years prior, Democrats comprised 48 percent of the registered electorate. The decline in registered Republicans is related to the marked drop in white registrants. In 1997, fully 81 percent of registrants were white. In 2017, 66 percent of Wake County registrants were white (an 18.5 percent drop). With respect to gender, the last two decades exhibit no detectable change in Wake County's majority female registrants (54 percent in 1997 and 53 percent in 2017). These changes to the Wake County population have certainly affected voter preferences. In 1996, 51 percent of the much smaller and less racially diverse Wake County electorate voted for Democratic President Bill Clinton's Republican opponent, Bob Dole. Twenty years hence, the much larger, less native, and more racially diverse Wake County electorate cast 61 percent of their votes for Democrat Hillary Clinton—a notably stronger performance than her husband's in 1996.

TABLE 9.4 ■ What a Difference a Couple of Decades Makes in Wake County, North Carolina

Year	Total Registration	Democratic Registered	Republican Registered	Unaffiliated Registered	White Registered	Women Registered	*Born Outside North Carolina	Democratic Pres. Vote
1997	349,854	48%	36%	17%	81%	54%	42%	1996 = 49%
2017	697,093	38%	27%	35%	66%	53%	56%	2016 = 61%
Difference	+347,239	−10	−9	+18	−15	−1	+14	+12

Sources: Voter registration data are from the following Wake County website: http://www.wakegov.com/elections/data/Pages/registrationstatistics.aspx; the presidential vote data are from the North Carolina State Board of Elections website: https://www.ncsbe.gov/Election-Results; *place of birth data are from the 1990 U.S. Census and the 1-year American Community Survey estimate for 2015, respectively.

Notes: The percentage of registered Democrats, Republicans, and Unaffiliated does not sum exactly to 100 percent because there are a small number of Libertarian Party registrants. The Democratic presidential vote is calculated out of the total votes cast for the major parties (Democratic and Republican). Bill Clinton won 49 percent of the vote in Wake County in 1996 and his wife Hillary Clinton won 61 percent of the vote in Wake County twenty years later.

Not only does it appear that recent white in-migrants are less Republican/more Democratic in their political behavior as compared to their native white counterparts, but in more recent decades the share of newcomers has increased and their demographic profile is more racially and geographically diverse (including an increasing number of in-migrants from other nations, particularly Latinos from Mexico, Central and South America). Figure 9.13 displays the percentage of native and in-migrant voters in the South from the 1950s to the 2000s. In the 1950s, the share of in-migrant voters was 14 percent and native southern voters were 86 percent of the electorate participating in national elections. This ratio of natives to in-migrant voters remains fairly steady until after the 1980s when there is an obvious decline in the portion of native voters and hence a concomitant rise in the percentage of in-migrant voters. By the 2000s, native southern voters account for 73 percent, and in-migrant voters 27 percent, of Dixie's electorate.

Because of the racial sorting of the southern electorate into opposing partisan camps, it bears considering whether the racial composition of native and in-migrant voters has changed over time. Figure 9.14 shows the percentage of white/nonwhite

---

FIGURE 9.13 ■ Percentage of Native and In-Migrant Voters in the South

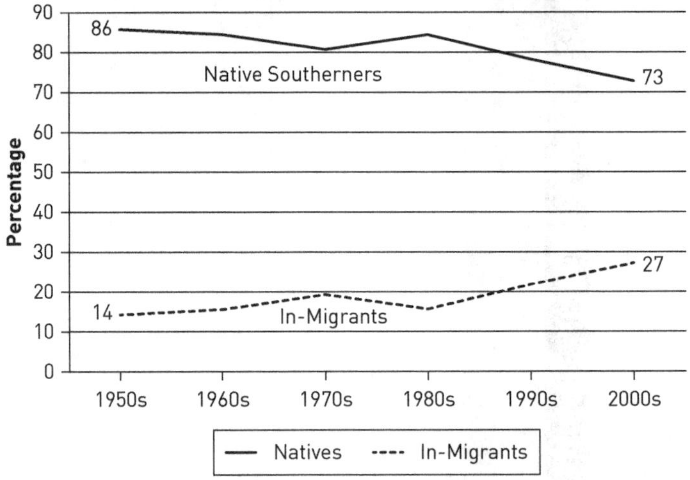

Source: ANES Time Series Cumulative Data File (1948–2012).

Notes: Self-reported voters in national elections. Specifically, the ANES asks a respondent in which state (or states) they grew up. In addition to the eleven former Confederate states, respondents are classified as native southerners if they grew up in the border states of Kentucky, Maryland, Oklahoma, West Virginia, and Washington, D.C. (or some combination of growing up in any of the aforementioned states). If respondents grew up anywhere else then they are classified as an in-migrant. The ANES did not ask the "where did respondent grow up" question in every year of the time series. The condensing of decades is as follows: 1950s = 1952, 1956, 1958; 1960s = 1960, 1964, 1966, 1968; 1970s = 1970, 1972, 1974, 1976, 1978; 1980s = 1980, 1982, 1984, 1986, 1988; 1990s = 1990, 1992, 1994, 1996; 2000s = 2000 and 2008. The appropriate ANES weight variable was used from 1994 to 2008.

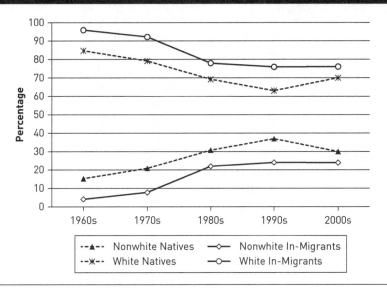

FIGURE 9.14 ■ Racial Composition of Native and In-Migrant Voters in the South

Source: ANES Time Series Cumulative Data File (1948–2012).

voters among natives and in-migrants. Especially for the first two decades, in the 1960s and 1970s, the data provide strong evidence for why in-migrants were likely to foster southern Republicanism: new arrivals were not just overwhelmingly white (96 percent white in the 1960s and 92 percent white in the 1970s), but in this period of time the South was still much more Democratic than the states outside the region from which most of these in-migrant voters left (Brown 1988). After the 1970s, there is a notable decline in the share of in-migrant voters who are white and thus a rise in the percentage of in-migrant voters who are nonwhite. With respect to in-migrant voters, in the 1960s only 4 percent were nonwhite, in the 2000s almost a quarter (24 percent) of in-migrant voters were nonwhite. The increasing number of in-migrants to the South and their changing demographic composition is a development that generally favors the Democratic Party. In the coming years this component of partisan change is likely to register an even greater effect on the state of southern party politics.

CONCLUDING THOUGHTS

When Alabama Governor George Wallace ran for president as a third-party candidate (American Independent Party) in 1968, he proclaimed that "there's isn't a dime's worth of difference" between the leading politicians of the Democratic and Republican parties (Nelson 2014, 134). If Wallace were alive today, chances are he would beg to differ with his own statement. As a vast and growing literature on party polarization shows, elected Democrats and Republicans are poles apart on a raft of political issues (Theriault 2008) and it is reflected in their voting behavior (Fleisher and Bond 2004). The disagreement and growing distance between Democrats and Republicans, especially among members of Congress, has not gone unnoticed by the mass electorate (Hetherington 2001). In this contemporary political environment legislative compromise is more difficult to achieve because Democrats and Republicans represent a set of constituents who look very different from each other and often hold preferences and political views that do not overlap.

As documented in this chapter, since the 1950s there have been wholesale changes to the coalitions of voters comprising the southern Democratic and Republican parties. White men, so long the bedrock of the southern Democracy, are now firmly aligned with the GOP. Republican white women account for practically the entire other half of a contemporary GOP, which is an overwhelmingly white coalition. But it is also the case that more white women than white men identify with the Democratic opposition and only African Americans outnumber their portion of the Democratic coalition. Since their punctuated and permanent shift to the Democratic Party in the 1960s, African Americans have become the plurality group and undisputed leaders of the modern southern Democratic coalition. And despite their relatively small share of the electorate, Latino voters are a growing constituency and they currently show a proclivity for the more racially and ethnically diverse and inclusive Democratic Party.

Demographic changes to the southern electorate, specifically in terms of growing racial diversity and the in-migration of voters who are less inclined to identify with the GOP and vote for its candidates, are obviously a concern for the current electorally dominant Republican Party. As the quote by Key (1949) that opened the chapter stresses, change is afoot, even if it is sometimes hard to detect. Indeed, shortly after Key's writing, in the 1950s changes to the southern electorate began to emerge from below the surface, and sixty years later the Solid Democratic South has been thoroughly replaced by a Republican Dixie that now must find a way to hold onto the reins of power. The Democratic threat may seem merely a nuisance, but it is real and GOP operatives are cognizant of it. As the next chapter demonstrates, Republicans are trying hard to stem the growing tide of demographic changes, which potentially have the force to wrest back political control for a very different looking contemporary version of the southern Democracy.

10 REPUBLICAN RESPONSES TO DEMOGRAPHIC CHANGE

I n the 2000 presidential election, the winner would be decided by the outcome of the popular vote in Florida. Absent the Sunshine State's 25 electoral votes, the partisan split in the Electoral College stood at 266 for the Tennessee Democrat Al Gore and 246 for the Texas Republican George W. Bush. After a controversial Supreme Court decision (*Bush v. Gore*), on December 12, 2000, by a 537-vote margin in Florida, George W. Bush became president with one electoral vote more (271) than the bare minimum needed to take office (270). Five hundred thirty-seven votes . . . a margin so slim a unified congregation in a Florida church could have delivered the victory. Indeed, if ever a contest was to find itself located within the bounds of the statistical margin of error then it was this presidential race (Ceaser and Busch 2001).[1] In fact, the election hinged on such a narrow razor's edge that voter confusion over the "butterfly ballot" in Palm Beach County alone accounted for enough votes to put Bush over the top (Wand et al. 2001).[2]

The "mal-administration" of the 2000 presidential election in Florida, with its arguably unlawful purging of the voter rolls (Flanigan et al. 2015), bewildering Palm Beach County butterfly ballots, dimpled and legions of hanging chads (Pleasants 2004), called such because they failed to completely dislodge themselves from their punch card ballots, spurred major electoral reform. And so, in 2002, via a bipartisan vote (Hicks et al. 2015), Congress passed the Help America Vote Act (HAVA). The legislation was crafted to bring some much-needed sanity, consistency, and uniformity to the administration of federal election contests.[3] Ironically though, in hindsight this congressional action, passed in the aftermath of the 2000 presidential election debacle, was perhaps the last politically unifying event of significance in the area of election administration law. At the state level in particular, the new millennium ushered in a wave of restrictive voting legislation, almost completely spearheaded by Republicans and opposed by Democrats.

This chapter lays out an empirically based political narrative that southern Republicans (not unlike many of their northern GOP colleagues) of late (especially since 2010), have concentrated most of their efforts at maintaining their political hold on Dixie's politics by pressing their advantage via aggressive election-related maneuvering and statutory-based electoral reforms. Piggybacking on the findings from the previous chapter, this one begins with another look at how demographic change stands to benefit Democrats while disadvantaging Republicans. It is from this backdrop (political context), that GOP efforts to seek an electoral edge through redistricting (partisan gerrymandering) and election reforms intended to curtail the eligible electorate (with stricter voter identification laws being perhaps the most salient example) have manifested in a rather blatant partisan driven electoral strategy. Control of state government was a necessary condition for southern Republicans to implement their strategy, and this materialized in most states following the Republican "tsunami" in the 2010 midterm elections. The ability of the southern GOP to pursue their electoral advantage by bending the institutional levers of government in their favor before any votes are cast, got a whole lot easier thanks to the fateful and monumental Supreme Court ruling in the 2013 Alabama case of *Shelby County v. Holder*. The significance of this decision is discussed and then the chapter wraps up with a brief recounting of its major findings.

DEMOGRAPHIC CHANGE IN THE SOUTHERN ELECTORATE

As the last chapter made clear, changes in the southern electorate have manifested in two rather distinct voting coalitions for the Democratic and Republican parties. Whereas the Republican coalition is overwhelmingly white (greater than 90 percent of its GOP identifiers; see Figure 9.9 in chapter 9), the Democratic coalition is remarkably diverse: at present, it is plurality African American with sizable numbers of white and Latino supporters (see Figure 9.8 in chapter 9). The astounding demographic transformation of the voters identifying as Democrats and Republicans in southern politics accounts for why the major parties appear diametrically opposed on most salient issues driving the political agenda. Further, the alteration in the *relative* size of the racial/ethnic groups participating in electoral politics (a subject left largely untouched in chapter 9), appears to shape the current political strategy of a now dominant southern GOP. Simply put, although southern Republicans have reached a hegemonic position in most elections from the top of the ballot to the bottom (see chapter 5), demographic change is not their friend because in relative terms the white population is declining.

Consider first the share of the voting age population (VAP) in the South that is black, Latino, and white, based on the 2000 and 2010 decennial census data. According to the 2000 Census, in the South the VAP for the black, Latino, and white population was, respectively, 17.8 percent, 11.8 percent, and 67.1 percent. Just a decade later, these VAP numbers had changed to 18.3 percent black, 15.6 percent Latino, and 61.7 percent white. Hence, the share of minority VAP increased, especially for Latinos (32 percent increase), while it dropped for the majority white population (8 percent decline). Additionally, the residual category of VAP for southern residents not classified as black, Latino, or white, went from 3.3 percent in 2000 to 4.4 percent in 2010. VAP data of course give only a rough approximation of demographic change because it often does not closely comport with participation rates (McDonald and Popkin 2001). A more important and direct political assessment is to track the

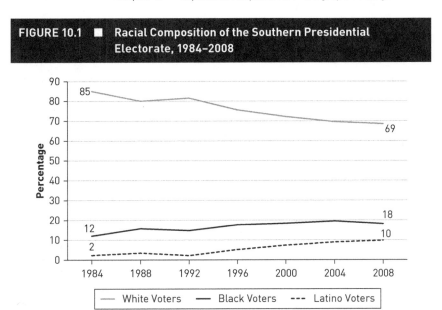

FIGURE 10.1 ■ Racial Composition of the Southern Presidential Electorate, 1984–2008

Source: Data compiled by the author from the national exit polls for the southern states.

share of black, Latino, and white voters in southern elections. Figure 10.1 charts the percentage of the southern electorate that is black, Latino, and white in presidential elections from the Ronald Reagan landslide in 1984 to the Barack Obama victory in 2008. The data are from the national exit polls (actual voters as opposed to survey respondents claiming to have voted) and thus should be very accurate measures of the racial composition of the southern electorate.

In the 1984 presidential contest, when the Democratic nominee Walter Mondale only managed to win the electoral votes of Minnesota and the District of Columbia, whites comprised 85 percent of southern voters, blacks were 12 percent, and Latinos a meager 2 percent. Almost twenty-five years later, in the historic election of Barack Obama—a contest in which the African American nominee won the southern states of Florida, North Carolina, and Virginia—the southern presidential electorate was now 69 percent white, 18 percent black, and 10 percent Latino. Obviously, the downward trend in the size of the white southern electorate is a cause of concern for the GOP because it is so heavily reliant on support from these voters. Figure 10.2 shows similar data on the composition of the southern electorate for midterm contests from 1986 to 2006. In 1986, the southern electorate was 84 percent white, 13 percent black, and 2 percent Latino. Twenty years hence, the southern electorate is 74 percent white, 16 percent black, and 8 percent Latino. Compared to presidential cycles, the long-term decline in the size of the white electorate in midterm years is not as severe and this is perhaps an explanation for why the GOP has generally performed better in midterm elections (with 2006 being an exception) from 2002 to 2014, even though

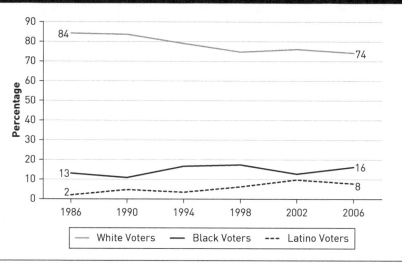

FIGURE 10.2 ■ Racial Composition of the Southern Midterm Electorate, 1986–2006

Source: Data compiled by the author from the national exit polls for the southern states.

it is still the case that the size of the minority electorate in the South is increasing (though at a slower pace versus presidential years).

Table 10.1 shows the changing demography of the southern electorate in partisan terms by documenting the relative size of black, Latino, and white voters who identify as Democrats, Independents, and Republicans, respectively, from 1984 to 2008. Starting with Democratic voters, in 1984 whites comprised 79 percent of these affiliates who participated in this presidential year, whereas blacks were 18 percent of Democratic identifiers and Latinos constituted 4 percent. In 2008, white Democratic voters were reduced to 62 percent of the total (a 22 percent decline) among Democratic identifiers, while African Americans were now 27 percent (a 50 percent increase), and Latinos had become 12 percent of the Democratic contingent (a 200 percent increase!). Although the decline in white voters is not as great, relatively speaking, among political Independents, the general pattern is the same: whites go from 93 percent of Independents in 1984 to 85 percent in 2008 (a 9 percent decline), blacks go from 5 percent in 1984 to 8 percent in 2008 (a 60 percent increase), and Latinos go from 2 percent in 1984 to 8 percent in 2008 (a 300 percent increase).

Finally, it is only among Republican identifiers where the long-term reduction in the share of white voters is trivial. In 1984, white voters comprised 96 percent of Republican identifiers, blacks were 2 percent of GOP affiliates, and Latinos were also 2 percent. By 2008, the demography of Republican-affiliated voters had changed very little; whites were 93 percent of GOP voters (a 3 percent decline compared to

TABLE 10.1 ■ Racial Composition of the Southern Voting Electorate According to Party Identification, 1984–2008								
	Democrats (%)			Independents (%)			Republicans (%)		
Election	White	Black	Latino	White	Black	Latino	White	Black	Latino
1984	79	18	4	93	5	2	96	2	2
1986	74	24	2	92	6	3	95	3	2
1988	75	20	5	92	5	2	96	3	2
1990	72	21	7	90	5	5	95	2	3
1992	81	16	3	94	4	2	97	2	2
1994	62	34	4	86	11	3	95	2	4
1996	75	18	7	91	6	3	94	3	3
1998	55	38	8	85	10	5	91	3	6
2000	70	20	10	91	5	4	93	2	5
2002	57	30	14	84	8	9	92	1	7
2004	66	24	10	85	7	8	91	2	7
2006	53	36	11	81	13	6	92	2	6
2008	62	27	12	85	8	8	93	2	6
2008–1984	−17	+9	+8	−8	+3	+6	−3	0	+4

Source: National exit poll data.

Notes: Data are weighted and sum to 100 percent (rounding to the nearest whole number) in each affiliation category (e.g., Democrats, Independents, Republicans). Midterm elections are shaded in gray.

1984), blacks remained 2 percent of voters who identified with the GOP, and the only notable growth was among Latino Republicans, who went from 2 percent in 1984 to 6 percent of Republican voters in 2008. In summary, since the mid-1980s and up through the first decade of the new millennium, demographic change has greatly impacted the relative size of the southern electorate in racial/ethnic terms, and the racial/ethnic composition of Democratic and politically Independent voters has undergone considerable change vis-à-vis Republican identifiers, the latter of whom have persisted in being an overwhelmingly white coalition.

Figure 10.3 gets to the heart of the matter as to why demographic changes are so important in southern politics by showing the Republican percentage of the two-party presidential vote cast by blacks, Latinos, and whites from 1984 to 2016. The dynamic in the GOP presidential vote is fairly stable for white and back participants.

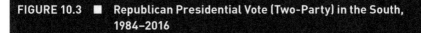

FIGURE 10.3 ■ Republican Presidential Vote (Two-Party) in the South, 1984–2016

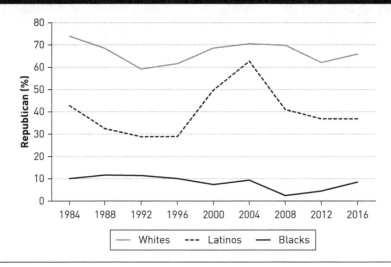

Sources: Data from 1984 to 2008 are from the national exit polls; data in 2012 and 2016 are from the Cooperative Congressional Election Study.

Indeed, for African Americans, the stated rule of thumb that 90 percent vote Democratic (see Black and Black 1987, 2002; Bullock and Gaddie 2009) is clearly evident in the figure. By comparison, white voting behavior is more variable, but only once does the white presidential vote dip below 60 percent Republican (59.2 percent in 1992), and as recent as 2016, almost two out of every three white voters cast a presidential vote for the Republican Donald Trump (65.9 percent).

By far, the greatest volatility in presidential preferences resides with Latinos. But due to Republican actions in more recent years (since 2004), however, the greater variability in Latino voting behavior may have settled down, and to the electoral benefit of southern Democrats. From 1984 to 2008, only once did a majority of southern Latinos back a Republican presidential nominee: in 2004, President Bush captured 62.7 percent of the southern Latino vote. In 1984, President Reagan received more than 40 percent of the Latino vote (42.8 percent), but then the Latino vote in presidential contests stayed under 40 percent until 2000, when Texas Governor George W. Bush won 49.9 percent among this group and then followed up with an impressive and perhaps historically high (for a Republican presidential nominee) 63 percent of Latino support in his successful 2004 presidential reelection bid. Post-President Bush, the Latino vote has strongly favored Democratic presidential candidates. In 2008, Barack Obama won 59 percent of the southern Latino vote and then increased his support among this segment of the southern electorate to 63 percent in 2012, a Democratic share that Hillary Clinton also secured in 2016.

The sharp drop in Republican support among southern Latinos in presidential contests since 2004 has a palpable explanation rooted in the public policy positioning of the major parties (Abrajano and Hajnal 2015). President Bush was the last Republican presidential nominee who had a moderate, in fact, liberal position with respect to immigration reform. In contrast, Bush's successors for the Republican presidential nomination, McCain in 2008 (who essentially ignored this salient issue) then Romney in 2012 (who advocated self-deportation for undocumented immigrants) and most recently Trump in 2016 (who embraced a policy of forcible removal of undocumented immigrants), have moved in a decidedly aggressive anti-immigrant direction. The recent departure from a position welcoming Latinos into the Republican Party, as embraced by President Bush (and previously during his tenure as governor of Texas from 1994–2000), to one that is openly hostile along the lines of that first pursued by California Governor Pete Wilson in his 1994 reelection campaign (see Monogan and Doctor 2017) and now essentially championed by southern and national Republicans since the rise of the Tea Party movement after the election of Barack Obama in 2008, is a turn of events that has definitely steered Latino voters in favor of the Democratic Party. This is arguably a curious development with regard to Republican electoral strategy because, as has already been shown, Latinos are the fastest growing segment of the southern electorate (see also Hood, Kidd, and Morris 2012).[4]

ELECTORAL VOLATILITY IN THE NEW MILLENNIUM

From the 1954 midterm until the 1994 midterm forty years later, the Democratic Party held the majority of seats in the U.S. House of Representatives. With the exception of a six-year interlude of Republican majorities in the upper chamber, commencing with the election of Ronald Reagan in 1980 (1980–1986), the Democrats also controlled the U.S. Senate dating back to 1954. The GOP managed to win a congressional majority in both chambers in the aftermath of the 1994 election, and held onto it until late spring after the 2000 election (June 2001) when a Republican Vermont Senator (James Jeffords) switched to political independence and in so doing, flipped what was a 50/50 partisan split with GOP control (because Republican Vice President Richard Cheney held the tiebreaking vote) to a one-vote Democratic majority because the erstwhile Republican decided to caucus with the Democratic Party (Nicholson 2005). The dawn of the new millennium accelerated a period of intense partisan warfare, and this is perhaps not surprising because of the growing ideological polarization between elected Democrats and Republicans (Fleisher and Bond 2004). Furthermore, and maybe even more important to explaining the intensity of partisan battles, is the increasing volatility in national elections.

The 2000–2008 Elections

A big reason why the Democratic Party managed to sustain its majority congressional status from the mid-1950s to mid-1990s, was because the South was such an overwhelmingly Democratic region. Thus, when northern Democrats suffered notable congressional defeats, the Democratic surplus of members of Congress in the South could often cover the shortfall (Black and Black 2002). But this became less tenable as Dixie gradually realigned to the GOP. Of course, now, when northern Republicans have become scarcer, the GOP surplus of congressional seats in the South has made up the difference (see chapter 11), but not always. Nationally, from 2000 to 2008, the Senate has changed partisan hands three times: first with the 2001 Jeffords switch giving Democrats control, then a Republican majority in the 2002 midterm that was lost two cycles later in the 2006 midterm (Democrats maintained their majority in 2008). Over this same span of elections, the GOP was the majority in the U.S. House until the 2006 midterm, when the Democrats recaptured majorities in both chambers of Congress (like in the Senate, House Democrats held onto their majority in 2008).

Although it is affirmed repeatedly throughout this book that the American South is politically distinct from the rest of the United States, this does not mean that Dixie is immune from the vicissitudes of national partisan tides (Prysby 2014). Therefore, because the GOP dominates southern electoral politics, in a notably good cycle for the national party, Republican gains are more pronounced in the South. In contrast, because the Democratic Party is electorally stronger in the North, a very promising national Democratic cycle is tempered in the South where Democrats are not as politically competitive.

Because congressional elections, especially U.S. House races, are an excellent barometer of short-term political conditions, consider the change in the partisan share of southern U.S. House seats for 2000–2004 versus 2006–2008. The 2000 to 2004 elections were either politically neutral at the national level (specifically the 2000 and 2004 contests) or favored the GOP (the first post-9/11 midterm of 2002; see Jacobson 2003). From 2000 to 2004, Republicans accounted for 59.6 percent of the seats in the southern U.S. House delegation. By comparison, from 2006 to 2008—two back-to-back elections that strongly favored the Democratic Party nationally—the southern Republican share of U.S. House seats declined to 56.9 percent.[5] Likewise, an impressive 82 percent Republican advantage in southern Senate seats (18 Republican Senators out of 22 total) attained in 2004, was subsequently reduced to a 73 percent GOP advantage from 2006 to 2008 (32 Republican Senators out of 44 for these two election cycles). Obviously, because the Democratic Party managed to win control of both congressional chambers in the 2006 midterm and then increased their seat shares in 2008 (see Jacobson 2009b), this national Democratic majority was not due to the South, where a short-term Republican downturn in these years fell far short of delivering a Democratic majority in the region.

Finally, another way to detect short-term partisan shifts is through an examination of macropartisanship. *Macropartisanship* is just a fancy word for the aggregate level of party identification among the mass public (MacKuen, Erikson, and Stimson 1989), e.g., the percentage of people who identify as Democrats, Independents,

FIGURE 10.4 ■ Macropartisanship of the Southern Electorate, 2000–2008

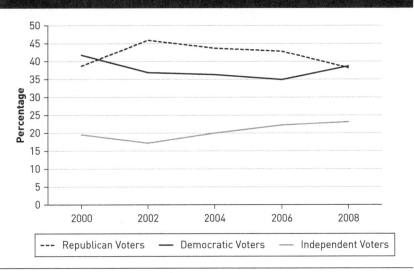

Source: Data compiled by the author from the national exit polls for the southern states.

and Republicans at any given time. Scholars have paid close attention to changes in macropartisanship because it is a strong indicator of which party will have the advantage in an election cycle.

Figure 10.4 charts the macropartisanship of southern voters from 2000 to 2008. The dynamic of party identification at the aggregate level is reflective of the short-term political conditions prevailing from 2000 to 2008. First, it is expected that Republican identification would increase between 2000 and 2002 because of the rally 'round the flag effect (Brody 1991) in the wake of the terrorist attacks on September 11, 2001. Republican control of redistricting in many states (Jacobson 2003), coupled with a strong response to the atrocities of 9/11 under the leadership of Republican President George W. Bush, contributed to the very unusual midterm seat *gains* for the president's party in 2002. In the South, the percentage of GOP identifiers went from 39 percent in 2000 to 46 percent in 2002 (the share of Democratic affiliates went from 42 percent in 2000 to 37 percent in 2002). After 2002, the percentage of Republican voters drops two points in 2004 and another point in 2006 (at 43 percent). Since 2002, Democratic voters decline about two percentage points through 2006 (from 37 to 35 percent), and therefore the one category displaying a notable rise over this period is among political Independents (increasing from 17 percent in 2002 to 22 percent in 2006).

After the GOP took a "thumping" (President Bush's characterization of his party's midterm loss, which returned majorities to the Democratic opposition) in 2006, the 2008 presidential election proved another very strong year for Democrats, with the historic election of African American Democratic nominee Barack Obama at a time of acute financial crisis and one of the highest disapproval ratings for a sitting president (see Jacobson 2009b). Indicative of the short-term drop in southern Republican congressional officeholding, the percentage of southern voters identifying with the GOP went from 43 percent in 2006 to 38 percent in 2008. In contrast, Democratic voters increased from 35 percent in 2006 to almost 39 percent in 2008. But the Democratic gains notched from 2006 to 2008 were short-lived, as the most electorally volatile U.S. House election in terms of partisan seat turnover since 1948 (Jacobson and Carson 2016, 183) was to take place two years later during President Obama's first midterm.

THE 2010 REPUBLICAN "TSUNAMI"

Not long after Barack Obama took office as the 44th president of the United States, the nation sunk deeper into a massive financial crisis that became known as the Great Recession. Obama entered the White House with an impressive honeymoon as indicated by an approval rating of 68 percent when he was sworn into office. But the public soon soured on the president who was once dubbed a rock star on the campaign trail. By the 2010 midterm, President Obama's approval rating had sunk to the mid-40s, a dangerously low number for congressional candidates running under the Democratic label.[6] Taking office with Democratic majorities in both chambers of Congress, the newly elected president promoted an ambitious agenda that in addition to enacting legislation intended to ease the financial damage of the economic crisis (the American Recovery and Reinvestment Act of 2009), also managed to pass one of the most sweeping health care reforms in the nation's history in March 2010: the Patient Protection and Affordable Care Act (ACA), more commonly referred to as Obamacare (Jacobson 2011).

Although experts continue to debate whether President Obama's legislative accomplishments fulfilled their objectives of mitigating the economic crisis while improving health care at an "affordable" cost to most Americans who were now insured, there is no question that in the realm of public opinion the president's agenda sharply divided voters. Indeed, most voters were split down the middle in their views toward Obamacare and the issue became a major bone of contention as the 2010 midterm neared. Further, Obama's legislative agenda was implemented almost entirely with Democratic support in the face of unified Republican congressional opposition. In the electorate, Republican detractors, in particular, exhibited remarkable animosity toward the nation's first minority president. In fact, survey data revealed that more than 30 percent of Republicans believed the president was foreign born and a Muslim (Jacobson 2011, 33).

Perhaps the most alarming development for the president and his party was the rise of the Tea Party movement, a loosely based and growing group of Republican-leaning voters who were fed up with the federal largesse purportedly necessary to stem the economic crisis, whereas Tea Party affiliates viewed it as exacerbating the problem at a time when fiscal belt-tightening seemed to be the sensible response. Reflecting the movement's roots in those places hit hardest by the economic downturn, especially in those cities reeling from the housing crisis (Cho, Gimpel, and Shaw 2012), Tea Party voters were hell-bent on punishing President Obama in the 2010 midterm elections.

Similar to macropartisanship, another very useful gauge of short-term political conditions is the measure of public policy mood, which is based on aggregating a bevy of public opinion data across a broad swath of domestic issue domains. Created by the political scientist James Stimson, the public policy mood exhibits a truly insightful dynamic of political movement. As argued by Stimson (2004), the public policy mood typically exerts countervailing pressure on American presidents. This means that the mood of the public tends to push in the opposite policy direction of the one pursued by the president. Empirically, for Republican presidents who generally push a conservative policy agenda, the public policy mood responds by moving in a liberal direction. Conversely, Democratic presidents generally push a liberal policy agenda and therefore the public policy mood reacts by moving in a conservative direction.

Figure 10.5 shows the annual measure of public policy mood for the entirety of Republican George W. Bush's presidency and the first two years of his successor's, Democrat Barack Obama. A higher public policy mood number indicates movement in a more liberal direction. It is apparent from the figure that Stimson's claim is strongly

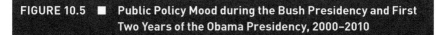

FIGURE 10.5 ■ Public Policy Mood during the Bush Presidency and First Two Years of the Obama Presidency, 2000–2010

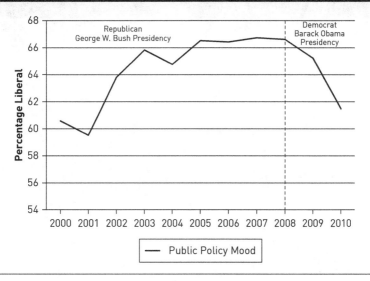

Source: Annual public policy mood data are from James A. Stimson's website (http://stimson.web .unc.edu/data).

supported: under Republican President Bush, with the exceptions of short-lived dips in the conservative direction in 2001 and then again in 2004, the public policy mood is generally and robustly moving in an increasingly liberal policy direction. Likewise, after Democratic President Obama takes office, the public policy mood runs sharply in a downward countervailing conservative direction.

An approval rating hovering around 45 percent, coupled with a public policy mood plunging in a conservative direction, are two robust indicators for a huge Democratic midterm loss in 2010, which President Obama dubbed a "shellacking." After the votes were counted on Election Day, November 2, 2010, the Democratic Party had lost 63 U.S. House seats to the GOP and dropped a half dozen in the U.S. Senate. It was the largest U.S. House seat loss for a major party since 1948, when the GOP shed 75 (Jacobson and Carson 2016, 183), and also the largest Republican U.S. House majority (242) since the GOP's ephemeral 246-seat majority was obtained in the 1946 midterm (Jacobson 2011, 27). In more recent times, the 2010 Democratic midterm loss was larger than the 1994 Democratic midterm loss of 1994 (under Democratic President Bill Clinton) when the GOP finally regained majority status in both chambers of Congress and in the process netted 52 U.S. House seats on Election Day and also picked up 8 U.S. Senate seats.

Southern seat gains in the wake of the 2010 Republican "tsunami" were extraordinary. Table 10.2 displays the Republican percentage of seats held by the two major parties in the South before and after the 2010 election, in other words, after the elections held in 2008 and 2010. Going down the rows starting at the top with Senate

TABLE 10.2 ■ Republican Share of Southern Seats in Selected Offices, 2008 versus 2010			
Office	2008	2010	Difference 2010–08
U.S. Senate	68.2%	72.7%	+4.5
U.S. House	55.0%	71.8%	+16.8
Statewide	63.5%	81.1%	+17.6
State Senate	49.8%	57.0%	+7.2
State House	49.4%	58.8%	+9.4
Total Rep (%)	50.6%	60.2%	+9.6
Total Rep Seats	1,010	1,200	+190

Source: Data compiled by author.

Note: All of the Republican seat percentages are out of the seats held by the major parties (Democrats plus Republicans). The data on state legislatures are based on the totals from January 2009 and January 2011, respectively, and are from the National Conference of State Legislatures (http://www.ncsl.org/research/about-state-legislatures/partisan-composition.aspx).

seats, the southern GOP held 15 out of 22 in 2008 (68 percent) and increased their share to 16 in 2010 (73 percent). For the remaining offices, the GOP gains were considerably more impressive and substantial. A whopping 17 percentage point increase in U.S. House seats between 2008 and 2010 (from 72 to 94 seats out of 131). In statewide elections (excluding the federal Senate contest, see chapter 5), the expansion in the share of Republican seats was the greatest, going from 64 percent of the total in 2008 to 81 percent in 2010 (from 47 seats to 60 out of 74). With respect to state legislative elections, in 2008 the GOP was on the cusp of a South-wide seat majority; in the aftermath of the 2010 midterm, southern Republicans now controlled 59 percent of state house seats (772 out of 1,313) and 57 percent of state senate seats (258 out of 453). Overall, for the various offices shown in Table 10.2, southern Republicans held a very slim majority in 2008 (50.6 percent of these seats), but after the 2010 election the GOP further tightened its grip on Dixie's politics, claiming ownership to 60 percent of these 1,993 seats.

For southern Republicans, their 2010 electoral surge could not have come at a more opportune time. In most southern states, the 2010 midterm was the last scheduled election for state legislative contests prior to the next round of decennial redistricting. This timing was critical because in southern states, the legislature is tasked with drawing new districts for their own chambers and for the U.S. House. With this in mind, Table 10.3 shows the Republican percentage of southern state legislative seats after the 2008 elections (as of January 2009) and after the 2010 elections (as of January 2011). Starting with state senates, between these two elections, Alabama and North Carolina's upper chambers shifted to Republican majorities. In five southern states (Florida, Georgia, South Carolina, Tennessee, and Texas), the GOP had state senate majorities in both election cycles and grew them in three of these states (Florida, Georgia, and Tennessee) and maintained their seat share in the other two (South Carolina and Texas). By January 2011, Arkansas, Louisiana, Mississippi, and Virginia still had state senates controlled by the Democratic Party. Interestingly, only in Virginia were Democrats in a better position in the state senate after the 2010 elections, but the Old Dominion holds its state legislative elections in odd years, and after the 2011 elections the state's upper chamber was evenly split, with 20 Democrats and 20 Republicans.

Turning to the state house, by January 2011, the GOP gained majority status in Alabama, Louisiana, and North Carolina. Arkansas and Mississippi were the only states in which the Democratic Party still held the majority, despite Republican gains in both states (especially in Arkansas). The half-dozen states (Florida, Georgia, South Carolina, Tennessee, Texas, and Virginia) that already had GOP state house majorities in January 2009 all increased their Republican majorities by January 2011. With the impressive Republican seat gains in state legislative elections on the eve of the 2010 decennial redistricting round, for the first time since the days of Reconstruction, the Grand Old Party would be in control of drawing district boundaries in most southern states.

TABLE 10.3 ■ Republican Share of Southern State Legislative Seats, 2009 versus 2011						
	State Senate (%)			State House (%)		
State	**2009**	**2011**	**Difference**	**2009**	**2011**	**Difference**
Alabama	40.6	**64.7**	+24.1	41.0	**62.9**	+21.9
Arkansas	22.9	42.9	+20.0	28.3	44.4	+16.1
Florida	65.0	70.0	+5.0	63.3	67.5	+4.2
Georgia	60.7	64.3	+3.6	58.3	63.1	+4.8
Louisiana	40.5	47.4	+6.9	49.0	**51.5**	+2.5
Mississippi	48.1	49.0	+0.9	39.3	41.0	+1.7
North Carolina	40.0	**62.0**	+22.0	43.3	**56.3**	+13.0
South Carolina	58.7	58.7	0.0	57.3	61.0	+3.7
Tennessee	57.6	59.4	+1.8	50.5	66.0	+15.5
Texas	61.3	61.3	0.0	50.7	67.3	+16.6
Virginia	47.5	45.0	**−2.5**	54.2	60.2	+6.0
South	49.8	**57.0**	+7.2	49.4	**58.8**	+9.4
Total Rep Seats	225	258	+33	651	772	+121

Source: Data compiled by author.

Note: Percentages are in bold for shifts from a Democratic to a Republican seat majority (Alabama, North Carolina, and the entire South for the State Senate in 2011; Alabama, Louisiana, North Carolina, and the entire South for the State House in 2011). The Republican State Senate seat percentage difference (2011 vs. 2009) is in bold for Virginia, the only state with a Democratic gain.

CONGRESSIONAL REDISTRICTING

Lest the reader get the wrong idea, redistricting is arguably the most political activity one can come across (Bullock 2010), and as such, if the circumstances are favorable, political parties have every incentive to push their advantage. For most of southern political history, this meant that white Democrats designed districts of severely uneven populations and spread the black population across various districts in order to dilute this group's voting power. But ever since the mandate of equal district populations handed down by the Supreme Court in the Tennessee case of *Baker v. Carr* (1962; made applicable to congressional redistricting in the 1964 Georgia case of *Wesberry v. Sanders*), followed many years later by the Supreme Court's prohibition against minority vote dilution in the 1986 North Carolina case of *Thornburg v. Gingles,* there are some definite limitations with respect to drawing districts to maximize partisan gains. Further, even if one party manages to control the redistricting process, there is often pressure to protect their incumbents, and this can detract from the competing objective of maximizing their seats under the new map.

In this section, the emphasis is on examining several features of congressional redistricting in southern states for the last two decennial redistricting rounds (2000 and 2010). First, it matters who is in charge of redistricting; after that it is worth looking at certain factors that are altered via the redistricting process, including the district presidential vote, the minority composition of districts (the black VAP and the Latino VAP in districts with substantial black and Latino populations), the percentage of redrawn constituents an incumbent inherits (i.e., the share of district residents that the incumbent did not represent until after redistricting), and a measure of partisan bias for each southern state's redistricting plan over the last two redistricting cycles.

Before focusing exclusively on the 2000 and 2010 redistricting rounds, Table 10.4 presents data on control of redistricting that goes back to the 1990 decennial reapportionment. The table starts with the 1990 redistricting in order to show that in the South, Democrats still dominated the process. With the exceptions of Alabama and Florida, whose maps were ultimately brokered by the courts, in the rest of the southern states, Democratic state legislators drew the congressional boundaries. As chapter 5 makes clear, however, even though Democrats drew the maps, it often did not redound to their partisan benefit because the Department of Justice (DOJ) through its oversight of redistricting via the Section 5 preclearance provision of the Voting Rights Act, pressured many of these states to maximize their number of majority-minority districts (Bullock 2010; Butler 2002; Cunningham 2001) and this made surrounding districts more favorable to Republican candidates. Thus, despite Democratic dominance of most southern state legislatures, the DOJ's directive to essentially pack the most loyal Democratic voters into a smaller number of districts increased Republican voting strength in the neighboring districts with reduced minority populations (Black and Black 2002).

Ten years later, in the 2000 redistricting round, Democrats maintained control of the process in most southern states.[7] This said, the GOP had attained majority status in the Florida, South Carolina, and Virginia state legislatures. Florida and Virginia Republicans finally had the opportunity to pursue partisan gerrymanders, but in South Carolina the governor was a Democrat and he vetoed the GOP plan, which ultimately led to a federal court drawing the boundaries. In Texas, the state had a Republican governor and a Republican state senate but Democrats held a slim majority of state house seats. There is no question that with split partisan control of the redistricting process, the court that enacted the Texas map approved of an incumbent protection plan that included two new Republican districts added through reapportionment (McKee and Shaw 2005). The 2002 map in Texas was not the last word because after the 2002 elections, Republicans won a majority of state house seats and then implemented a masterful Republican gerrymander for the 2004 contests (McKee, Teigen, and Turgeon 2006). Taking a page

TABLE 10.4 ■ Control of Congressional Redistricting and State Legislative Majorities: 1990, 2000, and 2010						
	Control of Redistricting and State Legislative Majority (Senate %–House %)					
State	1990		2000		2010	
Alabama	D-Court	80–78	D	69–65	R	65–63
Arkansas	D	89–92	D	77–70	D	57–56
Florida	D-Court	58–62	R	63–64	R	70–68
Georgia	D	80–81	D	57–58	R	64–63
Louisiana	D	85–82	*D	64–67	*R	56–51
Mississippi	D	83–85	D-Court	65–76	*Split-Court	52R–59D
North Carolina	D	72–68	D	70–52	R	62–56
South Carolina	D	76–65	*R-Court	52–56	R	59–61
Tennessee	D	58–58	D	55–59	R	59–66
Texas	D	74–62	Split-Court	52R–52D	R-Court	61–67
Virginia	D	75–60	R	54–53	*Split-R	50D/50R–60R

Source: Various editions of The Almanac of American Politics (1992, 1994, 2002, 2004, 2012, 2014).

Notes: The percentage for a party majority is out of the number of seats held by both major parties. *In 2000, Louisiana Democrats had majorities in both state legislative chambers, but the governor was a Republican with the power to veto an unfavorable plan. Ultimately, the Louisiana congressional map was designed by the Louisiana U.S. House delegation's six members (four Republicans and two Democrats) who sought reelection (Barone & Cohen 2003, 695). In 2000, South Carolina Republicans were the majority party in the state legislature, but the governor was a Democrat with veto power, which he exercised over a Republican plan, and the final map was drawn by a federal court (Barone & Cohen 2003, 1430–1431). The Virginia State Legislature had a 22 to 18 Democratic state senate majority in 2010 and Republicans a 59 to 39 state house majority, but the Old Dominion holds off-year elections, and in 2011 the Republicans ended up with a 20 to 20 split in the state senate. With control of the lower chamber and the governorship, Virginia Republicans actually controlled redistricting for the 2012 U.S. House elections (Barone and McCutcheon 2013, 1714). Finally, due to a handful of Democratic-to-Republican party switches in the Louisiana and Mississippi state senates after January 2011 (the date for compiling all of the Republican percentages in the state senates and state houses shown in the table for the other southern states in 2010; see the note under Table 10.2 and the data displayed in Table 10.3), at the time of congressional redistricting, Louisiana Republicans were in control, whereas in Mississippi, Republicans controlled the state senate while Democrats controlled the state house, with a Republican governor. Ultimately, a court drew the Mississippi congressional map, but it was not very different from the one favored by Mississippi Republicans (Barone and McCutcheon 2013, 938).

from the Texas Republicans' playbook, after the 2004 elections the Georgia GOP now controlled the legislature and governorship and also decided to undertake a mid-decade "re-redistricting" in 2006 (Hood and McKee 2009, 2013; see Box 10.1 for details on the Texas and Georgia cases).

BOX 10.1   PARTISAN GERRYMANDERING AND "RE-REDISTRICTING" IN THE NEW MILLENNIUM

Partisan gerrymandering is a frequent occurrence in American politics, and there is a long history of this activity in the South. Indeed, gerrymandering is certainly as old as the Republic and it has been alive and well wherever there have been multiple election districts in any given state. The term gerrymandering was coined in response to a curiously drawn district in colonial Massachusetts that resembled a salamander but was dubbed a gerrymander in "honor" of Governor Elbridge Gerry (Cox and Katz 2002).

Partisan gerrymandering is much more likely to be undertaken when one party controls redistricting and there is the opportunity to pick up additional seats by crafting district lines in a manner that clearly disadvantages the opposition. In the new millennium, Texas and Georgia were interesting examples where "re-redistricting" occurred because the Republican Party gained control of both the legislature and the governorship. In contrast, Florida and Virginia both redistricted prior to the 2016 elections because legal rulings compelled the redrawing of Republican maps in a manner that benefited Democrats.

At the time of the 2002 redistricting in Texas, Republicans controlled the governorship and the state senate, but Democrats had a majority of state house seats. The congressional map drawn for the 2002 elections was inarguably what is referred to as a "bipartisan incumbent protection plan." The Lone Star State added two districts through reapportionment and both of these were drawn to favor Republicans. In 2002, a 17 to 13 Democratic seat advantage was narrowed to 17 to 15 with the two new Republican pickups, and not a single incumbent of either party was in jeopardy of losing reelection. The Texas GOP found an opening to redistrict again after 2002 because they won a majority of the Texas House seats and therefore had control of the legislature in addition to the governorship. The U.S. House majority leader at the time was Tom DeLay (TX-22) and he pushed the Republican state legislators to draw a new congressional map for the sole purpose of gaining Republican seats. The new map for the 2004 elections was highly effective in achieving the GOP's objective of picking up seats. In fact, one endangered Democrat (Ralph Hall, TX-4), switched to the GOP before the 2004 contests, making for an evenly split (16 Democrats/16 Republicans) Texas U.S. House delegation. After the 2004 elections, Texas Republicans netted five seats, so that the Texas U.S. House delegation was now composed of 21 Republicans and 11 Democrats. The successful strategy employed by Texas Republicans was redrawing congressional district boundaries in a manner that flooded Anglo (non-Latino white) Democrats with Anglo voters they did not previously represent. Strong Republicans ran against these embattled Democratic incumbents and these redrawn Anglo voters were much more supportive of the Republican challengers. In two districts, incumbent Democrats faced off against incumbent Republicans and these Democrats had no chance because their Republican opponents retained a much larger share of the voters they represented prior to redistricting.

Taking a page out of the Texas Republicans' playbook, Republicans in the Peach State re-redistricted in the 2006 midterm. Like their Texas colleagues, Georgia

(Continued)

(Continued)

Republicans similarly had two of three levers of state power (governorship and the state senate) in 2002 and then won a majority of Georgia House seats after the 2004 elections, and with partisan control of the legislature, the Georgia GOP decided to redraw the Democratic congressional gerrymander implemented in 2002 (see Table 10.5). Where Georgia Republicans departed from their Texas counterparts, was the manner in which they redrew the congressional boundaries. There were two vulnerable white Democratic incumbents (Jim Marshall, GA-8 and John Barrow, GA-12), but the Georgia GOP line drawers did not go full bore in their goal of defeating these members and the reason why was very curious. In the lead-up to redrawing the congressional map, Georgia Republicans made it clear that their greatest complaint with the existing Democratic gerrymander was that the district boundaries were so convoluted, running all across the state and splitting numerous counties. Hence, when it came time to establish a new Republican map for the 2006 elections, a greater emphasis was placed on making the congressional districts more aesthetically appealing than ensuring that the two aforementioned vulnerable Democrats were defeated (see Hood and McKee 2009). Nonetheless, because Marshall and Barrow both inherited their fair share of white Republican-leaning redrawn constituents, Marshall lost two cycles later in the 2010 GOP "tsunami" and Barrow held on until 2014, when his defeat warranted considerable attention because he was the last white Democratic U.S. House Representative in the five-state Deep South delegation.

If purely partisan inspired maneuvers are not available, as is usually the case for the minority party, then legal recourse can be an avenue for accruing some electoral compensation. In the presidential swing states of Florida and Virginia, two states whose post-2010 congressional maps were engineered by Republicans (see Table 10.6), the court-drawn remaps prior to the 2016 U.S. House elections resulted in a one-seat Democratic gain in both states. In Florida and Virginia, questions related to the racial composition of two majority-minority districts (FL-5 and VA-3), came under legal scrutiny and it was evident that the district percentage of African Americans was decidedly higher than needed to ensure black representation. Florida District 5, represented by African American Democrat Corrine Brown since 1992 (it was FL-3 prior to 2012), was drawn in 2012 with a 49 percent black voting age population (BVAP) and 11 percent Latino VAP. In addition to Congresswoman Brown, Florida Republicans were staunch supporters of the configuration of FL-5 because of its odd shape, running in a predominantly north-south direction (capturing black neighborhoods from Jacksonville down to the Orlando area), had the electoral benefit of making multiple surrounding districts in north-central Florida favor Republican candidates (Altman and McDonald 2015).

Like Congresswoman Brown in Florida, African American Democratic Congressman Bobby Scott of Virginia District 3 had represented various permutations of VA-3 going back to 1992, when it was first created as a majority black district. In 2010, VA-3 had a 53 percent BVAP, but in the Republican-drawn map in 2012, VA-3 was given a 56 percent BVAP. Through a court-ordered redrawing of the Virginia Republicans' gerrymander, the BVAP in VA-3 was reduced to 45 percent and the neighboring VA-4 had its BVAP increased from 31 percent to 41 percent. Under the new map in 2016, the Republican who represented VA-4 sought reelection in VA-2 (its BVAP percent was

21 percent), while Representative Scott easily won reelection in the reconfigured VA-3 and Virginia's Democratic delegation netted one seat (4 out of 11) with the election of African American Donald McEachin in the newly drawn VA-4. Meanwhile, back in Florida, Representative Brown was defeated in the Democratic Primary by the eventual general election winner, African American Al Lawson; and for the first time in southern political history, an Asian Democrat won election to the U.S. House of Representatives and her surprise victory was in part due to the ripple effect of altered congressional boundaries with the massive changes made to FL-5, which affected the contours of FL-7, where Vietnamese-born Stephanie Murphy defeated the veteran Republican John Mica (giving Florida Democrats 11 out of 27 U.S. House seats).

In the 2000 round, Mississippi was the one southern state that because of slow population growth lost a seat through reapportionment, going from five districts to four.[8] Particularly in a small state like Mississippi, losing congressional representation can lead to a highly contentious process, and it certainly held true in this instance (see Glaser 2005). Going from five seats to four resulted in a district where a Democratic and Republican incumbent faced each other. In the redrawn District 3, Democratic Congressman Ronnie Shows ended up losing his reelection bid to Republican Congressman Chip Pickering, who captured more than 64 percent of the two-party vote (Barone and Cohen 2003, 908). Even though Mississippi Democrats commanded impressive state legislative majorities (as shown in Table 10.4) and the governorship, they could not settle on a congressional map and the one approved by a federal court clearly advantaged the GOP in District 3. First, in this redrawn district, Republican presidential nominee George W. Bush won 65 percent of the two-party vote in the 2000 election (Bush won 67 percent of the vote in Pickering's old District 3 and just 55 percent of the vote in Shows's old District 4; data are from Barone and Cohen 2001, 2003). Second, and perhaps more damaging than the Republican presidential vote favoring the GOP incumbent, was that Shows's share of redrawn constituents—meaning the district population new to the incumbent as a result of redistricting—was substantially higher than Pickering's: 62 percent for Shows versus 39 percent for Pickering. Put another way, after redistricting, Pickering had previously represented 61 percent of District 3 residents, whereas Shows had only represented 38 percent of the constituents in the new district.[9]

Finally, by the 2010 decennial redistricting, most southern states were under Republican control. In fact, in 2010, Arkansas was the only state in which Democrats controlled the redistricting process. In three southern states, their state legislative elections are held in odd-year cycles: Louisiana, Mississippi, and Virginia. This fact became very important at the time of congressional redistricting in these states. In Louisiana, the state legislature in January 2011 was split between a Democratic senate and a Republican house (see Table 10.3). But before the congressional map was to be decided upon, Louisiana Republicans took control of the state senate because a handful of Democrats switched to the Republican Party. Similarly, in Mississippi the legislature in January 2011 was controlled by Democrats, but very narrowly in the state senate (see Table 10.3), and like Louisiana, a handful of senate Democrats in 2011 switched allegiance to the GOP, so at the time of congressional redistricting, control was split between the parties and ultimately a court plan was implemented that was favorable to the map drafted by Mississippi Republicans (Barone and McCutcheon 2013). In Virginia, as shown in Table 10.3, Democrats had a senate majority in January 2011 and Republicans had a house majority. But after the 2011 elections and prior to implementing congressional redistricting, the Virginia Senate ended up being perfectly split with 20 Democrats and 20 Republicans, and with control of the governorship and the state house, the GOP actually steered congressional redistricting (Barone and McCutcheon 2013).

In 2010, Texas was once again embroiled in legal battles over its congressional redistricting (it seems as though the Lone Star State is perpetually involved in redistricting litigation). Nonetheless, because Texas Republicans successfully implemented a Republican gerrymander in 2004 that was somewhat altered thereafter through a court-drawn map that affected several districts in the south-central part of the state (McKee and McKenzie 2013), the court-approved plan for 2012 still had its roots firmly tied to a previous GOP plan. So, compared to the 2000 cycle in which Democrats were in charge of congressional redistricting in most southern states, by 2010, the tables had turned in favor of the GOP, with Republicans having complete control of the process in eight states and preponderant influence in two more (Mississippi and Texas). Only in Arkansas were Democrats unquestionably in charge, but as will be discussed, this reality was of little consolation to a declining Democratic party. In considering the bigger picture of partisan influence over congressional redistricting, in the subsections that follow it is important to keep in mind that Democrats held more sway over the process in 2000, whereas their GOP counterparts were decidedly in charge in an even greater number of southern states a decade later.

The District Presidential Vote

In recent decades, American elections have become increasingly nationalized. Briefly, this means that more high-profile national contests, especially presidential elections, shape outcomes in contests down the ballot, such as Senate, gubernatorial, and U.S. House races (McKee and Sievert 2017). The ramifications of this development are very clear: it has become more difficult for any candidate running under a major party label to run a campaign in which personal appeal to voters overshadows political party affiliation. Hence, the growing nationalization of American politics has served to weaken the electoral power of incumbency (Jacobson 2015). This reality is particularly salient in the context of redistricting because voters who are drawn into a new incumbent's district have little or no familiarity with their new representative (Hayes and McKee 2009; McKee 2008), and therefore they are more likely to cast a vote in line with their partisanship (Hood and McKee 2010b; McKee 2010).

A simple bivariate correlation of the district presidential vote and the U.S. House vote shows how this linkage has strengthened over the last two redistricting cycles. In every decennial redistricting, with hardly any exceptions (the state of Maine being one prior to the 2010 round), in states with multiple districts the new boundaries are set in place for the election ending in "2." Therefore, the new districts took effect in the 2000 redistricting cycle in the 2002 midterm and the new congressional boundaries took hold in the 2012 elections after the 2010 redistricting round, etc. The correlation between the two-party Democratic House vote in 2002 with the 2000 Democratic presidential vote cast in districts for 2002, was +0.68 and highly statistically significant ($p < .001$). Ten years later, the relationship between the House vote and presidential vote had become even stronger. The correlation between the two-party Democratic House vote in 2012 with the 2008 Democratic presidential vote cast in districts for 2012, was +0.85 and once again highly statistically significant ($p < .001$).[10]

These aforementioned correlations do not take into account incumbency. Incumbents have an incentive to cultivate a personal vote with their constituents (Cain, Ferejohn, and Fiorina 1987), in part to insulate themselves from the potentially negative association with their political affiliation (e.g., many Democratic incumbents saw the need to distance themselves from President Obama in the 2010 midterm) when short-term political conditions do not favor their party (see Petrocik and Desposato 2004). Thus, the correlation between the district presidential vote and the vote for the incumbent of the same party should not be as strong as the relationship between the district presidential vote and the vote cast for the candidate of the same party in an open seat contest. In other words, for a voter in an open seat race, because there is little to no familiarity with the candidates vis-à-vis the level of familiarity they would have *if* an incumbent was running, their vote is much more likely to be based on their partisanship and therefore how they voted for president (in accordance with their party affiliation). The data clearly support this expectation, but it is also the case that increasing nationalization is evident even in districts with an incumbent seeking reelection.

First, in districts with a Democratic incumbent seeking reelection in 2002, the correlation between the 2000 Democratic presidential vote and the 2002 Democratic House vote is +0.42 ($p < .01$). Ten years later, in districts with a Democratic incumbent seeking reelection in 2012, the correlation between the 2008 Democratic presidential vote and the 2012 Democratic House vote is +0.72 ($p < .001$). By comparison, in the case of open seat contests, the correlation between the 2000 Democratic presidential vote and the 2002 Democratic House vote is +0.92 ($p < .001$). And for open seat contests in 2012, the correlation between the 2008 Democratic presidential vote and the 2012 Democratic House vote is +0.98 ($p < .001$). In sum, although the correlation between the presidential vote and the vote for an incumbent of the same party is not nearly as strong as when this relationship is confined to open seats, over time the relationship between the district presidential vote and the House vote has become much stronger whether or not incumbency is taken into consideration.

Because the presidential vote and U.S. House vote are strongly linked and this association has strengthened over time, in the context of congressional redistricting, alterations to the district presidential vote can provide insight as to what line drawers intended. Table 10.5 shows the average of the district presidential vote cast in the 2000 election for districts held by Democrats (the Democratic presidential vote) and Republicans (the Republican presidential vote) before (in 2000) and after redistricting (in 2002) for the 2000 round. In addition, the table shows the statewide partisan split in the 2000 presidential vote for each state (in brackets) and indicates the control of redistricting for each state in the 2000 redistricting cycle.

Before proceeding with a discussion of each state, it is important to know how to detect evidence of a partisan gerrymander as compared to a redistricting plan that is more inclined to protect incumbents of both parties (a bipartisan incumbent protection plan). Nevertheless, the district presidential vote alone is not always enough to make these distinctions and that is why other factors will also be examined. If a party has control of redistricting and wants to implement a partisan gerrymander as a means to maximize its share of seats then the basic strategy is to pack the partisan opposition into a smaller number of districts and spread its own party's voters across a greater number of districts that the party hopes to win. With the use of the district presidential vote, therefore, it is expected that the party in charge of redistricting will increase the presidential vote for the opposition party in order to make these districts safer and this often means that the party in charge will actually reduce their own electoral security by reducing the average presidential vote for their party in the districts the party expects to win.

There is some clear evidence of partisan gerrymandering of the variety outlined above in Table 10.5. First, in the case of those states in which the Democrats controlled redistricting, partisan gerrymandering appears to be the preferred strategy. In Georgia, the Democratic presidential vote in Democratic districts is reduced by almost 5 percentage points (from 64 percent to 59 percent) while the Republican presidential vote in Republican districts is increased by more than 2 percentage points. Also, notice that between 2000 and 2002, Georgia Democrats managed to net two seats (going from three in 2000 to five in 2002). The Democratic gerrymander in Tennessee is equally impressive. Unlike Georgia, which gained two seats through reapportionment, the Volunteer State had nine total before and after redistricting. The Democratic presidential vote in Democratic districts in Tennessee is reduced by more than 4 percentage points while the Republican presidential vote in Republican districts is increased by almost 3 percentage points. Before redistricting, Tennessee Democrats had four of the nine House seats, but after redistricting the party gained one to take a 5 to 4 majority.

On the flip side, Virginia and Florida exhibit two impressive Republican gerrymanders. Like Tennessee, the Old Dominion had the same number of seats before and after redistricting, 11 total. In Democratic districts, the average Democratic presidential vote in Virginia increased more than two percentage points, but in Republican districts

TABLE 10.5 ■ Two-Party Presidential Vote (in 2000) in Southern Congressional Districts in 2000 and 2002						
State [R/D %]	**Democratic Districts (Dem Pres. Vote %)**			**Republican Districts (Rep Pres. Vote %)**		
	2000 (n)	2002 (n)	2002–2000	2000 (n)	2002 (n)	2002–2000
AL [58/42]	58.5 (2)	55.8 (2)	−2.7	62.8 (5)	62.6 (5)	−0.2
AR [53/47]	50.8 (3)	50.2 (3)	−0.6	61.5 (1)	61.5 (1)	0.0
FL [50/50]	64.2 (8)	68.5 (7)	+4.3	55.7 (15)	55.9 (18)	+0.2
GA [56/44]	64.0 (3)	59.3 (5)	−4.7	61.6 (8)	64.1 (8)	+2.5
LA [54/46]	61.1 (2)	53.8 (3)	−7.3	58.6 (5)	58.4 (4)	−0.2
MS [59/41]	46.1 (3)	45.7 (2)	−0.4	64.1 (2)	62.4 (2)	−1.7
NC [56/44]	51.4 (5)	52.2 (6)	+0.8	61.9 (7)	63.1 (7)	+1.2
SC [58/42]	53.0 (2)	51.6 (2)	−1.4	62.6 (4)	62.7 (4)	+0.1
TN [52/48]	58.9 (4)	54.5 (5)	−4.4	57.0 (5)	59.9 (4)	+2.9
TX [61/39]	49.6 (17)	50.1 (17)	+0.5	68.7 (13)	69.2 (15)	+0.5
VA [54/46]	54.7 (4)	57.0 (3)	+2.3	57.8 (6)	57.8 (8)	0.0
SOUTH [56/44]	54.6 (53)	54.6 (55)	0.0	61.0 (71)	61.6 (76)	+0.6

Source: Presidential vote data at the congressional district level was compiled by the author from *The Almanac of American Politics 2002* and *The Almanac of American Politics 2004.*

Notes: Statewide two-party presidential vote split data (the Republican percentage followed by the Democratic percentage in brackets next to each state abbreviation) is from Dave Leip's *Atlas of U.S. Presidential Elections.* With respect to control of redistricting (refer to Table 10.4), Democratic control is denoted by an italicized state abbreviation and highlighted in gray, Republican control has the state abbreviation in bold, and for states with court involvement the state abbreviation is underlined. There was a total of 125 southern U.S. House districts in 2000 and 131 in 2002 (following reapportionment the southern states gained six seats). Only a total of 124 districts are reported in 2000 because there was an Independent who won Virginia's Fifth District (Virgil Goode) and the presidential vote data from this district is omitted. Republicans controlled redistricting in Virginia in the 2000–2002 round, and in 2002 Representative Goode switched to the Republican Party and won reelection. Treating Congressman Goode as a Republican (he switched from Independent to Republican in February of 2002; see Barone and Cohen 2003, 1653) for the purpose of redistricting, the decline in the Republican share of the presidential vote between 2000 and 2002 comports with a Republican gerrymander because Goode's district cast a 58.3 percent GOP vote in 2000, which was reduced to 57.2 percent Republican in 2002. The number of districts won by each party is shown in parentheses.

the Republican presidential vote remained the same. Better yet for Republicans, the party's seats went from 6 in 2000 to 8 in 2002. As already stated, the number of seats in Virginia did not change due to reapportionment, but the partisan profile did. In 2000, there was one House member who was an Independent, Virgil Goode in District 5, and hence the delegation consisted of 4 Democrats, 1 Independent, and 6 Republicans. Goode switched to the GOP in 2002 and won reelection as a Republican. Congressional reapportionment awarded the Sunshine State with two new seats, which increased the Florida U.S. House delegation to twenty-five members. Not only did the average Democratic presidential vote in Democratic districts increase by more than 4 percentage points, but the Democrats lost a seat while the Republicans netted three and the average Republican presidential vote in Republican districts was barely changed (from 55.7 percent to 55.9 percent).

As mentioned, in Texas, the court-approved map for the 2002 elections was an obvious bipartisan incumbent protection gerrymander. The Lone Star State added two seats through reapportionment and both were drawn to favor Republicans while at the same time every Democratic and Republican incumbent had a district that was minimally changed. As shown in Table 10.5, the Democratic presidential vote in Democratic districts and the Republican presidential vote in Republican districts was hardly altered between 2000 and 2002, which reflects the objective of an incumbent protection plan. The GOP was given the two new districts through reapportionment, and the extant House delegation easily won reelection so that the partisan balance went from a 17 to 13 Democratic majority to a 17 to 15 Democratic majority.

Including the states discussed thus far, North Carolina is the remaining one that also increased its U.S. House delegation through reapportionment, going from 12 to 13 total seats. Democrats furthered a partisan gerrymander but it does not appear as blatant based on the changes in the district presidential vote. In fact, the Democratic presidential vote in Democratic districts increased slightly (+0.8), while the Republican presidential vote increased somewhat more in Republican districts (+1.2). Despite only marginal modifications in the district presidential vote, North Carolina Democrats did manage to net one seat, reducing a 7 to 5 Republican advantage in 2000 to 7 to 6 in 2002.

The 2002 Mississippi redistricting has already been discussed, so turning to the last four states of Alabama, Arkansas, Louisiana, and South Carolina, it should be noted that they all retained the same number of seats in the 2000 reapportionment. Arkansas Democrats made minimal changes to the state's four districts, basically making sure that they remained roughly equal in district population. Alabama Democrats intended to pick up at least one seat by spreading the Democratic presidential vote more widely (specifically making District 3 more Democratic; see Barone and Cohen 2003, 54), as indicated by the almost 3 percentage point drop in the Democratic presidential vote in Democratic districts. But after the 2002 midterm, the Alabama U.S. House delegation remained 5 Republicans and 2 Democrats. Similar to Arkansas, although South Carolina Republicans saw the court step in to approve the final plan, it made rather minimal changes and the partisan balance remained 4 to 2 Republican after the 2002 midterm. Finally, for all intents and purposes, Louisiana's congressional districts were redrawn to cater to the sitting incumbents of both parties, but it is evident from Table 10.5 that the Democratic presidential vote in Democratic districts was reduced an impressive 7 percentage

TABLE 10.6 ■ Two-Party Presidential Vote (in 2008) in Southern Congressional Districts in 2010 and 2012						
State [R/D %]	**Democratic Districts (Dem Pres. Vote %)**			**Republican Districts (Rep Pres. Vote %)**		
	2010 (n)	2012 (n)	2012–2010	2010 (n)	2012 (n)	2012–2010
AL [61/39]	74.0 (1)	72.0 (1)	−2.0	66.2 (6)	66.9 (6)	+0.7
AR [60/40]	40.4 (1)	N/A (0)	—	60.4 (3)	60.4 (4)	0.0
FL [49/51]	73.4 (6)	65.1 (10)	−8.3	53.4 (19)	55.2 (17)	+1.8
GA [53/47]	68.5 (5)	65.7 (5)	−2.8	64.6 (8)	63.9 (9)	−0.7
LA [54/46]	76.3 (1)	74.1 (1)	−2.2	63.5 (6)	66.0 (5)	+2.5
MS [57/43]	66.4 (1)	64.6 (1)	−1.8	63.8 (3)	64.3 (3)	+0.5
NC [50/50]	57.8 (7)	66.1 (4)	+8.3	58.9 (6)	56.7 (9)	−2.2
SC [55/45]	64.8 (1)	73.1 (1)	+8.3	58.2 (5)	59.3 (6)	+1.1
TN [58/42]	67.3 (2)	67.8 (2)	+0.5	64.2 (7)	65.1 (7)	+0.9
TX [56/44]	67.3 (9)	65.0 (12)	−2.3	62.2 (23)	63.4 (24)	+1.2
VA [47/53]	67.9 (3)	70.3 (3)	+2.4	52.4 (8)	53.2 (8)	+0.8
SOUTH [53/47]	66.3 (37)	66.3 (40)	0.0	59.9 (94)	60.7 (98)	+0.8

Source: Presidential vote data at the congressional district level was compiled by the author from *The Almanac of American Politics 2012* and *The Almanac of American Politics 2014*. Statewide two-party presidential vote split data (the Republican percentage followed by the Democratic percentage in brackets next to each state abbreviation) is from Dave Leip's *Atlas of U.S. Presidential Elections.*

Notes: With respect to control of redistricting (refer to Table 10.4), Democratic control is denoted by an italicized state abbreviation and highlighted in gray, Republican control has the state abbreviation in bold, and for states with court involvement the state abbreviation is underlined. There was a total of 131 southern U.S. House districts in 2010 and 138 in 2012 (following reapportionment, the southern states gained seven seats). The number of districts won by each party is shown in parentheses.

points. Spreading out Democratic strength, particularly in the redrawn District 5, enabled a Democrat to win this seat (Barone and Cohen 2003, 695), reducing the Republican advantage from 5 to 2 to 4 to 3.

Like Table 10.5, Table 10.6 displays the same data for the district presidential vote in 2010 and 2012. Just as the 2000 presidential vote was used to make comparisons before and after redistricting between 2000 and 2002, the 2008 presidential vote is used to make comparisons before and after redistricting between 2010 and 2012. It does not take as long to review the data in Table 10.6 as compared to Table 10.5 because of the political changes taking place since 2002. First, heading into the 2010 redistricting cycle, in four of the five Deep South states—Alabama, Louisiana, Mississippi, and

South Carolina—their U.S. House delegations consisted of a single African American Democrat, with the rest of the delegation consisting of Republicans (including a black Republican, Tim Scott, in District 1 in South Carolina). In these states with only one Democratic district, the Democratic presidential vote in the Democratic district only increased in South Carolina (+8.3), which was also the only state of the four to add a seat through reapportionment, going from 6 to 7 (Louisiana was the only southern state to lose a seat, going from 7 to 6).

Unfortunately, for Arkansas Democrats, the only southern state in 2010 to have Democrats in control of redistricting, despite drawing a plan intended to favor their party (Barone and McCutcheon 2013, 102), there was only one Democratic incumbent in 2010 and the seat left open by this representative (Mike Ross) in 2012 was won by a Republican. Hence, a 3 to 1 Republican U.S. House delegation in Arkansas in 2010 resulted in a 4 to 0 Republican sweep in 2012. Tennessee and Virginia did not gain or lose seats through reapportionment, and under the congressional plans drawn by Republicans the partisan balance in these states remained the same (7 to 2 Republican in Tennessee and 8 to 3 Republican in Virginia). Nonetheless, maintaining the Republican advantage in Virginia took a little more effort than in Tennessee, because Virginia has clearly been trending Democratic. With this in mind, consider that in 2008 Barack Obama won 53 percent of Virginia's presidential vote and yet in the three Democratic House districts, their 2008 Democratic presidential vote increased from 67.9 percent in 2010 to 70.3 percent in 2012.

Georgia and Texas both gained seats through the 2010 reapportionment, one for the Peach State and an astounding four for the Lone Star State (the largest gain in the 2010 cycle). As mentioned previously, because of Republican-directed re-redistricting that was implemented in both of these states after the initial 2002 redistricting cycle, Georgia and Texas Republicans continued to reap the electoral rewards from congressional maps that clearly advantaged their party. Thus, despite more than a 2 percentage point reduction in the Democratic presidential vote in Democratic districts in these states (-2.8 in Georgia and -2.3 in Texas), the GOP U.S. House seat advantage in Georgia went from 8 to 5 in 2010 to 9 to 5 in 2012. In Texas, its rapid population growth has been primarily fueled by a burgeoning Latino constituency, and this accounts for Texas Democrats netting 3 seats in 2012 (going from 9 to 12), but Texas Republicans also netted 1 additional seat (going from 23 to 24) in the South's largest U.S. House delegation, which now has 36 members.

It makes sense to discuss Florida and North Carolina last because of the interesting circumstances surrounding these states. Starting with Florida, based on the data in Table 10.6 it would seem that the state was controlled by Democrats and not Republicans. Indeed, the changes in the district presidential vote are reflective of a Democratic gerrymander because the Democratic presidential vote in Democratic districts is substantially reduced (-8.3), whereas the Republican presidential vote in Republican districts goes up 1.8 percentage points. More importantly, the Sunshine State added two seats through reapportionment (going from 25 to 27), and the

Democrats netted four seats (going from 6 to 10) while the Republicans dropped two (going from 19 to 17). What is going on? It turns out that there is a clear explanation for what otherwise would appear to be an illogical outcome. In the 2010 midterm elections, Florida voters approved of two amendments to the state constitution (one is germane to state legislative districting and the other to congressional districting), that placed considerable limitations on how Florida's state legislative and congressional districts can be drawn moving forward and starting with the 2012 elections. Briefly, districts are prohibited from being drawn to favor incumbents or to favor one party at the expense of the other (for details, see McKee 2015a, 4). So, despite the fact that Florida Republicans were technically in control of congressional redistricting, the so-called Fair Districts constitutional amendments hamstrung their efforts to maximize partisan gains.

Finally, the Tar Heel State in 2012 is deserving of the "Phil Burton Award" for the nation's most impressive partisan gerrymander.[11] Unlike Florida, which had Republican state legislative majorities dating back to the 1990s (1994 for the state senate and 1996 for the state house, Dubin 2007, 45), it was not until the 2010 midterm that North Carolina Republicans acquired majority control of *both* state legislative chambers at the same time (see Table 10.3), since the Reconstruction era. And although at the time of congressional redistricting, the North Carolina governor was a Democrat (Beverly Perdue), per North Carolina law, the governor cannot veto redistricting plans. Unimpeded, at least until the courts caught up with them (in the 2017 case of *Cooper v. Harris*), North Carolina Republicans drew a map that stuffed the Democratic opposition into a maximum of four districts out of a total of thirteen, and pulled this off despite the fact that in 2008, Barack Obama narrowly carried the state!

As shown in Table 10.6, the North Carolina redistricting exhibits the hallmarks of a Republican gerrymander because the Democratic presidential vote in Democratic districts went up substantially (+8.3) while the Republican presidential vote in Republican districts declined 2.2 percentage points. The Tar Heel state did not gain a seat through reapportionment, but a 7 to 6 Democratic congressional majority in 2010 flipped to a 9 to 4 Republican majority in 2012. In 2012, every district was contested by both major parties and the overall partisan split in the U.S. House vote was 51 percent Democratic and 49 percent Republican. From 2014 to 2016, the North Carolina U.S. House delegation has consisted of 3 Democrats and 10 Republicans.

Minority District Populations

Sometimes it can be difficult to discern a partisan motive based on the district presidential vote alone. By comparison, changes to district racial compositions typically shed more light on partisan intentions. This is especially true with respect to black voting age populations (BVAPs). Because African American voters are the most staunchly Democratic in their voting behavior, in the context of furthering Democratic and Republican gerrymanders the logic to do so is pretty straightforward. For the Democratic Party, it makes sense to reduce high black district VAPs, at least in those areas where Democratic candidates are winning elections in a landslide. In redistricting parlance, in those districts with high black populations where Democrats win easily, a large share of the vote (over the majority needed to win election) is *wasted* because it could be redistributed to surrounding districts to give Democrats a chance to win these contests (Stephanopoulos and McGhee 2015). In contrast, because so few African Americans vote for Republican candidates, the GOP has a clear incentive to pack black voters into as small a number of districts as they can, in order to increase the likelihood of winning all of the remaining districts with lower black populations.

The partisan logic discussed above is generally borne out by the data displayed in Table 10.7. Table 10.7 shows the average BVAP in districts with a BVAP of at least 35 percent and represented by a Democrat, in every southern state for 2000–2002 and 2010–2012 (Arkansas is excluded because none of its four districts have a BVAP as high as 35 percent). In addition, the average BVAP in the state is displayed in brackets for each state and South-wide, for the 2000 and 2010 Census. Of the five states in which the Democratic Party controlled redistricting in the 2000 round (Alabama, Georgia, Louisiana, North Carolina, and Tennessee), in all but North Carolina (+0.3) the BVAP in districts of at least 35 percent BVAP with a Democratic representative saw BVAP reductions, from a decline of 2.8 percentage points in Louisiana's majority black District 2 to almost 9 percentage points lower in Alabama's majority black District 7.

The court-approved plan in South Carolina reduced the BVAP in the majority black District 6 by four percentage points. Interestingly, and definitely a benefit to Republicans, in Mississippi (a court-approved, but Republican-inspired, plan) and Virginia (a Republican map), these states had two districts represented by Democrats in 2000 with BVAPs of at least 35 percent, but in 2002 each state only had one district represented by a Democrat with a BVAP of at least 35 percent (Mississippi's majority black District 2 and Virginia's majority black District 3). Florida was the only state whose redistricting Republicans controlled and the BVAP actually declined (–2.7 percentage points in its three districts all represented by African American Democrats with high black VAPs: District 3, District 17, and District 23). In the Texas court-drawn plan for 2002, its two districts represented by black Democrats (Districts 18 and 30) saw a slight increase in the BVAP (+1.7 percentage points). Overall, as to be expected, because Democrats controlled redistricting in most southern states in the 2000 round, South-wide the BVAP in districts with at least a 35 percent BVAP and a Democratic representative was reduced 1.8 percentage points (from 51.1 percent BVAP in 2000 to 49.3 percent BVAP in 2002).

Compared to the 2000 round, congressional redistricting in 2010 bears all the marks of Republican control. First, South-wide, the number of districts with a 35 percent BVAP or higher and a Democratic representative, declined by one (from 19 to 18 total districts). Second, the average BVAP in these districts went from 49 percent in 2010 to 52 percent in 2012, an increase of 3 percentage points, which is a strong

TABLE 10.7 ■ African American Composition of Majority-Minority and Minority Influence Districts Represented by Democrats

State [BVAP]	Black Voting Age Population (≥ 35%)			State [BVAP]	Black Voting Age Population (≥ 35%)		
	2000 (n)	2002 (n)	2002–2000		2010 (n)	2012 (n)	2012–2010
AL [23.9]	67.3 [1]	58.4 [1]	−8.9	AL [24.7]	58.4 [1]	60.2 [1]	+1.8
FL [12.5]	53.2 [3]	50.5 [3]	−2.7	FL [13.7]	50.5 [3]	49.8 [3]	−0.7
GA [26.6]	47.6 [3]	43.9 [5]	−3.7	*GA [28.8]	45.5 [5]	52.9 [4]	+7.4
LA [29.6]	63.3 [1]	60.5 [1]	−2.8	LA [29.9]	60.5 [1]	58.5 [1]	−2.0
MS [33.1]	52.1 [2]	59.5 [1]	+7.4	MS [34.6]	59.5 [1]	61.1 [1]	+1.6
NC [20.0]	45.2 [2]	45.5 [2]	+0.3	NC [20.4]	45.5 [2]	49.9 [2]	+4.4
SC [27.1]	58.1 [1]	54.1 [1]	−4.0	SC [26.3]	54.1 [1]	54.4 [1]	+0.3
TN [14.8]	61.9 [1]	55.6 [1]	−6.3	TN [15.5]	55.6 [1]	61.1 [1]	+5.5
TX [11.0]	40.0 [2]	41.7 [2]	+1.7	*TX [11.4]	39.8 [3]	41.3 [3]	+1.5
VA [18.4]	46.0 [2]	53.8 [1]	+7.8	VA [18.5]	53.8 [1]	55.3 [1]	+1.5
SOUTH [17.8]	51.1 [18]	49.3 [18]	−1.8	SOUTH [18.3]	49.0 [19]	52.0 [18]	+3.0

Source: Data for the district level black voting age population (BVAP) were compiled by the author from the decennial U.S. Census for 2000 and 2010, respectively. Likewise, the statewide BVAP in brackets next to each state abbreviation are also from the decennial U.S. Census for 2000 and 2010, respectively.

Notes: The BVAP for the South includes Arkansas, even though none of the state's four districts has a BVAP as high as 35 percent (the reason why Arkansas is omitted from the table). With respect to control of redistricting (refer to Table 10.4), Democratic control is denoted by an italicized state abbreviation and highlighted in gray, Republican control has the state abbreviation in bold, and for states with court involvement the state abbreviation is underlined. *For the 2004 election in Texas and the 2006 election in Georgia, the congressional districts were redrawn (see Box 10.1), and that accounts for why the BVAP over 35 percent with Democratic Representatives in 2002 and 2010 for these states are not the same (Texas created one more district for the 2004 elections with a BVAP of more than 35 percent, and it was won by a black Democrat, Al Green in Texas District 9).

indication that Republican line drawers were packing black voters. Indeed, apart from Florida, whose GOP mapmakers were necessarily constrained by the Fair Districts constitutional amendments, only in Louisiana did the BVAP also decline in a district with at least a 35 percent BVAP and a Democratic House member (majority black District 2). In the remaining eight states with Democratic members of Congress representing districts with BVAPs at 35 percent or higher, the average BVAP in these districts increased. Under its 2004 re-redistricting, Texas Republicans increased the number of 35 percent or higher BVAP districts from two to three, and between 2010 and 2012, the BVAP in these three districts increased 1.5 percentage points. Perhaps most impressive was Georgia Republicans' handiwork. In 2010, Georgia Democrats represented five districts with an average BVAP of 45.5 percent. In 2012, only four Democrats represented districts with a BVAP of at least 35 percent (all black Democrats in Districts 2, 4, 5, and 13), and compared to 2010, the average BVAP was increased by 7.4 percentage points (to 52.9 percent). Finally, in North Carolina and Tennessee, both states substantially increased the BVAP in its districts represented by Democrats with BVAPs of at least 35 percent (North Carolina Districts 1 and 12 and Tennessee District 9—the only majority black district in the South not represented by an African American); +4.4 points in North Carolina and +5.5 points in Tennessee.

This section concludes with a look at the changes made to congressional districts with majority Latino voting age populations (LVAPs) and/or those with LVAPs of 25 percent or higher. Whereas the last table only looked at districts with high black VAPs represented by Democratic representatives, given the more regionally concentrated nature of the southern Latino population—its numbers only exceed an LVAP of 25 percent in Florida and Texas—the data in Table 10.8 are shown for districts with Democratic and Republican representatives. The data also show the statewide Latino VAP for Florida and Texas (in brackets) based on the 2000 and 2010 census. South-wide, as Table 10.8 shows, the LVAP increased from 11.8 percent of the southern VAP in 2000 to 15.6 percent of the southern VAP in 2010. Starting with Democratic representatives, between 2000 and 2002, outside of Texas there was only one district in Florida with an LVAP that was at least 25 percent and it was a majority black district represented by an African American (District 17 in 2000). In 2002, only in Texas did Democrats represent districts with LVAPs of 25 percent or higher. Between 2000 and 2002, the average LVAP in these districts increased slightly, just 1.1 percentage points in the districts represented by Texas Democrats.

The 2010 round of congressional redistricting is very different from 2000, in the case of Democrats representing districts with LVAPs of at least 25 percent. Whereas there were no Florida Democrats in 2010 who represented high Latino VAP districts, in 2012 five Florida Democrats represented districts with LVAPs of 25 percent or more. In Texas, there were nine Democrats who represented these districts in 2010 (down two from 2002) and the number of Democrats representing high Latino VAP districts increased to twelve in 2012. Considering just Texas, the only state with Democrats who represented districts with high LVAPs between 2010 and 2012, the

TABLE 10.8 ■ Latino Composition of Majority-Minority and Minority Influence Districts Represented by Democrats and Republicans

State [LVAP] Democrats	Latino Voting Age Population (≥ 25%)			State [LVAP] Republicans	Latino Voting Age Population (≥ 25%)		
	2000 (n)	2002 (n)	2002–2000		2000 (n)	2002 (n)	2002–2000
FL [16.1]	29.1 (1)	N/A (0)	—	FL [16.1]	76.2 (2)	66.8 (3)	−9.4
TX [28.6]	49.3 (11)	50.4 (11)	+1.1	TX [28.6]	62.4 (1)	40.3 (3)	−22.1
SOUTH [11.8]	47.6 (12)	50.4 (11)	+2.8	SOUTH [11.8]	71.6 (3)	53.6 (6)	−18.0

State [LVAP] Democrats	Latino Voting Age Population (≥ 25%)			State [LVAP] Republicans	Latino Voting Age Population (≥ 25%)		
	2010 (n)	2012 (n)	2012–2010		2010 (n)	2012 (n)	2012–2010
FL [21.1]	N/A (0)	41.2 (5)	—	FL [21.1]	66.8 (3)	72.9 (2)	+6.1
*TX [33.6]	52.3 (9)	60.6 (12)	+8.3	*TX [33.6]	45.5 (4)	30.5 (6)	−15.0
SOUTH [15.6]	52.3 (9)	54.9 (17)	+2.6	SOUTH [15.6]	54.6 (7)	41.1 (8)	−13.5

Source: Data for the district level Latino voting age population (LVAP) were compiled by the author from the decennial U.S. Census for 2000 and 2010, respectively. Likewise, the statewide LVAP in brackets next to each state abbreviation are also from the decennial U.S. Census for 2000 and 2010, respectively.

Notes: The LVAP for the South includes every state, although obviously, Florida and Texas are the only ones in 2000–2002 and 2010–2012 with district LVAPs as high as 25 percent. With respect to control of redistricting (refer to Table 10.4), Republican control has the state abbreviation in bold (Florida), and for a state with court involvement (Texas) the state abbreviation is underlined. *For the 2004 and 2006 elections in Texas, the congressional districts were redrawn (see McKee and McKenzie 2013), and that partly accounts for why the average LVAP over 25 percent in 2002 and 2010 for this state is not the same.

average LVAP increased markedly in these two years: going from 52.3 percent in 2010 with 9 high LVAP districts to 60.6 percent in 2012 with 12 high LVAP districts (+8.3).

Turning to Republicans who represent high LVAP districts, a very different pattern is revealed. First, in the Sunshine State, the much higher percentage LVAP for Republicans (majority Latino districts) is tied to its unique history of Cuban settlement in South Florida (and primarily Miami-Dade County). These districts are located in the Miami metropolitan area where it is possible to pack large Cuban populations into majority Latino districts that are typically represented by Cuban-American Republicans who take a hard line against the communist regime of their native country. In contrast, very few of the Latinos in Texas hail from Cuba, the vast majority (not surprisingly) are of Mexican descent and most Texas Latinos of Mexican heritage lean in favor of the Democratic Party. Hence, since 2010, in the larger number of high LVAP districts represented by Republicans in Texas, it makes sense that under a court-drawn map that still favored the GOP in 2012, the percentage LVAP substantially declined (–15 percentage points) even though the number of high LVAP districts represented by Republicans increased from four to six.[12]

Redrawn District Populations

As explained, redrawn constituents refer to the residents in a district who are new to the incumbent seeking reelection as a direct consequence of redistricting. Hence, the term redrawn means that these constituents have been assigned a different representative because of a boundary change. When a redistricting occurs, most incumbents will seek reelection in the district that retains most of the voters they represented prior to redistricting. This makes sense because incumbents have cultivated a representational relationship with these voters that often spans many years and allows for the member to attract the votes of some constituents who would otherwise support another candidate if not for their familiarity with the incumbent. On rare occasions, incumbents will seek reelection in a district where they previously represented none of the voters because it appears a safer bet for winning another term (e.g., Republican Newt Gingrich did this in the 1992 election), but in most cases incumbents will prefer to retain as many of their voters as possible after the lines have been redrawn.

Simply put, redrawn constituents are not as likely to vote for the incumbent seeking reelection in their district. A simple correlation between the percentage of redrawn constituents and the U.S. House vote confirms this point. Pooling all the cases of incumbent southern Democrats running for reelection in 2002 and 2012 (77 cases) and then correlating their vote with the percentage of redrawn constituents produces a bivariate correlation of –0.26 ($p < .05$). Likewise, pooling all the cases of incumbent southern Republicans running for reelection in 2002 and 2012 (150 cases) and then correlating their vote with the percentage of redrawn constituents produces a bivariate correlation of –0.18 ($p < .05$). So, generally speaking, the higher the district percentage of redrawn constituents the lower the incumbent's share of the U.S. House vote, and this is true for Democrats and Republicans, though the impact is a bit more severe for Democrats in a region of the country where the GOP is electorally stronger.

Table 10.9 shows data on the percentage of redrawn constituents (mean and median) for Democratic and Republican incumbents running for reelection in the 2002 and 2012 U.S. House elections. Rather than get bogged down discussing the dynamics pertaining to incumbents of both major parties and in each state, it is more feasible and illuminating to highlight some of the broader patterns. Beginning with the 2002 elections, it is logical that collectively, southern Republicans have a higher percentage of redrawn constituents because in most states the Democrats controlled redistricting. South-wide, the mean and median percentage of redrawn constituents for Republican incumbents is 22.7 and 19.6 percent, respectively. For Democratic incumbents, their mean and median percentage of redrawn constituents is 14.7 and 10.9 percent, respectively. So, overall, in the 2002 elections, compared to the typical Democrat, the typical Republican had a redrawn district population that was 8 to 9 percentage points higher.

Compared to the 2000 redistricting cycle, in the 2010 redistricting round when most states were under GOP control, the mean and median percentage of redrawn constituents was higher for incumbents of both parties. Further, in contrast to the 2002 elections, in the 2012 elections now the mean and median percentage of redrawn constituents was higher for Democratic incumbents. South-wide, the mean and median percentage of redrawn constituents for Democratic incumbents is 26.8 and 22.7 percent, respectively. For Republican incumbents, their mean and median percentage of redrawn constituents is 24.6 and 20.9 percent, respectively. So, in the 2012 elections, compared to the typical Republican, the typical Democrat had a redrawn district population that was 2 percentage points higher. Overall, then, it would seem that despite notable state-level variation in the percentage of redrawn constituents, for the 2012 elections the Republicans were only made somewhat less electorally vulnerable because they inherited a slightly lower share of unfamiliar voters. However, this would be the wrong conclusion to draw. To be sure, Table 10.9 provides considerable detail in showing the percentage of redrawn constituents for incumbents of both parties in each state for the last two elections taking place after a decennial redistricting. But Table 10.9 does not break down the percentage of redrawn constituents according to the race/ethnicity and party of the incumbent; this is done in Table 10.10.

Showing the mean percentage of redrawn constituents according to the party affiliation and race/ethnicity of the incumbent running for re-election in 2002 and 2012 makes it much more evident which party was generally advantaged in these two elections. Once again, it is confirmed that the percentage of redrawn constituents for the typical incumbent, irrespective of party, was higher in 2012 (25 percent) than in 2002 (19 percent). In addition, starting with the party of the incumbent, in 2002, Democrats inherited a considerably lower share of unfamiliar voters (15 percent redrawn)

TABLE 10.9 ■ Percentage of Redrawn Constituents for Incumbents Seeking Reelection in 2002 and 2012

2002 Elections	Mean Redrawn (%)		Median Redrawn (%)	
	Democrats (n)	Republicans (n)	Democrats (n)	Republicans (n)
Alabama	4.8 (1)	11.5 (3)	4.8 (1)	8.6 (3)
Arkansas	4.6 (3)	0.0 (1)	5.7 (3)	0.0 (1)
Florida	30.6 (7)	29.0 (14)	32.1 (7)	31.3 (14)
Georgia	15.2 (2)	40.2 (6)	15.2 (2)	48.0 (6)
Louisiana	4.3 (2)	2.5 (4)	4.3 (2)	3.1 (4)
Mississippi	24.2 (2)	16.7 (1)	24.2 (2)	16.7 (1)
North Carolina	16.5 (4)	21.4 (7)	16.0 (4)	20.5 (7)
South Carolina	13.6 (2)	2.5 (3)	13.6 (2)	3.3 (3)
Tennessee	15.6 (3)	14.1 (3)	14.6 (3)	9.2 (3)
Texas	8.3 (16)	29.7 (12)	6.8 (16)	25.9 (12)
Virginia	22.5 (3)	17.6 (8)	26.7 (3)	15.6 (8)
South	14.7 (45)	22.7 (62)	10.9 (45)	19.6 (62)

2012 Elections	Mean Redrawn (%)		Median Redrawn (%)	
	Democrats (n)	Republicans (n)	Democrats (n)	Republicans (n)
Alabama	14.6 (1)	9.7 (6)	14.6 (1)	9.8 (6)
Arkansas	N/A (0)	1.9 (3)	N/A (0)	0.1 (3)
Florida	23.2 (6)	34.8 (16)	22.0 (6)	37.5 (16)
Georgia	28.1 (5)	36.2 (8)	22.8 (5)	33.8 (8)
Louisiana	37.7 (1)	23.0 (5)	37.7 (1)	24.4 (5)
Mississippi	11.9 (1)	3.4 (3)	11.9 (1)	3.1 (3)
North Carolina	42.5 (5)	46.3 (5)	35.7 (5)	48.5 (5)
South Carolina	31.4 (1)	14.0 (5)	31.4 (1)	13.5 (5)
Tennessee	16.9 (2)	31.5 (7)	16.9 (2)	34.2 (7)
Texas	24.6 (7)	23.3 (22)	21.5 (7)	19.9 (22)
Virginia	20.8 (3)	11.7 (8)	19.0 (3)	10.5 (8)
South	26.8 (32)	24.6 (88)	22.7 (32)	20.9 (88)

Source: Data compiled by the author from the MABLE/Geocorr program available through the Missouri Census Data Center.

Notes: With respect to control of redistricting (refer to Table 10.4), Democratic control is denoted by the state name in italics and highlighted in gray, Republican control shows the state name in bold, and for states with court involvement the state is underlined. The number of districts for each major party (Democrats and Republicans) incumbent seeking reelection is shown in parentheses. The data for 2002 exclude one district in Mississippi (MS-3) because two incumbents ran against each other (a Democrat and a Republican).

TABLE 10.10 ■ Percentage of Redrawn Constituents by Race/Ethnicity and Party of Incumbents Seeking Reelection in 2002 and 2012			
Incumbent Type	2002 (n)	2012 (n)	2012–2002
All Democrats	15 (45)	27 (32)	+12
White Democrats	13 (28)	32 (13)	+19
Black Democrats	21 (12)	23 (17)	+2
Latino Democrats	7 (5)	29 (2)	+22
All Republicans	23 (62)	25 (88)	+2
White Republicans	23 (59)	23 (82)	0
Latino Republicans	25 (3)	36 (4)	+11
Black Republicans	N/A (0)	51 (2)	N/A
All Incumbents	19 (107)	25 (120)	+6

Source: Data compiled by the author from the MABLE/Geocorr program available through the Missouri Census Data Center.

Note: The mean percentage of redrawn constituents is displayed with the corresponding number of districts in parentheses.

versus their Republican counterparts (23 percent redrawn). But in 2012, the typical Democratic incumbent faced a slightly higher share of redrawn constituents (27 percent) vis-à-vis their GOP colleagues (25 percent). But these statistics are far from telling the whole story, which becomes palpable once the share of redrawn constituents is viewed with respect to the party *and* race/ethnicity of the incumbent.

The most telling difference between the 2002 and 2012 elections resides among white Democrats versus white Republicans. In 2002, the typical white Democratic incumbent inherited a 13 percent redrawn district population, an amount ten percentage points lower than the average share of redrawn constituents for the typical white Republican (23 percent). So, in 2002, when Democrats were in charge of the redistricting process in most southern states, to no surprise, white Democratic incumbents were less electorally vulnerable than white Republican representatives, at least in terms of the number of voters in their districts they were not familiar with. In 2012, the partisan balance was drastically altered. In this election cycle, the typical white Democratic representative had a district that was 32 percent redrawn, whereas the typical white Republican had a district that was 23 percent redrawn, the same average redrawn percentage as in 2002. Thus, in 2012, when Republicans controlled the redistricting process in the vast majority of southern states, white Democrats were saddled with a much higher mean percentage of redrawn constituents. By isolating the party and race/ethnicity of the incumbent, we can see that the small number of minority Republican incumbents is driving up the mean percentage of redrawn constituents for Republicans in 2012, while just the opposite dynamic is taking place among Democrats; the lower percentage of redrawn constituents in minority Democratic districts is lowering the overall mean percentage of redrawn constituents for Democrats in 2012.

Partisan Bias

So far, congressional redistricting has been analyzed based on several important but distinct factors, including the district presidential vote, minority district populations, and redrawn district populations. In this section, a more holistic measure of congressional redistricting is considered. At this moment, the case law on redistricting is, quite frankly, a complicated mess, and there is no clear standard for what the courts would deem so blatant a partisan gerrymander that it would be declared unconstitutional. This said, scholars have invested substantial effort in devising statistical measures that are capable of detecting evidence of partisan gerrymandering. One that has gained traction in legal cases is known as *partisan symmetry*, and from this measure one can assess to what extent, if any, a redistricting plan exhibits partisan bias.

Although the mathematics behind it can be cumbersome (see Gelman and King 1994), the concept of partisan symmetry is very intuitive. Let us suppose that in a state, say Florida, the Republican Party won 60 percent of the U.S. House vote and this translated into winning 80 percent of the seats. On its face, this does not yield any evidence that the Florida GOP engaged in a Republican partisan gerrymander. In fact, if Florida Democrats were able to win 60 percent of the U.S. House vote and this also resulted in the Democrats taking 80 percent of the seats, then there is no partisan bias in this congressional plan because both parties are awarded the same exact share of seats based on winning the same percentage of the vote. In contrast, partisan bias rears its head if there is an asymmetric relationship between the percentage of the vote and the corresponding percentage of seats won on the basis of party. For example, if Florida Republicans win 60 percent of the U.S. House vote and 100 percent of the seats, but conversely Florida Democrats win 60 percent of the vote and 80 percent of the seats, then this congressional plan exhibits partisan bias that advantages the GOP. In other words, this plan is biased because at the same percentage of the vote, one party gets more electoral bang for its buck.

Table 10.11 displays the measure of partisan bias in each southern state for the 2002–2010 elections (the 2000 redistricting cycle) and the 2012 elections (the first election taking place under the 2010 redistricting cycle). Again, the states are identified with respect to control of redistricting. The measure of partisan bias is shown based on the assumption of what it would be if the statewide vote was split evenly between the major parties (50/50). A positive number denotes a Republican bias and a negative number signifies a Democratic bias. The seats ratio displays how the partisan bias registers with respect to the percentage of seats won by Republicans and

TABLE 10.11 ■ Partisan Bias at the 50% Vote Mark for 2002–2010 and 2012 Elections					
	2002–2010			2012	
State	Bias (+R/–D)	Seats Ratio (R/D)	State	Bias (+R/–D)	Seats Ratio (R/D)
AL	+12	62/38	**AL**	**+25**	75/25
AR	–13	37/63	AR	+1	51/49
FL	**+14**	64/36	**FL**	**+9**	59/41
*GA	**+8**	58/42	**GA**	**+14**	64/36
LA	+5	55/45	**LA**	**+19**	69/31
MS	+1	51/49	MS	**+23**	73/27
NC	–6	44/56	**NC**	**+20**	70/30
SC	+12	62/38	**SC**	**+16**	66/34
TN	–5	45/55	**TN**	**+14**	64/36
*TX	+6	56/44	TX	**+9**	59/42
VA	**+9**	59/41	**VA**	**+18**	68/32

Source: Data are originally from McGann et al. (2016, 90, 93).

Notes: For ease of presentation, the data have been rounded to the nearest whole number. Bias numbers in bold indicate the mean partisan bias estimate is significant at the .05 level. These measures of partisan bias were estimated via a simulation process (see McGann et al. 2016, 95–96) so that if we assume the major parties both capture 50 percent of the congressional vote then in the state of Alabama in 2012, the Republicans would win 75 percent of the districts and the Democrats would win the remaining 25 percent (the seats ratio). With respect to control of redistricting (refer to Table 10.4), Democratic control is denoted by an italicized state abbreviation and highlighted in gray, Republican control has the state abbreviation in bold, and for states with court involvement the state abbreviation is underlined. *For the 2004 election in Texas and the 2006 election in Georgia, the congressional districts were redrawn (see Box 10.1) and these new maps favored the Republican Party as GOP-controlled legislatures in these states produced these plans. Texas has been mired in legal disputes over its congressional redistricting, but the basic underlying map, which has been altered many times since 2004, stems from the Republican partisan gerrymander first enacted for the 2004 U.S. House elections.

Democrats when the statewide two-party vote is split 50/50. An example should help clarify things. Take North Carolina in 2012, a state that orchestrated a remarkably effective Republican gerrymander. Among states with a partisan bias that was statistically significant at the .05 level (those states in bold) in 2012, only Alabama had a Republican partisan bias (+25) that exceeded that of the Tar Heel State (+20). With a Republican bias of +20 points, with a statewide two-party vote split 50/50 between the parties, the North Carolina GOP is expected to win 70 percent of the seats (50 percent plus the 20-point partisan bias), and thus their Democratic opponents are left with the remaining 30 percent.

The North Carolina example is instructive because, as mentioned, in 2012, North Carolina Republicans won 49 percent of the U.S. House vote and took 9 of the 13 districts (69 percent) and the statewide presidential vote in 2008 was in fact almost evenly split between the major party candidates. Put differently, the estimated partisan bias for North Carolina in 2012 is very close to the actual results of the election with respect to the percentage of the vote won by Republicans and the attendant share of the seats awarded them when the statewide two-party vote was effectively at the 50/50 mark (whether one considers the U.S. House vote in 2012 or the presidential vote in 2008).

The biggest takeaway from Table 10.11 is how much more biased and one-sided Republican were the redistricting plans in the 2012 elections. Even in the 2002–2010 elections most southern states' redistricting plans exhibited bias in the Republican direction (the exceptions being Arkansas, North Carolina, and Tennessee), but only in two of them (Florida and Georgia) did the (Republican) partisan bias reach statistical significance. In contrast, in the 2012 elections in which only Democrats had control of redistricting in Arkansas, the partisan bias is uniformly Republican and attains statistical significance in eight states, including Texas, whose congressional plan was ultimately finalized by federal judges with a map not terribly different from the one promoted by the Texas GOP (Barone and McCutcheon 2013, 1567).

JIM CROW IN MINIATURE?
RESTRICTIVE VOTING LAWS

There is no question that, as of late, more and more states have busied themselves with passing restrictive voting legislation.[13] This activity has intensified since the 2010 midterm (see Box 10.2), when the GOP made historic gains in state legislative elections (see Table 10.3), giving Republicans control of numerous statehouses. With majority status in state legislatures, Republicans have the opportunity/ability to pass these electoral reforms, the most salient of which include curtailing early voting and tightening the requirements for voter identification (ID) when voting in person at the polls. But why expend precious political capital on legislation that has the potential to make it harder (raise the costs) to participate in the democratic process?

BOX 10.2   FLORIDA AND NORTH CAROLINA: GROUND ZERO FOR CURTAILING VOTING RIGHTS

As discussed in this chapter, the impressive GOP seat gains after the 2010 midterm elections emboldened the party to pursue restrictive voting reforms in those states where Republicans attained state legislative majorities and the competitiveness in these states was very high in various elective offices (e.g., a presidential battleground state). As McGann et al. (2016) contend, pushing a partisan advantage is much more likely when the party has the opportunity to do so by being in the majority and also because electoral competition is intense. In the South, of late, two states clearly satisfy McGann et al.'s criteria: Florida and North Carolina. Although Florida Republicans were in the majority prior to the 2010 midterm, like other very competitive states that had GOP state legislative majorities after the 2010 contests, tightening election laws became a major priority. As stated by McKee and Craig (2017–18, 114–115),

> [Florida] Republicans passed House Bill (H.B.) 1355 in July of 2011 . . . which was designed to increase the costs among Floridians more likely to vote Democratic, in particular, African Americans. The main provisions included reducing early voting from two weeks to eight days, with elimination of the Sunday before the election; the law also scaled back third-party registration drives to two days, with punitive consequences for turning in late petitions (this provision was overturned by the courts). Further, voters who had moved since the last election could no longer update their address at the polling place; instead they would have to cast a provisional ballot. In short, Florida Republicans used their lawmaking power to stack the deck in their favor by making it more difficult for likely Democratic voters to participate.

Research on the Florida case makes it clear that removing the Sunday before Election Day was done because blacks in the Sunshine State have exhibited a pattern of voting early on that day in previous election cycles (Herron and Smith 2012). In addition, before the punitive registration reform provision in H.B. 1355 was overturned, third-party organizations historically involved in voter registration drives markedly scaled back their activities or halted them altogether and most of these organizations mobilized voters who tended to favor the Democratic Party (Herron and Smith 2013). Finally, although most states disenfranchise convicted felons while they serve their sentences, unlike most states, felons who served their time in Florida essentially have no recourse to have their right to vote reinstated. This has become a point of considerable contention—recently, for example, the American Civil Liberties Union (ACLU) has devoted at least 5 million dollars on an advertising campaign intended to restore Florida ex-felons' voting rights via a constitutional amendment (Weigel 2017). Like this chapter's discussion of voter ID legislation, the partisan overtones of H.B. 1355 are reflected in the partisan breakdown of the vote on this measure: no Democrat voted in favor of the bill and only two Republicans voted against it (State Senators Paula Dockery and Mike Fasano).

Though Republicans in the Tar Heel State won majorities in both chambers of the legislature in the 2010 midterm, they did not overhaul their voting apparatus until after the *Shelby* decision was handed down (June 25, 2013) when Republican Governor Pat McCrory signed the Voter Information Verification Act (VIVA—H.B. 589) on August 12, 2013 (Herron and Smith 2016). Reflecting the partisan-charged nature of the VIVA legislation, not a single Democratic legislator in either chamber voted for it and not a single Republican voted against it. Like in Florida, North Carolina's VIVA shortened the early voting period, cutting it from "seventeen to ten days" (Herron and Smith 2016, 466). In addition, the law rolled back a handful of measures that were clearly hospitable to fostering political participation: voters used to be able to engage in one-stop

(Continued)

(Continued)

(same-day) registration and voting during the early voting period, those under the age of eighteen could register to vote, and voting could be done in person without a photo ID. VIVA got rid of all the aforementioned voting provisions and in addition to mandating a photo ID for in-person voting, the law reduced "the acceptable forms of voter photo identification" (Herron and Smith 2016, 474).

VIVA came under judicial scrutiny and it was eventually struck down by a federal appeals court that declared the North Carolina legislation "deliberately 'target[s] African-Americans with almost surgical precision" (Wines and Blinder 2016). Since Republicans took control of the legislature in the 2010 midterm, the political environment in North Carolina has been decidedly more tumultuous than the Sunshine State's. Perhaps this is due to the fact that North Carolina Democrats have had the upper hand for so long, despite the GOP's longstanding advantage in presidential elections. For instance, the Tar Heel State did not become a presidential battleground until 2008, when Barack Obama carried the state for the Democratic Party by a mere 14,177 votes (out of more than four million cast for the major parties) for the first time since Democrat Jimmy Carter was victorious in 1976. Over the same span of time, until Republican McCrory was elected in 2012, only one other Republican held the governorship, James G. Martin (1985–1993). The confluence of a recent Republican takeover of the legislature with the advent of presidential swing state status has resulted in a combustible state of politics, as the GOP has done its best to push every angle to gain an electoral advantage.

Besides the controversial but ultimately overturned VIVA legislation, as mentioned in this chapter, the most extreme partisan gerrymander in the 2010 redistricting round was far and away the one engineered by North Carolina Republicans. Consider that in 2010, the last U.S. House elections under the old congressional boundaries drawn by Democrats, all thirteen seats were contested by both major parties and the Democrats won 46 percent of the two-party vote and seven seats to the GOP's six. In 2012, when it was the North Carolina Republican legislators' chance to game the system, all thirteen seats were once again contested by both major parties and the Republicans won 49 percent of the two-party vote and nine seats to the Democrats' four. Thus, in both of these instances, the party that controlled redistricting actually garnered fewer votes overall but a majority of the seats, and the North Carolina GOP was much more adept at this than their Democratic predecessors.

In 2016, North Carolina Republicans managed to pass a very controversial piece of legislation referred to as the "bathroom bill," and it decreed that transgendered individuals must use the bathroom corresponding to the sex listed on their birth certificate. The state was in danger of losing millions (perhaps even billions) of dollars because of boycotts issued by the likes of the NCAA, which would seek other states for hosting college championships and related tournaments. Promotion of this law contributed to Governor McCrory's narrow reelection loss (10,277 two-party vote difference out of more than 4.5 million votes cast) to Democrat Roy Cooper, the state's attorney general.

Even prior to the 2010 GOP takeover of the North Carolina legislature, the state's branch of the NAACP had been instrumental in protesting against policies it deemed as extreme and out of step with the sentiments of most North Carolinians. But in the summer of 2013, after the North Carolina GOP had taken control of the governorship in addition to the legislature, a coalition of Democratic and left-leaning groups came together to hold "Moral Mondays," protesting the Republican policies emanating from the statehouse in Raleigh (Purdy 2017). In 2016, Republican Donald Trump won the Tar Heel State over Democrat Hillary Clinton by 3.8 percentage points. In this diverse and growing southern state with a large minority electorate and substantial northeastern in-migration (Hood and McKee 2010; McKee and Teigen 2016), expect two-party politics to continue to be cutthroat because neither Republicans nor Democrats have a definitive electoral advantage.

The Republican answer to this question, which has become their mantra (see von Spakovsky 2012), is that raising the requirements for voting is simply a means to safeguard the ballot box. Ostensibly, it is a necessary action to prevent voter fraud, so that the electorate can be assured and confident that election outcomes reflect the will of the people. The Democratic retort is that this raft of Republican-crafted restrictive voting legislation is designed and intended to discriminate against racial minorities. So, who is right? What is the motive behind these laws? To be sure, it is eminently possible that many Republicans believe that restrictive voting legislation is necessary to combat voter fraud (especially the party's voters because preventing voter fraud is the reason GOP elites have given to justify their promotion of these electoral reforms). Likewise, it is probable that Democrats have evidence (perhaps even firsthand accounts) that these electoral reforms are embraced to block minority participation.

The empirical record strongly suggests that the Republican justification of preventing voter fraud is baseless (see Keyssar 2009; Levitt 2012). The Democratic charge, on the other hand, holds much more sway but perhaps for a somewhat different intention. It is difficult to convince/prove that the GOP's motive for championing restrictive voting legislation is rooted in racism of the flavor witnessed during the days of the Jim Crow, racially segregated South.[14] No, making parallels between contemporary restrictive voting legislation and the brand of racially discriminatory laws that propped up the white Democratic Solid South of yesteryear (see chapter 3) is tied to one overriding motive: electoral competition. Just as southern Democrats once implemented a host of laws that had the effect of primarily discriminating against African Americans, these modern restrictive voting reforms appear to have racially disparate effects because, for example, it is a fact that minorities are less likely to have the necessary documentation (e.g., birth certificate, driver license) to qualify to vote at the polls in states with strict photo ID laws (Gaskins and Iyer 2012; Hood and Bullock 2008; Levitt 2012).

It is highly questionable, however, to impugn Republican motives on the grounds that an overwhelmingly white party has promoted restrictive voting legislation merely to punish minority groups. The most plausible objective of the GOP is to attain an electoral advantage by enacting legislation that has the *realized* effect of disproportionally reducing minority participation because minorities are overwhelmingly aligned with the Democratic Party. In other words, these election reforms are designed to raise the costs of minority participation, because minorities do not support the GOP, not because Republicans simply have it out for minorities. Admittedly, for many detractors of restrictive voting laws, this is a distinction without a difference. If these laws single out minority groups or have a racially disparate effect on minority participation, then who cares whether the nub of GOP maneuvering is electoral competition and not racial discrimination?

But the history of American politics is fundamentally tied to electoral competition. At one time, although now it seems very long ago, the Grand Old Party was revered by African Americans because it was the party of Lincoln, the party that freed the slaves. Likewise, the southern Democracy was a party whose raison d'être was the defense of white supremacy. My, how things have changed; now the southern GOP is practically a lily-white party and the Democratic opposition consists of a rainbow coalition of minority groups. Was the true motivation behind northern Republican military occupation of the American South during Reconstruction inextricably linked to Yankee sympathy for the plight of southern African Americans or was it mainly about ensuring a Republican national majority when the time came for white southern Democrats to re-enter the electorate? By all accounts, the answer was the latter. Likewise, did a man with salty language from the Texas Hill Country come to champion black civil rights, culminating in the passage of the 1964 Civil Rights Act and the 1965 Voting Rights Act, because President Johnson had a deep-rooted compassion for the struggle of African Americans or because he possessed indomitable political ambition?

Voter Identification Laws

Since the mid-2000s, a majority of states have either passed or proposed stricter voter ID laws (Underhill 2017). And, as mentioned, since Republican electoral gains in the 2010 midterm elections, restrictive voting measures like voter ID laws have become a more frequently pursued policy item on the GOP agenda. Curiously, however, once a critical mass of states passed stricter voter ID laws scholars set out to assess their suppressive effects on voter turnout, but the vast majority of studies have determined that they have no demonstrable impact on reducing turnout (Erikson and Minnite 2009; Highton 2017). Indeed, with few exceptions (see Hajnal, Lajevardi, and Nielson 2017), and these exceptions have come under justifiable attack for lacking empirical rigor (see Grimmer et al. 2017), it appears that despite the considerable evidence that Republicans desire stricter voter ID to gain an electoral advantage (Hicks et al. 2015; Hicks, McKee, and Smith 2016b; McKee 2015b), this goal has failed to materialize.

One reason why stricter voter ID laws have generally not proven to dampen participation is because of countermobilization undertaken by groups that otherwise would be placed at a disadvantage (Valentino and Neuner 2017). The scant and sometimes flimsy evidence for stricter voter ID laws reducing political participation is a somewhat remarkable revelation, if only because this reform has become the most salient, controversial, and litigated legislation in the Republicans' strategic electoral arsenal. Hence, despite the fact that Republicans and Democrats have poured impressive resources into their battle over voter ID, as one scholarly article concluded, this partisan feud, for all intents and purposes, has been "much ado about nothing" (Hood and Bullock 2012).

Of course, a partisan fight over what ultimately is a marginally and arguably inconsequential issue, at least with respect to its electoral effects, is not something new to American politics. And to the extent that the major parties devote considerable energy to waging a war over a reform like stricter voter ID legislation, the public is necessarily going to take notice (Schattschneider 1960) and divide over the issue based on the cues they receive from fellow partisan elites (Gronke et al., forthcoming; Zaller 1992). The purpose of this section is not to assess what effects if any does stricter voter ID have on political participation (as mentioned, it probably is trivial at best), nor is it to examine the positions/attitudes of the mass electorate toward voter ID legislation (on this, see Gronke et al., forthcoming; Wilson and Brewer 2013); instead, the objective is to simply demonstrate that in the South (and this is also true in the rest of the United States, see Hicks et al. 2015), the parties have polarized over the issue of stricter voter ID laws.

Figure 10.6 places in stark relief just how partisan the voter ID issue has become. After the 2010 Republican tsunami, from 2011 to 2013, seven southern states pushed for passage of stricter voter ID laws: Alabama, South Carolina, Tennessee, and Texas in 2011; Virginia in 2012; Arkansas, North Carolina, and Virginia (again) in 2013.

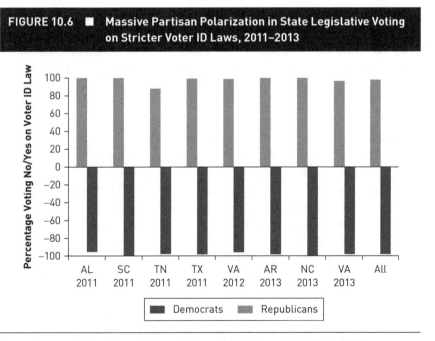

FIGURE 10.6 ■ Massive Partisan Polarization in State Legislative Voting on Stricter Voter ID Laws, 2011–2013

Source: Data compiled by the author from the *Research & Politics* article by McKee (2015).

Figure 10.6 shows the partisan breakdown of state legislative voting on voter ID laws in these southern states. Because of the massive partisan polarization over this legislation, the figure displays the percentage of Republican lawmakers who voted yes for stricter voter ID legislation and the portion of Democratic legislators who voted no. Only in Tennessee, in 2011, did less than 90 percent of Republicans vote yes on a stricter voter ID measure. With respect to Democrats, the least unified delegation was in Alabama, where 95 percent opposed a stricter voter ID law. Overall, summing all of these votes by party, in favor and against, 98 percent of GOP lawmakers voted yes for a stricter voter ID provision while 98 percent of their Democratic counterparts voted no. Regardless of whether such a voting reform has any appreciable electoral impact, Democratic and Republican lawmakers are behaving as though it will, and their votes reflect how they expect such legislation will alter political competition.

THE IMPORTANCE OF *SHELBY COUNTY V. HOLDER*

The 1965 Voting Rights Act (VRA), a towering piece of legislation that has mobilized black re-enfranchisement in the South and since then, protected African Americans' right to participate in the democratic process (as well as safeguarding the rights of other minority groups like Latinos and Native Americans), was extended for twenty-five years in 2006 by a bipartisan vote in Congress (98 to 0 in the Senate; 390 to 33 in the House; Rush 2013, 322). The VRA was renewed three times previously (1970, 1975, and 1982) and the extension of this landmark legislation is a strong statement regarding the need to protect minority groups from unfair treatment in exercising the right to vote. In the South in particular, the VRA has loomed large principally because of the frequent use of the Section 5 preclearance provision that required most southern jurisdictions (all of Alabama, Georgia, Louisiana, Mississippi, South Carolina, Texas, Virginia; five counties in Florida and forty counties in North Carolina)[15] to get approval from the Department of Justice (DOJ) when making changes to voting laws, including redistricting plans.

In the Alabama case of *Shelby County v. Holder* (2013), the Supreme Court rendered the Section 5 preclearance provision of the VRA inoperable and did so through an interesting maneuver. Section 4(b) of the VRA provided a technical formula for determining which states qualified for Section 5 oversight. But the coverage formula in Section 4 was woefully outdated, it was based on data gathered from 1964 to 1972 (Katz 2013, 329). As the political scientist and election law expert Bernard Grofman (2013, 332) put it, the data "were not just stale, they were incredibly stale." So, given the outdated formula of Section 4, the Supreme Court ruled that Section 5 could no longer be operable. This means that until Congress devises a new formula that sets a standard for detecting which political jurisdictions engage in election practices that rise to the level of discriminatory behavior, these heretofore Section 5 covered states can now make changes to their voting laws without getting approval from the DOJ. Thus, changes to election laws are basically implemented unless a court action can block them.

So, what is the significance of the *Shelby* decision? First, by removing the application of Section 5 to a large swath of southern political jurisdictions, state and local election administration will be pursued in a manner that furthers the interest of the political party in charge. In most states, this means that the GOP will proceed more aggressively with election laws and redistricting plans that further their political and strategic agenda. Also, in more localized areas, such as heavily black sections of the Mississippi delta, in this type of setting, it would not be surprising to find that black Democrats hold the political power (Bullock and Gaddie 2009). In short, without the credible deterrent effect of Section 5 coverage, expect partisans to be bolder in their pursuit of electoral advantage via manipulation of the various levers of the election administration apparatus.[16]

In the modern American South, race and partisanship have become inextricably linked. It is now virtually impossible to make a clean political distinction between a racially driven action versus a partisan driven motive. This reality has in turn tied the courts in knots. For instance, redistricting is a seemingly ever-evolving and unsettled area of case law. The recent North Carolina case of *Cooper v. Harris* (2017) highlights the legal mess the Supreme Court has managed to wade deeper into. The *Cooper* ruling was in response to the extraordinarily bold and successful gerrymander North Carolina Republicans enacted for the 2012 U.S. House elections (as detailed above). As Republicans have been wont to do, in North Carolina they justified their furtherance of a majority black (District 1) and plurality black (District 12)[17] district as a necessary action in compliance with the VRA, because to reduce these African American district populations would be an act of retrogression, which means these African American voters would be left worse off by not being able to elect the representative of their choice. But recent social science scholarship has found that in a state like North Carolina, enough white voters are willing to vote for a candidate favored by African Americans, so that districts can be drawn in which blacks are the plurality of the electorate but certainly not the majority of the constituency (see Lublin et al. 2009).

All this is to say that North Carolina Republicans disingenuously hid behind the VRA to justify the creation of two districts with highly concentrated black electorates in order to dilute their voting strength in neighboring districts. But the Court's ruling failed to bring some much-needed (and frankly overdue) clarity to the matter because it essentially ruled that the North Carolina congressional map was an unconstitutional racial gerrymander. But this legal language is not helpful because it is obvious to any social scientist that race had become the vehicle for furthering a partisan gerrymander, that is, African Americans were packed into Districts 1 and 12 in order to increase the odds that Republicans would be victorious in most of the other districts with much whiter voter populations. Like North Carolina Republicans, the Court also played the race card. The problem with this action is that the Court has declared partisan gerrymanders justiciable (subject to being overturned by the court; see *Davis v. Bandemer* 1986), but in a more recent decision (*Vieth v. Jubelirer* 2004) the Justices essentially threw up their hands by claiming they did not know what would constitute an unconstitutional partisan gerrymander (see McGann et al. 2016). So, in *Cooper,* instead of tackling head on the case of a blatant partisan gerrymander, because race and party are inextricably linked, the Court elided the issue by deeming the Republican plan in North Carolina a racial gerrymander.

Needless to say, with the Section 5 preclearance provision of the VRA effectively sidelined by the *Shelby* decision, there is an obvious incentive to push the electoral envelope in the realm of election administration and election reform, and this has led to a bevy of lawsuits. Unfortunately, recent Court rulings, like the *Cooper* case outlined above, seem to only complicate things and thus invite even more litigation. In more colloquial language, the *Shelby* ruling has opened the floodgates to a wild west in the arena of election law and election administration, and political and legal observers hang on every word of the Supreme Court's latest decision because it remains unclear what the political parties can and cannot do to gain an electoral advantage.

SUMMARY

This chapter began by showing recent demographic trends in the southern electorate. It is inescapable that the minority population and, by extension, the minority segment of the electorate (especially Latinos) is growing at a faster rate than the still majority and politically dominant Republican-leaning white population. This is an obvious cause of concern for southern Republicans who, even in the face of this demographic change, have failed to expand the GOP's appeal to minority voters. But rather than alter its course by making policy-based overtures that can attract an expanding minority electorate that is aligned with the Democratic opposition, favorable short-term conditions, like the 2010 midterm election, have bolstered GOP efforts to maintain the same policy agenda while aggressively pursuing an electoral advantage via redistricting and restrictive voting laws. The chapter ends with a discussion of the momentous 2013 Supreme Court decision in the Alabama case of *Shelby County v. Holder.* By rendering the Section 5 preclearance provision inoperable in the South, where most erstwhile covered jurisdictions reside, the *Shelby* ruling has unleashed a Pandora's box of highly contentious, rancorous, and sometimes plainly duplicitous legal maneuvering. In short, without legal clarity, both major parties have every incentive to maximize their position in the electoral arena. And this is something southern Republicans have done and continue to do, with a brashness that perhaps only white southern Democrats of the Jim Crow era could upstage.

11 THE SOUTH IN COMPARATIVE PERSPECTIVE

The South is different. It always has been. Of course, this statement is far from a revelation. Nonetheless, the historical trajectory of southern politics has thrown various top-flight scholars for a curve, particularly the closer one gets to analyzing Dixie's politics in real time. It would seem that the long span of Democratic dominance made it difficult for many observers to fathom the region eventually transforming into a Republican stronghold (but see Heard 1952). However, the evidence marshalled throughout this book leaves no doubt that the South went from a short-lived Republican-leaning system under the watchful eye of northern military occupation during Reconstruction (see chapter 2) to a one-party Democratic bastion persisting from the early 1900s to the 1950s (Key 1949) that then transitioned to a competitive two-party region (Lamis 1988) that has since been eclipsed by a palpable GOP electoral advantage (Hayes and McKee 2008; McKee 2012a; McKee and Yoshinaka 2015).

The gradual exodus of whites from the southern Democracy and into the contemporary GOP took decades to run its course. This slowly evolving transformation of the South's politics caught many by surprise because a large period of the transition toward the Republican Party was shrouded in dealignment. Indeed, writing in 1966, Philip Converse could hardly grasp any evidence that the decline in southern whites' Democratic affiliations necessarily precipitated the rise of the Republican Party. A decade later, assessing Dixie's party system at the height of white dealignment, Paul Allen Beck concluded with this pronouncement regarding a Republican takeover of southern politics:

> the evidence points consistently away from a forecast of partisan realignment. Gains in identification with the Republican party in the last two decades have been meager indeed, and the few which appeared through 1960 have been reversed since. With the potential for widespread black Republicanism gone, the impact of interregional population exchanges largely absorbed, and the lack of Republican support among the young, GOP prospects for the future seem dim. (1977, 495)

Beck (1977) goes on to say that a general weakening of both major parties appeared the most likely long-term course of southern politics (also an expectation for the national parties in the view of Wattenberg 1985). Were it to transpire, this development would be unfortunate because a lack of party competition was the historical bane of the American South—its absence of vigorous two-party competition meant that there could be no "popular influence on public policy" (Beck 1977, 495). This was V. O. Key's diagnosis when he began *Southern Politics in State and Nation* with this opening declaration: "The South may not be the nation's number one political problem, as some northerners assert, but politics is the South's number one problem" (1949, 3).

Nonetheless, Beck does point to a silver lining with respect to the race issue, noting that, "after years of presumably high salience, there is good reason to believe that the racial question is losing its position as an important issue to southern voters" (1977, 496). With the benefit of hindsight, not only has the racial question managed to remain the primary shaper of southern politics (see Black and Black 2002; Hood, Kidd, and Morris 2012; McKee and Springer 2015; Valentino and Sears 2005), but white dealignment ultimately served as a halfway house on the path to Republican realignment (Petrocik 1987). Furthermore, the young white voters who reached adulthood in the mid-1960s, when Converse (1966) saw no path for GOP ascendancy, became the principal architects of the modern day Republican South (see chapter 6, and Green, Palmquist, and Schickler 2002). To Beck's credit though, by their actions on civil rights (most telling in the case of Arizona Republican Senator Barry Goldwater voting against the 1964 Civil Rights Act, Carmines and Stimson 1989; Stimson 2004), the GOP did foreclose the possibility for a biracial Republican coalition (on this point, also see Black and Black 2002, 138–139) and southern in-migration in the 1950s and 1960s did register some effects favoring southern Republicans (but now in-migrants have proven a net benefit to southern Democrats, see chapter 9). In sum, Beck's general expectation of party decline was premature, or at least not the last word, because southern Republicans ultimately became ascendant in Dixie's electoral system. Alas, such are the perils of predicting the future state of southern politics.

Perhaps just as notable as the misguided prognostications launched in the 1960s and 1970s (and even in the 1980s) have been the more recent declarations that the politics of the South are converging with the rest of the nation (see Aistrup 2010; Shafer and Johnston 2006; Steed, Moreland, and Baker 1990). To be clear, to the extent that the collapse of the Solid Democratic South opened the door for Republican growth, it is not without merit to anticipate that GOP advancement would make the region come to resemble the more competitive politics of the North. However, as this chapter will demonstrate with various empirical evidence, the problem with the expectation of the South's politics gradually blending into the national fold is that Dixie has now become markedly more Republican than the rest of the United States. What at one time appeared to be partisan convergence, has eventually resulted in southern Republican divergence (Bullock 2014). It remains to be seen whether the Democratic Party can turn the southern political system back in its favor (see chapter 12), but at least for now, the sundry reports on the impending death of southern political exceptionalism are truly exaggerations.

Although there are of course notable intersectional differences in various parts of the non-South (see Black and Black 2007; Gimpel and Schuknecht 2004; McKee and Teigen 2009; Mellow 2008) and the South (e.g., the subregional distinction between the Deep South and Peripheral South, as detailed in chapter 8), in this chapter regional comparisons are limited to differences between the South and the North (in this chapter "non-South" and "North" are used interchangeably for any and all of the thirty-nine states that did not constitute the Confederacy during the Civil War). Simply put, if the politics of the South persist in being distinctive, this should manifest in comparisons with the rest of the nation—the most common approach to examining whether the South is a unique region in the broader scope of the American political system.

The chapter proceeds as follows. First, long-term patterns in the popular presidential vote and the partisan share of U.S. House seats are documented in a series of figures dating from 1868 to 2016. As one of the major analytical themes of the book, the chapter then compares the party identification of northerners and southerners and particularly with respect to race, with American National Election Studies (ANES) data from the 1950s to 2000s. The final analysis makes use of the Cooperative Congressional Election Study (CCES) surveys to assess the most recent regional voting patterns in presidential and congressional (U.S. House) contests, focusing again on party identification and the race of southern and northern respondents. The chapter concludes with a restatement of why the South's politics persist in their distinctiveness from the rest of the United States.

ELECTION PATTERNS IN THE SOUTH AND NON-SOUTH

The presidency is the biggest prize in American politics. There was a time when presidents were subservient to congressional majorities (particularly in the late 1800s), but the modernization of the executive office has permanently elevated the role of presidents from at least the time of Franklin Roosevelt (Neustadt 1991). As the most salient political position in the American system, the electoral dynamics of presidential politics sets the tone for all other contests and exerts the greatest direct influence in shaping the positions embraced by the major parties. U.S. House elections, by comparison, have always been more politically insulated, and this is by design because districts exhibit the strong flavor of the cultural milieu of their local environment. Nonetheless, the "presidential pulse," if you will (Campbell 1993, 1997), has come to cast a more notable impact in shaping the outcomes of congressional elections and most other contests because of the nationalization of American politics. In other words, in contemporary American elections the linkage between presidential voting behavior and that found in congressional preferences has grown stronger (Jacobson and Carson 2016). The South is not immune to this pattern, rather the region continues to show a partisan proclivity in presidential and congressional voting that continues to differ from the rest of the country.

In this section, the popular presidential vote and partisan seat shares in the U.S. House in the South and non-South are compared from 1868 to 2016. The 1868 election cycle is the first since the end of the Civil War in which most of the southern states have been readmitted to the Union and hence have constituencies once again participating in voting for federal offices. As mentioned, Republican top-down advancement in the South necessarily starts with presidential contests; they are the leading indicator of partisan change in the South and non-South. The empirical benefit of tracing partisan seat shares in U.S. House elections is because all of the offices are up for election every two years. This means that short-term political conditions are best captured in the election outcomes for this office.

In the respective graphical presentations for presidential and U.S. House elections, a series of five figures is shown. The first two figures illustrate the partisan balance within each region (the distribution of electoral power between the Democratic and Republican parties), showing the South first and then the non-South. Next, the Democratic side of the two-party battle is displayed (i.e., the popular presidential vote and the seat share in the U.S. House) for both regions (South vs. non-South). Then, the Republican pattern is illustrated for the South and non-South. In other words, it is useful to not only assess the balance of partisan power within the South and non-South, respectively, but also to view the relative strength of one party across regions.

Finally, the last graphical presentation for presidential and U.S. House contests illustrates the regional differences in partisan strength for these two federal offices from 1868 to 2016. For example, in every election year the Democratic percentage of the popular presidential vote in the South (percentage of Democratic U.S. House seats in the South) is subtracted from the Democratic percentage of the popular presidential vote cast in the non-South (percentage of Democratic U.S. House seats in the non-South). This difference is similarly computed and graphed for the Republican popular presidential vote (South minus non-South) and the GOP's share of U.S. House seats (South minus non-South).

Presidential Elections

Figure 11.1 charts the popular presidential vote cast in the South from 1868 to 2016 and Figure 11.2 displays the same data for the non-South. For all of the popular presidential vote data displayed in this section, the percentage of the Democratic and Republican vote is out of the two-party vote except for five elections: 1912, 1948, 1968, 1992, and 1996. In these years, the Democratic and Republican vote shares are calculated based on totals for the major party nominees and a third candidate: Teddy Roosevelt in 1912, Strom Thurmond in 1948, George Wallace in 1968, and Ross Perot in 1992 and 1996.

During Reconstruction, in the 1872 election when Republican Civil War hero Ulysses Grant won a second term by defeating the Democrat Horace Greeley, southerners cast a majority of their vote (53.6 percent) for the general-turned-president. Four

FIGURE 11.1 ■ Popular Presidential Vote in the South, 1868–2016

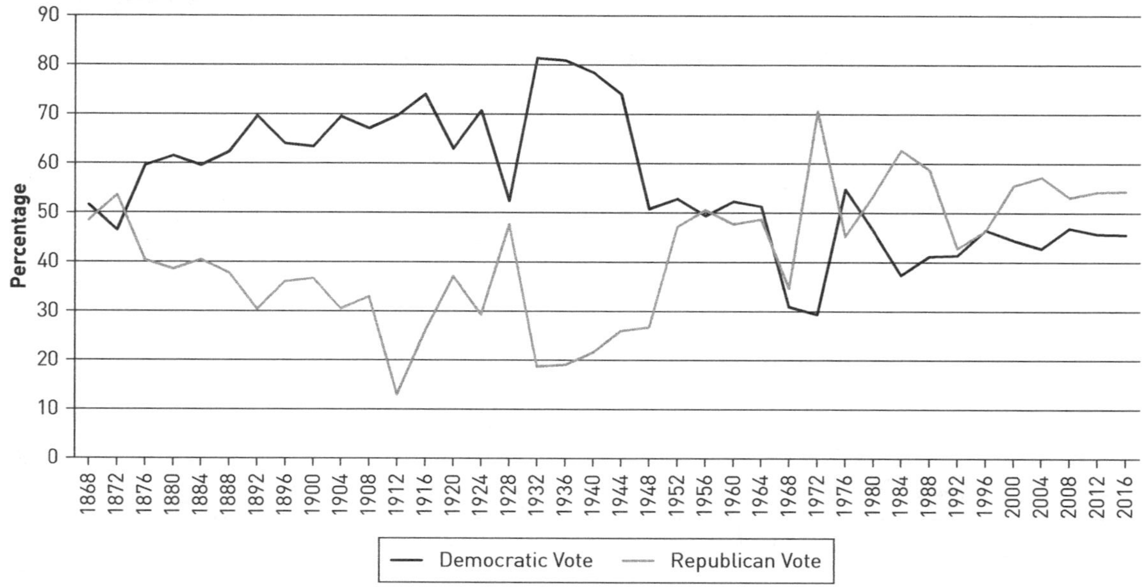

Source: Data compiled by the author from Dave Leip's *Atlas of U.S. Presidential Elections* (http://uselectionatlas.org/RESULTS/).

Notes: The popular vote is calculated for the two parties (Democratic and Republican) except in 1912, 1948, 1968, 1992, and 1996; in these contests the Democratic and Republican percentage is computed out of the vote cast for the major party candidates and a third candidate (Teddy Roosevelt in 1912, Strom Thurmond in 1948, George Wallace in 1968, and Ross Perot in 1992 and 1996).

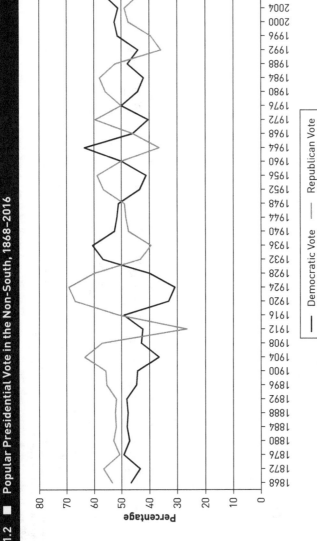

FIGURE 11.2 ■ Popular Presidential Vote in the Non-South, 1868–2016

Source: Data compiled by the author from Dave Leip's *Atlas of U.S. Presidential Elections* (http://uselectionatlas.org/RESULTS/).

Notes: The popular vote is calculated for the two parties (Democratic and Republican) except in 1912, 1948, 1968, 1992, and 1996; in these contests the Democratic and Republican percentage is computed out of the vote cast for the major party candidates and a third candidate (Teddy Roosevelt in 1912, Strom Thurmond in 1948, George Wallace in 1968, and Ross Perot in 1992 and 1996).

years later, in the disputed 1876 election, which resulted in a sectional compromise that officially ended Reconstruction (see chapter 2), southerners cast almost 60 percent of their votes for the national vote winner, the Democrat Samuel Tilden, who lost to the Republican Rutherford Hayes in the Electoral College by a single vote (185 to 184). Starting with 1876, Democratic presidential nominees simply dominated southern politics until the 1928 contest when a pronounced subregional split manifested in which the Rim South favored the Republican Herbert Hoover while the Deep South (and Arkansas) remained loyal to the Democrat Al Smith, a Catholic New Yorker (Key 1949). The peak of the presidentially Democratic Solid South occurred during the four Franklin Roosevelt elections from 1932 to 1944. White southerners were truly the backbone of the New Deal's national Democratic majority coalition (Petrocik 1981), casting the following historically impressive shares of the Democratic popular presidential vote in the South: 81 percent in 1932 and 1936, 78 percent in 1940, and 74 percent in 1944.

The fateful 1948 campaign dragged the southern Democratic vote for Harry Truman down to 51 percent primarily because of the 22 percent of the popular vote captured by the insurgent Dixiecrat Strom Thurmond (the Republican Thomas Dewey took 27 percent). Clearly, 1948 sounded the death knell of Democratic dominance in presidential elections. The Democratic and Republican shares of the southern presidential vote were remarkably close from 1952 through 1968. In his 1956 reelection, Republican President Dwight Eisenhower won a majority of the southern popular vote (51 percent), a first for the GOP since Grant way back in 1872. The third-party bid of Alabama Governor George Wallace in 1968 created a highly competitive three-way race, despite the fact that the Democrat Hubert Humphrey only carried the electoral votes of Texas. The 1968 southern Democratic vote went 35 percent for Republican Richard Nixon, 34 percent for George Wallace, and 31 percent for Humphrey. The 1972 election made history as President Nixon carried every southern state for the GOP, and his northern liberal opponent, Democrat George McGovern, captured only 29 percent of the southern popular vote. Since 1972, the Democratic Party has won the southern popular presidential vote just two times and in both instances the winner was a southerner: Jimmy Carter in 1976 with 55 percent and Bill Clinton in 1996 with 46.5 percent (Republican President George H. W. Bush won 46.4 percent, and Ross Perot won 7.1 percent of the southern presidential vote in 1996). From 2000 to 2016, a majority of the southern presidential vote has gone to every Republican nominee.

The popular presidential vote in the non-South exhibits a very different dynamic. Starting with the 1868 election, the first time the North delivered most of its votes for a Democratic presidential nominee was in 1912, because of the contentious third-party bid of Teddy Roosevelt, which siphoned off a huge chunk of votes from Republican President Howard Taft, which was also the case in the South (Taft won 27 percent of the northern vote, Roosevelt 31 percent, and the victorious Democrat Woodrow Wilson garnered 42 percent). In his successful 1916 reelection, President Wilson narrowly lost the northern popular vote to the Republican Charles Hughes, but GOP nominees dominated the non-South for the next three contests before the Democrat Franklin Roosevelt rode into office on a national wave in 1932. Two-party competition tightens in 1940 so that the 1964 presidential election is the only one since 1936 in which a major party nominee captures at least 60 percent of the vote (Democratic President Johnson won 64 percent of the northern vote). The Democrat Hubert Humphrey won the northern popular vote by a razor in 1968 (45.9 percent versus 45.8 percent for Nixon and 8.3 percent for Wallace). The GOP then won the northern popular vote in the next five consecutive elections (1972–1988), including the extremely close 1976 contest (50.03 percent for Republican President Gerald Ford versus 49.97 percent for the Democrat Jimmy Carter). Bill Clinton ushers in the contemporary Democratic electoral advantage in northern presidential elections in 1992. In retrospect, George H. W. Bush was the last Republican to win a northern popular vote majority (52 percent) in 1988; ever since, the non-South popular presidential vote has favored the Democratic Party.

Figure 11.3 presents the Democratic popular presidential vote from 1868 to 2016 for the South and non-South. Highlighting the regional distribution of the presidential vote for one party reveals that southern Democratic presidential voting behavior is more pronounced from 1868 until 1948 (eighty years), when Truman performs just a bit better in the North (51.1 percent versus 50.8 percent of the southern presidential vote) where the Dixiecrat Thurmond had hardly any appeal (0.03 percent of the northern presidential vote). In the next three elections, the South is more presidentially Democratic than the North in its support of the Democrat Adlai Stevenson in 1952 and 1956 and John Kennedy in 1960. In his landslide victory over Republican Barry Goldwater in 1964, Democratic President Johnson is much more popular among non-South voters (a difference of more than 12 percentage points). The South is slightly more Democratic than the North in the 1976 and 1980 elections, the last contests in which the share of the southern Democratic presidential vote exceeds the Democratic presidential vote cast by northerners.

Figure 11.4 presents the Republican popular presidential vote from 1868 to 2016 for the South and non-South. Looking at the other side of the partisan coin, it is evident that the northern popular Republican presidential vote has exceeded that of its southern GOP counterpart for almost an entire century, from 1868 to 1960. In 1964, the Republican Goldwater wins 49 percent of the southern popular vote versus 37 percent in the non-South. There is a general pattern of regional convergence in the Republican presidential vote from 1960 through the 1980s. Although the gap is not, at least in historical terms very substantial, a notable southern Republican advantage sets in by the 1990s. This said, the South has been more presidentially Republican in its popular vote for the last three decades (going back to 1984).

Last, Figure 11.5 shows the popular presidential vote margin between the South and non-South for the Democratic and Republican parties, respectively. The southern Democratic popular presidential vote advantage vis-à-vis the northern Republican advantage is on full display from the end of Reconstruction until the middle of the

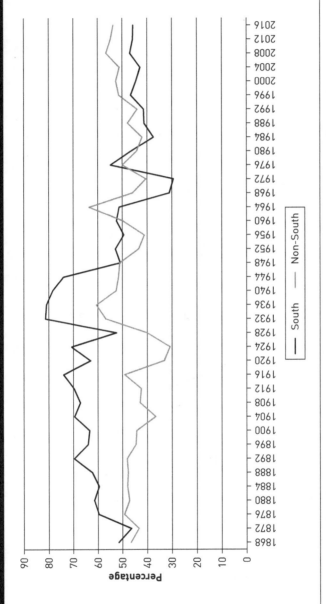

FIGURE 11.3 ■ Democratic Popular Presidential Vote by Region, 1868–2016

South — Non-South

Source: Data compiled by the author from Dave Leip's *Atlas of U.S. Presidential Elections* (http://uselectionatlas.org/RESULTS/).

Notes: The popular vote is calculated for the two parties (Democratic and Republican) except in 1912, 1948, 1968, 1992, and 1996; in these contests the Democratic and Republican percentage is computed out of the vote cast for the major party candidates and a third candidate (Teddy Roosevelt in 1912, Strom Thurmond in 1948, George Wallace in 1968, and Ross Perot in 1992 and 1996).

FIGURE 11.4 ■ Republican Popular Presidential Vote by Region, 1868–2016

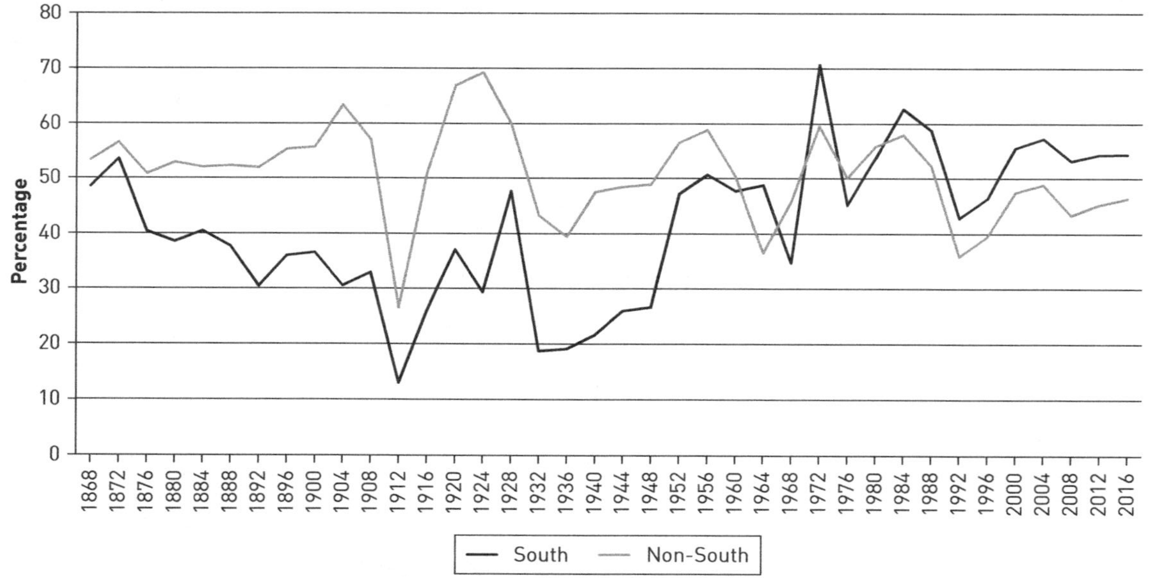

Source: Data compiled by the author from Dave Leip's *Atlas of U.S. Presidential Elections* (http://uselectionatlas.org/RESULTS/).

Notes: The popular vote is calculated for the two parties (Democratic and Republican) except in 1912, 1948, 1968, 1992, and 1996; in these contests the Democratic and Republican percentage is computed out of the vote cast for the major party candidates and a third candidate (Teddy Roosevelt in 1912, Strom Thurmond in 1948, George Wallace in 1968, and Ross Perot in 1992 and 1996).

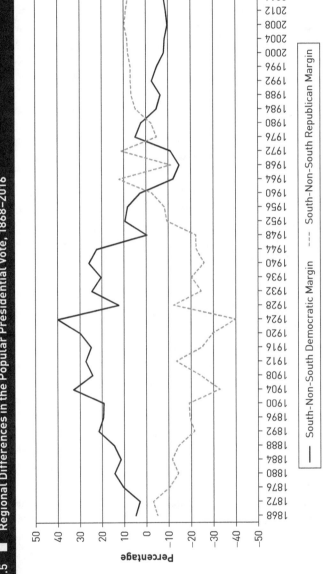

FIGURE 11.5 ■ Regional Differences in the Popular Presidential Vote, 1868–2016

— South–Non-South Democratic Margin   - - - South–Non-South Republican Margin

Source: Data compiled by the author from Dave Leip's *Atlas of U.S. Presidential Elections* [http://uselectionatlas.org/RESULTS/].

Note: The "South–Non-South Democratic Margin" is simply the percentage of the Democratic presidential vote in the South minus the percentage of the Democratic presidential vote in the non-South for a given election. The "South–Non-South Republican Margin" is calculated the same way.

twentieth century. Compared to the regional gulf in partisan presidential voting that prevails for these seven plus decades, it is understandable that scholars would push a political narrative of regional convergence in presidential voting behavior. Nonetheless, in the 1960s to 1980s, the regional differences in partisan presidential voting exhibit a high degree of political volatility. After Jimmy Carter exits the national scene in 1980, although the partisan voting gap by region is nothing like what existed in the first half of the twentieth century, there is an unmistakable southern Republican advantage offset by a northern Democratic advantage persisting since the mid-1980s. In 2016, the regional partisan presidential vote difference was 8 percentage points (in favor of the GOP in the South or, conversely, advantaging the Democratic Party in the North).

U.S. House Elections

In the previous section, the distorting effect of the distribution of the Electoral College vote (Edwards 2004) accounts for why a comparison of regional voting behavior in presidential elections is based on the popular vote. In contrast, it is not very useful to compare the popular share of the U.S. House vote by region because there are hundreds of contests, and in numerous districts only one of the major parties fields a candidate. Additionally, at any given time there is only one president, whereas an assessment of the popular U.S. House vote cannot necessarily tell us which party controls the most congressional seats, a much more useful piece of information. Therefore, in this section the partisan U.S. House balance within each region and across regions is based on the percentage of congressional seats held by Democrats and Republicans in two-year election cycles (every presidential and midterm contest) from 1868 to 2016.

Figure 11.6 displays the major party shares of southern U.S. House seats from 1868 to 2016, and Figure 11.7 displays the same data for the non-South. As was true for a briefer period in presidential elections (e.g., in 1868), the southern Democracy was the minority party in U.S. House contests during most of the Reconstruction era. Perhaps the single best depiction of the Solid Democratic South is the party's unprecedented reign in U.S. House elections—constituting a regional majority for 120 consecutive years—commencing in the 1874 midterm and ending with the 1994 midterm. For most of this period, the Democratic Party controlled more than 90 percent of Dixie's U.S. House seats. Notice, however, that in the two decades after the 1876 compromise, although the southern Democracy is unrivaled in its majority position, it is not until after the removal of the Populist electoral threat in 1896 (an 11-point drop in the Democratic seat share between 1894 and 1896) that the party locks down its hegemonic status until a gradual decline in Democratic seat holding takes root in the 1952 elections.

From the 1950s and into the late 1980s, the Democratic share of U.S. House seats generally declines with considerable fluctuations due to the vicissitudes of short-term political conditions (e.g., the Watergate scandal in 1974 buoys Democrats

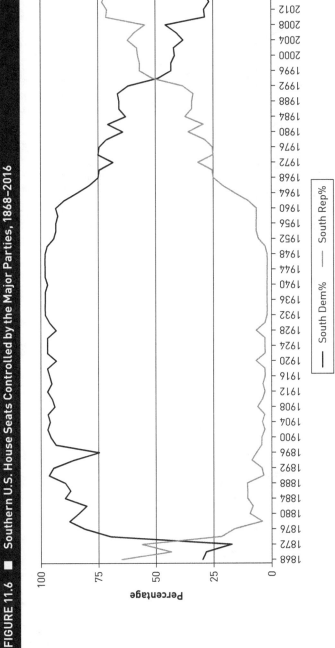

FIGURE 11.6 ■ Southern U.S. House Seats Controlled by the Major Parties, 1868–2016

—— South Dem% —— South Rep%

Sources: Data compiled by the author from CQ Press, *Guide to U.S. House Elections: Volume II,* 5th Edition (Washington, D.C.: CQ Press 2005), various volumes of *The Almanac of American Politics,* and the *New York Times* website for the 2016 elections.

Note: The percentage of Democratic and Republican seats is out of the total southern U.S. House seats.

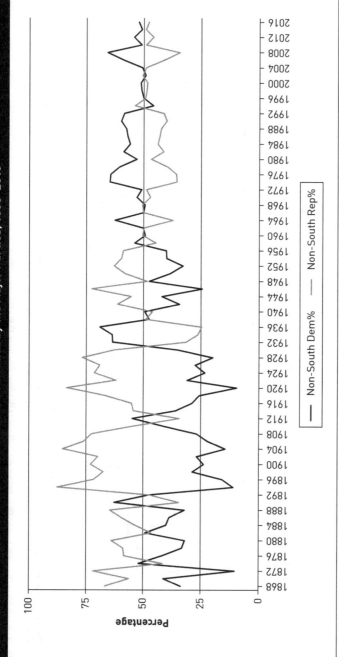

FIGURE 11.7 ■ Non-Southern U.S. House Seats Controlled by the Major Parties, 1868–2016

— Non-South Dem%   — Non-South Rep%

Sources: Data compiled by the author from CQ Press, *Guide to U.S. House Elections: Volume II*, 5th Edition (Washington, D.C.: CQ Press 2005), various volumes of *The Almanac of American Politics*, and the *New York Times* website for the 2016 elections.

Note: The percentage of Democratic and Republican seats is out of the total non-southern U.S. House seats.

and the election of Reagan in 1980 lifts Republicans). In the latter half of the 1980s, the partisan balance of southern U.S. House seats is essentially constant and then a Republican surge begins in the 1992 redistricting year (see chapter 5, and McKee 2010), which finally levels off in 1998. The two back-to-back Democratic national tide elections of 2006 and 2008 cut into the southern Republican congressional majority, but the GOP more than rebounds after the Republican wave election of 2010, which registered a 63-seat national Democratic midterm loss (Jacobson and Carson 2016). In 2016, Republicans comprised 72 percent of the southern U.S. House delegation and Democrats the remaining 28 percent, a smaller share of Democratic-held seats than in 1868–1870, during the days of Reconstruction when northern Republican intervention ensured a southern GOP congressional majority.

The northern pattern of partisan control of U.S. House seats is anything but a mirror image of the southern dynamic. The long period of southern Democratic dominance has no parallel in the more historically competitive North. Twice, northern Republicans held congressional majorities for sixteen consecutive years (from 1894 to 1910 and from 1914 to 1930), but the longest unbroken U.S. House majority belongs to northern Democrats who controlled the region's seats for twenty-two straight years, from 1970 to 1992. Only during the early years of the Democratic New Deal period (1932–1936), did northern Democrats hold a majority of non-South U.S. House seats. Indeed, for most of the 1940s and 1950s the GOP controlled a majority of northern U.S. House seats. The non-southern partisan seat balance has exhibited a general pattern of competitiveness since the late 1940s, with periods of remarkably narrow partisan seat majorities, such as from 1994 to 2004 and most recently from 2010 to 2016. In fact, with the exception of the particularly good Democratic cycles in 2006 and 2008, the partisan distribution of non-southern U.S. House seats has been historically competitive from 1994 to 2016.

Figure 11.8 shows the Democratic share of U.S. House seats in the South and non-South from 1868 to 2016. During the Reconstruction period the Democratic share of U.S. House seats is well below 50 percent in each region prior to 1874, and the regional difference at this time is the smallest seen until the late 1980s and early 1990s. In percentage terms, southern Democrats are more prominent than their northern Democratic peers from 1872 until 1996 (124 consecutive years). Since the 1996 election, the share of northern Democrats has exceeded the share of southern Democrats. Over these last two decades, the regional pattern of Democratic seat holding is very similar, except for the fact that the Democratic share of seats in the South is significantly lower. In 2016, Democrats were 52 percent of the non-southern U.S. House delegation, which was 24 percentage points higher than their seat share in the South.

Figure 11.9 presents the Republican share of U.S. House seats in the South and non-South from 1868 to 2016. By juxtaposing the share of GOP U.S. House seats by region, the lengthy period of southern Republican futility (the late 1870s through the 1950s) is captured in stark relief. Versus their southern GOP counterparts, northern

FIGURE 11.8 ■ Democratic U.S. House Seats by Region, 1868–2016

— South Dem%   — Non-South Dem%

Sources: Data compiled by the author from CQ Press, *Guide to U.S. House Elections*: Volume II, 5th Edition (Washington, D.C.: CQ Press 2005), various volumes of *The Almanac of American Politics*, and the *New York Times* website for the 2016 elections.

Note: The percentage of Democratic seats is out of the total U.S. House seats in each region.

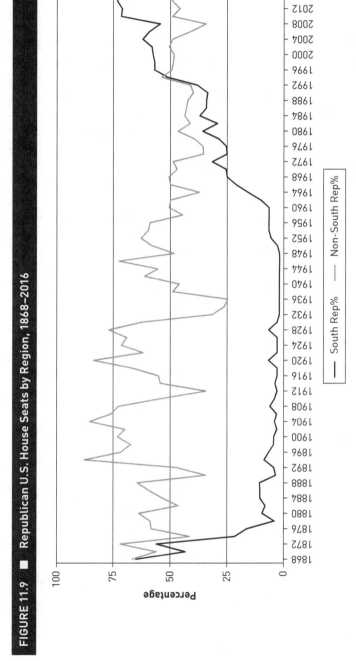

FIGURE 11.9 ■ Republican U.S. House Seats by Region, 1868–2016

—— South Rep%   —— Non-South Rep%

Sources: Data compiled by the author from CQ Press, *Guide to U.S. House Elections: Volume II*, 5th Edition (Washington, D.C.: CQ Press 2005), various volumes of *The Almanac of American Politics*, and the *New York Times* website for the 2016 elections.

Note: The percentage of Republican seats is out of the total U.S. House seats in each region.

Republicans constituted a higher share of their regional U.S. House delegation from 1868 until 1996 (128 consecutive years). Similar to the Democratic pattern in Figure 11.8, the regional pattern of GOP seat holding is very similar over the last twenty years, except that the southern Republican advantage has increased. In 2016, Republicans comprised more than 70 percent of the southern U.S. House delegation versus 48 percent of the northern U.S. House contingent.

Figure 11.10 displays the partisan U.S. House seat margins by region from 1868 to 2016. For most of the Reconstruction period (1868–1874), the partisan seat margins are fairly close—fewer than 20 percentage points. In 1876, the regional chasm opens up. From 1876 to 1970, the southern Democratic U.S. House seat margin was 20 points or more. Conversely, from 1876 to 1970, the northern Republican seat advantage was 20 points or greater. Since the 1950s, a gradual pattern of regional convergence is underway and it runs its course by 1994, when Republicans capture a national U.S. House majority for the first time in forty years. In 1994, the regional Democratic seat disparity and the regional Republican seat margin were fewer than 3 percentage points. For a brief moment, the South had rejoined the North, at least with respect to its partisan distribution of U.S. House seats. But this was short-lived; since 1994, regional divergence is the prevailing pattern. In percentage terms, southern Republicans now greatly outnumber northern Republicans and northern Democrats are substantially more prevalent than southern Democrats, the scions of a party that once virtually monopolized Dixie's congressional delegation for over a century.

Table 11.1 concludes this section on U.S. House elections by offering one more look at regional differences by decade, from the 1950s to the 2010s. First, the table documents the increasing size of the southern U.S. House delegation, a consequence of relatively higher population growth, resulting in a greater reallocation of congressional districts via the reapportionment process undertaken after each decennial census. In the 1950s, the South had 24 percent of all congressional districts (105 out of 435). After the 2010 reapportionment (valid for the 2012 elections), the South contained more than 31 percent of all U.S. House seats (138 out of 435). As the southern share of U.S. House seats has grown, there has been a long-term decline in the number of southerners in the Democratic U.S. House delegation. In the 1950s, southern Democrats constituted 42 percent of all U.S. House Democrats. Since then, the share of southern Democrats has declined by more than 50 percent; they are now just 20 percent of the entire Democratic delegation. By contrast, in the 1950s, southern Republicans were a paltry 3 percent of their party's U.S. House contingent. In the 2010s, the share of southern Republicans had ballooned to 41 percent, only one percentage point less than the portion of southern Democrats in the 1950s.

The last four rows of Table 11.1 present data on the percentage of congressional Democrats and Republicans in the South and non-South who won their districts without facing a major party opponent (e.g., a Democrat without a Republican opponent or a Republican without a Democratic opponent). The Solid South persists through the 1950s as just under three out of four Democrats (74 percent) won

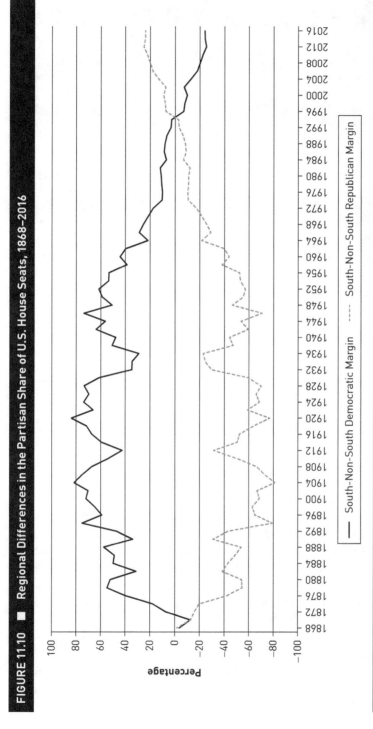

FIGURE 11.10 ■ Regional Differences in the Partisan Share of U.S. House Seats, 1868–2016

— South–Non-South Democratic Margin   ---- South–Non-South Republican Margin

Sources: Data compiled by the author from CQ Press, *Guide to U.S. House Elections: Volume II, 5th Edition* (Washington, D.C.: CQ Press 2005), various volumes of *The Almanac of American Politics*, and the *New York Times* website for the 2016 elections.

Note: The "South–Non-South Democratic Margin" is simply the percentage of Democratic U.S. House seats in the South minus the percentage of Democratic U.S. House seats in the non-South for a given election. The "South–Non-South Republican Margin" is calculated the same way.

TABLE 11.1 ■ Changes in U.S. House Elections by Region and Decade, 1950s–2010s								
Statistic	1950s	1960s	1970s	1980s	1990s	2000s	2010s	2010s–1950s
% of Districts								
In the South	24	24	25	26	28	30	31	+7
% of all Representatives								
Democrats: South	42	34	29	29	28	24	20	−22
Republicans: South	3	10	18	22	29	36	41	+38
% Unopposed								
Southern Dems	74	50	45	39	21	27	18	−56
Non-southern Dems	4	4	9	13	8	13	11	+7
Southern Reps	7	7	13	25	32	24	21	+14
Non-southern Reps	1	1	3	4	8	6	6	+5

Sources: Data compiled by the author from CQ Press, *Guide to U.S. House Elections:* Volume II, 5th Edition (Washington, D.C.: CQ Press 2005), various volumes of *The Almanac of American Politics,* and the *New York Times* website for the 2016 elections.

Notes: The percentage of Democratic and Republican seats is out of the total U.S. House seats and according to region, where applicable. Unopposed means that the Democratic (Republican) winner did not face opposition from a Republican (Democratic) opponent in the general election.

their U.S. House seats sans a GOP opponent. By comparison, the vast majority of northern Democrats (96 percent), southern Republicans (93 percent), and northern Republicans (99 percent) faced a major party opponent in the 1950s. The percentage of free rides (uncontested races) for southern Democrats shows a long-term decline since the 1950s, reaching its nadir at 18 percent uncontested elections in the 2010s (a 56-point decline since the 1950s). There is no discernible trend in uncontested races for northern Democrats, though the share of contests without a Republican opponent is 7 percentage points higher in the 2010s versus the 1950s. The share of uncontested northern Republican seats has increased since the 1950s, but remains very low at 6 percent in the 2010s. Finally, the percentage of uncontested southern Republican seats has tripled between the 1950s and 2010s (but notice the share of uncontested races was highest in the 1990s, at 32 percent). Compared to their northern colleagues, in contemporary U.S. House elections, southern Democrats and southern Republicans are much more likely to win their seats without a major party challenge.

PARTY IDENTIFICATION IN
THE SOUTH AND NON-SOUTH

Given the overriding importance of party affiliation in American voting behavior (Campbell et al. 1960), this section examines changes in the percentage of Democratic and Republican identifiers in the South and non-South, from the 1950s through the 2000s. The overall distribution of Democratic and Republican affiliates is tracked according to region, and then regional comparisons in party identification are displayed with respect to the three largest racial/ethnic groups in American politics: blacks, Latinos, and whites.

All of the analysis is contained in Table 11.2, which documents party identification by decade, from the 1950s to 2000s with American National Election Studies (ANES) data. The percentage of Democratic and Republican identifiers are shown out of all ANES respondents who placed themselves on the 7-point scale (Democratic percentage = strong and weak Democrats divided by all respondents on the scale; Republican percentage = strong and weak Republicans divided by all respondents on the scale). Each row presents the data on southern respondents for a given category immediately followed by the data on northern respondents. Then the South versus non-South difference is shown. Moving across the columns from left to right reveals the long-term changes in party identification for each respondent category. Finally, the last column displays the difference in party identification for the 2000s minus the 1950s (for Latinos, the partisan difference is the 2000s minus the 1970s).

Starting with all respondents in the South and non-South, the decline in southern Democratic identification is striking, going from 70 percent of southerners in the 1950s to 32 percent in the 2000s. In the 1950s, southern Democrats are much more prevalent than northern Democrats (70 percent versus 42 percent), but in the first decade of the new millennium the share of non-southern Democrats is larger (35 percent versus 32 percent). The decline of southern Democratic identification is of course the central storyline of southern political change. Although the rise is far from commensurate with the Democratic decline, the share of southern Republican identifiers has gone from 15 percent in the 1950s to 29 percent in the 2000s. By comparison, a third of northerners were Republicans in the 1950s and they decline to 26 percent in the 2000s. Hence, in the South the massive reduction in Democrats is only partially offset by an increase in Republicans whereas in the North, there is a 7-point drop in both Democratic and Republican identifiers between the 1950s and 2000s. In both regions, Democrats are still more numerous than Republicans (+3 points in the South and +9 in the North), but now there is a higher share of Democrats in the North than in the South and a greater percentage of southern Republicans than northern Republicans.

Turning to the relationship between race and identification, even in the 1950s when most southern blacks were disenfranchised and the civil rights movement was far from reaching its climax, a higher percentage of African Americans in the South identified with the Democratic Party (66 percent versus 59 percent in the case of

TABLE 11.2 ■ Party Identification by Region and Race, 1950s–2000s

	1950s	1960s	1970s	1980s	1990s	2000s	Difference
All Respondents							
S-Dems %	70	60	48	46	39	32	−38
NS-Dems %	42	44	37	36	35	35	−7
Difference	+28	+16	+11	+10	+4	−3	
S-Reps %	15	17	17	20	23	29	+14
NS-Reps %	33	30	25	28	28	26	−7
Difference	−18	−13	−8	−8	−5	+3	
Blacks							
S-Dems %	66	75	68	68	63	66	0
NS-Dems %	59	66	70	71	65	69	+10
Difference	+7	+9	−2	−3	−2	−3	
S-Reps %	22	12	6	6	5	4	−18
NS-Reps %	18	9	4	3	3	2	−16
Difference	+4	+3	+2	+3	+2	+2	
Latinos							
S-Dems %	—	—	40	43	46	36	−4
NS-Dems %	—	—	57	50	50	44	−13
Difference	—	—	−17	−7	−4	−8	
S-Reps %	—	—	17	17	18	20	+3
NS-Reps %	—	—	8	16	14	16	+8
Difference	—	—	+9	+1	+4	+4	
Whites							
S-Dems %	71	58	44	39	30	22	−49
NS-Dems %	41	42	34	32	32	30	−11
Difference	+30	+16	+10	+7	−2	−8	
S-Reps %	14	18	19	25	30	38	+24
NS-Reps %	34	32	27	31	31	30	−4
Difference	−20	−14	−8	−6	−1	+8	

Source: ANES Time Series Cumulative Data File.

Note: The last column displays the partisan difference for the 2000s minus the 1950s (1970s for Latinos). "S" = South, "NS" = Non-South. "Difference" is the southern entry minus the non-southern entry.

northern black Democrats). Since the 1970s, however, more non-southern African Americans identify as Democrats although the regional disparity in Democratic identification is not very large (a 3-point gap in the 2000s). Since the 1950s, the share of southern black Democrats has remained the same, but increased 10 percentage points with respect to northern African Americans (going from 59 percent to 69 percent in the 2000s). In regards to black Republican identification, it should be noted that it was a nontrivial segment of African Americans in the 1950s (22 percent southern black Republicans and 18 percent northern black Republicans). But the story since the 1950s has been one of marked decline so that in the 2000s just 4 percent of southern blacks and 2 percent of non-southern African Americans identify with the GOP.

Latino party identification can be assessed starting in the 1970s when the number of respondents is large enough to trust the data. Historically, northern Latinos have always been more Democratic than their southern peers and southern Latinos are always somewhat more Republican than their non-southern counterparts. Across party lines and region, Latinos are much more likely to be Democratic than Republican, although this gap has closed a bit as the share of Democrats has declined since the 1950s in both regions while the percentage of Latino Republicans has increased in the South and North. Finally, the regional gap in the percentage of Latino Democrats and Latino Republicans has narrowed since the 1950s (going from a 17-point northern Democratic advantage to an 8-point margin in the 2000s and a 9-point southern Republican margin in the 1950s to just a 4-point difference in the 2000s). Unlike African Americans, who are firmly aligned with the Democratic Party (irrespective of region), a large contingent of Latinos identify with neither major party: 44 percent of southern Latinos and 40 percent of northern Latinos are political independents in the 2000s.

The general pattern of Democratic decline and Republican growth in the South is amplified by looking specifically at changes in white party identification. Southern white Democrats go from 71 percent in the 1950s down to 22 percent in the 2000s, a 49-point decline. By comparison, there is an 11-point decline in northern white Democrats, going from 41 percent in the 1950s to 30 percent in the 2000s. Thus, the regional gap in Democratic identifiers went from a +30-point advantage in the South in the 1950s to an 8-point deficit in the 2000s. With respect to white Republicans, in the 1950s only 14 percent of southern whites identified with the GOP while 34 percent of northern whites were Republicans. By the 2000s, the share of southern white Republicans is now 38 percent whereas northern white Republicans are 30 percent. The regional difference in white Republican identifiers goes from a 20-point northern advantage to an 8-point southern Republican margin in the 2000s. Within the South, a 57-point Democratic advantage in the 1950s (71 percent Democratic versus 14 percent Republican) turned into a 16-point deficit by the 2000s (22 percent Democratic versus 38 percent Republican). Outside the South, a relatively modest Democratic advantage in the 1950s (41 percent Democratic versus 34 percent Republican) is reduced to a partisan stalemate in the 2000s (30 percent Democratic and 30 percent Republican).

Examining party identification from the 1950s to the 2000s, it is obvious that the cardinal regional difference is found within the white electorate. To be sure, in the case of Latinos, there are slightly more GOP adherents in the South, but in both regions the Democratic Party is considerably more popular. And in the case of African Americans, they overwhelmingly identify with the Democratic Party in the North and South. Black Democratic identification is simply unparalleled. Thus, the driver of Republican growth rests firmly with the partisan transformation of the white southern electorate. As noted above, white Democrats and white Republicans are both 30 percent of the northern population in the 2000s, whereas white southern Republicans outnumber white southern Democrats by a substantial margin. It remains to be seen, however, how these groups in the American electorate vote in contemporary presidential and U.S. House elections. That is the subject taken up in the next section.

VOTER PREFERENCES IN RECENT ELECTIONS

Going back to the late 1940s, the ANES data are the single most valuable source for tracking longitudinal changes in the American electorate. Unfortunately, though, the last ANES midterm survey was administered in 2002 and the subset of southern respondents for any single survey has never been terribly large (and then consider the further reduction in sample size for southerners with respect to race). On the bright side, the Cooperative Congressional Election Study (CCES) was launched for the 2006 midterm and one of its principal purposes (at least initially) was to fill the void left by the discontinuation of ANES midterm surveys. Compared to the ANES, the CCES survey samples are much larger. Whereas a typical ANES survey contains somewhere between 200 and 400 southern respondents, a CCES survey has more southern Latino voters, the smallest racial subgroup examined (around 600 in the 2006 CCES to almost 1,000 in the 2016 CCES), than the entire sample of ANES southern respondents for any given year; and the total sample of southern voters in a CCES survey ranges from around 6,000 to more than 12,000 voters. Finally, the CCES has been administered continuously for midterm and presidential elections from 2006 to the present.

In this section, the presidential and congressional voting behavior of southerners and northerners is chronicled from 2006 to 2016. Similar to the ANES data on party identification presented in Table 11.2, the 2006–2016 CCES data on presidential and congressional voting preferences are shown with respect to region (South and non-South), party identification, and race. In addition, unlike the last section, political independents are included in order to see if there is any regional variation in their vote choice. Sticking with the theme of examining changes in presidential and U.S. House elections, voter preferences are tracked for the 2008 through 2016 presidential contests and for every on- (presidential) and off-year (midterm) election in congressional races. Further, the presidential and congressional voting data are pooled for each span of elections (2008–2016 for president and 2006–2016 for the U.S. House). Over-time differences (e.g., 2016 versus 2008 in presidential elections) for each voter category (e.g., black southerners) are highlighted, as are regional differences within each voter category (e.g., black southerners versus black northerners). Lastly, all of the vote choice data are presented as the Republican share of the presidential/U.S. House vote.

Presidential Elections

Table 11.3 presents the Republican share of the presidential vote cast by region, according to party identification and race, from 2008 to 2016. Starting with all voters, southerners are more Republican in their presidential voting behavior for all three elections (2008–2016), registering a modest GOP majority in each year (51–52 percent). The regional gap narrows from 8 to 5 points between 2008 and 2016, but in this last contest it remains the case that the northern electorate casts a majority Democratic presidential vote (53 percent). In short, contemporary presidential voting indicates that the North is majority Democratic and the South is majority Republican, but neither section of voters in the aggregate is decidedly in favor of one party over the other.

Turning to party identification, the extreme contrast in voter preferences based on political affiliation is a hallmark of the contemporary electorate (Jacobson 2018). In the South and non-South, from 2008 to 2016, Democratic defection in favor of Republican presidential nominees is in the single digits. There is essentially no regional difference in the percentage of Democrats casting a Republican presidential vote, 6 percent of southern Democrats and 7 percent of northern Democrats in 2016. Conversely, southern and non-southern Republicans are historically loyal to their party nominee in recent presidential elections. As is the case with Democratic identifiers, there is no real regional distinction in the presidential voting behavior of Republicans. In 2016, fully 94 percent of the presidential vote cast by northern and southern Republicans went to their party's standard bearer.

In contrast to Democrats and Republicans, there is a sectional difference in the presidential preferences of Independent voters. Southern Independents are consistently more Republican in their presidential voting, an overall regional difference of 8 points from 2008 to 2016 (54 percent Republican in the South versus 46 percent Republican in the non-South). In 2012, Independents in both regions preferred the Democratic presidential nominee; southern Independents preferred the GOP nominee in 2008 and 2016, while non-southern Independents only cast a majority Republican vote in 2016. The regional gap is cut in half from 10 points in 2008 to 5 points in 2016. The more Republican-leaning voting behavior of southern Independents bolsters the general Republican tilt in the presidential preferences of southern voters.

TABLE 11.3 ■ Republican Presidential Vote in Recent Elections, 2008–2016					
	2008	2012	2016	Pooled	2016–2008
All Voters					
S	51	51	52	51	+1
NS	43	45	47	45	+4
Difference	+8	+6	+5	+6	
Democrats					
S	8	6	6	6	−2
NS	9	6	7	7	−2
Difference	−1	0	−1	−1	
Independents					
S	52	48	60	54	+8
NS	42	40	55	46	+13
Difference	+10	+8	+5	+8	
Republicans					
S	95	96	94	95	−1
NS	93	95	94	94	+1
Difference	+2	+1	0	+1	
Blacks					
S	5	5	8	6	+3
NS	7	4	9	7	+2
Difference	−2	+1	−1	−1	
Latinos					
S	44	37	37	39	−7
NS	35	26	26	28	−9
Difference	+9	+11	+11	+11	
Whites					
S	64	62	66	64	+2
NS	48	50	54	51	+6
Difference	+16	+12	+12	+13	

Source: Data are from the Cooperative Congressional Election Study (CCES) for multiple years.

Note: "Pooled" means all of the data for each year were combined. The last column displays the difference between 2016 and 2008. "S" = South, "NS" = Non-South. "Difference" is the southern entry minus the non-southern entry.

Similar to Democrats and Republicans, African Americans exhibit no regional difference in their presidential voting behavior. Of course, the majority of blacks are Democrats, but even if partisanship is not factored in, black voters' paltry Republican presidential support (irrespective of region) is equivalent to that of Democrats. From 2008 to 2016, both southern blacks and southern Democrats voted an average of 94 percent Democratic in presidential contests. Likewise, northern African Americans and northern Democrats each voted an average of 93 percent Democratic in these three presidential elections. It is no surprise that Democrats and African Americans (who are often one and the same), regardless of region, are the least likely groups to cast GOP presidential votes.

Contrary to African Americans, there is a regional difference in Latino voters' presidential preferences. As demonstrated in Table 11.2, southern Latinos are less Democratic/more Republican vis-à-vis northern Latinos (although overall both groups are much more likely to be Democrats than Republicans). In 2008, 44 percent of southern Latinos voted Republican for president versus a 35 percent GOP presidential vote cast by northern Latinos. Since 2008, the Republican share of the Latino vote has declined in the South and non-South, but the regional difference has widened by 2 points in 2016, amounting to an 11-point disparity in the Republican presidential vote (37 percent of southern Latinos voted Republican for president versus 26 percent of northern Latinos).

Finally, the largest and consistent regional gap in presidential voting behavior is found among whites. Since 2008, the Republican presidential vote cast among whites in the non-South has increased from 48 percent to 54 percent. By comparison, the GOP vote cast for president by southern whites has barely varied over these three elections: 64 percent in 2008, 62 percent in 2012, and 66 percent in 2016. Overall, the sectional difference in white voting for GOP presidential nominees has declined since 2008 (going from a 16-point gap to a 12-point margin favoring southern whites in 2016), but this still makes it the largest regional disparity in presidential voting behavior shown in Table 11.3. From 2008 to 2016, just over half of non-southern whites voted Republican for president (an average of 51 percent), while a little less than two-thirds (an average of 64 percent) of their southern counterparts marked GOP presidential ballots.

U.S. House Elections

Not surprisingly, Table 11.4 indicates that the general voting patterns found among the same categories of voters in U.S. House contests closely resemble presidential voting patterns. This said, for the decade of pooled U.S. House data (2006–2016), with the exception of Republican voters, in every other voter category the share of the Republican congressional vote is higher than the GOP presidential vote registered from 2008 to 2016. Even in the 2006 and 2008 elections, in which short-term political conditions strongly favored the Democratic Party, a majority of southern voters backed Republican U.S. House candidates (52 percent in 2006 and 53 percent in 2008).

TABLE 11.4 ■ Republican U.S. House Vote in Recent Elections, 2006–2016							
	2006	2008	2010	2012	2014	2016	Pooled	2016–2006
All Voters								
S	52	53	58	55	60	55	56	+3
NS	45	44	52	47	51	48	48	+3
Difference	+7	+9	+6	+8	+9	+7	+8	
Democrats								
S	16	10	9	10	11	11	11	−5
NS	10	9	8	8	9	10	9	0
Difference	+6	+1	+1	+2	+2	+1	+2	
Independents								
S	48	54	67	54	68	61	59	+13
NS	41	44	62	44	56	53	51	+12
Difference	+7	+10	+5	+10	+12	+8	+8	
Republicans								
S	89	93	96	95	95	93	94	+4
NS	86	90	94	93	93	92	92	+6
Difference	+3	+3	+2	+2	+2	+1	+2	
Blacks								
S	28	12	10	9	14	15	14	−13
NS	20	12	11	7	10	11	11	−9
Difference	+8	0	−1	+2	+4	+4	+3	
Latinos								
S	46	44	48	42	45	42	44	−4
NS	34	37	34	30	36	28	33	−6
Difference	+12	+7	+14	+12	+9	+14	+11	
Whites								
S	57	62	68	66	71	66	66	+9
NS	49	48	56	51	55	54	53	+5
Difference	+8	+14	+12	+15	+16	+12	+13	

Source: Data are from the Cooperative Congressional Election Study (CCES) for multiple years.

Note: "Pooled" means all of the data for each year were combined. The last column displays the difference between 2016 and 2006. "S" = South, "NS" = Non-South. "Difference" is the southern entry minus the non-southern entry.

By comparison, northern voters favored Democratic candidates for Congress in these elections (45 percent Republican in 2006 and 44 percent Republican in 2008). In fact, the northern U.S. House vote favored Democrats except in the very favorable Republican election cycles of 2010 and 2014. For the decade (2006–2016), the southern Republican congressional vote was 56 percent versus 48 percent for non-southerners (+8-point GOP margin favoring southern voters).

Although it is not much, except for the 16 percent Republican U.S. House vote registered by southern Democrats in 2006, the GOP congressional vote cast by Democrats hovers around 10 percent. There is no discernible regional variation among this group least likely to support opposing partisan candidates for Congress. From 2006 to 2016, 11 percent of southern Democrats vote for U.S. House Republicans and just 9 percent of northern Democrats did the same. With such a low rate of crossover voting, this is strong evidence that for a large segment of Republican incumbents (a plentiful group in the South) they accrue a meager incumbency advantage among their Democratic constituents.

Once again, similar to Democratic voters, there is no substantive regional difference in the congressional voting preferences of Republicans. The largest disparity is a mere 3 points in 2006 and 2008. In 2006, 89 percent of southern Republicans voted for GOP U.S. House candidates as compared to 86 percent of northern Republicans who supported GOP contenders. In every election after 2006, Republicans in the North and South vote 90 percent or higher for GOP congressional candidates.

As expected, the voting behavior of Independents is much more variable than that of party identifiers. Even though southern Independents favored Republican U.S. House candidates in five of the six elections (only going with the Democratic Party in 2006), the range in the Republican share of the vote is 20 points (a low of 48 percent in 2006 to a high of 68 percent in 2014). With regard to northern Independents, in three elections (2006, 2008, and 2012) they preferred Democratic candidates for Congress and in the other three they went Republican (2010, 2014, and 2016). The range in the Republican congressional vote cast by northern Independents is 21 points (a low of 41 percent in 2006 to a high of 62 percent in 2010). Despite the general volatility in the Independent vote, southern Independents are always more supportive of GOP U.S. House candidates, with an 8-point advantage over the ten-year span of elections (59 percent Republican in the South versus 51 percent Republican in the North).

Turning to race and congressional voting behavior, African Americans are not as one-sidedly Democratic in U.S. House voting as compared to presidential voting. In fact, it is somewhat hard to believe, but the CCES data have 28 percent of African Americans in the South voting Republican for the U.S. House in 2006 compared to a 20 percent Republican vote cast by northern blacks for the same office. After 2006, the reduction in black voting for GOP congressional candidates drops markedly to low double digits (even single digits in 2012) and the regional disparity in Republican voting is never more than a modest 4 points, although southern blacks are consistently more likely to vote Republican in the last three elections.

As was the case in presidential elections, Latinos lean decidedly in favor of Democratic U.S. House candidates. The same regional disparity in Republican voting is also present: southern Latinos are significantly more likely to vote for Republican congressional candidates than are northern Latinos. From 2006 to 2016, the southern Latino vote cast for GOP candidates for Congress is 44 percent versus 33 percent for northern Latinos (+11-point Republican advantage in the South). Nonetheless, the Democratic Party receives a higher share of the congressional vote registered by Latinos residing in the North and South and since 2006, the Republican share of the congressional vote cast by Latinos in both regions has declined (−4 points in the South and −6 points in the North).

Finally, similar to their presidential voting behavior, whites exhibit the greatest regional differences in Republican voting for Congress. Only in 2006 did less than 60 percent of southern whites vote Republican in U.S. House elections. In 2014, more than 7 out of 10 southern whites checked GOP for Congress. For the ten-year period (2006–2016), 66 percent of the southern white vote went to GOP U.S. House candidates, 2 points higher than the Republican presidential vote southern whites registered from 2008 to 2016. In contrast, northern whites leaned Democratic in the 2006 and 2008 elections, but consistently favor Republicans thereafter. In the Democratic cycle of 2006, the difference in Republican voting by region is smallest (8 points) and in the Republican midterm of 2014 the disparity is largest (16 points). From 2006 to 2016 (the pooled data), whites in the South and North favor the GOP in congressional elections, but southern whites are notably more supportive of the Republican Party (+13-point Republican advantage).

BOX 11.1   THE NORTH-SOUTH RELIGIOUS DIVIDE

Besides partisanship and voting behavior (documented in this chapter), and other notable divisions (e.g., racial composition, educational attainment, poverty rates), religiosity is a perennial dividing line between the more devout Dixie and the more secular North. Table 11.5 shows that not only are southerners more religious across a range of measures, but this is consistently true among the major racial/ethnic groups in the American electorate: whites, blacks, and Latinos. Table 11.5 presents data from the 2016 Cooperative Congressional Election Study for four religious variables: (1) whether a respondent is born again (percentage saying they are born again), (2) the importance of religion to the respondent (percentage saying religion is very important), (3) church attendance (percentage saying they attend once a week or more), and (4) the frequency of prayer (percentage saying they pray once a day or more).

Starting with the born again question, the North-South religious divide is palpable. Overall (across all three racial/ethnic groups), 44 percent of southerners claim to have experienced a born again religious conversion, whereas 28 percent of northerners concur. Among the four religious questions, this 16-point born again gap is the largest found in the table. A come to Jesus moment is clearly a much more frequent occurrence among southerners. With respect to race/ethnicity, African Americans are consistently the most religious, but the born again gap (16 points) is greatest among whites (42 percent in the South and 26 percent in the North).

There is another double digit regional difference with respect to the share of southerners and northerners who stated that religion is very important. Among all respondents, 48 percent in the South claim religion is very important versus 37 percent of northerners who stated the same. Only among African Americans do a majority claim religion is very important in both the South (64 percent) and North (55 percent), though the regional difference is a substantial 9 percentage points.

The last two questions, frequency of church attendance and frequency of prayer are indicators of religious devotion. Once again, southerners display a higher rate of religiosity as they report being more frequent religious practitioners. Three out of ten southerners report attending church at least once a week versus about one out of four northerners. A slight majority of southerners (51 percent) stated that they pray at least once a day while 42 percent of northerners pray at the same rate.

It is no surprise that religiosity is greater in the South, but it is less common to show that this regional gap is consistently present no matter whether an individual is white, black, or Latino. The more religious/churched culture of Dixie persists and it is evident regardless of race/ethnicity.

TABLE 11.5 ■ The Regional Religious Divide by Race/Ethnicity				
Variable	White (%)	Black (%)	Latino (%)	All (%)
Born Again				
South	42	54	36	44
North	26	43	27	28
S-N Difference	+16	+11	+9	+16
Religion Very Important				
South	44	64	45	48
North	34	55	41	37
S-N Difference	+10	+9	+4	+11
Church Every Week				
South	28	37	29	30
North	23	33	25	24
S-N Difference	+5	+4	+4	+6

(Continued)

(Continued)

Variable	White (%)	Black (%)	Latino (%)	All (%)
Pray Once a Day				
South	48	64	48	51
North	41	58	43	42
S-N Difference	+7	+6	+5	+9

Source: Data are from the 2016 Cooperative Congressional Election Study (CCES).

Notes: Data were weighted by the CCES common content weight variable. Whether a respondent is born again is a simple yes/no answer. The importance of religion variable has the following valid response options: 1 = very important (the frequency category displayed in the table), 2 = somewhat important, 3 = not too important, and 4 = not at all important. The church attendance variable has the following response options: 1 = more than once a week, 2 = once a week, 3 = once or twice a month, 4 = a few times a year, 5 = seldom, and 6 = never. The table presents the combined frequency of response options 1 and 2 (more than once a week and once a week). The frequency of prayer variable has the following valid response options: 1 = several times a day, 2 = once a day, 3 = a few times a week, 4 = once a week, 5 = a few times a month, 6 = seldom, and 7 = never. The table presents the frequency of response options 1 and 2 (several times a day and once a day). The percentages in the table were rounded up to the nearest whole number and then the South minus North difference was computed. The last column for "All" respondents is limited to the aggregation of responses registered by whites, blacks, and Latinos.

ENDURING SOUTHERN EXCEPTIONALISM

As demonstrated in this chapter, contrary to some of the leading accounts of partisan change in contemporary American elections (see Lublin 2004; Shafer and Johnston 2006), the evidence and argument strongly suggests that the South has, and continues to promulgate, a brand of politics that remains distinct from the rest of the nation.[1] In the 1960s and 1970s the African American electorate had already solidified its loyalty to the Democratic Party, but white southerners were undergoing a lengthy period of dealignment, moving from Democratic identification to political independence. As this decades-long process of partisan transformation unfolded, its gradual and incremental nature prompted political observers to conclude that the demise of the southern Democracy did not foretell a Republican future. Indeed, compared to the swift and permanent Democratic alignment of southern blacks, which transpired over no more than a few election cycles in the early to mid-1960s, the secular realignment (Key 1959) of southern whites to the Republican Party seemed glacial.

Although it is true that a segment of the white southern electorate demonstrated impressive political alacrity in switching to the GOP (mainly a group of hard core racial conservatives), for most white southerners the impediment of party identification proved too great a barrier to enter the waiting and open arms of the party of Lincoln. Instead, generational replacement (a naturally slow process) became the primary mechanism (Green, Palmquist, and Schickler 2002) through which southern Republicans eventually attained majority status among the white electorate. As Beck (1977) convincingly demonstrates, generations farther removed from the original crisis triggering a restructuring of the party system (e.g., the Great Depression preceding the Democratic takeover of national politics in the 1930s) are less vested in remaining loyal to their parentally inherited partisanship. Instead, the current state of politics holds more sway and as the parties shift on the most salient issues (e.g., civil rights in the 1960s) this can alter partisan loyalties and it is much easier for a voter who begins their formative years as an Independent to then make the move to the party more aligned with their political worldview. In other words, for most southern whites who came of age in the 1960s and 1970s, over the long term, dealignment from the Democratic Party eventually led to realignment to the GOP (see chapter 6).

Broadening the scope to national politics, the tumultuous political, social, and economic changes roiling and buffeting the American South from the mid-1950s through the 1980s did not have a non-South cognate of any comparable size or degree. The dynamics rippling through the South, if they existed outside the region (and sometimes did), were never commensurate in scale. For instance, the race question has always cast a longer shadow in Dixie and it is still the principal reason why the South's politics remain distinctive. Additionally, southerners (black and white) are a much more religious lot and for many white southerners the GOP's embrace of the Religious Right has made the party a more natural home. Finally, the more conservative political culture of the South not surprisingly leads to a greater share of conservative self-identifiers than those in the North and the increasing congruence between ideology and party identification has further fueled a more Republican South (Abramowitz and Saunders 1998).

As the period of southern white dealignment waned and strong overtures in favor of the GOP emerged (e.g., the jump in white Republican identification between 1980 and 1984), scholars were tempted to issue proclamations regarding the impending end of southern exceptionalism because growing Republicanism surely meant the South was rejoining the North. But Republican ascendancy did not halt once it mirrored the partisan balance of power prevailing in the North. Instead the southern GOP just kept on going and now Dixie is once again electorally out of step with the nation (Bullock 2014). With data on presidential elections, U.S. House elections, party identification, and voter preferences in the aforementioned contests, in contemporary American politics the fundamental distinction between the North and South is found among southern whites. In the early 1980s, the great southern sociologist John Shelton Reed (1982) penned a book (*One South: An Ethnic Approach to Regional Culture*) contending that white southerners in many ways resembled a distinct ethnic group (see also Black and Black 1987, 195–196). It appears he was on to something; even setting aside party identification, whites in the South are considerably more Republican than whites in the North and this is amplified in their voting preferences.

There is no question that observers of the South's politics will continue to speculate as to what extent and in which aspects is Dixie losing its regional distinctiveness. As will be considered in the next chapter, generational change, the impressive rates of northern in-migration in several southern states, and the growth of the Latino population appear to be the most obvious factors that favor a Democratic comeback. But at least for now, the aggregate political impact of recent Democratic gains is reminiscent of the once painstakingly slow advance of southern Republicans that took a permanent hold during the pivotal 1964 presidential election. The South is still exceptional. In its politics, Dixie was a veritable foreign outpost because of the hegemonic status of the Democratic Party from the early 1900s through the 1950s. Currently the American South again sticks out from the rest of the nation, but now because its brand of politics is decidedly more Republican.

12 THE FUTURE OF SOUTHERN POLITICS

The past and the present afford us only imperfect glimpses into the future. In his introduction to *The Strange Career of Jim Crow*, the great southern historian C. Vann Woodward opines with these words: "The people of the South should be the last Americans to expect indefinite continuity in their institutions and social arrangements" (2002, 3). Woodward goes on to quickly elaborate his point by noting that unlike the rest of the United States, the history of the nineteenth-century South was decidedly more tumultuous, with "breaks in the course of Southern history [that] go by the names of slavery and secession, independence and defeat, emancipation and reconstruction, redemption and reunion" (2002, 3–4). Although Woodward does not contend that southern history can be reduced to the station of African Americans, he makes it clear that at all of the above-mentioned turning points, blacks found themselves at the center of the controversy.

It is in the midst of "reunion" when V. O. Key (1949) takes up the historical narrative of southern politics. Scrutinizing the condition of Dixie's politics from roughly 1920 to the late 1940s, it was evident to Key that the party system was so dysfunctional as to not even be deserving of the name democratic with a small "d," as the Democratic Party (of the large "D" variety) had practically rendered the Republican opposition, an opposition in name only. With the exception found mainly in sections of Republican Appalachia, electoral competition was stifled by a Democratic Party whose only real diversity existed in varying degrees of localized factionalism most evident in primary contests, while the party proved remarkably united in blocking potential and actual outside interference into the South's Jim Crow system of racial segregation. Indeed, Key began his book with this critical observation: "The South may not be the nation's number one political problem, as some northerners assert, but politics is the South's number one problem" (1949, 3).

Key titled his final chapter, "Is There a Way Out?"; on page 675 (the last page) of *Southern Politics in State in Nation,* he concludes as follows: "The race issue broadly defined thus must be considered as the number one problem on the southern agenda. Lacking a solution for it, all else fails." To this day, it is difficult to argue against Key's pronouncement, despite it being almost seven decades old. Likewise, this work is bookended by the salience of race in structuring southern politics, from the starting point of Reconstruction to the 2016 election of Republican President Donald Trump. Admittedly, the civil rights movement wrought revolutionary changes to southern society, and greatly altered the character of southern politics (Black and

Black 1987; Woodward 2002; Wright 2013). Nonetheless, well into the second decade of the twenty-first century, the race issue continues to cast a long shadow over Dixie's political system and especially in shaping the dynamics of party politics.

Republican electoral dominance is the prevailing state of affairs in the contemporary American South (McKee 2012a), but this development has lasted for a very brief time as compared to the Democratic Solid South (circa 1900 to 1964). As documented and analyzed, below the presidential level, the southern GOP began its electoral ascendancy in the early 1990s (see chapter 5). Furthermore, even though Key (1949) did not envision the manifestation of what would become a full-blown southern civil rights movement in the 1960s (Black and Black 1987, 293), he was aware of the region's political fluidity[1] and had a keen eye regarding some of the factors that would conspire to break up the one-party Democratic political order of his day—factors that also play a role in the current weakening of GOP dominance in certain southern localities. Specifically, the size of the black population is a critical variable, along with urbanization and the transition from an old agriculture-based economy to a modernized industrial version (Key 1949, 672–673).[2] In addition to the presence of African Americans, it is necessary to consider generational change, the significance of northern in-migration, and the rising Latino population. These demographic developments are the principal drivers of potential and actual shifts in favor of a Democratic revival in southern electoral politics. As Key (1949, 673) understood, "an alteration of population composition . . . creates a new political setting that will eventually make itself felt."

This chapter starts with a very brief restatement of what southern politics looked like from the time of Reconstruction until the 1950s. Then the focus turns to providing analysis of trends in electoral competition South-wide and for each southern state, by making use of David's (1972) Index of Republican Party Strength along with presidential voting data. Next, the importance of race is assessed in terms of its fundamental role in the "re-segregation" of southern politics. Lastly, some of the indicators that point to a more electorally competitive future are highlighted and then the chapter concludes with some final thoughts.

THE OLD SOUTHERN POLITICS

In defeat, the American South united under the banner of the Democratic Party (Woodward 1960). In the wake of the Civil War, a vanquished Dixie was temporarily subordinate to the prerogatives of northern oversight that was enforced via military Reconstruction. Before the war, the political division within southern localities often found the slaveholding planters of the black belt counties affiliated with the Whig Party, whereas the middling and vastly larger lower class of whites sided with the Democratic Party. Interestingly, prior to the remarkably rapid dissolution of the Whigs in the mid-1850s, these two major parties exhibited a national pattern of two-party competition because of class differences that placed the "haves" with the Whigs and the "have-littles" and "have-nots" with the Democrats (Aldrich and Griffin 2017). The slavery issue doomed the Whig Party (Sundquist 1983), and it splintered into oblivion as the most salient moral issue of this era provided a political inroad for the northern-born GOP to consolidate votes above the Potomac while the Democratic Party was regionally split in two, with an anti-slavery northern wing offset by its pro-slavery southern counterparts. Just as a house divided against itself cannot stand, Abraham Lincoln's famous words regarding the sectional divide over slavery, a party divided against itself (the Democratic Party) cannot win elections and this explains how the Republican Lincoln won the 1860 presidential election.

In the early days following the South's military defeat, it appeared that President Lincoln would embrace a regional reconciliation that would have gone light on punishing the rebellious southern states, but of course his assassination closed the door to what might have been. In Lincoln's place was the Tennessean Andrew Johnson, a Democrat who had no intention of exacting retribution on the secessionist states of his homeland. Presidential Reconstruction under Johnson was brief, and his pro-southern sentiments rendered him just a single vote short of being removed from office through impeachment proceedings that commenced in February 1868. Northern outrage toward President Johnson, coupled with northern Republican congressional majorities, invoked a fairly rapid turn in favor of Radical Republican-led congressional Reconstruction. It was the winning (albeit ephemeral) electoral coalition of northern white carpetbaggers, recently freed native blacks (the Thirteenth Amendment abolishing slavery was passed in 1865), and southern scalawags (native southern whites who aligned with the GOP) that made Radical Reconstruction so unbearable for the erstwhile native white ruling class of the black belt counties.

But Radical Reconstruction also came to pass, and primarily because native white resistance was fierce. As more and more native white southerners were re-enfranchised and came to comprise voting majorities, it was only a matter of time before most, and eventually all, southern governments were "redeemed" in favor of a united, homegrown, and thoroughly white supremacist southern Democracy. And in the various settings where southern Democrats did not easily outnumber the Republican opposition, on numerous occasions political violence would serve the purpose of intimidating and suppressing otherwise majority Republican coalitions to the point of reducing them to functional voting minorities (Foner 1989). In fact, Democratic majorities were already present across Dixie in numerous localities a few years prior to the official end of Reconstruction in early 1877, when a bargain was struck to grant the GOP a presidential victory in the 1876 election in exchange for the removal of military oversight of the South's public affairs.

Return to native white control of the southern party system under the Democratic banner proved precarious and by no means a certainty so long as African Americans had the franchise. Their substantial presence throughout most of the South, and their numerical majorities in those places where the white Democratic opposition was most militant (in the black belt counties), made blacks the main target of statutorily implemented and often extra-legally enforced, disfranchisement measures (Kousser 1974). The Jim Crow system of racial segregation and the systematic removal of black voters from southern politics ensured that the mass of lower-class whites no longer had the opportunity and ability to construct biracial voting coalitions capable of winning electoral majorities of the sort that briefly prevailed in the 1890s in North Carolina. As was true in the Tar Heel State, it was the Populist Revolt of the 1890s that made it clear to the Democrats that fusion tickets combining the votes of dis-affected white and black farmers, the former proudly calling themselves Populists and the latter overwhelmingly Republican, were sometimes capable of defeating Democratic candidates. Democrats would not let this stand, and by marshaling all of the legal and extra-legal (intimidation, economic discrimination, social ostracism, and violence) means within their considerable powers, by the early 1900s, the one-party Democratic Solid South was erected and it would persist well into the middle of the twentieth century (Kousser 1974).

A LONGITUDINAL LOOK AT PARTY COMPETITION

First introduced in chapter 8, David's (1972) Index of party strength is an insight-ful way to gauge the competitiveness of a political system. In the context of southern politics, the GOP's steady rise is captured by a lengthy time series of Republican Party strength indexed for a sample of elective offices. As was the case in chapter 8, here, David's Index is in Composite B form, which is calculated as the Republican share of the vote earned in thirds (equal parts) across three offices: U.S. House, U.S. Senate, and Governor. To some degree this measure under-states Republican electoral strength because the GOP share of the vote is com-puted among all votes cast, as opposed to those tallied for just the major parties (Democrats and Republicans).

Aside from the aberrant 1928 contest, a Republican presence in post-Reconstruction southern politics takes permanent hold in the 1952 presidential election, the first to follow the Dixiecrat insurgence of 1948. Starting in 1952, the GOP has been competi-tive and then typically dominant in Dixie's presidential contests (Black and Black 1987, 1992, 2002, 2007; see chapter 5). But Republican success materialized in southern presi-dential elections long before it became commensurate in lower offices, a familiar pattern of top-down advancement distinctly captured in Figure 12.1. Figure 12.1 charts three data series from 1952 to 2016: (1) the Republican percentage of the two-party popu-lar vote cast in presidential elections; (2) David's Index of Republican Party Strength based on U.S. House, U.S. Senate, and gubernatorial returns; and (3) a ten-year moving average of the aforementioned GOP Index. The GOP Index is displayed with the ten-year moving average in order to smooth out the time series and thus dampen short-term political conditions that greatly favor one of the major parties.

At the start of the time series in the early 1950s, there is a massive gulf separating the GOP presidential vote share from Republican support obtained in lower offices

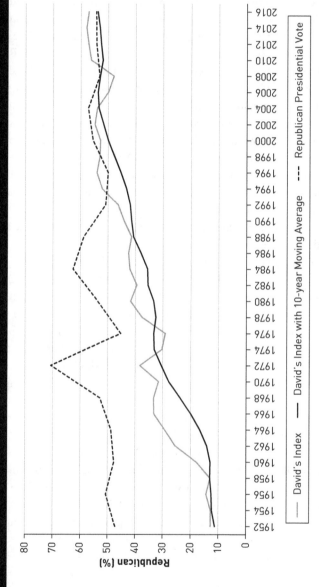

Republican (%)

—— David's Index   —— David's Index with 10-year Moving Average   --- Republican Presidential Vote

Sources: Presidential vote data compiled by the author from Dave Leip's *Atlas of U.S. Presidential Elections* (http://uselectionatlas.org/). David's Index data were compiled and computed by the author and Trey Hood at the University of Georgia.

Notes: The presidential vote is the Republican share out of the two-party total cast. The percentage of Republican Party strength is based on David's (1972) Composite B Index, which is the Republican percentage of the vote summed in thirds for gubernatorial, U.S. Senate, and U.S. House contests [percentage Republican Vote (Gubernatorial Election) + percentage Republican Vote (Senate Election) + percentage Republican Vote (Average Republican U.S. House Vote)] / 3. In this case (for David's Index), the Republican vote is out of all votes cast, not just the two-party vote.

according to David's Index. For instance, in 1952 the Republican Eisenhower captured 47 percent of the two-party popular presidential vote, whereas the Republican Index was a mere 13 percent. This huge disparity in Republican performance at the top of the ticket vis-à-vis lower offices, persists for decades, but it finally begins to close in the 1990s. By 1996, for the first time, the GOP Index (54 percent) exceeds the Republican share of the presidential vote (49.9 percent). Notice however, the lag in Republican strength as shown by the ten-year moving average. Near the end of the time series, commencing with the Republican wave election in the 2010 midterm, the GOP Index always slightly exceeds Republican presidential performance. In the second decade of the new millennium, Republican top-down advancement has run its course; the southern GOP is as successful in gubernatorial contests and congressional elections as it is in presidential politics.[3] The eventual consolidation of Republican electoral success from the top of the ballot down to state-level (e.g., gubernatorial elections), congressional, and even state-legislative races (see McKee and Yoshinaka 2015), speaks to the mature state of southern party politics. The days of massive split-ticket voting in favor of Republican presidential nominees and Democratic candidates for Congress and/or governor, have been over for the better part of two decades.

Table 12.1 provides a further look at the growing electoral prowess of the southern GOP by ranking the southern states according to David's Index of Republican Party Strength (highest to lowest) across decades, starting in 1952. The table shows the Deep South state abbreviations in bold and underlines the Index where GOP performance is 50 percent or higher. As was highlighted in chapter 8, over time, the rank order of southern states experiences almost a complete reversal according to subregion. For the first two decades (1952–1960 and 1962–1970), the traditional pattern of greater Republican success in the Rim South states with a GOP presence dating back to the Civil War (in the mountainous sections of North Carolina, Tennessee, and Virginia) or the 1890s Populist Revolt (e.g., in Texas) is evident. The Peripheral South state of Florida also ranks high on the GOP Index, but its relatively high level of Republican performance stems mainly from the substantial in-migration of Republican voters dating back to the end of World War II (Colburn 2007).

Indeed, until 1982, South Carolina is the only exception to the pattern of the top five most electorally Republican states hailing from the Peripheral South. From 1982–1990, Mississippi joins the Palmetto State as another one from the Deep South making it among the five most Republican (at number 4). Nonetheless, prior to 1992, not a single southern state obtains a GOP Index of 50 percent or more. Going back to the first decade (1952–1960), North Carolina is the most Republican state with a GOP Index of one-third, while Mississippi and South Carolina exhibit barely a trace of Republican competitiveness (both have a Republican Index registering 1 percent!). But the Solid Democratic South gradually fades away, and by the 1992–2000 decade, all but three states have a GOP Index of 50 percent or higher, with the Lone Star State leading the way at 56 percent. In the first decade of the twenty-first century (2002–2010) the rank order of states clearly reflects the advent of the Deep South as

TABLE 12.1 ■ Ranking Southern States Based on David's Index of Republican Party Strength						
1952–60	**1962–70**	**1972–80**	**1982–90**	**1992–00**	**2002–10**	**2012–16**
NC 33	NC 44	TN 49	VA 49	TX 56	AL 60	AL 69
VA 24	FL 41	VA 46	NC 49	TN 55	MS 58	TN 64
FL 23	TX 38	SC 42	SC 48	MS 54	SC 55	LA 60
TN 22	TN 37	NC 42	MS 46	SC 53	GA 55	MS 59
TX 18	VA 35	FL 40	FL 45	FL 53	LA 55	SC 58
AL 13	SC 33	TX 38	TX 45	VA 52	TX 53	AR 58
AR 12	AR 28	MS 32	AL 41	AL 50	VA 53	TX 57
LA 8	AL 27	AR 30	TN 41	GA 50	TN 51	GA 56
GA 2	GA 22	GA 28	AR 36	NC 49	FL 50	NC 52
SC 1	LA 16	AL 24	LA 31	AR 48	NC 49	FL 49
MS 1	MS 15	LA 20	GA 30	LA 47	AR 38	VA 49

Source: David's Index data were compiled and computed by the author and Trey Hood at the University of Georgia.

Notes: Table displays the percentage of Republican Party strength based on David's (1972) Composite B Index, which is the Republican percentage of the vote summed in thirds for gubernatorial, U.S. Senate, and U.S. House contests (percentage Republican Vote [Gubernatorial Election] + percentage Republican Vote [Senate Election] + percentage Republican Vote [Average Republican U.S. House Vote]) / 3. The Republican vote is out of all votes cast, not just the two-party vote. David's Index for each state was computed at two-year intervals for each decade and then averaged to get the numbers displayed in the table. Deep South states are in boldface. The Republican Party Strength Index is underlined in those cases where it is greater than or equal to 50.

the more Republican-dominant subregion, with the five most Republican states all residing from here (Alabama, Mississippi, South Carolina, Georgia, and Louisiana).

Over the entire time series in Table 12.1, in the aggregate, the GOP Index inexorably increases from the top of the ranking to the bottom. By the last (incomplete) decade (2012–2016), all the way down to the ninth-ranked Republican state, North Carolina (52 percent), David's Index of GOP Strength exceeds 50 percent. Only Florida and Virginia have indexes under 50 percent Republican. The rank order of Republican performance is notably altered in the most recent period, despite the fact that four of the five most Republican states still come from the Deep South. Alabama maintains the top spot at 69 percent, while the Rim South state of Tennessee goes from eighth place to second. Louisiana moves from number five to number three while its Deep South neighbor Mississippi drops from second to fourth. Likewise, South Carolina goes from number three to number five. Arkansas ascends from least Republican to sixth most Republican whereas Georgia and Virginia experience the greatest drops, going from number four down to eight and from number seven to last, respectively.

The descent in the rankings of South Carolina, Georgia, and Virginia deserve particular attention as these states are undergoing considerable demographic changes that are altering the profiles of their electorates. Similar to the model case of Florida, substantial in-migration and growing minority populations in these states located along the Eastern Seaboard (refer to Box 8.1 in chapter 8) suggests the Democratic Party can eventually assemble a viable voting coalition (this has already happened in Virginia). Texas, another state whose relative decline in its Republican ranking (from 6 to 7) is tied to demographic change (a burgeoning Latino population), still demonstrates that the reshuffling of GOP strength has generally occurred with almost every southern state's Republican Index actually gaining ground since 2002–2010. With the exception of the Democratic-leaning state of Virginia and the swing states of Florida and North Carolina, the contemporary Republican South remains very solid for the time being, but the changing order of Republican performance among the southern states points to certain factors that may generate a Democratic comeback.

THE RE-SEGREGATION OF SOUTHERN POLITICS

In the time between the 1954 landmark ruling in *Brown v. Board of Education*, which dealt the death blow to the South's Jim Crow caste system of racial segregation by declaring that "separate was inherently unequal," and the pivotal 1964 presidential election ten years later, less than 3 percent of southern public schools (K–12) were desegregated (Black and Black 1987; Woodward 2002). But the *Brown* decision prevailed, even if white massive resistance held firm until 1960, when the civil rights movement started to gain momentum and a series of significant victories finally culminated in passage of the 1964 Civil Rights Act and the 1965 Voting Rights Act (VRA). National Democratic leadership in furthering black civil rights, most politically evident in the tireless efforts of President Lyndon Johnson, resulted in a swift and permanent alignment of southern blacks to the Democratic Party in 1964, while their massive re-enfranchisement in the wake of VRA passage in 1965 meant that the historically racist southern Democracy would have to make room for an infusion of black voters.

The immediate effect of massive reentry of black Americans to the southern electorate[4] was a palpable shift in the campaign rhetoric of most politicians. As stated by Black and Black (1987, 142–143), "Old-style racism has not been completely eliminated, but the few remaining politicians who are still able to win elections by using flagrantly racist appeals as part of their repertoire are campaigning the hard way." As bluntly explained by Andrew Young in 1974, the first black Congressman from Georgia since Reconstruction:

> It used to be Southern politics was just "nigger" politics, who could
> "outnigger" the other—then you registered 10 to 15 percent in the

community and folk would start saying "Nigra," and then you get 35 to 40 percent registered and it's amazing how quick they learned how to say "Nee-grow," and now that we've got 50, 60, 70 percent of the black votes registered in the South, everybody's proud to be associated with their black brothers and sisters. (Bass and DeVries 1995, 47)

In the mid-1970s and throughout the 1980s, the Democratic Party maintained its hold over southern electoral politics by relying on biracial coalitions consisting of almost the entirety of black voters with varying but steadily declining segments of the white electorate (Lamis 1988). In the post-VRA South, with notable exceptions like Virginia Governor Linwood Holton and Arkansas Governor Winthrop Rockefeller (Black and Black 1987, 355), who sought and won large shares of the black vote, the southern GOP was not interested in constructing electoral majorities by cobbling together biracial coalitions. For decades after 1965, biracial coalitions ensured Democratic victories over what quickly emerged as a lily-white Republican opposition (Hood, Kidd, and Morris 2012). Cutting to the heart of the matter, Black and Black (2002, 138) succinctly explained the slow rise of southern Republicans below the presidential level:

> Why did it take such a long time for the southern Republicans to become a
> majority? Reduced to fundamentals, when Republican activists transformed
> the party of Abraham Lincoln into the party of Barry Goldwater,
> they foolishly wrote off black southerners at the very time when black
> participation was dramatically increasing.

Over the long run, however, the GOP's essentially all-white southern electoral strategy has proven very successful, though it may ultimately fail as current demographic changes are running in favor of the Democrats. The GOP's championing of policy positions that deter minority support while attracting conservative white voters is the root cause of the re-segregation of southern politics. The glaring lack of racial and ethnic diversity among the ranks of the southern Republican Party also accounts for the shift away from racially coded language to borderline, and now more frequently blatant, use of racist rhetoric. In 1981, the notorious Republican strategist Lee Atwater[5] of South Carolina explained the use of racially coded language to the late southern politics scholar Alexander Lamis:

> You start out in 1954 by saying, "Nigger, nigger, nigger." By 1968 you can't
> say "nigger"—that hurts you, backfires. So you say stuff like, uh, forced
> busing, states' rights, and all that stuff, and you're getting so abstract. Now,
> you're talking about cutting taxes, and all these things you're talking about
> are totally economic things and a byproduct of them is, blacks get hurt
> worse than whites . . ." We want to cut this," is much more abstract than
> even the busing thing, uh, and a hell of a lot more abstract than "Nigger,
> nigger." (quoted in Perlstein 2012)

But off-the-record comments like the one above (obviously, it was later released) reveal the racial divide between whites and blacks as they have re-segregated into different political parties that are polarizing along ideological and racial lines. Black and Black (1987, 313–314) also capture the raw racism found not far beneath the surface of coded language when some Republicans speak in confidence: "'Why don't you leave the niggers behind and come join us?' was the friendly invitation to one of the authors after he had addressed a gathering of South Carolina Republicans." In the aftermath of electing the nation's first African American president, instead of racial rhetoric becoming more abstract, it appears a harder edge has returned. Explicit racially hostile political messages are apparently less shocking and disturbing to the contemporary voter (Valentino, Neuner, and Vandenbroek, forthcoming), and this line of research is backed up by the tremendously salient anecdote of the racial rhetoric employed by 2016 Republican candidate and eventual President, Donald Trump.

The reemergence of racially charged and overtly hostile rhetoric of the kind perhaps not prevalent since the civil rights era (circa 1955–1965), tellingly reflects the reality of racial segregation in modern southern party politics. As masterfully analyzed by Hood, Kidd, and Morris (2012), the exodus of southern whites from the Democratic Party into the GOP in the post–civil rights South, is at its core a development stemming from racial conflict. Rather than engage in a precarious and conflict-ridden racial compromise under the banner of the same party, conservative white southerners have flocked to the GOP in order to maintain control of the political system; and nowhere is this dynamic clearer than in the Deep South as black mobilization (in voter registration) spurs GOP growth and Republican gains trigger further black mobilization (a recursive cause and effect relationship).

Table 12.2 shows one final time series of southern party identification according to race/ethnicity (whites, blacks, and Latinos) from American National Election Studies (ANES) surveys starting in the 1950s and ending in the 2010s. Among whites, Democrats outnumber Republicans more than 4 to 1 in the 1950s Solid South. But since then, the share of white Democrats declines while the percentage of white Republicans rises so that in the 2010s, GOP affiliates have a more than 2 to 1 presence over their white Democratic counterparts. It is this development that accounts for the bulk of the greatest transformation of a party system in American history.

With regard to African Americans, Democrats also vastly outnumber Republican adherents in the 1950s. In response to the pivot of the national parties on civil rights, as embodied by the Democratic and Republican presidential nominees in the 1964 election (Carmines and Stimson 1989), it is in the 1960s that the surge in black Democratic identification takes place. Black Democratic affiliation dips into the sixtieth percentile for the next four decades and then rebounds to an impressive three-quarters of this racial group in the 2010s. By contrast, after the 1950s, black Republican identification has been relegated to single digits and reaches its nadir of a mere 3 percent in the 2010s. Black Democrats currently outnumber black Republicans by an astounding 25 to 1!

Race/Ethnicity	1950s	1960s	1970s	1980s	1990s	2000s	2010s	Change
TABLE 12.2 ■ Percentage of Southern Party Affiliation by Race and Ethnicity, from the 1950s to 2010s								
Whites								
Democrats	68	54	43	38	27	22	18	−50
Republicans	16	17	20	24	33	40	41	+25
Blacks								
Democrats	63	82	67	67	63	67	75	+12
Republicans	24	7	6	6	5	4	3	−21
Latinos								
Democrats	—	—	45	41	45	37	42	−3
Republicans	—	—	17	18	17	23	20	+3

Source: All data are from the American National Election Studies (ANES).

Note: Percentage of Democrats and Republicans does not include independent-leaning partisans, but the percentage Democrat and Republican is out of all respondents registering identification on the seven-point scale. Decades start with years ending in "2" and end in years "00," except if it is later in the ANES time series when there is no midterm election data (e.g., data are for 2002–2008 for the 2000s because there are no data for the 2010 midterm).

Latino party identification cannot be registered until the 1970s, when the number of cases is finally large enough to trust the sample estimates. In the 1970s, Latino Democrats outnumber Latino Republicans by more than 2.6 to 1, and this ratio holds fairly steady until the 2000s, when Latino Democrats decline to 37 percent while Latino Republicans increase to 23 percent. In the 2010s, the share of Latino Democrats rebounds whereas Latino Republicans diminish—no doubt this most recent development speaks to a political environment in which the GOP has shifted in a rightward direction on issues like immigration, that hold great concern within the Latino community (see the brief discussion on this point in chapter 9).

The partisan sorting of the southern electorate along racial and ethnic lines is perhaps the most palpable evidence of the re-segregation of southern politics, but this development is even more pronounced in the case of officeholders. Figure 12.2 displays the median percentage of combined black and Latino voting age populations (VAPs) in southern U.S. House districts according to the party and race/ethnicity (for Democrats) of Representatives from 1990 to 2016. Because of the overall increase in the black and Latino VAPs in the South, the trend lines for every category of House Representative has increased since 1990. However, in the short term there has been a decline in the black and Latino VAPs of white Democrats holding office

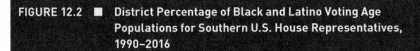

FIGURE 12.2 ■ District Percentage of Black and Latino Voting Age Populations for Southern U.S. House Representatives, 1990–2016

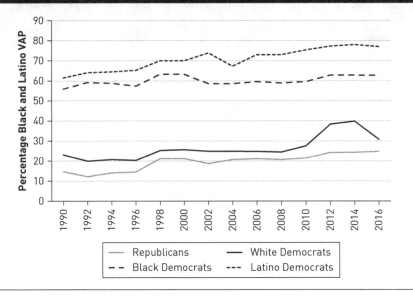

Source: U.S. Census Bureau data compiled by the author.

Note: Data show the median district percentage of black voting age population (VAP) plus the median district percentage of Latino VAP, according to the party and race/ethnicity (for Democrats) of southern U.S. House Representatives.

after 2014. Not surprisingly, Republicans represent districts with the smallest shares of black and Latino VAPs while black Democrats and Latino Democrats represent districts that are decidedly majority-minority in their racial/ethnic constituencies. The drawing of congressional boundaries in a fashion that consciously factors in the role of race/ethnicity in furthering political representation likely exacerbates the political differences between a contemporary Democratic Party that contains the bulk of minority voters and a Republican Party that continues to be overwhelmingly non-Latino white at the mass and elite levels.

What Figure 12.2 fails to capture is the total number of House Representatives according to party affiliation and race/ethnicity. Since 1990, the changing profile of Democratic officeholders juxtaposed with the stability found among Republicans is truly remarkable. Consider that in 1990, white Democrats were 59 percent of the southern U.S. House delegation (68 out of 116). Further, among Democratic Representatives, 88 percent were non-Latino white, 6.5 percent were black (5 total), and 5 percent were Latino (4 total). On the Republican side of the ledger, in 1990, 38 out of 39 GOP Congresspersons were non-Latino white (97 percent), with a single Latino Republican officeholder accounting for the one exception.

A quarter-century later in 2016, only 33 percent of the Democratic southern U.S. House delegation was non-Latino white. The number of black Democrats increased by 300 percent, from 5 members in 1990 to 20 in 2016. There was a 25 percent increase in Latino Democrats, going from 4 in 1990 to 5 in 2016. And for the first time in southern political history, in 2016 the Democratic Party also had an Asian officeholder. Of course, the most politically consequential developments center firmly on the impressive rise in the number of Republicans and the even more precipitous decline in white Democrats. The total number of Republicans went from 39 in 1990 to 99 in 2016, a 154 percent increase, making the GOP the unrivaled majority of the southern U.S. House delegation (72 percent of the 138 seats). Yet even with this massive increase in Republican officeholders, 96 percent were non-Latino white (three Latino Republicans and one black Republican account for the remainder). In contrast, the demise of white Democrats, almost the entire population of southern U.S. House members from the late 1800s through the 1950s, is simply dumbfounding. The population of 68 white Democrats in 1990 plunges to 13 in 2016, rendering them a political minority in a majority-minority Democratic southern U.S. House delegation in which black Democrats comprise a bare 51 percent majority. White Democrats are the indisputable principal casualty of the re-segregation of southern politics.

DEMOGRAPHIC CHANGE
AND DEMOCRATIC PROMISE

As mentioned, in his final chapter of *Southern Politics in State and Nation,* Key (1949) posed the question of whether there was a way out. He meant a way out of the dysfunctional politics of the one-party Democratic Solid South. Close to seven decades hence, because the politics of race remains the foremost molder of southern party competition, the way out has manifested in a presently dominant and overwhelmingly white GOP. But recent trends cast doubt on the sustainability of southern Republican electoral hegemony. For instance, because of compositional changes to the electorate in the Old Dominion, with each passing election cycle it is becoming more certain that Virginia is a state that now favors the Democratic Party. Consider that its three statewide offices (governor, lieutenant governor, and attorney general) up for election in the odd year after the presidential contest were swept by Virginia Republicans in 2009, but in the 2013 and 2017 contests Virginia Democrats won every office. In the 2017 elections for the 100-member Virginia House of Delegates (state house), what had been a 66-to-34 Republican majority was reduced to a 51-to-49 Republican advantage.[6] In presidential politics, Virginia is unique among the southern states, for it has awarded its electoral votes to the Democratic nominee for the last three consecutive elections (2008–2016). In this last substantive section, given the contemporary state of southern party politics, the question is whether there is a way back, that is, a way back to competitiveness for the Democratic Party. Virginia Democrats found a way back, and not surprisingly, the kinds of changes in the Old Dominion are transferable to fostering Democratic competitiveness in other southern states.

Three factors portend a Democratic comeback in southern politics: (1) racial and ethnic compositional change; (2) changing in-migration patterns; and (3) generational change. All three of these developments are altering the profile of the southern electorate in a fashion that at least on net, should redound to the electoral benefit of the Democratic Party.

Racial and Ethnic Compositional Change

Beginning with racial and ethnic changes to the southern electorate, there has been a marked tilt with respect to participants in presidential elections. It is a necessary caveat to acknowledge that the data about to be discussed are not from the same source and the former is a much more accurate gauge of participation than is the latter. Provided the sample is representative, exit poll data are a more reliable assessment of the demographic profile of actual voters than are survey self-reports, because it is highly unlikely that someone surveyed leaving the polling place did not in fact vote. Survey self-reports, on the other hand, are administered at a time most likely around but not on Election Day, and it is a certainty that a nontrivial number of respondents claim voting when in fact they abstained (the social desirability of wanting to claim voting because the action is looked upon favorably). Another issue is that the rate of misreporting voting is not equivalent across racial/ethnic groups (McKee, Hood, and Hill 2012). Nevertheless, because of the passage of a long span of time, the racial/ethnic profile of presidential voters in the South between 1984 and 2016, should be fairly accurate in painting a picture of the changing profile of the southern electorate.

Limiting the sample to only those southern respondents who identify as white, black, or Latino in the 1984 exit poll, among these presidential voters, 85 percent were white, 12 percent were black, and 2 percent were Latino. More than thirty years later, according to the data from self-reported presidential voters in the 2016 Cooperative Congressional Election Study (CCES), the southern electorate was 72 percent white, 21 percent black, and 7 percent Latino. Given the variation in voter preferences among these three groups, there is no question that a decline in white voters and an increase in black and Latino voters is a welcome development for the Democratic Party.

Although Latino voting behavior is relatively more of a wild card (Hood 2016) than the stalwart Democratic support African Americans have delivered since the mid-1960s (Fauntroy 2007), southern Latinos unquestionably favor the Democratic Party over the GOP (see chapter 11). Recall that compared to the 2000s, in the 2010s Latino affiliation with the Democratic Party has increased while Latino identification with the GOP has declined (see the discussion of Table 12.2). Citizenship remains the greatest hurdle in terms of the Latino electorate registering a significant impact in southern elections. With this in mind, Table 12.3 displays the share of the citizen voting age population (CVAP) in each southern state that consists of Latinos from 1980 to 2016. The first four decades

TABLE 12.3 ■ Percentage of Latino Citizen VAP in Southern States, 1980–2016						
State	1980	1990	2000	2010	2016	Change
Alabama	0.8	0.6	0.8	1.2	1.7	+0.9
Arkansas	0.6	0.7	1.3	2.1	3.0	+2.4
Florida	5.2	12.8	11.3	14.9	18.2	+13.0
Georgia	0.9	1.6	2.0	2.9	4.1	+3.2
Louisiana	2.0	2.3	1.8	2.4	2.9	+0.9
Mississippi	0.8	0.6	0.8	1.1	1.5	+0.7
North Carolina	0.8	1.1	1.6	2.4	3.5	+2.7
South Carolina	0.9	0.8	1.1	1.7	2.4	+1.5
Tennessee	0.7	0.6	1.0	1.5	2.1	+1.4
Texas	15.3	24.1	22.4	25.5	28.3	+13.0
Virginia	1.1	2.5	2.2	3.5	4.8	+3.7
South	4.9	8.6	8.1	10.1	12.2	+7.3

Source: Data are from the U.S. Census Bureau; decennial census for 1980, 1990, 2000, and 2010; 2016 data are the five-year estimates (2012–2016) from the American Community Survey.

Note: Data show the percentage of citizen VAP that is Latino in each southern state and South-wide.

(1980–2010) are actual decennial Census counts whereas the 2016 data are based on the five-year American Community Survey (2012–2016). With 1980 as the baseline, the growth in the Latino CVAP is impressive, but in most states, it is also true that the percentages are still rather meager even 36 years later. For instance, in 1980 only Florida and Texas had Latino CVAPs higher than 5 percent; three and a half decades later this is still true.

Florida and Texas have a Latino presence that has greatly increased in the years since 1980. The raw percentage increase in the Latino CVAPs in these two states (more than tripling in Florida and close to doubling in Texas) is quite remarkable when viewed in comparison with the other nine southern states, which all contain decidedly smaller Latino CVAPs. Nonetheless, Latino growth is evident across the board. In every southern state the Latino CVAP increased between 2010 and 2016. And South-wide, the percentage of the Latino CVAP goes from 5 percent in 1980 to 12 percent in 2016. The rising Latino population is definitely going to play a bigger role in the future of southern politics, and the data strongly suggest that this will translate into a Democratic advantage.

Changing In-Migration Patterns

In the twenty-first century, in-migration to the American South has been more robust than that occurring in any other region of the United States (Hillygus, McKee, and Young 2017). A shorthand way of confirming this development is by looking at the last two decennial congressional reapportionments in 2000 and 2010. Parceling the United States into five different regions based on the classification used by Black and Black (2007) (see the note under Table 12.4), because of higher population growth, due in part because of substantially more net in-migration, the South has been the big gainer in U.S. House seats. Between the 2000 and 1990 reapportionments, the Northeast and Midwest both shed 5 seats; the Mountains/Plains picked up 3; the Pacific Coast added 1; and the South netted 6. Between the 2000 and 2010 reapportionments, the Northeast lost another 5 seats and the Midwest dropped 6; once again the Mountains/Plains gained 3 and the Pacific Coast added 1, while the South netted 7.[7]

The data shown in Table 12.4, based on the one-year 2012 American Community Survey, suggest that the recent decline in congressional seats allocated to the Northeast and Midwest is partially attributable to the large immigration stream flowing from these regions to the South. Among the four non-southern regions of in-migration to the South, just under two-thirds originates from the Northeast (34 percent) and Midwest (31 percent). With respect to party politics, the Northeast and Pacific Coast are Democratic strongholds, while the Mountains/Plains favors the GOP, and the Midwest is the most politically competitive (Black and Black 2007). Just as recent racial and ethnic compositional changes to the southern electorate favor the Democratic Party, the current pattern of in-migration also benefits the Democrats.

It is not a coincidence that the only southern state that currently leans Democratic, Virginia, also has the highest percentage of northeastern in-migrants at 52 percent. Over the last quarter-century (going back to 1992), only two states have breached the formidable Northeast "blue wall" in presidential elections: New Hampshire went to the Republican George W. Bush in 2000 and in 2016 the Republican Donald Trump won Pennsylvania. Thus, over this span of seven presidential elections, the Granite State in 2000 and the Keystone State in 2016 were the only two that the GOP wrested from Democrats (out of a total of 84 state-level presidential races in the Northeast, including the District of Columbia).

It should also be pointed out that there is tremendous variation in the in-migration streams across the southern states. Therefore, in some of the states that have recently become even *more* Republican, like Arkansas and Tennessee (see Table 12.1), immigration from the Northeast is not nearly as prevalent as the in-migration from regions that do not strongly favor the Democratic Party (e.g., 83 percent of in-migrants to Arkansas are from the Midwest and Mountains/Plains). Still, the general pattern of recent in-migration to the South is on net, more favorable to the Democratic Party because most of these northern transplants hail from sections of the U.S. that are

TABLE 12.4 ■ Percentage of Southern In-Migration Based on Northern Region of Origin				
State	Northeast	Midwest	Mountains/Plains	Pacific Coast
Alabama	26	41	21	13
Arkansas	8	44	39	9
Florida	46	35	11	8
Georgia	30	38	19	13
Louisiana	22	30	27	21
Mississippi	20	42	19	20
North Carolina	46	27	12	15
South Carolina	48	28	14	11
Tennessee	19	52	16	13
Texas	16	24	36	24
Virginia	52	22	13	14
South	34	31	20	15

Source: Data are from the 2012 American Community Survey, as presented in graphical form by McKee and Teigen (2016, 229).

Notes: The states comprising each northern region is according to the classification scheme of Black and Black (2007). Northeast = Connecticut, Maine, Massachusetts, New Hampshire, Rhode Island, Vermont [New England], Delaware, District of Columbia, Maryland, New Jersey, New York, Pennsylvania [Mid-Atlantic]; Midwest = Illinois, Indiana, Iowa, Kentucky, Michigan, Minnesota, Missouri, Ohio, West Virginia, and Wisconsin; Mountains/Plains = Arizona, Colorado, Idaho, Kansas, Oklahoma, Montana, Nebraska, Nevada, New Mexico, North Dakota, South Dakota, Utah, and Wyoming; Pacific Coast = Alaska, California, Hawaii, Oregon, and Washington. According to this grouping of northern states, in presidential elections, the Northeast and Pacific Coast are Democratic strongholds, while the Mountains/Plains favor the GOP, and the Midwest is the most competitive because it contains the largest number of swing states (e.g., Iowa, Michigan, Missouri, Ohio, and Wisconsin).

considerably more Democratic than Dixie. The contemporary pattern of southern in-migration favoring the Democratic Party is a reversal of the longer previous pattern of in-migration generally benefiting the GOP from the 1950s through the 1980s (Black and Black 1987).

In racial terms, Table 12.5 charts the changing dynamic of white and black in-migration to the South from 1870–1880 to 2014–2015. With the end of Reconstruction, for decades the American South was a net exporter of population, white and black alike. For eighty years, 1880–1960, more white southerners left Dixie than did white northerners enter it. Similarly, from 1890 to 1970, the South experienced a deficit of black in-migration, a pattern hardly surprising because of Dixie's

TABLE 12.5 ■ Net White and Black Southern In-Migration, 1870–1880 to 2014–2015 (in Thousands)		
Years	White In-Migration	Black In-Migration
1870–1880	91	68
1880–1890	–271	88
1890–1900	–30	–185
1900–1910	–69	–194
1910–1920	–663	–555
1920–1930	–704	–903
1930–1940	–558	–408
1940–1950	–866	–1,581
1950–1960	–234	–1,202
1960–1970	1,807	–1,380
1970–1980	3,556	206
1980–1985	1,808	83
1985–1990	971	325
1990–1995	1,344*	358
1995–2000	1,127*	347
2000–2005	1,027*	318
2005–2010	731*	267
2014–2015	174*	62

Sources: Data from 1870 to 2010 are from Wright (2013, 143). Data for 2014–2015 are one-year estimates from the American Community Survey.

Notes: *Non-Latino White. The definition for South is the more expansive version used by the U.S. Census Bureau, which includes the eleven-state ex-Confederate South plus Delaware, the District of Columbia, Kentucky, Maryland, Oklahoma, and West Virginia.

oppressive Jim Crow system of racial segregation and its attendant disfranchising effects in the economic, social, and political realms. As the South finally shed its ugly past through the triumph of the black civil rights movement, Dixie has become very attractive to white and black in-migrants, with many of the latter group still holding ties to the region from their ancestral lineage to black southerners who were part of the so-called Great Migration to the North between the first and second World Wars (Woodward 2002). Additionally, it should be noted that Dixie is also the preferred relocation destination of Latinos. In 2014–2015, the South had a net Latino in-migration of 57,000 people, a number close to four times higher than the net Latino in-migration of 15,000 people to the Northeast (in the remaining two Census-defined regions, the Midwest and West, net Latino in-migration was negative).

Last, the 2016 ANES allows for an examination of the most recent southern transplants. Using the same method of classification for native southerners and in-migrants as that found in chapter 9 (see the note under Figure 9.13), the most recent in-migrants to the South possess a demographic profile more favorable to the Democratic Party than any previous data on this population. In terms of the share of native and in-migrant voters in 2016, 70 percent are southern natives and 30 percent are southern in-migrants—the highest percentage of southern in-migrant voters for the entire ANES time series going back to the 1950s (see Figure 9.13 in chapter 9).

In terms of racial composition, the share of nonwhite native southern voters (38 percent nonwhite/62 percent white) in 2016 is the highest recorded in the ANES. Likewise, the percentage of nonwhite southern in-migrant voters (32 percent non-white/68 percent white) in 2016 is the highest minority percentage for the entire ANES time series. So, in 2016, among native southern voters and southern in-migrant voters, these constituencies contained the greatest portion of minority voters ever documented since black disfranchisement was accomplished in the late 1800s to early 1900s (Kousser 1974).

Finally, with respect to voting behavior, native southern voters were four percent-age points more supportive of Trump, and this was the case even though there are significantly more African American native southern voters (23.5 percent) than black in-migrant voters (11.1 percent). Because the portion of Latino native southern voters (9.2 percent) is not markedly lower than the share of Latino in-migrant voters (13 per-cent Latino), there is a simple answer for why the most recent arrivals to Dixie are not as supportive of the GOP: white in-migrants. Out of the two-party 2016 presidential vote, 69 percent of in-migrant whites voted Republican versus 77 percent of native whites who marked their ballots for Trump.

Generational Change

Chapter 6 examined the role of generational change among white southern-ers in order to show that more recent generations had stronger attachments to the Republican Party. Most of the analysis was based on the ANES time series data that ended with the 2012 election. Importantly though, as the age cohorts were parceled, with the data terminating in 2012, the youngest groups of white southerners (those born from 1975–1990 and 1991 or later) were no longer the most Republican in their party affiliation (see Table 6.2 in chapter 6).

Table 12.6 cuts the southern electorate into four exhaustive and exclusive age groups similar to the recent analysis of Prysby (2017). Prysby makes use of the 2016 ANES, but given the massively larger sample size for the 2016 CCES, the latter survey

TABLE 12.6 ■ Vote Choice, Race/Ethnicity, and Party Identification of Four Generations of Southern Presidential Voters in 2016 (in Percentages)				
Category	Millennials (25%)	Generation X (28%)	Boomers (35%)	Seniors (12%)
Vote Choice				
Trump (R)	38	49	58	70
Clinton (D)	62	51	42	30
Difference	−24	−2	+16	+40
Race/Ethnicity				
White	58	65	73	87
Black	26	22	17	7
Latino	9	8	6	3
Other	7	5	4	3
Party ID				
Republican	26	32	37	44
Democrat	47	39	34	26
Independent	27	29	29	31
Cases	2,767	3,159	3,981	1,307

Source: Data compiled by the author from the 2016 Cooperative Congressional Election Study (CCES).

Notes: Birth years for each generation are as follows: Millennials = 1982–1998; Generation X = 1963–1981; Boomers = 1946–1962; Seniors = 1917–1945. Thus, Millennials are between 18 and 34 years old; Generation X voters are between 35 and 53 years old; Boomers are between 54 and 70 years old; and seniors are at least 71 years old. All data were weighted according to the CCES common content post-election weight variable ("commonweight_post").

is employed for this examination. The four generations of southern presidential voters profiled in Table 12.6, from youngest to oldest, consist of (1) Millennials (18- to 34-year-olds); (2) Generation X (35- to 53-year-olds); (3) Boomers (54- to 70-year-olds); and (4) Seniors (71 years old or older). The percentage of each age group is shown in the column heading for these four generations. In 2016, Millennials already outnumber Seniors by a 2-to-1 ratio, though Boomers (35 percent), followed by Generation X (28 percent), are the largest age groups.

Table 12.6 highlights three important pieces of information: (1) two-party presidential vote choice; (2) the race/ethnicity of these southern presidential voters; and (3) the party identification of these voters. A remarkably obvious pattern is present in the table; there is a consistent drop in southern Republicanism going from the oldest to youngest generation of southern presidential voters. Starting with vote choice, 70 percent of Seniors backed Trump, but this level of Republican support drops substantially, going from Boomers (58 percent) to Generation X (49 percent) to Millennials (38 percent). Another troubling sign for the southern GOP is the relationship between generations and race/ethnicity. White voters, the lion's share of Republican supporters, are not nearly as prevalent among millennials (58 percent). While the share of white voters increases with each older generation, the percentage of minority voters (black, Latino, and other) increases with each younger generation. Finally, among partisans, Republican adherents are more numerous in older generations, whereas moving in the direction of younger generations is associated with a higher percentage of Democrats—a strong plurality in the case of millennials (47 percent Democratic).

If the pattern captured in Table 12.6 continues to hold for many years to come, it could truly jeopardize Republican dominance in southern electoral politics. Combine this dynamic of generational change with the more generally favorable demographic changes regarding race and ethnicity and southern in-migration, and it becomes abundantly clear why the Republican Party has been busily altering the election administration apparatus (see chapter 10) so as to stem the steadily growing Democratic presence in Dixie's politics.

FINAL THOUGHTS

As chronicled in this final chapter, there are several factors that foretell a brighter electoral future for the currently outmatched Democratic Party. The broad sweep of demographic changes to the southern electorate exhibit an almost one-sided effect advantaging Democrats. As noted, a Democratic future already seems to be underway and in fact to some extent, has come to fruition in Virginia. The same kinds of dynamics causing a turn back to the Democratic Party in the Old Dominion are also present in several other states located along the Eastern Seaboard, which have also witnessed considerable in-migration from the most Democratic section of the United States, the Northeast. But rates of in-migration are hardly ever that substantial in the short run, comprising only a modest share of the southern electorate (Black and Black 1987; McKee and Teigen 2016). Viewed from this perspective, the most troublesome development facing the southern GOP is generational change. The certainty of aging highlights the reality that a growing and larger share of the electorate resides among voters under the age of 50, and the demographic profile and political behavior of these voters is markedly less Republican than that exhibited by their elders, who constitute a dwindling share of the southern polity.

The rise of the first African American president in U.S. political history has garnered so much attention in part because the widely held racial prejudice of voters led many experts to doubt such an outcome. Of course, not only did Barack Obama win in 2008, he was reelected in 2012. The understated, though far from ignored, significance of Obama's presidential victories is the coalition he constructed in his name. Provided turnout is healthy (it wasn't in 2016), the mobilization of minority groups, women, and young voters is the blueprint not only for national presidential majorities but also for a return to Democratic competitiveness in Dixie. But the American South remains exceptional because the partisan sorting of its voters is much more heavily predicated on race. Indeed, the southern Democracy and its GOP opposition both have a racial problem. Democrats need more white voters and Republicans desperately need more minority voters. The electoral system is not in a state of equilibrium; it is in a gradual state of transition, and at least for now, the smart money favors Democratic gains because the southern GOP continues to refuse to adopt a political strategy attractive to the growing ranks of black and Latino voters. The dynamics of southern politics live on.

REFERENCES

Abrajano, Marisa, and Zoltan L. Hajnal. 2015. *White Backlash: Immigration, Race, and American Politics*. Princeton, NJ: Princeton University Press.

Abramowitz, Alan I. 1994. "Issue Evolution Reconsidered: Racial Attitudes and Partisanship in the U.S. Electorate." *American Journal of Political Science 38*(1): 1–24.

Abramowitz, Alan I., and Kyle L. Saunders. 1998. "Ideological Realignment in the U.S. Electorate." *Journal of Politics 60*(3): 634–652.

Abramowitz, Alan I., and Kyle L. Saunders. 2008. "Is Polarization a Myth?" *Journal of Politics 70*(2): 542–555.

Abramson, Paul R. 1974. "Generational Change in American Electoral Behavior." *American Political Science Review 68*(1): 93–105.

Abramson, Paul R. 1976. "Generational Change and the Decline of Party Identification in America, 1952–1974." *American Political Science Review 70*(2): 469–478.

Abramson, Paul R. 1979. "Developing Party Identification: A Further Examination of Life-Cycle, Generational, and Period Effects." *American Journal of Political Science 23*(1): 78–96.

Adams, Greg D. 1997. "Abortion: Evidence of an Issue Evolution." *American Journal of Political Science 41*(3): 718–737.

Aistrup, Joseph A. 1996. *The Southern Strategy Revisited: Republican Top-Down Advancement in the South*. Lexington: University Press of Kentucky.

Aistrup, Joseph A. 2010. "Southern Political Exceptionalism? Presidential Voting in the South and Non-South." *Social Science Quarterly 91*(4): 906–927.

Aldrich, John H. 1995. *Why Parties? The Origin and Transformation of Political Parties in America*. Chicago: University of Chicago Press.

Aldrich, John H., and John D. Griffin. 2017. *Why Parties Matter: Political Competition and Democracy in the American South*. Chicago: University of Chicago Press.

Altman, Micah, and Michael P. McDonald. 2015. "Paradoxes of Political Reform: Congressional Redistricting in Florida." In *Jigsaw Puzzle Politics in the Sunshine State*, edited by Seth C. McKee, 163–182. Gainesville: University Press of Florida.

Anderson, R. Bruce, Zachary D. Baumann, and Matthew Geras. 2018. "Florida: The South, Border State, or Wild Frontier?" In *The New Politics of the Old South*, edited by Charles S. Bullock III and Mark J. Rozell, 275–301. Lanham, MD: Rowman & Littlefield.

Ansolabehere, Stephen, Alan Gerber, and James Snyder. 2002. "Equal Votes, Equal Money: Court-Ordered Redistricting and Public Expenditures in the American States." *American Political Science Review 96*(4): 767–777.

Ansolabehere, Stephen, and Eitan Hersh. 2012. "Validation: What Big Data Reveal About Survey Misreporting and the Real Electorate." *Political Analysis 20*(4): 437–459.

Ansolabehere, Stephen, and Eitan Hersh. 2013. "Gender, Race, Age, and Voting: A Research Note." *Politics and Governance 1*(2): 132–137.

Ansolabehere, Stephen, and James M. Snyder. 2008. *The End of Inequality: One Person, One Vote and the Transformation of American Politics*. New York: W. W. Norton & Company.

Arbour, Brian K., and Jeremy M. Teigen. 2011. "Barack Obama's 'American' Problem: Unhyphenated Americans in the 2008 Elections." *Social Science Quarterly 92*(3): 563–587.

Arsenault, Raymond. 2006. *Freedom Riders: 1961 and the Struggle for Racial Justice*. Oxford, UK: Oxford University Press.

Ayers, Edward L. 1992. *The Promise of the New South: Life After Reconstruction*. Oxford, UK: Oxford University Press.

Barbour, Henry, Sally Bradshaw, Ari Fleischer, Zori Fonalledas, and Glenn McCall. 2012. *Growth and Opportunity Project*. Washington, DC: Republican National Committee.

Barone, Michael, and Richard E. Cohen. 2001. *The Almanac of American Politics 2002*. Washington, DC: National Journal.

Barone, Michael, and Richard E. Cohen. 2003. *The Almanac of American Politics 2004*. Washington, DC: National Journal.

Barone, Michael, and Richard E. Cohen. 2005. *The Almanac of American Politics 2006*. Washington, DC: National Journal.

Barone, Michael, and Richard E. Cohen. 2007. *The Almanac of American Politics 2008*. Washington, DC: National Journal.

Barone, Michael, and Richard E. Cohen. 2009. *The Almanac of American Politics 2010*. Washington, DC: National Journal.

Barone, Michael, and Chuck McCutcheon. 2011. *The Almanac of American Politics 2012*. Chicago: University of Chicago Press.

Barone, Michael, and Chuck McCutcheon. 2013. *The Almanac of American Politics 2014*. Chicago: University of Chicago Press.

Barone, Michael, and Chuck McCutcheon. 2015. *The Almanac of American Politics 2016*. Bethesda, MD: Columbia Books Inc.

Barone, Michael, and Grant Ujifusa. 1991. *The Almanac of American Politics 1992*. Washington, DC: National Journal.

Barone, Michael, and Grant Ujifusa. 1993. *The Almanac of American Politics 1994*. Washington, DC: National Journal.

Barone, Michael, and Grant Ujifusa. 1995. *The Almanac of American Politics 1996*. Washington, DC: National Journal.

Barone, Michael, and Grant Ujifusa. 1997. *The Almanac of American Politics 1998*. Washington, DC: National Journal

Barone, Michael, and Grant Ujifusa. 1999. *The Almanac of American Politics 2000*. Washington, DC: National Journal.

Bartels, Larry M. 2000. "Partisanship and Voting Behavior, 1952–1996." *American Journal of Political Science 44*(1): 35–50.

Bartels, Larry M. 2002. "Beyond the Running Tally: Partisan Bias in Political Perceptions." *Political Behavior 24*(2): 117–150.

Bartels, Larry M. 2008. *Unequal Democracy: The Political Economy of the New Gilded Age*. Princeton, NJ: Princeton University Press.

Bartley, Numan V., and Hugh D. Graham. 1975. *Southern Politics and the Second Reconstruction*. Baltimore, MD: Johns Hopkins University Press.

Bass, Jack, and Walter DeVries. 1995. *The Transformation of Southern Politics: Social Change and Political Consequence Since 1945*. Athens: University of Georgia Press.

Bass, Jack, and Marilyn W. Thompson. 2003. *Ol' Strom: An Unauthorized Biography of Strom Thurmond*. Columbia: University of South Carolina Press.

Baum, Matthew A., and Angela S. Jamison. 2006. "The *Oprah* Effect: How Soft News Helps Inattentive Citizens Vote Consistently." *Journal of Politics* 68(4): 946–959.

Beck, Paul Allen. 1977. "Partisan Dealignment in the Postwar South." *American Political Science Review* 71(2): 477–496.

Bensel, Richard Franklin. 2008. *Passion and Preferences: William Jennings Bryan and the 1896 Democratic National Convention*. New York: Cambridge University Press.

Bernstein, Robert, Anita Chadha, and Robert Montjoy. 2001. "Overreporting Voting: Why It Happens and Why It Matters." *Public Opinion Quarterly* 65(1): 22–44.

Bernstein, Carl, and Bob Woodward. 1974. *All the President's Men*. New York: Simon & Schuster.

Bickerstaff, Steve. 2007. *Lines in the Sand: Congressional Redistricting in Texas and the Downfall of Tom DeLay*. Austin: University of Texas Press.

Bishop, Bill, and Robert G. Cushing. 2008. *The Big Sort: Why the Clustering of Like-Minded America is Tearing Us Apart*. Boston: Houghton Mifflin.

Black, Earl. 1976. *Southern Governors and Civil Rights: Racial Segregation as a Campaign Issue in the Second Reconstruction*. Cambridge, MA: Harvard University Press.

Black, Earl. 1998. "Presidential Address: The Newest Southern Politics." *Journal of Politics* 60(3): 591–612.

Black, Earl, and Merle Black. 1987. *Politics and Society in the South*. Cambridge, MA: Harvard University Press.

Black, Earl, and Merle Black. 1992. *The Vital South: How Presidents are Elected*. Cambridge, MA: Harvard University Press.

Black, Earl, and Merle Black. 2002. *The Rise of Southern Republicans*. Cambridge, MA: Harvard University Press.

Black, Earl, and Merle Black. 2007. *Divided America: The Ferocious Power Struggle in American Politics*. New York: Simon & Schuster.

Black, Merle. 2004. "Presidential Address: The Transformation of the Southern Democratic Party." *Journal of Politics* 66(4): 1001–1017.

Black, Merle, and Earl Black. 2012. "Deep South Politics: The Enduring Racial Divide in National Elections." In *The Oxford Handbook of Southern Politics*, edited by Charles S. Bullock III and Mark J. Rozell, 401–423. New York: Oxford University Press.

Box-Steffensmeier, Janet M., Suzanna De Boef, and Tse-Min Lin. 2004. "The Dynamics of the Partisan Gender Gap." *American Political Science Review* 98(3): 515–528.

Brody, Richard A. 1991. *Assessing the President: The Media, Elite Opinion, and Public Support*. Stanford, CA: Stanford University Press.

Browder, Glen, and Artemesia Stanberry. 2010. *Stealth Reconstruction: An Untold Story of Racial Politics in Recent Southern History*. Montgomery, AL: NewSouth Books.

Brown, Thad A. 1988. *Migration and Politics: The Impact of Population Mobility on American Voting Behavior*. Chapel Hill: University of North Carolina Press.

Buchanan, Scott E. 1997. "The Effects of the Abolition of the Georgia County-Unit System on the 1962 Gubernatorial Election." *Politics & Policy* 25(4): 687–704.

Bullock, Charles S., III. 1991. "The Nomination Process and Super Tuesday." In *The 1988 Election in the South: Continuity Amidst Change in Southern Party Politics*, edited by Laurence W. Moreland, Robert P. Steed, and Tod A. Baker, 3–19. New York: Praeger.

Bullock, Charles S., III. 1995. "Affirmative Action Districts: In Whose Faces Will They Blow Up?" *Campaigns & Elections* April: 22–23.

Bullock, Charles S., III. 2010. *Redistricting: The Most Political Activity in America*. Lanham, MD: Rowman & Littlefield.

Bullock, Charles S., III. 2014. "Introduction: Politics in the South: Out of Step with the Nation Once Again." In *The New Politics of the Old South*, edited by Charles S. Bullock III and Mark J. Rozell, 1–24. Lanham, MD: Rowman & Littlefield.

Bullock, Charles S., III, Donna R. Hoffman, and Ronald Keith Gaddie. 2005. "The Consolidation of the White Southern Congressional Vote." *Political Research Quarterly* 58(2): 231–243.

Bullock, Charles S., III, and Ronald Keith Gaddie. 2009. *The Triumph of Voting Rights in the South*. Norman: University of Oklahoma Press.

Bullock, Charles S., III, and M. V. Hood III. 2006. "A Mile-Wide Gap: The Evolution of Hispanic Political Emergence in the Deep South." *Social Science Quarterly* 87(5): 1117–1135.

Bullock, Charles S., III, and M. V. Hood III. 2015. "The Damnedest Mess: An Empirical Evaluation of the 1966 Georgia Gubernatorial Election." *Social Science Quarterly* 96(1): 104–118.

Burnham, Walter Dean. 1970. *Critical Elections and the Mainsprings of American Politics*. New York: W. W. Norton & Company.

Burnham, Walter Dean. 2010. *Voting in American Elections: The Shaping of the American Universe Since 1788*. Bethesda, MD: Academica Press.

Butler, Katharine Inglis. 2002. "Redistricting in a Post-*Shaw* Era: A Small Treatise Accompanied by Districting Guidelines for Legislators, Litigants, and Courts." *University of Richmond Law Review* 36(1): 137–270.

Butler, David, and Bruce E. Cain. 1992. *Congressional Redistricting: Comparative and Theoretical Perspectives*. New York: Macmillan.

Cain, Bruce E. 1984. *The Reapportionment Puzzle*. Berkeley: University of California Press.

Cain, Bruce E., John A. Ferejohn, and Morris P. Fiorina. 1987. *The Personal Vote: Constituency Service and Electoral Independence*. Cambridge, MA: Harvard University Press.

Cameron, Charles, David Epstein, and Sharyn O'Halloran. 1996. "Do Majority-Minority Districts Maximize Substantive Black Representation in Congress?" *American Political Science Review* 90(4): 794–812.

Campbell, Angus, Philip E. Converse, Warren E. Miller, and Donald E. Stokes. 1960. *The American Voter*. Chicago: University of Chicago Press.

Campbell, Bruce A. 1977. "Patterns of Change in the Partisan Loyalties of Native Southerners: 1952–1972." *Journal of Politics* 39(3): 730–761.

Campbell, James E. 1993. *The Presidential Pulse of Congressional Elections*. Lexington: University Press of Kentucky.

Campbell, James E. 1997. "The Presidential Pulse and the 1994 Midterm Congressional Election." *Journal of Politics* 59(3): 830–857.

Canon, David T. 1990. *Actors, Athletes, and Astronauts: Political Amateurs in the United States Congress*. Chicago: University of Chicago Press.

Canon, David T., and David J. Sousa. 1992. "Party System Change and Political Career Structures in the U.S. Congress." *Legislative Studies Quarterly 17*(3): 347–363.

Carmines, Edward G. 1991. "The Logic of Party Alignments." *Journal of Theoretical Politics* 3(1): 65–80.

Carmines, Edward G., and James A. Stimson. 1980. "The Two Faces of Issue Voting." *American Political Science Review 74*(1): 78–91.

Carmines, Edward G., and James A. Stimson. 1989. *Issue Evolution: Race and the Transformation of American Politics.* Princeton, NJ: Princeton University Press.

Carmines, Edward G., and James Woods. 2002. "The Role of Party Activists in the Evolution of the Abortion Issue." *Political Behavior* 24(4): 361–377.

Carsey, Thomas M., and Geoffrey C. Layman. 2006. "Changing Sides or Changing Minds? Party Identification and Policy Preferences in the American Electorate." *American Journal of Political Science 50*(2): 464–477.

Carson, Jamie L., and Jason M. Roberts. 2013. *Ambition, Competition, and Electoral Reform: The Politics of Congressional Elections Across Time.* Ann Arbor: University of Michigan Press.

Carter, Dan T. 1995. *The Politics of Rage: George Wallace, the Origins of the New Conservatism, and the Transformation of American Politics.* New York: Simon & Schuster.

Carter, Dan T. 1998. "Fact, Fiction, and Film: Frankenheimer's *George Wallace.*" *Perspectives on History 36*(1). Washington, DC: American Historical Association. https://www.historians.org/publications-and-directories/perspectives-on-history/january-1998/fact-fiction-and-film-frankenheimers-george-wallace (accessed July 20, 2017).

Carter, Dan T. 1999. *From George Wallace to Newt Gingrich: Race in the Conservative Counterrevolution, 1963–1994.* Baton Rouge: Louisiana State University Press.

Ceaser, James W., and Andrew E. Busch. 2001. *The Perfect Tie: The True Story of the 2000 Presidential Election.* Lanham, MD: Rowman & Littlefield.

Cecelski, David S., and Timothy B. Tyson, eds. 1998. *Democracy Betrayed: The Wilmington Race Riot of 1898 and Its Legacy.* Chapel Hill: University of North Carolina Press.

Cho, Wendy K. Tam, James G. Gimpel, and Daron R. Shaw. 2012. "The Tea Party Movement and the Geography of Collective Action." *Quarterly Journal of Political Science 7*(2): 105–133.

Colburn, David R. 2007. *From Yellow Dog Democrats to Red State Republicans: Florida and Its Politics since 1940.* Gainesville: University Press of Florida.

Converse, Philip E. 1964. "The Nature of Belief Systems in Mass Publics." In *Ideology and Discontent,* edited by David E. Apter, 206–261. New York: The Free Press of Glencoe.

Converse, Philip E. 1966. "On the Possibility of Major Political Realignment in the South." In *Elections and the Political Order,* edited by Angus Campbell, Philip E. Converse, Warren E. Miller, and Donald E. Stokes, 212–242. New York: John Wiley and Sons.

Converse, Philip E. 1976. *The Dynamics of Party Support: Cohort-Analyzing Party Identification.* Beverly Hills, CA: Sage.

Converse, Philip E. 2006. "The Nature of Belief Systems in Mass Publics (1964)." *Critical Review 18*(1–3): 1–74.

Cosman, Bernard. 1966. *Five States for Goldwater: Continuity and Change in Southern Presidential Voting Patterns.* Tuscaloosa: University of Alabama Press.

Cox, Gary W., and Jonathan N. Katz. 1996. "Why Did the Incumbency Advantage in U.S. House Elections Grow?" *American Journal of Political Science 40*(2): 478–497.

Cox, Gary W., and Jonathan N. Katz. 2002. *Elbridge Gerry's Salamander: The Electoral Consequences of the Reapportionment Revolution.* Cambridge: Cambridge University Press.

CQ Press, ed. 2005. *Guide to U.S. House Elections*. Volume 2, 5th ed. Washington, DC: CQ Press.

Cunningham, Maurice T. 2001. *Maximization, Whatever the Cost: Race, Redistricting and the Department of Justice*. Westport, CT: Praeger.

David, Paul T. 1972. *Party Strength in the United States: 1872–1970*. Charlottesville: University Press of Virginia.

David, Paul T., and Ralph Eisenberg. 1961. *Devaluation of the Urban and Suburban Vote: A Statistical Investigation of Long-Term Trends in State Legislative Representation*. Charlottesville: Bureau of Public Administration, University of Virginia.

Davidson, Chandler, ed. 1984. *Minority Vote Dilution*. Washington, DC: Howard University Press.

Delli Carpini, Michael X., and Scott Keeter. 1996. *What Americans Know about Politics and Why It Matters*. New Haven, CT: Yale University Press.

Dodd, Lawrence C. 2015. "Congress in a Downsian World: Polarization Cycles and Regime Change." *Journal of Politics 77*(2): 311–323.

Dowdle, Andrew, and Joseph D. Giammo. 2014. "Arkansas: As Red as the Rest?" In *The New Politics of the Old South*, edited by Charles S. Bullock III and Mark J. Rozell, 207–218. Lanham, MD: Rowman & Littlefield.

Downs, Anthony. 1957. *An Economic Theory of Democracy*. New York: Harper & Row.

Dubin, Michael J. 2007. *Party Affiliations in the State Legislatures: A Year by Year Summary, 1796–2006*. Jefferson, NC: McFarland & Company.

Edwards, George C., III. 2004. *Why the Electoral College is Bad for America*. New Haven, CT: Yale University Press.

Engstrom, Erik J. 2013. *Partisan Gerrymandering and the Construction of American Democracy*. Ann Arbor: University of Michigan Press.

Epstein, David, and Sharyn O'Halloran. 1999a. "A Social Science Approach to Race, Redistricting, and Representation." *American Political Science Review 93*(1): 187–191.

Epstein, David, and Sharyn O'Halloran. 1999b. "Measuring the Electoral and Policy Impact of Majority-Minority Voting Districts." *American Journal of Political Science 43*(2): 367–395.

Epstein, David, and Sharyn O'Halloran. 2000. "Majority-Minority Districts and the New Politics of Congressional Elections." In *Continuity and Change in House Elections*, edited by David W. Brady, John F. Cogan, and Morris P. Fiorina, 87–109. Stanford, CA: Stanford University Press.

Erikson, Robert S., and Lorraine C. Minnite. 2009. "Modeling Problems in the Voter Identification—Voter Turnout Debate." *Election Law Journal: Rules, Politics, and Policy 8*(2): 85–101.

Fauntroy, Michael K. 2007. *Republicans and the Black Vote*. Boulder, CO: Lynne Rienner.

Feinstein, Brain D., and Eric Schickler. 2008. "Platforms and Partners: The Civil Rights Realignment Reconsidered." *Studies in American Political Development 22*(Spring): 1–31.

Fenno, Richard F., Jr. 2000. *Congress at the Grassroots: Representational Change in the South, 1970–1998*. Chapel Hill: University of North Carolina Press.

Fiorina, Morris P. 1977. *Congress: Keystone of the Washington Establishment*. New Haven, CT: Yale University Press.

Fiorina, Morris P. 1981. *Retrospective Voting in American National Elections*. New Haven, CT: Yale University Press.

Fiorina, Morris P., Samuel A. Abrams, and Jeremy C. Pope. 2008. "Polarization in the American Public: Misconceptions and Misreadings." *Journal of Politics 70*(2): 556–560.

Flanigan, William H., Nancy H. Zingale, Elizabeth A. Theiss-Morse, and Michael W. Wagner. 2015. *Political Behavior of the American Electorate*. Washington, DC: CQ Press.

Fleisher, Richard, and Jon R. Bond. 2004. "The Shrinking Middle in the US Congress." *British Journal of Political Science 34*(3): 429–451.

Foner, Eric. 1988. *Reconstruction: America's Unfinished Revolution, 1863–1877*. New York: Harper & Row.

Foner, Eric. 1993. *Freedom's Lawmakers: A Directory of Black Officeholders during Reconstruction*. New York: Oxford University Press.

Frady, Marshall. 1996. *Wallace*. New York: Random House.

Frederickson, Kari. 2001. *The Dixiecrat Revolt and the End of the Solid South, 1932–1968*. Chapel Hill: University of North Carolina Press.

Gaddie, Ronald Keith. 2004. "The Texas Redistricting, Measure for Measure." *Extensions: A Journal of the Carl Albert Congressional Research and Studies Center* Fall: 19–24.

Garrow, David J. 1978. *Protest at Selma: Martin Luther King, Jr. and the Voting Rights Act of 1965*. New Haven, CT: Yale University Press.

Gaskins, Keesha, and Sundeep Iyer. 2012. *The Challenge of Obtaining Voter Identification*. New York: Brennan Center for Justice.

Gelman, Andrew, and Gary King. 1990. "Estimating Incumbency Advantage Without Bias." *American Journal of Political Science 34*(4): 1142–1164.

Gelman, Andrew, and Gary King. 1994. "A Unified Method of Evaluating Electoral Systems and Redistricting Plans." *American Journal of Political Science 38*(2): 514–554.

Gimpel, James G., and Jason E. Schuknecht. 2004. *Patchwork Nation: Sectionalism and Political Change in American Politics*. Ann Arbor: University of Michigan Press.

Glaser, James M. 1996. *Race, Campaign Politics, and the Realignment in the South*. New Haven, CT: Yale University Press.

Glaser, James M. 2001. "When Legislators Change Sides: The Implications of Party Defections in the South." In *Eye of the Storm: The South and Congress in an Era of Change*, edited by John C. Kuzenski, Laurence W. Moreland, and Robert P. Steed, 69–80. Westport, CT: Praeger.

Glaser, James M. 2005. *The Hand of the Past in Contemporary Southern Politics*. New Haven, CT: Yale University Press.

Glaser, James M. 2006. "The Primary Runoff as a Remnant of the Old South." *Electoral Studies 25*(4): 776–790.

Glass, Andrew. 2007. "Congress Runs Into 'Republican Revolution' Nov. 8, 1994." *Politico*, November 8. http://www.politico.com/story/2007/11/congress-runs-into-republican-revolution-nov-8-1994-006757 (accessed January 10, 2017).

Goodwyn, Lawrence. 1978. *The Populist Moment*. Oxford, UK: Oxford University Press.

Gould, Lewis L. 2003. *Grand Old Party: A History of the Republicans*. New York: Random House.

Grantham, Dewey W. 1983. *Southern Progressivism: The Reconciliation of Programs and Tradition*. Knoxville: University of Tennessee Press.

Green, John C., Lyman A. Kellstedt, Corwin E. Smidt, and James L. Guth. 2014. "The Soul of the South: Religion and Southern Politics in the New Millennium." In *The New Politics of the Old South*, edited by Charles S. Bullock III and Mark J. Rozell, 291–312. Lanham, MD: Rowman & Littlefield.

Green, Donald, Bradley Palmquist, and Eric Schickler. 2002. *Partisan Hearts and Minds: Political Parties and the Social Identities of Voters*. New Haven, CT: Yale University Press.

Grimmer, Justin, Eitan Hersh, Marc Meredith, Jonathan Mummolo, and Clayton Nall. 2017. "Comment on 'Voter Identification Laws and the Suppression of Minority Votes'" Manuscript. http://stanford.edu/~jgrimmer/comment_final.pdf (accessed June 30, 2017).

Grofman, Bernard. 2013. "Devising a Sensible Trigger for Section 5 of the Voting Rights Act." *Election Law Journal: Rules, Politics, and Policy 12*(3): 332–337.

Grofman, Bernard, and Thomas L. Brunell. 2005. "The Art of the Dummymander: The Impact of Recent Redistrictings on the Partisan Makeup of Southern House Seats." In *Redistricting in the New Millennium*, edited by Peter F. Galderisi, 183–199. Lanham, MD: Lexington Books.

Gronke, Paul, William D. Hicks, Seth C. McKee, Charles Stewart III, and James Dunham. Forthcoming. "Voter ID Laws: A View from the Public." *Social Science Quarterly*.

Grose, Christian R. 2004. "Is It Better to Join the Majority? The Electoral Effects of Party Switching by Incumbent Southern State Legislators, 1972 to 2000." *American Review of Politics 25*(Spring): 79–98.

Grose, Christian R., and Antoine Yoshinaka. 2003. "The Electoral Consequences of Party Switching by Incumbent Members of Congress, 1947–2000." *Legislative Studies Quarterly 28*(1): 55–75.

Gugliotta, Guy. 2012. "New Estimate Raises Civil War Death Toll." *New York Times*, April 2. http://www.nytimes.com/2012/04/03/science/civil-war-toll-up-by-20-percent-in-new-estimate.html (accessed September 22, 2017).

Hadley, Charles D., and Harold W. Stanley. 1989. "Super Tuesday 1988: Regional Results and National Implications." *Publius: The Journal of Federalism 19*(3): 19–37.

Hajnal, Zoltan, Nazita Lagevardi, and Lindsay Nielson. 2017. "Voter Identification Laws and the Suppression of Minority Votes." *Journal of Politics 79*(2): 363–379.

Hayes, Danny, and Seth C. McKee. 2004. "Booting Barnes: Explaining the Historic Upset in the 2002 Georgia Gubernatorial Election." *Politics & Policy 32*(4): 708–739.

Hayes, Danny, and Seth C. McKee. 2008. "Toward a One-Party South." *American Politics Research 36*(1): 3–32.

Hayes, Danny, and Seth C. McKee. 2009. "The Participatory Effects of Redistricting." *American Journal of Political Science 53*(4): 1006–1023.

Heard, Alexander. 1952. *A Two-Party South?* Chapel Hill: University of North Carolina Press.

Herron, Michael C., and Daniel A. Smith. 2012. "Souls to the Polls: Early Voting in Florida in the Shadow of House Bill 1355." *Election Law Journal: Rules, Politics, and Policy 11*(3): 331–347.

Herron, Michael C., and Daniel A. Smith. 2013. "The Effects of House Bill 1355 on Voter Registration in Florida." *State Politics & Policy Quarterly 13*(3): 279–305.

Herron, Michael C., and Daniel A. Smith. 2016. "Race, *Shelby County*, and the Voter Information Verification Act in North Carolina." *Florida State University Law Review 43*(2): 465–506.

Hetherington, Marc J. 2001. "Resurgent Mass Partisanship: The Role of Elite Polarization." *American Political Science Review 95*(3): 619–631.

Hetherington, Marc J. 2009. "Review Article: Putting Polarization in Perspective." *British Journal of Political Science* 39(2): 413–448.

Hicks, William D., Seth C. McKee, Mitchell D. Sellers, and Daniel A. Smith. 2015. "A Principle or a Strategy? Voter Identification Laws and Partisan Competition in the American States." *Political Research Quarterly* 68(1): 18–33.

Hicks, William D., Seth C. McKee, and Daniel A. Smith. 2016a. "A Bipartisan Election Reform? Explaining Support for Online Voter Registration in the American States." *American Politics Research* 44(6): 1008–1036.

Hicks, William D., Seth C. McKee, and Daniel A. Smith. 2016b. "The Determinants of State Legislator Support for Restrictive Voter ID Laws." *State Politics and Policy Quarterly* 16(4): 411–431.

Highton, Benjamin. 2017. "Voter Identification Laws and Turnout in the United States." *Annual Review of Political Science* 20: 149–167.

Hill, Kevin A. 1995. "Does the Creation of Majority Black Districts Aid Republicans? An Analysis of the 1992 Congressional Elections in Eight Southern States." *Journal of Politics* 57(2): 384–401.

Hillygus, D. Sunshine, Seth C. McKee, and McKenzie Young. 2017. "Reversal of Fortune: The Political Behavior of White Migrants to the South." *Presidential Studies Quarterly* 47(2): 354–364.

Hillygus, D. Sunshine, and Todd G. Shields. 2009. *The Persuadable Voter: Wedge Issues in Presidential Campaigns*. Princeton, NJ: Princeton University Press.

Holbrook, Thomas M. 2002. "Did the Whistle-Stop Campaign Matter?" *PS: Political Science and Politics* 35(1): 59–66.

Hood, M. V., III. 2016. "Race, Class, Religion and the Southern Party System: A Field Report from Dixie." *The Forum* 14(1): 83–96.

Hood, M. V., III, and Charles S. Bullock III. 2008. "Worth a Thousand Words? An Analysis of Georgia's Voter Identification Statute." *American Politics Research* 36(4): 555–579.

Hood, M. V., III, and Charles S. Bullock III. 2012. "Much Ado about Nothing? An Empirical Assessment of the Georgia Voter Identification Statute." *State Politics and Policy Quarterly* 12(4): 394–414.

Hood, M.V., III, Quentin Kidd, and Irwin L. Morris. 2012. *The Rational Southerner: Black Mobilization, Republican Growth, and the Partisan Transformation of the American South*. New York: Oxford University Press.

Hood, M. V., III, and Seth C. McKee. 2009. "Trying to Thread the Needle: The Effects of Redistricting in a Georgia Congressional District." *PS: Political Science and Politics* 42(4): 679–687.

Hood, M. V., III, and Seth C. McKee. 2010a. "What Made Carolina Blue? In-Migration and the 2008 North Carolina Presidential Vote." *American Politics Research* 38(2): 266–302.

Hood, M. V., III, and Seth C. McKee. 2010b. "Stranger Danger: Redistricting, Incumbent Recognition, and Vote Choice." *Social Science Quarterly* 91(2): 344–358.

Hood, M. V., III, and Seth C. McKee. 2013. "Unwelcome Constituents: Redistricting and Countervailing Partisan Tides." *State Politics and Policy Quarterly* 13(2): 203–224.

Huffmon, Scott H., H. Gibbs Knotts, and Seth C. McKee. 2017. "First in the South: The Importance of South Carolina in Presidential Politics." *Journal of Political Science* 45: 7–31.

Jacobson, Gary C. 1990. *The Electoral Origins of Divided Government: Competition in U.S. House Elections, 1946-1988*. Boulder, CO: Westview Press.

Jacobson, Gary C. 2003. "Terror, Terrain, and Turnout: Explaining the 2002 Midterm Elections." *Political Science Quarterly 118*(1): 1–22.

Jacobson, Gary C. 2004. "Partisan and Ideological Polarization in the California Electorate." *State Politics and Policy Quarterly 4*(2): 113–139.

Jacobson, Gary C. 2007a. *A Divider, Not a Uniter: George W. Bush and the American People.* New York: Pearson/Longman.

Jacobson, Gary C. 2007b. "Referendum: The 2006 Midterm Congressional Elections." *Political Science Quarterly 122*(1): 1–24.

Jacobson, Gary C. 2009a. *The Politics of Congressional Elections.* New York: Pearson/ Longman.

Jacobson, Gary C. 2009b. "The 2008 Presidential and Congressional Elections: Anti-Bush Referendum and Prospects for the Democratic Majority." *Political Science Quarterly 124*(1): 1–30.

Jacobson, Gary C. 2011. "The Republican Resurgence in 2010." *Political Science Quarterly 126*(1): 27–52.

Jacobson, Gary C. 2014. "Congress: Partisanship and Polarization." In *The Elections of 2012,* edited by Michael Nelson, 145–171. Washington, DC: CQ Press.

Jacobson, Gary C. 2015. "It's Nothing Personal: The Decline of the Incumbency Advantage in U.S. House Elections." *Journal of Politics 77*(3): 861–873.

Jacobson, Gary C., and Jamie L. Carson. 2016. *The Politics of Congressional Elections.* Lanham, MD: Rowman & Littlefield.

Jacobson, Gary C., and Samuel Kernell. 1983. *Strategy and Choice in Congressional Elections.* New Haven, CT: Yale University Press.

Justesen, Benjamin R. 2001. *George Henry White: An Even Chance in the Race of Life.* Baton Rouge: Louisiana State University Press.

Katz, Ellen D. 2013. "What Was Wrong with the Record?" *Election Law Journal: Rules, Politics, and Policy 12*(3): 329–331.

Kaufmann, Karen M. 2006. "The Gender Gap." *PS: Political Science and Politics 39*(3): 447–453.

Kaufmann, Karen M., and John R. Petrocik. 1999. "The Changing Politics of American Men: Understanding the Sources of the Gender Gap." *American Journal of Political Science 43*(3): 864–887.

Keith, Bruce E., David B. Magleby, Candice J. Nelson, Elizabeth Orr, Mark C. Westlye, and Raymond E. Wolfinger. 1992. *The Myth of the Independent Voter.* Berkeley: University of California Press.

Kernell, Samuel, Gary C. Jacobson, and Thad Kousser. 2009. *The Logic of American Politics.* Washington, DC: CQ Press.

Kernell, Samuel, Gary C. Jacobson, Thad Kousser, and Lynn Vavreck. 2015. *The Logic of American Politics.* Washington, DC: CQ Press.

Key, V. O., Jr. 1949. *Southern Politics in State and Nation.* New York: Alfred A. Knopf.

Key, V. O., Jr. 1955. "A Theory of Critical Elections." *Journal of Politics 17*(1): 3–18.

Key, V. O., Jr. 1959. "Secular Realignment and the Party System." *Journal of Politics 21*(2): 198–210.

Keyssar, Alexander. 2009. *The Right to Vote: The Contested History of Democracy in the United States*. New York: Basic Books.

Kleppner, Paul. 1982. *Who Voted? The Dynamics of Electoral Turnout, 1870–1980*. New York: Praeger.

Kousser, J. Morgan. 1974. *The Shaping of Southern Politics: Suffrage Restriction and the Establishment of the One-Party South, 1880–1910*. New Haven, CT: Yale University Press.

Kousser, J. Morgan. 1996. "Estimating the Partisan Consequences of Redistricting Plans—Simply." *Legislative Studies Quarterly 21*(4): 521–541.

Ladewig, Jeffrey W., and Matthew P. Jasinski. 2008. "On the Causes and Consequences of and Remedies for Interstate Malapportionment of the U.S. House of Representatives." *Perspectives on Politics 6*(1): 89–107.

Ladewig, Jeffrey W., and Seth C. McKee. 2014. "The Devil's in the Details: Evaluating the One Person, One Vote Principle in American Politics." *Politics and Governance 2*(1): 4–31.

Lamis, Alexander P. 1988. *The Two-Party South*. Oxford, UK: Oxford University Press.

Lamis, Alexander P., ed. 1999. *Southern Politics in the 1990s*. Baton Rouge: Louisiana State University Press.

Lau, Richard R., David J. Andersen, and David P. Redlawsk. 2008. "An Exploration of Correct Voting in Recent U.S. Presidential Elections." *American Journal of Political Science 52*(2): 395–411.

Lau, Richard R., and David P. Redlawsk. 1997. "Voting Correctly." *American Political Science Review 91*(3): 585–598.

Levendusky, Matthew. 2009. *The Partisan Sort: How Liberals Became Democrats and Conservatives Became Republicans*. Chicago: University of Chicago Press.

Levitt, Justin. 2012. "Election Deform: The Pursuit of Unwarranted Electoral Regulation." *Election Law Journal: Rules, Politics, and Policy 11*(1): 97–117.

Lewis, Jeffrey B., Brandon DeVine, Lincoln Pitcher, and Kenneth C. Martis. 2013. *Digital Boundary Definitions of United States Congressional Districts, 1789–2012*. http://cdmaps.polisci.ucla.edu.

Lublin, David. 1997. *The Paradox of Representation: Racial Gerrymandering and Minority Interests in Congress*. Princeton, NJ: Princeton University Press.

Lublin, David. 1999. "Racial Redistricting and African-American Representation: A Critique of 'Do Majority-Minority Districts Maximize Substantive Black Representation in Congress?'" *American Political Science Review 93*(1): 183–186.

Lublin, David. 2004. *The Republican South: Democratization and Partisan Change*. Princeton, NJ: Princeton University Press.

Lublin, David, Thomas L. Brunell, Bernard Grofman, and Lisa Handley. 2009. "Has the Voting Rights Act Outlived its Usefulness? In a Word, 'No.'" *Legislative Studies Quarterly 34*(4): 525–553.

Lublin, David, and D. Stephen Voss. 2000. "Racial Redistricting and Realignment in Southern State Legislatures." *American Journal of Political Science 44*(4): 792–810.

Lupia, Arthur. 1994. "Shortcuts Versus Encyclopedias: Information and Voting Behavior in California Insurance Reform Elections." *American Political Science Review 88*(1): 63–76.

Lupton, Robert N., William M. Myers, and Judd R. Thornton. 2015. "Political Sophistication and the Dimensionality of Elite and Mass Attitudes, 1980–2004." *Journal of Politics 77*(2): 368–380.

MacKuen, Michael B., Robert S. Erikson, and James A. Stimson. 1989. "Macropartisanship." *American Political Science Review 83*(4): 1125–1142.

MacManus, Susan A. 2011. "V. O. Key Jr.'s *Southern Politics*: Demographic Changes Will Transform the Region; In-migration and Generational Shifts Speed Up the Process." In *Unlocking V. O. Key Jr.: Southern Politics for the Twenty-First Century*, edited by Angie Maxwell and Todd G. Shields, 185–206. Fayetteville: University of Arkansas Press.

Matthews, Donald R., and James W. Prothro. 1966. *Negroes and the New Southern Politics*. New York: Harcourt, Brace & World.

Mayhew, David R. 1974. *Congress: The Electoral Connection*. New Haven, CT: Yale University Press.

Mayhew, David R. 2002. *Electoral Realignments: A Critique of an American Genre*. New Haven, CT: Yale University Press.

McDonald, Michael P. 2004. "A Comparative Analysis of Redistricting Institutions in the United States, 2001–02." *State Politics and Policy Quarterly 4*(4): 371–395.

McDonald, Michael P., and Samuel L. Popkin. 2001. "The Myth of the Vanishing Voter." *American Political Science Review 95*(4): 963–974.

McGann, Anthony J., Charles Anthony Smith, Michael Latner, and Alex Keena. 2016. *Gerrymandering in America: The House of Representatives, the Supreme Court, and the Future of Popular Sovereignty*. New York: Cambridge University Press.

McGinniss, Joe. 1969. *The Selling of the President 1968*. New York: Trident Press.

McGlennon, John J. 2014. "Virginia: Obama's Unexpected Firewall." In *Second Verse, Same as the First: The 2012 Presidential Election in the South*, edited by Scott E. Buchanan and Branwell DuBose Kapeluck, 213–231. Fayetteville: University of Arkansas Press.

McKee, Seth C. 2007. "Rural Voters in Presidential Elections, 1992–2004." *The Forum 5*(2), Article 2.

McKee, Seth C. 2008. "Redistricting and Familiarity with U.S. House Candidates." *American Politics Research 36*(6): 962–979.

McKee, Seth C. 2010. *Republican Ascendancy in Southern U.S. House Elections*. Boulder, CO: Westview Press.

McKee, Seth C. 2012a. "The Past, Present, and Future of Southern Politics." *Southern Cultures 18*(3): 95–117.

McKee, Seth C. 2012b. "Demanding Deliverance in Dixie: Race, The Civil Rights Movement, and Southern Politics." In *The Oxford Handbook of Southern Politics*, edited by Charles S. Bullock III and Mark J. Rozell, 153–178. New York: Oxford University Press.

McKee, Seth C. 2013. "Political Conditions and the Electoral Effects of Redistricting." *American Politics Research 41*(4): 623–650.

McKee, Seth C. 2015a. "Introduction: Redistricting in Florida." In *Jigsaw Puzzle Politics in the Sunshine State*, edited by Seth C. McKee, 1–14. Gainesville: University Press of Florida.

McKee, Seth C. 2015b. "Politics is Local: State Legislator Voting on Restrictive Voter Identification Legislation." *Research & Politics* July-September: 1–7.

McKee, Seth C. 2017. "Race and Subregional Persistence in a Changing South." *Southern Cultures 23*(2): 134–159.

McKee, Seth C., and Stephen C. Craig. 2017-18. "A Political History of Florida Elections, 1866–2016." *Florida Political Chronicle 25*(2): 93–122.

McKee, Seth C., and Danny Hayes. 2010. "The Transformation of Southern Presidential Primaries." In *Presidential Elections in the South: Putting 2008 in Political Context*, edited by

Branwell DuBose Kapeluck, Robert P. Steed, and Laurence W. Moreland, 39–69. Boulder, CO: Lynne Rienner.

McKee, Seth C., M. V. Hood III, and David Hill. 2012. "Achieving Validation: Barack Obama and Black Turnout in 2008." *State Politics and Policy Quarterly 12*(1): 3–22.

McKee, Seth C., and Mark J. McKenzie. 2013. "Analyzing Redistricting Outcomes." In *Rotten Boroughs, Political Thickets, and Legislative Donnybrooks: Redistricting in Texas*, edited by Gary A. Keith, 95–146. Austin: University of Texas Press.

McKee, Seth C., and Daron R. Shaw. 2003. "Suburban Voting in Presidential Elections." *Presidential Studies Quarterly 33*(1): 125–144.

McKee, Seth C., and Daron R. Shaw. 2005. "Redistricting in Texas: Institutionalizing Republican Ascendancy." In *Redistricting in the New Millennium*, edited by Peter F. Galderisi, 275–311. Lanham, MD: Lexington Books.

McKee, Seth C., and Joel Sievert. 2017. *Nationalization in U.S. Senate and Gubernatorial Elections*. Paper presented at the annual meeting of the Midwest Political Science Association, Chicago, IL, April 2017.

McKee, Seth C., and Melanie J. Springer. 2015. "A Tale of 'Two Souths': White Voting Behavior in Contemporary Southern Elections." *Social Science Quarterly 96*(2): 588–607.

McKee, Seth C., and Jeremy M. Teigen. 2009. "Probing the Reds and Blues: Sectionalism and Voter Location in the 2000 and 2004 U.S. Presidential Elections." *Political Geography 28*(8): 484–495.

McKee, Seth C., and Jeremy M. Teigen. 2016. "The New Blue: Northern In-Migration in Southern Presidential Elections." *PS: Political Science and Politics 49*(2): 228–233.

McKee, Seth C., Jeremy M. Teigen, and Mathieu Turgeon. 2006. "The Partisan Impact of Congressional Redistricting: The Case of Texas, 2001–2003." *Social Science Quarterly 87*(2): 308–317.

McKee, Seth C., and Antoine Yoshinaka. 2015. "Late to the Parade: Party Switchers in Contemporary US Southern Legislatures." *Party Politics 21*(6): 957–969.

McKee, Seth C., Antoine Yoshinaka, Keith E. Lee, Jr., and Richard McKenzie. 2016. "Party Switchers and Reelection: A Precinct-Level Analysis." *American Review of Politics 35*(2): 1–26.

Mellow, Nicole. 2008. *The State of Disunion: Regional Sources of Modern American Partisanship*. Baltimore, MD: Johns Hopkins University Press.

Miller, Gary, and Norman Schofield. 2008. "The Transformation of the Republican and Democratic Party Coalitions in the U.S." *Perspectives on Politics 6*(3): 433–450.

Miller, Warren E. 1991. "Party Identification, Realignment, and Party Voting: Back to the Basics." *American Political Science Review 85*(2): 557–568.

Monmonier, Mark S. 2001. *Bushmanders and Bullwinkles: How Politicians Manipulate Electronic Maps and Census Data to Win Elections*. Chicago: University of Chicago Press.

Monogan, James E., and Austin C. Doctor. 2017. "Immigration Politics and Partisan Realignment: California, Texas, and the 1994 Election." *State Politics and Policy Quarterly 17*(1): 3–23.

Moore, Donald Matthew. 2014. *The Economic Impact of South Carolina's 2012 Republican Presidential Primary*. Master's thesis, University of South Carolina.

Nadeau, Richard, and Harold W. Stanley. 1993. "Class Polarization in Partisanship among Native Southern Whites, 1952–90." *American Journal of Political Science 37*(3): 900–919.

Nelson, Michael. 2014. *Resilient America: Electing Nixon in 1968, Channeling Dissent, and Dividing Government*. Lawrence: University Press of Kansas.

Neustadt, Richard E. 1991. *Presidential Power and the Modern Presidents: The Politics of Leadership from Roosevelt to Reagan*. New York: Simon & Schuster.

Nicholson, Stephen P. 2005. "The Jeffords Switch and Public Support for Divided Government." *British Journal of Political Science* 35(2): 343–356.

Nixon, H. C. 1948. "The Southern Legislature and Legislation." *Journal of Politics* 10(2): 410–417.

Page, Benjamin I., and Robert Y. Shapiro. 1992. *The Rational Public: Fifty Years of Trends in Americans' Policy Preferences*. Chicago: University of Chicago Press.

Parent, Wayne, and Huey Perry. 2018. "Louisiana: Deep Red, Yet Unpredictable." In *The New Politics of the Old South*, edited by Charles S. Bullock III and Mark J. Rozell, 144–164. Lanham, MD: Rowman & Littlefield.

Parker, Frank R. 1990. *Black Votes Count: Political Empowerment in Mississippi After 1965*. Chapel Hill: University of North Carolina Press.

Parry, Janine A., and Jay Barth. 2014. "Arkansas: Another Anti-Obama Aftershock." In *Second Verse, Same as the First: The 2012 Presidential Election in the South*, edited by Scott E. Buchanan and Branwell DuBose Kapeluck, 123–141. Fayetteville: University of Arkansas Press.

Perlstein, Rick. 2012. "Exclusive: Lee Atwater's 1981 Interview on the Southern Strategy." *The Nation*, November 13. https://www.thenation.com/article/exclusive-lee-atwaters-infamous-1981-interview-southern-strategy (accessed September 27, 2017).

Pearson, Kathryn, and Eric Schickler. 2009. "The Transition to Democratic Leadership in a Polarized House." In *Congress Reconsidered*, edited by Lawrence C. Dodd and Bruce I. Oppenheimer, 165–188. Washington, DC: CQ Press.

Petrocik, John R. 1981. *Party Coalitions: Realignment and the Decline of the New Deal Party System*. Chicago: University of Chicago Press.

Petrocik, John R. 1987. "Realignment: New Party Coalitions and the Nationalization of the South." *Journal of Politics* 49(2): 347–375.

Petrocik, John R. 1996. "Issue Ownership in Presidential Elections, With a 1980 Case Study." *American Journal of Political Science* 40(3): 825–850.

Petrocik, John R., and Scott W. Desposato. 1998. "The Partisan Consequences of Majority-Minority Redistricting in the South, 1992 and 1994." *Journal of Politics* 60(3): 613–633.

Petrocik, John R., and Scott W. Desposato. 2004. "Incumbency and Short-Term Influences on Voters." *Political Research Quarterly* 57(3): 363–373.

Pfiffner, James P. 1988. "The President's Legislative Agenda." *Annals of the American Academy of Political and Social Science* 499(1): 22–35.

Phillips, Derek L., and Kevin J. Clancy. 1972. "Some Effects of 'Social Desirability' in Survey Studies." *American Journal of Sociology* 77(5): 921–940.

Phillips, Kevin P. 1969. *The Emerging Republican Majority*. New Rochelle, NY: Arlington House.

Pleasants, Julian M. 2004. *Hanging Chads: The Inside Story of the Presidential Recount in Florida*. New York: Palgrave Macmillan.

Polsby, Nelson W. 1968. "The Institutionalization of the U.S. House of Representatives." *American Political Science Review* 62(1): 144–168.

Popkin, Samuel L. 1991. *The Reasoning Voter: Communication and Persuasion in Presidential Campaigns*. Chicago: University of Chicago Press.

Prysby, Charles. 2014. "North Carolina: The Shifting Sands of Tar Heel Politics." In *The New Politics of the Old South*, edited by Charles S. Bullock III and Mark J. Rozell, 157–180. Lanham, MD: Rowman & Littlefield.

Prysby, Charles. 2017. "The Newest Southerners: Generational Differences in Electoral Behavior in the Contemporary South." *American Review of Politics* 36(1): 53–74.

Purdy, Jedediah. 2017. "North Carolina's Long Moral March and Its Lessons for the Trump Resistance." *The New Yorker*, February 17. http://www.newyorker.com/news/news-desk/north-carolinas-long-moral-march-and-its-lessons-for-the-trump-resistance (accessed August 2, 2017).

Reed, John Shelton. 1982. *One South: An Ethnic Approach to Regional Culture*. Baton Rouge: Louisiana State University Press.

Reiter, Howard L., and Jeffrey M. Stonecash. 2011. *Counter Realignment: Political Change in the Northeastern United States*. Cambridge, UK: Cambridge University Press.

Reston, James, Jr. 2016. "Clark and Pritchett: A Comparison of Two Notorious Southern Lawmen." *Southern Cultures* 22(4): 50–62.

Rintala, Marvin. 1968. "Political Generations." In *International Encyclopedia of the Social Sciences*. New York: Macmillan.

Rozell, Mark J. 2018. "Virginia: From Red to Blue?" In *The New Politics of the Old South*, edited by Charles S. Bullock III and Mark J. Rozell, 167–185. Lanham, MD: Rowman & Littlefield.

Rush, Mark. 2013. "*Shelby County v. Holder*: A Case of Judicial Hubris or a Clash of Ancient Principles?" *Election Law Journal: Rules, Politics, and Policy* 12(3): 322–323.

Russ, William A., Jr. 1934. "Registration and Disfranchisement Under Radical Reconstruction." *Mississippi Valley Historical Review* 21(2): 163–180.

Russ, William A., Jr. 1935. "Radical Disfranchisement in Georgia, 1867–71." *Georgia Historical Quarterly* 19(3): 175–209.

Scammon, Richard M., and Ben J. Wattenberg. 1970. *The Real Majority: An Extraordinary Examination of the American Electorate*. New York: Coward-McCann.

Schattschneider, E. E. 1960. *The Semisovereign People: A Realist's View of Democracy in America*. New York: Holt, Reinhart, and Winston.

Scher, Richard K. 1997. *Politics in the New South: Republicanism, Race and Leadership in the Twentieth Century*. Armonk, NY: M. E. Sharpe.

Schlesinger, Joseph A. 1966. *Ambition and Politics: Political Careers in the United States*. Chicago: University of Chicago Press.

Shafer, Byron E. 2016. *The American Political Pattern: Stability and Change, 1932–2016*. Lawrence: University Press of Kansas.

Shafer, Byron E., and Richard G. C. Johnston. 2001. "The Transformation of Southern Politics Revisited: The House of Representatives as a Window." *British Journal of Political Science* 31(4): 601–625.

Shafer, Byron E., and Richard Johnston. 2006. *The End of Southern Exceptionalism: Class, Race, and Partisan Change in the Postwar South*. Cambridge, MA: Harvard University Press.

Sides, John, Daron Shaw, Matt Grossmann, and Keena Lipsitz. 2015. *Campaigns and Elections: Rules, Reality, Strategy, Choice*. New York: W. W. Norton and Company.

Silver, James W. 2012. *Mississippi: The Closed Society*. Jackson: University Press of Mississippi.

Skowronek, Stephen. 2011. *Presidential Leadership in Political Time: Reprise and Reappraisal*. Lawrence: University Press of Kansas.

Stanley, Harold W. 1988. "Southern Partisan Changes: Dealignment, Realignment or Both?" *Journal of Politics 50*(1): 64–88.

Stanley, Harold W. 2010. "The Latino Vote in 2008." In *Presidential Elections in the South: Putting 2008 in Political Context*, edited by Branwell DuBose Kapeluck, Robert P. Steed, and Laurence W. Moreland, 137–151. Boulder, CO: Lynne Rienner.

Steed, Robert P., Laurence W. Moreland, and Tod A. Baker, eds. 1990. *The Disappearing South? Studies in Regional Change and Continuity*. Tuscaloosa: University of Alabama Press.

Stephanopoulos, Nicholas O., and Eric M. McGhee. 2015. "Partisan Gerrymandering and the Efficiency Gap." *University of Chicago Law Review 82*(2): 831–900.

Stimson, James A. 2004. *Tides of Consent: How Public Opinion Shapes American Politics*. Cambridge, UK: Cambridge University Press.

Stonecash, Jeffrey M. 2008. *Reassessing the Incumbency Effect*. New York: Cambridge University Press.

Sundquist, James L. 1983. *Dynamics of the Party System: Alignment and Realignment of Political Parties in the United States*. Washington, DC: Brookings Institution Press.

Theriault, Sean M. 2008. *Party Polarization in Congress*. Cambridge, UK: Cambridge University Press.

Theriault, Sean M., and David W. Rohde. 2011. "The Gingrich Senators and Party Polarization in the U.S. Senate." *Journal of Politics 73*(4): 1011–1024.

Timpone, Richard J. 1995. "Mass Mobilization or Government Intervention? The Growth of Black Registration in the South." *Journal of Politics 57*(2): 425–442.

Traugott, Michael W., Santa Traugott, and Stanley Presser. 1992. "Revalidation of Self-Reported Vote." ANES Technical Report Series, No. nes010160.

Underhill, Wendy. 2017. "Voter Identification Requirements/Voter ID Laws." *National Conference of State Legislatures*, June 5. http://www.ncsl.org/research/elections-and-campaigns/voter-id.aspx (accessed July 2, 2017).

Valentino, Nicholas A., and Fabian G. Neuner. 2017. "Why the Sky Didn't Fall: Mobilizing Anger in Reaction to Voter ID Laws." *Political Psychology 38*(2): 331–350.

Valentino, Nicholas A., Fabian G. Neuner, and L. Matthew Vandenbroek. Forthcoming. "The Changing Norms of Racial Political Rhetoric and the End of Racial Priming." *Journal of Politics*. Ahead of Print: https://www.journals.uchicago.edu/doi/full/10.1086/694845

Valentino, Nicholas A., and David O. Sears. 2005. "Old Times There Are Not Forgotten: Race and Partisan Realignment in the Contemporary South." *American Journal of Political Science 49*(3): 672–688.

Verba, Sidney, and Norman H. Nie. 1987. *Participation in America: Political Democracy and Social Equality*. Chicago: University of Chicago Press.

von Spakovsky, Hans A. 2012. "Protecting the Integrity of the Election Process." *Election Law Journal: Rules, Politics, and Policy 11*(1): 90–96.

Voss, D. Stephen, and David Lublin. 2001. "Black Incumbents, White Districts: An Appraisal of the 1996 Congressional Elections." *American Politics Research 29*(2): 141–182.

Wand, Jonathan N., Kenneth W. Shotts, Jasjeet S. Sekhon, Walter R. Mebane, Jr., Michael C. Herron, and Henry E. Brady. 2001. "The Butterfly Did It: The Aberrant Vote for Buchanan in Palm Beach County, Florida." *American Political Science Review 95*(4): 793–810.

Wattenberg, Martin P. 1985. *The Decline of American Political Parties, 1952–1980.* Cambridge: Harvard University Press.

Weigel, David. 2017. "ACLU Investing Millions of Dollars in Florida to Restore Ex-Felons' Voting Rights." *Washington Post*, July 2017. https://www.washingtonpost.com/news/ powerpost/wp/2017/07/31/aclu-investing-millions-in-florida-to-restore-felons-voting-rights/?utm_term=.ff177531ee32 (accessed August 2, 2017).

Whalen, Charles, and Barbara Whalen. 1985. *The Longest Debate: A Legislative History of the 1964 Civil Rights Act.* Cabin John, MD: Seven Locks Press.

White, Steven. 2014. "The Heterogeneity of Southern White Distinctiveness." *American Politics Research 42*(4):551–78.

Wilcox, Clyde, and Carin Robinson. 2011. *Onward Christian Soldiers? The Religious Right in American Politics.* Boulder, CO: Westview Press.

Wilson, David C., and Paul R. Brewer. 2013. "The Foundations of Public Opinion on Voter ID Laws: Political Predispositions, Racial Resentment, and Information Effects." *Public Opinion Quarterly 77*(4): 962–984.

Wines, Michael, and Alan Blinder. 2016. "Federal Appeals Court Strikes Down North Carolina Voter ID Requirement." *New York Times*, July 29. https://www.nytimes.com/ 2016/07/30/us/federal-appeals-court-strikes-down-north-carolina-voter-id-provision .html (accessed August 2, 2017).

Wolfinger, Raymond E., and Steven J. Rosenstone. 1980. *Who Votes?* New Haven, CT: Yale University Press.

Woodman, Spencer. 2016. "How White Georgia Republicans are Derailing an African-American Candidate." *New Republic*, April 5. https://newrepublic.com/article/132398/white-georgia-republicans-derailing-african-american-candidate (accessed August 2, 2017).

Woodward, C. Vann. 1960. *The Burden of Southern History.* Baton Rouge: Louisiana State University Press.

Woodward, C. Vann. 2002. *The Strange Career of Jim Crow.* Oxford, UK: Oxford University Press.

Wright, Gavin. 2013. *Sharing the Prize: The Economics of the Civil Rights Revolution in the American South.* Cambridge, MA: Belknap Press of Harvard University Press.

Yoshinaka, Antoine. 2012. "Party Building in the South through Conversion." In *The Oxford Handbook of Southern Politics*, edited by Charles S. Bullock III and Mark J. Rozell, 355–381. New York: Oxford University Press.

Yoshinaka, Antoine. 2016. *Crossing the Aisle: Party Switching by U.S. Legislators in the Postwar Era.* New York: Cambridge University Press.

Yoshinaka, Antoine, and Christian R. Grose. 2005. "Partisan Politics and Electoral Design: The Enfranchisement of Felons and Ex-Felons in the United States, 1960–99." *State and Local Government Review 37*(1): 49–60.

Yoshinaka, Antoine, and Seth C. McKee. 2017. "Short-Term Pain for Long-Term Gain: The Logic of Legislative Party Switching in the Contemporary American South." Manuscript.

Zaller, John R. 1992. *The Nature and Origins of Mass Opinion.* Cambridge, UK: Cambridge University Press.

NOTES

Preface

1. Lest the reader be confused, the Mason-Dixon Line is the border dividing Pennsylvania and Maryland, which are (at least according to this author) two northern states. Nonetheless, it is common parlance to speak of the South when referring to the area found below this boundary. A more accurate but similarly simple geographic descriptor of the region is captured by the phrase "south of the Potomac," the river separating Virginia and Maryland. The state-based definition of the American South is provided in chapter 2.

Chapter 1

1. In both of his articles explaining electoral realignment (Key 1955, 1959), Key was examining presidential voting data on New England townships leading up to the 1932 election. At first Key thought the evidence showed a sharp reversal (a critical election) in which certain townships altered their voting behavior in favor of the opposite party (resembling a widening scissor-like pattern), but the longer trend toward the other party became the emphasis for stressing a more gradual pattern of realignment that might show up more prominently in a single election. Interestingly, even though 1932 is widely considered a critical election, the strong reversal in voting patterns for many of these New England townships shows up in 1928, lending support to a lengthier period of partisan change. Because Key lacked individual-level survey data, he was compelled to make some plausible inferences about voting behavior. A common pattern emerged throughout his analysis: rural townships became increasingly Republican in presidential elections, whereas urban townships were becoming more Democratic in presidential voting. These differences were rooted in the compositional profiles of rural and urban New England electorates. Over time, rural townships had become more native, with more descendants of northern European stock, Protestants, and voters supportive of the GOP. By comparison, urban townships had become increasingly more foreign-born migration destinations, with more descendants of eastern European stock, Catholics, and voters supportive of the Democratic Party.

Chapter 2

1. The Democratic Party was split by the presence of a northern (Douglas-Johnson) and southern (Breckinridge-Lane) presidential ticket. Further, the Constitutional Union ticket (Bell-Everett) prevailed in Kentucky, Tennessee, and Virginia. The southern Democrats were victorious in the rest of the South, while Douglas carried Missouri and New Jersey and the rest of the North went to Lincoln. The breakdown of the 1860 presidential vote in the Electoral College was as follows: Lincoln 180 (49.5 percent); Breckenridge 72 (23.8 percent); Bell 39 (12.9 percent); and Douglas 12 (4.0 percent). These data were retrieved from Dave Leip's *Atlas of U.S. Presidential Elections* (http://uselectionatlas.org/RESULTS/).
2. Historical party divisions in the U.S. House of Representatives can be found here: http://history.house.gov/Institution/Party-Divisions/Party-Divisions/.

3. Historical party divisions in the U.S. Senate can be found here: http://www.senate.gov/history/partydiv.htm.

4. As in other reviews of southern politics, in this study the South is divided into two common subregions: the Deep and Peripheral/Rim South. The Deep South consists of Alabama, Georgia, Louisiana, Mississippi, and South Carolina. The Peripheral South includes Arkansas, Florida, North Carolina, Tennessee, Texas, and Virginia. Because more of the black belt region is located in the Deep South, and hence the percentage of African Americans is higher there, the greater militancy and racial conservatism of southern whites vis-à-vis their Peripheral South counterparts persists to this day. A more systematic accounting of this subregional delineation will be made in chapter 8.

5. To be clear, although Key (1949) acknowledged their political skill, he bemoaned the political power of the black-belt whites because their success was responsible for the perpetuation of a notably undemocratic one-party Democratic South that oppressed almost the entirety of the black population and a large share of poor whites from the late 1800s until the 1960s.

6. The Republican Party supplanted the Whig Party, making it the only instance in American history when a third party managed to take the place of one of the major parties. Unlike the GOP, the Whig Party had a national presence, and many southern black-belt whites were affiliated with it before uniting under the Democratic banner.

7. By trading off admission to the United States such that a slave state must be paired with a free state, the Missouri Compromise prolonged a political stalemate in the U.S. Senate, ensuring that southern senators had enough votes to block any legislation that might undermine slavery. In 1820, the slave state of Missouri entered the Union with the free state of Maine. Interestingly, although almost the entire state of Missouri lay above the 36^0 30′ latitude line, under the compromise, slavery was only allowed for territories organized below.

8. A full accounting of the Reconstruction Acts can be found online at the North Carolina American Republic Resource Library (www.ncrepublic.org/lib_reconstruction.php#4).

9. Here is the text of congressional action dismantling Section 3 of the Fourteenth Amendment:

> Be it enacted by the Senate and House of Representatives of the United States of America in Congress assembled (two-thirds of each house concurring therein), That all political disabilities imposed by the third section of the fourteenth article of amendments of the Constitution of the United States are hereby removed from all persons whomsoever, except Senators and Representatives of the thirty-sixth and thirty-seventh Congresses, officers in the judicial, military, and naval service of the United States, heads of departments, and foreign ministers of the United States. APPROVED, May, 1872.

> Document was accessed from the Cornell Law School Legal Information Institute (www.law.cornell.edu).

10. Republicans held onto a majority of Senate seats; their numbers reduced from 47 to 46. Nonetheless, Democrats did make gains between 1872 and 1874, going from 19 to 28 seats, or 37 percent of the Senate delegation (a total of 76 seats). Recall that Senators were not popularly elected until passage of the Seventeenth Amendment in 1913.

11. Perhaps the most infamous, and indisputably the most deadly, act of terror occurred in Colfax, Louisiana, in 1873. Armed Louisiana blacks chose to take a stand against white Redeemer violence. According to Foner (1988, 437), "the Colfax massacre taught many lessons, including the lengths to which some opponents of Reconstruction would go to regain their accustomed authority." Quoting African American John G. Lewis, a "Louisiana black teacher and legislator":

They attempted [armed self-defense] in Colfax. The result was that on Easter Sunday of 1873, when the sun went down that night, it went down on the corpses of two hundred and eighty negroes.

12. To be sure, in many northern cities with a strong union presence, blacks were denied employment (Woodward 2002).
13. These numbers slightly understate the Populist presence in Congress because there were also a handful of similarly aligned third-party members who served under the Silver Party or the fusion Silver Republican label.

Chapter 3

1. Using the case of Texas, here is what Key said:

    By the time the Texas poll tax became effective not only had Negroes been disfranchised but a substantial proportion of the white population had begun to stay away from the polls. Party conflict had been repressed; Populist leaders had almost completely given up the battle. Conservative Democratic forces and whites of the black-belt counties had joined forces to kill off dissent. Should the poll tax be held responsible for low levels of voting interest consistently maintained since 1904? Apparently the poll tax merely reflected a fait accompli; opposition had been discouraged and suppressed. The solidification of economic power, characteristic of the one-party system, had been accomplished and the electoral abdication of a substantial part of the white population signed and sealed. (1949, 535)

2. This section makes extensive reference to J. Morgan Kousser's classic work, *The Shaping of Southern Politics: Suffrage Restriction and the Establishment of the One-Party South, 1880–1910* (1974).
3. Elaborating on the point, Key (1949, 560) explained,

    In the South registration assumes special importance because of the peculiar regional suffrage qualifications. Registration authorities determine whether applicants meet literacy and understanding tests and thus have functioned as the principal governmental agency for Negro disfranchisement.

4. Here is Key's (1949, 16) description of the South's faction-laden one-party political system:

    unlike most of the rest of the democratic world, [the South] really has no political parties . . . A single party . . . dominates the South, but in reality the South has been Democratic only for external purposes, that is, presidential and congressional elections. The one-party system is purely an arrangement for national affairs. The legend prevails that within the Democratic party in the southern states factional groups are the equivalent of political parties elsewhere. In fact, the Democratic party in most states of the South is merely a holding-company for a congeries of transient squabbling factions, most of which fail by far to meet the standards of permanence, cohesiveness, and responsibility that characterize the political party.

5. As Key (1949, 620) noted, Virginia had a white primary law on its books but a lower federal court struck it down in *West v. Bliley* (1929). In some settings a handful of blacks might be allowed to vote in the Democratic Primary, but their presence amounted to a miniscule share of the electorate.
6. Instead of being subjugated to the Jim Crow system, thousands of blacks left the South to find work in northern states that provided greater economic and political freedom. This "Great Migration" of southern blacks to northern cities, which occurred from the end of

World War I and lasted into the 1960s, had the effect of making several non-southern states political battlegrounds in presidential elections. According to Woodward (2002, 128), "In the decade of the 'forties alone the number of Negroes living outside the South jumped from 2,360,000 to 4,600,000, an increase of nearly 100 per cent."

7. Here is the breakdown of the 1948 popular vote for president: 49.55 percent for Democrat Truman (24,179,347); 45.07 percent for Republican Dewey (21,991,292); 2.41 percent for Dixiecrat Thurmond (1,175,946). The remainder of the vote was cast for Progressive Henry Wallace and Socialist Norman Thomas. Data are from Dave *Leip's Atlas of U.S. Presidential Elections*.

Chapter 4

1. The NAACP (National Association for the Advancement of Colored People), founded in 1909, is the oldest and most successful organization advocating for civil rights. Prior to *Brown*, the NAACP's primary legal strategy consisted of exposing the absence of equality in the separation of the races in institutions of higher learning. For instance, because there was not an equivalent black graduate school in Texas and Oklahoma, the NAACP was successful in helping to desegregate graduate schools in these states in the cases of *Sweatt v. Painter* (1950) and *McLaurin v. Oklahoma* (1950). What made the *Brown* decision different is that it overturned the separate but equal precedent established in *Plessy*. Thus, the NAACP's argument in favor of desegregation, which the Court adopted, was now based on the principle that separate was inherently unequal.

2. The ANES has been surveying the American electorate since 1948. In 1952 the ANES began including a state indicator, which allows for dividing the electorate into the South and non-South. The ANES was run consecutively for midterm and presidential years from 1952 to 2004. Since 2004, due to a decline in funding, the ANES has been only conducted regularly in presidential years.

3. According to southern subregion, in 1962, 64 percent of Peripheral South whites opposed federally imposed school integration and an astounding 94 percent of Deep South whites opposed such an action. In 1972, the number of white southerners expressing disagreement with federal intervention to promote school integration by subregion was 62 percent of Rim South whites and 69 percent of Deep South whites (see Table 7.2, p. 163 in McKee 2012b).

4. For instance, as the SNCC dissolved, some of its members would go on to create and lead the Black Panthers, an openly militant organization not afraid to engage in violence to push their "Black Power" agenda. Unlike the primary civil rights organizations mentioned above, the Black Panthers were headquartered outside the South (in Oakland, California) and pressed an aggressive agenda in other sections of the United States.

5. In the period of white massive resistance, Ms. Autherine Lucy attempted to integrate the University of Alabama in 1956—the effort failed and sparked a violent reaction that was greatly overshadowed by the Ole Miss riot in 1962 and Alabama Governor Wallace's 1963 stand in the schoolhouse door (Woodward 2002).

6. In this discussion, the author analyzed the ANES data of interest. In the case of party identification, the ANES uses a seven-point scale with the following responses from left to right: 1 = Strong Democrat, 2 = Not very strong (weak) Democrat, 3 = Independent-leaning Democrat, 4 = Independent, 5 = Independent-leaning Republican, 6 = Weak Republican, 7 = Strong Republican. In the data shown in the chapter, following common practice, and because independent leaners behave similarly to weak partisans (Keith et al. 1992), they are included as partisans in reporting the percentages identifying as Democrats, Republicans, and Independents.

7. Lest the reader be uncertain, Goldwater had a much more substantial impact on the voting behavior of Deep South whites, who immediately responded to the racially conservative appeals of the Republican presidential standard bearer. For instance, not since northern-enforced military Reconstruction did a Republican nominee have a chance of winning Mississippi's electoral votes, but in 1964, fully 87 percent of the state's popular vote went to Goldwater (a vote cast almost entirely by whites). Likewise, in 1962, under U.S. House contests that were held at large (all statewide races as opposed to separate district-based elections) in Alabama, Democrats won all eight of the state's seats. But after the 1964 election, Goldwater's coattails were significant, with the Alabama delegation consisting of three Democrats and five Republicans (who all ran in district-based contests). As a final example, Goldwater's coattails helped elect Republican Howard "Bo" Callaway to a Georgia congressional district, and two years later Callaway won a plurality of the popular vote in the 1966 Georgia gubernatorial election, but he was denied the office because the Democratic-controlled legislature selected the avowed racist Democrat Lester Maddox as the next governor, an authority the Georgia General Assembly had if the top candidate fell short of capturing a popular vote majority (see Bullock and Hood 2015; Hayes and McKee 2004).
8. As the Georgia County Clerks Association (GCCA) website (http://georgiacca.com) explains,

    > There were 410 County unit votes. The eight most populous counties had six unit votes each (a total of 48), the 30 next most populous counties had four votes each (a total of 120) and the remaining 121 counties had two votes each (a total of 242). The counties with two votes therefore had a majority of the votes, despite only making up one-third of the population in 1962 when the system was abolished by the courts.

9. The entirety of LBJ's address can be found at http://lbjlib.utexas.edu.
10. One Ford elector cast his presidential vote for Ronald Reagan and vice presidential vote for Robert Dole (http://uselectionatlas.org/RESULTS/).
11. Choosing this location was viewed as a blatant invocation of the southern strategy, and it generated considerable media controversy because Philadelphia, Mississippi, was where the civil rights workers James Chaney, Andrew Goodman, and Michael Schwerner were abducted and murdered during the 1964 Freedom Summer.
12. Independent John Anderson failed to garner a single EC vote, but he managed to take 6.6 percent of the popular presidential vote.
13. A Dukakis elector in West Virginia cast her presidential vote for Lloyd Bentsen and vice presidential vote for Michael Dukakis (http://uselectionatlas.org/RESULTS/).
14. In 1988, South Carolina Republicans conducted a primary on March 5, whereas South Carolina Democrats held a caucus on March 12 (http://frontloading.blogspot.com/2009/02/1988-presidential-primary-calendar.html). In 1980, South Carolina Republicans held their inaugural "First in the South" presidential primary. Thanks to the effort and leadership of the notorious and legendary campaign operative Lee Atwater (a native South Carolinian) and Republican Governor James B. Edwards (1975–1979), the first Republican governor of South Carolina since the Reconstruction period, the South Carolina GOP managed to establish the Palmetto State as the first to hold its Republican primary in the South, although Georgia did go first in 1992 (see Huffmon, Knotts, and McKee 2017; Moore 2014). Since 2004, it has also been the case that South Carolina Democrats are the first to hold their party's presidential preference primary in the southern states.

Chapter 5

1. In 2013, in the Alabama case of *Shelby County v. Holder*, the U.S. Supreme Court essentially rendered inoperable the Section 5 preclearance provision of the VRA because the formulas that were established for determining evidence of minority

vote dilution in Section 4 of the VRA were based on data from the 1960s and were therefore obsolete. In the absence of preclearance enforcement and with southern Republicans in charge of most state and local jurisdictions (outside of heavily black settings), expect to see the GOP favor the large concentration of minority voters into a small number of districts so that the surrounding majority white districts can be carried by Republicans.

2. Leading up to the 1992 elections, there were Republican governors in Alabama, Mississippi, North Carolina, and South Carolina. The presence of a Republican executive in the Tar Heel State did not serve as an impediment to the plans of North Carolina legislators because the governor does not possess veto power with regard to redistricting legislation.

3. Playing off the term *gerrymander*, which simply means to draw district boundaries to further a political objective, Grofman and Brunell (2005) coined the term *dummymander* to account for the distinct species of southern Democratic-drawn district boundaries that directly contributed to an increase in Republican electoral victories.

4. It is also the case that because redrawn constituents are less familiar with the incumbent running in their district (McKee 2008), they are more inclined to abstain from voting for that particular contest (Hayes and McKee 2009).

5. Pursuant to court order, Florida, North Carolina, and Virginia all redrew their congressional boundaries prior to the 2016 elections. Unlike in North Carolina, where the districts were redrawn but the Republican gerrymander (see chapter 10) essentially remained intact, at least based on the election returns (maintaining a 10 to 3 Republican majority in the North Carolina U.S. House delegation), compared to the existing plans, the Florida and Virginia maps were drawn to be more favorable to the Democrats (in 2016, Democrats netted one seat apiece in these states, the only Democratic gains in the South), and this was accomplished by reducing minority populations in some districts. In Florida, this actually resulted in an increase in the number of majority white districts from 18 to 20 (out of 27 total). Demographic reports of the redrawn congressional boundaries in Florida and Virginia can be found at these websites: https://www.flsenate.gov/Session/Redistricting; http://redistricting.dls.virginia.gov/2010/RedistrictingPlans.aspx. All of the voting age population (VAP) data discussed in this section come from the 2010 U.S. Census.

6. In case the student is wondering about the one Asian Republican who shows up in Table 5.2 in 2008, this was a remarkable occurrence. Heading into the 2008 election, the veteran black incumbent Democrat William Jefferson of the New Orleans–based black majority District 2 (61 percent black VAP) was in deep trouble for bribery and was indicted before the general election. In one of the most incredible upsets in the history of congressional elections, Joseph Cao, a Vietnamese immigrant and Republican, defeated a black incumbent Democrat in a majority black district by a margin of 1,814 votes (see Barone and Cohen 2009, 658–660). In 2010, Cao was easily defeated in his reelection bid by a quality African American Democratic challenger, Cedric Richmond, a former Louisiana state representative. Although the Louisiana case above is perhaps unrivaled, one of the twenty African American Democrats in the 2016 southern congressional delegation represents a district with a majority Latino VAP: Marc Veasey of Texas District 33, which has a 60 percent Latino VAP and a 17 percent black VAP. Veasey was first elected to Congress in 2012.

7. In 2004 in Georgia, there was a Democratic seat pickup, but it was canceled out by a Republican seat pickup in Louisiana (see Table 5.4). This brief account of the 2004 Texas congressional redistricting is too short to do justice to such an intriguing case study of partisan politics; for additional information and analysis, see the works by Bickerstaff (2007), Gaddie (2004), McKee and McKenzie (2013), McKee and Shaw (2005), and McKee, Teigen, and Turgeon (2006).

8. After 1996, from 1998 through 2002, among the twenty-three newly elected southern Republicans, nineteen had previously held elective office (83 percent), which clearly speaks to a more normal pattern of politics in which fewer candidates are newly elected and among them, most have previous officeholding experience. Only one of these twenty-three newly elected Republicans was victorious outside of an open-seat district. In 2002, former Florida state senator Ginny Brown-Waite defeated the Democratic incumbent Karen Thurman in Florida District 5, which contained a 53 percent redrawn voting age population (McKee 2015a, 7) and the district's share of the two-party Republican presidential vote (in the 2000 election) went from 48 percent in 2000 to 54 percent in the redrawn district in 2002. Lest the student get the wrong idea, even in these rare periods of electoral upheaval (i.e., 1992–1996 in southern U.S. House elections), all else equal, candidates with previous elective office-holding experience perform better at the ballot box, but there just happens to be fewer of them compared to the number of political amateurs. Within the population of political amateurs, as a group they perform relatively better if they are aligned with the rising party in a period of electoral upheaval because voters are more inclined to support their party.

9. In the history of the southern United States, there has never been an African American Democratic U.S. Senator. With regard to scandal, it took a scandal for a Democrat (Doug Jones) to wrest back an Alabama Senate seat in the 2017 special election. There is almost no doubt that if the Republican nominee Roy Moore had not been mired in allegations of preying on teenaged girls while in his thirties, he would have won the 2017 special Senate election. Alabama is currently the most electorally Republican state in the South (see chapter 12).

10. Speaking to the importance of running under a major party label (a lesson that Bernie Sanders and Donald Trump both understood in 2016), Perot won 19 percent of the national popular vote in 1992 and yet failed to win a single EC vote because he was not the popular vote winner in any of the fifty states.

11. Although most southern states impose a consecutive two-term limit, when this limit is reached, unlike the presidency, after sitting out a term, a former governor can serve again (e.g., North Carolina Democratic Governor James B. Hunt served from 1976 to 1984 and then from 1992 to 2000). As Earl and Merle Black (1987, 285) point out, because of the importance of the incumbency advantage, southern Democrats changed the rules so that "between 1966 and 1984 nine southern states revised their constitutions to permit governors to serve a second consecutive four-year term."

12. David Vitter was a deeply flawed, disliked candidate, with few friends and plenty of Republican opponents who openly endorsed the Democrat Edwards. Senator Vitter was caught in the 2007 "D.C. Madam" scandal and publicly apologized for his actions (with his wife present). Edwards ran a scathing commercial against Vitter that became known as the "Prostitutes over Patriots" ad (https://www.youtube.com/watch?v=RpzMQ-z-QsY). I thank Joshua Stockley (University of Louisiana Monroe) for explaining to me just how poor a candidate Senator Vitter was by the time of the 2015 gubernatorial election.

13. Unlike its southern neighbors, Texas does have a statewide elective position (railroad commissioner) with staggered six-year terms, so that only one of these three positions is up for election every two years. All of the other southern statewide elective positions have four-year terms.

Chapter 6

1. Here is just one notable quote in which Beck (1977, 487) contends that there is no reason to anticipate a realignment of white southerners to the GOP:

> By 1972, the Postwar Generation was less Democratic than Independent—a fact which portends a volatile future for southern politics. That only 13 per cent of this generation was Republican by 1972, furthermore, implies that GOP domination of the region is a highly unlikely prospect.

2. Georgia was the only southern state that allowed 18-year-olds to vote (setting this voting age in 1943) prior to passage of the Twenty-sixth Amendment in 1971, which lowered the voting age (set in most states at 21) to a minimum age of 18.

3. For more details on the Youth-Parent Socialization Panel Study, see the study description on the website provided by the Inter-university Consortium for Political and Social Research (ICPSR): http://www.icpsr.umich.edu/icpsrweb/ICPSR/studies/4037.

4. According to Green, Palmquist, and Schickler (2002, 140), "Party attachments tend to be stable because the social group imagery associated with the parties tends to change slowly over time." With this in mind, the massive influx of enfranchised black southerners after passage of the VRA in 1965 constituted a direct threat to white southerners because these African Americans overwhelmingly identified with the Democratic Party.

Chapter 7

1. Converse (1964) did, however, point out that among the mass electorate exists various so-called issue publics, which are in fact very knowledgeable about certain political issues because they are directly affected with respect to their employment. For instance, in *Who Votes?*, authors Raymond E. Wolfinger and Steven J. Rosenstone (1980) make a point of demonstrating that farmers, as a group, vote at a surprisingly high rate given their relatively low socioeconomic status because their livelihoods are intimately tied to federally constructed and enforced farm policies.

Chapter 8

1. Compliance with the equal population ruling swiftly increased Republican representation in Florida state legislative districts. Before reapportionment, in 1964, Florida Republicans were 8.9 percent of the state house and 4.5 percent of the state senate. After reapportionment and redistricting was implemented three years later, Florida Republicans comprised 32.8 percent of the state house and 41.7 percent of the state senate (McKee 2015a, 2).

2. It should be pointed out that to this day, across states with more than one congressional district there are great disparities in district populations (Ladewig and Jasinski 2008), and there are currently seven states whose populations are relatively so small that they contain only one congressional district, which is of course the entire state (Alaska, Delaware, Montana, North Dakota, South Dakota, Vermont, and Wyoming).

3. According to the 2010 Census, the entire United States population was 81 percent urban, while the non-South population was 83 percent urban.

4. The county level 2010 Census data show 140 persons per square mile of land area in the Deep South versus 275 persons per square mile of land area in the Peripheral South (226 persons per square mile of land area South-wide).

5. Based on the 2010 Census, the percentage black for each Deep South state and Rim South state was as follows: AL = 26, GA = 30, LA = 32, MS = 37, SC = 28 (Deep South); and AR = 15, FL = 16, NC = 21, TN = 17, TX = 12, VA = 19 (Rim South).

6. In terms of population size, the Rim South has grown at a much greater clip. In 1960, the Deep South U.S. House delegation had 39 Representatives and in 2016 it had 38 (a 2.6 percent decline). In 1960, the Rim South U.S. House delegation had 67 Representatives and in 2016 it had 100 (a 49 percent increase).

7. In case the student is wondering why there is no comparable subregional analysis of black voting behavior, with respect to this racial group's partisan preferences, their one-sided support for Democratic candidates is such that "there are so few 'deviant' black southerners that exploration of differences among blacks would not take us far" (Black and Black 1987, 272).

8. Pooling the ANES data by decade (1952–1960, 1962–1970, etc.) results in an average sample size of 2,455 respondents, while the average Pew survey for each year (from 2002 to 2016) includes 2,554 respondents.

9. In the 2016 national exit poll of 24,558 respondents, the Republican Trump's vote share by location was as follows: urban = 34 percent, suburban = 49 percent, and rural = 61 percent (the denominator for these GOP percentages include voters who backed the Democrat Clinton and respondents who declined to answer the question or voted for another presidential candidate).

10. Four states' electoral votes in 1876 were called into question: Florida, Louisiana, Oregon, and South Carolina. To consummate the grand bargain officially ending military Reconstruction of the South in exchange for declaring a Republican presidential victory, all four of these states had to be declared GOP wins.

11. Before 1964, a majority of the Mississippi popular presidential vote last favored a Republican in 1872 (Union Civil War General Ulysses Grant).

12. As a former resident of St. Petersburg, FL, I should note that the western terminus of Interstate-4 is in Tampa, but St. Petersburg (on the western side of Tampa Bay) is considered part of the I-4 corridor in presidential politics because Pinellas County (St. Petersburg) is one of the most presidentially competitive counties in the Sunshine State. For instance, in 2016, four counties flipped in favor of Trump, and Pinellas was one of them, and its two-party split mirrored the statewide split of 51 to 49 percent Republican.

Chapter 9

1. In fact, Key (1949) did not foresee a 1960s civil rights movement, and despite Black (2004, 1010) quoting Key (1955, 165) in observing that "southern Democratic party unity 'probably could not survive another New Deal,'" it is not exactly clear what the dissolution of the southern Democracy would ultimately lead to. Of course, thanks to hindsight, instead of the Democratic Party being opposed by a more politically inclusive and moderate Republican opposition, an antithetical result transpired as white conservatives fled their native party and became the leaders of the perennially moribund but eventually ascending GOP.

2. There is no state indicator for the 1954 American National Election Study (ANES), and hence it is not possible to analyze the segment of southern respondents.

3. This chapter relies heavily on the simple, elegant, and vastly insightful work of Merle Black (2004) in his *Journal of Politics* article ("The Transformation of the Southern Democratic Party") that served as the basis of his Southern Political Science Association Presidential Address. Black focused specifically on changes to the southern Democratic coalition, and this chapter covers that too, but it also examines the other side of the ledger, the transformation of the southern Republican Party.

4. The percentage of Asians in the city of Houston is based on the one-year American Community Survey estimate in 2015.

5. Because the raft of restrictive and prohibitive voting laws was still firmly in place in the 1950s (Woodward 2002), most southern African Americans could not vote, let alone register to vote, at this time. But black mobilization was rapid after the 1965 Voting Rights Act removed most of the legal impediments to black participation, and the empirical evidence suggests two primary dynamics at work that led to the unusually swift and permanent alignment of southern blacks with the Democratic Party: (1) a conversion of many black voters from Republican to Democratic identification and (2) a comparatively larger mobilization of black voters who went from being politically independent/apolitical to Democratic when they first exercised the franchise (see Campbell 1977).

6. All of the data on Latinos presented in this section are from the decennial U.S. Census counts from 1980 to 2010. Further complicating any discussion of the Latino electorate is that growth rates and residential patterns are remarkably varied. For example, in Florida the bulk of the Cuban population, with the exception of a nontrivial number of Cubans in Tampa, resides in South Florida, specifically Miami-Dade County. Puerto Ricans are a much more geographically dispersed population and most of them are located in Central Florida, especially the greater Orlando area. Whereas the rate of Cuban growth appears to be leveling off, Puerto Rican growth continues to climb (e.g., consider the exodus of Puerto Ricans to Florida in the wake of Hurricane Maria, which wreaked havoc on the small island of Puerto Rico in September of 2017), and because these Latinos are American citizens by birthright and they are markedly less Republican in identification, their increasing presence advantages the Democratic Party. Doing justice to the kaleidoscopic nature of the southern Latino electorate requires another book (something the author intends to write in the near future).

7. Although Ansolabehere and Hersh (2013) examine a national sample of the voting electorate, there is no reason to suspect that turnout rates among blacks in the South are markedly different than the entire black electorate (if anything, *eligible* black turnout in the South may be higher due to the much higher rate of black male incarceration rates in the South; southern black men are a substantially smaller segment of Dixie's black voting electorate; see Yoshinaka and Grose 2005). Estimating registration and turnout based on a 1 percent sample of the national registered voter population in the 2008 general election (almost 2 million registrants), among registered African Americans, Ansolabehere and Hersh (2013, 134, Table 1) find that 75.1 percent of black men were registered and their turnout rate was 61 percent. By contrast, 90.9 percent of black women were registered and 69 percent of them voted in the 2008 election.

8. Florida, Louisiana, and North Carolina hold closed presidential primaries, restricted only to registered voters of the party holding the primary contest (e.g., only registered Democrats can vote in the Democratic presidential primary). The other eight southern states hold open primaries: any registered voter (and these states do not have party registration) can participate in either the Democratic or Republican presidential primary, but not both.

9. Fortunately, the 2016 Democratic presidential primary exit polls in Alabama, Georgia, Mississippi, and South Carolina break down the share of voters according to race and gender. Here is the percentage of white men, white women, black men, and black women for all four states (these data were accessed at the following CNN website: http://www.cnn.com/election/primaries/polls):

   Alabama: white men = 20 percent, white women = 20 percent, black men = 17 percent, black women = 37 percent

   Georgia: white men = 16 percent, white women = 22 percent, black men = 19 percent, black women = 33 percent

   Mississippi: white men = 10 percent, white women = 14 percent, black men = 23 percent, black women = 47 percent

   South Carolina: white men = 14 percent, white women = 21 percent, black men = 24 percent, black women = 37 percent.

10. South Carolina holds its elections for statewide offices (e.g., governor and state treasurer) in even-year midterms; congressional and state legislative primaries are held on the same primary date (as are statewide contests in midterm years). Like U.S. House Representatives, South Carolina state representatives serve two-year terms. South Carolina state senators serve four-year terms, with elections taking place in presidential years.

11. Although in 2016 more voters participated in the Republican presidential primary than the Democratic presidential primary in South Carolina (67 percent of all major party voters), this was not the case in 2008, when a slightly higher percentage of voters participated in the Democratic presidential primary (54 percent of all major party voters).

Chapter 10

1. There are, of course, some other federal elections that have gone down in the annals for being breathtakingly close. Consider the 1948 U.S. Senate Democratic runoff primary election in Texas, which Lyndon Johnson won over Governor Coke Stevenson with a margin of 87 votes and under a cloud of ballot stuffing voter fraud in some counties that delivered a suspiciously lopsided vote for the future president. V. O. Key (1949, 258) had this to say about the contest: "With approximately a million votes cast [988,295 to be exact], this was surely one of the closest elections in American history." More recently, in a recount that changed the outcome, in the 2008 Minnesota general election for U.S. Senate, former comedian and Democrat Al Franken upset the Republican incumbent, Norm Coleman, by 312 votes out of 2,424,946 cast for these major party nominees (election data are from Dave Leip's *Atlas of U.S. Presidential Elections* website).

2. In the article by Wand et al. (2001), the authors conclude that around 2,000 Palm Beach County votes that would have gone to Al Gore mistakenly went to Reform Party candidate Patrick Buchanan because these voters did not understand how to line up their vote correctly for Gore due to the unusual design of the butterfly ballot.

3. Here is a quote from the U.S. Election Assistance Commission (EAC) website that briefly outlines the purpose of HAVA: "HAVA was passed by the U.S. Congress in 2002 to make sweeping reforms to the nation's voting process. HAVA addresses improvements to voting systems and voter access that were identified following the 2000 election. HAVA mandates that EAC test and certify voting equipment, maintain the National Voter Registration form and administer a national clearinghouse on elections that includes shared practices, information for voters and other resources to improve elections. Section 803 of HAVA transferred the functions of the FEC's [Federal Election Commission] National Clearinghouse on Election Administration to an Election Assistance Commission (EAC)" (https://www.eac.gov/about/help-america-vote-act/). In short, because of multiple issues regarding the administration of the 2000 presidential election in Florida, the U.S. Congress saw a need to enter the breach in order to ensure an electoral experience that would restore voter confidence in the integrity and reliability of American elections. The desire to achieve this objective made HAVA a nonpartisan reform, and it led to certain changes in Florida election administration that voters demanded, like the elimination of punch card ballots (no more dimpled/pregnant and hanging chads) and the inclusion of a paper trail for every completed ballot that was filled out via an electronic voting machine.

4. Speaking directly to the GOP's problem with cultivating the support of minority voters in recent presidential elections, after the 2012 election in which President Obama won 71 percent of the national Latino vote (according to the 2012 exit poll), the Republican National Committee (RNC) published a document that explicitly addressed the GOP's need to attract more minority support (Barbour et al. 2012). But alas, then along came Donald Trump, who shocked the world by not only capturing the 2016 Republican presidential nomination with incendiary racially charged and racially divisive rhetoric, but went on to win the presidency even though his Democratic rival Hillary Clinton won over 2.8 million more popular votes. In fact, in California alone, the most populous and racially diverse state, Clinton bested Trump by a margin of well over 4 million votes (4,269,978 votes to be exact; data are from Dave Leip's *Atlas of U.S. Presidential Elections*). According to the 2016 presidential exit poll of California voters, Clinton won a majority of the major party vote among every racial/ethnic group in the state: 50 to 45

among whites (48 percent of voters), 88 to 9 among blacks (6 percent of voters), 71 to 24 among Latinos (31 percent of voters), and 70 to 17 among Asians (12 percent of voters). It warrants mentioning California in the 2016 presidential election because southern states like Florida, North Carolina, and Virginia are becoming much more racially and ethnically diverse, and the changing demographic patterns in these states are certainly contributing to their shift toward the Democratic Party in more recent elections.

5. The 2006 midterm was unique in American history; it was the only election in which every Democratic incumbent was victorious and every seat vacated by a Democratic member of Congress (Democratic open seat) was subsequently won by a Democratic candidate (Jacobson 2007b).

6. These presidential approval numbers were retrieved from the data made available through the American Presidency Project (APP), hosted at the University of California, Santa Barbara (http://www.presidency.ucsb.edu).

7. Speaking to the enduring split-level alignment of Republican strength in the South and the slow movement of GOP top-down electoral advancement, even though Democrats controlled congressional redistricting in most southern states in the 2000 round by virtue of their state legislative majorities, at this time, only three states had Democratic majority U.S. House delegations (Arkansas, Mississippi, and Texas); the other eight were majority Republican.

8. In 2010, principally due to migration out of the state because of Hurricane Katrina, Louisiana lost a seat, going from seven to six.

9. The redrawn district percentages were calculated through the MABLE/Geocorr Geographic Correspondence Engine from the Missouri Census Data Center website (http://mcdc2.missouri.edu/websas/geocorr2k.html).

10. Because these correlations are based on the two-party vote, showing the relationship between the Republican presidential vote and the Republican House vote is exactly the same.

11. Phil Burton was a California Democratic Congressman known for his deftness at crafting partisan gerrymanders, like the one he designed for the Democrats in the 1982 California U.S. House elections (see Cain 1984). In 1992, Texas Democrats implemented such an impressive partisan congressional gerrymander that the authors of *The Almanac of American Politics* praised it as worthy of the "Phil Burton Award" (Barone and Ujifusa 1993, 1209).

12. In 2000, District 23, a massive and sprawling district running along the Texas-Mexico border from the San Antonio suburbs in the east to the edge of El Paso in the west, was the one majority Latino district in Texas represented by a Republican (Latino Henry Bonilla).

13. There is a notable exception to a trend in favor of restrictive voting legislation fostered disproportionately by Republican lawmakers, and it is online voter registration (OVR). OVR has taken hold in the majority of states and it has been passed by Democrats and Republicans alike, although in some contexts its passage, or resistance to passage, is tied to partisan competition (see Hicks, McKee, and Smith 2016a).

14. Short of delving into a critical race theory explanation for racial division in the South, it is difficult to deny that the current structuring of partisan politics in Dixie centers on race; the self-segregating of most whites and almost all African Americans into separate parties because of fundamental differences (perceived or actual) among these groups, whether rooted in racial prejudice or something else (economic competition), continues to keep whites and blacks sharply at odds in the political arena.

15. Five counties in Florida and all of Texas were placed under the VRA in 1975 when the act was amended to cover language minorities; in these states, Latinos became the covered minority group. In practice, a partially covered state like Florida (or North Carolina) was treated as though it was completely covered for state-level changes to voting administration (e.g., implementing a new redistricting plan). Section 5 preclearance was never made applicable to Arkansas and Tennessee.

16. For instance, in perhaps one of the most blatant power plays in this post-*Shelby* period, in March of 2016, a Democratic African American candidate who intended to challenge the white Republican incumbent in a Georgia state legislative district (House District 151) had his residence drawn out of the district (living in the district is a necessary qualification for holding the office) when the Georgia Secretary of State slightly altered the district boundary without giving any prior notice (Woodman 2016). Before the *Shelby* ruling, changing the district boundary would have required approval from the Department of Justice under Section 5 of the VRA.

17. As shown in Table 10.7, the black voting age populations in these two North Carolina districts increased 4.4 percentage points between 2010 and 2012 (District 1 went from a BVAP of 48.1 percent in 2010 to 50.7 in 2012; District 12 went from a BVAP of 42.9 percent in 2010 to 49.0 in 2012).

Chapter 11

1. Not only do scholars continue to disagree on whether the South remains distinct from the rest of the United States, but even when scholars have agreed that the South persists in its political exceptionalism, there is still considerable disagreement regarding which factors are most responsible for Dixie realigning in favor of the Republican Party and how much weight to assign to those factors.

Chapter 12

1. Key (1949, 664) observes in the first paragraph of his last chapter in *Southern Politics in State and Nation*, "Not only is there diversity within the South; the region is also changing. Its rate of evolution may seem glacial, but fundamental shifts in the conditions underlying its politics are taking place." This is the same quote highlighted in the introductory section of chapter 9.

2. In his final chapter, Key (1949, 671–672) shows that there was an across-the-board decline in majority black counties in southern states from 1900 to 1940. With the repressive system of Jim Crow segregation and severe marginalization of African American participation in most states (especially in the Deep South), it was no surprise to see that black populations were in decline, as so many blacks migrated to northern cities (exit became the preferred option for those with the means to "vote with their feet"). The contemporary South has witnessed a pronounced reversal in black migration patterns, with the lifting of Jim Crow opening the door to a lengthy pattern of net black in-migration (see Figure 12.3). Hence, whereas Key expected the share of African Americans to continue to decline and thus reduce the hard edge on the South's race-conscious political system, as a share of the electorate, blacks have increased. Likewise, Key was optimistic about the coming biracial coalition of lower-class whites and African Americans, an arrangement that would apparently be reminiscent of the short-lived Populist uprising of the late 1800s. This also has not come to pass, and it is the primary reason why the Democratic Party has declined in electoral prowess.

3. In 2016, David's Index of GOP Strength closely matches the presidential vote in every state (a difference of less than 4 percentage points), and this holds true even based on the ten-year moving average, with the exception of two states that have recently experienced a surge in Republicanism: Arkansas and Tennessee. In the Natural State, the ten-year moving average GOP Index was 42.9 percent in 2016, whereas the 2016 Republican presidential vote was 64.3 percent. In the Volunteer State, the ten-year moving average GOP Index was 56.8 percent in 2016, whereas the 2016 Republican presidential vote was 63.6 percent. However, like the other nine southern states, the difference between the raw Republican Index and the GOP presidential vote in 2016 was also under 4 percentage points in Arkansas and Tennessee.

4. In the words of Black and Black (1987, 136), "The Voting Rights Act was the grand turning point in modern times for the reentry of blacks into southern politics. By 1966 2.6 million blacks were registered, about 52 percent of the black voting age population." In comparison, after the *Smith v. Allwright* decision struck down the white (Democratic) primary in 1944, by 1952 the share of southern black registrants had increased to a very modest 20 percent of the black voting age population (Black and Black 1987, 85).

5. Atwater was also the brains behind the highly racially charged Willie Horton ad, which aired during the 1988 presidential campaign. The ad can be accessed at this link: https://www.youtube.com/watch?v=Io9KMSSEZ0Y.

6. The National Conference of State Legislatures (NCSL) provides the total number of seats held by each party after the 2017 state legislative elections in the following document: http://www.ncsl.org/Portals/1/Documents/Elections/Legis_Control_2017_111017_1pm.pdf. There was, however, one contest in Virginia that was still undecided when the NCSL compiled their data, and thus the NCSL had the Virginia House at 50 Republicans and 49 Democrats. After a recount, the Virginia House District 94 contest resulted in a perfect tie, and according to Virginia election law, the winner is chosen by lot (chance). The Republican prevailed in a random drawing, resulting in a 51-to-49 GOP majority (for more information, see the Ballotpedia passage on Virginia's 2017 state house elections: https://ballotpedia.org/Virginia_House_of_Delegates_elections,_2017).

7. Data on the total number of U.S. House districts for each state for the 1990, 2000, and 2010 reapportionments are from the United States House of Representatives website (http://history.house.gov/Institution/Apportionment/Apportionment).

INDEX

Note: Page numbers in *italic* refer to tables, figures, and boxes. Page numbers followed by an 'n' refer to notes.